A PANORAMA OF CO[...]

This superb anthology presents the com[...] of the world's greatest comedies, classic plays by major dramatists from Aristophanes to Shaw. Each play represents an important style or tradition of comedy, as well as a different aspect of the comic view.

The editors have contributed explanatory essays that set the plays in context. They have also included analytical and critical essays by G. K. Chesterton, Susanne K. Langer, Bonamy Dobrée, and Northrop Frye, which provide penetrating insights into the meaning and roots of the comic drama.

Each of the three editors holds a Ph.D. from Harvard University and has taught in the Boston area, Sylvan Barnet at Tufts University, Morton Berman at Boston University, and William Burto at the University of Lowell. They have edited a companion volume, *Eight Great Tragedies*, as well as *The Genius of the Early English Theater*, and Sylvan Barnet served as the general editor of the Signet Classic Shakespeare editions.

Eight
Great Comedies

Edited by
SYLVAN BARNET
MORTON BERMAN
WILLIAM BURTO

A MERIDIAN BOOK

MERIDIAN
Published by the Penguin Group
Penguin Books USA Inc., 375 Hudson Street, New York,
New York 10014, U.S.A.
Penguin Books Ltd, 27 Wrights Lane, London W8 5TZ, England
Penguin Books Australia Ltd, Ringwood, Victoria, Australia
Penguin Books Canada Ltd, 10 Alcorn Avenue, Toronto, Ontario,
Canada M4V 3B2
Penguin Books (N.Z.) Ltd, 182-190 Wairau Road, Auckland 10, New Zealand

Penguin Books Ltd, Registered Offices: Harmondsworth, Middlesex, England

Published by Meridian, an imprint of Dutton Signet, a division of Penguin
Books USA Inc. Previously published in a Mentor edition.

First Meridian Printing, July, 1996
10   9   8   7   6   5

REGISTERED TRADEMARK—MARCA REGISTRADA

ISBN: 0-452-01170-1
CIP data is available.

Printed in the United States of America

Grateful acknowledgment is made to the following for permission to quote from the works listed.

G. Bell and Sons, Ltd. (London) for Aristophanes' *The Clouds*, translated by Benjamin Bickley Rogers.

Kenneth Burke for a passage from *Attitudes toward History*, Copyright, 1937 by Editorial Publications, Inc.

The Clarendon Press (Oxford) for a selection from *Restoration Comedy*, by Bonamy Dobrée.

Miss Dorothy Collins for "On the Comic Spirit," from *Generally Speaking*, by G. K. Chesterton.

Bonamy Dobrée for a selection from *Restoration Comedy*, by Bonamy Dobrée.

Gerald Duckworth and Company, Ltd. (London) for Chekhov's *Uncle Vanya*, from *Six Famous Plays* by Anton Tchekov, translated by Marian Fell.

J. R. Hale, Jesus College, Oxford University, for his translation of Machiavelli's *Mandragola*.

Macmillan and Co., Ltd. (London) for a passage from *Autobiographies* by W. B. Yeats.

The Macmillan Company of Canada Ltd. (Toronto) for a passage from *Autobiographies* by W. B. Yeats.

Methuen and Company, Ltd. (London) for "On the Comic Spirit," from *Generally Speaking*, by G. K. Chesterton.

Princeton University Press (Princeton, N.J.) for a selection from *Anatomy of Criticism*, by Northrop Frye, Copyright © 1957, by Princeton University Press.

The Public Trustee and the Society of Authors (London) for *Arms and the Man*, by George Bernard Shaw. *Arms and the Man* is published in the United States by Dodd, Mead and Company in Volume III of *Selected Plays by Bernard Shaw* and in *Seven Plays* by Bernard Shaw.

Routledge & Kegan Paul, Ltd. (London) for a selection from *Feeling and Form*, by Susanne K. Langer.

William Sargant for a passage from *Battle for the Mind*, Copyright © 1957 by William Sargant.

Charles Scribner's Sons (New York) for Chekhov's *Uncle Vanya*, translated by Marian Fell, Copyright 1912, by Charles Scribner's Sons; and for a selection from *Feeling and Form*, by Susanne K. Langer, Copyright, 1953, by Charles Scribner's Sons.

A. P. Watt and Son (London) for a passage from *Autobiographies*, by W. B. Yeats.

E. B. White for a passage from *A Subtreasury of American Honor*, Copyright, 1941, by E. B. White and Katharine S. White.

Mrs. William Butler Yeats for a passage from *Autobiographies*, by W. B. Yeats. All the translated plays, and George Bernard Shaw's *Arms and the Man*, are protected against unauthorized publication or performance, in whole or in part. Application for reproducing these plays in any medium should be made to the copyright holder, the translation of Moilère's *The Miser* is copyrighted by the editors. Request for performing rights to the Marian Fell translation of *Uncle Vanya* should be directed either to Samuel French, Ltd., 16 Southampton St., London W. C. 2, or Samuel French, Inc., 25 West 45th St., New York, New York 10036.

Eight
Great Comedies

CONTENTS

The Comic View: An Introduction   **7**

PART ONE: THE COMEDIES

ARISTOPHANES: The Clouds, translated by Benjamin Bickley Rogers   13

NICCOLÒ MACHIAVELLI: Mandragola, translated by J. R. Hale   66

WILLIAM SHAKESPEARE: Twelfth Night   107

MOLIÈRE: The Miser, translated by Sylvan Barnet, Morton Berman, and William Burto   173

JOHN GAY: The Beggar's Opera   229

OSCAR WILDE: The Importance of Being Earnest   286

ANTON CHEKHOV: Uncle Vanya, translated by Marian Fell   344

GEORGE BERNARD SHAW: Arms and the Man   388

PART TWO: THE ESSAYS

G. K. CHESTERTON: On the Comic Spirit   450

BONAMY DOBRÉE: Comedy   453

SUSANNE K. LANGER: The Comic Rhythm   456

NORTHROP FRYE: The Structure of Comedy   461

Bibliography   470

THE COMIC VIEW:

An Introduction

"A fool lifteth up his voice with laughter," writes the author of Ecclesiasticus, "but a wise man doth scarce smile a little." The ancient Hebrews strove to live righteously in Jehovah's eyes, and they felt that problems of good and evil were no laughing matter. If they had seen a comic play, however, they might have granted that drama which evokes laughter is not wholly foolish. The Greeks, people of broader sensibilities than the Hebrews, honored their comic as well as their tragic dramatists. There was something about comedy, the Greeks felt, which plumbed an essential human quality. Greek philosophers usually defined man as the only animal who reasons, but Aristotle once defined him as the only animal who laughs. And not only is man able to laugh; perhaps he *must* laugh if he is to remain a healthy specimen. The beneficial effect of comedy has been variously stated for over two thousand years: comedy cures us of our folly by showing it to us on the stage; or, less extravagantly, comedy affords us a chance to laugh at our neighbors, and it is healthier for social man to laugh at his neighbors when he sees them on the stage than when he meets them on the street. Recently an eminent psychiatrist has suggested that a sense of humor may help us withstand great tensions and pressures: "The safety of the free world . . . seems to lie in the cultivation, not only of courage, moral virtue and logic, but of humor: humor which produces the well-balanced state in which emotional excess is laughed at as ugly and wasteful." [1]

Most of the great dramas of the Western world can be fitted into one of two classes, tragedy or comedy. There seem to be two general patterns of life which most plays

[1] William Sargant, *Battle for the Mind* (New York: Doubleday and Co., 1957), p. 231.

7

imitate: one culminates in a tragic defeat, usually death, and the other in a joyous procession or union, frequently a marriage (the Greek word *komoidia* or "revel-song" gives us our word "comedy"). And the comedies which dramatize (or, to use Aristotle's word, imitate) the pattern of revelry may be derived ultimately from animal masquerades or from primitive fertility rituals. The ancient peoples who lived around the Mediterranean enacted in ritual dances the power and fertility of a Vegetation Spirit, and celebrated in a ribald yet religious manner the miracle of generation.

Primitive men usually enact ritual dances in order to make something happen: if they want the crops to grow tall, they may *imitate* the desired growth by leaping high into the air. If they want the land to be fertile, they may enact a celebration of the disappearance of winter and the coming of spring. If they want the power or cunning of an animal, they may claim relationship with the beast, wearing its skin and imitating its gait. But if and when they gradually realize that their rituals do not in fact bring something about, they may nevertheless continue imitative acts, partly (it seems) out of the same sheer delight that children get from imitating cowboys and Indians. The primitive fear, for example, that perhaps winter will triumph and spring will not flourish fades away, and the villainous or threatening representative of winter is no longer fearful but grotesque, not a terrifying object but a comic figure who in these performances is unable to prevent the inevitably fruitful union of lovers. Or perhaps even when the antagonist was still feared, he was abused and derided by representatives of the fertile force, in the hope that by jeering at him and treating him as laughable they would in fact cause him to become trivial and laughable.

Aristotle suggests that man is instinctively imitative, and that the artist imitates the essential qualities of reality. The word "imitation" (*mimesis*) is not pejorative; a Greek might say that a sculptor imitates men in marble, and we might say that Beethoven's *Eroica* imitates heroism (heroic action). As Thomas De Quincey put it, though no one whistled at Waterloo, one could whistle Waterloo. The drama, Aristotle says in the *Poetics*, imitates the actions of men; comedy, he says, imitates the actions of men worse than the average. If, however, we bypass this specific statement about the subject matter of Greek comedy of the fourth century B.C., we can retain Aristotle's concept of imitation and say that most comedy imitates man's effort to stave off death and to renew life, even as the primitive rituals did. Comedy often dramatizes the ejection of barrenness—obdurate parents who oppose their children's marriages either soften at the end or are laughed off the stage—and the reassertion of fertility. Shake-speare knew nothing of ancient rituals or ancient drama, yet his comedies, no less than those of Aristophanes, are rejections of impediments to joy, and celebrations of life's abundance. In *As You Like It*, for example, the reverence for a fertile community becomes explicit:

> Wedding is great Juno's crown
> O blessed bond of board and bed!
> 'Tis Hymen peoples every town;
> High wedlock then be honored.
> Honor, high honor, and renown,
> To Hymen, god of every town,

and the characters troop off "to a long and well-deserved bed." Comedy from Aristophanes to Shaw imitates the joy of social life (and, correlatively, it imitates the follies of those who try to maintain their own foolish ways against the community), a joy usually signaled by a social act such as a marriage or a feast (or both) at the conclusion of the play.

The dramas in this book are works of art, not primitive rituals, and we ought now to look less conjecturally at the chief pattern which they partly imitate, and consider generally the pleasure which comedy affords. The examination must be general because, as E. B. White has observed, "humor can be dissected, as a frog can, but the thing dies in the process and the innards are discouraging to any but the pure scientific mind."

Although most tragedy assumes that there is something priceless in the struggles of a man who is, in a spiritual way, greater than the society around him, much comedy assumes that the norms of society ought to be respected, and that the individual who attempts to go beyond the confines of the world of his fellows is not noble but foolish or even vicious. Comedy is thus frequently critical of the individual; it accepts as valid the codes of society, and is amused to see individuals set themselves up as exceptional. It finds laughable, for example, the amorous passion of an old man. Though love is a fit activity for the young, old men ought to realize that their efforts to behave coltishly are grotesque. The mistakes of the tragic hero arouse our sympathy—we admire him, and to a considerable degree we identify ourselves with him; the mistakes of the comic figure arouse our critical laughter —we observe him and his foibles with an intelligent aware-ness of their shortcomings. We feel the importance and va-lidity of the tragic figure's values and goals, but we perceive the gap between the comic figure's concept of life and life itself. This gap or mistake often exists in the comic character's false evaluation of himself (the world of comedy abounds in the self-deceived), but it is also present in the disguises (a man as a woman, in *Charley's Aunt*) or mere mistaken identities which have been the stock in trade of comic writers for two thousand years.

When we attend a comedy we have a godlike vision of the action, and we are amused by the bumbling fellows who are partially blinded to reality either by folly or by ignorance. Homer's gods laugh, and Jehovah (the Old Testament tells us) holds fools in derision. At a comedy, from our place overlooking the stage, we laugh at human absurdity. Our laughter is only rarely derisive (we are seldom *that* detached from the humanity on the stage), but we are comfortably "above" the comic figures. We may even regard these figures affectionately, for affection is sometimes based on an assuring, if unconscious, sense of superiority. At a comedy we delight in the antics before us, and our delight ranges from derision to affection for fallible man, but in some degree we feel with Puck (a supernatural creature, incidentally), "What fools these mortals be!" Puck's comment is not cruel, however, because in comedy folly is banished laughingly, and goodwill finally prevails. We laugh at the "obstacle race to the altar," but we are pleased by the outcome: "Jack shall have Jill," Puck assures us midway in the play,

> Nought shall go ill;
> The man shall have his mare again, and all shall be well.

"All shall be well." The phrase covers a multitude of comic plots. Sometimes the central character is not absurd but rather is a shrewd manipulator of the absurdities of others. He may, for example, be a rogue whose exuberant chicanery amuses us when we contrast it with the stifling jealousy of a husband or the parsimony of a merchant. Or perhaps we enjoy a rogue's deceits because his declaration that the world is his oyster which he will open with his sword expresses our rebellious desire to cast off impediments to life, to live fully, and not to be tyrannized by the boss. And for a few minutes, in the theater at least, all is well.

Perhaps comedy's best justification is that it refreshes or renews us and helps us face our daily world. More exalted claims, however, are usually made for comedy. Moralists and comic dramatists generally assert comedy's curative power. In the Preface to his *Complete Plays*, George Bernard Shaw summed up his job: "If I make you laugh at yourself, remember that my business as a classic writer of comedies is 'to chasten morals with ridicule'; and if I sometimes make you feel like a fool, remember that I have by the same action cured your folly, just as the dentist cures your toothache by pulling out your tooth. And I never do it without giving you plenty of laughing gas." But it is doubtful that people really go to the theater to be corrected, however entertaining the chastisement. Shakespeare makes an apter, more modest, and no less important claim for comedy when he suggests that it induces a playful mood, and that such a mood may be life-giving:

> Frame your mind to mirth and merriment,
> Which bars a thousand harms and lengthens life.

The entire problem of comic theory is complicated by the fact that analyses of laughter are not necessarily analyses of comedy. Freud, for example, in *Wit and Its Relation to the Unconscious*, distinguishes between comedy, humor, and wit (twenty-three varieties), and never discusses dramatic comedy. While a comedy is expected to evoke laughter, not all laughter is comic. We laugh, of course, when tickled, when subjected to laughing gas, and sometimes when nervous or hysterical. And a comic drama is not merely a play with jokes; *Hamlet* contains witticisms, but is not a comedy. It is impossible to conceive of a great comedy as a mere collection of jokes, however funny each joke might be. Jokes may be appropriate and even necessary to the action of a comedy, but they do not of themselves make a comedy. The relative unimportance of wit is suggested in a story told about Menander, a Greek comic dramatist. Asked by a friend how his play was progressing, he replied that he had finished it, though he had not yet written the dialogue—an indication that comedy consists not of a mere exhibition of wit but of characters in action.

The characters who amuse us in comedy are usually mildly abnormal figures to whom we feel superior, for by their folly they set themselves against the judgment of society. But because society's norms change, comedy often loses its appeal to later generations. We might note, by way of contrast, that because men have over the centuries suffered in much the same way, and for much the same things, great tragedy is highly communicable. Its problems are still our problems, its lamentations and exultations are still ours. Comedy, too, of course, often deals with universal characters—the avaricious, the boastful, the foolhardy, but it is more likely than tragedy to focus on a peculiarly local problem, and thus it may write its own closing notice. That is, because comedy assumes the validity of a particular society's code of behavior, it is easily dated. Things laughable to the Renaissance may not amuse us, for Renaissance common sense is not always the same as ours. Witty jibes at Jews, for example, do not always delight us today, for we do not all believe that Jews are funny by being in some ways apart from a dominant Christian society. We tend to understand and to sympathize with Shylock and therefore we lose a great deal of the humor of *The Merchant of Venice.*

A word about the ending of comedies is relevant at the end of this introduction. Though comedy usually concludes happily, at least for the "good" characters, only in a superficial view is comedy purely optimistic. Just as close study suggests that tragedy is not merely pessimistic but partakes, by virtue of its affirmation of the human spirit, of optimism, so similar study may show a touch of pessimism in comedy. Comedy touches on pessimism when it notes (as it generally does) the melancholy fact that men of ideals—men who seek to live by some one principle—are frequently ridiculous because of their inadequate view of reality. When, for example, Molière's Miser attempts to order and reduce to money the complexity of the world, his efforts are laughable. Similarly, the puritan, the businessman, the philosopher, the clergyman —anyone who attempts to arrange experience into a meaningful pattern—runs the risk of straitjacketing existence. And because existence cannot be straitjacketed, because life is so complex that it eludes the pattern which even the most sophisticated would impose on it, the one-sided effort is mistaken and comic. "The progress of humane enlightenment," Kenneth Burke says in *Attitudes toward History,* "can go no further than in picturing people not as *vicious,* but as *mistaken.* When you add that people are *necessarily* mistaken, that *all* people are exposed to situations in which they must act as fools, that *every* insight contains its own special kind of blindness, you complete the comic circle, returning again to the lesson of humility that underlies great tragedy."

PART ONE

THE COMEDIES

Aristophanes:

THE CLOUDS

"Humor," says James Thurber, "is a serious thing. I like to think of it as one of our greatest natural resources which must be preserved at all costs. One of the things that worry me is the diminishing of political satire. In the heyday of Henry Mencken and Will Rogers . . . they were not afraid to make fun of public figures. I think we are a little bit now."[1] No comic writer ever made fun of public figures more harshly and more beautifully than did Aristophanes. And it is to the credit of Athens that his bold dramas encountered almost no censorship. It is the duty of the dramatist, he says in one play, "to teach the city what is best," and the city agreed by staging his plays on holidays and by tolerating—and laughing at—these dramas whose frankness of language is unthinkable on any other stage. A legend—doubtless false, but enlightening—says that when a Syracusan tyrant asked Plato to describe the Athenian constitution, Plato sent him the plays of Aristophanes, for these dramas are striking documents of Athens' liberty.

The outspoken drama of Aristophanes (*c.* 445–*c.* 385 B.C.) owes a good deal to the tradition behind it. The precise origins of Athenian comedy are lost, but it seems to have begun in licentious revelry. Perhaps men masquerading as animals, or the reveling worshipers of Dionysus, god of the vine, indulged in song and dance which became formalized into a procession of devotees (i.e., a chorus) singing the praises of the phallus and heaping abuse on impediments to fertility, or perhaps they satirized jeering bystanders. Aristotle tells us (though he may have been wrong) that comedy was originated by the leader of a phallic chorus. Meanwhile non-choral farces or crudely amusing scenes were acted elsewhere in Greece

[1] *Atlantic Monthly* (August, 1956), p. 39.

13

and in Italy, and somehow in the sixth century B.C. these farces came to be joined to the reveling procession with its joyful and satirical songs. Perhaps, then, in the sixth century some costumed revelers would enter, sing, banter or debate, and finally clown a bit. This hypothesis is highly conjectural, but it may account for some elements discernible in extant Greek comedy. Looking at the problem in another way, we can say that even if the plotting in the plays seems chaotic, the dramas are in part extremely formal and elaborate, thus suggesting a ritual origin brought into conjunction with alien farces. Although it is not known precisely how or why this or that element got into the comic form, the dramas have a definite structure—with some variations from play to play. The typical Aristophanic comedy opens with a *prologos* wherein a situation or problem is sketched (in *The Clouds* we see a father decide to visit Socrates in the hope of learning how to avoid paying debts); then in the *parodos* a fantastically dressed chorus enters, usually garbed as animals, thereby lending support to the theory that the chorus may be derived from rituals involving totem animals (though in this play the chorus is one of clouds). Next there is usually a debate or *agon* (in *The Clouds* it is between Right and Wrong Logic) relevant to the opening situation, followed by the Chorus Leader's direct address to the audience. In the Leader's elaborately structured address (called the *parabasis* or "coming-forward") the poet harangues the crowd, airing his views on art or politics or whatever pleases him. The *parabasis* in *The Clouds*, for example, is partly devoted to praising the author and criticizing the audience. The *parabasis*, as has just been suggested, usually follows the *agon* (debate), but in *The Clouds* it untypically precedes the *agon* between Right Logic and Wrong Logic.

Although there are variations, then, in the structure of the individual plays, the plays are nevertheless highly structured, some parts rivaling a sonnet in their complexity. As a small example, it is worth mentioning that just prior to the *agon* the Leader of the Chorus always asks—in exactly two lines— one contender to present his argument, and it is this contender who always loses. The argument itself follows a complex form, and at its conclusion the Leader asks—again in two lines—the second party to speak. After these formal sections, Greek comedies do in fact have a formless part, a series of loose episodes whose origin most scholars attribute to the farces which somehow got attached to the basic ritual procession of singing revelers who satirized onlookers. Such, then, is the general pattern of Aristophanic comedy, a highly

satiric comedy which died at the close of the fifth century B.C.
and was ultimately replaced in Greece by a compassionate
comedy anticipating the modern stock comic theme of boy
meets girl.

The Clouds (produced in 423 B.C., but extant only in a
revised version) is an attack on Socrates in particular and philosophers in general. The conflict between poets and philosophers became increasingly sharp during the fifth century,
when the philosophers more and more took on the role of
teacher, a role earlier held by the poets. The attack on
Socrates is thus not only a personal lampoon, but an indict-
ment of the philosophers' attempts to value only logic and
science. Logical and scientific analysis is, in Aristophanes' view,
a narrow-minded effort to stifle the breadth, complexity,
beauty, and joy of experience, for it substitutes clever thinking for full wholesome living. That a philosophic view of man
can be funny—the basic comic situation in *The Clouds*—
is admirably explained by Lucien Price in a conversation
with the late Alfred North Whitehead (who, though himself
a philosopher-scientist, insisted on "the necessity of irrever-
ence"): "Laughter," Price says, "is our reminder that our
theories are an attempt to make existence intelligible, but
necessarily only an attempt; and does not the irrational, the
instinctive, burst in to keep the balance true by laughter?" [1]

It is true, as Thurber suggests in the sentence quoted
above, that satire of public figures is generally wholesome;
and it is true, as Price suggests, that life is bigger than any
philosopher's theories. Socrates, because he walked about the
streets of Athens talking to anyone who wished to search
for the truth, was a convenient figure by whom Aristophanes
could represent the new philosophers who doubted the traditional teachings of the poets. Unlike the "Socrates" in
The Clouds, Socrates did not teach for money. He would
not have helped a man avoid paying debts, and was not
(except in his youth) interested in scientific speculation.
Despite these differences between the real and the Aristophanic Socrates, twenty-four years after the production of
The Clouds the Athenian public confused the two, and the
populace which had guaranteed freedom of speech to Aristophanes withdrew it from Socrates. When *The Clouds* was
performed in 423 B.C., Socrates (according to legend) stood
up so that the spectators could compare him with the image
on the stage. But in 399 B.C., when he showed himself to

[1] Lucien Price, *Dialogues of Alfred North Whitehead* (Boston: Little,
Brown and Company—Atlantic Monthly Press, 1954), p. 62; (New
York: The New American Library [Mentor Books] 1956), p. 55.

a court of 501 Athenians, he could not convince them that he was not the dishonest and irreverent creature whom they had seen in Aristophanes' comedy. It is one of the purposes of comedy to criticize eccentricity, but comedy may inadvertently help produce tragedy when the eccentric happens to be a genius misunderstood and condemned to death by insecure mediocrities who will tolerate no variations, however noble. *The Clouds* is both a great comedy and an illustration of the dangers of the comic view.

The Clouds

TRANSLATED BY BENJAMIN BICKLEY ROGERS

Characters

STREPSIADES

PHEIDIPPIDES, *his son*

SERVANT-BOY *of Strepsiades*

STUDENTS *of Socrates*

SOCRATES

CHORUS OF CLOUDS

RIGHT LOGIC

WRONG LOGIC

PASIAS ⎱
AMYNIAS ⎰ *creditors*

A WITNESS

CHAEREPHON

*There are two buildings at the back of the stage, the resi-
dence of* STREPSIADES, *and the Phrontisterion, or thinking-
establishment of the Sophists. The opening scene discloses the
interior of the house of* STREPSIADES. *We see* STREPSIADES
*and his son lying within, each on his own pallet. It is still
dark, but the day is about to dawn. The son,* PHEIDIPPIDES,
is sound asleep, but the father is tossing on his couch.

STREPSIADES: O dear! O dear!
O Lord! O Zeus! these nights, how long they are.
Will they ne'er pass? will the day never come?
Surely I heard the cock crow, hours ago.
Yet still my servants snore. These are new customs.
O 'ware of war for many various reasons;
One fears in war even to flog one's servants.
And here's this hopeful son of mine wrapped up
Snoring and sweating under five thick blankets.
Come, we'll wrap up and snore in opposition.

                              (*Tries to sleep.*)
But I can't sleep a wink, devoured and bitten
By ticks, and bugbears, duns, and race-horses,
All through this son of mine. *He* curls his hair,
And sports his thoroughbreds, and drives his tandem;
Even in dreams he rides: while I—I'm ruined,
Now that the Moon has reached her twentieths,
And paying-time comes on.[1] Boy! light a lamp,
And fetch my ledger: now I'll reckon up
Who are my creditors, and what I owe them.
Come, let me see then. *Fifty pounds to Pasias!*
Why fifty pounds to Pasias? what were they for?
O, for the hack from Corinth. O dear! O dear!
I wish my eye had been hacked out before—

PHEIDIPPIDES (*in his sleep*): You are cheating, Philon; keep
   to your own side.

STREPSIADES: Ah! there it is! that's what has ruined me!
Even in his very sleep he thinks of horses.

PHEIDIPPIDES (*in his sleep*): How many heats do the war-
   chariots run?

STREPSIADES: A pretty many heats you have run your
   father.
Now then, what debt assails me after Pasias?
A curricle and wheels. Twelve pounds. Amynias.

PHEIDIPPIDES (*in his sleep*): Here, give the horse a roll,
   and take him home.

---

[1] The month is almost over, and interest will soon be payable.

STREPSIADES: You have rolled me *out* of house and home,
> my boy,
Cast in some suits already, while some swear
They'll seize my goods for payment.
PHEIDIPPIDES: Good, my father,
What makes you toss so restless all night long?
STREPSIADES: There's a bumbailiff from the mattress bites
> me.
PHEIDIPPIDES: Come now, I prithee, let me sleep in peace.
STREPSIADES: Well then, you sleep; only be sure of this,
These debts will fall on your own head at last.
Alas, alas! For ever cursed be that same matchmaker,
Who stirred me up to marry your poor mother.
Mine in the country was the pleasantest life,   *opposites*
Untidy, easy-going, unrestrained,
Brimming with olives, sheepfolds, honey-bees.
Ah! then I married—I a rustic—her
A fine town-lady, niece of Megacles.
A regular, proud, luxurious, Coesyra.
This wife I married, and we came together,
I rank with wine-lees, fig-boards, greasy woolpacks;
She all with scents, and saffron, and tongue-kissings,
Feasting, expense, and lordly modes of loving.
She was not idle though, she was too fast.
I used to tell her, holding out my cloak,
Threadbare and worn; *Wife, you're too fast by half.*
SERVANT-BOY: Here's no more oil remaining in the lamp.
STREPSIADES: O me! what made you light the tippling
> lamp?
Come and be whipp'd.
SERVANT-BOY: Why, what would you whip me for?
STREPSIADES: Why did you put one of those thick wicks in?
Well, when at last to me and my good woman
This hopeful son was born, our son and heir,
Why then we took to wrangle on the name.
She was for giving him some knightly name,
"Callippides," "Xanthippus," or "Charippus:"
I wished "Pheidonides," [1] his grandsire's name.
Thus for some time we argued: till at last
We compromised it in Pheidippides.
This boy she took, and used to spoil him, saying,
Oh! when you are driving to the Acropolis, clad
Like Megacles, in your purple; whilst I said
Oh! when the goats you are driving from the fells,
Clad like your father, in your sheepskin coat.

[1] The name means "a son of thrift."

Well, he cared nought for my advice, but soon
A galloping consumption caught my fortunes.
Now cogitating all night long, I've found
One way, one marvellous transcendent way,
Which if he'll follow, we may yet be saved.
So,—but, however, I must rouse him first;
But how to rouse him kindliest? that's the rub.
Pheidippides, my sweet one.

 PHEIDIPPIDES: Well, my father.

 STREPSIADES: Shake hands, Pheidippides, shake hands and
  kiss me.

 PHEIDIPPIDES: There; what's the matter?

 STREPSIADES: Dost thou love me, boy?

 PHEIDIPPIDES: Ay! by Poseidon there, the God of horses.

 STREPSIADES: No, no, not that: miss out the God of horses,
That God's the origin of all my evils.
But if you love me from your heart and soul,
My son, obey me.

 PHEIDIPPIDES: Very well: what in?

 STREPSIADES: Strip with all speed, strip off your present
  habits,
And go and learn what I'll advise you to.

(*Here the two leave the bedroom and come out upon the
stage.*)

 PHEIDIPPIDES: Name your commands.

 STREPSIADES: Will you obey?

 PHEIDIPPIDES: I will,
By Dionysus!

 STREPSIADES: Well then, look this way.
See you that wicket and the lodge beyond?

 PHEIDIPPIDES: I see: and prithee what is that, my father?

 STREPSIADES: That is the thinking-house of sapient souls.
There dwell the men who teach—aye, who persuade us,
That Heaven is one vast fire-extinguisher
Placed round about us, and that we're the cinders.
Aye, and they'll teach (only they'll want some money),[1]
How one may speak and conquer, right or wrong.

 PHEIDIPPIDES: Come, tell their names.

 STREPSIADES: Well, I can't quite remember,
But they're deep thinkers, and true gentlemen.

  [1] The Sophistical teachers always required a money payment. Socrates
never did.

PHEIDIPPIDES: Out on the rogues! I know them. Those rank
  pedants,
Those palefaced, barefoot vagabonds you mean:
That Socrates, poor wretch, and Chaerephon.
  STREPSIADES: Oh! Oh! hush! hush! don't use those foolish
  words;
But if the sorrows of my barley touch you,
Enter their Schools and cut the Turf for ever.
  PHEIDIPPIDES: I wouldn't go, so help me Dionysus,
For all Leogoras's breed of Phasians! [1]

  STREPSIADES: Go, I beseech you, dearest, dearest son,
Go and be taught.
  PHEIDIPPIDES: And what would you have me learn?
  STREPSIADES: 'Tis known that in their Schools they keep
  two Logics,
The Worse, Zeus save the mark, the Worse and Better.
This Second Logic then, I mean the Worse one,
They teach to talk unjustly and—prevail.   *Sophists*
Think then, you only learn that Unjust Logic,
And all the debts, which I have incurred through you,—
I'll never pay, no, not one farthing of them.
  PHEIDIPPIDES: I will not go. How could I face the knights
With all my colour worn and torn away!
  STREPSIADES: O! then, by Earth, you have eat your last
  of mine,
You, and your coach-horse, and your sigma-brand:
Out with you! Go to the crows, for all I care.
  PHEIDIPPIDES: But uncle Megacles won't leave me long
Without a horse: I'll go to him: good-bye.

  (*Exit* PHEIDIPPIDES.)

  STREPSIADES: I'm thrown, by Zeus, but I won't long lie
  prostrate.
I'll pray the Gods and send myself to school:
I'll go at once and try their thinking-house.
Stay: how can I, forgetful, slow, old fool,
Learn the nice hair-splittings of subtle Logic?
Well, go I must. 'Twont do to linger here.
Come on, I'll knock the door. Boy! Ho there, boy!
  STUDENT (*within*): O, hang it all! who's knocking at the
  door? (*He opens the door.*)
  STREPSIADES: Me! Pheidon's son: Strepsiades of Cicynna.
  STUDENT: Why, what a clown you are! to kick our door,
In such a thoughtless, inconsiderate way!

[1] Probably "horses."

You've made my cogitation to miscarry.[1]

STREPSIADES: Forgive me: I'm an awkward country fool.
But tell me, what was that I made miscarry?

STUDENT: 'Tis not allowed: Students alone may hear.

STREPSIADES: O that's all right: you may tell *me:* I'm come
To be a student in your thinking-house.

STUDENT: Come then. But they're high mysteries, re-
            member.
'Twas Socrates was asking Chaerephon,
How many feet of its own a flea could jump.
For one first bit the brow of Chaerephon,
Then bounded off to Socrates's head.

STREPSIADES: How did he measure this?

STUDENT: Most cleverly.
He warmed some wax, and then he caught the flea,
And dipped its feet into the wax he'd melted:
Then let it cool, and there were Persian slippers!
These he took off, and so he found the distance.

STREPSIADES: O Zeus and king, what subtle intellects!

STUDENT: What would you say then if you heard another,
Our Master's own?

STREPSIADES: O come, do tell me that.

STUDENT: Why, Chaerephon was asking him in turn,
Which theory did he sanction; that the gnats
Hummed through their mouth, or backwards, through the tail?

STREPSIADES: Aye, and what said your Master of the gnat?

STUDENT: He answered thus: the entrail of the gnat
Is small: and through this narrow pipe the wind
Rushes with violence straight towards the tail;
There, close against the pipe, the hollow rump
Receives the wind, and whistles to the blast.

STREPSIADES: So then the rump is trumpet to the gnats!
O happy, happy in your entrail-learning
Full surely need he fear nor debts nor duns,
Who knows about the entrails of the gnats.

STUDENT: And yet last night a mighty thought we lost
Through a green lizard.

STREPSIADES: Tell me, how was that?

STUDENT: Why, as Himself, with eyes and mouth wide
            open,
Mused on the moon, her paths and revolutions,
A lizard from the roof squirted full on him.

[1] Socrates' mother was a midwife, and he described himself as an
intellectual *accoucheur.*

STREPSIADES: He, he, he, he. I like the lizard's spattering Socrates.

STUDENT: Then yesterday, poor we, we'd got no dinner.

STREPSIADES: Hah! what did he devise to do for barley?

STUDENT: He sprinkled on the table—some fine ash—
He bent a spit—he grasped it compass-wise—
And—filched a mantle from the Wrestling School.[1]

STREPSIADES: Good heavens! Why Thales was a fool to this!
O open, open, wide the study door,
And show me, show me, show me Socrates.
I die to be a student. Open, open!

(*Not the door only, but the whole house opens, exposing to the view of the audience, the inner court of the Phrontisterion. High up in the air we behold* SOCRATES *suspended in a basket, whilst below are a number of miserable half-starved wretches, all stooping forward as if anxiously examining something on the ground. They look so little like ordinary specimens of humanity, that* STREPSIADES, *in amazement, invokes Heracles the destroyer of monsters.*)

O Heracles, what kind of beasts are these!

STUDENT: Why, what's the matter? what do you think they're like?

STREPSIADES: Like? why those Spartans whom we brought from Pylus:
What makes them fix their eyes so on the ground?

STUDENT: They seek things underground.

STREPSIADES: O! to be sure,
Truffles! You there, don't trouble about that!
I'll tell you where the best and finest grow.
Look! why do those stoop down so very much?

STUDENT: They're diving deep into the deepest secrets.

STREPSIADES: Then why's their rump turned up towards the sky?

STUDENT: It's taking private lessons on the stars. (*To the other Students*) Come, come: get in: *he'll* catch us presently.

STREPSIADES: Not yet! not yet! just let them stop one moment,
While I impart a little matter to them.

STUDENT: No, no: they must go in: 'twould never do

[1] Socrates, instead of drawing a geometric problem in the ash, hooks (to sell for food) a garment discarded by a wrestler.

To expose themselves too long to the open air.

STREPSIADES: O! by the Gods, now, what are these? do tell me.

STUDENT: This is Astronomy.

STREPSIADES: And what is this?

STUDENT: Geometry.

STREPSIADES: Well, what's the use of that?

STUDENT: To mete out lands.

STREPSIADES: What, for allotment grounds?

STUDENT: No, but all lands.

STREPSIADES: A choice idea, truly.

Then every man may take his choice, you mean.

STUDENT: Look; here's a chart of the whole world. Do you see?

This city's Athens.

STREPSIADES: Athens? I like that.

I see no dicasts[1] sitting. That's not Athens.

STUDENT: In very truth, this is the Attic ground.

STREPSIADES: And where then are my townsmen of Cicynna?

STUDENT: Why, thereabouts; and here, you see, Euboea:

Here, reaching out a long way by the shore.

STREPSIADES: Yes, overreached by us and Pericles.

But now, where's Sparta?

STUDENT: Let me see: O, here.

STREPSIADES: Heavens! how near us. O do please manage this,

To shove her off from us, a long way further.

STUDENT: We can't do that, by Zeus.

STREPSIADES: The worse for you.

Hallo! who's that? that fellow in the basket?

STUDENT: That's *he.*

STREPSIADES: Who's *he?*

STUDENT: Socrates.

STREPSIADES: Socrates!

You sir, call out to him as loud as you can.

STUDENT: Call him yourself: I have not leisure now. (*Exit.*)

STREPSIADES: Socrates! Socrates!

Sweet Socrates!

SOCRATES: Mortal! why call'st thou me?

STREPSIADES: O, first of all, please tell me what you are doing.

SOCRATES: I walk on air, and contem-plate the Sun.

[1] Paid Athenian jurors.

STREPSIADES: O then from a basket you contemn the Gods,
And not from the earth, at any rate?
SOCRATES: Most true.
I could not have searched out celestial matters
Without suspending judgement, and infusing
My subtle spirit with the kindred air.
If from the ground I were to seek these things,
I could not find: so surely doth the earth
Draw to herself the essence of our thought.
The same too is the case with water-cress.[1]
STREPSIADES: Hallo! what's that?
Thought draws the essence into water-cress?
Come down, sweet Socrates, more near my level,
And teach the lessons which I come to learn.

(SOCRATES *descends, joining* STREPSIADES.)

SOCRATES: And wherefore art thou come?
STREPSIADES: To learn to speak.
For owing to my horrid debts and duns,
My goods are seized, I'm robbed, and mobbed, and plundered.
SOCRATES: How did you get involved with your eyes open?
STREPSIADES: A galloping consumption seized my money.
Come now: do let me learn the unjust Logic
That can shirk debts: now do just let me learn it.
Name your own price, by all the Gods I'll pay it.
SOCRATES: The Gods! why you must know the Gods with us
Don't pass for current coin.
STREPSIADES: Eh? what do you use then?
Have you got iron, as the Byzantines have?
SOCRATES: Come, would you like to learn celestial matters,
How their truth stands?
STREPSIADES: Yes, if there's any truth.
SOCRATES: And to hold intercourse with yon bright Clouds,
Our virgin Goddesses?
STREPSIADES: Yes, that I should.
SOCRATES: Then sit you down upon that sacred bed.
STREPSIADES: Well, I am sitting.
SOCRATES: Here then, take this chaplet.
STREPSIADES: Chaplet? why? why? now, never, Socrates:
Don't sacrifice poor me, like Athamas.[2]
SOCRATES: Fear not: our entrance-services require
All to do this.
STREPSIADES: But what am I to gain?
SOCRATES: You'll be the flower of talkers, prattlers, gossips:
Only keep quiet. (*Initiates* STREPSIADES *by sprinkling grain.*)

---

[1] A parody of Socrates' homely imagery.
[2] Strepsiades confuses the ritual of initiation with that of sacrifice.

STREPSIADES: Zeus! your words come true!
I shall be flour indeed with all this peppering.
  SOCRATES: Old man sit you still, and attend to my will,
       and hearken in peace to my prayer,
O Master and King, holding earth in your swing, O meas-
       ureless infinite Air;
And thou glowing Ether, and Clouds who enwreathe her
       with thunder, and lightning, and storms,
Arise ye and shine, bright Ladies Divine, to your student in
       bodily forms.
  STREPSIADES: No, but stay, no, but stay, just one moment
       I pray, while my cloak round my temples I wrap.
To think that I've come, stupid fool, from my home, with
       never a waterproof cap!
  SOCRATES: Come forth, come forth, dread Clouds, and to
       earth your glorious majesty show;
Whether lightly ye rest on the time-honoured crest of Olympus
       environed in snow,
Or tread the soft dance 'mid the stately expanse of Ocean,
       the nymphs to beguile,
Or stoop to enfold with your pitchers of gold, the mystical
       waves of the Nile,
Or around the white foam of Maeotis ye roam, or Mimas
       all wintry and bare,
O hear while we pray, and turn not away from the rites which
       your servants prepare.
  CHORUS (*Heard in the distance*): Clouds of all hue,
Rise we aloft with our garments of dew.
Come from old Ocean's unchangeable bed,
Come, till the mountain's green summits we tread,
Come to the peaks with their landscapes untold,
Gaze on the Earth with her harvests of gold,
Gaze on the rivers in majesty streaming,
  Gaze on the lordly, invincible Sea,
Come, for the Eye of the Ether is beaming,
  Come, for all Nature is flashing and free.
    Let us shake off this close-clinging dew
    From our members eternally new,
    And sail upwards the wide world to view.
      Come away! Come away!
  SOCRATES: O Goddesses mine, great Clouds and divine, ye
       have heeded and answered my prayer.
Heard ye their sound, and the thunder around, as it thrilled
       through the tremulous air?
  STREPSIADES: Yes, by Zeus, and I shake, and I'm all of a
       quake, and I fear I must sound a reply,
Their thunders have made my soul so afraid, and those ter-
       rible voices so nigh:

So if lawful or not, I must run to a pot, by Zeus, if I stop
    I shall die.

SOCRATES: Don't act in our schools like those Comedy-
    fools with their scurrilous scandalous ways.
Deep silence be thine: while this Cluster divine their soul-
    stirring melody raise.

CHORUS: Come then with me,
Daughters of Mist, to the land of the free.
Come to the people whom Pallas hath blest,
Come to the soil where the Mysteries rest;
Come, where the glorified Temple invites
The pure to partake of its mystical rites:
Holy the gifts that are brought to the Gods,
    Shrines with festoons and with garlands are crowned,
Pilgrims resort to the sacred abodes,
    Gorgeous the festivals all the year round.
       And the Bromian rejoicings in Spring,[1]
       When the flutes with their deep music ring,
       And the sweetly-toned Choruses sing
           Come away! Come away!

STREPSIADES: O Socrates pray, by all the Gods, say, for I
    earnestly long to be told,
Who are these that recite with such grandeur and might?
    are they glorified mortals of old?

SOCRATES: No mortals are there, but Clouds of the air,
    great Gods who the indolent fill:
These grant us discourse, and logical force, and the art of
    persuasion instil,
And periphrasis strange, and a power to arrange, and a
    marvellous judgement and skill.

STREPSIADES: So then when I heard their omnipotent word,
    my spirit felt all of a flutter,
And it yearns to begin subtle cobwebs to spin and about
    metaphysics to stutter,
And together to glue an idea or two, and battle away in
    replies:
So if it's not wrong, I earnestly long to behold them myself
    with my eyes.

SOCRATES: Look up in the air, towards Parnes out there,
    for I see they will pitch before long
These regions about.

STREPSIADES: Where? point me them out.

SOCRATES: They are drifting, an infinite
    throng,

---

[1] Spring festivals honoring Dionysus.

And their long shadows quake over valley and brake.

STREPSIADES: Why, whatever's the matter to-day?
I can't see, I declare.

SOCRATES: By the Entrance; look there!

STREPSIADES: Ah, I just got a glimpse, by the
way.

(*During the following conversation the* CLOUDS *silently
take their places in the orchestra; they do not break silence
until* STREPSIADES *earnestly begs them to speak.*)

SOCRATES: There, now you must see how resplendent they
    be, or your eyes must be pumpkins, I vow.

STREPSIADES: Ah! I see them proceed; I should think so
    indeed: great powers! they fill everything now.

SOCRATES: So then till this day that celestials were they,
    you never imagined or knew?

STREPSIADES: Why, no, on my word, for I always had heard
    they were nothing but vapour and dew.

SOCRATES: O, then I declare, you can't be aware that 'tis
    these who the sophists protect,
Prophets sent beyond sea, quacks of every degree, fops signet-
    and-jewel-bedecked,
Astrological knaves, and fools who their staves of dithyrambs
    proudly rehearse—
'Tis the Clouds who all these support at their ease, because
    they exalt them in verse.

STREPSIADES: 'Tis for this then they write of "the on-rushin'
    might o' the light-stappin' rain-drappin' Cloud,"
And the "thousand black curls whilk the Tempest-lord whirls,"
    and the "thunder-blast stormy an' loud,"
And "birds o' the sky floatin' upwards on high," and "air-
    water leddies" which "droon
Wi' their saft falling dew the gran' Ether sae blue," [1] and then
    in return they gulp doon
Huge gobbets o' fishes an' bountifu' dishes o' mavises prime
    in their season.

SOCRATES: And is it not right such praise to requite?

STREPSIADES: Ah, but tell me then what is the
    reason
That if, as you say, they are Clouds, they to-day as women
    appear to our view?
For the ones in the air are not women, I swear.

---

[1] Strepsiades in the original is probably using genuine quotations from
the effusions of the dithyrambic poets.

SOCRATES: Why, what do they seem then to
    you?

STREPSIADES: I can't say very well, but they straggle and
    swell like fleeces spread out in the air;

Not like women they flit, no, by Zeus, not a bit, but these
    have got noses to wear.

SOCRATES: Well, now then, attend to this question, my
    friend.

STREPSIADES: Look sharp, and propound it to me.

SOCRATES: Didst thou never espy a Cloud in the sky, which
    a centaur or leopard might be,

Or a wolf, or a cow?

STREPSIADES: Very often, I vow: and show me
    the cause, I entreat.

SOCRATES: Why, I tell you that these become just what they
    please, and whenever they happen to meet

One shaggy and wild, like the tangle-haired child of old
    Xenophantes, their rule

Is at once to appear like Centaurs, to jeer the ridiculous
    look of the fool.

STREPSIADES: What then do they do if Simon they view,
    that fraudulent harpy to shame?

SOCRATES: Why, his nature to show to us mortals below, a
    wolfish appearance they frame.

STREPSIADES: O, they then I ween having yesterday seen
    Cleonymus quaking with fear,

(Him who threw off his shield as he fled from the field),
    metamorphosed themselves into deer.

SOCRATES: Yes, and now they espy soft Cleisthenes nigh,
    and therefore as women appear.

STREPSIADES: O then without fail, All hail! and All hail!
    my welcome receive; and reply

With your voices so fine, so grand and divine, majestical
    Queens of the Sky!

CHORUS: Our welcome to thee, old man, who wouldst see
    the marvels that science can show:

And thou, the high-priest of this subtlety feast, say what would
    you have us bestow?

Since there is not a sage for whom we'd engage our wonders
    more freely to do,

Except, it may be, for Prodicus: he for his knowledge may
    claim them, but you,

For that sideways you throw your eyes as you go, and are all
    affectation and fuss;

No shoes will you wear, but assume the grand air on the
    strength of your dealings with us.

STREPSIADES: Oh Earth! what a sound, how august and
    profound! it fills me with wonder and awe.

SOCRATES: These, these then alone, for true Deities own,
the rest are all God-ships of straw.

STREPSIADES: Let Zeus be left out: He's a God beyond
doubt: come, that you can scarcely deny.

SOCRATES: Zeus, indeed! there's no Zeus: don't you be so
obtuse.

STREPSIADES: No Zeus up aloft in the sky!

Then, you first must explain, who it is sends the rain; or I
really must think you are wrong.

SOCRATES: Well then, be it known, these send it alone: I can
prove it by arguments strong.

Was there ever a shower seen to fall in an hour when the sky
was all cloudless and blue?

Yet on a fine day, when the Clouds are away, he might send
one, according to you.

STREPSIADES: Well, it must be confessed, that chimes in
with the rest: your words I am forced to believe.

Yet before, I had dreamed that the rain-water streamed from
Zeus and his chamber-pot sieve.

But whence then, my friend, does the thunder descend? that
does make me quake with affright!

SOCRATES: Why 'tis they, I declare, as they roll through the
air.

STREPSIADES: What the Clouds? did I hear you aright?

SOCRATES: Ay: for when to the brim filled with water they
swim, by Necessity carried along,

They are hung up on high in the vault of the sky, and so by
Necessity strong

In the midst of their course, they clash with great force, and
thunder away without end.

STREPSIADES: But is it not He who compels this to be? does
not Zeus this Necessity send?

SOCRATES: No Zeus have we there, but a Vortex of air.

STREPSIADES: What! Vortex? that's something, I own.

I knew not before, that Zeus was no more, but Vortex was
placed on his throne!

But I have not yet heard to what cause you referred the
thunder's majestical roar.

SOCRATES: Yes, 'tis they, when on high full of water they
fly, and then, as I told you before,

By Compression impelled, as they clash, are compelled a
terrible clatter to make.

STREPSIADES: Come, how can that be? I really don't see.

SOCRATES: Yourself as my proof I will take.

Have you never then eat the broth-puddings you get when
the Panathenaea comes round,

And felt with what might your bowels all night in turbulent
tumult resound?

STREPSIADES: By Apollo, 'tis true, there's a mighty to-do,
and my belly keeps rumbling about;
And the puddings begin to clatter within and kick up a
wonderful rout:
Quite gently at first, papapax, papapax, but soon pappapappax
away,
Till at last, I'll be bound, I can thunder as loud, papapappap-
papappax, as They.
SOCRATES: Shalt thou then a sound so loud and profound
from thy belly diminutive send,
And shall not the high and the infinite Sky go thundering on
without end?
For both, you will find, on an impulse of wind and similar
causes depend.
STREPSIADES: Well, but tell me from Whom comes the bolt
through the gloom, with its awful and terrible flashes;
And wherever it turns, some it singes and burns, and some
it reduces to ashes!
For this 'tis quite plain, let who will send the rain, that Zeus
against perjurers dashes.
SOCRATES: And how, you old fool of a dark-ages school,
and an antediluvian wit,
If the perjured they strike, and not all men alike, have they
never Cleonymus hit?
Then of Simon again, and Theorus explain: known perjurers,
yet they escape.
But he smites his own shrine with his arrows divine, and
"Sunium, Attica's cape,"
And the ancient gnarled oaks: now what prompted those
strokes? *They* never forswore I should say.
STREPSIADES: Can't say that they do: your words appear
true. Whence comes then the thunderbolt, pray?
SOCRATES: When a wind that is dry, being lifted on high,
is suddenly pent into these,
It swells up their skin, like a bladder, within, by Necessity's
changeless decrees:
Till, compressed very tight, it bursts them outright, and away
with an impulse so strong,
That at last by the force and the swing of its course, it takes
fire as it whizzes along.
STREPSIADES: That's exactly the thing that I suffered one
Spring, at the great feast of Zeus, I admit:
I'd a paunch in the pot, but I wholly forgot about making
the safety-valve slit.
So it spluttered and swelled, while the saucepan I held, till
at last with a vengeance it flew:
Took me quite by surprise, dung-bespattered my eyes, and
scalded my face black and blue!

CHORUS: O thou who wouldst fain great wisdom attain, and comest to us in thy need,

All Hellas around shall thy glory resound, such a prosperous life thou shalt lead:

So thou art but endued with a memory good, and accustomed profoundly to think,

And thy soul wilt inure all wants to endure, and from no undertaking to shrink,

And art hardy and bold, to bear up against cold, and with patience a supper thou losest:

Nor too much dost incline to gymnastics and wine, but all lusts of the body refusest:

And esteemest it best, what is always the test of a truly intelligent brain,

To prevail and succeed whensoever you plead, and hosts of tongue-conquests to gain.

STREPSIADES: But as far as a sturdy soul is concerned and a horrible restless care,

And a belly that pines and wears away on the wretchedest, frugalest fare,

You may hammer and strike as long as you like; I am quite invincible there.

SOCRATES: Now then you agree in rejecting with me the Gods you believed in when young,

And *my* creed you'll embrace "*I believe in wide Space, in the Clouds, in the eloquent Tongue.*"

STREPSIADES: If I happened to meet other Gods in the street, I'd show the cold shoulder, I vow.

No libation I'll pour: not one victim more on their altars I'll sacrifice now.

CHORUS: Now be honest and true, and say what we shall do: since you never shall fail of our aid,

If you hold us most dear in devotion and fear, and will ply the philosopher's trade.

STREPSIADES: O Ladies Divine, small ambition is mine: I only most modestly seek,

Out and out for the rest of my life to be best of the children of Hellas to speak.

CHORUS: Say no more of your care, we have granted your prayer: and know from this moment, that none

More acts shall pass through in the People than you: such favour from us you have won.

STREPSIADES: Not acts, if you please: I want nothing of these: this gift you may quickly withdraw;

But I wish to succeed, just enough for my need, and to slip through the clutches of law.

CHORUS: This then you shall do, for your wishes are few: not many nor great your demands,

So away with all care from henceforth, and prepare to be
    placed in our votaries' hands.

    STREPSIADES: This then will I do, confiding in you, for
        Necessity presses me sore,

And so sad is my life, 'twixt my cobs and my wife, that I
    cannot put up with it more.

So now, at your word, I give and afford

My body to these, to treat as they please,

To have and to hold, in squalor, in cold,

In hunger and thirst, yea by Zeus, at the worst,

To be flayed out of shape from my heels to my nape

So along with my hide from my duns I escape,

And to men may appear without conscience or fear,

Bold, hasty, and wise, a concocter of lies,

A rattler to speak, a dodger, a sneak,

A regular claw of the tables of law,

A shuffler complete, well worn in deceit,

A supple, unprincipled, troublesome cheat;

A hang-dog accurst, a bore with the worst,

In the tricks of the jury-courts thoroughly versed.

If all that I meet this praise shall repeat,

Work away as you choose, I will nothing refuse,

Without any reserve, from my head to my shoes.

You shan't see me wince though my gutlets you mince,

And these entrails of mine for a sausage combine,

Served up for the gentlemen students to dine.

    CHORUS: Here's a spirit bold and high Ready-armed for any
        strife.

(*To* STREPSIADES) If you learn what I can teach Of the
    mysteries of speech,

Your glory soon shall reach To the summit of the sky.

    STREPSIADES: And what am I to gain?

    CHORUS: With the Clouds you will
    obtain

The most happy, the most enviable life.

    STREPSIADES: Is it possible for me Such felicity to see?

    CHORUS: Yes, and men shall come and wait In their thou-
        sands at your gate,

        Desiring consultations and advice

On an action or a pleading From the man of light and leading,
    And you'll pocket many talents in a trice.

(*To* SOCRATES) Here, take the old man, and do all that you
    can, your new-fashioned thoughts to instil,

And stir up his mind with your notions refined, and test him
    with judgement and skill.

    SOCRATES: Come now, you tell me something of your
    habits:

For if I don't know them, I can't determine
What engines I must bring to bear upon you.

STREPSIADES: Eh! what? Not going to storm me, by the
    Gods?

SOCRATES: No, no: I want to ask you a few questions.
First: is your memory good?

STREPSIADES: Two ways, by Zeus:
If I'm owed anything, I'm mindful, very:
But if I owe, (Oh, dear!) forgetful, very.

SOCRATES: Well then: have you the gift of speaking in you?

STREPSIADES: The gift of speaking, no: of cheating, yes.

SOCRATES: No? how then can you learn?

STREPSIADES: O, well enough.

SOCRATES: Then when I throw you out some clever notion
About the laws of nature, you must catch it.

STREPSIADES: What! must I snap up sapience, in dog-
    fashion?

SOCRATES: O! why the man's an ignorant old savage:
I fear, my friend, that you'll require the whip.
Come, if one strikes you, what do you do?

STREPSIADES: I'm struck:
Then in a little while I call my witness:
Then in another little while I summon him.

SOCRATES: Put off your cloak.

STREPSIADES: Why, what have I done wrong?

SOCRATES: O, nothing, nothing: all go in here naked.

STREPSIADES: Well, but I have not come with a search-
    warrant.[1]

SOCRATES: Fool! throw it off.

STREPSIADES: Well, tell me this one thing;
If I'm extremely careful and attentive,
Which of your students shall I most resemble?

SOCRATES: Why Chaerephon. You'll be his very image.

STREPSIADES: What! I shall be half-dead! O luckless me!

SOCRATES: Don't chatter there, but come and follow me;
Make haste now, quicker, here.

STREPSIADES: O, but do first
Give me a honeyed cake: Zeus! how I tremble,
To go down there, as if to see Trophonius.[2]

SOCRATES: Go on! why keep you pottering round the door.
(SOCRATES *and* STREPSIADES *go into the Phrontisterion.*)

CHORUS: Yes! go, and farewell; as your courage is great,
So bright be your fate.

---

[1] A searcher for stolen goods had to enter a suspected house stripped of his upper garments, lest he "plant" the thing asserted to be stolen.

[2] Visitors to the oracle of Trophonius took honeyed cakes to appease serpents which haunted the place.

May all good fortune his steps pursue,
　Who now, in his life's dim twilight haze,
Is game such venturesome things to do,
To steep his mind in discoveries new,
　To walk, a novice, in wisdom's ways.

Parabaeis

O Spectators, I will utter honest truths with accents free,
Yea! by mighty Dionysus, Him who bred and nurtured me.
So may I be deemed a poet; and this day obtain the prize,
As till that unhappy blunder I had always held you wise,
And of all my plays esteeming this the wisest and the best,
Served it up for your enjoyment, which had, more than all
　　the rest,
Cost me thought, and time, and labour: then most scandal-
　　ously treated,
I retired in mighty dudgeon, by unworthy foes defeated.
This is why I blame your critics, for whose sake I framed
　　the play:
Yet the clever ones amongst you even now I won't betray.
No! for ever since from judges unto whom 'tis joy to speak,
Brothers Profligate and Modest gained the praise we fondly
　　seek,[1]
When, for I was yet a Virgin, and it was not right to bear,
I exposed it, and Another did the foundling nurse with care,[2]
But 'twas ye who nobly nurtured, ye who brought it up with
　　skill;—
From that hour I proudly cherish pledges of your sure good
　　will.
Now then comes its sister hither, like Electra in the play,[3]
Comes in earnest expectation kindred minds to meet to-day;
She will recognize full surely, if she find, her brother's tress.
And observe how pure her morals: who, to notice first her
　　dress,
Enters not with filthy symbols on her modest garments hung,
Jeering bald-heads, dancing ballets, for the laughter of the
　　young.

[1] Characters in Aristophanes' first (now lost) comedy.

[2] The comedy was produced under another's name.

[3] As Electra in Aeschylus' *Choephoroe* found a lock of her brother's
hair, so may this play find the applause which greeted its predecessor.

In this play no wretched grey-beard with a staff his fellow
    pokes,
So obscuring from the audience all the poorness of his jokes.
No one rushes in with torches, no one groans, *"Oh, dear!*
    Oh, dear!"
Trusting in its genuine merits comes this play before you
    here.
Yet, though such a hero-poet, I, the bald-head, do not grow
Curling ringlets: neither do I twice or thrice my pieces show.
Always fresh ideas sparkle, always novel jests delight,
Nothing like each other, save that all are most exceeding
    bright.
I am he who floored the giant, Cleon, in his hour of pride,
Yet when down I scorned to strike him, and I left him when
    he died!
But the others, when a handle once Hyperbolus did lend,
Trample down the wretched caitiff, and his mother, without
    end.
In his Maricas the Drunkard, Eupolis the charge began,
Shamefully my "Knights" distorting, as he is a shameful man,
Tacking on the tipsy beldame, just the ballet-dance to keep,
Phrynichus's prime invention, eat by monsters of the deep.
Then Hermippus on the caitiff opened all his little skill,
And the rest upon the caitiff are their wit exhausting still;
And my simile to pilfer "of the Eels" they all combine.[1]
Whoso laughs at their productions, let him not delight in
    mine.
But for you who praise my genius, you who think my writings
    clever,
Ye shall gain a name for wisdom, yea! for ever and for ever.
  O mighty God, O heavenly King,
  First unto Thee my prayer I bring,
    O come, Lord Zeus, to my choral song;—
  And Thou, dread Power, whose resistless hand
  Heaves up the sea and the trembling land,
    Lord of the trident, stern and strong;—
  And Thou who sustainest the life of us all
  Come, Ether, our parent, O come to my call;—
  And Thou who floodest the world with light,
  Guiding thy steeds through the glittering sky,
  To men below and to Gods on high
    A Potentate heavenly-bright!

[1] In *The Knights* Aristophanes compares the demagogues troubling
the city with wars, to eel-fishers who can catch nothing while the water
is clear, but when they have troubled the water, then make their catch.

O most sapient wise spectators, hither turn attention due,
We complain of sad ill-treatment, we've a bone to pick with
  you:
We have ever helped your city, helped with all our might and
  main;
Yet you pay us no devotion, that is why we now complain.
We who always watch around you. For if any project seems
Ill-concocted, then we thunder, then the rain comes down in
  streams.
And, remember, very lately, how we knit our brows together,
"Thunders crashing, lightnings flashing," never was such
  awful weather;
And the Moon in haste eclipsed her, and the Sun in anger
  swore
He would curl his wick within him and give light to you no
  more,
Should you choose that mischief-worker, Cleon, whom the
  Gods abhor,
Tanner, Slave, and Paphlagonian, to lead out your hosts to
  war.
Yet you chose him! yet you chose him! For they say that
  Folly grows
Best and finest in this city, but the gracious Gods dispose
Always all things for the better, causing errors to succeed:
And how this sad job may profit, surely he who runs may
  read.
Let the Cormorant be convicted, in command, of bribes and
  theft,
Let us have him gagged and muzzled, in the pillory chained
  and left,
Then again, in ancient fashion, all that ye have erred of late,
Will turn out your own advantage, and a blessing to the State.

"Phoebus, my king, come to me still,"
Thou who holdest the Cynthian hill,
  The lofty peak of the Delian isle;—
And Thou, his sister, to whom each day
Lydian maidens devoutly pray
  In Thy stately gilded Ephesian pile;—
And Athene, our Lady, the queen of us all,
With the Aegis of God, O come to my call;—
And Thou whose dancing torches of pine
Flicker, Parnassian glades along,
Dionysus, Star of Thy Maenad throng,
  Come, Reveller most divine!

We, when we had finished packing, and prepared our journey
  down,

Met the Lady Moon, who charged us with a message for
    your town.
First, All hail to noble Athens, and her faithful true Allies;
Then, she said, your shameful conduct made her angry
    passions rise,
Treating her so ill who always aids you, not in words, but
    clearly;
Saves you, first of all, in torchlight every month a drachma
    nearly,
So that each one says, if business calls him out from home
    by night,
"Buy no link, my boy, this evening, for the Moon will lend
    her light."
Other blessings too she sends you, yet you will not mark your
    days
As she bids you, but confuse them, jumbling them all sorts of
    ways.
And, she says, the Gods in chorus shower reproaches on her
    head,
When in bitter disappointment, they go supperless to bed,
Not obtaining festal banquets duly on the festal day;
Ye are badgering in the law-courts when ye should arise and
    slay!
And full oft when we celestials some strict fast are duly
    keeping,
For the fate of mighty Memnon, or divine Sarpedon weeping,
Then you feast and pour libations: and Hyperbolus of late
Lost the crown he wore so proudly as Recorder of the Gate,
Through the wrath of us immortals: so perchance he'll rather
    know
Always all his days in future by the Lady Moon to go.

(*Enter* SOCRATES, *who has been examining* STREPSIADES *in the Phrontisterion.*)

SOCRATES: Never by Chaos, Air, and Respiration,
Never, no never have I seen a clown
So helpless, and forgetful, and absurd!
Why if he learns a quirk or two he clean
Forgets them ere he has learnt them: all the same,
I'll call him out of doors here to the light.
Take up your bed, Strepsiades, and come!

(*Enter* STREPSIADES.)

STREPSIADES: By Zeus, I can't: the bugs make such re-
    sistance.
SOCRATES: Make haste. There, throw it down, and listen.

STREPSIADES: **Well!**
SOCRATES: Attend to me: what shall I teach you first
That you've not learnt before? Which will you have,
Measures or rhythms or the right use of words?
STREPSIADES: O! measures to be sure: for very lately
A grocer swindled me of full three pints.
SOCRATES: I don't mean that: but which do you like the
    best
Of all the measures; six feet, or eight feet?
STREPSIADES: Well, I like nothing better than the yard.
SOCRATES: Fool! don't talk nonsense.
STREPSIADES: What will you bet me
    now
That two yards don't exactly make six feet?
SOCRATES: Consume you! what an ignorant clown you are!
Still, perhaps you can learn tunes more easily.
STREPSIADES: But will tunes help me to repair my fortunes?
SOCRATES: They'll help you to behave in company:
If you can tell which kind of tune is best
For the sword-dance, and which for finger music.[1]
STREPSIADES: For fingers! aye, but I know that.
SOCRATES: Say on,
    then.
STREPSIADES: What is it but this finger? though before,
Ere this was grown, I used to play with that.
SOCRATES: Insufferable dolt!
STREPSIADES: Well but, you goose,
I don't want to learn this.
SOCRATES: What *do* you want then?
STREPSIADES: Teach me the Logic! teach me the unjust
    Logic!
SOCRATES: But you must learn some other matters first:
As, what are males among the quadrupeds.
STREPSIADES: I should be mad indeed not to know that.
The Ram, the Bull, the Goat, the Dog, the Fowl.
SOCRATES: Ah! there you are! there's a mistake at once!
You call the male and female fowl the same.
STREPSIADES: How! tell me how.
SOCRATES: Why fowl and fowl of
    course.
STREPSIADES: That's true enough! what then shall I say in
    future?
SOCRATES: Call one a fowless and the other a fowl.
STREPSIADES: A fowless? Good! Bravo! Bravo! by Air.

[1] By "finger music" Socrates means a poetic measure, but Strepsiades
interprets him obscenely.

Now for that one bright piece of information
I'll give you a barley bumper in your trough.

SOCRATES: Look there, a fresh mistake; you called it trough,
Masculine, when it's feminine.

STREPSIADES: How, pray?
How did I make it masculine?

SOCRATES: Why "trough,"
Just like "Cleonymus."

STREPSIADES: I don't quite catch it.

SOCRATES: Why "trough," "Cleonymus," both masculine.

STREPSIADES: Ah, but Cleonymus has got no trough,
His bread is kneaded in a rounded mortar:
Still, what must I say in future?

SOCRATES: What! why call it
A "troughess," female, just as one says "an actress."

STREPSIADES: A "troughess," female?

SOCRATES: That's the way to call it.

STREPSIADES: O "troughess" then and Miss Cleonymus.

SOCRATES: Still you must learn some more about these
names;
Which are the names of men and which of women.

STREPSIADES: Oh, I know which are women.

SOCRATES: Well, repeat
some.

STREPSIADES: Demetria, Cleitagora, Philinna.

SOCRATES: Now tell me some men's names.

STREPSIADES: O yes, ten thousand.
Philon, Melesias, Amynias.[1]

SOCRATES: Hold! I said men's names: these are women's
names.

STREPSIADES: No, no, they're men's.

SOCRATES: They are *not* men's, for how
Would you address Amynias if you met him?

STREPSIADES: How? somehow thus: "Here, here, Amynia!"

SOCRATES: Amynia! a woman's name, you see.

STREPSIADES: And rightly too; a sneak who shirks all
service!
But all know this: let's pass to something else.

SOCRATES: Well, then, you get into the bed.

STREPSIADES: And then?

SOCRATES: Excogitate about your own affairs.

---

[1] Aristophanes elsewhere satirizes Amynias' effeminacy. The joke here
is based on the fact that in Greek the vocative of Amynias is Amynia,
a feminine form.

STREPSIADES: Not there: I do beseech, not there: at least
Let me excogitate on the bare ground.
SOCRATES: There is no way but this.
STREPSIADES (*getting into bed*): O luckless me!
How I shall suffer from the bugs to-day.
SOCRATES: Now then survey in every way, with airy judge-
　　　ment sharp and quick:
Wrapping thoughts around yo ι thick:
And if so be in one you stick,
Never stop to toil and bother,
　　Lightly, lightly, lightly leap,
To another, to another;
　　Far away be balmy sleep.
STREPSIADES: Ugh! Ugh! Ugh! Ugh! Ugh!
CHORUS: What's the matter? where's the pain?
STREPSIADES: Friends! I'm dying. From the bed
Out creep bugbears scantly fed
And my ribs they bite in twain,
And my life-blood out they suck,
And my manhood off they pluck,
And my loins they dig and drain,
And I'm dying, once again.
CHORUS: O take not the smart so deeply to heart.
STREPSIADES:　　　　　　　Why, what can I do?
Vanished my skin so ruddy of hue,
Vanished my life-blood, vanished my shoe,
Vanished my purse, and what is still worse
As I hummed an old tune till my watch should be past,
I had very near vanished myself at the last.
SOCRATES: Hallo there, are you pondering?
STREPSIADES:　　　　　　　　　　　Eh! what? I?
Yes to be sure.
SOCRATES:　　　And what have your ponderings come to?
STREPSIADES: Whether these bugs will leave a bit of me.
SOCRATES: Consume you, wretch!
STREPSIADES:　　　　　　　　Faith, I'm consumed al-
　　　ready.
SOCRATES: Come, come, don't flinch: pull up the clothes
　　　again:
Search out and catch some very subtle dodge
To fleece your creditors.
STREPSIADES:　　　　　　　O me, how can I
Fleece any one with all these fleeces on me?

(*Puts his head under the clothes.*)

SOCRATES: Come, let me peep a moment what he's doing.
Hey! he's asleep!

STREPSIADES: No, no! no fear of that!

SOCRATES: Caught anything?

STREPSIADES: No, nothing.

SOCRATES: Surely, something.

STREPSIADES: Well, I had something in my hand, I'll own.

SOCRATES: Pull up the clothes again, and go on pondering.

STREPSIADES: On what? now do please tell me, Socrates.

SOCRATES: What is it that you want? first tell me that.

STREPSIADES: You have heard a million times what 'tis I
want:

My debts! my debts! I want to shirk my debts.

SOCRATES: Come, come, pull up the clothes: refine your
thoughts

With subtle wit: look at the case on all sides:

Mind you divide correctly.

STREPSIADES: Ugh! O me.

SOCRATES: Hush: if you meet with any difficulty

Leave it a moment: then return again

To the same thought: then lift and weigh it well.

STREPSIADES: O, here, dear Socrates!

SOCRATES: Well, my old friend.

STREPSIADES: I've found a notion how to shirk my debts.

SOCRATES: Well then, propound it.

STREPSIADES: What do you think of
this?

Suppose I hire some grand Thessalian witch

To conjure down the Moon, and then I take it

And clap it into some round helmet-box,

And keep it fast there, like a looking-glass,—

SOCRATES: But what's the use of that?

STREPSIADES: The use, quotha:

Why if the Moon should never rise again,

I'd never pay one farthing.

SOCRATES: No! why not?

STREPSIADES: Why, don't we pay our interest by the month?

SOCRATES: Good! now I'll proffer you another problem.

Suppose an action: damages, five talents:

Now tell me how you can evade that same.

STREPSIADES: How! how! can't say at all: but I'll go seek.

SOCRATES: Don't wrap your mind for ever round yourself,

But let your thoughts range freely through the air,

Like chafers with a thread about their feet.

STREPSIADES: I've found a bright evasion of the action:

Confess yourself, 'tis glorious.

SOCRATES: But what is it?

STREPSIADES: I say, haven't you seen in druggists' shops

That stone, that splendidly transparent stone,

By which they kindle fire?

SOCRATES: The burning glass?

STREPSIADES: That's it: well then, I'd get me one of these,
And as the clerk was entering down my case,
I'd stand, like this, some distance towards the sun,
And burn out every line.

SOCRATES: By the Three Graces,
A clever dodge!

STREPSIADES: O me, how pleased I am
To have a debt like that clean blotted out.

SOCRATES: Come, then, make haste and snap up this.

STREPSIADES: Well, what?

SOCRATES: How to prevent an adversary's suit
Supposing you were sure to lose it; tell me.

STREPSIADES: O, nothing easier.

SOCRATES: How, pray?

STREPSIADES: Why thus,
While there was yet one trial intervening,
Ere mine was cited, I'd go hang myself.

SOCRATES: Absurd!

STREPSIADES: No, by the Gods, it isn't though:
They could not prosecute me were I dead.

SOCRATES: Nonsense! Be off: I'll try no more to teach you.

STREPSIADES: Why not? do, please: now, please do, Socrates.

SOCRATES: Why you forget all that you learn, directly.
Come, say what you learnt first: there's a chance for you.

STREPSIADES: Ah! what was first?—Dear me: whatever was
    it?—
Whatever's that we knead the barley in?—
Bless us, what was it?

SOCRATES: Be off, and feed the crows,
You most forgetful, most absurd old dolt!

STREPSIADES: O me! what will become of me, poor wretch!
I'm clean undone: I haven't learnt to speak.—
O gracious Clouds, now do advise me something.

CHORUS: Our counsel, ancient friend, is simply this,
To send your son, if you have one at home,
And let him learn this wisdom in your stead.

STREPSIADES: Yes! I've a son, quite a fine gentleman:
But he won't learn, so what am I to do?

CHORUS: What! is he master?

STREPSIADES: Well: he's strong and vigorous,
And he's got some of the Coesyra blood within him:[1]
Still I'll go for him, and if he won't come
By all the Gods I'll turn him out of doors.

[1] Pheidippides inherited lofty notions from his mother's side.

Go in one moment, I'll be back directly.

(STREPSIADES *goes into his house.*)

CHORUS: Dost thou not see how bounteous we our favours
    free
    Will shower on you,
Since whatsoe'er your will prepare
    This dupe will do.
But now that you have dazzled and elated so your man,
Make haste and seize whate'er you please as quickly as you
    can,
For cases such as these, my friend, are very prone to change
    and bend.

(*Exit* SOCRATES *into Phrontisterion. Enter* STREPSIADES *and*
PHEIDIPPIDES.)

STREPSIADES: Get out! you shan't stop here: so help me Mist!
Be off, and eat up Megacles's columns.
    PHEIDIPPIDES: How now, my father? what's i'the wind
    to-day?
You're wandering; by Olympian Zeus, you are.
    STREPSIADES: Look there! Olympian Zeus! you blockhead
    you,
Come to *your* age, and yet believe in Zeus!
    PHEIDIPPIDES: Why prithee, what's the joke?
    STREPSIADES: 'Tis so preposterous
When babes like you hold antiquated notions.
But come and I'll impart a thing or two,
A wrinkle, making you a man indeed.
But, mind: don't whisper this to any one.
    PHEIDIPPIDES: Well, what's the matter?
    STREPSIADES: Didn't you swear by Zeus?
    PHEIDIPPIDES: I did.
    STREPSIADES: See now, how good a thing is learning.
There is no Zeus, Pheidippides.
    PHEIDIPPIDES: Who then?
    STREPSIADES: Why Vortex reigns, and he has turned out
    Zeus.
    PHEIDIPPIDES: Oh me, what stuff.
    STREPSIADES: Be sure that this is so.
    PHEIDIPPIDES: Who says so, pray?
    STREPSIADES: The Melian—Socrates,
And Chaerephon, who knows about the flea-tracks.
    PHEIDIPPIDES: And are you come to such a pitch of madness
As to put faith in brain-struck men?
    STREPSIADES: O hush!

See P 30

And don't blaspheme such very dexterous men
And sapient too: men of such frugal habits
They never shave, nor use your precious ointment,
Nor go to baths to clean themselves: but you
Have taken *me* for a corpse and cleaned me out.
Come, come, make haste, do go and learn for me.

PHEIDIPPIDES: What can one learn from them that is worth
knowing?

STREPSIADES: Learn! why whatever's clever in the world:
And you shall learn how gross and dense you are.
But stop one moment: I'll be back directly. (*He leaves.*)

PHEIDIPPIDES: O me! what must I do with my mad father?
Shall I indict him for his lunacy,
Or tell the undertakers of his symptoms?

(STREPSIADES *returns with a cock and a hen.*)

STREPSIADES: Now then! you see this, don't you? what do you
call it?

PHEIDIPPIDES: That? why a fowl.

STREPSIADES: Good! now then, what is this?

PHEIDIPPIDES: That's a fowl too.

STREPSIADES: What both! Ridiculous!
Never say that again, but mind you always
Call this a fowless and the other a fowl.

PHEIDIPPIDES: A fowless! These then are the mighty secrets
You have picked up amongst those earth-born fellows.

STREPSIADES: And lots besides: but everything I learn
I straight forget: I am so old and stupid.

PHEIDIPPIDES: And this is what you have lost your mantle
for?

STREPSIADES: It's very absent sometimes: 'tisn't lost.

PHEIDIPPIDES: And what have you done with your shoes, you
dotard you!

STREPSIADES: Like Pericles, all for the best, I've lost them.[1]
Come, come; go with me: humour me in this,
And then do what you like. Ah! I remember
How I to humour you, a coaxing baby,
With the first obol which my judgeship fetched me
Bought you a go-cart at the great Diasia.[2]

PHEIDIPPIDES: The time will come when you'll repent of this.

(*Enter* SOCRATES.)

STREPSIADES: Good boy to obey me. Hallo! Socrates.

See p 39

[1] Pericles (*c.* 445 B.C.) vaguely accounted for an expenditure as "all
for the best."
[2] A festival.

Come here; come here; I've brought this son of mine,
Trouble enough, I'll warrant you.

SOCRATES: Poor infant
Not yet aware of my suspension-wonders.

PHEIDIPPIDES: You'd make a wondrous piece of ware, suspended.

STREPSIADES: Hey! Hang the lad! Do you abuse the Master?

SOCRATES: And look, "suthspended!" In what foolish fashion
He mouthed the word with pouting lips agape.
How can *he* learn evasion of a suit,
Timely citation, damaging replies?
Hyperbolus, though, learnt them for a talent.

STREPSIADES: O never fear! he's very sharp, by nature.
For when he was a little chap, *so* high,
He used to build small baby-houses, boats,
Go-carts of leather, darling little frogs
Carved from pomegranates, you can't think how nicely!
So now, I prithee, teach him both your Logics,
The Better, as you call it, and the Worse
Which with the worse cause can defeat the Better;
Or if not both, at all events the Worse.

SOCRATES: Aye, with his own ears he shall hear them argue.
I shan't be there.

STREPSIADES: But please remember this,
Give him the knack of reasoning down all Justice.

(*Exit* SOCRATES; *enter* RIGHT LOGIC *and* WRONG LOGIC.)

RIGHT LOGIC: Come show yourself now with your confident
brow.
—To the stage, if you dare!

WRONG LOGIC: "Lead on where you please:" I shall smash
you with ease,
If an audience be there.

RIGHT LOGIC: *You'll* smash me, you say! And who are *you,*
pray?

WRONG LOGIC: A Logic, like you.

RIGHT LOGIC: But the Worst of the two.

WRONG LOGIC: Yet you I can drub whom my Better they
dub.

RIGHT LOGIC: By what artifice taught?

WRONG LOGIC: By original thought.

RIGHT LOGIC: Aye truly your trade so successful is made
By means of these noodles of ours, I'm afraid.

WRONG LOGIC: Not noodles, but wise.

RIGHT LOGIC: I'll smash you and your lies!

WRONG LOGIC: By what method, forsooth?

RIGHT LOGIC: By speaking the Truth.
WRONG LOGIC: Your words I will meet, and entirely defeat:
There never *was* Justice or Truth, I repeat.
RIGHT LOGIC: No Justice! you say?
WRONG LOGIC: Well, where does it stay?
RIGHT LOGIC: With the Gods in the air.
WRONG LOGIC: If Justice be there,
How comes it that Zeus could his father reduce,
Yet live with their Godships unpunished and loose?
RIGHT LOGIC: Ugh! Ugh! These evils come thick, I feel
     awfully sick,
A basin, quick, quick!
WRONG LOGIC: You're a useless old drone with one foot in
     the grave!
RIGHT LOGIC: You're a shameless, unprincipled, dissolute
     knave!
WRONG LOGIC: Hey! a rosy festoon.
RIGHT LOGIC: And a vulgar buffoon!
WRONG LOGIC: What! Lilies from *you?*
RIGHT LOGIC: And a parricide too!
WRONG LOGIC: 'Tis with gold (you don't know it) you
     sprinkle my head.
RIGHT LOGIC: O gold is it now? but it used to be lead!
WRONG LOGIC: But now it's a grace and a glory instead.
RIGHT LOGIC: You're a little too bold.
WRONG LOGIC: You're a good deal too old.
RIGHT LOGIC: 'Tis through you I well know not a stripling
     will go
To attend to the rules which are taught in the Schools;
But Athens one day shall be up to the fools.
WRONG LOGIC: How squalid your dress!
RIGHT LOGIC: Yours is fine, I confess,
Yet of old, I declare, but a pauper you were;
And passed yourself off, our compassion to draw
     As a Telephus, (Euripidéan)[1]
Well pleased from a beggarly wallet to gnaw
     At inanities Pandeletéan.
WRONG LOGIC: O me! for the wisdom you've mentioned in
     jest!
RIGHT LOGIC: O me! for the folly of you, and the rest
Who you to destroy their children employ!
WRONG LOGIC: *Him* you never shall teach; you are quite out
     of date.
RIGHT LOGIC: If not, he'll be lost, as he'll find to his cost:

[1] Euripides' Telephus was a beggar; Aristophanes accuses Euripides of plagiarizing lines from Pandeletus.

Taught nothing by you but to chatter and prate.

    WRONG LOGIC: He raves, as you see: let him be, let him be.

    RIGHT LOGIC: Touch him if you dare! I bid you beware.

    CHORUS: Forbear, forbear to wrangle and scold!
      Each of you show
You what you taught their fathers of old,
    You let us know
Your system untried, that hearing each side
From the lips of the Rivals the youth may decide
    To which of your schools he will go.

    RIGHT LOGIC: This then will I do.

    WRONG LOGIC: And so will I too.

    CHORUS: And who will put in his claim to begin?

    WRONG LOGIC: If *he* wishes, he may: I kindly give way:
And out of his argument quickly will I
Draw facts and devices to fledge the reply
Wherewith I will shoot him and smite and refute him.
And at last if a word from his mouth shall be heard
My sayings like fierce savage hornets shall pierce
    His forehead and eyes,
Till in fear and distraction he yields and he—dies!

    CHORUS: With thoughts and words and maxims pondered
      well
    Now then in confidence let both begin:
Try which his rival can in speech excel:
    Try which this perilous wordy war can win,
Which all my votaries' hopes are fondly centred in.
O Thou who wert born our sires to adorn with characters
    blameless and fair,
Say on what you please, say on and to these your glorious
    Nature declare.

    RIGHT LOGIC: To hear then prepare of the Discipline rare
    which flourished in Athens of yore
When Honour and Truth were in fashion with youth and
    Sobriety bloomed on our shore;
First of all the old rule was preserved in our school that
    "boys should be seen and not heard:"
And then to the home of the Harpist would come decorous
    in action and word
All the lads of one town, though the snow peppered down,
    in spite of all wind and all weather:
And they sang an old song as they paced it along, not
    shambling with thighs glued together:
"O the dread shout of War how it peals from afar," or
    "Pallas the Stormer adore,"
To some manly old air all simple and bare which their fathers
    had chanted before.

And should any one dare the tune to impair and with intricate
    twistings to fill,
Such as Phrynis is fain, and his long-winded train, perversely
    to quaver and trill,
Many stripes would he feel in return for his zeal, as to
    genuine Music a foe.
And every one's thigh was forward and high as they sat to
    be drilled in a row,
So that nothing the while indecent or vile the eye of a stranger
    might meet;
And then with their hand they would smooth down the sand
    whenever they rose from their seat,
To leave not a trace of themselves in the place for a vigilant
    lover to view.
They never would soil their persons with oil but were in-
    artificial and true.
Nor tempered their throat to a soft mincing note and sighs to
    their lovers addressed:
Nor laid themselves out, as they strutted about, to the wanton
    desires of the rest:
Nor would any one dare such stimulant fare as the head
    of the radish to wish:
Nor to make over bold with the food of the old, the anise,
    and parsley, and fish:
Nor dainties to quaff, nor giggle and laugh, nor foot within
    foot to enfold.
    WRONG LOGIC: Faugh! this smells very strong of some musty
    old song, and Chirrupers mounted in gold;[1]
And Slaughter of beasts, and old-fashioned feasts.
    RIGHT LOGIC: Yet these are the precepts which taught
The heroes of old to be hardy and bold, and the Men who
    at Marathon fought!
But now must the lad from his boyhood be clad in a Man's
    all-enveloping cloak:
So that, oft as the Panathenaea returns, I feel myself ready
    to choke
When the dancers go by with their shields to their thigh, not
    caring for Pallas a jot.
You therefore, young man, choose me while you can; cast in
    with my Method your lot;
And then you shall learn the forum to spurn, and from dis-
    solute baths to abstain,
And fashions impure and shameful abjure, and scorners
    repel with disdain:

---

[1] "Chirrupers" were golden grasshoppers worn in the hair of Athenians of a previous age.

And rise from your chair if an elder be there, and respect-
fully give him your place,
And with love and with fear your parents revere, and shrink
from the brand of Disgrace,
And deep in your breast be the Image imprest of Modesty,
simple and true,
Nor resort any more to a dancing-girl's door, nor glance at
the harlotry crew,
Lest at length by the blow of the Apple they throw from the
hopes of your Manhood you fall.[1]
Nor dare to reply when your Father is nigh, nor "musty old
Japhet" to call
In your malice and rage that Sacred Old Age which lovingly
cherished your youth!
   WRONG LOGIC: Yes, yes, my young friend, if to him you
attend, by Bacchus I swear of a truth
You will scarce with the sty of Hippocrates vie, as a mammy-
suck known even there!
   RIGHT LOGIC: But then you'll excel in the games you love
well, all blooming, athletic and fair:
Not learning to prate as your idlers debate with marvellous
prickly dispute,
Nor dragged into Court day by day to make sport in some
small disagreeable suit:
But you will below to the Academe go, and under the olives
contend
With your chaplet of reed, in a contest of speed with some
excellent rival and friend:
All fragrant with woodbine and peaceful content, and the leaf
which the lime blossoms fling,
When the plane whispers love to the elm in the grove in the
beautiful season of Spring.
If then you'll obey and do what I say,
And follow with me the more excellent way,
Your chest shall be white, your skin shall be bright,
Your arms shall be tight, your tongue shall be slight,
And everything else shall be proper and right.
But if you pursue what men nowadays do,
You will have, to begin, a cold pallid skin,
Arms small and chest weak, tongue practised to speak,
Special laws very long, and the symptoms all strong
Which show that your life is licentious and wrong.
And your mind he'll prepare so that foul to be fair
And fair to be foul you shall always declare;
And you'll find yourself soon, if you listen to him,
With the filth of Antimachus filled to the brim!

---

[1] Throwing an apple was a love-challenge.

CHORUS: O glorious Sage! with loveliest Wisdom teeming!
    Sweet on thy words does ancient Virtue rest!
Thrice happy they who watched thy Youth's bright beaming!
    Thou of the vaunted genius, do thy best;
This man has gained applause: His Wisdom stands confest.
And you with clever words and thoughts must needs your
    case adorn
Else he will surely win the day, and you retreat with scorn.

WRONG LOGIC: Aye, say you so? why I have been half-burst;
    I do so long
To overthrow his arguments with arguments more strong.
I am the Lesser Logic? True: these Schoolmen call me so,
Simply because I was the first of all mankind to show
How old established rules and laws might contradicted be:
And this, as you may guess, is worth a thousand pounds to
    me,

Sophist

To take the feebler cause, and yet to win the disputation.
And mark me now, how I'll confute his boasted Education!
You said that always from warm baths the stripling must
    abstain:
Why must he? on what grounds do you of these warm baths
    complain?

RIGHT LOGIC: Why it's the worst thing possible, it quite un-
    strings a man.

WRONG LOGIC: Hold there: I've got you round the waist:
    escape me if you can.
And first: of all the sons of Zeus which think you was the
    best?
Which was the manliest? which endured more toils than all
    the rest?

RIGHT LOGIC: Well, I suppose that Heracles was bravest and
    most bold.

WRONG LOGIC: And are the baths of Heracles so wonder-
    fully cold?
Aha! you blame warm baths, I think.

RIGHT LOGIC: This, this is what they say:
This is the stuff our precious youths are chattering all the day!
This is what makes them haunt the baths, and shun the
    manlier Games!

WRONG LOGIC: Well then, we'll take the Forum next: I
    praise it, and he blames.
But if it *was* so bad, do you think old Homer would have
    made
Nestor and all his worthies ply a real forensic trade?
Well: then he says a stripling's tongue should always idle be:
I say it should be used of course: so there we disagree.
And next he says you must be chaste. A most preposterous
    plan!

Come, tell me did you ever know one single blessed man
Gain the least good by chastity? come, prove I'm wrong:
  make haste.

RIGHT LOGIC: Yes, many, many! Peleus gained a sword by
  being chaste.

WRONG LOGIC: A sword indeed! a wondrous meed the unlucky fool obtained.
Hyperbolus the Lamp-maker hath many a talent gained
By knavish tricks which I have taught: but not a sword,
  no, no!

RIGHT LOGIC: Then Peleus did to his chaste life the bed of
  Thetis owe.

WRONG LOGIC: And then she cut and ran away! for nothing
  so engages
A woman's heart as forward warmth, old shred of those dark
  Ages!
For take this chastity, young man: sift it inside and out:
Count all the pleasures, all the joys, it bids you live without:
No kind of dames, no kind of games, no laughing, feasting,
  drinking,—
Why life itself is little worth without these joys, I'm thinking.
Well I must notice now the wants by Nature's self implanted;
You love, seduce, you can't help that, you're caught, con-
  victed. Granted.
You're done for; you can't say one word: while if you follow
  me
Indulge your genius, laugh and quaff, hold nothing base to be.
Why if you're in adultery caught, your pleas will still be
  ample:
You've done no wrong, you'll say, and then bring Zeus as
  your example.
He fell before the wondrous powers by Love and Beauty
  wielded:
And how can you, the Mortal, stand, where He, the Immortal,
  yielded?

RIGHT LOGIC: Aye, but suppose in spite of all, he must be
  wedged and sanded: [1]
Won't he be probed, or else can you prevent it? now be candid.

WRONG LOGIC: And what's the damage if it should be so?

RIGHT LOGIC: What greater damage can the young man
  know?

WRONG LOGIC: What will you do, if this dispute I win?

RIGHT LOGIC: I'll be for ever silent.

WRONG LOGIC: Good, begin.

[1] Punishments for adulterers.

The Counsellor: from whence comes he?
RIGHT LOGIC: From probed adulterers.
WRONG LOGIC: I agree.
The Tragic Poets: whence are they?
RIGHT LOGIC: From probed adulterers.
WRONG LOGIC: So I say.
The Orators: what class of men?
RIGHT LOGIC: All probed adulterers.
WRONG LOGIC: Right again.
You feel your error, I'll engage,
But look once more around the stage,
Survey the audience, which they be,
Probed or not Probed.
RIGHT LOGIC: I see, I see.
WRONG LOGIC: Well, give your verdict.
RIGHT LOGIC: It must go
For probed adulterers: him I know,
And him, and him: the Probed are most.
WRONG LOGIC: How stand we then?
RIGHT LOGIC: I own, I've lost.
O Cinaeds, Cinaeds, take my robe!
Your words have won, to you I run
To live and die with glorious Probe!

(*The two* LOGICS *go out.* SOCRATES *enters from the Phrontisterion;* STREPSIADES *enters from his own house to see how his son's education is progressing.*)

SOCRATES: Well, what do you want? to take away your son
At once, or shall I teach him how to speak?
STREPSIADES: Teach him, and flog him, and be sure you well
Sharpen his mother wit, grind the one edge
Fit for my little law-suits, and the other
Why make that serve for more important matters.
SOCRATES: O, never fear! He'll make a splendid sophist.
STREPSIADES: Well, well, I hope he'll be a poor pale rascal.

(*Exeunt* SOCRATES *and* STREPSIADES. *The following Chorus represents a period long enough for* PHEIDIPPIDES *to have gone through the entire course of training.*)

CHORUS: Go: but in us the thought is strong, you will repent
of this ere long.
Now we wish to tell the Judges all the blessings they shall gain
If, as Justice plainly warrants, we the worthy prize obtain.
First, whenever in the Season ye would fain your fields renew,
All the world shall wait expectant till we've poured our rain
on you:

Then of all your crops and vineyards we will take the utmost
    care
So that neither drought oppress them, nor the heavy rain
    impair.
But if any one amongst you dare to treat our claims with scorn,
Mortal he, the Clouds immortal, better had he ne'er been born!
He from his estates shall gather neither corn, nor oil, nor wine,
For whenever blossoms sparkle on the olive or the vine
They shall all at once be blighted: we will ply our slings
    so true.
And if ever we behold him building up his mansions new,
With our tight and nipping hailstones we will all his tiles
    destroy.
But if he, his friends or kinsfolk, would a marriage-feast enjoy,
All night long we'll pour in torrents, so perchance he'll rather
    pray
To endure the drought of Egypt, than decide amiss today!

(STREPSIADES *comes out of his house.*)

STREPSIADES: The fifth, the fourth, the third, and then the
    second,
And then that day which more than all the rest
I loathe and shrink from and abominate,
Then comes at once that hateful Old-and-New day.[1]
And every single blessed dun has sworn
He'll stake his gage, and ruin and destroy me.
And when I make a modest small request,
"O my good friend, part don't exact at present,
And part defer, and part remit," they swear
So they shall never touch it, and abuse me
As a rank swindler, threatening me with actions.
Now let them bring their actions! Who's afraid?
Not I: if these have taught my son to speak.
But here's the door: I'll knock and soon find out.
Boy! Ho there, boy!

(*Enter* SOCRATES.)

SOCRATES: I clasp Strepsiades.
STREPSIADES: And I clasp you: but take this meal-bag first.
'Tis meet and right to glorify one's Tutors.
But tell me, tell me, has my son yet learnt
That Second Logic which he saw just now?
SOCRATES: He hath.
STREPSIADES: Hurrah! great Sovereign Knavery!
SOCRATES: You may escape whatever suit you please.
STREPSIADES: What, if I borrowed before witnesses?

---

[1] The last day of the month, when debts were due.

SOCRATES: Before a thousand, and the more the merrier.
STREPSIADES: "Then shall my song be loud and deep."
Weep, obol-weighers, weep, weep, weep,
Ye, and your principals, and compound interests,
For ye shall never pester me again.
Such a son have I bred,
(He is within this door),
Born to inspire my foemen with dread,
Born his old father's house to restore:
Keen and polished of tongue is he,
He my Champion and Guard shall be,
He will set his old father free,
Run you, and call him forth to me.
"O my child! O my sweet! come out, I entreat;
'Tis the voice" of your sire.

(*Enter* PHEIDIPPIDES.)

SOCRATES: Here's the man you require.
STREPSIADES: Joy, joy of my heart!
SOCRATES: Take your son and depart.
STREPSIADES: O come, O come, my son, my son,
O dear! O dear!
O joy, to see your beautiful complexion!
Aye now you have an aspect Negative
And Disputative, and our native query
Shines forth there "What d'ye say?" You've the true face
Which rogues put on, of injured innocence.
You have the regular Attic look about you.
So now, you save me, for 'twas you undid me.
PHEIDIPPIDES: What is it ails you?
STREPSIADES: Why the Old-and-New day.
PHEIDIPPIDES: And is there such a day as Old-and-New?
STREPSIADES: Yes: that's the day they mean to stake their
gages.
PHEIDIPPIDES: They'll lose them if they stake them. What!
do you think
That one day can be two days, both together?
STREPSIADES: Why, can't it be so?
PHEIDIPPIDES: Surely not; or else
A woman might at once be old and young.
STREPSIADES: Still, the law says so.
PHEIDIPPIDES: True: but I believe
They don't quite understand it.
STREPSIADES: You explain it.
PHEIDIPPIDES: Old Solon had a democratic turn.
STREPSIADES: Well, but that's nothing to the Old-and-New.
PHEIDIPPIDES: Hence then he fixed that summonses be issued

For these two days, the old one and the new one,
So that the gage be staked on the New-month.

STREPSIADES: What made him add "the old" then?
PHEIDIPPIDES: I will tell you.
He wished the litigants to meet on *that* day
And compromise their quarrels: if they could not,
Then let them fight it out on the New-month.

STREPSIADES: Why then do Magistrates receive the stakes
On the Old-and-New instead of the New-month?
PHEIDIPPIDES: Well, I believe they act like the Foretasters.
They wish to bag the gage as soon as possible,
And thus they gain a whole day's foretaste of it.

STREPSIADES: Aha! poor dupes, why sit ye mooning there,
Game for us Artful Dodgers, you dull stones,
You ciphers, lambkins, butts piled up together!
O! my success inspires me, and I'll sing
Glad eulogies on me and thee, my son.
   "*Man, most blessed, most divine,*
      What a wondrous wit is thine,
      What a son to grace thy line,"
      Friends and neighbors day by day
            Thus will say,
When with envious eyes my suits they see you win:
But first I'll feast you, so come in, my son, come in.

(STREPSIADES *and* PHEIDIPPIDES *re-enter their house. Enter*
PASIAS, *a creditor, and a* WITNESS.)

PASIAS: What! must a man lose his own property!
No: never, never. Better have refused
With a bold face, than be so plagued as this.
See! to get paid my own just debts, I'm forced
To drag you to bear witness, and what's worse
I needs must quarrel with my townsman here.
Well, I won't shame my country, while I live,
I'll go to law, I'll summon him.

(*Enter* STREPSIADES.)

STREPSIADES: Hallo!
PASIAS: To the next Old-and-New.
STREPSIADES: Bear witness, all!
He named two days. You'll summon me; what for?
PASIAS: The fifty pounds I lent you when you bought
That iron-grey.
STREPSIADES: Just listen to the fellow!
The whole world knows that I detest all horses.
PASIAS: I swear you swore by all the Gods to pay me.

Logic and religion joined through money

STREPSIADES: Well, now I swear I won't: Pheidippides
Has learnt since then the unanswerable Logic.

PASIAS: And will you therefore shirk my just demand?

STREPSIADES: Of course I will: else why should he have
    learnt it?

PASIAS: And will you dare forswear it by the Gods?

STREPSIADES: The Gods indeed! What Gods?

PASIAS: Poseidon, Hermes, Zeus.

STREPSIADES: By Zeus I would,
Though I gave twopence halfpenny for the privilege.

PASIAS: O then confound you for a shameless rogue!

STREPSIADES: Hallo! this butt should be rubbed down with
    salt.

PASIAS: Zounds! you deride me!

STREPSIADES: Why 'twill hold four gallons.

PASIAS: You 'scape me not, by Mighty Zeus, and all
The Gods!

STREPSIADES: I wonderfully like the Gods;
An oath by Zeus is sport to knowing ones.

PASIAS: Sooner or later you'll repent of this.
Come do you mean to pay your debts or don't you?
Tell me, and I'll be off.

STREPSIADES: Now do have patience;
I'll give you a clear answer in one moment.

PASIAS: What do you think he'll do?

WITNESS: I think he'll pay you.

STREPSIADES: Where is that horrid dun? O here: now tell me
What you call this.

PASIAS: What I call that? a trough.

STREPSIADES: Heavens! what a fool: and do *you* want your
    money?
I'd never pay one penny to a fellow
Who calls my troughess, trough. So there's your answer.

PASIAS: Then you won't pay me?

STREPSIADES: No, not if I know it.
Come put your best foot forward, and be off:
March off, I say, this instant!

PASIAS: May I die
If I don't go at once and stake my gage!

STREPSIADES: No don't: the fifty pounds are loss enough:
And really on my word I would not wish you
To lose this too just for one silly blunder.

(*Exeunt* PASIAS *and* WITNESS.)

AMYNIAS (*Off stage*): Ah me! Oh! Oh! Oh!

STREPSIADES: Hallo! who's that making that horrible noise?

Not one of Carcinus's snivelling Gods?

AMYNIAS (*Entering with a limp*): Who cares to know what
    I am? what imports it?
An ill-starred man.

STREPSIADES: Then keep it to yourself.

AMYNIAS: "O heavy fate!" "O Fortune, thou hast broken
My chariot wheels!" "Thou hast undone me, Pallas!"

STREPSIADES: How! has Tlepolemus been at you, man?

AMYNIAS: Jeer me not, friend, but tell your worthy son
To pay me back the money which I lent him:
I'm in a bad way and the times are pressing.

STREPSIADES: What money do you mean?

AMYNIAS: Why what he borrowed.

STREPSIADES: You *are* in a bad way, I really think.

AMYNIAS: Driving my four-wheel out I fell, by Zeus.

STREPSIADES: You rave as if you'd fall'n times out-of-mind.

AMYNIAS: I rave? how so? I only claim my own.

STREPSIADES: You can't be quite right, surely.

AMYNIAS: Why what mean you?

STREPSIADES: I shrewdly guess your brain's received a shake.

AMYNIAS: I shrewdly guess that you'll receive a summons
If you don't pay my money.

STREPSIADES: Well then tell me,
Which theory do you side with, that the rain
Falls fresh each time, or that the Sun draws back
The same old rain, and sends it down again?

AMYNIAS: I'm very sure I neither know nor care.

STREPSIADES: Not care! good heavens! And do *you* claim
    your money,
So unenlightened in the Laws of Nature?

AMYNIAS: If you're hard up then, pay me back the Interest
At least.

STREPSIADES: Int-er-est? what kind of a beast is that?

AMYNIAS: What else than day by day and month by month
Larger and larger still the silver grows
As time sweeps by.

STREPSIADES: Finely and nobly said.
What then! think you the Sea is larger now
Than 'twas last year?

AMYNIAS: No surely, 'tis no larger:
It is not right it should be.

STREPSIADES: And do you then,
Insatiable grasper! when the Sea,
Receiving all these Rivers, grows no larger,
Do you desire your silver to grow larger?
Come now, you prosecute your journey off!
Here, fetch the whip.

AMYNIAS: Bear witness, I appeal.
STREPSIADES: Be off! what won't you? Gee up, sigma-brand!
AMYNIAS: I say! a clear assault!
STREPSIADES: You won't be off?
I'll stimulate you; Zeus! I'll goad your haunches.
Aha! you run: I thought I'd stir you up
You and your phaetons, and wheels, and all!

(*Exit* AMYNIAS; STREPSIADES *departs to the feast celebrating his son's ability to "reason down all justice.*")

CHORUS: What a thing it is to long for matters which are
    wrong!
    For you see how this old man
    Is seeking, if he can
    His creditors trepan:
    And I confidently say
    That he will this very day
        Such a blow
Amid his prosperous cheats receive, that he will deeply
        deeply grieve.
    For I think that he has won what he wanted for his son,
    And the lad has learned the way
    All justice to gainsay,
    Be it what or where it may:
    That he'll trump up any tale,
    Right or wrong, and so prevail.
        This I know.
Yea! and perchance the time will come when he shall wish
    his son were dumb.

(*Enter* STREPSIADES, *followed by* PHEIDIPPIDES.)

STREPSIADES: Oh! Oh!
Help! Murder! Help! O neighbours, kinsfolk, townsmen,
Help, one and all, against this base assault,
Ah! Ah! my cheek! my head! O luckless me!
Wretch! do you strike your father?
PHEIDIPPIDES: Yes, Papa.
STREPSIADES: See! See! he owns he struck me.
PHEIDIPPIDES: To be sure.
STREPSIADES: Scoundrel! and parricide! and house-breaker!
PHEIDIPPIDES: Thank you: go on, go on: do please go on.
I am quite delighted to be called such names!
STREPSIADES: O probed Adulterer.
PHEIDIPPIDES: Roses from your lips.
STREPSIADES: Strike you your father?
PHEIDIPPIDES: O dear yes: what's more,

I'll prove I struck you justly.

STREPSIADES: Struck me justly!

Villain! how can you strike a father justly?

PHEIDIPPIDES: Yes, and I'll demonstrate it, if you please.

STREPSIADES: Demonstrate this?

PHEIDIPPIDES: O yes, quite easily.

Come, take your choice, which Logic do you choose?

STREPSIADES: Which what?

PHEIDIPPIDES: .   Logic: the Better or the Worse?

STREPSIADES: Ah, then, in very truth I've had you taught
To reason down all Justice, if you think
You can prove this, that it is just and right
That fathers should be beaten by their sons!

PHEIDIPPIDES: Well, well, I think I'll prove it, if you'll listen,
So that even you won't have one word to answer.

STREPSIADES: Come, I should like to hear what you've
    to say.

CHORUS: 'Tis yours, old man, some method to contrive
    This fight to win:
He would not without arms wherewith to strive
    So bold have been.
    He knows, be sure, whereon to trust.
    His eager bearing proves he must.

So come and tell us from what cause this sad dispute began;
Come, tell us how it first arose: do tell us if you can.

STREPSIADES: Well from the very first I will the whole con-
    tention show:
'Twas when I went into the house to feast him, as you know,
I bade him bring his lyre and sing, the supper to adorn,
Some lay of old Simonides, as, how the Ram was shorn:
But he replied, to sing at meals was coarse and obsolete;
Like some old beldame humming airs the while she grinds
    her wheat.

PHEIDIPPIDES: And should you not be thrashed who told
    your son, from food abstaining
To sing! as though you were, forsooth, cicalas [1] entertaining.

STREPSIADES: You hear him! so he said just now or e'er
    high words began:
And next he called Simonides a very sorry man.
And when I heard him, I could scarce my rising wrath com-
    mand;
Yet so I did, and him I bid take myrtle in his hand

[1] Grasshoppers were supposed always to sing and to live on dew
alone.

And chant some lines from Aeschylus, but he replied with ire,
"Believe me, I'm not one of those who Aeschylus admire,
That rough, unpolished, turgid bard, that mouther of bom-
    bast!"
When he said this, my heart began to heave extremely fast;
Yet still I kept my passion down, and said, "Then prithee you,
Sing one of those new-fangled songs which modern strip-
    lings do."
And he began the shameful tale Euripides has told
How a brother and a sister lived incestuous lives of old.
Then, then I could no more restrain, but first I must confess
With strong abuse I loaded him, and so, as you may guess,
We stormed and bandied threat for threat: till out at last
    he flew,
And smashed and thrashed and thumped and bumped and
    bruised me black and blue.

PHEIDIPPIDES: And rightly too, who coolly dared Euripides
    to blame,
Most sapient bard.

STREPSIADES: Most sapient bard! you, what's your fitting
    name?
Ah! but he'll pummel me again.

PHEIDIPPIDES: He will: and justly too.

STREPSIADES: What! justly, heartless villain! when 'twas
    I who nurtured you.
I knew your little lisping ways, how soon, you'd hardly think,
If you cried "bree!" I guessed your wants, and used to give
    you drink:
If you said "mamm!" I fetched you bread with fond discern-
    ment true,
And you could hardly say "Cacca!" when through the door
    I flew
And held you out a full arm's length your little needs to do:
    But now when I was crying
    That I with pain was dying,
    You brute! you would not tarry
    Me out of doors to carry,
    But choking with despair
    I've been and done it there.

CHORUS: Sure all young hearts are palpitating now
    To hear him plead,
Since if those lips with artful words avow
    The daring deed,
And once a favouring verdict win,
A fig for every old man's skin.
O thou! who rakest up new thoughts with daring hands pro-
    fane,

Try all you can, ingenious man, that verdict to obtain.

PHEIDIPPIDES: How sweet it is these novel arts, these clever
    words to know,
And have the power established rules and laws to overthrow.
Why in old times when horses were my sole delight, 'twas
    wonder
If I could say a dozen words without some awful blunder!
But now that he has made me quit that reckless mode of
    living,
And I have been to subtle thoughts my whole attention giving,
I hope to prove by logic strict 'tis right to beat my father.

STREPSIADES: O! buy your horses back, by Zeus, since I
    would ten times rather
Have to support a four-in-hand, so I be struck no more.

PHEIDIPPIDES: Peace. I will now resume the thread where
    I broke off before.
And first I ask: when I was young, did you not strike me
    then?

STREPSIADES: Yea: for I loved and cherished you.

PHEIDIPPIDES: Well, solve me this again,
Is it not just that I your son should cherish you alike,
And strike you, since, as you observe, to cherish means to
    strike?
What! must my body needs be scourged and pounded black
    and blue
And yours be scathless? was not I as much freeborn as you?
"Children are whipped, and shall not sires be whipped?"
Perhaps you'll urge that children's minds alone are taught by
    blows:—
Well: Age is Second Childhood then: that everybody knows.
And as by old experience Age should guide its steps more
    clearly,
So when they err, they surely should be punished more
    severely.

STREPSIADES: But Law goes everywhere for me: deny it,
    if you can.

PHEIDIPPIDES: Well was not he who made the law, a man,
    a mortal man,
As you or I, who in old times talked over all the crowd?
And think you that to you or me the same is not allowed,
To change it, so that sons by blows should keep their fathers
    steady?
Still, we'll be liberal, and blows which we've received already
We will forget, we'll have no ex-post-facto legislation.
—Look at the game-cocks, look at all the animal creation,
Do not *they* beat their parents? Aye: I say then, that in fact
They are as we, except that they no special laws enact.

STREPSIADES: Why don't you then, if always where the
game-cock leads you follow,
Ascend your perch to roost at night, and dirt and ordure
swallow?

PHEIDIPPIDES: The case is different there, old man, as
Socrates would see.

STREPSIADES: Well then you'll blame yourself at last, if you
keep striking me.

PHEIDIPPIDES: How so?

STREPSIADES: Why, if it's right for me to punish you my
son,
You can, if you have got one, yours.

PHEIDIPPIDES: Aye, but suppose I've none.
Then having gulled me you will die, while I've been flogged
in vain.

STREPSIADES: Good friends! I really think he has some
reason to complain.
I must concede he has put the case in quite a novel light:
I really think we should be flogged unless we act aright!

PHEIDIPPIDES: Look to a fresh idea then.

STREPSIADES: He'll be my death I vow.

PHEIDIPPIDES: Yet then perhaps you will not grudge ev'n
what you suffer now.

STREPSIADES: How! will you make me like the blows which
I've received to-day?

PHEIDIPPIDES: Yes, for I'll beat my mother too.

STREPSIADES: What! What is that you say!
Why this is worse than all.

PHEIDIPPIDES: But what, if as I proved the other,
By the same Logic I can prove 'tis right to beat my mother?

STREPSIADES: Aye! what indeed! if this you plead,
   If this you think to win,
Why then, for all I care, you may
To the Accursed Pit convey
Yourself with all your learning new,
Your master, and your Logic too,
   And tumble headlong in.
O Clouds! O Clouds! I owe all this to you!
Why did I let you manage my affairs!

CHORUS: Nay, nay, old man, you owe it to yourself.
Why didst thou turn to wicked practices?

STREPSIADES: Ah, but ye should have asked me that before,
And not have spurred a poor old fool to evil.

CHORUS: Such is our plan. We find a man
   On evil thoughts intent,
Guide him along to shame and wrong,
   Then leave him to repent.

STREPSIADES: Hard words, alas! yet not more hard than just.
It was not right unfairly to keep back
The money that I borrowed. Come, my darling,
Come and destroy that filthy Chaerephon
And Socrates; for they've deceived us both!

PHEIDIPPIDES: No. I will lift no hand against my Tutors.

STREPSIADES: Yes do, come, reverence Paternal Zeus.

PHEIDIPPIDES: Look there! Paternal Zeus! what an old fool.
Is there a Zeus?

STREPSIADES: There is.

PHEIDIPPIDES: There is *no* Zeus.
Young Vortex reigns, and he has turned out Zeus.

STREPSIADES: No Vortex reigns: that was my foolish thought
All through this vortex here. Fool that I was,
To think a piece of earthenware a God.[1]

PHEIDIPPIDES: Well rave away, talk nonsense to yourself.

STREPSIADES: O! fool, fool, fool, how mad I must have been
To cast away the Gods, for Socrates.
Yet Hermes, gracious Hermes, be not angry
Nor crush me utterly, but look with mercy
On faults to which his idle talk hath led me.
And lend thy counsel; tell me, had I better
Plague them with lawsuits, or how else annoy them.

(*Affects to listen.*)

Good: your advice is good: I'll have no lawsuits,
I'll go at once and set their house on fire,
The prating rascals. Here, here, Xanthias,
Quick, quick here, bring your ladder and your pitchfork,
Climb to the roof of their vile thinking-house,
Dig at their tiles, dig stoutly, an' thou lovest me,
Tumble the very house about their ears.
And some one fetch me here a lighted torch,
And I'll soon see if, boasters as they are,
They won't repent of what they've done to me.

STUDENT 1: O dear! O dear!

STREPSIADES: Now, now, my torch, send out a lusty flame.

STUDENT 1: Man! what are you at there?

STREPSIADES: What am I at? I'll tell you.
I'm splitting straws with your house-rafters here.

STUDENT 2: Oh me! who's been and set our house on fire?

STREPSIADES: Who was it, think you, that you stole the
       cloak from?

---

[1] The Greek word meaning "vortex" also means "earthenware bowl."

STUDENT 3: O murder! Murder!

STREPSIADES: That's the very thing,
Unless this pick prove traitor to my hopes,
Or I fall down, and break my blessed neck.

SOCRATES: Hallo! what are you at, up on our roof?

STREPSIADES: I walk on air, and contemplate the Sun.

SOCRATES: O! I shall suffocate. O dear! O dear!

CHAEREPHON: And I, poor devil, shall be burnt to death.

STREPSIADES: For with what aim did ye insult the Gods,
And pry around the dwellings of the Moon?
Strike, smite them, spare them not, for many reasons,
But most because they have blasphemed the Gods!

CHORUS: Lead out of the way: for I think we may say
We have acted our part very fairly to-day.

Niccolò Machiavelli:

MANDRAGOLA

Man, according to the Hebrew psalmist, is a little lower than the angels. Machiavelli (1469-1527) preferred not to talk about angels, but to concentrate on more observable phenomena. "We are," said Francis Bacon, "beholden to Machiavel and writers of that kind who openly and unmasked declare what men do in fact, and not what they ought to do." Machiavelli's summary of what men do is directly stated in *The Prince*, his philosophy of statecraft, and is amusingly dramatized in *Mandragola (Mandrake Root)*. "All men," he says in Chapter 17 of *The Prince*, "are ungrateful, fickle, dissimulating, cowardly in the face of danger, greedy for gain." In the eighteenth chapter he says that a ruler can break a treaty whenever convenient, Machiavelli's assumption and justification being that the other party is always about to break it anyway. "If all men were good, this precept would not be a good one; but since they are bad, and would not keep faith with you, you are not obliged to keep faith with them." Success in life, he believed, comes from a clear recognition of man's base nature and a cold willingness to manipulate it. Thus, in *Mandragola (c.* 1518), when asked who will persuade a priest to advise a virtuous wife to have an illicit affair, the engineer of the deception replies, "You, me, money, our baser selves—and his." Men are bad, and most are foolish, too; hence the deceiver will never lack for dupes.

Machiavelli assumed that men have always been the same. "Whoever compares the present with the past," he writes in the First Book of his *Discourses*, "will soon perceive that there prevail and always have prevailed the same desires and passions." It is not surprising, then, that like many of his contemporaries he found no difficulty in adapting to contemporary Florence the form and, to some degree, the characters and ideas of Roman comedy. His static view of mankind allowed him to assume that the materials of Roman comedy were satisfactory mirrors of the follies of his own day. As in the Roman plays of Plautus and Terence, *Mandragola* is set in an open square onto which face three houses. And, again as in Plautus and Terence, it has a prologue and consists of an action which

covers less than twenty-four hours. More important, like much
Roman comedy, it has a parasite—a man who lives by spong-
ing dinners—and it is the parasite who engineers the plot. How
to seduce Lucrezia is the problem; the young lover is be-
fuddled, but the parasite Ligurio knows how to handle people,
and it is his ingenuity and knowledge of human weakness
which keep the play going.

The most significantly Roman quality of the play, however,
is its concept of love—or rather, the lack of a concept of love
and the substitution for it of mere sex. Roman literature knew
little of love; Ovid's *Art of Love* is really a witty handbook on
practical seduction. But in some of the literature of the late
Middle Ages, perhaps partly because of the Christian assumption that the human body houses an immortal soul, we find
a respect for the body which was foreign to Roman drama.
In Terence's *Eunuch* (*c.* 161 B.C.), for example, a girl offers
herself to a man to further her and her lover's plans, and a
man pretends to be a eunuch in order to gain access to a
woman whom he then rapes. In the poetry of Dante (1265–
1321), however, physical love is transformed into an earthly
image of divine love. The sight of Dante's Beatrice (her
name, incidentally, means "blessed") drives out all foul
thoughts, her presence ennobles, and her discourse is an aid
to salvation:

> this virtue owns she, by God's will:
> Who speaks with her can never come to ill.

Similarly, Castiglione, a contemporary of Machiavelli's, writes
that true love strikes through the eye but reaches to the soul
and creates a thirst for spiritual rather than fleshly beauty.
The Middle Ages and Renaissance were not, of course, devoid
of bawdy tales, and *Mandragola* owes a good deal to such
native material. But one of the profoundest changes in man's
thinking was the spiritualization of his attitude toward women;
and Machiavelli wrote as though it had never occurred. Against
spiritualized medieval and early Renaissance concepts of love,
Machiavelli's play of sex is strikingly pagan.

Machiavelli is not so much anti-Christian as indifferent to
the essential value of Christianity. He does not scorn religion;
in a way, he does worse, for he says in his *Discourses* that
religion is valuable as a means of controlling men. He cheapens
it so that it becomes a useful tool for the man who wishes
to control. In *Mandragola* Fra Timoteo is simply another
agent whom Ligurio employs to persuade Lucrezia to be un-
chaste. Lucrezia's infidelity (urged, incidentally, by her foolish
husband) produces consequences delightful to all—including
the cuckolded Messer Nicia.

The play is about seduction, but if we were to take Machiavelli to task as an immoralist, he might reply (as he does in *The Prince*, Chapter 15): "If one considers everything thoroughly, one will find something which seems to be virtue, and following it would lead to ruin; and something else which seems to be vice, and following it would lead to security and prosperity." *Mandragola* is surely meant to delight rather than to edify by distinguishing between vice and virtue, and even persons offended by its immorality (notably the dramatist Goldoni) have been entertained by its vigor. Somerset Maugham, in his novel about Machiavelli, *Then and Now,* aptly describes the plot as "ribald, extravagant, and comic." We can, however, read a justification of comedy in *Clizia,* another of Machiavelli's plays: "It is certainly useful to men, and especially to youths, to know the avarice of an old man, the fury of a lover, the tricks of a servant, the gullet of a parasite, . . . the little faith there is in everyone; with these examples comedies are filled, and all these things may with greatest integrity be represented." But to take this speech as indicative of a pious hope to reform man's moral nature would be a piece of folly worthy of comic representation in Machiavelli's own play.

Mandragola

TRANSLATED BY J. R. HALE

Characters

CALLIMACO, *a young Florentine.*

SIRO, *his servant.*

LIGURIO, *a parasite.*

MESSER NICIA, *a lawyer.*

LUCREZIA, *his wife.*

SOSTRATA, *her mother.*

FRA TIMOTEO.

A YOUNG WIDOW.

PROLOGUE

God save you, gentle audience—that is
If you have come to smile and not to hiss.
And if you hold your tongue and persevere
We'll show you something new that happened—here!
Florence—your home—the setting of the play
(Pisa, perhaps, or Rome, another day);
And have no fear—
You'll split your sides with laughing if you stay.

2

Here on my right hand where you see that door
There lives a bookish doctor of the law.
On that side is the Street of Love, a lane
Where, if you slip, you don't get up again.
And soon, if you're still here, you'll see the friar—
You'll know him straight away, for his attire
Will make it plain.
The church that faces you is where he's prior.

3

A youth, Callimaco Guadagni, dwells
There on the left, and his appearance tells
Of honourable qualities he shares
With other gallants. Paris and his affairs
He's left: he loves a girl—a girl, it's true,
Of wit—but still he'll catch her; what he'll do
Our play declares—
Ladies, I wish the same sweet fate on you!

4

The play is called Mandragola, and why?
You'll see the reason soon enough, say I.
The author is of no great fame, and will,
If you are not diverted, foot the bill.
So here we offer you for your delight
A lover wan, a lawyer none too bright,
And two more still:
A wicked friar, a scheming parasite.

5

And if this seems too light and frivolous
For one who likes to be thought serious,
Forgive him: for he tries with idle dreams

To make the hour less bitter than it seems.
—Bitter, for he can turn no other way
To show a higher worth, do what he may;
For graver themes
He sees no chance of patronage or pay.

6

The payment he expects is jeers and spite,
For everyone to damn his work outright.
Such treatment is a proof the present day
Declines from ancient worth in every way.
And who will strain, when all they get is scorn,
To achieve a work of art?—A work that's born
To fade away,
Hidden in mist, or by the tempest torn.

7

But he who thinks *this* author can be wrung
By malice, or be made to hold his tongue,
I warn him: this man is malicious too;
Malice, indeed, his earliest art, and through
The length and limits of all Italy
He owes respect to none; though I agree
He'll fawn and do
Service to richer, smarter folk than he.

8

Well, let who will speak evil; you and I
Must turn to what's in hand, for time goes by.
Words are but air; the wise man will ignore
A monster whose existence is not sure.[1]
Callimaco comes out, and Siro, too,
His servant; they will tell you what's to do.
And so no more
From me—I leave them and the play to you.

Song

*(To be sung before the play by a chorus of Nymphs
and Shepherds.)*

We know that life is brief,
With no reward but pain,

---

[1] Translator's note: The prologue may well have been spoken by
some mythological creature, like the centaur who sounds his lyre on the
title page of one of the earliest editions (*c.* 1520) of this play. I owe
this suggestion to Mr. Cecil Grayson.

So we desert the fight
And give Desire rein.

The man who turns away
From pleasure and desire
Is ignorant of life,
Of all the strains that tire,

Of traps that lie in wait
To catch his weary feet;
His chosen way will bring
Misfortune and deceit.

To fly such pain, we live
As nymphs and shepherds gay:
Far from the world, we keep
Perpetual holiday.

But leaving our retreat,
With mirth and harmony
We come in honour of
This day and company.

This also drew us here:
Your Governor's great name.[1]
In him united are
All gifts the Gods can claim.

For such a happy lot—
Content and peace and cheer—
You should rejoice—and thank
Its gracious author here.

(*A square in Florence, in* 1504.)

ACT I

CALLIMACO; SIRO *about to leave*

CALLIMACO: Oh Siro, don't go. I want you.

[1] Translator's note: Francesco Guicciardini, President of the Romagna. This song was written for a performance at Modena in 1526 at which he was present.

SIRO: Well, here I am.

CALLIMACO: I know you were surprised when I left Paris so suddenly, and I think you are wondering now why I have been here doing nothing for a month.

SIRO: You're right—I am.

CALLIMACO: If I haven't told you this before, it is not because I don't trust you, but because I think the best way to keep a thing secret is not to say a word about it until you have to. Now I need your help, so I am going to tell you how matters stand.

SIRO: I am your servant, and it's not for servants to meddle with their master's affairs, or try to find out what they are up to, but when they are *told* to take an interest, then it is their business to act faithfully. That's how I've behaved, and so I always shall.

CALLIMACO: Exactly. Well, you must have heard me say a thousand times—so it does not matter if you have to listen for the thousand and first—how I lost my parents when I was ten, how my guardians sent me to Paris, where I stayed for twenty years; and because after ten of them King Charles began the wars that laid Italy waste, I decided to stay on in Paris and not come home—life there seemed safer than it did here.

SIRO: Yes, I know.

CALLIMACO: I had all my possessions sold except this house, and lived on in perfect happiness for another ten years in France—

SIRO: Yes, I know that too.

CALLIMACO: —passing the time in study, in business and in pleasure. And I managed to keep the three things separate as they should be. So I spent my time, as you know, peacefully enough, offending no one and helping whoever I could. Shopkeepers and gentlemen, foreigners and locals, the rich and the poor—I got on with all of them.

SIRO: That's right enough.

CALLIMACO: But Fortune, thinking that I was too happy, sent Cammillo Calfucci to Paris.

SIRO: Now I'm beginning to see what the trouble is.

CALLIMACO: I often entertained him just as I did the other Florentines, and one day we happened to be discussing where the loveliest women were to be found—in Italy or in France —and as I could not speak for the Italians, because I was too young when I left, another Florentine took the French side, while Cammillo stood up for the Italians. When they had argued back and forth for some time, Cammillo, who was losing his temper by then, said that even if all the other women of Italy were monsters, he had a relative who would make up for them all.

SIRO: And I know what is coming next.

CALLIMACO: Yes—he named Madonna Lucrezia, the wife of Nicia Calfucci. He heaped on her such praises for beauty and for sweetness of nature that he left us all without a word to say, and every idea vanished from my head but one: to come here, whether Italy was at peace or at war. And since I arrived I have found something rare enough: that the fame of Madonna Lucrezia is pale beside the truth; and I long for her so desperately that I am nearly out of my mind.

SIRO: If you'd told me about this in Paris, I should have known what advice to give you, but as it is I don't know what to say.

CALLIMACO: I want a good listener, not good advice. And besides, you must be ready to help whenever I need you.

SIRO: I will do my best. But do you think you have any hope?

CALLIMACO: That is the trouble—almost none. I will tell you: in the first place, her whole character is against me— she is virtuous and won't let herself think of love. Then she has a rich husband who lets her dominate him completely, and if he is not exactly young, it seems he's not quite past it yet. There aren't even the usual chances of meeting her with people of her own age, at people's houses or dances, because she has no friends or relations to chaperone her. No workmen are allowed in the house and her virtuousness keeps all the servants in awe of her. In fact there's not a chink for corruption to creep through.

SIRO: What are you going to do then?

CALLIMACO: Things are never so bad that there is no reason for hope; it may be weak, it may be an illusion—but desire, and your determination to succeed, blind you to that.

SIRO: But have you got any reason for hope?

CALLIMACO: Yes, two: one—Messer Nicia's foolishness; for all that he's got a degree, he's the most blockheaded and simple-minded man in Florence; the other—they badly want children. They have been married six years without any, they are rich, and so they are all the more anxious not to die without heirs. And there is a third—her mother. She used to be easy-going enough; now she's rich, of course, I'm not so sure how to get round her.

SIRO: Have you tried to do anything about it yet?

CALLIMACO: Yes I have—but nothing much.

SIRO: But what?

CALLIMACO: You know Ligurio, who often comes round to eat. He used to be a marriage broker; now he simply sponges for meals, and because he is good company Messer Nicia has grown quite fond of him, and Ligurio pulls his leg, and although he never gets asked to dinner he manages

parasite

to touch him for a little money now and again. I have got to know him well, and have told him that I love her, and he has promised to help in every way he can.

SIRO: Look out he doesn't cheat you; these spongers don't make a habit of keeping promises.

CALLIMACO: I know. All the same, if you've put yourself in someone's hands you've got to trust him. I've promised he'll be well paid if he succeeds; if he doesn't—well, I hate eating alone, and he'll still get his lunch and supper.

SIRO: And what has he promised to do so far?

CALLIMACO: He has promised to persuade Messer Nicia to take his wife to the baths this May!

SIRO: But how does this affect you?

CALLIMACO: Me? It might lead to some change in her outlook: you've got to be gay in these resorts: there's nothing else to do. I would go too, and arrange all sorts of festivities, and show myself off as splendidly as possible; and I would work my way into their acquaintance. Who knows? One thing leads to another, and time will tell.

SIRO: It's not a bad idea.

CALLIMACO: Ligurio went off this morning to talk to Messer Nicia about it and said he would let me know what happened.

SIRO: Here they come together.

CALLIMACO: I'll keep out of the way so I can see Ligurio when he's left Messer Nicia. You go inside and get on with your work; if I want anything I'll call you. (*He retires.*)

SIRO: I'm off then. (*He goes.*)

(*Enter* LIGURIO *with* MESSER NICIA.)

MESSER NICIA: I think your counsel is good and I spoke of it last night to my wife. She said she would let me have her answer today; but to tell you the truth, I am not altogether happy myself.

LIGURIO: But why?

MESSER NICIA: Because I am not the sort of man who shifts his ground easily. And then, having to drag my wife after me, and servants, and baggage—it doesn't suit me. And another thing. I was talking to some doctors last night. One said I should go to San Filippo, another to Porretta, and another to Villa—like so many squawking birds. If you want my opinion, these doctors don't even know their own trade.

LIGURIO: You might well hesitate for the first reason you gave me—that you aren't used to being out of sight of the Cathedral dome.

MESSER NICIA: Oh, that's just where you are wrong! When I was younger I was a positive globe-trotter. Whenever there was a fair at Prato—there I was! There is not a castle in the neighbourhood I've not been to. Ah, but that's not all: I've been to Pisa and Leghorn. There now!

LIGURIO: Then in Pisa you must have seen the Campo Sanitro.

MESSER NICIA: You mean the Campo *Santo*.

LIGURIO: Oh, yes, the Campo Santo. And at Leghorn did you see the sea?

MESSER NICIA: Of course I saw the sea.

LIGURIO: How much bigger is it than the Arno?

MESSER NICIA: Than the Arno? It's four times—more than six—I'd even go so far as to say more than seven times as big; you can't see a thing but water, water, water.

LIGURIO: Then if you are such a great traveller, I can't see what frightens you about these baths.

MESSER NICIA: You talk like a green boy. Do you think the upheaval of a whole household is a mere joke? Still, be that as it may, I'm so anxious for an heir I would do anything at all. Now have a word with these doctors, and try and find out which is really the best place. I will go home to my wife, and we will see you there later.

LIGURIO: As you like. (MESSER NICIA *goes*.) Now you can't tell me there's more of a fool to be found—but just look at his luck! He's rich. He's got a wife who's beautiful, amiable, discreet and fit to be a queen. You don't come across many marriages that bear out the proverb so well: "Man can't choose his birth, but he can choose his mate." It's usually the woman with all her wits falls for a man without one; the shrewdest of men picks himself—a shrew. But this fellow's stupidity has got this to be said for it—it's a handle for Callimaco—and here he is. Callimaco! what are you doing?

(CALLIMACO *comes forward*.)

CALLIMACO: I saw you were with Messer Nicia and waited till he'd left to find out how things were going.

LIGURIO: You know what sort of man he is—silly and cautious: he hates the idea of leaving Florence. I got him worked up a little, though, till he said he was ready for anything. I think if there were really nothing else for it but to go, he would do it. But I'm not sure now that's what we really want.

CALLIMACO: Why not?

LIGURIO: Well, this is how I see it: you know that all sorts of people go to these watering places, and among them might be someone who fancies Lucrezia as much as you do: and he might be richer than you, he might be more attractive than you; in which case the fruits of our labours would be picked by someone else. Then it might be that faced by a number of rivals she will become colder than ever, or, if she likes the situation, she may decide on another man and not on you.

CALLIMACO: You are right: I can see that. But what can I do? Is there any other way out? What else can I try? I've got to do something, even if it seems mad or dangerous or scandalous—even if it's criminal. I'd rather die than go on living like this. If I could sleep, if I could eat, if I could enjoy a conversation—if I could find any sort of relief, then I'd have the patience to wait. But as it is there is no way out: if I can't see a single ray of hope, then I shall die. And if death's the only alternative, I won't stop at anything, however violent, or wrong.

his obsession

LIGURIO: Don't carry on like this: try to be more calm.

CALLIMACO: It's to keep calm that I feed on these wild ideas. You can see that well enough. We must either carry on with sending him to the baths or else work out some other plan, however fanciful it is, just to keep me from complete despair.

LIGURIO: We must—and I will do all I can.

CALLIMACO: I know you will, and though I'm well enough aware that men like you live by deception, I do not think you'll deceive me, because if you did and I caught you at it you would no longer have the run of my house or the hope of getting what I have promised you.

LIGURIO: You shouldn't be suspicious. Even if nothing comes of the reward you're promising—and which I want right enough—I'm so much of your mind that I'm almost as eager to get what you want as you are. But enough of that. Messer Nicia has commissioned me to find a doctor and discover which baths would be best to visit. Now I want you to do as I tell you. Say that you have studied medicine and have practised in Paris. He will easily believe that, he's so simple, and what is more, you're educated and can bandy a bit of Latin with him.

CALLIMACO: What good will that do?

LIGURIO: It would help us send him to whatever baths we chose—or—to try another plan of mine, one that would yield quicker returns and have more chance of success than going to the baths.

CALLIMACO: What do you mean?

LIGURIO: I mean, if you are prepared to trust me and take a risk, I will see that you have what you want before this time tomorrow. And even if he were the sort of man who could tell whether or not you were a doctor—which he isn't —my plan won't allow him the time or the chance to suspect you. And if he does discover who you actually are, it will only be when it's too late to spoil the plot.

CALLIMACO: You are bringing me back to life. But the idea is fantastic—and it offers too much. What are you going to do?

LIGURIO: You'll learn soon enough. That's all you need to know for the present; as it is there's too little time to work in, and we can talk later. Go home and wait for me, and I'll find Messer Nicia. If I bring him to see you, take your cue from me and fall in with the plot.

CALLIMACO: Well, I'll do as you say, but these fine hopes of yours—I'm afraid they will just vanish in a puff of smoke.

Song at the end of Act I

> Oh mighty Love, your power
> Alone will show a man
> A joy more blest
> Than all the rest
> In realms elysian.
>
> Who loves not cannot feel
> The mingled pain and bliss,
> The peril sweet
> We run to meet,
> The self-forgetting kiss;
>
> How fear and hope by turns
> Can freeze and burn the heart;
> Nor does he know
> The gods also
> Do dread your fatal dart.

ACT II

(*Enter* LIGURIO *and* MESSER NICIA.)

LIGURIO: And as I said before, I believe God himself has sent us this man, that your desire may be fulfilled. He has done wonders in Paris, and don't be surprised that he hasn't practised in Florence: he is rich and doesn't need to—and at any moment he may be returning to France.

MESSER NICIA: That's just it, my friend! That is the very thing that worries me. I have no intention of letting myself become involved only to be left high and dry.

LIGURIO: Oh, *that* needn't trouble you. Your only fear should be that he won't accept the case: but if he does take it, then he will stand by you until it is all over.

MESSER NICIA: That side I am prepared to leave to you. As for his learning, once I have had a few words with him I shall be able to tell you if he is well grounded or not; I am not the man to be taken in by a mere cap and gown!

LIGURIO: It is just because I know what sort of a man you are that I am giving you the opportunity of meeting him. And if when you have spoken to him, you don't agree that for presence, learning and eloquence he is a man to put your last ducat on—my name's not Ligurio!

MESSER NICIA: Well then, in God's name, let us go. Where does he live?

LIGURIO: He is staying here, over in that house.

MESSER NICIA: Good. Good.

LIGURIO: (*Knocks*) There.

SIRO: (*within*)—Who is it?

LIGURIO: Is Callimaco at home?

SIRO: Yes he is.

MESSER NICIA: Why don't you say Doctor Callimaco?

LIGURIO: He's above that sort of thing.

MESSER NICIA: Don't say that! Address him properly. If he doesn't like it—so much the worse.

(*Enter* CALLIMACO, *dressed as a doctor.*)

CALLIMACO: Who wants to see me?

MESSER NICIA: *Bona dies, domine magister.*

CALLIMACO: *Et vobis bona, domine doctor.*

LIGURIO: What do you think of that?

MESSER NICIA: My word! It's phenomenal!

LIGURIO: But if you want me to stay, you must speak a language I understand, otherwise I might as well take myself off.

CALLIMACO: To what do I owe the pleasure of this visit?

MESSER NICIA: I hardly know where to start: I am looking for two things most men would probably try to avoid—namely to bring trouble to myself, and to other people. I have no children but want them, and to bring this trouble on my head I have come to trouble you.

CALLIMACO: I can wish for nothing better than to be of service to you, as to all like-minded persons of merit and standing. And I would not have fatigued myself with study so long in Paris if it had not enabled me to assist men of worth like yourself.

MESSER NICIA: I am much obliged; and if you should stand in need of *my* skill, I should be pleased to place it at your disposition. But let us return *ad rem nostram*. Have you thought which of the baths is most likely to help my wife conceive? I know Ligurio has told you how the matter stands.

CALLIMACO: That is true, but for your wish to be gratified, it is necessary to know the origin of your wife's sterility, for this can rise from several causes. *Nam causae sterilitatis sunt: aut in semine, aut in matrice, aut in instrumentis seminariis, aut in virga, aut in causa extrinseca.*

MESSER NICIA: (This is the most admirable man we could have found!)

CALLIMACO: Then again—and if this were the case, then there could be no cure at all—this sterility could be caused by your impotence.

Manhood honor

MESSER NICIA: Me, impotent! My dear sir, you amuse me! I do not think that in all Florence there is a man more brisk and virile than I.

CALLIMACO: If that is the case, then rest assured we shall find some remedy.

MESSER NICIA: Might there not be some other cure than the baths? There's all the inconvenience, and my wife has no wish to leave Florence.

LIGURIO: There is indeed. I can answer for that myself. Callimaco is so courteous that he finds it difficult to get down to business. Haven't you told me that you can mix a certain potion that invariably leads to conception?

CALLIMACO: Yes I can. But in case I should be thought a mountebank I only disclose it to men I am entirely sure of.

MESSER NICIA: You can count on me. I would never question a scholar of your standing.

LIGURIO: I expect you need to see a specimen of urine.

CALLIMACO: Certainly. One can hardly do without that.

LIGURIO: Call Siro: he can go home with Messer Nicia and come straight back, while we wait here.

(*Enter* SIRO.)

CALLIMACO: Siro, go with him. And, if you are agreeable, Messere, come back as soon as possible, and we shall try to satisfy you.

MESSER NICIA: Agreeable? Are you serious? I shall be back in a twinkling! I have more confidence in you than a Janissary in his sword.

(CALLIMACO *and* LIGURIO *go out.*)

MESSER NICIA: Your master is a most worthy man.
SIRO: Oh he's all of that.
MESSER NICIA: The king of France must esteem him.
SIRO: Yes.
MESSER NICIA: That must make his residence in France very pleasant.
SIRO: Oh yes.

Standard satire
of local customs and
anti-feminine attitudes
etc.
81

MESSER NICIA: And he is quite right. In this city there's nothing but numbskulls who don't know quality when they see it. If he stayed here there is no one who would respect him. I know what I am talking about: why I've worn myself out to get up a little Latin; but if I had to depend on that for my bread and butter, I'd soon go hungry, I can tell you!

SIRO: Do you earn a hundred ducats a year?

MESSER NICIA: Ducats? not even a hundred pennies! I tell you: you've got to be in with the Government in this city before even a dog will bark at you. Men of learning like us are good for nothing but funerals and weddings and lounging about all day on the Bench. But it doesn't bother me: I'm not dependent on anyone: there are others worse off than I. All the same I wouldn't like what I've just said to get about or I would be made to feel it either in my pocket or on my backside.

SIRO: You would indeed.

MESSER NICIA: Here we are: wait for me here. I will be back in a minute.

SIRO: Right. (MESSER NICIA *goes.*) If all learned men were like that one, we might as well be living in Bedlam. I should say that Ligurio and that crazy master of mine are leading him by the nose straight into trouble. I'm all for it as long as we're sure of getting away with it—if we're caught out, my life's not going to be worth much—and the same goes for my master's life and his goods too. He's already turned doctor; I don't know what the idea is or where it's leading. But here is the Messere with a bottle in his hand: dirty old man—he'd make a cat laugh!

(*Enter* MESSER NICIA.)

MESSER NICIA (*To* LUCREZIA, *off*): I have always considered your wishes. In this matter I intend you to consider mine. If I had known I was going to be left without children I would have taken a peasant girl for a wife. Oh! there you are, Siro. Follow me. The trouble I have had getting that foolish girl to give me a specimen! It is not that she does not care about having children, she wants them more than I do, but when I ask her to do the slightest thing about it—then the trouble starts!

SIRO: Have a little patience. Women will let themselves be led—as long as you do it with soft words.

MESSER NICIA: Soft words! She nearly drives me mad! Run on and tell your master and Ligurio that I am here.

SIRO: They are coming now.

(*Enter* CALLIMACO *and* LIGURIO.)

LIGURIO: (It shouldn't be hard to persuade Messer Nicia: the problem will be his wife, but we still have something up our sleeves.)

CALLIMACO: Have you the specimen?

MESSER NICIA: Siro has it under there.

CALLIMACO: Let me see. Oh! this specimen shows great weakness in the kidneys.

MESSER NICIA: It does appear a trifle clouded to me, yet it has only just been provided.

CALLIMACO: Don't let that surprise you. *Nam mulieris urinae sunt semper maioris grossitiei et albedinis et minoris pulchritudinis quam virorum. Huius autem in caetera, causa est amplitudo canalium, mixtio eorum quae ex matrice exeunt cum urina.*

MESSER NICIA: Oh, oh! By the beard of the Baptist! He blossoms under my very eyes! See how learnedly he speaks of such matters!

CALLIMACO: I am afraid that she is not well covered at night, and that causes the cloudiness.

MESSER NICIA: She has a good counterpane over her, but she kneels four hours at a time stringing paternosters together before she gets into bed. She's like an animal the way she stands the cold.

CALLIMACO: Look now, Messer Nicia, either you have confidence in me or you don't; either I can tell you a sure remedy, or I won't. For my part, I am willing to give you the remedy. If you believe in me you will take it, and, a year from today, if your wife has not a son in her arms, I will gladly make you present of two thousand ducats.

MESSER NICIA: Tell me then; I will follow you in everything and trust you more than I do my confessor.

CALLIMACO: Then you must understand this: that there is nothing more certain to bring a woman to pregnancy than to give her a potion made from mandragola. It is an experiment I have made on several occasions and it has always succeeded; if it were not for this the Queen of France would be childless, and so would innumerable other princesses in that land.

MESSER NICIA: Is it possible?

CALLIMACO: It is as I tell you. And fortune has favoured you to such an extent that I have brought with me everything that the potion needs, and it can be yours whenever you wish.

MESSER NICIA: When should she take it?

CALLIMACO: This evening after dinner; the moon is in a favourable aspect and the time could not be more propitious.

MESSER NICIA: Don't worry about that. You just get it ready; I will see that she takes it.

CALLIMACO: However, one thing you must face: the man who first has to do with a woman who has taken this potion dies within eight days, and nothing in this world can save him.

MESSER NICIA: Death and damnation! I wouldn't touch the filthy stuff! You'll not play your tricks on me! A fine fix you'd be putting me in!

CALLIMACO: Keep calm: there is an alternative.

MESSER NICIA: Well, what is it?

CALLIMACO: To make someone else sleep with her. In a night he will have drawn off all the infection from the mandragola. Then you can resume your rights again without any danger.

MESSER NICIA: No, that I won't do.

CALLIMACO: Why not?

MESSER NICIA: Because I don't want to make my wife a whore and myself a cuckold.

CALLIMACO: Is that how you feel? I took you for a wiser man. So you hesitate to follow the King of France in this— and the whole of his court?

MESSER NICIA: But who do you think I could find to take part in such madness? If I tell him the truth he will refuse; if I don't, I shall be deceiving him, and putting a noose round my own neck. I don't want to look for trouble.

CALLIMACO: If that is all that worries you, leave everything to me.

MESSER NICIA: What will you do?

CALLIMACO: I will tell you. I will let you have the potion this evening after dinner; you give it her to drink, and put her straight to bed about four hours after dark. Then we shall disguise ourselves, you, Ligurio, Siro and I, and we will scour the New Market and the Old Market, and the streets round here, and the first idle young lout we find, we'll throw a cloak over his head and whip him along in the dark into your house and up to your room. Then we will put him into bed, tell him what to do—and there won't be any difficulty at all. Afterwards, in the morning, pack him off before daybreak, get your wife to wash, and you can do what you like with her without the slightest danger.

MESSER NICIA: Well, since you say that the King and princes and great lords have done the same, I am content. But, above all, as you value my life, let no one know of it!

CALLIMACO: Who do you think would tell?

MESSER NICIA: There is still one obstacle: and it's a tricky one.

CALLIMACO: What is that?

MESSER NICIA: To bring my wife round to it—and I can't believe that she would ever agree.

CALLIMACO: Very well then. But I should not pretend to the name of husband if I couldn't make my wife do as I wanted.

LIGURIO: I have thought of a way.

MESSER NICIA: How?

LIGURIO: Through her confessor.

CALLIMACO: But who will persuade the confessor?

LIGURIO: You, me, money, our baser selves—and his.

MESSER NICIA: None the less, I fear that if I suggest it, she will refuse to speak to her confessor.

LIGURIO: There's a remedy for that, too.

CALLIMACO: Tell me.

LIGURIO: Get her mother to take her to him.

MESSER NICIA: She certainly confides in her.

LIGURIO: And I know her mother will see things our way. Come now, we mustn't delay; it is getting late. You can go for a walk, Callimaco, but make sure that we find you at home with the potion ready two hours after nightfall. Messer Nicia and I will go to his mother-in-law's house to warn her; she and I understand one another. Then we will go to the friar, and we will let you know what happens.

CALLIMACO: But I beg you—don't leave me alone.

LIGURIO: You're in a fine state!

CALLIMACO: Where am I to go?

LIGURIO: Here, there—anywhere. Florence is a great city.

CALLIMACO: O God, the thought of her . . .

Song at the end of Act II

How happy the man
To stupidity born,
A gullible, credulous,
Innocent pawn.
Unmoved by ambition,
Untroubled by doubt,
Untouched by suspicion,
He lives his life out.
Your grey-beard Messere
So anxious for heirs,
Would believe pigs could fly,
If it helped his affairs;
Conception's a blessing—
All else is forgot
In erecting his hopes
On the thing he has not.

ACT III

(Enter SOSTRATA: MESSER NICIA, *and* LIGURIO.)

SOSTRATA: I have always heard it said that it is the part of a wise man to choose the lesser of two evils. If there is no other way to have children, then, conscience permitting, you must take this one.

MESSER NICIA: That is how it is.

LIGURIO: You go and find your daughter, and we will get hold of her confessor, Fra Timoteo, and explain the business to him, so that you won't have to tell him yourself. Then you will see what he has to say.

SOSTRATA: That's what we'll do then; you go that way; and I will look for Lucrezia, and come what may I will bring her along to speak to the friar. *(She goes.)*

MESSER NICIA: You may be surprised, Ligurio, that we have to go such a long way round to persuade my wife; but if you knew the whole story you would cease to marvel.

LIGURIO: Surely it's because all women are suspicious.

MESSER NICIA: It is not that. She was the gentlest creature in the world, and the easiest to manage, but since one of her neighbors said that if she vowed to hear the first mass at the Servites for forty mornings running she would conceive, she swore to do it, and went there about twenty times. Well then, let me tell you that one day those horrid monks began to sidle round about her so that she did not want to go back again. It is really too bad that those who ought to set a good example should behave like that. Don't you agree?

See P. 90

LIGURIO: Hell fire. Of course I do.

MESSER NICIA: From that moment to this she's on her guard —all ears and as touchy as a hare; and if one ventures a word, up come a hundred objections.

LIGURIO: Well, now I can see why. And what became of her vow?

MESSER NICIA: She got herself dispensed from it.

LIGURIO: Good. But tell me—have you got twenty-five ducats? If our plan is to succeed we shall need them to make a good friend of the friar, and give him hope of something still better to come.

MESSER NICIA: Take them; it does not worry me; I shall get it back in other ways.

LIGURIO: These friars are sly and cunning; and that is only to be expected, for they know all about our sins as well as their own: and someone who was not familiar with them might easily go about getting their support in the wrong way. So I am anxious that you should not spoil anything in talk-

85

ing to him—for men like you, who spend all day studying
their books, understand the wisdom of the ages, but don't
know how to handle the business of the world—(He's such
a half-wit—I'm afraid he might ruin everything.)

MESSER NICIA: Tell me what you want me to do.

LIGURIO: Just leave all the talking to me, and don't say a
word unless I make a sign to you.

MESSER NICIA: Very well. What sign will you make?

LIGURIO: I'll wink and bite my lip. No, no! We'll have to
think of something else. How long is it since you spoke to
the friar?

MESSER NICIA: More than ten years.

LIGURIO: Good: then I'll tell him that you've gone deaf;
and you are not to answer or say anything unless we shout.

MESSER NICIA: Very well.

LIGURIO: Don't be upset if I seem to be talking off the
point; everything will turn out all right.

MESSER NICIA: Till we meet again, then.

(LIGURIO *and* MESSER NICIA *go out*.)

(*Enter* FRA TIMOTEO *and the* YOUNG WIDOW.)

FRA TIMOTEO: If you wish to confess, I am ready to serve
you.

WIDOW: Not today: I've got someone waiting for me; and
it will be enough to get one or two things off my mind just
walking along with you like this. Have you said those masses
of Our Lady?

FRA TIMOTEO: Yes, madonna.

WIDOW: Now, take this florin, and say the mass of the
dead for my husband's soul every Monday for two months.
For even if he was a bit demanding—the flesh is sometimes
too strong for us: I can't help feeling . . . a bit . . . when I
think of him. But do you really think he is in purgatory?

FRA TIMOTEO: Beyond all doubt.

WIDOW: I wouldn't be too sure. You know very well what
he did to me sometimes. You must have got quite tired of me
and my troubles. I kept him off as long as I could; but he
was so importunate. Lordy me!

FRA TIMOTEO: Never fear: God's clemency is great; if the
will is not lacking, there will always be time for repentance.

WIDOW: Do you think the Turk will come into Italy this
year?

FRA TIMOTEO: If you do not say your prayers, yes.

WIDOW: Glory be! Lord preserve us from their devilments.
I have a mortal fear of being impaled like that. But I can
see that my friend is waiting for me there in the church—
she's got some stuff of mine—Well, good day to you.

FRA TIMOTEO: God keep you. (YOUNG WIDOW *goes*.) Women are the most charitable creatures in the world, and the most trying. Whoso renounces them avoids trouble, but also certain advantages; who lives with them has plenty of both. But true it is that where the honey is there will the flies be gathered together.

(*Enter* LIGURIO *and* MESSER NICIA.)

And what brings you here, my good people? Do I not recognise Messer Nicia?

LIGURIO: Speak louder; he is so deaf that he can't hear a thing.

FRA TIMOTEO: You are welcome, Messere!

LIGURIO: Louder.

FRA TIMOTEO: Welcome!!

MESSER NICIA: I am glad to see you, father.

FRA TIMOTEO: What brings you here?

MESSER NICIA: Very well, thank you.

LIGURIO: Speak to me, father—if you want to make him understand you, you will have to shout these houses down.

FRA TIMOTEO: What do you want of me?

LIGURIO: Messer Nicia here, and another gentleman whom you will hear about later on, intend to distribute some hundreds of ducats in alms.

MESSER NICIA: Death and damnation!

LIGURIO: (Hold your tongue, curse you. He won't get much out of it.) Don't be surprised at anything he says, father; he doesn't hear, but he sometimes thinks he does, and he answers quite off the point.

FRA TIMOTEO: Tell me, then, and let him ramble on.

LIGURIO: I've some of this money with me, and they have decided that you are to be in charge of its distribution.

FRA TIMOTEO: Most willingly.

LIGURIO: But before the alms are made over, you must help Messer Nicia in a rather strange business he has got involved in: you are the only man who can help us; you see, it's a matter that concerns the honour of his whole family.

FRA TIMOTEO: Tell me what it is.

LIGURIO: I don't know if you are acquainted with Cammillo Calfucci, Messer Nicia's nephew?

FRA TIMOTEO: Yes, I know him.

LIGURIO: A year ago he went to France on business and as his wife was dead, he left his daughter, who was just old enough to marry, in the care of a certain convent—I don't think it's necessary to mention the name.

FRA TIMOTEO: And what happened?

LIGURIO: What happened was that as a result either of the carelessness of the nuns or some piece of light-headedness on the part of the girl, she finds herself four months gone with child; so that, unless the accident is remedied, Messer Nicia, the nuns, the girl herself, Cammillo, the whole house of Calfucci will be disgraced; and Messer Nicia is so sensitive about scandal, that he has promised, if it can be kept secret, to give three hundred ducats for the love of God.

MESSER NICIA: Nothing of the sort!

LIGURIO: (Be quiet!) He wants them to be distributed by your hands. It is a situation that can only be dealt with by the Abbess and yourself.

FRA TIMOTEO: How is that?

LIGURIO: You could persuade the Abbess to give the girl a drug that would bring about an abortion.

FRA TIMOTEO: That would need consideration.

LIGURIO: Think how much good would come from doing this: you would preserve the reputation of the convent, and of the girl and her family; you would restore a daughter to her father, relieve Messer Nicia here, and his whole family, distribute alms to the tune of three hundred ducats; and on the other hand you harm nothing but an unborn piece of flesh, something that might come to grief in a thousand other ways; and I believe that what benefits and satisfies the majority is itself good.

FRA TIMOTEO: So be it, and in God's name. Let what you wish be done, and all for God's sake and charity's. Tell me the name of the convent, give me the potion, and, if you like, give me the money too, so that I can start by putting it to some good use.

LIGURIO: Now I see that you are the truly religious man I took you for. Here is part of the money. The name of the convent is—But wait a moment; someone's beckoning to me from the church there: I'll be back in a moment; don't leave Messer Nicia—this won't take more than a couple of words. (He goes.)

FRA TIMOTEO: How far is the girl gone?

MESSER NICIA: My head is going round and round.

FRA TIMOTEO: I said, how far is the girl gone with child?

MESSER NICIA: Devil take them!

FRA TIMOTEO: But why?

MESSER NICIA: And good riddance!

FRA TIMOTEO: I might as well address the beasts of the field. One of the men I have to deal with is deaf and the other is out of his wits. One can't hear and the other has run away. But if this is sound money I can beat them at their own game. —Here is Ligurio coming back.

(Re-enter LIGURIO.)

LIGURIO: (Hold your tongue, Messere). Oh, I have great news, father.

FRA TIMOTEO: What is it?

LIGURIO: The woman I have been speaking with tells me the girl has miscarried.

FRA TIMOTEO: Good. These alms will go into the general treasury.

LIGURIO: What do you mean?

FRA TIMOTEO: I mean that you have all the more cause to give these alms.

LIGURIO: Oh, they shall be given as soon as you like. But meanwhile there is one other thing that you must do to help Messer Nicia.

FRA TIMOTEO: What is that?

LIGURIO: Something less urgent, not so scandalous, but more advantageous to us, and more profitable to you.

FRA TIMOTEO: What is it? We seem to be on such good terms, and understand one another so well, that I'd be pleased to oblige you in any way.

LIGURIO: I would like to talk about it in the church, just between ourselves, and Messer Nicia will be good enough to wait for us here.—We shall soon be back.

MESSER NICIA: (As the bailiff said to the bankrupt.)

FRA TIMOTEO: Come then.

(LIGURIO *and* FRA TIMOTEO *go out.*)

MESSER NICIA: What is going on? Is it night or day? Am I awake or dreaming? I might be drunk—but I haven't been able to touch a drop all day because of this damned talk talk talk. We arranged what to say to the friar, then he says something else—and he makes me pretend to be deaf, and stuff up my ears as if there were Sirens about, just so I have to pretend I haven't heard all his tomfoolery. And to what end —Lord only knows. I find myself twenty-five ducats to the bad, and my business not even mentioned, and now they have left me here to stew. . . . But here they are again. Lord help them if it wasn't my business they were discussing.

(LIGURIO *and* FRA TIMOTEO *return.*)

FRA TIMOTEO: Get the ladies to come along here. I know what I have to do; and if my authority has any weight with them, we will conclude this little family affair this evening.

LIGURIO: Messer Nicia, Fra Timoteo will do everything we want. It is up to you to see that the ladies come.

MESSER NICIA: You make me very happy. And will it be a son?

LIGURIO: Oh yes.

MESSER NICIA: A boy. I'm quite overcome.

FRA TIMOTEO: Now you go to church; I will wait here for the ladies. Keep out of the way so they don't see you; and when they are gone, I will tell you what they have said.

(LIGURIO *and* MESSER NICIA *go.*)

FRA TIMOTEO: I really don't know who is tricking whom. That rogue Ligurio only produced the first story to try me out, so that if I refused to help with that he wouldn't have told me about this business at all, and given away their plot for nothing; they aren't concerned with the bogus one. Well, they caught me all right: but I can still turn the trap to my own use. Messer Nicia and Callimaco are rich, and by one means or another I shall do well out of both of them; the whole affair must be kept secret—that is as much in their interest as mine. Come what may I have no regrets. I expect there will be difficulties, it is true; Madonna Lucrezia is a sensible woman, and a good one; but I'll make that goodness work for me. All women are a little light in the head; if one of them can string two words together she is considered a marvel—in the country of the blind the one-eyed man is king. Here she is with her mother—a good sort of woman; she will be a great help in working her daughter round to my way of thinking. (*He goes.*)

(*Enter* SOSTRATA *and* LUCREZIA.)

SOSTRATA: I am sure you know, Lucrezia, that no one in the world values your honour more than I do, and that I would never advise you to do anything against your own interests. I have already told you, and I tell you again: if Fra Timoteo says there is nothing to burden your conscience with, then you needn't think twice about it.

LUCREZIA: This is what I have always been afraid of, that Messer Nicia's longing for an heir would make him do something outrageous; so I get anxious whenever he starts explaining some new idea—especially since what you know happened when I went to the Servites. But of all the ideas he has had, this is the strangest. That I should have to be ravished, and that a man should die for having ravished me— If I were the only woman left in all the world, and responsible for replenishing the whole human race, I can't think I would be justified in doing this.

SOSTRATA: I haven't so many fine words, my girl. Talk to the friar, see what he has to say, and then do whatever you are advised by him, by us, and by all who love you.

LUCREZIA: Oh God, my heart is bursting.

(FRA TIMOTEO *returns.*)

FRA TIMOTEO: You are welcome. I know what you have come to see me about; Messer Nicia has spoken to me. To tell you the truth I have been poring over my books for hours, studying the case, and after careful research I find that there are numerous considerations on our side, both general and particular.

LUCREZIA: Do you mean it, or are you laughing at me?

FRA TIMOTEO: Ah, Madonna Lucrezia. Is this a laughing matter? Am I such a stranger to you?

LUCREZIA: No, father; but this is the most fantastic idea I ever heard.

FRA TIMOTEO: I believe you, madonna, but I do not want you to continue in this strain. There are many things which, afar off, seem strange, terrifying, intolerable, which when you come close appear natural, bearable, homely; because of this one says that fear of the evil is greater than the evil itself. And this is such a matter.

LUCREZIA: Please God it is.

FRA TIMOTEO: I want to go back to what I first said to you. As far as conscience is concerned, you have to accept this common rule: that where there is a certain good and an uncertain evil, the good must never be sacrificed for fear of the evil. Here we have a certain good—that you will conceive a child, gaining a soul for our Almighty Saviour: the uncertain evil is that the man who shares your bed after you have taken the potion might die; but it may well turn out that he does not die. Nevertheless, as there is some doubt, it is better for Messer Nicia not to run any risk. As for the act itself, it is foolish to call that a sin, for it is the will that commits a sin, not the body; the real sin is to displease your husband, and you will be pleasing him; or to take pleasure in the act, and you will not take pleasure in it. Besides this, it is the outcome of any action that we have to bear in mind: the outcome of yours will be to content your husband and fill a place in Paradise. The Bible says that Lot's daughters, believing themselves left alone in the world, lay with their father; and, because their intention was good they did not sin.

the fate of the man considered first — death —

an ancient principle twisted

LUCREZIA: What advice do you give me then?

SOSTRATA: Just let yourself *be* advised, girl. Don't you realize that a childless wife is a homeless wife? When her husband is dead she is like a mere wild creature, abandoned by the world.

FRA TIMOTEO: I swear to you, madonna, by this sacred cloth that by obeying your husband in this matter your conscience will be no more burdened than if you were to eat meat on a Friday, and that is a sin which can be washed away with holy water.

LUCREZIA: Where are you leading me, father?

FRA TIMOTEO: I am leading you to an action for which you will always want to pray God's blessing on me, and which will please you more in a year's time than it does now.

note irony

SOSTRATA: She will do what you wish. I am going to put her to bed myself. What are you frightened of, you silly girl? There are fifty women in this city who would give their eyes to be in your place.

LUCREZIA: Well, I consent—but I know I'll die before the morning comes.

FRA TIMOTEO: Have no fears, my child: I will pray God for you; I will intercede with the angel Raphael so that he will be with you. Go with God's blessing, and prepare yourself for the mystery, for it is already growing dark.

SOSTRATA: Peace be with you, father.

LUCREZIA: God and our Lady protect me and keep me from harm!

(LUCREZIA *and* SOSTRATA *go out.*)

FRA TIMOTEO: Oh Ligurio, come here.

(*Enter* LIGURIO.)

LIGURIO: How did it go?

FRA TIMOTEO: Very well. They have gone home prepared to do what we want, and there will be no difficulty: her mother intends to stay with her and put her to bed herself.

MESSER NICIA: Is that the truth?

FRA TIMOTEO: What's this? So you've got over your deafness!

LIGURIO: St. Clement has vouchsafed him this favour.

FRA TIMOTEO: You will want to donate an ex voto. It will draw other offerings, and we shall share together in this blessing.

MESSER NICIA: We are straying from the point. Is my wife going to make difficulties about doing as I wish?

FRA TIMOTEO: As I tell you, no.

MESSER NICIA: I am the happiest man alive!

FRA TIMOTEO: I believe it—and if a bonny boy isn't soon yours—well, there aren't any to be had.

LIGURIO: Father, go back to your prayers, and if we need you again we'll come for you. You, Messere, go after your wife and keep her resolution firm, while I find Maestro Callimaco and get him to send you the potion. Come back after sunset, so that we can arrange what is to be done at midnight.

MESSER NICIA: Wisely spoken. Farewell.

FRA TIMOTEO: God be with you.

Song at the end of Act III

How sweet when the decision's made,
The trap for your desires laid:
Anticipation softens grief,
And stratagems afford relief.

Oh solace lofty, sweet and sure,
When the uncertain plagues no more;
Enriching love, rewarding care—
Such is the plot, the pleasing snare,

Whose mighty power and sacred lore
Rocks, spells and poisons yield before.

ACT IV

(*Enter* CALLIMACO.)

CALLIMACO: I only wish I knew what the others had done. Am I never going to find Ligurio? I'm sure it's after eleven— it must be nearly midnight! The agonies I have been suffering —and still do! It's all too true that fortune and nature balance our accounts between them: nothing good happens but something bad is sure to follow—the higher my hopes, the greater my fears. I'm so miserable! How can I go on like this, living in despair, with these hopes and fears torturing me? I am like a ship tossed by contrary winds: the nearer I get to port, the more I am afraid of being lost. For while Messer Nicia's stupidity gives me hope, the prudence and coldness of Lucrezia make me lose heart. Oh God! if only I could get some rest. I've tried to be calm, and laugh myself out of this mood. I say: What do you think you're doing? Have you lost your senses? And when you have won her, what then? You'll see your folly and regret all the anguish and pain it has cost. Don't you know how little pleasure a man gets from the things he desires compared to what he hoped to find? And on the other hand, the worst that can happen to you is that you'll die and go to hell; so many others are dead there must be plenty of good company down below! Surely you aren't ashamed to join them? Look fortune in the face: avoid danger, but if you cannot, confront it like a man; don't grovel, don't degrade yourself like a woman. So I try to encourage myself; but it has little effect, for the longing comes over me to be with the girl I love; it shakes me and changes my whole being—even my legs are trembling, my stomach fluttering, my heart is pounding as though it would burst, and my arms feel useless, my tongue wordless, my eyes dazzled, my brain awhirl. If only I could find Ligurio I could at least tell someone about it. But here he is—and in a hurry. What he says will either give me life for a little longer or kill me at once.

(*Enter* LIGURIO.)

LIGURIO: Never have I wanted Callimaco so much, and never have I had such a business finding him. If it had been bad news I was bringing I would have come upon him all too soon. I've been to his house, to the Piazza, to the market, outside the Spini, to the Loggia of the Tornaquinci, and no sign of him. These lovers are made of quicksilver and can't keep still.

CALLIMACO: (Well, why not call out to him? He seems to be cheerful after all.) Oh, Ligurio! Ligurio!

LIGURIO: Oh Callimaco, where have you been?

CALLIMACO: What news?

LIGURIO: Good.

CALLIMACO: Really good?

LIGURIO: The best.

CALLIMACO: Has Lucrezia agreed?

LIGURIO: Yes.

CALLIMACO: And the friar will do what we need?

LIGURIO: He will.

CALLIMACO: Oh blessed friar! I will always pray to God for him!

LIGURIO: Oh, magnificent! So God grants the prayers of the wicked as well as the good! The friar will want something more than prayers.

CALLIMACO: Well, what?

LIGURIO: Cash.

CALLIMACO: Let him have it then. How much have you promised him?

LIGURIO: Three hundred ducats.

CALLIMACO: Excellent.

LIGURIO: And Messer Nicia has handed over twenty-five of them.

CALLIMACO: Messer Nicia?

LIGURIO: Never mind. He has.

CALLIMACO: And Lucrezia's mother—what has she done?

LIGURIO: Just about everything. When she found that her daughter could have this pleasant night without any sin, she didn't stop begging, ordering, and then reassuring Lucrezia until she had led her to the friar, and then went on until she gave in.

CALLIMACO: Oh God! What am I to deserve all this? I could die for joy.

LIGURIO: What sort of a man is this? First it's grief he's dying for, then joy. Have you got the potion ready?

CALLIMACO: Yes, I have.

LIGURIO: What are you sending her?

CALLIMACO: A draught of hippocras, ideal for calming the

stomach and stimulating the mind.—Oh, God! Oh fool, fool, fool that I am!

LIGURIO: What is it? What's the matter?

CALLIMACO: And there's no way out.

LIGURIO: What the devil is wrong with you?

CALLIMACO: There is nothing to be done; and the thought is like fire.

LIGURIO: But why? Why don't you say what's the matter? Take your hands from your face.

CALLIMACO: Oh—don't you know that I told Messer Nicia that you, he, Siro and *I* would kidnap someone to put to bed with his wife?

LIGURIO: What is wrong with that?

CALLIMACO: What is wrong? Why, if I am with you, I can't be the man you take; if I'm not with you he will see through the plot.

LIGURIO: That is true. But isn't there some way out?

CALLIMACO: Not that I can see.

LIGURIO: Oh, there must be.

CALLIMACO: Well, what?

LIGURIO: You'll have to let me think.

CALLIMACO: Oh, if you've got to start thinking about it now, I'm lost.

LIGURIO: I've got it!

CALLIMACO: What?

LIGURIO: I will work it so that the friar, who has helped us as far as this, will take care of the rest as well.

CALLIMACO: How?

LIGURIO: We've all got to be disguised! I'll dress up the friar; he will change his voice, his face and his habit, and I'll tell Messer Nicia that it's you—and he'll believe it.

CALLIMACO: Yes, I like that. But what shall I do?

LIGURIO: Make sure you've got a tattered old cloak on, and pass by his house with a lute in your hand, singing some song or other.

CALLIMACO: With my face uncovered?

LIGURIO: Yes: if you wear a mask he'll be suspicious.

CALLIMACO: Then he'll recognize me.

LIGURIO: No he won't, because you're going to screw your face up—hang your mouth open, grimace, suck your lips in, or show your teeth—close one eye. Try it out.

CALLIMACO: Like this?

LIGURIO: No.

CALLIMACO: This way?

LIGURIO: Not good enough.

CALLIMACO: Like this, then?

LIGURIO: Yes, good; keep that in mind. I've got a false nose at home, and you can stick that on.

CALLIMACO: Good—and what then?

LIGURIO: When you arrive at the corner, we shall be there, and we'll seize your lute, lay hold of you, spin you round, take you indoors and put you to bed. And the rest is up to you.

CALLIMACO: But that is just the point—what do I do then?

LIGURIO: That is your affair—and to manage it so that you can go back again—that's your worry, not ours.

CALLIMACO: What do you mean?

LIGURIO: That you should make her yours tonight, and before you leave, let her know who you are, explain the plot, declare your love for her, tell her how much you adore her; show her that she could remain your ally without any scandal, or with a great deal of scandal become your enemy. But there'll be no question of that—she won't want tonight to be the last.

CALLIMACO: You really believe that?

LIGURIO: I am sure of it. But don't let's lose any more time; it's ten already. Call Siro, send the potion to Messer Nicia, and wait for me at home. I will fetch the friar and disguise him; we'll get him here, find Messer Nicia, and do whatever else needs doing.

CALLIMACO: Good. Wonderful. Go on then.

(LIGURIO *goes. Enter* SIRO.)

CALLIMACO: Oh Siro!

SIRO: Messere!

CALLIMACO: Come here.

SIRO: And here I am.

CALLIMACO: Bring me the silver goblet which is in the cupboard in my room. Cover it with a napkin, and be careful not to spill it on the way.

SIRO: Right away. (*He goes.*)

CALLIMACO: Siro has been with me for ten years now and he's never let me down. I think I can trust him in this business too. I haven't said anything but he's no fool—he knows something's going on; and he seems to be playing up to it.

(SIRO *returns.*)

SIRO: Here it is.

CALLIMACO: Good. Now, go to Messer Nicia's house and tell him that this is the medicine his wife is to take straight after dinner—the sooner she dines now the better; and tell him that we will be in our place without fail at the time he is to join us here. Now hurry.

SIRO: I'm off.

CALLIMACO: And listen. If he wants you to wait, then come back with him; otherwise come back as soon as you've delivered it.

SIRO: Yes, messere. (*He goes.*)

CALLIMACO: Now I have to wait for Ligurio to come back with the friar—and whoever said waiting was a hard task told no lie. I must lose pounds every hour, thinking where I am now and where I might be in two hours' time, and afraid all the time that something will happen to ruin our plans. If it did, this would be the last night of my life; I would drown myself in the Arno, or hang myself, or throw myself out of that window, or stab myself in her very doorway—anything to end it all. But isn't that Ligurio coming? It is—yes—and someone with him, someone limping, with a humpback; it must be that friar in disguise. Lord, friars— know one and you know them all! Who is the other man who has joined them? It seems to be Siro—he must have finished his errand to Messer Nicia; yes, it is. I'll wait to meet them here.

(*Re-enter* SIRO *with* LIGURIO, *and* FRA TIMOTEO, *disguised.*)

SIRO: Who's that with you, Ligurio?

LIGURIO: An honest man if ever there was one.

SIRO: Is he really lame or is he faking it?

LIGURIO: Mind your own business.

SIRO: Lord! He's got the face of a proper villain!

LIGURIO: For God's sake be quiet; you'll spoil everything. Where is Callimaco?

CALLIMACO: I am here. It's good to see you back!

LIGURIO: Oh Callimaco, warn this idiot Siro. He has made enough trouble already.

CALLIMACO: Siro, listen to me: this evening you are to do everything Ligurio tells you, and when he gives you an order behave as though it was I; and keep secret whatever you see or hear, if you respect my concerns, my honour, my life— and your own interests.

SIRO: I'll do as you say.

CALLIMACO: Did you give the goblet to Messer Nicia?

SIRO: Yes, messere.

CALLIMACO: And what did he say?

SIRO: That he'll soon be at your disposal.

FRA TIMOTEO: Is this Callimaco?

CALLIMACO: At your service. Let us be quite clear about terms; you may dispose of me and all my fortune as if your own.

FRA TIMOTEO: I thank you—For my part, I have undertaken to do for you what I would not do for any other man.

CALLIMACO: It will be worth your while.

FRA TIMOTEO: Enough that I have your good wishes.

LIGURIO: Let's leave ceremony out of this. Siro and I will

go and disguise ourselves. You, Callimaco, come and get
ready to play your part. The friar can wait for us here; we'll
soon be back and then go for Messer Nicia.

CALLIMACO: Well said. Let us go.

FRA TIMOTEO: I will wait for you.

(*All go but the friar.*)

FRA TIMOTEO: It has been truly said that bad company
leads men to the gallows: an excess of good nature as well as
evil nature can bring you to a bad end. God knows that I
have never thought of bringing harm to anyone; that I have
kept in my cell, said my office, looked after my parishioners.
Then comes this devil Ligurio, who made me first dip my
finger into mischief, then my arm, and then my whole body
—and I still don't know where it's all going to end. But my
consolation is this: that when a thing concerns many, the
responsibility can't be laid at the door of anyone in particular.
But here is Ligurio again with the servant.

(*Enter* LIGURIO *and* SIRO.)

FRA TIMOTEO: I am glad to see you back.

LIGURIO: Are we ready?

FRA TIMOTEO: All prepared.

LIGURIO: We still need Messer Nicia. Let's go towards his
house; it's already past eleven. Come on.

SIRO: Someone's opening his door. Is it a servant?

LIGURIO: No, it's himself. Oh!

SIRO: What are you laughing at?

LIGURIO: Well, who wouldn't? He is wearing some sort of
cloak that doesn't even cover his bottom. What the devil has
he got on his head? It looks like one of these canon's hoods,
and he's got some sort of little sword sticking out—eh?—he's
muttering something, I don't know what. Stand back and let's
hear something of what his wife has to put up with.

(*Enter* MESSER NICIA, *disguised.*)

MESSER NICIA: The way that jade carries on! She has sent
her maid off to her mother's, and the porter to the country.
I approve of that; but I do not approve of all the fuss she
made before she would consent to go to bed—I don't want
to! . . . What will become of me? . . . What are you forcing
me to do? . . . Alas! Oh my mama! And if her mother hadn't
got round her with her tongue she would not have gone to
bed at all. A plague on her! I am all for women being a little
difficult to please—but within reason: She has driven me out
of my wits, the silly, affected creature! If you were to say:
"Damn you, for all that you are the paragon of Florence!"
she would only reply "What have I done?"—But I know that

the wooden horse has got to break into Troy, and before
I leave the field of action I am going to be able to say, with
Monna Ghinga: "I've seen it all right—with my two hands!"
I really look rather fine. Who would recognize me? I look
taller, younger, slenderer—there isn't a girl in the town who
wouldn't have me for nothing! But where have the others
got to?

LIGURIO: Good evening, messere!

MESSER NICIA: Oh, oh, oh!

LIGURIO: Don't be afraid, it's us.

MESSER NICIA: Oh! you are all here! If I had not recognized
you at once, I would have had at you with my sword in a
flash! This is Ligurio, and you, Siro, and the other is your
master? Ah!

LIGURIO: Quite right, messere.

MESSER NICIA: Let's see. Oh, his disguise is good; the town
marshal himself would not know him.

LIGURIO: I have made him put a couple of walnuts in his
mouth, so that he won't be recognized by his voice.

MESSER NICIA: Dear me now—silly boy!

LIGURIO: What?

MESSER NICIA: Why didn't you tell me about it before? I
would have used two of them myself: you know it's most
important people shouldn't recognize our voices.

LIGURIO: Here, then, put this in your mouth.

MESSER NICIA: What is it?

LIGURIO: A bit of wax.

MESSER NICIA: Give it me . . . ca, pu, ca, co, co, cu, cu,
spu . . . Plague take you, you filthy scoundrel.

LIGURIO: Oh, forgive me, I must have given you the wrong
one by mistake.

MESSER NICIA: Ca, ca, pu, pu, . . . What . . . What was it?

LIGURIO: Bitter aloes.

MESSER NICIA: Be damned to you! spu, spu . . . Doctor,
can't you say something?

FRA TIMOTEO: I am very annoyed with Ligurio.

MESSER NICIA: Oh! How well you have changed your voice!

LIGURIO: Don't let's lose any more time here. I will be
captain and draw up the plan of campaign. We'll use the
crescent formation. Callimaco, you be the right horn, I'll be
the left, and Messer Nicia can support us in the middle. Siro
be rearguard and come to the help of whichever side gives
way. The password shall be: Saint Cuckoo.

MESSER NICIA: Saint Cuckoo? Who is Saint Cuckoo?

LIGURIO: The most celebrated saint in France. Come now,
to our positions; we will lay the ambush in this corner. Keep
still—listen: I can hear a lute.

MESSER NICIA: It's a man. What are we going to do?

LIGURIO: Send forward a spy to find out who it is, and then act on his report.

MESSER NICIA: Who will go?

LIGURIO: You go, Siro. You know what you have to do: investigate, observe, hurry back, and report to us.

SIRO: Very well.

MESSER NICIA: I would not want us to make some mistake, and get some weak old man or a cripple, so that we'd have to play this game all over again tomorrow evening.

LIGURIO: Don't worry, Siro's reliable. He is on his way back now. Siro, what have you found?

SIRO: He's the prettiest young man you ever saw! He's barely twenty-five, all alone, dressed like a beggar, and playing a lute.

MESSER NICIA: If you're telling the truth, he's just the man —but remember you'll be to blame if anything goes wrong.

SIRO: He's just as I say.

LIGURIO: We will wait till he is round the corner, then set on him suddenly.

MESSER NICIA: Doctor, come on over here; you're as silent as a post this evening! Here he is!

(*Enter* CALLIMACO, *disguised.*)

CALLIMACO: "—And so may the devil get into your bed, As I can no longer come there—"

LIGURIO: Hold him tight! Hand over the lute.

CALLIMACO: Help! What have I done?

MESSER NICIA: You'll soon see. Cover his head—muffle him up!

LIGURIO: Spin him round!

MESSER NICIA: Give him another turn! Give him another! Home with him!

FRA TIMOTEO: Messer Nicia, I am going home to get some rest: my head is aching enough to kill me; and I won't come back tomorrow morning unless you need me.

MESSER NICIA: Certainly, Maestro. Don't come back; we can manage on our own.

(*They all go, except the friar.*)

FRA TIMOTEO: And now they have gone indoors, and I am off to my monastery. But you, spectators, don't complain; because tonight none of us will be asleep; and although this act is over, the action, I assure you, will be continuous. I am going to say my office. Ligurio and Siro will have supper, as they have not eaten all day. Messer Nicia will go from room to room, keeping an eye on things. And Callimaco and Madonna Lucrezia won't sleep, because I know that if I were in his place and you were in hers—we wouldn't sleep either.

Song at the end of Act IV

O tender night, O holy
Serene and quiet hour,
So many joys fulfilling
With your uniting power;

You are for hopeful lovers
The sole source of all pleasure,
For you can make a mortal
Blessèd beyond all measure.

You crown them at the ending
Of the hard way they've chosen—
Soft night! that can enkindle
Even the heart that's frozen.

ACT V

(*Enter* FRA TIMOTEO.)

FRA TIMOTEO: I have been so longing to know how Callimaco and the others got on that I couldn't close an eye all
night. I tried to kill time in one way after another: I said
matins, read a life of one of the Fathers, went into the church
and lit a lamp that had gone out, and changed the veil on a
Madonna who works miracles.——How many times have I told
these monks to keep her clean! And then they are surprised
when devotion falls off! I remember when she had five hundred ex votos, and today there aren't twenty; and this is our
own fault, for not knowing how to keep up her reputation.
Why, we used to go there in procession every evening after
compline, and have lauds sung there every Saturday. We used
to make ex votos ourselves so that there were always fresh
ones to be seen; we used to get offerings for her out of the
ladies through the confessional—and out of the men too.
There's nothing like that now—and then we marvel that devotion is so cold! Oh, what a stupid lot my brother monks
are! But I can hear a great uproar in Messer Nicia's house.
There they are, by my faith; they are turning out their victim.
I have come at just the right moment. They are in a hurry
to get rid of him, though it's hardly dawn. I think I'll stay
and hear what they are saying—no need to show myself. (*He
retires.*)

(*Enter* MESSER NICIA, LIGURIO *and* SIRO *with* CALLIMACO.)
MESSER NICIA: You hold him that side and I on this: and
you, Siro, hold him at the back, by his doublet.

CALLIMACO: Don't hurt me!

LIGURIO: You've nothing to be afraid of, but be off with you.

MESSER NICIA: We had better not go any further.

LIGURIO: You are right, let him go here. Turn him round a couple of times, so that he can't tell where he's been. Turn him, Siro.

SIRO: There.

MESSER NICIA: Give him another turn!

SIRO: There!

CALLIMACO: My lute!

LIGURIO: Now you, make yourself scarce! And if I hear you babbling about this, I'll cut your dirty throat!

(CALLIMACO goes.)

MESSER NICIA: Well, he's gone. Now we can be ourselves again and we must all be out early so that it does not look as if we were up all night.

LIGURIO: You are right.

MESSER NICIA: You and Siro go and find Maestro Callimaco and tell him that the affair went off well.

LIGURIO: But what can we tell him? We don't know anything. Once we got inside the house we went straight down to drink in the cellar—you know we did. You and your mother-in-law stayed up to deal with him, and we didn't see you again until just now, when you called us to put him out.

MESSER NICIA: That is true. Oh! I can tell you some fine things! My wife was in bed in the dark. Sostrata was waiting up by the fire. I arrived with our young clodhopper, and, so that I should not be left in doubt about anything, I took him into that dim little room over the hall, and cast the light so that he could not see my face.

LIGURIO: Wisely done.

MESSER NICIA: I had him undress: he made a bit of trouble, but I turned on him like a dog, so that he jumped to it, I can tell you, and had his things off in a trice. He'd got an ugly sort of face. He had a great brute of a nose, a mouth all askew—but you never saw such a good skin: white, smooth, tender; and as for the rest, there is no need to ask.

LIGURIO: No, you've got to see that sort of thing with your own eyes; what is the good of talking about it?

MESSER NICIA: Now you are joking. Once I had put my hand to the plough I wasn't going to let go. I wanted to make sure he was all right. Why, if he had had the pox, where should I have been? What would you have done?

LIGURIO: Yes, you are quite right.

MESSER NICIA: When I was sure he was healthy, then I made him follow me and led him in the dark to the bedroom, and got him into bed. And before I left I wanted to make sure with my own hands how things were going: I was never one to be fooled by appearances.

LIGURIO: With what excellent judgement you have managed this whole affair!

MESSER NICIA: So when I had touched and felt everything, I left the room and shut the door, and went to my mother-in-law who was still waiting up, and we spent the whole night in conversation.

LIGURIO: And what were you talking about?

MESSER NICIA: About Lucrezia's foolishness, and how much better it would have been if she had given in at the start without making so much trouble. Then we talked about the heir that I felt was already mine, the little rascal!—and then I heard five o'clock striking, and was afraid it would soon be light, so I went into the bedroom. And would you believe it? —I couldn't wake the fellow up!

LIGURIO: I believe you!

MESSER NICIA: It had just about finished him. However, I got him up, called you, and we took him outside.

LIGURIO: Everything went off very well.

MESSER NICIA: What would you say if I told you I was worried about something?

LIGURIO: About what?

MESSER NICIA: About that poor young man, because he has to die so soon, and because the night's escapade is going to cost him so dear.

LIGURIO: You can't have much to worry about! Let him look after himself.

MESSER NICIA: You are right. But I can't wait till I find Maestro Callimaco and congratulate him.

LIGURIO: He will be out in an hour or so. But the sun's up already and we must get out of these things. What about you?

MESSER NICIA: I will go home too, and put on fresh clothes. I will get my wife up and washed, and make her come to the friar's to be churched. I would like you and Callimaco to be there, so that we can speak to the friar, to thank him and repay him for the good he has done us.

LIGURIO: Well and good, and so be it.

(*All go out except the friar.*)

FRA TIMOTEO (*coming forward*): I heard everything they said, and I can't help smiling when I think of Messer Nicia's foolishness; but it is the conclusion of the matter that has really rejoiced my heart. And since they are off to find me I must not stay here any longer but be waiting for them in

church, where I can get the best value for my goods. But
who is coming out of the house? It looks like Ligurio, and
that must be Callimaco with him. As I've said, I do not want
to be discovered here; after all, if they don't come to see
me, I can always go looking for them. (*He goes.*)

(*Enter* CALLIMACO *with* LIGURIO.)

CALLIMACO. As I told you, Ligurio, till after one o'clock I
wasn't really happy about it, and though my pleasure was
great, I was not able to enjoy it. But after I had told her who
I was, and had made her understand how much I loved her,
and how easily we could live happily without it involving any
scandal, thanks to the foolishness of her husband, and had
promised that when God had other plans for him I would
marry her at once—and when on top of all this she had felt
the difference between my love and Messer Nicia's, and between the kisses of a young lover and an old husband, then,
after a sigh or two, she said: "Since your cunning, the folly
of my husband, my mother's lack of scruple and the wickedness of my confessor have combined to make me do what I
would never have done on my own, I can only believe that
some divine influence has willed this, and, as it is not for me
to resist what heaven decrees, I surrender. And so I take you
for my lord, and master, and guide. You must be everything
to me—father, defender, and the sole source of all my happiness: and what my husband wanted for a night, I want him
to have for ever. Seek his friendship, then: go to church this
morning, then come home to dine with us; you shall come
and go as you will, and we shall be able to be together at
any time without suspicion." When I heard this I was overwhelmed with tenderness, and hardly able to express anything
of what I felt. But the result is that I am the happiest and
most contented man in all the world, and if neither death
nor time destroy my happiness—the saints themselves shall
call me blessed!

LIGURIO: And your happiness is my happiness; everything's
fallen out just as I said it would. And what do we do now?

CALLIMACO: Go to the church; I promised I'd be there,
and she is coming, with her mother and Messer Nicia.

LIGURIO: I can hear the door opening; there they are—with
Messer Nicia behind.

CALLIMACO: Come on, then, and wait for them. (*They go.*)

(*Enter* MESSER NICIA, LUCREZIA, SOSTRATA.)

MESSER NICIA: Lucrezia, I believe that everything should be
done, not rashly, but out of the fear of God.

LUCREZIA: And now what is there to do?

MESSER NICIA: Look how she answers! Perky as a peacock.

SOSTRATA: Don't be surprised at that: she's a bit over-
excited.

LUCREZIA: What have you got to say?

MESSER NICIA: I say that it is right that I should go on ahead to speak to the friar, and tell him to meet you at the church door so that he can sanctify you—for this morning it is just as though you had been reborn.

LUCREZIA: Why don't you go then?

MESSER NICIA: Well, well! How lively you are this morning. Last night you seemed half-dead.

LUCREZIA: It's you I have to thank for it.

SOSTRATA: Go along and find the friar—oh, there's no need: he's coming out of the church.

MESSER NICIA: So he is.

(*Enter* FRA TIMOTEO.)

FRA TIMOTEO: I come because I have been told by Callimaco and Ligurio that Messer Nicia and his wife are on the way to church.

MESSER NICIA: *Bona dies,* father!

FRA TIMOTEO: You are welcome; may fortune favor you, madonna, and may God grant you a fine male child!

LUCREZIA: As God wills.

FRA TIMOTEO: Oh, He wills it, He certainly wills it.

MESSER NICIA: Is that Ligurio and Callimaco I can see in church?

FRA TIMOTEO: It is.

MESSER NICIA: Ask them to come here.

FRA TIMOTEO: Come!

(*Enter* CALLIMACO *and* LIGURIO.)

CALLIMACO: God save you!

MESSER NICIA: Maestro, take my wife's hand.

CALLIMACO: I will.

MESSER NICIA: Lucrezia, this is the man thanks to whom we shall have a staff to support our old age.

LUCREZIA: I am most grateful to him and I hope he will consider himself our friend.

MESSER NICIA: May heaven bless you! And I hope that he and Ligurio will come to dine with us this morning.

LUCREZIA: I should be most pleased.

MESSER NICIA: And I am going to give them the key of the ground floor room off the loggia, so that they can come whenever they like; they have no women to look after them and must live like animals.

CALLIMACO: Thank you: and I shall make good use of it.

FRA TIMOTEO: And am I to have the money to give in alms?

MESSER NICIA: You are, father, you are; it will be sent to you without delay.

LIGURIO: Doesn't Siro get anything out of this?

MESSER NICIA: Let him but ask! What I have is his. You, Lucrezia, how much shall we give the friar for churching you?

LUCREZIA: Oh—ten ducats.

MESSER NICIA: (I can't breathe!)

FRA TIMOTEO: And you, Madonna Sostrata, seem to me to have recovered your own youth!

SOSTRATA: Today everyone is happy.

FRA TIMOTEO: Let us all go into church, and there join together in prayer, and after the service go off to dinner as you please. You spectators, do not wait for us to come out any more; the service is long, and I shall remain in church, and when they go home they will leave from the door on the other side. Farewell!

William Shakespeare:

TWELFTH NIGHT

On January 6, 1663, Samuel Pepys made an entry in his famous diary: "Saw *Twelfth Night* acted well, though it be but a silly play, and not related at all to the name or day." Pepys' two criticisms are understandable. For a busy Englishman a play about the confusion resulting when twins are shipwrecked can easily be silly, and such a plot has no apparent connection with the holiday of Twelfth-night, the twelfth day after Christmas, commemorating the visit of the Magi to the infant Jesus. But the "silliness" of Shakespeare's *Twelfth Night* (c. 1601) was part of the holiday spirit, and a play such as this was just the sort often performed to mark the close of the Christmas revels. Perhaps foreseeing Pepys' kind of criticism, Shakespeare (1564–1616) provided a subtitle, *What You Will*, though George Bernard Shaw insisted (underscoring *You*) that this second title indicated Shakespeare's recognition of, and contempt for, the public's demand for silliness.

A bare retelling of the plot would confirm Pepys' view that the play was silly, and Shakespeare himself seems to have been aware of the comedy's wild improbabilities, for at one point a character comments, "If this were played upon a stage now, I could condemn it as an improbable fiction." And yet tales of the mishaps of twins, perhaps *because* they are foolish, have, in various forms, persisted from the Greeks through the Romans to the Italians of the Renaissance, then to the Elizabethans, and down to the present. Rodgers and Hart, for example, built their musical comedy, *The Boys from Syracuse*, on the twins in Shakespeare's *Comedy of Errors* (adapted in turn from Plautus' *The Menaechmus Twins*), and recently Jean Anouilh's *Ring Round the Moon* used this ancient gambit. But Shakespeare's comedy is more than simply a couple of hours of hodgepodge: it is, among other things, a masterpiece of organization, complex, yet easy to follow, with every part harmonizing (the musical analogy is intentional) with the whole. Viola and Sebastian are shipwrecked and separated, and Viola is forced by circumstances to adopt a boy's apparel. She calls herself "Cesario," and finds herself in love (but, of course, unable in her male disguise to reveal her love) with Duke Orsino;

107

Orsino, however, is in love with the Lady Olivia, who falls in love with "Cesario." Superficially this is silliness, but, even if it were no more, its madness would be its own excuse for being; yet it is more than that.

Some idea of the nature of Elizabethan comedy can be gained from a passage in *An Apology for Actors* (1612), by Thomas Heywood, a dramatist whom Shakespeare must have known well. Comedy, Heywood writes, "is pleasantly contrived with merry accidents, and intermixed with apt and witty jests . . . merrily fitted to the stage. And what is then the subject of this harmless mirth? Either in the shape of a Clown, to show others their slovenly and unhandsome behavior, that they may reform that simplicity in themselves, which others make their sport, lest they happen to become the like subject of general scorn to an auditory, . . . or [secondly] to refresh such weary spirits as are tired with labor, or study, to moderate the cares and heaviness of the mind, that they may return to their trades and faculties with more zeal and earnestness, after some small soft and pleasant retirement." Heywood, then, gives comedy two functions: to reform by exposing bad behavior, and "to refresh." Whether anyone ever saw himself on the stage and therefore amended his behavior is dubious (though most comic dramatists insist on the therapeutic function of comedy), but, to begin with this first point of Heywood's, Shakespeare in *Twelfth Night* offers those of us who are proud a chance to see ourselves and repent. Olivia's steward, Malvolio, suffers from the disease of self-love, or pride, is encouraged in his suit for his lady's hand by an agreeable bunch of tricksters, and is finally rudely awakened. Before we take a look at the non-satiric or "refreshing" elements in *Twelfth Night*, we might examine Malvolio and see why his plight is comic rather than tragic; see, that is, why we smile at this figure in distress, yet feel pity for a tragic hero who out of pride may have reached too high.

Like a tragic hero, Malvolio suffers from pride, the *hybris* of the Greeks, and, again like a tragic hero, he finds that self-assertion brings him into conflict with his environment. In tragedy, the protagonist by a heroic and exhausting endeavor readjusts the balance, wringing significance out of his life—though usually at the expense of that life. But in *Twelfth Night* Malvolio merely continues to defy his antagonists, who are not great forces but jovial tipplers. He is "a kind of Puritan," anxious to impose his will on others, thinking that because he is virtuous there shall be no more cakes and ale. His struggle is unworthy as well as unheroic. Our sympathies are all with his foes, who represent an easy way of life which, at least within the playhouse, gains our approval. The corrupt world which surrounds some of Shakespeare's tragic heroes we reject, and our sympathy goes out to the man partly entrapped in it; but the Illyria of *Twelfth Night* is another thing, and he who would war against it forfeits our approval, since he has forfeited his love for humanity.

It is love of humanity that characterizes most of the other figures in the play, and if the Malvolios of the audience decide to abandon their self-love, they can best see how they ought to live by looking at Viola. And this brings us to the second part of Heywood's definition of the aims of comedy, for when we turn from the deformity of Malvolio, we find not only good models to imitate, but also characters who are delightful simply to see and hear. Shakespearean comedy shows us not merely a way of life to shun, but an exuberant world richer than our own, a world filled with beauty. Appropriately, the play begins with a reference to music, "If music be the food of love, play on," and concludes with a song, for music is perhaps the closest analogy to Shakespeare's melodious comic world. Shakespeare's comedy, like music, has an "outgoingness" which swells beyond a merely rational view; when Duke Orsino rewards Feste's song with money "for thy pains," and Feste replies, "No pains, sir, I take pleasure in singing, sir," we dwell in a world larger than that of good business relations.

Shakespeare's world is not, however, a mere fantasy world; it is rooted in reality. Olivia's household must have seemed to the Elizabethan much like any great household; along with song it harbors drinking, folly, and cowardice. In *Much Ado about Nothing* Shakespeare noted that music, though it hales forth men's souls, is produced from sheep-guts, and in *Twelfth Night* we see a world more beautiful than our own but one which is rooted in the raw material of ours. And even in Viola's world something must be left to Providence:

> O Time! thou must untangle this, not I;
> It is too hard a knot for me to untie!

Time does untangle the knot, and, after a while, "journeys end in lovers meeting." And yet, while we perceive that Viola's realm is not totally removed from our own world, we nevertheless are conscious of a difference: hence, at the end of the play the clown gently brings us back to everyday existence. Life must be taken for what it is; youth may dream of Illyria, but maturity teaches us (the clown says with pardonable hyperbole) that "the rain it raineth every day."

Twelfth Night: or What You Will

Characters

ORSINO, *Duke of Illyria.*

SEBASTIAN, *brother to Viola.*

ANTONIO, *a sea captain, friend to Sebastian.*

A SEA CAPTAIN, *friend to Viola.*

VALENTINE,
CURIO, } *gentlemen attending on the Duke.*

SIR TOBY BELCH, *uncle to Olivia.*

SIR ANDREW AGUECHEEK.

MALVOLIO, *steward to Olivia.*

FABIAN,
FESTE, *a clown,* } *servants to Olivia.*

OLIVIA, *a Countess.*

VIOLA, *sister to Sebastian.*

MARIA, *Olivia's woman.*

LORDS, PRIESTS, SAILORS, OFFICERS, MUSICIANS, *and other* ATTENDANTS.

Scene: *A city in Illyria, and the seacoast near it.*

ACT I
SCENE I
(The DUKE'S *palace.)*

(Enter ORSINO [DUKE OF ILLYRIA], CURIO, *and other* LORDS; MUSICIANS.*)*

DUKE: If music be the food of love, play on.
Give me excess of it, that, surfeiting,
The appetite may sicken, and so die.
That strain again! it had a dying fall:[1]
O, it came o'er my ear like the sweet sound
That breathes upon a bank of violets,
Stealing and giving odor! Enough; no more!
'Tis not so sweet now as it was before.
O spirit of love, how quick[2] and fresh art thou!
That, notwithstanding thy capacity
Receiveth as the sea, nought enters there,
Of what validity and pitch[3] soe'er,
But falls into abatement and low price,
Even in a minute! So full of shapes is fancy,[4]
That it alone is high fantastical.[5]
CURIO: Will you go hunt, my Lord?
DUKE: What, Curio?
CURIO: The hart.
DUKE: Why, so I do, the noblest that I have.
O, when mine eyes did see Olivia first,
Methought she purged the air of pestilence!
That instant was I turn'd into a hart;[6]
And my desires, like fell and cruel hounds,
E'er since pursue me.

(Enter VALENTINE.*)*

                                    How now! what news from her?
VALENTINE: So please my lord, I might not be admitted;
But from her handmaid do return this answer:

[1] Cadence.
[2] Alive.
[3] Value and height.
[4] Love.
[5] Highly imaginative.
[6] Actaeon, having seen Diana bathing, was turned into a hart and killed by his own hounds.

111

The element[1] itself, till seven years' heat,

Shall not behold her face at ample view;
But, like a cloistress, she will veiled walk
And water once a day her chamber round
With eye-offending brine: all this to season[2]

A brother's dead love, which she would keep fresh
And lasting in her sad remembrance.

    DUKE: O, she that hath a heart of that fine frame
To pay this debt of love but to a brother,
How will she love, when the rich golden shaft[3]

Hath kill'd the flock of all affections else
That live in her; when liver, brain and heart,
These sovereign thrones, are all supplied, and fill'd
Her sweet perfections with one self king![4]

Away before me to sweet beds of flowers:
Love-thoughts lie rich when canopied with bowers.

    (*Exeunt.*)

SCENE II
(*The seacoast.*)

(*Enter* VIOLA, *a* CAPTAIN, *and* SAILORS.)
    VIOLA: What country, friends, is this?
    CAPTAIN: This is Illyria, lady.
    VIOLA: And what should I do in Illyria?
My brother he is in Elysium.
Perchance he is not drown'd. What think you, sailors?
    CAPTAIN: It is perchance that you yourself were saved.
    VIOLA: O my poor brother! and so perchance may he be.
    CAPTAIN: True, madam: and, to comfort you with chance,
Assure yourself, after our ship did split,
When you and those poor number saved with you
Hung on our driving boat, I saw your brother,
Most provident in peril, bind himself,
Courage and hope both teaching him the practice,
To a strong mast that lived upon the sea;
Where, like Arion[5] on the dolphin's back,
I saw him hold acquaintance with the waves
So long as I could see.
    VIOLA: For saying so, there's gold.
Mine own escape unfoldeth to my hope,
Whereto thy speech serves for authority,
The like of him. Know'st thou this country?

[1] Sky.
[2] To preserve.
[3] Cupid's arrow which causes love.
[4] One ruler only: love for one person.
[5] Greek poet who leaped into the sea to escape robbers. His music enchanted a dolphin who carried him safely to shore.

CAPTAIN: Aye, madam, well; for I was bred and born
Not three hours' travel from this very place.

VIOLA: Who governs here?

CAPTAIN: A noble Duke, in nature as in name.

VIOLA: What is his name?

CAPTAIN: Orsino.

VIOLA: Orsino! I have heard my father name him:
He was a bachelor then.

CAPTAIN: And so is now, or was so very late;
For but a month ago I went from hence,
And then 'twas fresh in murmur (as, you know,
What great ones do the less will prattle of)
That he did seek the love of fair Olivia.

VIOLA: What's she?

CAPTAIN: A virtuous maid, the daughter of a count
That died some twelvemonth since, then leaving her
In the protection of his son, her brother.
Who shortly also died; for whose dear love,
They say, she hath abjured the company
And sight of men.

VIOLA: O that I served that lady,
And might not be delivered to the world
Till I had made mine own occasion mellow,
What my estate is!

CAPTAIN: That were hard to compass,[1]
Because she will admit no kind of suit,
No, not the Duke's.

VIOLA: There is a fair behavior in thee, captain;
And though that nature with a beauteous wall
Doth oft close in pollution, yet of thee
I will believe thou hast a mind that suits
With this thy fair and outward character.
I prithee (and I'll pay thee bounteously)
Conceal me what I am, and be my aid
For such disguise as haply shall become
The form of my intent. I'll serve this Duke:
Thou shalt present me as an eunuch to him:
It may be worth thy pains; for I can sing,
And speak to him in many sorts of music
That will allow me very worth his service.
What else may hap to time I will commit;
Only shape thou thy silence to my wit.

CAPTAIN: Be you his eunuch, and your mute I'll be:
When my tongue blabs, then let mine eyes not see.

VIOLA: I thank thee. Lead me on.

(Exeunt.)

[1] To bring about.

SCENE III
(OLIVIA'S *house.*)

(*Enter* SIR TOBY BELCH *and* MARIA.)

SIR TOBY: What a plague means my niece, to take the death of her brother thus? I am sure care's an enemy to life.

MARIA: By my troth, Sir Toby, you must come in earlier o' nights. Your cousin,[1] my lady, takes great exceptions to your ill hours.

SIR TOBY: Why, let her except, before excepted.[2]

MARIA: Aye, but you must confine yourself within the modest limits of order.

SIR TOBY: Confine! I'll confine myself no finer than I am. These clothes are good enough to drink in, and so be these boots too. An they be not, let them hang themselves in their own straps.

MARIA: That quaffing and drinking will undo you. I heard my lady talk of it yesterday; and of a foolish knight that you brought in one night here to be her wooer.

SIR TOBY: Who, Sir Andrew Aguecheek?

MARIA: Aye, he.

SIR TOBY: He's as tall[3] a man as any's in Illyria.

MARIA: What's that to the purpose?

SIR TOBY: Why, he has three thousand ducats a year.

MARIA: Aye, but he'll have but a year in all these ducats; he's a very fool and a prodigal.

SIR TOBY: Fie that you'll say so! He plays o' the viol-de-gamboys, and speaks three or four languages word for word without book, and hath all the good gifts of nature.

MARIA: He hath indeed, almost natural,[4] for besides that he's a fool, he's a great quarreler; and but that he hath the gift of a coward to allay the gust[5] he hath in quarreling, 'tis thought among the prudent he would quickly have the gift of a grave.

SIR TOBY: By this hand, they are scoundrels and subtractors[6] that say so of him. Who are they?

MARIA: They that add, moreover, he's drunk nightly in your company.

SIR TOBY: With drinking healths to my niece. I'll drink to her as long as there is a passage in my throat and drink in Illyria. He's a coward and a coystrill[7] that will not drink to my niece till his brains turn o' the toe like a parish-top.[8] What,

---

1 Relative; here, niece.
2 A legal phrase meaning "except for exceptions."
3 Valiant.
4 Like a born fool.

5 Taste.
6 Slanderers.
7 Knave.
8 Spin like a top.

114

wench! Castiliano vulgo![1] for here comes Sir Andrew Ague-
face.

(*Enter* SIR ANDREW AGUECHEEK.)

SIR ANDREW: Sir Toby Belch! how now, Sir Toby Belch!

SIR TOBY: Sweet Sir Andrew!

SIR ANDREW: Bless you, fair shrew.

MARIA: And you too, sir.

SIR TOBY: Accost, Sir Andrew, accost.

SIR ANDREW: What's that?

SIR TOBY: My niece's chambermaid.

SIR ANDREW: Good Mistress Accost, I desire better acquaintance.

MARIA: My name is Mary, sir.

SIR ANDREW: Good Mistress Mary Accost,—

SIR TOBY: You mistake, knight. "Accost" is front her, board
her, woo her, assail her.

SIR ANDREW: By my troth, I would not undertake her in this
company. Is that the meaning of "accost"?

MARIA: Fare you well, gentlemen.

SIR TOBY: An thou let part so, Sir Andrew, would thou
mightst never draw sword again.

SIR ANDREW: An you part so, mistress, I would I might
never draw sword again. Fair lady, do you think you have
fools in hand?

MARIA: Sir, I have not you by the hand.

SIR ANDREW: Marry, but you shall have; and here's my hand.

MARIA: Now, sir, thought is free. I pray you, bring your
hand to the buttery-bar and let it drink.

SIR ANDREW: Wherefore, sweetheart? what's your metaphor?

MARIA: It's dry,[2] sir.

SIR ANDREW: Why, I think so. I am not such an ass but I
can keep my hand dry. But what's your jest?

MARIA: A dry jest, sir.

SIR ANDREW: Are you full of them?

MARIA: Aye, sir, I have them at my fingers' ends. Marry,
now I let go your hand, I am barren. (*Exit.*)

SIR TOBY: O knight, thou lackest a cup of canary.[3] When did
I see thee so put down?

SIR ANDREW: Never in your life, I think, unless you see
canary put me down. Methinks sometimes I have no more wit
than a Christian or an ordinary man has. But I am a great
eater of beef and I believe that does harm to my wit.

SIR TOBY: No question.

SIR ANDREW: An I thought that, I'ld forswear it. I'll ride
home to-morrow, Sir Toby.

---

[1] Gibberish to alert Maria of Sir Andrew's approach.
[2] A pun on "dry" meaning "debilitated" and "not moist."
[3] Sweet wine.

SIR TOBY: Pourquoi, my dear knight?

SIR ANDREW: What is "pourquoi"? Do, or not do? I would I had bestowed that time in the tongues[1] that I have in fencing, dancing and bear-baiting. O, had I but followed the arts!

SIR TOBY: Then hadst thou had an excellent head of hair.

SIR ANDREW: Why, would that have mended my hair?

SIR TOBY: Past question; for thou seest it will not curl by nature.

SIR ANDREW: But it becomes me well enough, does't not?

SIR TOBY: Excellent. It hangs like flax on a distaff; and I hope to see a housewife take thee between her legs and spin it off.

SIR ANDREW: Faith, I'll home to-morrow, Sir Toby. Your niece will not be seen; or if she be, it's four to one she'll none of me. The Count himself here hard by woos her.

SIR TOBY: She'll none o' the Count. She'll not match above her degree, neither in estate, years, nor wit; I have heard her swear't. Tut, there's life in 't,[2] man.

SIR ANDREW: I'll stay a month longer. I am a fellow o' the strangest mind i' the world. I delight in masques and revels sometimes altogether.

SIR TOBY: Art thou good at these kickshawses,[3] knight?

SIR ANDREW: As any man in Illyria, whatsoever he be, under the degree of my betters,[4] and yet I will not compare with an old man.

SIR TOBY: What is thy excellence in a galliard,[5] knight?

SIR ANDREW: Faith, I can cut a caper.

SIR TOBY: And I can cut the mutton to 't.

SIR ANDREW: And I think I have the back-trick[6] simply as strong as any man in Illyria.

SIR TOBY: Wherefore are these things hid? Wherefore have these gifts a curtain before 'em? Are they like to take dust, like Mistress Mall's picture? Why dost thou not go to church in a galliard and come home in a coranto?[7] My very walk should be a jig. I would not so much as make water but in a sink-a-pace.[8] What dost thou mean? Is it a world to hide virtues in? I did think, by the excellent constitution of thy leg, it was formed under the star of a galliard.

SIR ANDREW: Aye, 'tis strong, and it does indifferent well in a dun-colored stock. Shall we set about some revels?

SIR TOBY: What shall we do else? Were we not born under Taurus?

SIR ANDREW: Taurus! That's sides and heart.

SIR TOBY: No, sir; it is legs and thighs. Let me see thee caper. Ha! Higher! Ha, ha! Excellent! (*Exeunt.*)

---

[1] In his next speech Sir Toby puns on curling tongs.
[2] There's still hope.
[3] Trifles.
[4] Of lower rank than me.
[5] A lively dance.
[6] Elaborate backward step.
[7] Rapid dance.
[8] Five-step dance.

SCENE IV
(*The* DUKE'S *palace.*)

(*Enter* VALENTINE, *and* VIOLA *in man's attire.*)

VALENTINE: If the Duke continue these favors towards you,
Cesario, you are like to be much advanced. He hath known
you but three days, and already you are no stranger.

VIOLA: You either fear his humor[1] or my negligence, that
you call in question the continuance of his love. Is he inconstant, sir, in his favors?

VALENTINE: No, believe me.

VIOLA: I thank you. Here comes the count.

(*Enter* DUKE, CURIO, *and* ATTENDANTS.)

DUKE: Who saw Cesario, ho?

VIOLA: On your attendance, my lord, here.

DUKE: Stand you a while aloof. Cesario,
Thou know'st no less but all. I have unclasp'd
To thee the book even of my secret soul.
Therefore, good youth, address thy gait unto her;
Be not denied access, stand at her doors,
And tell them, there thy fixed foot shall grow
Till thou have audience.

VIOLA: Sure, my noble lord,
If she be so abandon'd to her sorrow
As it is spoke, she never will admit me.

DUKE: Be clamorous and leap all civil bounds
Rather than make unprofited[2] return.

VIOLA: Say I do speak with her, my lord, what then?

DUKE: O, then unfold the passion of my love;
Surprise her with discourse of my dear faith.
It shall become thee well to act my woes.
She will attend[3] it better in thy youth
Than in a nuncio's[4] of more grave aspect.

VIOLA: I think not so, my lord.

DUKE: Dear lad, believe it;
For they shall yet belie thy happy years,
That say thou art a man. Diana's lip
Is not more smooth and rubious,[5] thy small pipe
Is as the maiden's organ, shrill and sound;[6]
And all is semblative a woman's part.
I know thy constellation[7] is right apt

1 Capriciousness.
2 Unsuccessful.
3 Listen to.
4 Messenger's.

5 Rosy.
6 High and clear.
7 Nature.

117

For this affair. Some four or five attend him;
All, if you will; for I myself am best
When least in company. Prosper well in this,
And thou shalt live as freely as thy lord,
To call his fortunes thine.

VIOLA: I'll do my best
To woo your lady. (*Aside*) Yet, a barful[1] strife!
Whoe'er I woo, myself would be his wife.

(*Exeunt.*)

SCENE V
(OLIVIA'S *house.*)

(*Enter* MARIA *and* CLOWN.)

MARIA: Nay, either tell me where thou hast been, or I will
not open my lips so wide as a bristle may enter in way of thy
excuse. My lady will hang thee for thy absence.

CLOWN: Let her hang me! He that is well hanged in this
world needs to fear no colors.[2]

MARIA: Make that good.

CLOWN: He shall see none to fear.

MARIA: A good lenten[3] answer: I can tell thee where that
saying was born, of "I fear no colors."

CLOWN: Where, good Mistress Mary?

MARIA: In the wars; and that may you be bold to say in
your foolery.

CLOWN: Well, God give them wisdom that have it; and
those that are fools, let them use their talents.

MARIA: Yet you will be hanged for being so long absent; or,
to be turned away, is not that as good as a hanging to you?

CLOWN: Many a good hanging prevents a bad marriage;
and, for turning away, let summer bear it out.

MARIA: You are resolute, then?

CLOWN: Not so, neither; but I am resolved on two points.[4]

MARIA: That if one break, the other will hold; or, if both
break, your gaskins fall.

CLOWN: Apt, in good faith; very apt. Well, go thy way! If
Sir Toby would leave drinking, thou wert as witty a piece of
Eve's flesh as any in Illyria.

MARIA: Peace, you rogue, no more o' that. Here comes my
lady: make your excuse wisely, you were best. (*Exit.*)

---

[1] Full of impediments.
[2] "Colors" probably means "hostile flag," hence "fear no foe." There
is also a pun on hangman's collar or noose.
[3] Scanty.
[4] Pun on laces supporting breeches.

CLOWN: Wit, an't be thy will, put me into good fooling!
Those wits, that think they have thee, do very oft prove fools;
and I, that am sure I lack thee, may pass for a wise man. For
what says Quinapalus? "Better a witty fool than a foolish wit."

(*Enter* LADY OLIVIA *with* MALVOLIO.)

God bless thee, lady.

OLIVIA: Take the fool away.

CLOWN: Do you not hear, fellows? Take away the lady.

OLIVIA: Go to, you're a dry[1] fool! I'll no more of you.
Besides, you grow dishonest.

CLOWN: Two faults, madonna,[2] that drink and good counsel
will amend: for give the dry fool drink, then is the fool not
dry: bid the dishonest man mend himself; if he mend, he is
no longer dishonest; if he cannot, let the botcher[3] mend him.
Anything that's mended is but patched: virtue that trans-
gresses is but patched with sin; and sin that amends is but
patched with virtue. If that this simple syllogism will serve, so;
if it will not, what remedy? As there is no true cuckold but
calamity, so beauty's a flower. The lady bade take away the
fool; therefore I say again, take her away.

OLIVIA: Sir, I bade them take away you.

CLOWN: Misprision[4] in the highest degree! Lady, cucullus
non facit monachum;[5] that's as much to say as I wear not
motley in my brain. Good madonna, give me leave to prove
you a fool.

OLIVIA: Can you do it?

CLOWN: Dexteriously, good madonna.

OLIVIA: Make your proof.

CLOWN: I must catechize you for it, madonna. Good my
mouse of virtue, answer me.

OLIVIA: Well, sir, for want of other idleness, I'll bide your
proof.

CLOWN: Good madonna, why mournest thou?

OLIVIA: Good fool, for my brother's death.

CLOWN: I think his soul is in hell, madonna.

OLIVIA: I know his soul is in heaven, fool.

CLOWN: The more fool, madonna, to mourn for your
brother's soul being in heaven. Take away the fool, gentlemen.

OLIVIA: What think you of this fool, Malvolio? Doth he not
mend?[6]

MALVOLIO: Yes, and shall do till the pangs of death shake
him. Infirmity, that decays the wise, doth ever make the better
fool.

---

[1] Dull.
[2] My lady.
[3] Tailor.
[4] Misapprehension.
[5] A cowl doesn't make a monk.
[6] Improve.

CLOWN: God send you, sir, a speedy infirmity, for the better increasing your folly! Sir Toby will be sworn that I am no fox; but he will not pass his word for twopence that you are no fool.

OLIVIA: How say you to that, Malvolio?

MALVOLIO: I marvel your ladyship takes delight in such a barren rascal. I saw him put down the other day with an ordinary fool that has no more brain than a stone. Look you now, he's out of his guard already. Unless you laugh and minister occasion to him, he is gagged. I protest, I take these wise men, that crow so at these set kind of fools, no better than fools' zanies.[1]

OLIVIA: O, you are sick of self-love, Malvolio, and taste with a distempered appetite. To be generous, guiltless and of free disposition, is to take those things for bird-bolts[2] that you deem cannon-bullets. There is no slander in an allowed[3] fool, though he do nothing but rail; nor no railing in a known discreet man, though he do nothing but reprove.

CLOWN: Now Mercury endue thee with leasing,[4] for thou speakest well of fools!

(*Re-enter* MARIA.)

MARIA: Madam, there is at the gate a young gentleman much desires to speak with you.

OLIVIA: From the Count Orsino, is it?

MARIA: I know not, madam: 'tis a fair young man, and well attended.

OLIVIA: Who of my people hold him in delay?

MARIA: Sir Toby, madam, your kinsman.

OLIVIA: Fetch him off, I pray you. He speaks nothing but madman. Fie on him! (*Exit* MARIA.) Go you, Malvolio: if it be a suit from the count, I am sick, or not at home. What you will, to dismiss it. (*Exit* MALVOLIO.) Now you see, sir, how your fooling grows old, and people dislike it.

CLOWN: Thou hast spoke for us, madonna, as if thy eldest son should be a fool; whose skull Jove cram with brains! for,— here he comes,—one of thy kin has a most weak pia mater.[5]

(*Enter* SIR TOBY.)

OLIVIA: By mine honor, half drunk. What is he at the gate, cousin?[6]

SIR TOBY: A gentleman.

OLIVIA: A gentleman! What gentleman?

SIR TOBY: 'Tis a gentleman here. (*Belches*.) A plague o' these pickle-herring! How now, sot!

---

[1] Minor fools.	[4] Lying.
[2] Blunt arrows.	[5] Brain.
[3] Licensed.	[6] Kinsman; here, uncle.

CLOWN: Good Sir Toby!

OLIVIA: Cousin, cousin, how have you come so early by this lethargy?

SIR TOBY: Lechery! I defy lechery. There's one at the gate.

OLIVIA: Aye, marry, what is he?

SIR TOBY: Let him be the devil, an he will, I care not. Give me faith, say I. Well, it's all one. (*Exit.*)

OLIVIA: What's a drunken man like, fool?

CLOWN: Like a drowned man, a fool and a madman. One draught above heat makes him a fool, the second mads him, and a third drowns him.

OLIVIA: Go thou and seek the crowner,[1] and let him sit o' my coz,[2] for he's in the third degree of drink, he's drowned: go look after him.

CLOWN: He is but mad yet, madonna, and the fool shall look to the madman. (*Exit.*)

(*Re-enter* MALVOLIO.)

MALVOLIO: Madam, yond young fellow swears he will speak with you. I told him you were sick; he takes on him to understand so much, and therefore comes to speak with you. I told him you were asleep; he seems to have a foreknowledge of that too, and therefore comes to speak with you. What is to be said to him, lady? He's fortified against any denial.

OLIVIA: Tell him he shall not speak with me.

MALVOLIO: Has been told so; and he says, he'll stand at your door like a sheriff's post,[8] and be the supporter to a bench, but he'll speak with you.

OLIVIA: What kind o' man is he?

MALVOLIO: Why, of mankind.

OLIVIA: What manner of man?

MALVOLIO: Of very ill manner: he'll speak with you, will you or no.

OLIVIA: Of what personage and years is he?

MALVOLIO: Not yet old enough for a man, nor young enough for a boy; as a squash[4] is before 'tis a peascod, or a codling[5] when 'tis almost an apple: 'tis with him in standing water,[6] between boy and man. He is very well-favored, and he speaks very shrewishly. One would think his mother's milk were scarce out of him.

OLIVIA: Let him approach. Call in my gentlewoman.

MALVOLIO: Gentlewoman, my lady calls. (*Exit.*)

---

[1] Coroner.
[2] Let him hold an inquest on my kinsman.
[8] Post for public notices.
[4] Unripe peapod.
[5] Unripe apple.
[6] Between ebb and flood tides.

(*Re-enter* MARIA.)

OLIVIA: Give me my veil; come, throw it o'er my face.
We'll once more hear Orsino's embassy.

(*Enter* VIOLA, *and* ATTENDANTS.)

VIOLA: The honorable lady of the house, which is she?

OLIVIA: Speak to me; I shall answer for her. Your will?

VIOLA: Most radiant, exquisite and unmatchable beauty,—I
pray you, tell me if this be the lady of the house, for I never
saw her. I would be loath to cast away my speech, for besides
that it is excellently well penned, I have taken great pains to
con[1] it. Good beauties, let me sustain no scorn; I am very
comptible,[2] even to the least sinister usage.

OLIVIA: Whence came you, sir?

VIOLA: I can say little more than I have studied, and that
question 's out of my part. Good gentle one, give me modest
assurance if you be the lady of the house, that I may proceed
in my speech.

OLIVIA: Are you a comedian?

VIOLA: No, my profound heart; and yet (by the very fangs
of malice I swear) I am not that I play. Are you the lady of
the house?

OLIVIA: If I do not usurp myself, I am.

VIOLA: Most certain, if you are she, you do usurp[8] yourself;
for what is yours to bestow is not yours to reserve. But this is
from my commission. I will on with my speech in your praise,
and then show you the heart of my message.

OLIVIA: Come to what is important in 't. I forgive you the
praise.

VIOLA: Alas, I took great pains to study it, and 'tis poetical.

OLIVIA: It is the more like to be feigned. I pray you, keep it
in. I heard you were saucy at my gates, and allowed your
approach rather to wonder at you than to hear you. If you be
not mad, be gone; if you have reason, be brief. 'Tis not that
time of moon with me to make one in so skipping[4] a dialogue.

MARIA: Will you hoist sail, sir? Here lies your way.

VIOLA: No, good swabber,[5] I am to hull here a little longer.
Some mollification for your giant, sweet lady.

OLIVIA: Tell me your mind.

VIOLA: I am a messenger.

[1] Memorize.   [4] Incoherent.
[2] Sensitive.   [5] Petty officer.
[8] Counterfeit.

OLIVIA: Sure, you have some hideous matter to deliver, when the courtesy of it is so fearful. Speak your office.

VIOLA: It alone concerns your ear. I bring no overture of war, no taxation[1] of homage. I hold the olive in my hand; my words are as full of peace as matter.

OLIVIA: Yet you began rudely. What are you? What would you?

VIOLA: The rudeness that hath appeared in me have I learned from my entertainment. What I am, and what I would, are as secret as maiden-head: to your ears, divinity, to any other's, profanation.

OLIVIA: Give us the place alone. We will hear this divinity. (*Exeunt* MARIA *and* ATTENDANTS.) Now, sir, what is your text?

VIOLA: Most sweet lady,—

OLIVIA: A comfortable doctrine, and much may be said of it. Where lies your text?

VIOLA: In Orsino's bosom.

OLIVIA: In his bosom! In what chapter of his bosom?

VIOLA: To answer by the method,[2] in the first of his heart.

OLIVIA: O, I have read it: it is heresy. Have you no more to say?

VIOLA: Good madam, let me see your face.

OLIVIA: Have you any commission from your lord to negotiate with my face? You are now out of your text. But we will draw the curtain and show you the picture. Look you, sir, such a one I was this present.[8] Is't not well done? (*Unveiling.*)

VIOLA: Excellently done, if God did all.

OLIVIA: 'Tis in grain,[4] sir; 'twill endure wind and weather.

VIOLA: 'Tis beauty truly blent, whose red and white
Nature's own sweet and cunning hand laid on.
Lady, you are the cruel'st she alive,
If you will lead these graces to the grave
And leave the world no copy.

OLIVIA: O, sir, I will not be so hard-hearted. I will give out divers schedules of my beauty: it shall be inventoried, and every particle and utensil labeled to my will: as, item, two lips indifferent red; item, two gray eyes, with lids to them; item, one neck, one chin, and so forth. Were you sent hither to praise[5] me?

VIOLA: I see you what you are, you are too proud;
But if you were the devil, you are fair.
My lord and master loves you. O, such love

[1] Demand.
[2] In this preaching style.
[8] Moment.

[4] Dyed in fast colors.
[5] Appraise.

Could be but recompensed, though you were crown'd
The nonpareil of beauty!

OLIVIA: How does he love me?

VIOLA: With adorations, fertile tears,
With groans that thunder love, with sighs of fire.

OLIVIA: Your lord does know my mind; I cannot love him.
Yet I suppose him virtuous, know him noble,
Of great estate, of fresh and stainless youth;
In voices well divulged,[1] free, learn'd and valiant;
And in dimension and the shape of nature
A gracious person. But yet I cannot love him.
He might have took his answer long ago.

VIOLA: If I did love you in my master's flame,
With such a suffering, such a deadly life,
In your denial I would find no sense;
I would not understand it.

OLIVIA: Why, what would you?

VIOLA: Make me a willow cabin at your gate,
And call upon my soul within the house;
Write loyal cantons[2] of contemned love
And sing them loud even in the dead of night;
Halloo your name to the reverberate hills,
And make the babbling gossip of the air
Cry out "Olivia!" O, you should not rest
Between the elements of air and earth,
But you should pity me!

OLIVIA: You might do much.
What is your parentage?

VIOLA: Above my fortunes, yet my state[3] is well:
I am a gentleman.

OLIVIA: Get you to your lord.
I cannot love him. Let him send no more;
Unless, perchance, you come to me again,
To tell me how he takes it. Fare you well.
I thank you for your pains. Spend this for me.

VIOLA: I am no fee'd post,[4] lady; keep your purse:
My master, not myself, lacks recompense.
Love make his heart of flint that you shall love;
And let your fervor, like my master's, be
Placed[5] in contempt! Farewell, fair cruelty. (*Exit.*)

OLIVIA: "What is your parentage?"
"Above my fortunes, yet my state is well:
I am a gentleman." I'll be sworn thou art.
Thy tongue, thy face, thy limbs, actions, and spirit,

---

[1] Highly spoken of.
[2] Songs.
[3] Condition.
[4] Hired messenger.
[5] Held.

Do give thee five-fold blazon.[1] Not too fast: soft, soft!
Unless the master were the man.[2] How now!
Even so quickly may one catch the plague?
Methinks I feel this youth's perfections
With an invisible and subtle stealth
To creep in at mine eyes. Well, let it be.
What ho, Malvolio!

(*Re-enter* MALVOLIO.)

MALVOLIO: Here, madam, at your service.
OLIVIA: Run after that same peevish messenger,
The county's[3] man. He left this ring behind him,
Would I or not. Tell him I'll none of it.
Desire him not to flatter with[4] his lord,
Nor hold him up with hopes. I am not for him.
If that the youth will come this way to-morrow,
I'll give him reasons for 't. Hie thee, Malvolio.
MALVOLIO: Madam, I will. (*Exit.*)
OLIVIA: I do I know not what, and fear to find
Mine eye too great a flatterer for my mind.
Fate, show thy force. Ourselves we do not owe.[5]
What is decreed must be, and be this so. (*Exit.*)

ACT II

SCENE I
(*The seacoast.*)

(*Enter* ANTONIO *and* SEBASTIAN)

ANTONIO: Will you stay no longer? nor will you not that I
go with you?

SEBASTIAN: By your patience, no. My stars shine darkly
over me; the malignancy of my fate might perhaps distemper[6]
yours. Therefore I shall crave of you your leave that I may
bear my evils alone. It were a bad recompense for your love,
to lay any of them on you.

ANTONIO: Let me yet know of you whither you are bound.

SEBASTIAN: No, sooth, sir. My determinate voyage is mere
extravagancy.[7] But I perceive in you so excellent a touch of
modesty, that you will not extort from me what I am willing to
keep in; therefore it charges me in manners the rather to
express myself. You must know of me then, Antonio, my

---

[1] Coat of arms.
[2] Unless Orsino were as attractive as the servant.
[3] Count's, Duke's.
[4] Falsely encourage.
[5] Own.
[6] Infect.
[7] My planned voyage is mere wandering.

name is Sebastian, which I called Roderigo. My father was that Sebastian of Messaline, whom I know you have heard of. He left behind him myself and a sister, both born in an hour. If the heavens had been pleased, would we had so ended! But you, sir, altered that, for some hour before you took me from the breach[1] of the sea was my sister drowned.

ANTONIO: Alas the day!

SEBASTIAN: A lady, sir, though it was said she much resembled me, was yet of many accounted beautiful. But though I could not with such estimable wonder[2] overfar believe that, yet thus far I will boldly publish her: she bore a mind that envy could not but call fair. She is drowned already, sir, with salt water, though I seem to drown her remembrance again with more.

ANTONIO: Pardon me, sir, your bad entertainment.

SEBASTIAN: O good Antonio, forgive me your trouble!

ANTONIO: If you will not murder me for my love, let me be your servant.

SEBASTIAN: If you will not undo what you have done, that is, kill him whom you have recovered, desire it not. Fare ye well at once. My bosom is full of kindness, and I am yet so near the manners of my mother, that upon the least occasion more, mine eyes will tell tales of me. I am bound to the Count Orsino's court. Farewell. (*Exit.*)

ANTONIO: The gentleness of all the gods go with thee!
I have many enemies in Orsino's court,
Else would I very shortly see thee there.
But, come what may, I do adore thee so,
That danger shall seem sport, and I will go. (*Exit.*)

SCENE II
(*A street.*)

(*Enter* VIOLA, MALVOLIO *following.*)

MALVOLIO: Were not you even now with the Countess Olivia?

VIOLA: Even now, sir. On a moderate pace I have since arrived but hither.

MALVOLIO: She returns this ring to you, sir. You might have saved me my pains, to have taken it away yourself. She adds, moreover, that you should put your lord into a desperate[3] assurance she will none of him. And one thing more, that you be never so hardy to come again in his affairs, unless it be to report your lord's taking of this. Receive it so.

VIOLA: She took the ring of me: I'll none of it.

MALVOLIO: Come, sir, you peevishly threw it to her; and her

---

[1] Breakers.   [2] Such admiring judgment.   [3] Hopeless

will is, it should be so returned. If it be worth stooping for,
there it lies in your eye; if not, be it his that finds it. (*Exit.*)
  VIOLA: I left no ring with her: what means this lady?
Fortune forbid my outside have not charm'd her!
She made good view of me; indeed, so much
That, methought, her eyes had lost her tongue,
For she did speak in starts distractedly.
She loves me, sure; the cunning of her passion
Invites me in this churlish messenger.
None of my lord's ring! Why, he sent her none.
I am the man.[1] If it be so, as 'tis,
Poor lady, she were better love a dream.
Disguise, I see, thou art a wickedness,
Wherein the pregnant enemy[2] does much.
How easy is it for the proper-false[3]
In women's waxen hearts to set their forms!
Alas, our frailty is the cause, not we!
For such as we are made of, such we be.
How will this fadge?[4] My master loves her dearly;
And I, poor monster, fond[5] as much on him;
And she, mistaken, seems to dote on me.
What will become of this? As I am man,
My state is desperate for my master's love;
As I am woman,—now alas the day!—
What thriftless sighs shall poor Olivia breathe!
O Time! thou must untangle this, not I;
It is too hard a knot for me to untie! (*Exit.*)

SCENE III
(OLIVIA'S *house.*)

(Enter SIR TOBY *and* SIR ANDREW.*)*

SIR TOBY: Approach, Sir Andrew. Not to be abed after midnight is to be up betimes; and "diluculo surgere,"[6] thou
know'st,—
  SIR ANDREW: Nay, by my troth, I know not: but I know, to
be up late is to be up late.
  SIR TOBY: A false conclusion! I hate it as an unfilled can.
To be up after midnight and to go to bed then, is early: so
that to go to bed after midnight is to go to bed betimes. Does
not our life consist of the four elements?
  SIR ANDREW: Faith, so they say; but I think it rather consists of eating and drinking.

---

1 I am the man she loves.   4 Fit.
2 Clever enemy, the Devil.   5 Dote.
3 Handsome, deceitful men.   6 To rise early (is most healthful).

SIR TOBY: Thou 'rt a scholar! Let us therefore eat and drink. Marian, I say! a stoup[1] of wine!

(*Enter* CLOWN.)

SIR ANDREW: Here comes the fool, i' faith.

CLOWN: How now, my hearts! Did you never see the picture of "we three"?[2]

SIR TOBY: Welcome, ass. Now let's have a catch.

SIR ANDREW: By my troth, the fool has an excellent breast.[3] I had rather than forty shillings I had such a leg, and so sweet a breath to sing, as the fool has. In sooth, thou wast in very gracious fooling last night, when thou spokest of Pigrogromitus, of the Vapians passing the equinoctial of Queubus:[4] 'twas very good, i' faith. I sent thee sixpence for thy leman:[5] hadst it?

CLOWN: I did impeticos thy gratillity;[6] for Malvolio's nose is no whipstock. My lady has a white hand, and the Myrmidons are no bottle-ale houses.

SIR ANDREW: Excellent! why, this is the best fooling, when all is done. Now, a song.

SIR TOBY: Come on; there is sixpence for you. Let's have a song.

SIR ANDREW: There's a testril[7] of me, too: If one knight give a—

CLOWN: Would you have a love-song, or a song of good life?

SIR TOBY: A love-song, a love-song.

SIR ANDREW: Aye, aye: I care not for good life.

CLOWN (*Sings*):

> O mistress mine, where are you roaming?
> O, stay and hear; your true love's coming,
>   That can sing both high and low.
> Trip no further, pretty sweeting;
> Journeys end in lovers meeting,
>   Every wise man's son doth know.

SIR ANDREW: Excellent good, i' faith.

SIR TOBY: Good, good.

CLOWN (*Sings*):

> What is love? 'tis not hereafter.
> Present mirth hath present laughter;
>   What's to come is still unsure.
> In delay there lies no plenty;
> Then come kiss me, sweet and twenty,
>   Youth's a stuff will not endure.

SIR ANDREW: A mellifluous voice, as I am true knight.

---

[1] Cup.
[2] A picture of two asses; the viewer is the third.
[3] Voice.
[4] Gibberish.
[5] Sweetheart.
[6] Pocket your gratuity.
[7] Sixpence.

SIR TOBY: A contagious breath.[1]

SIR ANDREW: Very sweet and contagious, i' faith.

SIR TOBY: To hear by the nose, it is dulcet in contagion. But shall we make the welkin dance indeed? shall we rouse the night-owl in a catch that will draw three souls out of one weaver? shall we do that?

SIR ANDREW: An you love me, let's do 't. I am dog at a catch.

CLOWN: By 'r lady, sir, and some dogs will catch well.

SIR ANDREW: Most certain. Let our catch be, "Thou knave."

CLOWN: "Hold thy peace, thou knave," knight? I shall be constrained in 't to call thee knave, knight.

SIR ANDREW: 'Tis not the first time I have constrained one to call me knave. Begin, fool: it begins "Hold thy peace."

CLOWN: I shall never begin if I hold my peace.

SIR ANDREW: Good, i' faith. Come, begin.

(*Catch sung.*)

(*Enter* MARIA.)

MARIA: What a caterwauling do you keep here! If my lady have not called up her steward Malvolio and bid him turn you out of doors, never trust me.

SIR TOBY: My lady's a Cataian,[2] we are politicians, Malvolio 's a Peg-a-Ramsey,[3] and "Three merry men be we." Am not I consanguineous? Am I not of her blood? Tillyvally. Lady! (*Sings*) "There dwelt a man in Babylon, lady, lady!"

CLOWN: Beshrew me, the knight's in admirable fooling.

SIR ANDREW: Aye, he does well enough if he be disposed, and so do I too: he does it with a better grace, but I do it more natural.

SIR TOBY (*sings*): "O, the twelfth of December,"—

MARIA: For the love o' God, peace!

(*Enter* MALVOLIO.)

MALVOLIO: My masters, are you mad? or what are you? Have you no wit, manners, nor honesty, but to gabble like tinkers at this time of night? Do ye make an alehouse of my lady's house, that ye squeak out your coziers'[4] catches without any mitigation or remorse of voice? Is there no respect of place, persons, nor time in you?

SIR TOBY: We did keep time, sir, in our catches. Sneck up![5]

---

[1] Pun on "a catchy song."   [4] Cobblers'.
[2] Scoundrel.   [5] Be hanged.
[3] Wench (figure in a ballad). Sir Toby proceeds to quote fragments of ballads.

MALVOLIO: Sir Toby, I must be round with you. My lady bade me tell you, that, though she harbors you as her kinsman, she's nothing allied to your disorders. If you can separate yourself and your misdemeanors, you are welcome to the house. If not, an it would please you to take leave of her, she is very willing to bid you farewell.

SIR TOBY: "Farewell, dear heart, since I must needs be gone."

MARIA: Nay, good Sir Toby.

CLOWN: "His eyes do show his days are almost done."

MALVOLIO: Is't even so?

SIR TOBY: "But I will never die."

CLOWN: Sir Toby, there you lie.

MALVOLIO: This is much credit to you.

SIR TOBY: "Shall I bid him go?"

CLOWN: "What an if you do?"

SIR TOBY: "Shall I bid him go, and spare not?"

CLOWN: "O no, no, no, no, you dare not."

SIR TOBY: Out o' tune, sir: ye lie. Art any more than a steward? Dost thou think, because thou art virtuous, there shall be no more cakes and ale?

CLOWN: Yes, by Saint Anne, and ginger shall be hot i' the mouth too.

SIR TOBY: Thou'rt i' the right. Go, sir, rub your chain[1] with crumbs. A stoup of wine, Maria!

MALVOLIO: Mistress Mary, if you prized my lady's favor at any thing more than contempt, you would not give means for this uncivil rule.[2] She shall know of it, by this hand. (*Exit.*)

MARIA: Go shake your ears.

SIR ANDREW: 'Twere as good a deed as to drink when a man's a-hungry, to challenge him the field, and then to break promise with him and make a fool of him.

SIR TOBY: Do 't, knight. I'll write thee a challenge; or I'll deliver thy indignation to him by word of mouth.

MARIA: Sweet Sir Toby, be patient for to-night. Since the youth of the Count's was to-day with my lady, she is much out of quiet. For Monsieur Malvolio, let me alone with him. If I do not gull him into a nayword,[3] and make him a common recreation, do not think I have wit enough to lie straight in my bed. I know I can do it.

SIR TOBY: Possess[4] us, possess us! Tell us something of him.

MARIA: Marry, sir, sometimes he is a kind of Puritan.

SIR ANDREW: O, if I thought that, I'ld beat him like a dog!

---

[1] Steward's badge of office.   [3] A byword (for a fool).
[2] Disorderly conduct.   [4] Tell.

SIR TOBY: What, for being a Puritan? Thy exquisite reason, dear knight?

SIR ANDREW: I have no exquisite reason for 't, but I have reason good enough.

MARIA: The devil a Puritan that he is, or any thing constantly, but a time-pleaser; an affectioned [1] ass, that cons state without book [2] and utters it by great swarths: the best persuaded of himself, so crammed, as he thinks, with excellencies, that it is his grounds of faith that all that look on him love him; and on that vice in him will my revenge find notable cause to work.

SIR TOBY: What wilt thou do?

MARIA: I will drop in his way some obscure epistles of love, wherein, by the color of his beard, the shape of his leg, the manner of his gait, the expressure [3] of his eye, forehead, and complexion, he shall find himself most feelingly personated. I can write very like my lady your niece; on a forgotten matter we can hardly make distinction of our hands.

SIR TOBY: Excellent! I smell a device.

SIR ANDREW: I have 't in my nose too.

SIR TOBY: He shall think, by the letters that thou wilt drop, that they come from my niece, and that she's in love with him.

MARIA: My purpose is, indeed, a horse of that color.

SIR ANDREW: And your horse now would make him an ass.

MARIA: Ass, I doubt not.

SIR ANDREW: O, 'twill be admirable!

MARIA: Sport royal, I warrant you. I know my physic will work with him. I will plant you two, and let the fool make a third, where he shall find the letter. Observe his construction of it. For this night, to bed, and dream on the event. Farewell. (*Exit.*)

SIR TOBY: Good night, Penthesilea. [4]

SIR ANDREW: Before me, she's a good wench.

SIR TOBY: She's a beagle, true-bred, and one that adores me. What o' that?

SIR ANDREW: I was adored once too.

SIR TOBY: Let's to bed, knight. Thou hadst need send for more money.

SIR ANDREW: If I cannot recover [5] your niece, I am a foul way out.

SIR TOBY: Send for money, knight. If thou hast her not i' the end, call me cut. [6]

SIR ANDREW: If I do not, never trust me, take it how you will.

SIR TOBY: Come, come, I'll go burn some sack, [7] 'tis too

---

1 Affected.
2 Memorizes stately language.
3 Expression.
5 Win.
6 Perhaps an obscene pun.
7 Heat some sherry.

late to go to bed now: come, knight; come, knight. (*Exeunt.*)

SCENE IV
(*The* DUKE'S *palace.*)

(*Enter* DUKE, VIOLA, CURIO, *and others.*)

DUKE: Give me some music. Now, good morrow, friends,
Now, good Cesario, but[1] that piece of song,
That old and antique song we heard last night.
Methought it did relieve my passion much,
More than light airs and recollected[2] terms
Of these most brisk and giddy-paced times.
Come, but one verse.
    CURIO: He is not here, so please your lordship, that should
sing it.
    DUKE: Who was it?
    CURIO: Feste, the jester, my lord; a fool that the lady
Olivia's father took much delight in.
He is about the house.
    DUKE: Seek him out, and play the tune the while.
    (*Exit* CURIO. *Music plays.*)
Come hither, boy. If ever thou shalt love,
In the sweet pangs of it remember me.
For such as I am all true lovers are,
Unstaid and skittish in all motions[3] else,
Save in the constant image of the creature
That is beloved. How dost thou like this tune?
    VIOLA: It gives a very echo to the seat
Where love is throned.
    DUKE: Thou dost speak masterly.
My life upon 't, young though thou art, thine eye
Hath stay'd upon some favor[4] that it loves:
Hath it not, boy?
    VIOLA: A little, by your favor.
    DUKE: What kind of woman is 't?
    VIOLA: Of your complexion.
    DUKE: She is not worth thee, then. What years, i' faith?
    VIOLA: About your years, my lord.
    DUKE: Too old, by heaven! Let still[5] the woman take
An elder than herself; so wears she to him,
So sways she level in her husband's heart.
For, boy, however we do praise ourselves,
Our fancies are more giddy and unfirm,

---

1 Only.   4 Face.
2 Elaborately studied (?).   5 Always.
3 Emotions.

More longing, wavering, sooner lost and worn,
Than women's are.
   VIOLA: I think it well, my lord.
   DUKE: Then let thy love be younger than thyself,
Or thy affection cannot hold the bent.[1]
For women are as roses, whose fair flower
Being once display'd, doth fall that very hour.
   VIOLA: And so they are: alas, that they are so;
To die, even when they to perfection grow!

(*Re-enter* CURIO *and* CLOWN.)

   DUKE: O, fellow, come, the song we had last night.
Mark it, Cesario, it is old and plain.
The spinsters and the knitters in the sun
And the free[2] maids that weave their thread with bones[3]
Do use to chant it. It is silly sooth,[4]
And dallies with the innocence of love,
Like the old age.[5]
   CLOWN: Are you ready, sir?
   DUKE: Aye; prithee, sing.
(*Music.*)

                Song

CLOWN: Come away, come away, death,
        And in sad cypress[6] let me be laid.
    Fly away, fly away, breath;
        I am slain by a fair cruel maid.
    My shroud of white, stuck all with yew,
          O, prepare it!
    My part of death, no one so true
          Did share it.
    Not a flower, not a flower sweet,
        On my black coffin let there be strown;
    Not a friend, not a friend greet
        My poor corpse, where my bones shall be
        thrown.
    A thousand thousand sighs to save,
        Lay me, O, where
    Sad true lover never find my grave,
        To weep there!

DUKE: There's for thy pains.

[1] Maintain its tension.
[2] Carefree.
[3] Bone bobbins.
[4] Plain truth.
[5] Olden times.
[6] Cypress coffin.

CLOWN: No pains, sir. I take pleasure in singing, sir.

DUKE: I'll pay thy pleasure then.

CLOWN: Truly, sir, and pleasure will be paid, one time or another.

DUKE: Give me now leave to leave thee.

CLOWN: Now, the melancholy god protect thee; and the tailor make thy doublet of changeable taffeta, for thy mind is a very opal. I would have men of such constancy put to sea, that their business might be every thing and their intent everywhere; for that's it that always makes a good voyage of nothing. Farewell. (*Exit.*)

DUKE: Let all the rest give place.

(CURIO *and* ATTENDANTS *leave.*)

          Once more, Cesario,
Get thee to yond same sovereign cruelty.
Tell her, my love, more noble than the world,
Prizes not quantity of dirty lands.
The parts that fortune hath bestow'd upon her,
Tell her, I hold as giddily [1] as fortune;
But 'tis that miracle and queen of gems
That nature pranks [2] her in attracts my soul.

VIOLA: But if she cannot love you, sir?

DUKE: I cannot be so answer'd.

VIOLA: Sooth, but you must.
Say that some lady, as perhaps there is,
Hath for your love as great a pang of heart
As you have for Olivia. You cannot love her.
You tell her so. Must she not then be answer'd?

DUKE: There is no woman's sides
Can bide the beating of so strong a passion
As love doth give my heart; no woman's heart
So big, to hold so much; they lack retention.
Alas, their love may be call'd appetite,
No motion of the liver, but the palate, [8]
That suffer surfeit, cloyment and revolt.
But mine is all as hungry as the sea
And can digest as much. Make no compare
Between that love a woman can bear me
And that I owe Olivia.

VIOLA: Aye, but I know,—

DUKE: What dost thou know?

VIOLA: Too well what love women to men may owe:
In faith, they are as true of heart as we.
My father had a daughter loved a man,

---

[1] Indifferently.
[2] Adorns.
[8] Not real passion, but casual interest.

As it might be, perhaps, were I a woman,
I should your lordship.
    DUKE: And what's her history?
    VIOLA: A blank, my lord. She never told her love,
But let concealment, like a worm i' the bud,
Feed on her damask[1] cheek. She pined in thought;
And with a green and yellow[2] melancholy

She sat like Patience on a monument,
Smiling at grief. Was not this love indeed?
We men may say more, swear more: but indeed
Our shows are more than will,[3] for still we prove

Much in our vows, but little in our love.
    DUKE: But died thy sister of her love, my boy?
    VIOLA: I am all the daughters of my father's house,
And all the brothers too: and yet I know not.
Sir, shall I to this lady?
    DUKE: Aye that's the theme.
To her in haste; give this jewel; say,
My love can give no place, bide no denay.[4] (*Exeunt.*)

SCENE V
(OLIVIA'S *garden.*)

(*Enter* SIR TOBY, SIR ANDREW, *and* FABIAN.)

SIR TOBY: Come thy ways, Signior Fabian.
FABIAN: Nay, I'll come: if I lose a scruple[5] of this sport,
let me be boiled to death with melancholy.
SIR TOBY: Wouldst thou not be glad to have the niggardly
rascally sheep-biter come by some notable shame?
FABIAN: I would exult, man. You know he brought me out
o' favor with my lady about a bear-baiting here.
SIR TOBY: To anger him we'll have the bear again and we
will fool him black and blue. Shall we not, Sir Andrew?
SIR ANDREW: An we do not, it is pity of our lives.
SIR TOBY: Here comes the little villain.

(*Enter* MARIA.)

How now, my metal of India!
MARIA: Get ye all three into the box-tree. Malvolio's coming down this walk. He has been yonder i' the sun practising

----

[1] Red and white.
[2] Hopeful and pale.
[3] We profess more than we feel.
[4] Denial.
[5] Tiny bit.

behavior to his own shadow this half hour. Observe him, for the love of mockery; for I know this letter will make a contemplative idiot of him. Close, in the name of jesting! (*The others conceal themselves*) Lie thou there (*throws down a letter*); for here comes the trout that must be caught with tickling.[1] (*Exit.*)

(*Enter* MALVOLIO.)

MALVOLIO: 'Tis but fortune; all is fortune. Maria once told me she[2] did affect me: and I have heard herself come thus near, that, should she fancy, it should be one of my complexion. Besides, she uses me with a more exalted respect than any one else that follows her. What shoud I think on 't?

SIR TOBY: Here's an overweening rogue!

FABIAN: O, peace! Contemplation makes a rare turkey-cock of him: how he jets[3] under his advanced plumes!

SIR ANDREW: 'Slight, I could so beat the rogue!

SIR TOBY: Peace, I say.

MALVOLIO: To be Count Malvolio!

SIR TOBY: Ah, rogue!

SIR ANDREW: Pistol him, pistol him.

SIR TOBY: Peace, peace!

MALVOLIO: There is example for 't; the lady of the Strachy married the yeoman of the wardrobe.

SIR ANDREW: Fie on him, Jezebel!

FABIAN: O, peace! now he's deeply in: look how imagination blows him.

MALVOLIO: Having been three months married to her, sitting in my state,[4]—

SIR TOBY: O, for a stone-bow, to hit him in the eye!

MALVOLIO: Calling my officers about me, in my branched[5] velvet gown; having come from a day-bed, where I have left Olivia sleeping,—

SIR TOBY: Fire and brimstone!

FABIAN: O, peace, peace!

MALVOLIO: And then to have the humor of state[6]; and after a demure travel of regard,[7] telling them I know my place as I would they should do theirs, to ask for my kinsman Toby,—

SIR TOBY: Bolts and shackles!

FABIAN: O, peace, peace, peace! Now, now.

MALVOLIO: Seven of my people, with an obedient start, make out for him: I frown the while; and perchance wind up my watch, or play with my[8]—some rich jewel. Toby

---

1 *I.e.*, by flattery.
2 Olivia.
3 Struts.
4 Chair of state.
5 Embroidered with figures of leaves and branches.

6 To have a magisterial demeanor.
7 After gravely looking around.
8 Malvolio fingers his chain, then remembers he will be more than a steward.

approaches; courtesies there to me,—

SIR TOBY: Shall this fellow live?

FABIAN: Though our silence be drawn from us with cars, yet peace.

MALVOLIO: I extend my hand to him thus, quenching my familiar smile with an austere regard of control,—

SIR TOBY: And does not Toby take you a blow o' the lips then.

MALVOLIO: Saying, "Cousin Toby, my fortunes having cast me on your niece give me this prerogative of speech."

SIR TOBY: What, what?

MALVOLIO: "You must amend your drunkenness."

SIR TOBY: Out, scab!

FABIAN: Nay, patience, or we break the sinews of our plot.

MALVOLIO: "Besides, you waste the treasure of your time with a foolish knight,"—

SIR ANDREW: That's me, I warrant you.

MALVOLIO: "One Sir Andrew,"—

SIR ANDREW: I knew 'twas I, for many do call me fool.

MALVOLIO: What employment have we here? (*Taking up the letter.*)

FABIAN: Now is the woodcock near the gin.[1]

SIR TOBY: O, peace! and the spirit of humors intimate reading aloud to him!

MALVOLIO: By my life, this is my lady's hand: these be her very C's, her U's, and her T's; and thus makes she her great P's. It is, in contempt of question,[2] her hand.

SIR ANDREW: Her C's, her U's and her T's: why that?

MALVOLIO (*reads*): "To the unknown beloved, this, and my good wishes." Her very phrases! By your leave, wax. Soft! and the impressure her Lucrece, with which she uses to seal: 'tis my lady. To whom should this be?

FABIAN: This wins him, liver and all.

MALVOLIO (*reads*): "Jove knows I love:
　　　　　　But who?
　　　　Lips, do not move;
　　　　No man must know."

"No man must know." What follows? the numbers[3] altered! "No man must know:" if this should be thee, Malvolio?

SIR TOBY: Marry, hang thee, brock![4]

MALVOLIO (*reads*): "I may command where I adore;
　　　　　　But silence, like a Lucrece knife,
　　　　With bloodless stroke my heart doth gore:
　　　　M, O, A, I, doth sway my life."

[1] The bird is near the trap.　　[3] Meter.
[2] Doubtless.　　[4] Badger.

FABIAN: A fustian[1] riddle!

SIR TOBY: Excellent wench, say I.

MALVOLIO: "M, O, A, I, doth sway my life." Nay, but first, let me see, let me see, let me see.

FABIAN: What dish o' poison has she dressed him!

SIR TOBY: And with what wing the staniel checks at it![2]

MALVOLIO: "I may command where I adore." Why, she may command me: I serve her; she is my lady. Why, this is evident to any formal capacity;[3] there is no obstruction in this: and the end,—what should that alphabetical position portend? If I could make that resemble something in me,—Softly! M, O, A, I,—

SIR TOBY: O, aye, make up that: he is now at a cold scent.

FABIAN: Sowter will cry upon 't for all this,[4] though it be as rank as a fox.

MALVOLIO: M,—Malvolio; M,—why, that begins my name.

FABIAN: Did not I say he would work it out? the cur is excellent at faults.[5]

MALVOLIO: M,—but then there is no consonancy in the sequel; that suffers under probation: A should follow, but O does.

FABIAN: And O shall end, I hope.

SIR TOBY: Aye, or I'll cudgel him, and make him cry O!

MALVOLIO: And then I comes behind.

FABIAN: Aye, an you had any eye behind you, you might see more detraction at your heels than fortunes before you.

MALVOLIO: M, O, A, I; this simulation[6] is not as the former: and yet, to crush this a little, it would bow to me, for every one of these letters are in my name. Soft! here follows prose. (*Reads*) "If this fall into thy hand, revolve. In my stars I am above thee; but be not afraid of greatness: some are born great, some achieve greatness, and some have greatness thrust upon 'em. Thy Fates open their hands; let thy blood and spirit embrace them; and, to inure thyself to what thou art like to be, cast thy humble slough[7] and appear fresh. Be opposite with a kinsman, surly with servants; let thy tongue tang arguments of state; put thyself into the trick of singularity. She thus advises thee that sighs for thee. Remember who commended thy yellow stockings, and wished to see thee ever cross-gartered. I say, remember. Go to, thou art made, if thou desirest to be so. If not, let me see thee a steward still, the fellow of servants, and not worthy to touch Fortune's fingers. Farewell. She that would alter

---

[1] Nonsensical.
[2] How the hawk is led astray.
[3] Normal understanding.
[4] The dog will follow the scent.
[5] Cold scent.
[6] Disguise.
[7] Snakeskin.

services with thee, The Fortunate-Unhappy." Daylight and champain[1] discovers not more; this is open. I will be proud, I will read politic authors, I will baffle Sir Toby, I will wash off gross acquaintance, I will be point-devise[2] the very man. I do not now fool myself, to let imagination jade[3] me; for every reason excites to this, that my lady loves me. She did commend my yellow stockings of late, she did praise my leg being cross-gartered; and in this she manifests herself to my love, and with a kind of injunction drives me to these habits of her liking. I thank my stars I am happy. I will be strange, stout,[4] in yellow stockings, and cross-gartered, even with the swiftness of putting on. Jove and my stars be praised! Here is yet a postscript. (*Reads*) "Thou canst not choose but know who I am. If thou entertainest my love, let it appear in thy smiling; thy smiles become thee well; therefore in my presence still smile, dear my sweet, I prithee." Jove, I thank thee: I will smile; I will do everything that thou wilt have me. (*Exit.*)

FABIAN: I will not give my part of this sport for a pension of thousands to be paid from the Sophy.[5]

SIR TOBY: I could marry this wench for this device,—

SIR ANDREW: So could I too.

SIR TOBY: And ask no other dowry with her but such another jest.

SIR ANDREW: Nor I neither.

FABIAN: Here comes my noble gull-catcher.

(*Re-enter* MARIA.)

SIR TOBY: Wilt thou set thy foot o' my neck?

SIR ANDREW: Or o' mine either?

SIR TOBY: Shall I play my freedom at tray-trip,[6] and become thy bond-slave?

SIR ANDREW: I' faith, or I either?

SIR TOBY: Why, thou hast put him in such a dream, that when the image of it leaves him he must run mad.

MARIA: Nay, but say true; does it work upon him?

SIR TOBY: Like aqua-vitæ with a midwife.

MARIA: If you will then see the fruits of the sport, mark his first approach before my lady. He will come to her in yellow stockings, and 'tis a color she abhors, and cross-gartered, a fashion she detests; and he will smile upon her, which will now be so unsuitable to her disposition, being

---

[1] Open field.
[2] Exactly.
[3] Trick.
[4] Haughty.
[5] Persian shah.
[6] Dice.

addicted to a melancholy as she is, that cannot but turn him into a notable contempt. If you will see it, follow me.

SIR TOBY: To the gates of Tartar, thou most excellent devil of wit!

SIR ANDREW: I'll make one too. (*Exeunt.*)

ACT III

SCENE I
(OLIVIA'S *garden.*)

(*Enter* VIOLA, *and* CLOWN *with a tabor.*[1])

VIOLA: Save thee, friend, and thy music! Dost thou live by thy tabor?

CLOWN: No, sir, I live by the church.

VIOLA: Art thou a churchman?

CLOWN: No such matter, sir. I do live by the church; for I do live at my house, and my house doth stand by the church.

VIOLA: So thou mayst say, the king lies by a beggar, if a begger dwell near him; or, the church stands by thy tabor, if thy tabor stand by the church.

CLOWN: You have said, sir. To see this age! A sentence is but a cheveril[2] glove to a good wit: how quickly the wrong side may be turned outward!

VIOLA: Nay, that's certain; they that dally nicely[3] with words may quickly make them wanton.

CLOWN: I would, therefore, my sister had had no name, sir.

VIOLA: Why, man?

CLOWN: Why, sir, her name's a word; and to dally with that word might make my sister wanton. But indeed words are very rascals since bonds disgraced them.[4]

VIOLA: Thy reason, man?

CLOWN: Troth, sir, I can yield you none without words; and words are grown so false I am loath to prove reason with them.

VIOLA: I warrant thou art a merry fellow and carest for nothing.

CLOWN: Not so, sir, I do care for something; but in my conscience, sir, I do not care for you. If that be to care for nothing, sir, I would it would make you invisible.

VIOLA: Art not thou the Lady Olivia's fool?

CLOWN: No, indeed, sir! the Lady Olivia has no folly. She will keep no fool, sir, till she be married; and fools are

---

1 Drum.
2 Kid.

3 Precisely.
4 Words are no longer as good as bonds.

as like husbands as pilchards[1] are to herrings; the husband's the bigger: I am indeed not her fool, but her corrupter of words.

VIOLA: I saw thee late at the Count Orsino's.

CLOWN: Foolery, sir, does walk about the orb like the sun, it shines everywhere. I would be sorry, sir, but the fool should be as oft with your master as with my mistress. I think I saw your wisdom there.

VIOLA: Nay, an thou pass upon me,[2] I'll no more with thee. Hold, there's expenses for thee. (*Gives him money.*)

CLOWN: Now Jove, in his next commodity[3] of hair, send thee a beard!

VIOLA: By my troth, I'll tell thee, I am almost sick for one; (*Aside*) though I would not have it grow on my chin. Is thy lady within?

CLOWN: Would not a pair of these have bred, sir?

VIOLA: Yes, being kept together and put to use.

CLOWN: I would play Lord Pandarus of Phrygia, sir, to bring a Cressida to this Troilus.

VIOLA: I understand you, sir; 'tis well begged. (*Gives more money.*)

CLOWN: The matter, I hope, is not great, sir, begging but a beggar: Cressida was a beggar. My lady is within, sir. I will conster[4] to them whence you come; who you are and what you would are out of my welkin, I might say "element," but the word is overworn. (*Exit.*)

VIOLA: This fellow is wise enough to play the fool;
And to do that well craves a kind of wit.
He must observe their mood on whom he jests,
The quality of persons, and the time,
And, like the haggard,[5] check at every feather
That comes before his eye. This is a practice
As full of labor as a wise man's art.
For folly that he wisely shows is fit;
But wise men, folly-fall'n, quite taint their wit.

(*Enter* SIR TOBY *and* SIR ANDREW.)

SIR TOBY: Save you, gentleman.

VIOLA: And you, sir.

SIR ANDREW: Dieu vous garde, monsieur.

VIOLA: Et vous aussi; votre serviteur.

SIR ANDREW: I hope, sir, you are; and I am yours.

SIR TOBY: Will you encounter the house? my niece is desirous you should enter, if your trade be to her.

VIOLA: I am bound to your niece, sir. I mean, she is the list[6] of my voyage.

[1] A fish.
[2] If you make witty thrusts at me.
[3] Shipment.
[4] Explain.
[5] Untrained hawk.
[6] Destination.

SIR TOBY: Taste[1] your legs, sir; put them to motion.

VIOLA: My legs do better understand me, sir, than I understand what you mean by bidding me taste my legs.

SIR TOBY: I mean, to go, sir, to enter.

VIOLA: I will answer you with gait and entrance. But we are prevented.

(*Enter* OLIVIA *and* MARIA.)

Most excellent accomplished lady, the heavens raid odors on you!

SIR ANDREW: That youth's a rare courtier: "Rain odors"; well.

VIOLA: My matter hath no voice, lady, but to your own most pregnant and vouchsafed[2] ear.

SIR ANDREW: "Odors," "pregnant," and "vouchsafed"; I'll get 'em all three all ready.

OLIVIA: Let the garden door be shut, and leave me to my hearing. (*Exeunt* SIR TOBY, SIR ANDREW, *and* MARIA.) Give me your hand, sir.

VIOLA: My duty, madam, and most humble service.

OLIVIA: What is your name?

VIOLA: Cesario is your servant's name, fair princess.

OLIVIA: My servant, sir! 'Twas never merry world Since lowly feigning ws call'd compliment. You're servant to the Count Orsino, youth.

VIOLA: And he is yours, and his must needs be yours. Your servant's servant is your servant, madam.

OLIVIA: For him, I think not on him; for his thoughts, Would they were blanks, rather than fill'd with me!

VIOLA: Madam, I come to whet your gentle thoughts On his behalf.

OLIVIA:　　　　　　　O, by your leave, I pray you! I bade you never speak again of him; But, would you undertake another suit, I had rather hear you to solicit that Than music from the spheres.

VIOLA:　　　　　　　Dear lady,—

OLIVIA: Give me leave, beseech you. I did send, After the last enchantment you did here, A ring in chase of you. So did I abuse[3] Myself, my servant and, I fear me, you. Under your hard construction must I sit, To force that on you, in a shameful cunning, Which you knew none of yours. What might you think? Have you not set mine honor at the stake

---

[1] Try out.　　　[2] Ready and receptive　　　[3] Deceive.

And baited it with all the unmuzzled thoughts
That tyrannous heart can think?[1] To one of your receiving
Enough is shown; a cypress,[2] not a bosom,
Hides my heart. So, let me hear you speak.
   VIOLA: I pity you.
   OLIVIA: That's a degree to love.
   VIOLA: No, not a grize;[3] for 'tis a vulgar proof,[4]
That very oft we pity enemies.
   OLIVIA: Why, then, methinks 'tis time to smile again.
O world, how apt the poor are to be proud!
If one should be a prey, how much the better
To fall before the lion than the wolf! (*Clock strikes.*)
The clock upbraids me with the waste of time.
Be not afraid, good youth, I will not have you;
And yet, when wit and youth is come to harvest,
Your wife is like to reap a proper man.
There lies your way, due west.
   VIOLA: Then westward-ho!
Grace and good disposition attend your ladyship!
You'll nothing, madam, to my lord by me?
   OLIVIA: Stay:
I prithee, tell me what thou think'st of me.
   VIOLA: That you do think you are not what you are.
   OLIVIA: If I think so, I think the same of you.
   VIOLA: Then think you right: I am not what I am.
   OLIVIA: I would you were as I would have you be!
   VIOLA: Would it be better, madam, than I am?
I wish it might, for now I am your fool.
   OLIVIA: O, what a deal of scorn looks beautiful
In the contempt and anger of his lip!
A murderous guilt shows not itself more soon
Than love that would seem hid. Love's night is noon.
Cesario, by the roses of the spring,
By maidhood, honor, truth and every thing,
I love thee so, that, mauger[5] all thy pride,
Nor wit nor reason can my passion hide.
Do not extort thy reasons from this clause,
For that I woo, thou therefore hast no cause;[6]
But rather reason thus with reason fetter:
Love sought is good, but given unsought is better.
   VIOLA: By innocence I swear, and by my youth,

---

[1] In the sport of bear-baiting, a bear was tied to a stake and attacked (baited) by large dogs.
[2] Veil of transparent crepe.
[3] Step.
[4] Common thing.
[5] Despite.
[6] Do not conclude, from this declaration of love, that you should not woo me.

I have one heart, one bosom and one truth,
And that no woman has; nor never none
Shall mistress be of it, save I alone.
And so adieu, good madam. Never more
Will I my master's tears to you deplore.

OLIVIA: Yet come again; for thou perhaps mayst move
That heart, which now abhors, to like his love. (*Exeunt.*)

SCENE II
(OLIVIA'S *house.*)

(*Enter* SIR TOBY, SIR ANDREW, *and* FABIAN.)

SIR ANDREW: No, faith, I'll not stay a jot longer.

SIR TOBY: Thy reason, dear venom, give thy reason.

FABIAN: You must needs yield your reason, Sir Andrew.

SIR ANDREW: Marry, I saw your niece do more favors to
the Count's serving-man than ever she bestowed upon me.
I saw 't i' the orchard.

SIR TOBY: Did she see thee the while, old boy? Tell me that.

SIR ANDREW: As plain as I see you now.

FABIAN: This was a great argument[1] of love in her toward
you.

SIR ANDREW: 'Slight, will you make an ass o' me?

FABIAN: I will prove it legitimate, sir, upon the oaths of
judgment and reason.

SIR TOBY: And they have been grand-jurymen since before
Noah was a sailor.

FABIAN: She did show favor to the youth in your sight
only to exasperate you, to awake your dormouse valor, to
put fire in your heart, and brimstone in your liver. You
should then have accosted her; and with some excellent jests,
fire-new from the mint, you should have banged the youth
into dumbness. This was looked for at your hand, and this
was balked.[2] The double gilt of this opportunity you let time
wash off, and you are now sailed into the north of my lady's
opinion; where you will hang like an icicle on a Dutchman's
beard, unless you do redeem it by some laudable attempt
either of valor or policy.

SIR ANDREW: An 't be any way, it must be with valor, for
policy I hate: I had as lief be a Brownist[3] as a politician.

SIR TOBY: Why, then, build me thy fortunes upon the basis
of valor. Challenge me the count's youth to fight with him;
hurt him in eleven places. My niece shall take note of it;
and assure thyself, there is no love-broker in the world can

1 Proof.   3 Unpopular sect.
2 This chance was missed.

more prevail in man's commendation with woman than report of valor.

FABIAN: There is no way but this, Sir Andrew.

SIR ANDREW: Will either of you bear me a challenge to him?

SIR TOBY: Go, write it in a martial hand; be curst and brief; it is no matter how witty, so it be eloquent and full of invention. Taunt him with the license of ink. If thou thou'st him some thrice, it shall not be amiss; and as many lies as will lie in thy sheet of paper, although the sheet were big enough for the bed of Ware[1] in England, set 'em down. Go, about it. Let there be gall enough in thy ink, though thou write with a goose-pen, no matter. About it.

SIR ANDREW: Where shall I find you?

SIR TOBY: We'll call thee at the cubiculo:[2] go.

(*Exit* SIR ANDREW.)

FABIAN: This is a dear manikin to you, Sir Toby.

SIR TOBY: I have been dear to him, lad, some two thousand strong, or so.

FABIAN: We shall have a rare letter from him: but you'll not deliver 't?

SIR TOBY: Never trust me, then; and by all means stir on the youth to an answer. I think oxen and wainropes cannot hale them together. For Andrew, if he were opened, and you find so much blood in his liver as will clog the foot of a flea, I'll eat the rest of the anatomy.

FABIAN: And his opposite, the youth, bears in his visage no great presage of cruelty.

(*Enter* MARIA.)

SIR TOBY: Look, where the youngest wren of nine comes.

MARIA: If you desire the spleen,[3] and will laugh yourselves into stitches, follow me. Yond gull Malvolio is turned heathen, a very renegado; for there is no Christian, that means to be saved by believing rightly, can ever believe such impossible passages of grossness. He's in yellow stockings.

SIR TOBY: And cross-gartered?

MARIA: Most villainously; like a pedant that keeps a school i' the church. I have dogged him, like his murderer. He does obey every point of the letter that I dropped to betray him. He does smile his face into more lines than is in the

---

[1] A famous huge bed.　　[3] If you want a laugh.
[2] Private room.

new map with the augmentation of the Indies. You have not
seen such thing as 'tis. I can hardly forbear hurling things
at him. I know my lady will strike him. If she do, he'll smile
and take 't for a great favor.

SIR TOBY: Come, bring us, bring us where he is. (*Exeunt.*)

SCENE III
(*A street.*)

(*Enter* SEBASTIAN *and* ANTONIO.)

SEBASTIAN: I would not by my will have troubled you;
But, since you make your pleasure of your pains,
I will no further chide you.

ANTONIO: I could not stay behind you. My desire,
More sharp than filed steel, did spur me forth;
And not all love to see you, though so much
As might have drawn one to a longer voyage,
But jealousy[1] what might befall your travel,
Being skilless in these parts; which to a stranger,
Unguided and unfriended, often prove
Rough and unhospitable: my willing love
The rather by these arguments of fear,
Set forth in your pursuit.

SEBASTIAN: My kind Antonio,
I can no other answer make but thanks,
And thanks, and ever thanks; and oft good turns
Are shuffled off with such uncurrent pay.
But, were my worth[2] as is my conscience firm,
You should find better dealing. What's to do?
Shall we go see the relics of this town?

ANTONIO: To-morrow, sir: best first go see your lodging.

SEBASTIAN: I am not weary, and 'tis long to night.
I pray you, let us satisfy our eyes
With the memorials and the things of fame
That do renown this city.

ANTONIO: Would you'ld pardon me.[8]
I do not without danger walk these streets.
Once, in a sea-fight, 'gainst the Count his galleys[4]
I did some service; of such note indeed
That were I ta'en here it would scarce be answer'd.

SEBASTIAN: Belike you slew great number of his people?

ANTONIO: The offense is not of such a bloody nature;
Albeit the quality of the time and quarrel
Might well have given us bloody argument.

1 Anxiety.
2 My wealth.
8 Excuse me from going with you.
4 Against the Count's ships.

It might have since been answer'd in repaying
What we took from them; which, for traffic's[1] sake,
Most of our city did. Only myself stood out;
For which, if I be lapsed in this place,
I shall pay dear.

SEBASTIAN: Do not then walk too open.

ANTONIO: It doth not fit me. Hold, sir, here's my purse.
In the south suburbs, at the Elephant,
Is best to lodge. I will bespeak our diet,
Whiles you beguile the time and feed your knowledge
With viewing of the town. There shall you have me.

SEBASTIAN: Why I your purse?

ANTONIO: Haply your eye shall light upon some toy
You have desire to purchase; and your store,
I think, is not for idle markets, sir.

SEBASTIAN: I'll be your purse-bearer and leave you
For an hour.

ANTONIO: To the Elephant.

SEBASTIAN: I do remember. (*Exeunt.*)

SCENE IV
(OLIVIA'S *garden.*)

(*Enter* OLIVIA *and* MARIA.)

OLIVIA: I have sent after him: he says he'll come;
How shall I feast him? what bestow of him?
For youth is bought more oft than begg'd or borrow'd.
I speak too loud.
Where is Malvolio? He is sad[2] and civil,
And suits well for a servant with my fortunes:
Where is Malvolio?

MARIA: He's coming, madam; but in very strange manner.
He is, sure, possessed,[3] madam.

OLIVIA: Why, what's the matter? does he rave?

MARIA: No, madam, he does nothing but smile. Your
ladyship were best to have some guard about you, if he come;
for, sure, the man is tainted in's wits.

OLIVIA: Go call him hither. (*Exit* MARIA.) I am as mad
     as he,
If sad and merry madness equal be.

(*Enter* MARIA, *with* MALVOLIO.)

How now, Malvolio!

MALVOLIO: Sweet lady, ho, ho.

---

[1] To resume trade relations.
[2] Serious.
[3] Possessed by the devil.

OLIVIA: Smilest thou?
I sent for thee upon a sad occasion.

MALVOLIO: Sad, lady? I could be sad. This does make some obstruction in the blood, this cross-gartering; but what of that? If it please the eye of one, it is with me as the very true sonnet is, "Please one, and please all."

OLIVIA: Why, how dost thou, man? What is the matter with thee?

MALVOLIO: Not black in my mind, though yellow in my legs. It did come to his hands, and commands shall be executed: I think we do know the sweet Roman hand.[1]

OLIVIA: Wilt thou go to bed, Malvolio?

MALVOLIO: To bed! Aye, sweetheart, and I'll come to thee.

OLIVIA: God comfort thee! Why dost thou smile so and kiss thy hand so oft?

MARIA: How do you, Malvolio?

MALVOLIO: At your request! yes; nightingales answer daws.

MARIA: Why appear you with this ridiculous boldness before my lady?

MALVOLIO: "Be not afraid of greatness": 'twas well writ.

OLIVIA: What meanest thou by that, Malvolio?

MALVOLIO: "Some are born great"—

OLIVIA: Ha!

MALVOLIO: "Some achieve greatness"—

OLIVIA: What sayest thou?

MALVOLIO: "And some have greatness thrust upon them."

OLIVIA: Heaven restore thee!

MALVOLIO: "Remember who commended thy yellow stockings"—

OLIVIA: Thy yellow stockings!

MALVOLIO: "And wished to see thee cross-gartered."

OLIVIA: Cross-gartered!

MALVOLIO: "Go to, thou art made, if thou desirest to be so"—

OLIVIA: Am I made?

MALVOLIO: "If not, let me see thee a servant still."

OLIVIA: Why, this is very midsummer madness.

(*Enter* SERVANT.)

SERVANT: Madam, the young gentleman of the Count Orsino's is returned. I could hardly entreat him back: he attends your ladyship's pleasure.

OLIVIA: I'll come to him. (*Exit* SERVANT.) Good Maria, let this fellow be looked to. Where's my cousin Toby? Let some of my people have a special care of him: I would not have him miscarry[2] for the half of my dowry.

(*Exeunt* OLIVIA *and* MARIA.)

---

[1] Italian-style handwriting. [2] Come to harm.

MALVOLIO: O, ho! do you come near me now? No worse man than Sir Toby to look to me! This concurs directly with the letter. She sends him on purpose, that I may appear stubborn to him; for she incites me to that in the letter. "Cast thy humble slough," says she; "be opposite with a kinsman, surly with servants; let thy tongue tang with arguments of state; put thyself into the trick of singularity"; and consequently sets down the manner how: as, a sad face, a reverend carriage, a slow tongue, in the habit[1] of some sir of note, and so forth. I have limed[2] her; but it is Jove's doing, and Jove make me thankful! And when she went away now, "Let this fellow be looked to": "fellow"! not "Malvolio," nor after my degree, but "fellow." Why, every thing adheres together, that no dram of a scruple,[3] no scruple of a scruple, no obstacle, no incredulous or unsafe circumstance—What can be said? Nothing that can be can come between me and the full prospect of my hopes. Well, Jove, not I, is the doer of this, and he is to be thanked.

(*Re-enter* MARIA, *with* SIR TOBY *and* FABIAN.)

SIR TOBY: Which way is he, in the name of sanctity? If all the devils of hell be drawn in little, and Legion[4] himself possessed him, yet I'll speak to him.

FABIAN: Here he is, here he is. How is 't with you, sir? how is 't with you, man?

MALVOLIO: Go off; I discard you. Let me enjoy my private. Go off.

MARIA: Lo, how hollow the fiend speaks within him! Did not I tell you? Sir Toby, my lady prays you to have a care of him.

MALVOLIO: Ah, ha! does she so?

SIR TOBY: Go to, go to; peace, peace! We must deal gently with him. Let me alone. How do you, Malvolio? how is 't with you? What, man! defy the devil! Consider, he's an enemy to mankind.

MALVOLIO: Do you know what you say?

MARIA: La you, an you speak ill of the devil, how he takes it at heart! Pray God, he be not bewitched!

FABIAN: Carry his water to the wise woman.

MARIA: Marry, and it shall be done to-morrow morning, if I live. My lady would not lose him for more than I'll say.

MALVOLIO: How now, mistress!

MARIA: O Lord!

SIR TOBY: Prithee, hold thy peace. This is not the way.

---

1 Clothes.   3 Pun on scruple meaning (1) small amount, (2) doubt.
2 Snared.   4 A host of devils.

Do you not see you move him? Let me alone with him.

FABIAN: No way but gentleness; gently, gently. The fiend is rough, and will not be roughly used.

SIR TOBY: Why, how now, my bawcock! How dost thou, chuck?[1]

MALVOLIO: Sir!

SIR TOBY: Aye, Biddy, come with me. What, man! 'tis not for gravity to play at cherrypit[2] with Satan. Hang him, foul collier!

MARIA: Get him to say his prayers, good Sir Toby, get him to pray.

MALVOLIO: My prayers, minx!

MARIA: No, I warrant you, he will not hear of godliness.

MALVOLIO: Go, hang yourselves all! You are idle shallow things. I am not of your element. You shall know more hereafter. (*Exit.*)

SIR TOBY: Is 't possible?

FABIAN: If this were played upon a stage now, I could condemn it as an improbable fiction.

SIR TOBY: His very genius[3] hath taken the infection of the device, man.

MARIA: Nay, pursue him now, lest the device take air and taint.

FABIAN: Why, we shall make him mad indeed.

MARIA: The house will be the quieter.

SIR TOBY: Come, we'll have him in a dark room and bound. My niece is already in the belief that he's mad. We may carry it thus, for our pleasure and his penance, till our very pastime, tired out of breath, prompt us to have mercy on him: at which time we will bring the device to the bar and crown thee for a finder of madmen. But see, but see.

(*Enter* SIR ANDREW.)

FABIAN: More matter for a May morning.

SIR ANDREW: Here's the challenge; read it. I warrant there's vinegar and pepper in 't.

FABIAN: Is 't so saucy?

SIR ANDREW: Aye, is 't, I warrant him. Do but read.

SIR TOBY: Give me. (*Reads*) "Youth, whatsoever thou art, thou art but a scurvy fellow."

FABIAN: Good, and valiant.

SIR TOBY (*Reads*): "Wonder not, nor admire[4] not in thy mind, why I do call thee so, for I will show thee no reason for 't."

FABIAN: A good note! that keeps you from the blow of the law.

SIR TOBY (*Reads*): "Thou comest to the lady Olivia, and

---

[1] Terms of affection.   [3] Guardian spirit.
[2] A child's game.   [4] Wonder.

in my sight she uses thee kindly. But thou liest in thy throat; that is not the matter I challenge thee for."

FABIAN: Very brief, and to exceeding good sense—less.

SIR TOBY (*Reads*): "I will waylay thee going home; where if it be thy chance to kill me,"—

FABIAN: Good.

SIR TOBY (*Reads*): "Thou killest me like a rogue and a villain."

FABIAN: Still you keep o' the windy side of the law: good.

SIR TOBY (*Reads*): "Fare thee well; and God have mercy upon one of our souls! He may have mercy upon mine; but my hope is better, and so look to thyself. Thy friend, as thou usest him, and thy sworn enemy, Andrew Aguecheek." If this letter move him not, his legs cannot. I'll give 't him.

MARIA: You may have very fit occasion for 't. He is now in some commerce with my lady, and will by and by depart.

SIR TOBY: Go, Sir Andrew! Scout me for him at the corner of the orchard like a bum-baily.[1] So soon as ever thou seest him, draw; and, as thou drawest, swear horrible; for it comes to pass oft that a terrible oath, with a swaggering accent sharply twanged off, gives manhood more approbation than ever proof itself would have earned him. Away!

SIR ANDREW: Nay, let me alone for swearing. (*Exit.*)

SIR TOBY: Now will not I deliver his letter: for the behavior of the young gentleman gives him out to be of good capacity and breeding; his employment between his lord and my niece confirms no less. Therefore this letter, being so excellently ignorant, will breed no terror in the youth. He will find it comes from a clodpoll. But, sir, I will deliver his challenge by word of mouth; set upon Aguecheek a notable report of valor; and drive the gentleman, as I know his youth will aptly receive it, into a most hideous opinion of his rage, skill, fury and impetuosity. This will so fright them both, that they will kill one another by the look, like cockatrices.[2]

(*Re-enter* OLIVIA, *with* VIOLA.)

FABIAN: Here he comes with your niece. Give them way till he take leave, and presently[3] after him.

SIR TOBY: I will meditate the while upon some horrid message for a challenge. . (*Exeunt* SIR TOBY, FABIAN, *and* MARIA.)

OLIVIA: I have said too much unto a heart of stone, And laid mine honor too unchary[4] out.

---

[1] Like a bailiff lurking to make an arrest.
[2] Mythical animal.

[3] Immediately.
[4] Too heedlessly.

There's something in me that reproves my fault;
But such a headstrong potent fault it is,
That it but mocks reproof.

VIOLA: With the same 'havior that your passion bears
Goes on my master's grief.

OLIVIA: Here, wear this jewel for me; 'tis my picture.
Refuse it not; it hath no tongue to vex you.
And I beseech you come again to-morrow.
What shall you ask of me that I'll deny,
That honor saved may upon asking give?

VIOLA: Nothing but this;—your true love for my master.

OLIVIA: How with mine honor may I give him that
Which I have given to you?

VIOLA: I will acquit you.

OLIVIA: Well, come again to-morrow: fare thee well:
A fiend like thee might bear my soul to hell. (*Exit.*)

(*Re-enter* SIR TOBY *and* FABIAN.)

SIR TOBY: Gentleman, God save thee.

VIOLA: And you, sir.

SIR TOBY: That defense thou hast, betake thee to 't. Of
what nature the wrongs are thou hast done him, I know
not; but thy intercepter, full of despite, bloody as the hunter,
attends thee at the orchard-end. Dismount thy tuck,[1] be yare[2]
in thy preparation, for thy assailant is quick, skillful and
deadly.

VIOLA: You mistake, sir; I am sure no man hath any quarrel to me. My remembrance is very free and clear from any
image of offense done to any man.

SIR TOBY: You'll find it otherwise, I assure you. Therefore,
if you hold your life at any price, betake you to your guard;
for your opposite hath in him what youth, strength, skill and
wrath can furnish man withal.

VIOLA: I pray you, sir, what is he?

SIR TOBY: He is knight, dubbed with unhatched rapier and
on carpet consideration;[3] but he is a devil in private brawl:
souls and bodies hath he divorced three; and his incensement
at this moment is so implacable, that satisfaction can be none
but by pangs of deaths and sepulcher. "Hob, nob," is his
word; "give 't or take 't."

VIOLA: I will return again into the house and desire some
conduct[4] of the lady. I am no fighter. I have heard of some

1 Unsheathe your sword.
2 Ready.
8 Dubbed with a sword never used in battle, and knighted for court
reasons.
4 Escort.

kind of men that put quarrels purposely on others, to taste their valor: belike this is a man of that quirk.

SIR TOBY: Sir, no; his indignation derives itself out of a very competent injury: therefore, get you on and give him his desire. Back you shall not to the house, unless you undertake that with me which with as much safety you might answer him. Therefore, on, or strip your sword stark naked; for meddle[1] you must, that's certain, or forswear to wear iron about you.

VIOLA: This is as uncivil as strange. I beseech you, do me this courteous office, as to know of the knight what my offense to him is. It is something of my negligence, nothing of my purpose.

SIR TOBY: I will do so. Signior Fabian, stay you by this gentleman till my return. (*Exit.*)

VIOLA: Pray you, sir, do you know of this matter?

FABIAN: I know the knight is incensed against you, even to a mortal arbitrement,[2] but nothing of the circumstance more.

VIOLA: I beseech you, what manner of man is he?

FABIAN: Nothing of that wonderful promise, to read him by his form, as you are like to find him in the proof of his valor. He is, indeed, sir, the most skillful, bloody and fatal opposite that you could possibly have found in any part of Illyria. Will you walk towards him? I will make your peace with him if I can.

VIOLA: I shall be much bound to you for 't. I am one that had rather go with sir priest than sir knight. I care not who knows so much of my mettle. (*Exeunt.*)

(*Re-enter* SIR TOBY, *with* SIR ANDREW.)

SIR TOBY: Why, man, he's a very devil; I have not seen such a firago.[3] I had a pass with him, rapier, scabbard and all, and he gives me the stuck in with such a mortal motion, that it is inevitable; and on the answer, he pays you as surely as your feet hit the ground they step on. They say he has been fencer to the Sophy.

SIR ANDREW: Pox on 't, I'll not meddle with him.

SIR TOBY: Aye, but he will not now be pacified: Fabian can scarce hold him yonder.

SIR ANDREW: Plague on 't, an I thought he had been valiant and so cunning in fence I'ld have seen him damned ere I'ld have challenged him. Let him let the matter slip, and I'll give him my horse, gray Capilet.

SIR TOBY: I'll make the motion. Stand here, make a good

---

1 Engage.   3 Virago.
2 A decision of death.

show on 't. This shall end without the perdition of souls.
(*Aside*) Marry, I'll ride your horse as well as I ride you.

(*Re-enter* FABIAN *and* VIOLA.)

(*To* FABIAN) I have his horse to take up the quarrel. I have
persuaded him the youth's a devil.

FABIAN: He is as horribly conceited of him;[1] and pants and
looks pale, as if a bear were at his heels.

SIR TOBY (*to* VIOLA): There's no remedy, sir; he will fight
with you for's oath sake. Marry, he hath better bethought
him of his quarrel, and he finds that now scarce to be worth
talking of. Therefore draw, for the supportance of his vow.
He protests he will not hurt you.

VIOLA (*aside*): Pray God defend me! A little thing would
make me tell them how much I lack of a man.

FABIAN: Give ground, if you see him furious.

SIR TOBY: Come, Sir Andrew, there's no remedy. The
gentleman will, for his honor's sake, have one bout with you;
he cannot by the duello[2] avoid it: but he has promised me, as
he is a gentleman and a soldier, he will not hurt you. Come
on; to 't.

SIR ANDREW: Pray God, he keep his oath!

VIOLA: I do assure you, 'tis against my will. (*They draw.*)

(*Enter* ANTONIO.)

ANTONIO: Put up your sword. If this young gentleman
Have done offense, I take the fault on me.
If you offend him, I for him defy you.

SIR TOBY: You, sir! why, what are you?

ANTONIO: One, sir, that for his love dares yet do more
Than you have heard him brag to you he will.

SIR TOBY: Nay, if you be an undertaker,[3] I am for you.
(*They draw.*)

(*Enter* OFFICERS.)

FABIAN: O good Sir Toby, hold! Here come the officers.

SIR TOBY (*to* ANTONIO): I'll be with you anon.

VIOLA (*to* SIR ANDREW): Pray, sir, put your sword up, if
you please.

SIR ANDREW: Marry, will I, sir; and, for that I promised
you, I'll be as good as my word: he will bear you easily and
reins well.

FIRST OFFICER: This is the man; do thy office.

---

[1] He has as horrible a conception of him.   [2] Rules of dueling.
[3] Meddler.

SECOND OFFICER: Antonio, I arrest thee at the suit of Count
Orsino.

ANTONIO: You do mistake me, sir.

FIRST OFFICER: No, sir, no jot; I know your favor[1] well,
Though now you have no sea-cap on your head.
Take him away: he knows I know him well.

ANTONIO: I must obey. (To VIOLA.) This comes with seek-
     ing you:
But there's no remedy; I shall answer it.
What will you do, now my necessity
Makes me to ask you for my purse? It grieves me
Much more for what I cannot do for you
Than what befalls myself. You stand amazed;
But be of comfort.

SECOND OFFICER: Come, sir, away.

ANTONIO: I must entreat of you some of that money.

VIOLA: What money, sir?
For the fair kindness you have show'd me here,
And, part, being prompted by your present trouble,
Out of my lean and low ability
I'll lend you something. My having is not much.
I'll make division of my present with you:
Hold, there's half my coffer.

ANTONIO: Will you deny me now?
Is 't possible that my deserts to you
Can lack persuasion? Do not tempt my misery,
Lest that it make me so unsound[2] a man
As to upbraid you with those kindnesses
That I have done for you.

VIOLA: I know of none,
Nor know I you by voice or any feature.
I hate ingratitude more in a man
Than lying vainness, babbling drunkenness,
Or any taint of vice whose strong corruption
Inhabits our frail blood.

ANTONIO: O heavens themselves!

SECOND OFFICER: Come, sir, I pray you, go.

ANTONIO: Let me speak a little. This youth that you see here
I snatch'd one half out of the jaws of death;
Relieved him with such sanctity of love,
And to his image, which methought did promise
Most venerable worth, did I devotion.

FIRST OFFICER: What's that to us? The time goes by. Away!

ANTONIO: But, O, how vile an idol proves this god!
Thou hast, Sebastian, done good feature shame.
In nature there's no blemish but the mind;

---

1 Features.   2 Unmanly.

None can be call'd deform'd but the unkind:
Virtue is beauty; but the beauteous evil
Are empty trunks, o'erflourish'd[1] by the devil.

FIRST OFFICER: The man grows mad. Away with him!
Come, come, sir.

ANTONIO: Lead me on. (*Exit with* OFFICERS.)

VIOLA: Methinks his words do from such passion fly,
That he believes himself; so do not I.
Prove true, imagination, O prove true,
That I, dear brother, be now ta'en for you!

SIR TOBY: Come hither, knight; come hither, Fabian. We'll
whisper o'er a couplet or two of most sage saws.

VIOLA: He named Sebastian. I my brother know
Yet living in my glass.[2] Even such and so
In favor was my brother, and he went
Still in this fashion, color, ornament,
For him I imitate. O, if it prove,
Tempests are kind and salt waves fresh in love! (*Exit.*)

SIR TOBY: A very dishonest paltry boy, and more a coward
than a hare. His dishonesty appears in leaving his friend here
in necessity and denying him; and for his cowardship, ask
Fabian.

FABIAN: A coward, a most devout coward, religious in it.

SIR ANDREW: 'Slid, I'll after him again and beat him.

SIR TOBY: Do; cuff him soundly, but never draw thy sword.

SIR ANDREW: An I do not,— (*Exit.*)

FABIAN: Come, let's see the event.

SIR TOBY: I dare lay any money 'twill be nothing yet.
(*Exeunt.*)

ACT IV

SCENE I
(*Before* OLIVIA'S *house.*)

(*Enter* SEBASTIAN *and* CLOWN.)

CLOWN: Will you make me believe that I am not sent for
you?

SEBASTIAN: Go to, go to, thou art a foolish fellow. Let me
be clear of thee.

CLOWN: Well held out, i' faith! No, I do not know you; nor
I am not sent to you by my lady, to bid you come speak with
her; nor your name is not Master Cesario; nor this is not
my nose neither. Nothing that is so is so.

SEBASTIAN: I prithee, vent thy folly[3] somewhere else. Thou
know'st not me.

---

[1] Decorated.   [2] Mirror.   [3] Utter your foolish talk.

CLOWN: Vent my folly! He has heard that word of some great man and now applies it to a fool. Vent my folly! I am afraid this great lubber, the world, will prove a cockney.[1] I prithee now, ungird thy strangeness and tell me what I shall vent to my lady. Shall I vent to her that thou art coming?

SEBASTIAN: I prithee, foolish Greek[2] depart from me. There's money for thee. If you tarry longer, I shall give worse payment.

CLOWN: By my troth, thou hast an open hand. These wise men that give fools money get themselves a good report—after fourteen years' purchase.[8]

(*Enter* SIR ANDREW, SIR TOBY, *and* FABIAN.)

SIR ANDREW: Now, sir, have I met you again? there's for you. (*Strikes* SEBASTIAN.)

SEBASTIAN: Why, there's for thee, and there, and there. (*Strikes* SIR ANDREW.) Are all the people mad?

SIR TOBY: Hold, sir, or I'll throw your dagger o'er the house. (*Seizes* SEBASTIAN.)

CLOWN: This will I tell my lady straight. I would not be in some of your coats for two pence. (*Exit.*)

SIR TOBY: Come on, sir; hold.

SIR ANDREW: Nay, let him alone. I'll go another way to work with him. I'll have an action of battery against him, if there be any law in Illyria. Though I struck him first, yet it's no matter for that.

SEBASTIAN: Let go thy hand.

SIR TOBY: Come, sir, I will not let you go. Come, my young soldier, put up your iron. You are well fleshed.[4] Come on.

SEBASTIAN: I will be free from thee. What wouldst thou now? If thou darest tempt me further, draw thy sword. (*Draws.*)

SIR TOBY: What, what? Nay, then I must have an ounce or two of this malapert[5] blood from you. (*Draws.*)

(*Enter* OLIVIA.)

OLIVIA: Hold, Toby! On thy life, I charge thee, hold!

SIR TOBY: Madam!

OLIVIA: Will it be ever thus? Ungracious wretch,
Fit for the mountains and the barbarous caves,
Where manners ne'er were preach'd! Out of my sight!
Be not offended, dear Cesario.
Rudesby,[6] be gone!

(*Exeunt* SIR TOBY, SIR ANDREW, *and* FABIAN.)
                I prithee, gentle friend,
Let thy fair wisdom, not thy passion, sway

---

1 This stupid world will be foppish.   4 You have tasted blood.
2 Jester.   5 Saucy.
8 At a high price.   6 Ruffian.

In this uncivil and unjust extent
Against thy peace. Go with me to my house;
And hear thou there how many fruitless pranks
This ruffian hath botch'd up,[1] that thou thereby
Mayst smile at this. Thou shalt not choose but go;
Do not deny. Beshrew his soul for me!
He started one poor heart of mine, in thee.
SEBASTIAN: What relish is in this? how runs the stream?
Or I am mad, or else this is a dream.
Let fancy still my sense in Lethe steep;
If it be thus to dream, still let me sleep!
OLIVIA: Nay, come, I prithee. Would thou'ldst be ruled by
me!
SEBASTIAN: Madam, I will.
OLIVIA: O, say so, and so be!

(*Exeunt.*)

SCENE II
(OLIVIA'S *house.*)

(*Enter* MARIA *and* CLOWN.)

MARIA: Nay, I prithee, put on this gown and this beard;
make him believe thou art Sir[2] Topas the curate: do it quickly.
I'll call Sir Toby the whilst. (*Exit.*)
CLOWN: Well, I'll put it on, and I will dissemble myself in
't; and I would I were the first that ever dissembled in such a
gown. I am not tall[3] enough to become the function well,
nor lean enough to be thought a good student; but to be said
an honest man and a good housekeeper goes as fairly as to
say a careful man and a great scholar. The competitors[4] enter.

(*Enter* SIR TOBY *and* MARIA.)

SIR TOBY: Jove bless thee, Master Parson.
CLOWN: Bonos dies,[5] Sir Toby; for, as the old hermit of
Prague, that never saw pen and ink, very wittily said to a
niece of King Gorboduc, "That that is is;" so I, being Master
Parson, am Master Parson; for, what is "that" but "that," and
"is" but "is"?
SIR TOBY: To him, Sir Topas.
CLOWN: What, ho, I say! Peace in this prison!
SIR TOBY: The knave counterfeits well; a good knave.
MALVOLIO (*within*): Who calls there?

---

[1] Patched clumsily.
[2] Priests were called "Sir."
[3] Robust.
[4] Confederates.
[5] Good day.

CLOWN: Sir Topas the curate, who comes to visit Malvolio the lunatic.

MALVOLIO: Sir Topas, Sir Topas, good Sir Topas, go to my lady.

CLOWN: Out, hyperbolical[1] fiend! How vexest thou this man! Talkest thou nothing but of ladies?

SIR TOBY: Well said, Master Parson.

MALVOLIO: Sir Topas, never was man thus wronged. Good Sir Topas, do not think I am mad. They have laid me here in hideous darkness.

CLOWN: Fie, thou dishonest Satan! I call thee by the most modest terms; for I am one of those gentle ones that will use the devil himself with courtesy. Sayest thou that house is dark?

MALVOLIO: As hell, Sir Topas.

CLOWN: Why, it hath bay windows transparent as barricadoes, and the clearstories[2] toward the south north are as lustrous as ebony; and yet complainest thou of obstruction?

MALVOLIO: I am not mad, Sir Topas. I say to you, this house is dark.

CLOWN: Madman, thou errest. I say, there is no darkness but ignorance, in which thou art more puzzled than the Egyptians in their fog.

MALVOLIO: I say, this house is as dark as ignorance, though ignorance were as dark as hell; and I say, there was never man thus abused. I am no more mad than you are. Make the trial of it in any constant[3] question.

CLOWN: What is the opinion of Pythagoras concerning wild fowl?

MALVOLIO: That the soul of our grandam might haply inhabit a bird.

CLOWN: What thinkest thou of his opinion?

MALVOLIO: I think nobly of the soul, and no way approve his opinion.

CLOWN: Fare thee well. Remain thou still in darkness. Thou shalt hold the opinion of Pythagoras ere I will allow of thy wits, and fear to kill a woodcock, lest thou dispossess the soul of thy grandam. Fare thee well.

MALVOLIO: Sir Topas, Sir Topas!

SIR TOBY: My most exquisite Sir Topas!

CLOWN: Nay, I am for all waters.[4]

MARIA: Thou mightst have done this without thy beard and gown. He sees thee not.

SIR TOBY: To him in thine own voice, and bring me word how thou findest him. (*To* MARIA.) I would we were well rid

---

1 Raging.   3 Logical.
2 Upper windows.   4 I can turn my hand to anything.

of this knavery. If he may be conveniently delivered, I would he were; for I am now so far in offense with my niece, that I cannot pursue with any safety this sport to the upshot. (*To the* CLOWN.) Come by and by to my chamber.

(*Exeunt* SIR TOBY *and* MARIA.)

CLOWN (*singing*): Hey, Robin, jolly Robin,
　　　　　　　　　Tell me how thy lady does.
MALVOLIO: Fool,—
CLOWN: My lady is unkind, perdy.
MALVOLIO: Fool,—
CLOWN: Alas, why is she so?
MALVOLIO: Fool, I say,—
CLOWN: She loves another—Who calls, ha?
MALVOLIO: Good fool, as ever thou wilt deserve well at my hand, help me to a candle, and pen, ink, and paper. As I am a gentleman, I will live to be thankful to thee for 't.
CLOWN: Master Malvolio!
MALVOLIO: Aye, good fool.
CLOWN: Alas, sir, how fell you besides your five wits?[1]
MALVOLIO: Fool, there was never man so notoriously abused. I am as well in my wits, fool, as thou art.
CLOWN: But as well? Then you are mad indeed, if you be no better in your wits than a fool.
MALVOLIO: They have here propertied me;[2] keep me in darkness, send ministers to me, asses, and do all they can to face[3] me out of my wits.
CLOWN: Advise you what you say. The minister is here. —Malvolio, Malvolio, thy wits the heavens restore! Endeavor thyself to sleep, and leave thy vain bibble babble.
MALVOLIO: Sir Topas,—
CLOWN: Maintain no words with him, good fellow.—Who, I, sir? not I, sir. God be wi' you, good Sir Topas.—Marry, amen.—I will, sir, I will.
MALVOLIO: Fool, fool, fool, I say,—
CLOWN: Alas, sir, be patient. What say you, sir? I am shent[4] for speaking to you.
MALVOLIO: Good fool, help me to some light and some paper. I tell thee, I am as well in my wits as any man in Illyria.
CLOWN: Well-a-day that you were, sir!
MALVOLIO: By this hand, I am. Good fool, some ink, paper and light; and convey what I will set down to my lady. It

---

[1] The five are common wit, imagination, fantasy, estimation, and memory.
[2] Made me a mere utensil.　　　　[3] Bluff.　　　　[4] Rebuked.

shall advantage thee more than ever the bearing of letter did.

CLOWN: I will help you to 't. But tell me true, are you not mad indeed? or do you but counterfeit?

MALVOLIO: Believe me, I am not. I tell thee true.

CLOWN: Nay, I'll ne'er believe a madman till I see his brains. I will fetch you light and paper and ink.

MALVOLIO: Fool, I'll requite it in the highest degree. I prithee, be gone.

CLOWN (*singing*):   I am gone, sir,
                  And anon, sir,
              I'll be with you again,
                  In a trice,
                  Like to the old Vice,[1]
          Your need to sustain;
          Who, with dagger of lath,
          In his rage and his wrath,
                  Cries, "ah, ha!" to the devil:
          Like a mad lad,
      "Pare thy nails, dad;"
              Adieu, goodman devil.

SCENE III
(OLIVIA'S *garden.*)

(*Enter* SEBASTIAN.)

SEBASTIAN: This is the air; that is the glorious sun;
This pearl she gave me, I do feel't and see't;
And though 'tis wonder that enwraps me thus,
Yet 'tis not madness. Where's Antonio, then?
I could not find him at the Elephant:
Yet there he was;[2] and there I found this credit,[8]
That he did range the town to seek me out.
His counsel now might do me golden service;
For though my soul disputes well with my sense,
That this may be some error, but no madness,
Yet doth this accident and flood of fortune
So far exceed all instance, all discourse,[4]
That I am ready to distrust mine eyes
And wrangle with my reason, that persuades me
To any other trust but that I am mad,
Or else the lady's mad. Yet, if 'twere so,
She could not sway her house, command her followers,
Take and give back affairs and their dispatch
With such a smooth, discreet, and stable bearing

---

1 Jester in old plays.   3 Report.
2 Had been.   4 All example, all reasoning.

As I perceive she does. There's something in 't
That is deceivable.[1] But here the lady comes.

(*Enter* OLIVIA *and* PRIEST.)

OLIVIA: Blame not this haste of mine. If you mean well,
Now go with me and with this holy man
Into the chantry[2] by. There, before him,
And underneath that consecrated roof,
Plight me the full assurance of your faith;
That my most jealous and too doubtful soul
May live at peace. He shall conceal it
Whiles you are willing it shall come to note,
What[3] time we will our celebration keep
According to my birth. What do you say?
　　SEBASTIAN: I'll follow this good man, and go with you;
And having sworn truth, ever will be true.
　　OLIVIA: Then lead the way, good father; and heavens so
　　　　shine,
That they may fairly note this act of mine! (*Exeunt.*)

ACT V

SCENE I
(*Before* OLIVIA'S *house.*)

(*Enter* CLOWN *and* FABIAN.)

FABIAN: Now, as thou lovest me, let me see his letter.
CLOWN: Good Master Fabian, grant me another request.
FABIAN: Any thing.
CLOWN: Do not desire to see this letter.
FABIAN: This is, to give a dog, and in recompense desire my
dog again.

(*Enter* DUKE, VIOLA, CURIO, *and* LORDS.)

DUKE: Belong you to the lady Olivia, friends?
CLOWN: Aye, sir; we are some of her trappings.
DUKE: I know thee well. How dost thou, my good fellow?
CLOWN: Truly, sir, the better for my foes and the worse for
my friends.
DUKE: Just the contrary; the better for thy friends.
CLOWN: No, sir, the worse.
DUKE: How can that be?

---

1 Deceptive.　　　　　2 Chapel.　　　　　8 At which.

CLOWN: Marry, sir, they praise me and make an ass of me. Now my foes tell me plainly I am an ass; so that by my foes, sir, I profit in the knowledge of myself; and by my friends I am abused; so that, conclusions to be as kisses,[1] if your four negatives make your two affirmatives, why then, the worse for my friends, and the better for my foes.

DUKE: Why, this is excellent.

CLOWN: By my troth, sir, no; though it please you to be one of my friends.

DUKE: Thou shalt not be the worse for me. There's gold.

CLOWN: But that it would be double-dealing, sir, I would you could make it another.

DUKE: O, you give me ill counsel.

CLOWN: Put your grace in your pocket, sir, for this once, and let your flesh and blood obey it.

DUKE: Well, I will be so much a sinner, to be a double-dealer. There's another.

CLOWN: Primo, secundo, tertio, is a good play; and the old saying is, "The third pays for all." The triplex, sir, is a good tripping measure; or the bells of Saint Bennet, sir, may put you in mind—one, two, three.

DUKE: You can fool no more money out of me at this throw:[2] if you will let your lady know I am here to speak with her, and bring her along with you, it may awake my bounty further.

CLOWN: Marry, sir, lullaby to your bounty till I come again. I go, sir; but I would not have you to think that my desire of having is the sin of covetousness. But, as you say, sir, let your bounty take a nap, I will awake it anon. (*Exit.*)

VIOLA: Here comes the man, sir, that did rescue me.

(*Enter* ANTONIO *and* OFFICERS.)

DUKE: That face of his I do remember well;
Yet, when I saw it last, it was besmear'd
As black as Vulcan in the smoke of war.
A bawbling[3] vessel was he captain of,
For shallow draught and bulk and unprizable,[4]
With which such scathful[5] grapple did he make
With the most noble bottom of our fleet,
That very envy and the tongue of loss
Cried fame and honor on him. What's the matter?

FIRST OFFICER: Orsino, this is that Antonio
That took the Phœnix and her fraught[6] from Candy;

---

[1] Two people make a kiss, and two premises make one conclusion.
[2] At this throw of the dice, *i.e.*, at this stage of the game.
[3] Insignificant.   [4] Worthless.   [5] Harmful.   [6] Freight.

And this is he that did the Tiger board,
When your young nephew Titus lost his leg.
Here in the streets, desperate of shame and state,
In private brabble[1] did we apprehend him.
   VIOLA: He did me kindness, sir, drew on my side;
But in conclusion put strange speech upon me.
I know not what 'twas but distraction.
   DUKE: Notable pirate! thou salt-water thief!
What foolish boldness brought thee to their mercies,
Whom thou, in terms so bloody and so dear,[2]
Hast made thine enemies?
   ANTONIO: Orsino, noble sir,
Be pleased that I shake off these names you give me.
Antonio never yet was thief or pirate,
Though I confess, on base and ground enough,
Orsino's enemy. A witchcraft drew me hither.
That most ingrateful boy there by your side,
From the rude sea's enraged and foamy mouth
Did I redeem. A wreck past hope he was.
His life I gave him, and did thereto add
My love, without retention or restraint,
All his in dedication. For his sake
Did I expose myself, pure for his love,
Into the danger of this adverse town;
Drew to defend him when he was beset;
Where being apprehended, his false cunning,
Not meaning to partake with me in danger,
Taught him to face me out of his acquaintance,
And grew a twenty years removed thing
While one would wink; denied me mine own purse,
Which I had recommended to his use
Not half an hour before.
   VIOLA: How can this be?
   DUKE: When came he to this town?
   ANTONIO: To-day, my lord; and for three months before,
No interim, not a minute's vacancy,
Both day and night did we keep company.

(*Enter* OLIVIA *and* ATTENDANTS.)

   DUKE: Here comes the Countess: now heaven walks on
      earth!
But for thee, fellow: fellow, thy words are madness:
Three months this youth hath tended upon me;
But more of that anon. Take him aside.
   OLIVIA: What would my lord, but that he may not have,

---

[1] Brawl.   [2] Grievous.

Wherein Olivia may seem serviceable?
Cesario, you do not keep promise with me.
    VIOLA: Madam!
    DUKE: Gracious Olivia—
    OLIVIA: What do you say, Cesario? Good my lord—
    VIOLA: My lord would speak; my duty hushes me.
    OLIVIA: If it be aught to the old tune, my lord,
It is as fat [1] and fulsome to mine ear
As howling after music.
    DUKE: Still so cruel?
    OLIVIA: Still so constant, lord.
    DUKE: What, to perverseness? You uncivil lady,
To whose ingrate and unauspicious altars
My soul the faithfull'st offerings hath breathed out
That e'er devotion tender'd! What shall I do?
    OLIVIA: Even what it please my lord, that shall become him.
    DUKE: Why should I not, had I the heart to do it,
Like to the Egyptian thief at point of death,
Kill what I love?—a savage jealousy
That sometimes savors nobly. But hear me this:
Since you to non-regardance cast my faith,
And that I partly know the instrument
That screws me from my true place in your favor,
Live you the marble-breasted tyrant still.
But this your minion,[2] whom I know you love,
And whom, by heaven I swear, I tender [3] dearly,
Him will I tear out of that cruel eye,
Where he sits crowned in his master's spite.[4]
Come, boy, with me; my thoughts are ripe in mischief:
I'll sacrifice the lamb that I do love,
To spite a raven's heart within a dove. (*Leaving.*)
    VIOLA: And I, most jocund, apt and willingly,
To do you rest,[5] a thousand deaths would die. (*Following.*)
    OLIVIA: Where goes Cesario?
    VIOLA: After him I love
More than I love these eyes, more than my life,
More, by all mores, than e'er I shall love wife.
If I do feign, you witnesses above
Punish my life for tainting of my love!
    OLIVIA: Aye me, detested! how am I beguiled!
    VIOLA: Who does beguile you? Who does do you wrong?
    OLIVIA: Hast thou forgot thyself? Is it so long?
Call forth the holy father. (*Exit a* SERVANT.)
    DUKE (*to* VIOLA):   Come, away!

---

1 Distasteful.
2 Favorite.
3 Cherish.

4 With Olivia's scorn of his master.
5 To give you ease.

OLIVIA: Whither, my lord? Cesario, husband, stay.
DUKE: Husband!
OLIVIA: Aye, husband. Can he that deny?
DUKE: Her husband, sirrah?
VIOLA: No, my lord, not I.
OLIVIA: Alas, it is the baseness of thy fear
That makes thee strangle thy propriety.[1]
Fear not, Cesario; take thy fortunes up;
Be that thou know'st thou art, and then thou art
As great as that thou fear'st.[2]
    (*Enter* PRIEST.)

                            O, welcome, father!
Father, I charge thee, by thy reverence,
Here to unfold, though lately we intended
To keep in darkness what occasion now
Reveals before 'tis ripe, what thou dost know
Hath newly pass'd between this youth and me.
    PRIEST: A contract of eternal bond of love,
Confirm'd by mutual joinder of your hands,
Attested by the holy close of lips,
Strengthen'd by interchangement of your rings;
And all the ceremony of this compact
Seal'd in my function,[3] by my testimony:
Since when, my watch hath told me, toward my grave
I have travel'd but two hours.
    DUKE: O thou dissembling cub! What wilt thou be
When time hath sow'd a grizzle [4] on thy case?
Or will not else thy craft so quickly grow,
That thine own trip[5] shall be thine overthrow?
Farewell, and take her; but direct thy feet
Where thou and I henceforth may never meet.
    VIOLA: My lord, I do protest—
    OLIVIA: O, do not swear!
Hold little faith, though thou hast too much fear.

    (*Enter* SIR ANDREW.)

    SIR ANDREW: For the love of God, a surgeon! Send one
presently to Sir Toby.
    OLIVIA: What's the matter?
    SIR ANDREW: He has broke my head across and has given
Sir Toby a bloody coxcomb[6] too. For the love of God, your

---

1 Suppress your identity.   4 Beard.
2 As great as the Duke whom you fear.   5 Wrestler's trick.
3 *I.e.*, in my official capacity as chaplain.   6 Head.

help! I had rather than forty pound I were at home.

OLIVIA: Who has done this, Sir Andrew?

SIR ANDREW: The count's gentleman, one Cesario: we took him for a coward, but he's the very devil incardinate.

DUKE: My gentleman, Cesario?

SIR ANDREW: 'Od's lifelings, here he is! You broke my head for nothing; and that that I did, I was set on to do 't by Sir Toby.

VIOLA: Why do you speak to me? I never hurt you.
You drew your sword upon me without cause;
But I bespake you fair, and hurt you not.

SIR ANDREW: If a bloody coxcomb be a hurt, you have hurt me. I think you set nothing by a bloody coxcomb.

(*Enter* SIR TOBY *and* CLOWN.)

Here comes Sir Toby halting; you shall hear more: but if he had not been in drink, he would have tickled you other-gates[1] than he did.

DUKE: How now, gentleman! how is 't with you?

SIR TOBY: That's all one. Has hurt me, and there's the end on 't. Sot, didst see Dick surgeon, sot?

CLOWN: O, he's drunk, Sir Toby, an hour agone. His eyes were set at eight i' the morning.

SIR TOBY: Then he's a rogue, and a passy measures pavin.[2] I hate a drunken rogue.

OLIVIA: Away with him! Who hath made this havoc with them?

SIR ANDREW: I'll help you, Sir Toby, because we'll be dressed together.

SIR TOBY: Will you help? an ass-head and a coxcomb and a knave, a thin-faced knave, a gull!

OLIVIA: Get him to bed, and let his hurt be look'd to.

(*Exeunt* CLOWN, FABIAN, SIR TOBY *and* SIR ANDREW.)

(*Enter* SEBASTIAN.)

SEBASTIAN: I am sorry, madam, I have hurt your kinsman;
But, had it been the brother of my blood,
I must have done no less with wit and safety.
You throw a strange regard[3] upon me, and by that
I do perceive it hath offended you.
Pardon me, sweet one, even for the vows
We made each other but so late ago.

---

1 Otherwise.   3 Look.
2 Stately dance.

DUKE: One face, one voice, one habit, and two persons!
A natural perspective,[1] that is and is not!

SEBASTIAN: Antonio, O my dear Antonio!
How have the hours rack'd and tortured me,
Since I have lost thee!

ANTONIO: Sebastian are you?

SEBASTIAN: Fear'st [2] thou that, Antonio?

ANTONIO: How have you made division of yourself?
An apple, cleft in two, is not more twin
Than these two creatures. Which is Sebastian?

OLIVIA: Most wonderful!

SEBASTIAN: Do I stand there? I never had a brother;
Nor can there be that deity in my nature,
Of here and every where.[3] I had a sister,
Whom the blind waves and surges have devour'd.
Of charity, what kin are you to me?
What countryman? what name? what parentage?

VIOLA: Of Messaline: Sebastian was my father;
Such a Sebastian was my brother too,
So went he suited[4] to his watery tomb.
If spirits can assume both form and suit,
You come to fright us.

SEBASTIAN: A spirit I am indeed,
But am in that dimension[5] grossly clad
Which from the womb I did participate.[6]
Were you a woman, as the rest goes even,
I should my tears let fall upon your cheek,
And say, "Thrice-welcome, drowned Viola!"

VIOLA: My father had a mole upon his brow.

SEBASTIAN: And so had mine.

VIOLA: And died that day when Viola from her birth
Had number'd thirteen years.

SEBASTIAN: O, that record is lively in my soul!
He finished indeed his mortal act
That day that made my sister thirteen years.

VIOLA: If nothing lets[7] to make us happy both
But this my masculine usurp'd attire,
Do not embrace me till each circumstance
Of place, time, fortune, do cohere and jump
That I am Viola; which to confirm,
I'll bring you to a captain in this town,
Where lie my maiden weeds; by whose gentle help

---

1 An illusion produced by nature.
2 Doubtest.
3 I am not a god who can be everywhere.
4 Dressed.

5 Bodily shape.
6 Possess.
7 Hinders.

I was preserved to serve this noble Count.
All the occurrence[1] of my fortune since
Hath been between this lady and this lord.

SEBASTIAN (*to* OLIVIA): So comes it, lady, you have been
    mistook.
But nature to her bias drew in that.[2]
You would have been contracted to a maid;
Nor are you therein, by my life, deceived:
You are betroth'd both to a maid and man.

DUKE: Be not amazed; right noble is his blood.
If this be so, as yet the glass[3] seems true,
I shall have share in this most happy wreck.
(*To* VIOLA) Boy, thou hast said to me a thousand times
Thou never shouldst love woman like to me.

VIOLA: And all those sayings will I over-swear;
And all those swearings keep as true in soul
As doth that orbed continent[4] the fire
That severs day from night.

DUKE: Give me thy hand,
And let me see thee in thy woman's weeds.

VIOLA: The captain that did bring me first on shore
Hath my maid's garments. He upon some action
Is now in durance, at Malvolio's suit,
A gentleman, and follower of my lady's.

OLIVIA: He shall enlarge him. Fetch Malvolio hither.
And yet, alas, now I remember me,
They say, poor gentleman, he's much distract.

(*Re-enter* CLOWN *with a letter, and* FABIAN.)

A most extracting frenzy of mine own
From my remembrance clearly banish'd his.
How does he, sirrah?

CLOWN: Truly, madam, he holds Belzebub at the stave's
end[5] as well as a man in his case may do. Has here writ a
letter to you; I should have given 't you to-day morning.
(*Showing a letter.*) But as a madman's epistles are no gospels,
so it skills[6] not much when they are delivered.

OLIVIA: Open 't and read it.

CLOWN: Look then to be well edified when the fool de-
livers the madman. (*Reads in loud voice*) "By the Lord,
madam"—

OLIVIA: How now! art thou mad?

CLOWN: No, madam, I do but read madness. An your ladyship will have it as it ought to be, you must allow Vox.[7]

---

[1] Course of events.
[2] Nature obeyed her course by making
Olivia fall in love with Sebastian's image.
[3] Magical mirror producing this illusion.

[4] Sun.
[5] Arm's length.
[6] Matters.
[7] Loud voice.

OLIVIA: Prithee, read i' thy right wits.

CLOWN: So I do, madonna; but to read his right wits is to read thus: therefore perpend,[1] my princess, and give ear.

OLIVIA (*to* FABIAN): Read it you, sirrah.

FABIAN (*reads*): "By the Lord, madam, you wrong me and the world shall know it. Though you have put me into darkness and given your drunken cousin rule over me, yet have I the benefit of my senses as well as your ladyship. I have your own letter that induced me to the semblance I put on; with the which I doubt not but to do myself much right, or you much shame. Think of me as you please. I leave my duty a little unthought of, and speak out of my injury. The madly-used Malvolio."

OLIVIA: Did he write this?

CLOWN: Aye, madam.

DUKE: This savors not much of distraction.

OLIVIA: See him deliver'd, Fabian; bring him hither.

(*Exit* FABIAN.)

My lord, so please you, these things further thought on,
To think me as well a sister as a wife,
One day shall crown the alliance on 't, so please you,
Here at my house and at my proper[2] cost.

DUKE: Madam, I am most apt to embrace your offer.
(*To* VIOLA) Your master quits[3] you; and for your service
          done him,
So much against the mettle[4] of your sex,
So far beneath your soft and tender breeding,
And since you call'd me master for so long,
Here is my hand: you shall from this time be
Your master's mistress.

OLIVIA: A sister! you are she.

(*Re-enter* FABIAN, *with* MALVOLIO.)

DUKE: Is this the madman?

OLIVIA: Aye, my lord, this same.
How now, Malvolio!

MALVOLIO: Madam, you have done me wrong,
Notorious wrong.

OLIVIA: Have I, Malvolio? No.

MALVOLIO: Lady, you have. Pray you, peruse that letter.
You must not now deny it is your hand.
Write from it,[5] if you can, in hand or phrase.

---

1 Attend.   4 Temperament.
2 Own.   5 Differently from it.
8 Releases.

Or say 'tis not your seal, not your invention.
You can say none of this. Well, grant it then
And tell me, in the modesty of honor,
Why you have given me such clear lights of favor,
Bade me come smiling and cross-garter'd to you,
To put on yellow stockings and to frown
Upon Sir Toby and the lighter[1] people;
And, acting this in an obedient hope,
Why have you suffer'd me to be imprison'd,
Kept in a dark house, visited by the priest,
And made the most notorious geck[2] and gull
That e'er invention play'd on? Tell me why.

   OLIVIA: Alas, Malvolio, this is not my writing,
Though, I confess, much like the character:
But out of question 'tis Maria's hand.
And now I do bethink me, it was she
First told me thou wast mad. Thou camest in smiling,
And in such forms which here were presupposed[3]
Upon thee in the letter. Prithee, be content.
This practice[4] hath most shrewdly pass'd upon thee;
But when we know the grounds and authors of it,
Thou shalt be both the plaintiff and the judge
Of thine own cause.

   FABIAN: Good madam, hear me speak,
And let no quarrel nor no brawl to come
Taint the condition of this present hour,
Which I have wonder'd at. In hope it shall not,
Most freely I confess, myself and Toby
Set this device against Malvolio here,
Upon some stubborn and uncourteous parts
We had conceived against him. Maria writ
The letter at Sir Toby's great importance,[5]
In recompense whereof he hath married her.
How with a sportful malice it was follow'd
May rather pluck on[6] laughter than revenge;
If that the injuries be justly weigh'd
That have on both sides pass'd.

   OLIVIA: Alas, poor fool, how have they baffled thee!

   CLOWN: Why, "some are born great, some achieve greatness, and some have greatness thrown upon them." I was one, sir, in this interlude; one Sir Topas, sir; but that's all one. "By the Lord, fool, I am not mad." But do you remember? "Madam, why laugh you at such a barren rascal? an you smile not, he's gagged:" and thus the whirligig of time brings in his revenges.

---

1 Inferior.
2 Dupe.
3 Suggested.
4 Trick.
5 Importunity.
6 Excite.

MALVOLIO: I'll be revenged on the whole pack of you.
(*Exit.*)

OLIVIA: He hath been most notoriously abused.

DUKE: Pursue him, and entreat him to a peace:
He hath not told us of the captain yet.
When that is known, and golden time convents,[1]
A solemn combination shall be made
Of our dear souls. Meantime, sweet sister,
We will not part from hence. Cesario, come;
For so you shall be, while you are a man;
But when in other habits you are seen,
Orsino's mistress and his fancy's queen.

(*Exeunt all, except* CLOWN.)

CLOWN (*sings*):
　When that I was and a little tiny boy,
　　With hey, ho, the wind and the rain,
　A foolish thing was but a toy,
　　For the rain it raineth every day.

　But when I came to man's estate,
　　With hey, ho, the wind and the rain,
　'Gainst knaves and thieves men shut their gate,
　　For the rain it raineth every day.

　But when I came, alas! to wive,
　　With hey, ho, the wind and the rain,
　By swaggering could I never thrive,
　　For the rain it raineth every day.

　But when I came unto my beds,
　　With hey, ho, hte wind and the rain,
　With toss-pots still had drunken heads,
　　For the rain it raineth every day.

　A great while ago the world begun,
　　With hey, ho, the wind and the rain,
　But that's all one, our play is done,
　　And we'll strive to please you every day.

(*Exit.*)

---

1 Is convenient.

Molière:

THE MISER

Among Molière's best-known plays are *The Misanthrope, The Would-Be Gentleman,* and *The Miser* (1668). The titles serve to warn us that the plays present highly generalized characters—almost stock types—rather than characters who are as complex as life itself. A long tradition lies behind such drama. According to Aristotle, the aim of drama is to imitate or to represent on the stage the doings of men. The artist, Aristotle says, shows us life, but, unlike the historian, he does not do this simply by telling what happened. The historian merely narrates what has occurred, but the artist depicts what ought to occur, for he dramatizes (to take the specific instance of the playwright) a unified, probable story with consistent characters. Thus, when Aristotle says that art depicts what "ought" to occur, he is speaking not of morality but of probability. The dramatic characters, that is, must act consistently; or if they suddenly alter their personalities, we must feel that in real life they would probably have altered themselves in just this manner. A question naturally arises, however: If drama depicts the "universal" or generalized and probable figure (the very idea of miserliness) rather than a unique detailed figure capable of surprising us by unexpected actions, how can it hold our interest?

The seventeenth and eighteenth centuries in France had no difficulty in enjoying generalized characters, but since the early nineteenth century, with its emphasis on abundant detail, writing has increasingly approached reportage, and today we are apt to assume that the best writing is that which sounds most like the talk we hear in the street. This modern premise is, of course, false, just as photographic art and wax fruit are not necessarily the best pieces of painting and sculpture. The artist who is concerned with catching the exact words he hears may as well simply play back his tape recorder. When Aristotle said that the comic dramatist depicts characters who act consistently, he was saying that art does not depict the odds and ends of the confusion around us, does not portray this particular person whom we half-know, but rather penetrates through the jumble to an essential truth or probability in human experience.

The pattern which comedy generally depicts is the steady flow of the life-force, a flow which may be momentarily interrupted or diverted but which finally triumphs over sterile forces and comes to fruition. As the introduction to this book suggests, comedy seems to be derived from fertility celebrations. Though it has left its ritual origin far behind, it nevertheless frequently retains the basic praise and joy of life's abundance. When we understand that comedy is a celebration of the fullness of life, we understand why it so often depicts lovers, or, to put it more directly, why it is frequently based on sex. Opposed to the stock lovers (who are almost always youthful, even as the spring is the youth of the year) there is generally someone who seeks to interrupt the happy flow of fertile nature: an old father, for example, may disapprove of his son's passion, and may, in fact, himself covet the young girl courted by the boy, and thus, as in *The Miser,* the wintry father grotesquely tries to couple December with May. But the sterile force in comedy is inevitably defeated, and the play ends with a reassertion of the indomitableness of those human emotions which favor (as, it is felt, nature herself favors), expansiveness, generosity, and generation.

About the time of Aristotle's death (322 B.C.), Greek comedy settled into the job of entertainingly depicting this pattern, and the Romans continued the tradition. Literary drama died after the fall of Rome, but wandering players probably kept alive debased playlets on this theme. The basic types or characters—lovers and would-be frustrators of love—in the comedies of Aristotle's last days, survived, or perhaps were reborn, when the theater was only four players at a crossroad in a medieval village. By the end of the sixteenth century these wandering players had gained in prestige and performed not only for villagers but for the nobility. In Italy the *commedia dell' arte*—the humble professional rather than literary and courtly drama—acquired such fame in its improvised playlets on a stock tale that it won the eye of the French court; the young lovers of the *commedia dell' arte,* continually triumphing over crabbed fathers and old pedants, were the players whom Molière (1622-1673) saw as a youth in Paris. The actors in the *commedia dell' arte* were experts who spent a lifetime developing one stock role, and their performances depended more heavily on bits of business (*lazzi*) than on speeches of literary value. They represented generalized types and sought to capture the essence of, say, the old man—not this or that old man, but the universal old man. Molière inherited the tradition of the *commedia dell' arte,* and, fortified with a knowledge of Plautus and Terence, he raised it to a level where it was not only great acting but great literature. His plays evoke laughter, but they also evoke an inner response which is more lasting. " 'Tis a good thing," John Dryden wrote, "to laugh at any rate; and if a straw can tickle a man, it is an instrument of happiness." But there are degrees of happiness, and a comedy need not be judged merely by the dial of a laughmeter. When the French dramatist Racine gibed that only Boileau, the critic, laughed at a performance of Molière's *Miser*, Boileau replied that he thought too highly of Racine to believe that he was not laughing inwardly.

Molière's plays deal with types—though with types which are not mere signboards but are fully as vigorous as anything created by the contemporary realistic stage. His miser is consistently avaricious, but no matter how deformed, he is always a human being. He is vivified by a few details—he has a cough, he is subject to flattery, he wishes to wed a pretty girl—but always he is the essence of avarice. His avarice almost destroys the happiness of his children, and it drives them to a variety of subterfuges. But love and life will not be frustrated, and the miser's avarice can finally destroy only his own peace of mind. "Spare all that I have and take my life," says a character in Farquhar's *Beaux' Stratagem*. This is the quintessence of miserliness, the sterile principle embodied in Molière's miser; this is the spirit that must always be defeated in its narrow-minded, selfish struggle against the fecundity of nature.

The Miser

TRANSLATED BY SYLVAN BARNET,
MORTON BERMAN AND WILLIAM BURTO

Characters

HARPAGON, *father of Cléante and Élise, infatuated with Mariane.*

CLÉANTE, *Harpagon's son, in love with Mariane.*

ÉLISE, *Harpagon's daughter, in love with Valère.*

VALÈRE, *Anselm's son, in love with Élise.*

MARIANE, *Anselm's daughter, courted by Harpagon but in love with Cléante.*

ANSELM, *father of Valère and Mariane.*

FROSINE, *a woman of intrigue.*

SIMON, *a broker.*

JACQUES, *Harpagon's cook and coachman.*

LA FLÈCHE, *Cléante's valet.*

DAME CLAUDE, *Harpagon's servant.*

BRINDAVOINE, *Harpagon's lackey.*

LA MERLUCHE, *Harpagon's lackey.*

An OFFICER *and his* CLERK.

The place: Paris. A room in Harpagon's house. In the rear, a door leads to a garden.

176

ACT I

(Enter VALÈRE *and* ÉLISE.)

VALÈRE: What is the matter, my dear Élise? Why so sad? And after the kind assurances you have given me of your faith? Alas! You sigh in the midst of my joy! Tell me, do you regret having made me happy? Do you repent the promise which my ardor has forced from you?

ÉLISE: No, Valère, I could not repent of anything that I have done for you. I feel enthralled by too pleasant a power, and I have not even the strength to wish that things were different. But, to tell you the truth, I am afraid of what may happen; and I am quite afraid of loving you a little more than I ought.

VALÈRE: Élise! what is there to fear in the affection you have for me?

ÉLISE: Alas! a hundred things: my father's anger, my family's reproaches, the world's censure; but most of all, Valère, a change in your heart and that criminal coldness with which those of your sex most often repay the too ardent professions of innocent love.

VALÈRE: Ah! do not wrong me by judging me according to others. Suspect me of anything, Élise, rather than of failing in my duty to you. I love you too much for that, and my love for you will last as long as I live.

ÉLISE: Ah! Valère, everyone makes the same speeches. All men are alike in their promises; it is only their actions which reveal their differences.

VALÈRE: Since actions alone show what we are, at least wait and judge my heart by mine. Do not search out faults in me that exist only in the unjust fears of a foolish foreboding. Do not kill me, I beg of you, with the sharp blows of outrageous suspicion. Give me time and I will convince you, by a thousand and one proofs, that my affections are sincere.

ÉLISE: Alas! how easily we are persuaded by those we love! Yes, Valère, I think your heart is incapable of deceiving me. I believe you really love me and will be faithful. I have not the slightest wish to doubt you; I confine my fears to dreading that others will blame me.

VALÈRE: But why this uneasiness?

ÉLISE: I should have nothing to fear if everyone saw you

177

as I do, for I see in you enough to justify all I have done. My heart, for its defense, pleads your worth, and even Heaven has bound me to you with gratitude. Every hour I picture to myself the terrible disaster which brought us together; the wonderful generosity that made you risk your life to save mine from the fury of the waves; the tender care you took of me after rescuing me from the water; the unceasing attention of your ardent love which neither time nor difficulties have discouraged and which causes you to neglect both parents and country to remain in this place, your true rank disguised for my sake, reduced to wearing the livery of a servant in my father's house—in order to see me. All this has made a wonderful impression on me and is enough to justify to me the pledge I have consented to. But it is perhaps not enough to justify it to others, and I am not certain they share my feelings.

VALÈRE: Of all you have said of me, it is my love alone which gives me the right to merit anything from you. As for your scruples, your father himself has been only too careful to justify you before the world. His excessive avarice and the austere manner in which he lives with his children might authorize far stranger things. Forgive me, dear Élise, for talking this way in front of you, but you surely know that in this respect nothing good can be said of him. But if, as I hope, I can find my parents, we shall not have much difficulty winning him over. I impatiently await news of them, and if it is late in coming, I shall search it out myself.

ÉLISE: Oh! Valère, do not leave, I beg you. Think only of winning my father's confidence.

VALÈRE: You see how I go about it; the clever schemes I have had to put into practice in order to ingratiate myself into his service; what a mask of sympathy and of agreement I assume in order to please him; and what a role I daily play before him to gain his affection. I am making admirable progress. And I find that, in order to win men over, there is no better way than to seem to be of their inclinations, than to fall in with their maxims, flatter their faults, and applaud everything they do. There is no fear of overdoing flattery; the manner of fooling may be the most open—the shrewdest are always made the greatest dupes by flattery. There is nothing so impertinent or so ridiculous that they cannot be made to swallow, provided it is seasoned with praise. Sincerity suffers a little in this business. But when one has need of men, it is necessary to adjust oneself to them. Since there is no other way to win them over except by this means, it is not the fault of those who flatter, but of those who wish to be flattered.

ÉLISE: But why not also try to gain my brother's help, in case my maid decides to reveal our secret?

VALÈRE: I cannot manage both of them at once. The temperaments of father and son are so opposed that it would be hard to retain the confidence of both at the same time. But you could approach your brother and avail yourself of his friendship to get him to act in our interest. Here he comes now. I'll withdraw. Take this opportunity to speak with him. Don't reveal any more of our situation to him than you think proper. (*Exit* VALÈRE.)

ÉLISE: I do not know if I shall have the courage to confide in him.

(*Enter* CLÉANTE.)

CLÉANTE: I am delighted to find you alone, Élise. I have been anxious to speak to you, to reveal a secret.

ÉLISE: Here I am, ready to listen, Cléante. What have you to tell me?

CLÉANTE: Many things, Élise, but in a word: I'm in love.

ÉLISE: You're in love?

CLÉANTE: Yes, I am in love. But, before going any further, I know that I am dependent on father, and that as his son I am subject to his wishes; that we ought never to make vows without the consent of those who gave us life; that Heaven has made them masters of our affections; and that we are charged not to bestow them except by their counsel; that unaffected by foolish passion themselves, they are far less likely to be deceived than we and can see much better what is right for us. We should rather trust the light of their prudence than the blindness of our passion, for the eagerness of youth leads us most often toward troublesome precipices. I tell you all this, Élise, so you won't take the trouble of telling it to me. For, in a word, my passion will listen to nothing, and I beg you to forgo any remonstrances.

ÉLISE: Are you engaged to her whom you love?

CLÉANTE: No, but I am resolved to be. And I ask you again not to attempt to dissuade me.

ÉLISE: Am I so strange a person, Cléante?

CLÉANTE: No, dear sister, but you are not in love. You do not understand the sweet violence which tender love does to our hearts, and I fear your prudence.

ÉLISE: Alas! let us not speak of my prudence, Cléante. There is no one who does not lack it at least once in his life; and if I opened my heart to you, perhaps I should appear in your eyes much less prudent than you.

CLÉANTE: Ah! May Heaven grant that your heart, like mine—

ÉLISE: Let us first finish your difficulties. Tell me whom you love.

CLÉANTE: A young girl who has been living nearby for a short time, and who seems created to inspire love in all who see her. Nature has fashioned nothing more lovable. I felt enthralled from the moment I saw her. Her name is Mariane and she lives under the protection of her mother, a good woman who is nearly always ill, and for whom this dear girl shows the greatest kindness imaginable. She waits upon her, sympathizes with her, and consoles her with a tenderness that would touch your soul. She has the most charming way in the world in whatever she does, and her every action shines with a thousand graces. Such attractive gentleness, such engaging goodness, such adorable modesty, such— Ah! Élise, if you could only see her.

ÉLISE: I see a great deal of her, Cléante, in what you tell me. And to understand what she is, it is enough for me that you love her.

CLÉANTE: I have found out, secretly, that they are not very well off, and that, even though they live frugally, they have a difficult time making ends meet. Imagine, Élise, what joy it would be to be able to raise the fortune of the person one loves, discreetly to give some slight help to the modest needs of a virtuous family. Just think how miserable it makes me to find myself powerless, because of my father's avarice, to taste that pleasure, or to show the dear girl any evidence of my love.

ÉLISE: Yes, Cléante, I can see how grieved you must be.

CLÉANTE: Ah! Élise, far more than you can imagine. Have you ever seen anything more cruel than this rigorous economy exercised over us, than this unheard-of stinginess we are made to languish under? What good will wealth do us, if it comes only when we are no longer young enough to enjoy it; if even to maintain myself, I am forced on every side to run into debt; if you and I are reduced to obtaining daily help from tradesmen to keep decent clothes on our backs? So, I have wanted to talk with you, to ask you to help me sound father out about my present feelings. If he disapproves, I am resolved to go away with this dear girl, and enjoy whatever fortune Heaven may offer us. I am trying now to obtain money everywhere for this purpose; and if your difficulties resemble mine, Élise, if father insists on opposing our desires, we shall both leave him and free ourselves from the tyranny his unbearable avarice has so long imposed on us.

ÉLISE: It is certainly true that every day he gives us more and more reason to regret mother's death, and that—

CLÉANTE: I hear his voice. Let us go somewhere else to

finish our discussion. Later we will join forces and attack his hard heart. (*Exeunt* CLÉANTE *and* ÉLISE.)

(*Enter* HARPAGON *and* LA FLÈCHE.)

HARPAGON: Get out of here immediately, and don't talk back! Go on, get out of my house! You master-crook! You gallows-bird!

LA FLÈCHE (*aside*): I have never seen anyone so wicked as this accursed old scoundrel, and I believe, without a doubt, he is possessed of the devil.

HARPAGON: What are you muttering?

LA FLÈCHE: Why are you chasing me out of the house?

HARPAGON: It's just like you, you rogue, to ask for reasons. Be off before I beat you.

LA FLÈCHE: What have I done to you?

HARPAGON: Enough to make me want you to leave.

LA FLÈCHE: My master, your son, gave me orders to wait for him.

HARPAGON: Wait for him out in the street, not here in my house, planted as stiff as a post to watch what goes on and profit from everything. I won't have someone constantly near me, spying on my affairs, a traitor whose accursed eyes peer into everything I do, coveting everything I own, and ferreting in every corner to see if there is anything he can rob.

LA FLÈCHE: How the deuce could you be robbed of anything? Can a man be robbed who locks up everything and stands guard day and night?

HARPAGON: I will lock up everything I think fit, and stand guard as I please. (*To audience*) Doesn't he sound like a spy watching everything you do? I'm afraid that he suspects where my money is. (*To* LA FLÈCHE) Aren't you the kind of man who would go about spreading rumors that I have money hidden in my house?

LA FLÈCHE: You *have* money hidden in the house?

HARPAGON: No, you villain, I didn't say that! (*Aside*) I shall go mad. (*To* LA FLÈCHE) I am asking whether you wouldn't go around maliciously spreading tales that I do have some hidden?

LA FLÈCHE: Ah! what difference does it make to us whether you have any or not? It's all the same.

HARPAGON: Argue, will you! I'll knock your arguments about your ears. (*He raises his hand to give* LA FLÈCHE *a box on the ear.*) Once more—get out of here!

LA FLÈCHE: All right, I'm going.

HARPAGON: Wait! Are you taking anything of mine?

LA FLÈCHE: What could I take of yours?

HARPAGON: Come here. I'll see. Show me your hands.

LA FLÈCHE: There they are.

HARPAGON: The others.[1]

LA FLÈCHE: The others?

HARPAGON: Yes.

LA FLÈCHE: There they are.

HARPAGON: Have you put anything down there? (*He points to* LA FLÈCHE'S *breeches.*)

LA FLÈCHE: Look for yourself.

HARPAGON (*kneeling, feels the bottoms of* LA FLÈCHE'S *breeches*): These baggy breeches are just right for hiding stolen goods, and I wish people could be hanged for wearing them.

LA FLÈCHE (*aside*): Ah! doesn't such a man as this deserve everything he fears! What joy I'd have in robbing him!

HARPAGON (*hearing "robbing," jumps up*): Eh?

LA FLÈCHE: What?

HARPAGON: What did you say about robbing?

LA FLÈCHE: I said that you poke about everywhere to see if I'm robbing you.

HARPAGON: That's just what I intend to do. (*He feels in* LA FLÈCHE'S *pockets.*)

LA FLÈCHE (*aside*): A plague on avarice and the avaricious.

HARPAGON: What's that? What did you say?

LA FLÈCHE: What did I say?

HARPAGON: Yes! What did you say about avarice and the avaricious?

LA FLÈCHE: I said, a plague on avarice and the avaricious.

HARPAGON: Whom are you talking about?

LA FLÈCHE: About avaricious men.

HARPAGON: And who are these avaricious men?

LA FLÈCHE: They are scoundrels and skinflints.

HARPAGON: But whom do you mean by that?

LA FLÈCHE: What are *you* so upset about?

HARPAGON: I'm upset about what I should be upset about.

LA FLÈCHE: Do you think I'm talking about you?

HARPAGON: I think what I think. But tell me whom you were speaking to when you said that.

LA FLÈCHE: I was speaking to . . . to my cap.

HARPAGON: And I may knock your cap right off your head.

LA FLÈCHE: Would you stop me from cursing avaricious men?

HARPAGON: No, but I'll stop you from chattering and being insolent. Keep quiet!

---

[1] Doubtless there was some stage business here, perhaps obscene, but it is lost.

LA FLÈCHE: I didn't mention anyone's name.

HARPAGON: If you talk any more, I'll give you a thrashing.

LA FLÈCHE: If the cap fits, wear it.

HARPAGON: Will you hold your tongue?

LA FLÈCHE: Yes, in spite of myself.

HARPAGON: Ah! Ah! (HARPAGON *raises his cane to strike* LA FLÈCHE, *who wards off the blow by pointing to one of the pockets of his coat.*)

LA FLÈCHE: Look, here's another pocket. Are you satisfied?

HARPAGON: Come, give it back to me without all this searching.

LA FLÈCHE: What?

HARPAGON: What you've taken from me.

LA FLÈCHE: I've taken nothing at all from you.

HARPAGON: Positively?

LA FLÈCHE: Positively.

HARPAGON: Goodbye, and go to the devil.

LA FLÈCHE (*aside*): That's a fine send-off.

HARPAGON: Your conscience knows the truth, at least. (*Exit* LA FLÈCHE.) That scoundrel of a valet really upsets me. I don't like to see that lame cur around at all. It's certainly no small worry guarding a large sum of money in the house. Happy is the man who has all his money well invested and keeps only what is necessary for his current expenses. It's hard to find a safe hiding place anywhere in the house. To my way of thinking, strong-boxes are suspect; I could never trust them. I see them as nothing but an open invitation to thieves; they are always the first thing pounced on. Still, I don't know whether it was wise to bury in the garden the ten thousand écus I was paid yesterday. Ten thousand gold écus is a pretty large sum to have in one's house. . . . (CLÉANTE *and* ÉLISE, *speaking in low voices, appear at the door to the garden but hesitate before entering.*) Oh! Heavens! I have given myself away! My anxiety has undone me! I think I spoke aloud while thinking to myself. (*To* CLÉANTE *and* ÉLISE.) What do you want?

CLÉANTE: Nothing, father.

HARPAGON: Have you been there long?

ÉLISE: We have just arrived.

HARPAGON: You heard—

CLÉANTE: What, father?

HARPAGON: There—

ÉLISE: What?

HARPAGON: What I just said.

CLÉANTE: No.

HARPAGON: Yes, you did, you did.

ÉLISE: I beg your pardon, but we didn't, father.

HARPAGON: I can see quite well that you heard something. The fact is I was talking to myself about how hard it is these days to find money, and I was saying how happy a man must be who has ten thousand écus about the house.

CLÉANTE: We hesitated to come near for fear of interrupting you.

HARPAGON: I'm anxious to tell you what I said so that you won't get things mixed up and imagine I said it is *I* who have ten thousand écus.

CLÉANTE: We don't mix into your affairs.

HARPAGON: Would to Heaven I had that much money . . . ten thousand écus!

CLÉANTE: I do not believe—

HARPAGON: It would be a fortunate thing for me.

ÉLISE: These are things—

HARPAGON: I could use it.

CLÉANTE: I think that—

HARPAGON: It would suit me exactly.

ÉLISE: You are—

HARPAGON: Then I wouldn't complain, as I do now, that times are hard.

CLÉANTE: My God, father, you have no cause to complain. Everyone knows you are well off.

HARPAGON: What? I, well off? Whoever says that is a liar. Nothing is further from the truth. And those who spread such reports around are villains.

ÉLISE: Don't get angry.

HARPAGON: It's strange that my own children should betray me and become my enemies!

CLÉANTE: Am I your enemy because I say you are well off?

HARPAGON: Yes! Such talk, and the expenses you run up, will, one of these days, cause somebody to come here and cut my throat, in hope that they will find me stuffed with gold.

CLÉANTE: What great expenses have I run up?

HARPAGON: What? Can anything be more scandalous than the sumptuous apparel you parade around the city in? Yesterday I criticized your sister, but this is even worse. This cries aloud to Heaven for vengeance. From head to toe there is enough on your body to buy a good annuity. Son, I have told you twenty times that your ways greatly displease me. You outrageously give yourself the airs of a marquis, and to be able to go about dressed as you are, you must certainly be robbing me.

CLÉANTE: What! How can I be robbing you?

HARPAGON: How do I know? Where, then, do you get the means to keep up your fashionable dress?

CLÉANTE: I, father? I gamble, and, since I am very lucky, I put all the money I win on my back.

HARPAGON: That's badly done. If you are lucky at cards, you ought to profit by it and invest at good interest the money that you win, so that you'll have it on a rainy day. Without troubling about anything else, I'd really like to know what good are all those ribbons you are bedecked with from head to foot, and if a half-dozen laces are not enough to hold up your breeches. Is it really necessary to spend money on wigs when you can wear the hair of your own head, which costs nothing? I'll wager that your wigs and ribbons alone are worth at least twenty pistoles; and twenty pistoles bring in eighteen livres, six sous, and eight deniers a year, even at only eight per cent interest.

CLÉANTE: You are right.

HARPAGON: Enough of this. Let's talk of something else. Eh? (HARPAGON, *seeing* CLÉANTE *and* ÉLISE *signalling to each other "You speak," "No, you speak," mutters in a low voice*) I think they are signalling each other to steal my purse. (*Aloud*) What do those signs mean?

ÉLISE: Cléante and I are debating who shall speak first. Both of us have something to say to you.

HARPAGON: And I, too, have something to say to both of you.

CLÉANTE: It is about marriage, father, that we wish to speak to you.

HARPAGON: And it is also about marriage that I wish to speak to you.

ÉLISE: Ah! father!

HARPAGON: Why this cry? Are you afraid, my daughter, of the word or the thing?

CLÉANTE: Marriage, at least in the way you understand it, frightens both of us. We are afraid that our feelings may not agree with your choice.

HARPAGON: A little patience. Do not alarm yourselves. I know what is best for both of you; and neither of you will have cause to complain of anything that I intend to do. To begin at the beginning: tell me, have you ever seen a young person named Mariane, who lives not far from here?

CLÉANTE: Yes, father.

HARPAGON: And you?

ÉLISE: I have heard of her.

HARPAGON: Well, my son, what do you think of this girl?

CLÉANTE: A most charming person.

HARPAGON: Her looks?

CLÉANTE: Very honest and full of intelligence.

HARPAGON: Her air and manner?

CLÉANTE: Admirable, without a doubt.

HARPAGON: Don't you think that a girl like that is quite worthy of serious consideration?

CLÉANTE: Yes, father.

HARPAGON: That she would make a desirable match?

CLÉANTE: Very desirable.

HARPAGON: That she has all the appearances of making a good housewife?

CLÉANTE: Without a doubt.

HARPAGON: And that a husband would be satisfied with her?

CLÉANTE: Surely.

HARPAGON: But there is one little difficulty; I am afraid that she does not have as much money as one might expect.

CLÉANTE: Ah! father, money should not be a consideration when it is a question of marrying a respectable person.

HARPAGON: Pardon me, pardon me! But there is this to be said: if one does not find all the wealth one wishes, one can try to make up for it in some other way.

CLÉANTE: Quite so.

HARPAGON: Ah, I am so happy to find you agree with me, because her modest bearing and her gentleness have won my heart, and I am resolved to marry her, provided she has some means.

CLÉANTE: What?

HARPAGON: What?

CLÉANTE: You say you have resolved—

HARPAGON: To marry Mariane.

CLÉANTE: Who, you, you?

HARPAGON: Yes, I, I, I. What do you mean by that?

CLÉANTE: I suddenly feel dizzy. I must go. (*Exit* CLÉANTE.)

HARPAGON: Oh, that's nothing. Go into the kitchen immediately and drink a large glass of plain water. (*To* ÉLISE) These are your effeminate dandies, who have no more strength than a chicken. That's what I have resolved to do, my daughter. As for your brother, I intend for him a certain widow that someone mentioned to me this morning. And for you, I am giving you to Signor Anselm.

ÉLISE: To Signor Anselm?

HARPAGON: Yes! A mature, prudent, wise man, who is not more than fifty, and who is said to have great wealth.

ÉLISE: (*She makes a curtsy.*) If you please, father, I do not want to marry.

HARPAGON: (*He imitates her curtsy.*) If *you* please, my little girl, my pet, I want you to marry.

ÉLISE: (*She makes another curtsy.*) I beg your pardon, father.

HARPAGON: (*He again imitates her curtsy.*) I beg *your* pardon, daughter.

ÉLISE: I am Signor Anselm's most humble servant, but (*making another curtsy*), with your permission, I will not marry him.

HARPAGON: I am *your* most humble servant, but (*imitating her curtsy*), with your permission, you *shall* marry him, and this very evening.

ÉLISE: This very evening?

HARPAGON: This very evening.

ÉLISE: That shall not be, father. (*She curtsies.*)

HARPAGON: That *shall* be, daughter. (*He curtsies.*)

ÉLISE: No!

HARPAGON: Yes!

ÉLISE: No, I tell you.

HARPAGON: Yes, I tell you.

ÉLISE: This is something you cannot force me to do.

HARPAGON: This is something I can force you to do.

ÉLISE: I would rather kill myself than marry such a husband.

HARPAGON: You will not kill yourself, and you will marry him. What impudence! Have you ever heard a daughter talk to her father like that?

ÉLISE: But have you ever heard of a father marrying off his daughter like that?

HARPAGON: Nothing can be said against such a match, and I'll wager that everyone will approve my choice.

ÉLISE: And I'll wager that it will not be approved by any reasonable person.

HARPAGON (*seeing* VALÈRE *approach*): Here is Valère. Are you willing to let him judge between us in this matter?

ÉLISE: I consent.

HARPAGON: Will you submit to his judgment?

ÉLISE: Yes, I will abide by his decision.

HARPAGON: Then it is agreed. (VALÈRE *enters.*) Here, Valère. We have elected you to decide who is in the right, my daughter or I.

VALÈRE: You, sir, without a doubt.

HARPAGON: You know, then, what we have been talking about?

VALÈRE: No, but you couldn't be wrong; you are reason itself.

HARPAGON: Tonight I wish to give her a husband as rich as he is wise, and the hussy tells me to my face that she scorns to take him. What do you say to that?

VALÈRE: What do I say to that?

HARPAGON: Yes.

VALÈRE: Ahem!

HARPAGON: What?

VALÈRE: I say that fundamentally I am of your opinion; and you cannot but be right. But I cannot say she is entirely wrong, and—

HARPAGON: What? Signor Anselm is a desirable match. He is a gentleman, noble, refined, poised, wise, and well off; furthermore, he has no children left from his first marriage. Could she meet anyone more desirable?

VALÈRE: That's true. But she might tell you that you were rushing matters a bit and that she ought at least to be allowed a little time to see if she could accommodate her feelings to—

HARPAGON: This is an opportunity which must be grasped by the forelock. I find in this match an advantage which I would not find elsewhere, for he promises to take her without a dowry.

VALÈRE: Without a dowry?

HARPAGON: Yes.

VALÈRE: Ah! Then I will say no more. Don't you see? Here is the absolutely conclusive reason; one must submit to it.

HARPAGON: For me it means a considerable saving.

VALÈRE: Certainly. There's no denying that. It's true that your daughter might suggest to you that marriage is a far more serious matter than most people believe; that it means being happy or unhappy all her life; and that a union which ought to last until death ought never to be made without the greatest precautions.

HARPAGON: But—without a dowry!

VALÈRE: You are right. That settles everything, of course. There are some people who might say to you that in such matters the feelings of the daughter ought, unquestionably, to be considered, and that this great difference in age, disposition, and sentiment might subject the marriage to most unfortunate accidents.

HARPAGON: Without a dowry!

VALÈRE: Ah! Everyone knows there's no reply to that. Who the deuce would argue the contrary? It isn't that there are not some fathers who would prefer to think more of their daughters' happiness than of the money they might have to give them; who would never sacrifice them for interest, and who would seek, above everything else, to secure for them in a marriage that gentle harmony which unfailingly produces honor, tranquillity, and joy, and which—

HARPAGON: But—without a dowry!

VALÈRE: True. That shuts every mouth: without a dowry. How can one resist an argument like that?

HARPAGON (looking toward the garden): What was that?

I thought I heard a dog barking. (*Aside*) Is someone trying to find my money? (*To* VALÈRE *and* ÉLISE) Don't budge from here; I'll be right back. (*Exit.*)

ÉLISE: Are you joking, Valère, talking to him as you have done?

VALÈRE: I don't want to anger him, for then I shall better achieve my purpose. To oppose his wishes to his face is a sure way to spoil everything. There are certain natures which can be overcome only by indirect means; temperaments which are enemies of all resistance; restive minds, who rear at truth, who always stiffen against the straight path of reason. Only by leading them in an indirect way can you guide them where you want them to go. Pretend to consent to his wishes; you will better gain your ends, and—

ÉLISE: But this marriage, Valère.

VALÈRE: We will find some expedient to break it off.

ÉLISE: But what pretense can we find, if it is to be concluded tonight?

VALÈRE: You must ask for a delay. Feign some sickness.

ÉLISE: But they will discover the feint, if they call in doctors.

VALÈRE: Are you joking? What do doctors know? Come, come, as for them, you can have whatever sickness you please; they will find you reasons for having it and tell you where it came from.

(*Enter* HARPAGON, *unseen.*)

HARPAGON (*aside*): It was nothing, thank God.

VALÈRE: Our last resort could be flight, which will shelter us from everything. And if your love, fair Élise, is capable of such strength— (*He sees* HARPAGON.) Yes, a girl ought to obey her father. She ought not to concern herself with what her husband is like. And when the powerful argument "without a dowry" is presented to her, she ought to be ready to accept all that is given her.

HARPAGON: Good! That was well spoken.

VALÈRE: Sir, I beg your pardon if I have been too forward in taking the liberty of speaking to her as I have.

HARPAGON: Why, I am delighted. I want you to assume absolute control over her. (*To* ÉLISE, *who has moved to the back of the stage*) Yes, try running away. I give him the authority over you that God gave me, and I expect you to do everything he tells you.

VALÈRE: After that, just try to resist my remonstrances! Sir, I will follow her and continue the lessons I was giving her.

HARPAGON: Yes, you will oblige me greatly. By all means—
VALÈRE: It's a good idea to hold her in with a tight rein.
HARPAGON: That's right. You must—
VALÈRE: Do not trouble yourself. I know I shall get things right.
HARPAGON: Do, go on. I'm going for a stroll through the town, and I'll be back soon.
VALÈRE: Yes, money is more precious than anything else in the world, and you ought to thank God for the honest father He has given you. He knows what life is; when someone offers to take a daughter without a dowry, there's no need to look further. Everything is contained in that; "without a dowry" takes the place of beauty, youth, birth, honor, wisdom, and integrity. (*Exeunt* VALÈRE *and* ÉLISE.)
HARPAGON: Ah! Such a fine fellow. Spoken like an oracle. Happy the man who can have such a servant.

ACT II

(*On stage*: CLÉANTE. *Enter* LA FLÈCHE.)

CLÉANTE: Ah! you rogue! Where have you been hiding? Didn't I order you to—
LA FLÈCHE: Yes, sir! And I came here with every intention of waiting for you, but your father, the crudest man in the world, chased me out of the house, in spite of myself, and I ran the risk of a beating.
CLÉANTE: How is our affair going? Things are more pressing than ever. Since I last saw you, I have discovered that my father is my rival.
LA FLÈCHE: Your father is in love?
CLÉANTE: Yes, and I had all the trouble in the world hiding from him how much this news pained me.
LA FLÈCHE: Mixing himself up with love! What the devil is he thinking of? Is he making a mockery of the world? Was love made for people built like him?
CLÉANTE: This passion had to take hold of him as a result of my sins.
LA FLÈCHE: But why do you keep your love a secret from him?
CLÉANTE: To make him less suspicious, and to keep the way open more easily so that I can, if necessary, prevent his marriage.—What answer did they give you?
LA FLÈCHE: Good Lord, sir, those who borrow are most unhappy. A man has to put up with strange things when, like

you, he has to pass through the hands of the money-lenders.

CLÉANTE: The matter cannot be managed?

LA FLÈCHE: Not quite. Our Master Simon, the broker, who was recommended to us as an active, zealous man, says he has worked furiously for you; and he swears that your appearance alone has won his heart.

CLÉANTE: Will I get the fifteen thousand francs I asked for?

LA FLÈCHE: Yes, but with several little conditions attached, which you must accept, if you want things to go well.

CLÉANTE: Did he let you speak to the man who is to lend the money?

LA FLÈCHE: Ah! It's not quite that simple. He takes even more care than you to remain unknown, for such dealings are much more mysterious than you realize. They would not even mention his name, and they are going to bring you face to face today in a house rented for the occasion, to learn, from your own lips, what your means are and who your family is. I have not the slightest doubt that the mere name of your father will make things easy.

CLÉANTE: Especially as my mother is dead, and I cannot be deprived of her property.

LA FLÈCHE: Here are some of the conditions he himself dictated to our go-between, to be shown you before anything can be done. "Provided that the lender find all the securities satisfactory, and that the borrower be of age, and of a family whose estate is ample, solid, assured, clear, and free from all encumbrances, a valid and exact contract shall be drawn up in the presence of a notary, the most honest man available, who, on this account, shall be chosen by the lender, to whom it is of the utmost importance that the contract shall be properly executed."

CLÉANTE: There's nothing to say against that.

LA FLÈCHE: "In order not to burden his conscience with any scruple, the lender proposes to charge no more than five and a half per cent interest."

CLÉANTE: No more than five and a half per cent? Well, that's honest enough. There is no reason to complain about that.

LA FLÈCHE: That's true. "But, as the said lender does not have on hand the sum in question, and in order to please the borrower, he himself is compelled to borrow it from someone else at the rate of twenty per cent, it shall be agreed that the said first borrower shall pay this interest, without prejudice to the other, since it is only to oblige him that the said lender himself borrows the money."

CLÉANTE: What the devil! What Jew, what Arab is this? That's more than twenty-five per cent.

LA FLÈCHE: Quite true. That's what I said. You had better look into it.

CLÉANTE: What can I do? Since I need the money, I have to consent to everything.

LA FLÈCHE: That's what I said.

CLÉANTE: Is there anything else?

LA FLÈCHE: Only one small condition. "Of the fifteen thousand francs asked, the lender can only pay out twelve thousand, and in place of the remaining one thousand écus, the borrower must take furniture, clothing, and jewels, according to the following memorandum, the said lender attaching to them, in good faith, the lowest price possible."

CLÉANTE: What does that mean?

LA FLÈCHE: Listen to the memorandum. "First, one four-poster bed, with strips of Hungarian lace elegantly embroidered on olive-colored cloth, with six chairs and a counterpane to match; all in good condition and lined with iridescent red and blue silk. In addition, one canopy, of good, pale rose-colored Aumale serge, with silken tassels and fringes."

CLÉANTE: What does he expect me to do with that?

LA FLÈCHE: Wait. "In addition, a set of tapestries showing the loves of Gombaut and Macaea. In addition, one large walnut table, with twelve columns or turned legs, which pulls out at either end, complete with six stools underneath."

CLÉANTE: Good Heavens, what good is that to me!

LA FLÈCHE: Be patient. "In addition, three large muskets inlaid with mother-of-pearl, with three assorted rests. In addition, one brick furnace with two retorts and three receivers, very useful for those interested in distilling."

CLÉANTE: This is infuriating.

LA FLÈCHE: Easy now. "In addition, a lute from Bologna with all its strings, or very nearly all. In addition, one gaming table, one checker board, with a game of goose, revived from the Greeks, quite fit for passing the time when one has nothing to do. In addition, one lizard skin, three and a half feet long, stuffed with straw, a pleasant curiosity to hang from the ceiling of a room. The total mentioned above, easily worth more than four thousand five hundred francs, is reduced to the value of one thousand écus at the discretion of the lender."

CLÉANTE: May the plague choke the scoundrel and his discretion! Cut-throat that he is! Have you ever heard of such usury? Isn't he content with the outrageous interest he exacts, without wanting to make me take, for three thousand francs, all the old junk he's collected? I won't get two hundred écus for the lot. Nevertheless, I must give in, for he is in a position to make me accept anything, and so the villain has me, with a knife at my throat.

LA FLÈCHE: Sir, if I may say so, I see you on the same broad road that Panurge travelled to his ruin, taking money in advance, buying dear, selling cheap, and eating your wheat while it's still in the blade.

CLÉANTE: What would you have me do? This is what young men are reduced to by the cursed avarice of their fathers. And yet people are astonished when sons wish that their fathers would die.

LA FLÈCHE: I must confess that yours would arouse the most placid man in the world against his stinginess. I have, thank God, no strong desire for the gallows, and among my colleagues, whom I see mixed up in many petty schemes, I am clever enough to keep out of scrapes, and to drop out prudently from any gallantries that smell even slightly of the gallows. But, to tell you the truth, your father's actions would tempt *me* to rob him; and I believe that if I did I would be performing a good deed.

CLÉANTE: Give me the memorandum a moment; I want to look it over again.

(*Enter* SIMON *and* HARPAGON.)

SIMON: Yes, sir, he is a young man in need of money. His affairs force him to find some, and he will agree to everything you demand.

HARPAGON: But are you certain, Simon, that I run no risk? Do you know the name, the fortune, and the family of the client you represent?

SIMON: No, I cannot really tell you anything definite; it was only by chance that he was recommended to me. But he will explain everything to you himself; and his servant has assured me that you will be satisfied when you meet him. All I can tell you is that his family is very rich, that his mother is dead, and that he will guarantee, if you wish, that his father will die before eight months are over.

HARPAGON: Well, that's something. Charity, Simon, requires us to please people, when we can.

SIMON: Quite so.

LA FLÈCHE (*low to* CLÉANTE): What does this mean? Simon's talking to your father!

CLÉANTE (*low to* LA FLÈCHE): Can anyone have told him who I am? Have you betrayed me?

SIMON (*seeing* CLÉANTE *and* LA FLÈCHE): Aha! you certainly are in a hurry! Who told you this was the house? (*To* HARPAGON) It was not I, sir, in any event, who revealed your

name and residence. But, in my opinion, there's no great
harm done. They are discreet fellows, and you can discuss
things together here.

HARPAGON: What do you mean?

SIMON (*pointing to* CLÉANTE): This gentleman is the one I
have mentioned to you, the person who wants to borrow the
fifteen thousand francs.

HARPAGON: What! rogue! It is you who abandon yourself
to such sinful excesses?

CLÉANTE: What! father! It is you who deal in such shameful actions?

HARPAGON: It is you who want to ruin yourself by such
detestable borrowing?

CLÉANTE: It is you who seek to enrich yourself by such
criminal usury?

HARPAGON: How dare you, after this, appear before me?

CLÉANTE: How dare you, after this, show yourself to the
world?

HARPAGON: Tell me, have you no shame at all, to indulge
in such debauchery? to throw yourself into such horrible
expenses? to squander shamelessly the wealth your parents
have amassed for you by the sweat of their brows?

CLÉANTE: Do you not blush at dishonoring your rank by
this trade you carry on? sacrificing glory and reputation to
the insatiable desire of heaping up gold upon gold, and out-
doing by your rate of interest the most infamous schemes ever
invented by the most notorious usurers?

HARPAGON: Get out of my sight, you villain, get out of my
sight!

CLÉANTE: Who is the greater criminal in your opinion: the
man who buys money he needs, or the man who steals money
he does not need?

HARPAGON: Get out of here, I tell you; you make my blood
boil. (*Exeunt* CLÉANTE, LA FLÈCHE, *and* SIMON.) I am not
sorry this has happened; it is a warning to me to keep a
stricter eye than ever on all his actions.

(*Enter* FROSINE.)

FROSINE: Sir—

HARPAGON: Just a moment. I'll be right back to talk to you.
(*Aside*) It's time to take a little look at my money. (*Exit.*)

(*Enter* LA FLÈCHE.)

LA FLÈCHE (*without seeing* FROSINE): The whole thing is
most amusing. Somewhere he certainly must have a large

storehouse of junk, for we couldn't recognize anything from here in that inventory list.

FROSINE: Ah! it's you, my good La Flèche! How do you happen to be here?

LA FLÈCHE: Aha! it's you, Frosine! What are *you* doing here?

FROSINE: What I do everywhere else: play the go-between in affairs, make myself useful to people, and profit as best I can from the little talent I possess. In this world, you know, you have to live by your wits. Heaven has not endowed people like me with any resources other than intrigue and cleverness.

LA FLÈCHE: Have you some business with the master of the house?

FROSINE: Yes, I am negotiating a trifling matter for him, for which I hope to be compensated.

LA FLÈCHE: By him? Aha! you will be very clever indeed if you get anything from him. I warn you that around here money is very scarce.

FROSINE: There are certain services that have a wonderful effect.

LA FLÈCHE: I am your humble servant, but you don't know Monsieur Harpagon yet. Monsieur Harpagon is of all humans the least human, of all mortals the hardest and tightest. There is not one single service that can rouse his gratitude to the point of making him put his hand into his purse. Praise, esteem, kind words, and friendship, as much as you like. But money, out of the question! Nothing is drier and more withered than his favors and caresses, and "give" is a word for which he has such an aversion that he never says "I give you" but "I lend you good day."

FROSINE: Heavens! But I know the art of drawing men out; I have the secret for opening up their tenderness to me, for tickling their hearts, for finding their sensitive spots.

LA FLÈCHE: No use here! I defy you to soften the man in question when it comes to money. In that matter he is a Turk, but he out-Turks a Turk to the despair of everyone. You could be dying and he wouldn't lift a finger. In a word, he loves money more than reputation, than honor, than virtue, and the mere sight of anyone asking for money sends him into convulsions. It's a mortal wound. It pierces his heart. It rips out his entrails. And if— He's coming back! I must be off! (*Exit.*)

(*Enter* HARPAGON.)

HARPAGON (*aside, low*): All's well. (*To* FROSINE) Well now! What is it, Frosine?

FROSINE: Ah! My, how well you look! You are the very picture of health!

HARPAGON: Who? I?

FROSINE: I've never seen your complexion so fresh and sparkling.

HARPAGON: Really?

FROSINE: Really. You've never in your life looked so young as you do now. I see men of twenty-five who are older than you.

HARPAGON: Nevertheless, Frosine, I'm over sixty.

FROSINE: Well, what is sixty? A mere trifle! It's the flower of one's age, and you are now entering upon the prime of manhood.

HARPAGON: That's true. But twenty years younger wouldn't do me any harm.

FROSINE: You're joking! You don't need them. You're the type that will live to be a hundred.

HARPAGON: Do you think so?

FROSINE: Certainly. You show every sign of it. Hold still a moment! Oh! most certainly, there between your eyes—a sign of long life.

HARPAGON: Do you really know what you're talking about?

FROSINE: Without a doubt. Let me see your hand. My goodness! What a life line!

HARPAGON: Where?

FROSINE: Don't you see how far that line goes?

HARPAGON: Well! But what does it mean?

FROSINE: Upon my word! I said a hundred, but you'll survive one hundred and twenty!

HARPAGON: Is it possible?

FROSINE: They'll have to club you to death, I tell you. You'll bury your children and your children's children.

HARPAGON: So much the better!—But how is our little business going along?

FROSINE: Need you ask? Has anyone ever seen me start anything I didn't finish? I have a marvellous talent, especially for matchmaking. There aren't two people in the world that I couldn't join in a short time. I believe, if I took it into my head, that I could marry the Grand Turk to the Republic of Venice. Of course, there weren't any such great difficulties in your case. As I have business in their house, I have often spoken to both of them about you, and I have told the mother about the future you've been planning for Mariane, since you saw her pass by in the street and take the air at her window.

HARPAGON: What answer did—

FROSINE: She received the proposition with pleasure. And when I told her you greatly desired that her daughter be present this evening at the signing of the marriage contract here at your house, she consented willingly, and even entrusted her daughter to me for that purpose.

HARPAGON: I have to give a supper for Signor Anselm, Frosine, and I should like her to be present.

FROSINE: You are quite right. After dinner she has to pay your daughter a visit; then she plans to go to the fair, and will return here for supper.

HARPAGON: Very well. They can go together in my coach, which I shall lend them.

FROSINE: That will suit her exactly.

HARPAGON: But, Frosine, have you talked to the mother about the money she can give her daughter? Have you told her that she ought to help a little, if only slightly; that she should make some attempt; that she should bleed herself for an occasion such as this? For, after all, a man does not marry a girl unless she brings along something.

FROSINE: What? This girl will bring you twelve thousand francs a year.

HARPAGON: Twelve thousand francs a year?

FROSINE: Yes. First of all: she has been brought up and nourished on a very sparing diet. She is a girl accustomed to live on salads, milk, cheese, and apples; and, consequently, she does not need elaborate meals, or exquisite broths, or barley syrups all the time, nor all the rest of the delicacies other women need. And they are no slight matter, for year after year they mount up to three thousand francs at least. Besides this, she cares only for what is simple in dress, and does not like gorgeous clothes, expensive jewels, or sumptuous furniture, to which her contemporaries are so much addicted. This saving is worth more than four thousand francs a year. Furthermore, she has a positive loathing for cards, a taste not common in women today. I know of one in our neighborhood who has lost twenty thousand francs at cards this year! But let us figure it at a quarter of that. Five thousand francs a year for cards, four thousand francs for clothes and jewels, make nine thousand francs. And three thousand francs which we set aside for food. Doesn't that make your twelve thousand francs a year all accounted for?

HARPAGON: Yes, that's not bad. But your figures have no reality.

FROSINE: I beg your pardon. Isn't perfect sobriety a real asset in marriage? Or her inheritance of a great love for simplicity in dress? Or the acquisition of a deep well of hatred for gambling?

HARPAGON: It's mockery to make up her dowry with the expenses that she *won't* run up. I give no receipt for something I don't actually get. I have to put my hands on something.

FROSINE: Great Heavens! you'll put your hands on enough. And they did mention to me some property they own in a foreign country of which you will become the master.

HARPAGON: I'll have to see it. But, Frosine, there is something else that upsets me. The girl is young, as you know, and the young generally like only those of their own age, and seek only their company. I'm afraid that a man of my age won't be to her liking, and that this can only produce in my house certain little vexations which wouldn't please me.

FROSINE: Ah! how little you know her! This was one other characteristic that I was going to tell you about. She has a frightful aversion to all young men, and only likes old ones.

HARPAGON: She?

FROSINE: Yes, she. I wish you had heard her on that subject. She cannot bear the sight of a young man. But she says that nothing delights her more than the sight of a handsome old man with a majestic beard. The older they are, the more charming they are for her, and I warn you not to make yourself appear younger than you are. She likes a man to be at least sixty. Not four months ago, on the point of getting married, she promptly broke off the match, when she found out that her lover was only fifty-six and didn't need glasses to sign the marriage contract.

HARPAGON: Just for that?

FROSINE: Yes! She said that she wasn't satisfied with a man of only fifty-six, and, above all, she likes noses with spectacles on them.

HARPAGON: Really, this is something quite new!

FROSINE: It goes even further than I have told you. There are a few pictures and engravings in her room, but what do you think they are? Adonis? Cephalus? Paris? Apollo? Not at all! Fine portraits of Saturn, of King Priam, of old Nestor, and of good father Anchises on his son's shoulders.

HARPAGON: That *is* admirable! I should never have thought it. And my mind is eased to learn she has that attitude. In fact, if I had been a woman, I wouldn't have liked young men either.

FROSINE: I quite believe it. Love young men! What are they but worthless trash! They are mere puppies, show-offs that make you envy their complexions. I'd really like to know who likes them!

HARPAGON: As for me, I don't understand it either. I don't know how some women can like them so much.

FROSINE: One has to be an utter fool to find youth charming! Is that common sense? Are they men, these young fops? Can one really be attached to such animals?

HARPAGON: That's what I say day after day: with their effeminate voices, and their three little wisps of beard turned up like cat's whiskers, their straw-colored wigs, their baggy pants, and their fancy waistcoats.

FROSINE: They make a fine comparison next to a man like you. (*To the audience*) Here is a man. There's something here that satisfies the eye. This is the way a man should be made, and dressed, to inspire love.

HARPAGON: You find me attractive?

FROSINE: What? Ah! you are stunning, and your portrait ought to be painted. Turn around a bit, if you please. Nothing could be better. Let me see you walk. (*To the audience*) Here is a body that is trim, free, and easy in its motions, as it should be, without a trace of any physical weakness.

HARPAGON: Nothing much ‹ is the matter with me, thank God. (*He coughs.*) That's only my catarrh, which bothers me occasionally.

FROSINE: That's nothing. Your catarrh is not unbecoming, since you cough with such grace.

HARPAGON: Tell me something. Hasn't Mariane ever seen me yet? Hasn't she ever noticed me in passing?

FROSINE: No, but we have often talked about you. I've sketched a portrait of your person and I've not failed to extol your merits and the advantage it would be to her to have a husband such as you.

HARPAGON: You have done well and I thank you for it.

FROSINE: I have, sir, a small favor to ask of you. There's a lawsuit I am about to lose for want of a little money; and you could easily enable me to win this lawsuit if you would show me some kindness. (HARPAGON *frowns.*) You would not believe how pleased she will be to see you. (HARPAGON *smiles.*) Ah! how you will please her. How admirable an effect on her your old-fashioned ruff will have. But above all, she will be charmed by your breeches, attached to your doublet with laces; that will make her mad for you. And a laced-up lover will be a marvellous treat for her.

HARPAGON: Really! I am delighted to hear you say so.

FROSINE: To tell the truth, sir, this lawsuit is of the greatest consequence to me. I shall be ruined if I lose it. Some slight aid would set right my affairs. (HARPAGON *frowns.*) I wish you could see her rapture when I talk to her of you. (HARPAGON *smiles again.*) Her eyes shone with joy at the recitation of your qualities. In fact, I have made her extremely impatient to see this marriage completed.

HARPAGON: You have given me great pleasure, Frosine, and I assure you, I am deeply indebted to you.

FROSINE: I beg you, sir, to give me the slight help I ask

for. (HARPAGON *frowns again.*) It will set me back on my feet, and I shall be eternally obligated to you.

HARPAGON: Goodbye! I am going to finish my letters.

FROSINE: I assure you, sir, you could never assist me in a greater need.

HARPAGON: I will give orders for my carriage to be ready to drive you to the fair.

FROSINE: I would not trouble you, if I were not forced by necessity.

HARPAGON: And I'll take care that we dine early so that you won't get sick.

FROSINE: Do not refuse me the favor I beg of you. You would not believe, sir, the pleasure that—

HARPAGON: I am going. There! Someone is calling me. Until later. (*Exit.*)

FROSINE: May a fever burn you up! Thieving dog! The devil take you! The skinflint has fended off all my attacks. But I mustn't drop the business now. In any case, there's the other party; I'm sure to be well rewarded there.

ACT III

(*On stage*: HARPAGON, CLÉANTE, ÉLISE, VALÈRE, DAME CLAUDE, JACQUES, BRINDAVOINE, *and* LA MERLUCHE.)

HARPAGON: All right! Come here, all of you! I want to give you orders for the rest of the day, and assign each of you to your tasks! Come, Dame Claude, I'll begin with you. (*She approaches, carrying a broom.*) Good, you carry your arms along with you. To you I assign the task of cleaning the entire house; but above all take care not to rub the furniture too hard, or you'll wear it out. In addition you're assigned to look after the bottles during supper; and if any are lost, or if anything is broken, I shall hold you responsible and deduct it from your wages.

JACQUES (*aside*): A shrewd punishment.

HARPAGON (*to* DAME CLAUDE): Go. (*Exit* DAME CLAUDE.) You, Brindavoine, and you, La Merluche, I put in charge of rinsing the glasses, and serving the drinks, but only when someone is thirsty. And don't be like those impertinent lackeys who deliberately encourage people to drink when they had no intention at all of doing so. Wait until they have asked you more than once, and always remember to keep plenty of water at hand.

JACQUES (*aside*): Yes, undiluted wine goes to the head.

LA MERLUCHE: Shall we serve without aprons, sir?

HARPAGON: Yes, when you see the guests coming, but be careful not to soil your clothes.

BRINDAVOINE: But, sir, you know that one of the lapels of my doublet is covered with a large stain of lamp-oil.

LA MERLUCHE: And I, sir, have a large hole in the back of my breeches, and, begging your pardon, people can see my—

HARPAGON: That's enough! Keep that side discreetly to the wall and always show people your front only. (HARPAGON *holds his hat in front of his doublet to show* BRINDAVOINE *how to hide the oil-stain.*) And you must always hold your cap like this when you serve. (*Exeunt* LA MERLUCHE *and* BRINDAVOINE.) As for you, my daughter, you must keep an eye on what is cleared away from the table and take care that nothing is wasted. That's a daughter's proper work. But meanwhile, prepare yourself to receive my fiancée, who is coming to visit you and to take you to the fair. Did you hear what I said?

ÉLISE: Yes, father.

HARPAGON: And you, my son, the dandy, whose latest escapade I have been kind enough to pardon, be careful not to make sour faces at her.

CLÉANTE: I, father, a sour face? Why should I?

HARPAGON: My God, we all know the attitude of children when their fathers remarry and how they look upon what is called a stepmother. But, if you want me to forget your last prank, I recommend above all that you receive this lady pleasantly and give her the best welcome you possibly can.

CLÉANTE: To tell you the truth, father, I can't promise you I'll be very glad she is to become my stepmother. I would be lying if I were to tell you so. But as for welcoming her and receiving her pleasantly, I promise to obey you to the letter.

HARPAGON: Take care you do that, at least.

CLÉANTE: You'll see that you will have no cause for complaint.

HARPAGON: That will be wise. (*Exeunt* CLÉANTE *and* ÉLISE.) Valère, help me with this. Ho there, Jacques! Come here! I have kept you for the last.

JACQUES: Do you wish to speak to your coachman, sir, or to your cook, for I am both?

HARPAGON: To both of you.

JACQUES: But to which one first?

HARPAGON: The cook.

JACQUES: One moment, then, if you please. (*He takes off his coachman's livery and appears dressed as a cook.*)

HARPAGON: What the deuce does this ceremony mean?

JACQUES: I am at your service, sir.

HARPAGON: Jacques, I am committed to give a supper tonight.

JACQUES (*aside*): What a miracle!

HARPAGON: Tell me, can you serve us something good?

JACQUES: Yes, if you give me plenty of money.

HARPAGON: What the devil! Always money! It seems they have nothing else to say than money, money, money. Always talking of money. Money is their best friend.

VALÈRE: I have never heard a more impertinent answer than that. What kind of miracle is it to be able to provide a fine feast with plenty of money? That's the easiest thing in the world to do; any poor fool could do as much. But it's the work of a clever man to arrange good fare with little money.

JACQUES: Good fare with little money?

VALÈRE: Yes.

JACQUES: Upon my word, Monsieur Steward, you would oblige us if you'd let us in on your secret and take my place as cook. You interfere with so much that you might as well be the factotum.

HARPAGON: Hold your tongue! What shall we need?

JACQUES: There's your steward who will provide you with fine dishes for little money.

HARPAGON: Stop that! I want you to answer me.

JACQUES: How many will there be?

HARPAGON: We will be eight or ten; but you need only provide for eight. When there's enough for eight, there's plenty for ten.

VALÈRE: Of course.

JACQUES: Very well. We will need four good soups, and five dishes. Soups, entrées—

HARPAGON: What the devil! that's enough to feed an entire city.

JACQUES: Roast—

HARPAGON (*putting his hand over Jacques's mouth*): Ah, spendthrift, you are eating up all my money!

JACQUES: Side dishes—

HARPAGON (*again putting his hand over Jacques's mouth*): More?

VALÈRE: Do you want to make everyone burst? Has our master invited people here to murder them by overeating? Go and read the manual of health, and ask a doctor if there's anything more harmful to a man than eating to excess.

HARPAGON: He's right.

VALÈRE: You must learn, Jacques, you and your kind, that an overladen table is a cut-throat; that to prove yourself a friend of those you invite, frugality must reign over the meals you serve; and, following the sayings of the ancients, "One should eat to live, and not live to eat."

HARPAGON: Ah! that is well said! Come here; I want to embrace you for those words. That is the most beautiful sentence I've ever heard in my life. "One should live to eat, and not eat to li—" No, that's not it. How did you say it?

VALÈRE: "One should eat to live, and not live to eat."

HARPAGON (*to* JACQUES): Yes! Do you hear that? (*To* VALÈRE) Who is the great man who said that?

VALÈRE: I don't remember his name offhand.

HARPAGON: Don't forget to write those words down for me: I shall have them engraved in gold letters above the mantelpiece of my dining room.

VALÈRE: I shall not forget. And as for your supper, just leave it to me. I'll arrange everything as it should be.

HARPAGON: Do so.

JACQUES: So much the better; there will be less trouble for me.

HARPAGON: We should have those things people don't eat much of, and which will fill them up quickly—a rather fatty mutton stew, with a meat pie well stuffed with chestnuts.

VALÈRE: Leave everything to me.

HARPAGON: Now, Jacques, my coach must be cleaned.

JACQUES: Just a moment. This concerns the coachman. (*Exit, and reappears in coachman's livery.*) You were saying . . . ?

HARPAGON: That my coach must be cleaned, and my horses made ready to drive to the fair. . . .

JACQUES: Your horses, sir? My goodness, they are not in a fit state to walk. I won't tell you that they can't get up from their straw; the poor beasts have none at all—so that would be a lie. But you make them observe such strict fasts that they are no more than ideas or ghosts—mere shadows of horses.

HARPAGON: Why should they be sick? They never *do* anything.

JACQUES: And because they do nothing, sir, is that any reason why they shouldn't eat? It would be much better for them, poor beasts, if they worked a lot and were fed accordingly. It breaks my heart to see them so emaciated, for I have such affection for my horses that when I see them suffering, it's as if I myself were suffering. Everyday I feed them food out of my own mouth. It's a very hard nature, sir, that feels no pity for a fellow creature.

HARPAGON: It won't be too hard work for them to go as far as the fair.

JACQUES: No, sir, I haven't the heart to drive them, and

my conscience would bother me if I gave them a lash of the whip, the state they're in. How can you expect them to draw a carriage when they can't drag themselves?

VALÈRE: Sir, I will ask our neighbor Picard if he will drive them. Besides, we shall need him here to help us prepare the supper.

JACQUES: Very well. I'd much rather they died under someone else's hands than mine.

VALÈRE: Jacques is becoming an arguer.

JACQUES: Monsieur Steward is becoming a busybody.

HARPAGON: Enough!

JACQUES: Sir, I cannot endure flatterers. I see what he is doing. His perpetual surveillance over the bread, wine, wood, salt, and candles has no other end than to inch up to you, to win your favor. It makes me mad, and it grieves me to hear what people are saying about you every day. For I do have a real affection for you, in spite of myself, and, after my horses, you are the person I like most.

HARPAGON: Might I know, Jacques, what people are saying about me?

JACQUES: Yes, sir, if I could be sure it wouldn't make you angry.

HARPAGON: No, not in the least.

JACQUES: Begging your pardon, I know only too well I shall make you angry.

HARPAGON: Not at all. On the contrary, it will give me pleasure. I shall be most glad to learn what they say about me.

JACQUES: Since you wish it, sir, I will tell you frankly that everyone everywhere laughs at you. On all sides, they make a hundred jokes about you. And nothing pleases them more than to pull you to pieces and to tell endless stories of your stinginess. One person says you have special almanacs printed, in which you double the ember days and vigils, in order to profit from the fasts you make your household keep. Another says you always have a quarrel ready with your servants when it's time to give New Year's gifts or when one of them is leaving, so that you can find an excuse for not giving them something. This one tells the story that you once brought a lawsuit against a neighbor's cat for having eaten the remains of a leg of mutton. That one says you were caught one night stealing the hay from your own horses, and that your coachman—the one who preceded me—gave you I don't know how many blows with his stick in the dark, about which you never said a word. Shall I go on? We can't go anywhere without hearing you pulled inside out. You are the joke and laughingstock of the whole world. And they never talk of you except by the name of miser, skinflint, villain, or usurer.

HARPAGON (*beating him*): You're an idiot, a scoundrel, a rascal, and an impudent knave.

JACQUES: Oh! Oh! didn't I predict it? You wouldn't believe me. I warned you that I'd make you angry if I told you the truth.

HARPAGON: That will teach you how to talk. (*Exit.*)

VALÈRE (*laughing*): From what I can see, Jacques, your frankness has paid off rather badly.

JACQUES: By God! Monsieur Newcomer—who thinks he's a man of importance—it's none of your business. Laugh at your own beatings, when you get them, and don't come laughing at mine.

VALÈRE: Ah! Jacques, don't be angry, I beg of you.

JACQUES (*aside*): He's backing down. I'll bully him, and if he's fool enough to be afraid of me, I'll thrash him a bit. (*To* VALÈRE) Do you know, Monsieur Laugher, that I never laugh? And that if you arouse my anger, I'll make you laugh out of the other side of your mouth? (JACQUES *pushes* VALÈRE *to the back of the stage, threatening him.*)

VALÈRE: Gently, now!

JACQUES: What do you mean gently? I don't want to be gentle.

VALÈRE: Pray—

JACQUES: You're an impudent fellow.

VALÈRE: My dear Monsieur Jacques!

JACQUES: There's no "my dear Monsieur Jacques" for a nobody like you. If I had a club, I'd beat the importance out of you.

VALÈRE: What! a club? (VALÈRE *picks up a stick and makes* JACQUES *retreat.*)

JACQUES: Er, I didn't mean that.

VALÈRE: Do you know, Monsieur Fool, that I'm just the man to give you a good beating?

JACQUES: I don't doubt it.

VALÈRE: And that, for all your soups, you're nothing at all but a pot-washing cook?

JACQUES: I know it.

VALÈRE: And that you don't know me yet?

JACQUES: Pardon me.

VALÈRE: You'll thrash me, you said?

JACQUES: I was only joking.

VALÈRE: I don't care at all for your jokes. (*He thrashes him with the stick.*) Learn what a poor joker you are. (*Exit.*)

JACQUES: A plague on sincerity. It's a bad business. I give it up from now on, and I'll no longer tell the truth. My master, at least, has some right to beat me, but as for this steward, I'll get revenge on him if I can.

(*Enter* FROSINE *and* MARIANE.)

FROSINE: Jacques, do you know if your master is at home?

JACQUES: Yes, indeed, he is. I know only too well.

FROSINE: Tell him, if you please, that we are here. (*Exit* JACQUES.)

MARIANE: Ah, Frosine, what a strange position I am in. And, if I may speak out my thoughts, how I dread this meeting.

FROSINE: But why? What makes you uneasy?

MARIANE: Alas! Need you ask me? Can you not imagine the fears of a girl about to see the rack on which she is to be bound?

FROSINE: I see well enough that Harpagon is not the rack you'd willingly embrace for a pleasant death, and I can tell from your face that you are thinking again of the fair young man you spoke to me about.

MARIANE: Yes. I do not wish to deny that, Frosine. The respectful visits he has paid us have, I admit, made some impression on my heart.

FROSINE: But have you found out who he is?

MARIANE: No, I do not know who he is, but I know he is made to be loved; that, if things were up to me, I would have him rather than any other man, and that he contributes not a little to my vision of horrible torment in the arms of the man chosen for me.

FROSINE: Oh, Lord, all these fair young men are agreeable, and play their roles quite well; but most of them are poor as church-mice. It's best for you to take an old husband who can give you material comfort. I admit that the senses aren't fully satisfied by the course I advise, and that there are several petty revulsions to overcome with such a husband. But that won't last, and his death, I assure you, will soon put you in a position to take a more agreeable husband, who will make things all right.

MARIANE: Oh, my goodness, Frosine, it is a strange business where, to be happy, one must wish and wait for the death of someone. And death does not always come to suit our plans.

FROSINE: Are you jesting? You are marrying him only on the condition that he will soon make you a widow; that ought to be one of the articles in the marriage contract. It would be most impertinent of him not to die within three months.— Here he comes in person.

MARIANE: Oh, Frosine, what a figure!

(*Enter* HARPAGON.)

HARPAGON: Do not be offended, my pretty one, if I come to you wearing spectacles. I know that your charms strike the unaided eye—that they are visible in themselves—and that spectacles are not necessary in order to see them. But after all, it is with lenses that one observes the stars, and I claim and guarantee that you are a star, the most beautiful star in the world of stars. Frosine, she makes no reply, and displays, I think, no joy in seeing me.

FROSINE: Because she is still taken by surprise. Furthermore, girls are ashamed to display immediately what their hearts feel.

HARPAGON: You are right. (*To* MARIANE) Here, my little one, is my daughter, who comes to welcome you.

(*Enter* ÉLISE.)

MARIANE: I have delayed my visit too long, Madam.

ÉLISE: *You* have done, Madam, what *I* ought to have done. I ought to have come first to you.

HARPAGON: You can see how tall she is; but weeds always flourish.

MARIANE (*whispering to* FROSINE): What a horrid man!

HARPAGON: What is the lovely creature saying?

FROSINE: That she finds you admirable.

HARPAGON: You do me too great an honor, adorable darling.

MARIANE (*aside*): What a beast!

HARPAGON: I am most obliged to you for these sentiments.

MARIANE (*aside*): I cannot bear any more.

(*Enter* CLÉANTE.)

HARPAGON: Here is my son, who also comes to pay you his respects.

MARIANE (*looks at* CLÉANTE *and whispers to* FROSINE): Ah, Frosine, what a coincidence! It is the very young man I told you of.

FROSINE (*to* MARIANE): What odd luck!

HARPAGON: I see you are astonished to see me with such grown-up children. But I shall soon be rid of both of them.

CLÉANTE: Madam, to tell the truth, I certainly did not expect this encounter. My father surprised me not a little when he recently told me of the plans he had made.

MARIANE: I may say the same. This is an unforeseen meeting which surprises me as well as you; I was not at all prepared for such an occurrence.

CLÉANTE: Madam, it is true that my father could not make a better choice, and the honor of seeing you gives me heartfelt joy. But, for all that, I cannot assure you that I rejoice in the plan to make you my stepmother. That congratulation, I confess, is beyond me. It is a title, if you please, that I do not wish for you. This greeting will seem brutal to some eyes, but I am confident that you will be one to take it as it was intended. This is a marriage, Madam, which you can well imagine I have an aversion to. You cannot be ignorant, knowing who I am, how it conflicts with my interests. And you will allow me to tell you, with my father's permission, that if matters depended on me, this marriage would not take place.

HARPAGON: This is a most impertinent congratulation! What a fine admission to make to her!

MARIANE: And I, in reply, must say the same to you. If you have an aversion to seeing me your stepmother, I feel no less at seeing you my stepson. Do not think, I beg you, it is I who sought to cause you this uneasiness. I would be most disturbed to cause you any displeasure. And, if I am not forced to it by despotic power, I give you my word that I will not consent to a marriage which grieves you.

HARPAGON: She's right. A foolish compliment deserves an answer of the same sort. I beg your pardon, my fair lady, for my son's impertinence. He's a young fool who has not yet learned the consequences of the words he speaks.

MARIANE: I assure you that what he has told me is not at all offensive. On the contrary, he pleased me by thus explaining his real feelings. I like such an open avowal as his, and if he had spoken otherwise, I should think less of him.

HARPAGON: It is too good of you to wish thus to excuse his faults. Time will make him wiser, and you will see that he will change his sentiments.

CLÉANTE: No, father, I am incapable of changing them, and I urgently beg Madam to believe me.

HARPAGON: What madness! He's worse than ever.

CLÉANTE: Would you want me to betray my heart?

HARPAGON: Again? Let's change the conversation.

CLÉANTE: Well, since you wish me to speak in a different manner, allow me, Madam, to put myself in my father's place and to tell you that in all the world I have seen nothing so charming as you. I can conceive of nothing equal to the happiness of pleasing you, and the title of your husband is a glory, a felicity which I would prefer to the fates of the greatest princes of the earth. Yes, Madam, the happiness of possessing you is, in my eyes, the most beautiful of fortunes. All my ambition is directed to that. There is nothing that I am incapable of in order to make so precious a conquest, and the most insuperable obstacles—

HARPAGON: Easy, son, if you please.

CLÉANTE: I am complimenting Madam on your behalf.

HARPAGON: My God, I have a tongue to talk for myself,

and I don't need any intermediary like you. Come, bring some chairs.

FROSINE: No. It would be best to go to the fair now, so that we can return sooner and have the remaining time for conversation.

HARPAGON: Have the horses hitched to the carriage.—I beg you, fair lady, to excuse me for not having thought to offer you some refreshment before leaving.

CLÉANTE: I have provided for some, father, and have ordered some bowls of China oranges, candied lemons, and preserves, which I have sent for in your name.

HARPAGON (*in a low voice, to* VALÈRE): Valère!

VALÈRE (*to* HARPAGON): He's out of his mind.

CLÉANTE: Father, do you think this is not enough? Madam will have the kindness to forgive it, I trust.

MARIANE: It was quite unnecessary.

CLÉANTE (*as* HARPAGON *offers his hand to lead* MARIANE *to the carriage*): Madam, have you ever seen a diamond more brilliant than the one on my father's finger?

MARIANE: It sparkles brightly, indeed.

CLÉANTE (*taking the ring from his father's finger and placing it on* MARIANE'S): You must see it close up.

MARIANE: It is most handsome, indeed, and full of fire.

CLÉANTE (*placing himself before* MARIANE, *who wishes to return the ring*): No, no, Madam, it is on too beautiful a hand. It is a gift which my father gives you.

HARPAGON: I?

CLÉANTE: Father, isn't it true that you wish Madam to keep it for your love's sake?

HARPAGON (*aside, to his son*): What?

CLÉANTE: A charming request. He indicates to me that I should make you accept it.

MARIANE: But I do not wish—

CLÉANTE: Are you jesting? He does not wish to take it back.

HARPAGON (*aside*): I'm furious!

MARIANE: It would be—

CLÉANTE (*still preventing* MARIANE *from returning the ring*): No, I tell you, you will offend him.

MARIANE: For pity's sake—

CLÉANTE: Not at all.

HARPAGON (*aside*): May the plague—

CLÉANTE: See how shocked he is by your refusal?

HARPAGON (*low, to his son*): Ah, traitor!

CLÉANTE: You see how he is driven to despair.

HARPAGON (*low, threatening his son*): Scoundrel!

CLÉANTE: Madam, you are making my father angry with me.

HARPAGON (*low, continues to threaten* CLÉANTE): You rogue!

CLÉANTE: You will make him ill. Pray, Madam, do not resist any further.

FROSINE: My God, what a fuss! Keep the ring, since Monsieur wishes you to.

MARIANE: In order not to anger you, I shall keep it for now, and I will take some other opportunity to return it to you.

(*Enter* BRINDAVOINE.)

BRINDAVOINE: Sir, there is a man who wishes to speak to you.

HARPAGON: Tell him I'm busy; tell him to come back some other time.

BRINDAVOINE: He says he brings you some money.

HARPAGON (*to* MARIANE): I shall return immediately.

LA MERLUCHE (*running in, knocks* HARPAGON *over*): Sir—

HARPAGON: Oh, I'm killed!

CLÉANTE: What is it, father? Have you hurt yourself?

HARPAGON: This traitor must have been bribed by my debtors to break my neck.

VALÈRE (*to* HARPAGON): It's nothing.

LA MERLUCHE: Sir, I beg your pardon; I meant well in hurrying.

HARPAGON: Well, what are you here for, you wretch?

LA MERLUCHE: To tell you your two horses are shoeless.

HARPAGON: Have them taken to the blacksmith immediately.

CLÉANTE: While we're waiting to have them shod, father, I will do the honors of your house for you, and show Madam to the garden, where the refreshments shall be brought. (*Exeunt all but* HARPAGON *and* VALÈRE.)

HARPAGON: Valère, keep your eye on them, and take care, please, to save as much as you can to return to the shop.

VALÈRE (*leaving*): I understand. (*Exit.*)

HARPAGON (*alone*): Impertinent son! Have you set out to ruin me?

ACT IV

(*Enter* CLÉANTE, MARIANE, ÉLISE, *and* FROSINE.)

CLÉANTE: Let us go in here; we shall be safer. There are no suspicious people around, and we can talk freely.

ÉLISE: Yes, Madam, my brother has confided to me the

love he feels for you. I know the grief and the unpleasantness such obstacles can cause, and, I assure you, I am deeply sympathetic to your difficulties.

MARIANE: It is a pleasant consolation when someone like you sympathizes with one's problems. And I beg you, Madam, always to preserve your generous affection for me—an affection so capable of softening the cruelties of fate.

FROSINE: On my word, you are both unlucky people, not to have told me of the situation sooner. I would undoubtedly have warded off this mishap and not brought things as far as they are now.

CLÉANTE: How could we help it? My evil destiny has willed this. But, fair Mariane, what have you resolved to do?

MARIANE: Alas! Can I resolve to do anything? Dependent as I am, can I do more than wish?

CLÉANTE: Can I find no other encouragement within your heart but simple wishes? No tender pity? No helpful goodwill? No lively affection?

MARIANE: What can I say to you? Put yourself in my place and see what I might do. Advise me, command me yourself! I will place myself in your hands; I think you are too fair-minded a person to demand from me more than what honor and decency permit.

CLÉANTE: Alas! To what am I reduced when you bind me with the vexing sentiments of rigorous honor and scrupulous decency!

MARIANE: But what would you have me do? Even if I could disregard many of the restrictions which bind my sex, I must have some consideration for my mother. She brought me up most tenderly, and I could never make up my mind to cause her pain. You do something with her; deal with her; do your utmost to win her sympathy. I give you permission to do and say what you will; and if nothing is lacking except my approval, I am willing to avow to her all that I feel for you.

CLÉANTE: Frosine, dear Frosine, won't you help us?

FROSINE: Good Lord, need you ask? I want to, with all my heart. My nature, you know, is pretty human. Heaven didn't give me a heart of iron, and I am only too well disposed to render little services to people decently and honestly in love. But what can we do about this situation?

CLÉANTE: Give it a little thought, I beg you.

MARIANE: Show us some way out.

ÉLISE: Find some means to undo what you have done.

FROSINE: That's quite difficult. (*To* MARIANE) As for your mother, she's not unreasonable; perhaps we could win her over and induce her to give the son the gift she plans to give the father. (*To* CLÉANTE) But the real trouble here is—that your father is your father.

CLÉANTE: Too true!

FROSINE (*to* MARIANE): I mean that he will be spiteful if he's rejected, and he will not be willing, later, to consent to the marriage. The best thing would be for the rejection to come from himself and for you to attempt in some way to make him disgusted with you.

CLÉANTE: You're right.

FROSINE: Yes, I'm right, I know that well enough. That's the only way, but how the deuce can we find the means.— Wait! Suppose we found a woman, somewhat along in years, and who had my talent, who acted well enough to counterfeit a lady of quality, with the help of a hastily collected entourage, and some bizarre name of a marchioness or viscountess, say from Lower Brittany. I've enough skill to make your father think her rich, with a hundred thousand écus in cash as well as great houses, and so madly in love with him and so determined to be his wife, that she would give all her wealth for a marriage contract. I've not the slightest doubt that he'd lend an ear to the proposition, for, though he loves you well, I know he loves money a little more. And, dazzled by this bait, when he once consents to your wishes, it won't matter much if later he is disabused when he wants to see more precisely our marchioness' property.

CLÉANTE: Excellently planned!

FROSINE: Leave it to me. I've just thought of a friend of mine who'll suit our purpose exactly.

CLÉANTE: Frosine, you can be sure of my gratitude if you succeed. But, charming Mariane, let us begin, I beg you, by winning over your mother; it will be something to break off this marriage. I beg you to make every possible effort. Use over her all the power which her affection for you gives you; display, without reserve, the eloquent graces, the all-powerful charms which Heaven placed in your eyes and on your lips. And I beg of you, overlook none of those soft words, those gentle prayers, those sweet caresses to which, I am sure, nothing can be refused.

MARIANE: I shall do all I can; I will overlook nothing.

(*Enter* HARPAGON, *unseen.*)

HARPAGON (*aside*): What! My son kissing the hand of his intended stepmother, and his intended stepmother not objecting very strongly! Can there be something behind all this?

ÉLISE: Here comes father!

HARPAGON: The carriage is ready. You can leave as soon as you like.

CLÉANTE: Since you are not going, father, I will accompany them.

HARPAGON: No, you stay here. They will be all right by themselves, and I need you.

(*Exeunt* MARIANE, ÉLISE, *and* FROSINE.)

Well, now, putting aside the question of a stepmother, what do you think of the lady?

CLÉANTE: What do I think of her?

HARPAGON: Yes! Of her manner, her figure, her beauty, her mind?

CLÉANTE: So-so.

HARPAGON: Be more precise.

CLÉANTE: To speak frankly, I have not found her to be what I expected. Her manner is that of an out-and-out coquette, her figure rather awkward, her beauty very mediocre, and her mind most ordinary. Don't think, father, that this is said to disgust you with her, for, stepmother for stepmother, I like this one as well as another.

HARPAGON: But just now you were telling her—

CLÉANTE: I was saying sweet nothings in your name, but only to please you.

HARPAGON: Then you don't feel any inclination for her?

CLÉANTE: I? None at all!

HARPAGON: That's too bad, for it spoils a plan that had occurred to me. Seeing her here, I reflected on my age, and I thought that people might talk about my marrying so young a girl. This consideration made me drop the idea, but, as I have asked for her hand and have given her my word, I would have given her to you if you hadn't shown your aversion.

CLÉANTE: To me?

HARPAGON: To you.

CLÉANTE: In marriage?

HARPAGON: In marriage.

CLÉANTE: Listen: it's true that she isn't much to my taste, but to please you, father, I will resign myself to marrying her, if you wish.

HARPAGON: I? I am more reasonable than you think; I will not force your inclinations.

CLÉANTE: Pardon me; I will make this effort out of affection for you.

HARPAGON: No, no: a marriage can't be happy if the heart isn't in it.

CLÉANTE: Perhaps it will be, later, father; they say that love is often the fruit of marriage.

HARPAGON: The man ought to risk nothing in such a situa-

tion; grievous consequences may follow which I don't want
to be responsible for. If you had felt a liking for her, fine;
I would have had her marry you instead of me; but, that
not being the case, I'll follow my original plan and marry
her myself.

CLÉANTE: Look, father. Since things have come to this, I
must disclose our secret. The truth is that I have loved her
since the day I first saw her taking a walk. My plan, until
just recently, was to ask your permission to make her my
wife, and only your declaration of your feelings and my fear
of displeasing you restrained me.

HARPAGON: Have you paid her any visits?

CLÉANTE: Yes, father.

HARPAGON: Often?

CLÉANTE: Enough, considering how little time there has
been.

HARPAGON: Have you been well received?

CLÉANTE: Very well, but without her knowing who I was.
That is why Mariane was so surprised just now.

HARPAGON: Have you declared your love and your intention
to marry her?

CLÉANTE: Certainly, and I've even made some overtures
to her mother about it.

HARPAGON: Did she listen to your proposal for her
daughter?

CLÉANTE: Yes, most civilly.

HARPAGON: And does the daughter return your love?

CLÉANTE: If I can believe appearances, father, I think she
has some affection for me.

HARPAGON (softly, aside): I am delighted to have learned
this secret; it's just what I wanted to know. (Aloud) Now,
my son, do you know what you have to do? You must think,
if you please, of getting rid of your love, of ceasing to pursue
a lady I intend for myself, and of marrying shortly the one
I have decided on for you.

CLÉANTE: So, father, this is how you trick me! Very well.
Since it's come to this, I declare to you that I will never give
up my love for Mariane, that there is no extremity from
which I will shrink to prevent your triumph, and that if you
have the mother's consent on your behalf, I shall have other
resources, perhaps, which will fight on mine.

HARPAGON: What, you rogue! You dare to hunt my game?

CLÉANTE: It's you who are hunting mine; I was there first.

HARPAGON: Am I not your father? Don't you owe me
respect?

CLÉANTE: This is not a matter where children are obliged
to defer to their parents; love is no respecter of persons.

HARPAGON: I'll make you respect me with a good stick.

CLÉANTE: All your threats will accomplish nothing.

HARPAGON: You shall renounce Mariane.

CLÉANTE: I will do nothing of the sort.

HARPAGON *(calling out)*: Quick, give me a stick.

JACQUES *(entering)*: Ah, ah, gentlemen, what's all this? What can you be thinking of?

CLÉANTE: I couldn't care less.

JACQUES: *(to* CLÉANTE*)*: Ah, sir, gently.

HARPAGON: To talk so impudently to me!

JACQUES *(to* HARPAGON*)*: Ah, sir, for Heaven's sake.

CLÉANTE: I won't yield an inch.

JACQUES *(to* CLÉANTE*)*: What! This to your father?

HARPAGON: Let me get at him.

JACQUES *(to* HARPAGON*)*: What! This to your son? You're not dealing with me, you know.

HARPAGON: Jacques, I'll make you the judge in this affair, to prove I'm right.

JACQUES: I'm agreeable. *(To* CLÉANTE*)* Stand away a little, please.

HARPAGON: I love a girl whom I want to marry—and this rogue has the insolence to love her, too—and despite my orders, he wants to marry her.

JACQUES: Ah! He is wrong.

HARPAGON: Isn't it frightful for a son to wish to compete with his father? Shouldn't he, out of respect, refrain from meddling with my intentions?

JACQUES: You are right. Let me speak to him while you stay here. *(He goes to* CLÉANTE *at the other end of the stage.)*

CLÉANTE: Well, all right, if he wants to appoint you as judge, I won't hold back. I don't care who the judge is, and I am willing to refer our differences to you, Jacques.

JACQUES: I am honored.

CLÉANTE: I love a young lady who returns my affection and who tenderly accepts the offer of my love. But my father decides to come along and interfere in our love by making her an offer himself.

JACQUES: He's certainly wrong.

CLÉANTE: Shouldn't he be ashamed, at his age, to think of marrying? Does it still become him to be amorous? Shouldn't he leave that to younger people?

JACQUES: You're right. He's joking. Let me have a word with him. *(He goes back to* HARPAGON.*)* Well, your son isn't as difficult as you think, and he will be reasonable. He says that he knows the respect he owes you, that he was only carried away by momentary passion, and that he will not refuse to submit to your wishes, provided that you will treat him better than you now do, and will give him someone in marriage with whom he will be content.

HARPAGON: Ah! In that case, Jacques, tell him that he can expect everything of me, and that, except for Mariane, I give him freedom to choose whomever he wishes.

JACQUES: Let me handle it. (*He goes to* CLÉANTE.) Well, your father isn't so unreasonable as you make out. He explained that your violence angered him; that he objects only to your behavior, and that he is quite willing to agree to what you wish, provided you behave gently and show him the deference, the respect, and the submission a son owes a father.

CLÉANTE: Ah! Jacques, you may assure him that if he will give me Mariane, he will always find me the most submissive of men, and I shall never do anything against his wishes.

JACQUES (*to* HARPAGON): Everything's arranged. He agrees to what you say.

HARPAGON: Then things will go excellently.

JACQUES (*to* CLÉANTE): Everything's arranged. He is satisfied with your promise.

CLÉANTE: Heaven be praised!

JACQUES: Gentlemen, you have only to talk together. You are in agreement now; you were about to quarrel simply for want of understanding each other.

CLÉANTE: Good Jacques, I am indebted to you for the rest of my life.

JACQUES: It is nothing, sir.

HARPAGON: You have pleased me, Jacques, and you deserve a reward. (HARPAGON *reaches into his pocket;* JACQUES *extends his hand, but* HARPAGON *only pulls out a handkerchief.*) Go, now, I'll keep it in mind, I assure you.

JACQUES: Your servant, sir. (*Exit.*)

CLÉANTE: I ask your pardon, father, for the anger I've shown.

HARPAGON: It's nothing.

CLÉANTE: I assure you that I am filled with regret.

HARPAGON: And I, I am filled with joy to see you so reasonable.

CLÉANTE: How generous of you to forget my fault so quickly!

HARPAGON: A father easily forgets his children's faults when they return to their duty.

CLÉANTE: Ah, then you harbor no resentment for all my outrageous behavior?

HARPAGON: You force me not to, by the submission and respect which you show.

CLÉANTE: Father, I promise you that to my death I will preserve the memory of your kindness.

HARPAGON: And as for me, I promise that there is nothing which you shall not obtain from me.

CLÉANTE: Oh, father, I ask no more of you; you have given me enough in giving me Mariane.

HARPAGON: What?

CLÉANTE: I say, father, that I am quite content, and that you give me everything when you give me Mariane.

HARPAGON: Who's talking about giving you Mariane?

CLÉANTE: You, father.

HARPAGON: Me?

CLÉANTE: Certainly.

HARPAGON: What! *You* are the one who promised to renounce her!

CLÉANTE: Me? Renounce her?

HARPAGON: Yes!

CLÉANTE: Not at all!

HARPAGON: Then you haven't given up your claim to her?

CLÉANTE: On the contrary, I hold to it now more than ever.

HARPAGON: What! Again, you scoundrel?

CLÉANTE: Nothing can change me!

HARPAGON: Let me at you, you wretch!

CLÉANTE: Do whatever you please.

HARPAGON: I forbid you from ever coming into my sight.

CLÉANTE: Fine.

HARPAGON: I disown you.

CLÉANTE: Disown me.

HARPAGON: I renounce you as my son.

CLÉANTE: So be it.

HARPAGON: I disinherit you.

CLÉANTE: Whatever you please.

HARPAGON (*rushing out*): I give you my curse. (*Exit.*)

CLÉANTE (*shouting after him*): I don't want any of your gifts.

LA FLÈCHE (*entering from the garden with a money box in his hand*): Ah! sir, I've found you just in the nick of time. Follow me, quickly!

CLÉANTE: What's the matter?

LA FLÈCHE: Follow me, I say. Everything's all right.

CLÉANTE: How do you mean?

LA FLÈCHE: Here's your answer. (*Shows him a money box.*)

CLÉANTE: What?

LA FLÈCHE: I've kept my eye on this all day.

CLÉANTE: What is it?

LA FLÈCHE: Your father's money—which I've got hold of.

CLÉANTE: How did you get it?

LA FLÈCHE: You'll hear everything. Let's get away—I hear him calling. (*Exeunt.*)

HARPAGON (*enters from the garden, hatless and shouting*): Thieves, thieves! Assassins! Murderers! Justice, merciful Heaven! I am lost, I am killed! They've cut my throat, they've stolen my money! Who can it be? What has become of him? Where is he? Where is he hiding? What shall I do to find him? Where shall I run? Where shall I not run? Is he there? Is he here? (*Seeing his own shadow on the wall.*) Who is that? Stop! (*Seizing his own arm.*) Give me back my money, villain! Ah! It's me. My mind's in a turmoil and I don't know where I am, who I am, or what I'm doing. Alas! My poor money, my poor money, my dear friend, they have deprived me of you. And with you taken away from me, I have lost my support, my consolation, my joy; all is over for me, and I have nothing further to do on earth. Without you, life is impossible. All is over, I can bear no more, I am dying, I am dead, I am buried. Will no one revive me by returning my dear money or by telling me who took it? Eh? (*To someone in the audience*) What are you saying? There's no one. Whoever did this must have been watching for exactly the right moment, and he chose just the time when I was speaking to that treacherous son of mine. I must go out! I must find the police and have the whole household examined: servants, valets, son, daughter—and myself, too. What a mob! Everyone I look at is suspect, and they all look like thieves. Eh? What are they talking about over there? Of the man who robbed me? What's that noise up there? Is the thief there? For Heaven's sake, if anyone knows anything about the thief, I implore him to tell me. Isn't he hiding down there among you? They are all looking up at me and beginning to laugh. You'll see, doubtless, that they all had a share in the theft. Come, quickly, police, provosts, judges, thumbscrews and racks, gibbets and executioners. I'll have everybody hanged—and if I don't get back my money, I'll hang myself afterwards.

ACT V

(*Enter* HARPAGON, *an Officer, and his Clerk.*)

OFFICER (*calmly*): Let me handle it. I know my business, thank Heaven. Today isn't the first time I've dealt with robbery. I wish I had a bag of a thousand francs for every person I've had hanged.

HARPAGON (*excitedly*): Every magistrate is involved in this affair; and if they don't get my money back, I'll demand justice of Justice itself.

OFFICER: We shall take all the necessary steps. There was, you said, in the box . . . ?

HARPAGON: Exactly ten thousand écus!

OFFICER: Ten thousand écus?

HARPAGON: Ten thousand écus.

OFFICER: A considerable theft.

HARPAGON: No torture is too great for such an enormous crime; and if it goes unpunished, the most sacred things are no longer safe.

OFFICER: What denominations was this sum in?

HARPAGON: In good louis d'or and solid pistoles.

OFFICER: Whom do you suspect of the theft?

HARPAGON: Everyone. I want you to arrest the whole city and the suburbs.

OFFICER: Take my word for it, we must not frighten anybody, but must try to get the evidence quietly so that later we can rigorously act to recover the money stolen from you.

JACQUES (*enters at the far end of the stage, speaking over his shoulder*): I'll be back soon. Meanwhile, have them slit his throat, scorch his feet, put him in boiling water, and hang him from the ceiling.

HARPAGON: Who? The man who robbed me?

JACQUES: I'm talking about the suckling pig your steward has just sent in for supper, and I want to prepare it for you in my own special way.

HARPAGON: That's not the problem; here is a gentleman to whom you must talk about another matter.

OFFICER: Don't be alarmed. I'm not the man to accuse you unfairly, and matters will be handled gently.

JACQUES: Is the gentleman a dinner guest?

OFFICER: You must hide nothing from your master, my friend.

JACQUES: Good Lord, sir, I'll show all I know, and serve you the best I can.

HARPAGON: That's not the problem.

JACQUES: If I don't give you as sumptuous a dinner as I'd like to, it's your steward's fault, who clipped my wings with the scissors of his economy.

HARPAGON: Wretch, it concerns something other than supper; I want you to give me some information about the money someone has stolen from me.

JACQUES: Someone has taken your money?

HARPAGON: Yes, scoundrel. And I'll have you hanged if you don't give it back.

OFFICER: Heavens, don't abuse him. I see by his face that

he's an honest man and that without being jailed he will tell you what you want to know. Yes, my friend, if you tell us, no harm will come to you, and your master will reward you appropriately. Today someone stole his money, and you must know something about the affair.

JACQUES (*aside*): Here's just what I need to be revenged on the steward: ever since he came into the house he's been favored; they listen only to his advice. And I won't forget the beating I got.

HARPAGON: What are you mumbling?

OFFICER: Let him alone. He's getting ready to do as you wish. I told you he was an honest man.

JACQUES: Sir, if you want the truth, I think that your steward is responsible.

HARPAGON: Valère?

JACQUES: Yes.

HARPAGON: He, who seemed so faithful?

JACQUES: The very same! I think he's the one who robbed you.

HARPAGON: On what grounds do you think so?

JACQUES: On what grounds?

HARPAGON: Yes.

JACQUES: I think so on the grounds . . . that I think so.

OFFICER: But it is necessary to cite what evidence you have.

HARPAGON: Have you seen him prowling around the place where I put my money?

JACQUES: Yes, indeed. Where was your money?

HARPAGON: In the garden.

JACQUES: Exactly. I saw him prowling around in the garden. What was the money in?

HARPAGON: In a money box.

JACQUES: That's it. I saw him with a money box.

HARPAGON: What was this money box like? I'll soon see if it is mine.

JACQUES: What was it like?

HARPAGON: Yes!

JACQUES: It was like . . . it was like a money box.

OFFICER: Naturally, that's understood. But describe it a little, so we can visualize it.

JACQUES: It is a large money box.

HARPAGON: The one they stole from me is small.

JACQUES: Yes! it *is* small, if you consider its size. But I call it large considering its contents.

OFFICER: What color is it?

JACQUES: What color?

OFFICER: Yes.

JACQUES: Its color is . . . well, a certain color. Can't you help me express it?

HARPAGON: Ah!

JACQUES: Isn't it red?

HARPAGON: No, gray.

JACQUES: Ah, yes, grayish red; that's what I meant.

HARPAGON: There's no doubt about it. That's absolutely it. Write, sir, write down his testimony. Heavens! Whom can I trust from now on? One can no longer swear to anything. After this I could believe that I would rob myself.

JACQUES: Sir, here he comes. Be sure not to tell him that it was I who revealed this to you.

(*Enter* VALÈRE.)

HARPAGON: Come here! Come and confess the blackest deed, the most horrible crime ever committed.

VALÈRE: What do you mean, sir?

HARPAGON: What, traitor! You do not blush for your crime?

VALÈRE: What crime are you talking about?

HARPAGON: What crime am I talking about? Infamous wretch! As though you don't know what I mean. You seek to cover up in vain. The deed is revealed; I have just learned all. Ah! To abuse my kindness like this and to get yourself into my house expressly to betray me, to play such a trick on me!

VALÈRE: Sir, since everything has been revealed to you, I will not sidestep or deny the matter.

JACQUES (*aside*): Aha! Could I have unconsciously guessed right?

VALÈRE: I planned to speak to you, and I wanted to wait for a favorable moment, but since this is the way things are, I implore you not to be angry, and to listen to my motives.

HARPAGON: And what fine motives can you give me, infamous thief?

VALÈRE: Ah, sir, I do not deserve these names. True, I have committed an offense against you, but, after all, the fault is pardonable.

HARPAGON: What? Pardonable? A sneak attack, a murder like that?

VALÈRE: For Heaven's sake, don't get angry. When you have heard me out, you will see that the harm isn't as great as you make it.

HARPAGON: The harm isn't as great as I make it! What! My blood! My vitals! Villain!

VALÈRE: Sir, your blood has not fallen into evil hands. I

am of a rank not to wrong it, and there is nothing in all this that I cannot fully repair.

HARPAGON: That is fully my intention; you must restore to me what you have robbed me of.

VALÈRE: Sir, your honor will be fully satisfied.

HARPAGON: There is no question of honor involved. But tell me, who drove you to such a deed?

VALÈRE: Ah, you have to ask me that?

HARPAGON: I most certainly do.

VALÈRE: A god who is his own excuse for all that he makes us do: Love.

HARPAGON: Love?

VALÈRE: Yes.

HARPAGON: A fine love, a fine love, indeed. Love of my louis d'or.

VALÈRE: No, sir, your wealth did not tempt me at all; that does not dazzle me, and I insist that I care nothing for all your property, provided you let me keep what I have.

HARPAGON: By the devil, I'll do no such thing! I will not let you keep it. What insolence to want to keep what he has stolen!

VALÈRE: You call it stealing?

HARPAGON: Yes, I call it stealing. A treasure like that!

VALÈRE: It is indeed a treasure, and doubtless the most precious you have; but it is not losing it to let me have it. On my knees I ask for this treasure full of charms. And, indeed, you must award it to me.

HARPAGON: I'll do nothing of the sort. Why talk like this?

VALÈRE: We have pledged our mutual faith; we have sworn never to be parted.

HARPAGON: The pledge is admirable, and the promise amusing.

VALÈRE: Yes, we are bound to one another, forever.

HARPAGON: I'll prevent that, I guarantee you.

VALÈRE: Nothing but death can separate us.

HARPAGON: You are devilishly set on my money.

VALÈRE: Sir, I have already told you that your money did not drive me to do what I have done. My heart was not at all moved by the motives you think; a more noble goal inspired my resolution.

HARPAGON: Next you'll see that it is from Christian charity that he wants my money. But I'll take care of that; and the law, you outrageous scoundrel, will give me justice.

VALÈRE: Do what you please, and I shall readily suffer all the violence you like; but I beg you to believe, at least, that if harm has been done, I alone am to blame, and that your daughter is in no way guilty.

HARPAGON: I'm sure of that! It would certainly be strange if my daughter were involved in this crime. But I want to regain my property and I want you to confess where you've carried my treasure off to.

VALÈRE: I? I haven't carried your treasure out of the house.

HARPAGON (*aside*): Ah, my dear money box. (*Aloud*) Not left my house?

VALÈRE: No, sir.

HARPAGON: Ah! Tell me now, you haven't tampered . . . ?

VALÈRE: I? Tamper? Ah, you wrong us. I burn with a wholly pure and respectful ardor.

HARPAGON (*aside*): Burn for my money box?

VALÈRE: I would rather die than express any offensive thought. Your treasure is too wise and too modest for that.

HARPAGON (*aside*): My money box too modest!

VALÈRE: All my desires are limited to the pleasures of gazing, and nothing criminal has profaned the passion those beautiful eyes have inspired in me.

HARPAGON (*aside*): My money box's beautiful eyes? He talks like a lover about his mistress.

VALÈRE: Sir, Dame Claude knows the whole truth, and she can testify—

HARPAGON: What? My servant is an accomplice?

VALÈRE: Yes, sir, she was a witness to our engagement, and after seeing the purity of my love, she helped me persuade your daughter to give me her pledge and to accept mine.

HARPAGON (*aside*): Ah! Does the fear of justice make him rave? (*To* VALÈRE.) Why do you bring in this nonsense about my daughter?

VALÈRE: Sir, I say that I have labored greatly to persuade her modesty to accept my love.

HARPAGON: Whose modesty?

VALÈRE: Your daughter's. And only yesterday she consented to sign a marriage agreement.

HARPAGON: My daughter signed a promise of marriage?

VALÈRE: Yes, sir, just as I signed one to her.

HARPAGON: Heavens! Another disgrace!

JACQUES (*to the* OFFICER): Write, sir, write it down.

HARPAGON: More trouble! Further agony! (*To the* OFFICER) Come, sir, do your duty and arraign him as a thief and a seducer.

VALÈRE: These are names which do not apply to me; and when you all know who I am—

(*Enter* ÉLISE, MARIANE, *and* FROSINE.)

HARPAGON (*to* ÉLISE): Ah! Shameless daughter, daughter unworthy of a father like me! This is how you put into practice the lessons I taught you. You let yourself fall in love with an infamous thief, and you pledge yourself to him without my consent. But both of you will see what a mistake you have made. Four solid walls will answer for your conduct; (*to* VALÈRE) and a solid gibbet will satisfy me for your audacity.

VALÈRE: It will not be your rage which will judge this affair; at least the law will give me a hearing before condemning me.

HARPAGON: I was wrong to say a gibbet; you will be broken alive on the rack.

ÉLISE (*kneeling before her father*): Oh, father, show some human feeling, I beg you, and do not push matters with all the violence of paternal power. Do not yield to the first impulses of your rage, but give yourself time to consider what you will do. Take the trouble to know better who he is who angers you. He is quite different from what your eyes judge, and you will find it less strange that I have given myself to him when you know that without him you would not have me now. Yes, father, he is the man who saved me from the great danger I encountered in the ocean, and to whom you owe the life of this very daughter who—

HARPAGON: All this is nothing, and it would have been better for me if he had let you drown, than do what he has done.

ÉLISE: Father, I implore you by your paternal love to—

HARPAGON: No, no. I don't want to hear anything. The law must do its duty.

JACQUES (*aside*): You'll pay me for the beating I got.

FROSINE (*aside*): What a strange situation.

(*Enter* SIGNOR ANSELM.)

ANSELM: What is this, Signor Harpagon? I see you are quite upset.

HARPAGON: Ah, Signor Anselm, you see here the most unfortunate of men. A lot of trouble and disorder has come up about the contract you have come to sign. They have murdered my fortune, they have murdered my honor; and there is the traitor, the wretch who has violated the most sacred rights, who sneaked into my house disguised as a servant in order to steal my money and seduce my daughter.

VALÈRE: Who is even thinking about the money which you are making such a fuss over?

HARPAGON: Yes, they have exchanged promises of marriage. This affront concerns you, Signor Anselm; it is you who should retaliate with the law, and it is you who should undergo the legal expenses to get revenge for his insolence.

ANSELM: It is not my intention to marry anyone by force or to claim a heart which has given itself elsewhere. But, as for your interests, I am ready to defend them as my own.

HARPAGON: Monsieur, here is a worthy officer, who neglects, he told me, none of the functions of his office. (*To the* OFFICER) Indict him, sir, as necessary, and make the charges very criminal.

VALÈRE: I do not see what crime can be made out of my love for your daughter, nor to what punishment I can be condemned for our marriage engagement. When you know who I am——

HARPAGON: I scorn all these stories. Nowadays society is full of fake noblemen, impostors who take advantage of their obscurity to cloak themselves insolently in the first illustrious name that pops into their heads.

VALÈRE: I would have you know that I have too noble a heart to deck myself out in something not my own, and that all Naples can bear witness to my birth.

ANSELM: One moment, please. Be careful of what you say. You risk more than you realize, for you speak before a man who knows all Naples, and who can easily see through any tale you make up.

VALÈRE (*putting on his hat with dignity*): I am not a man who has anything to fear. If Naples is well known to you, you know who was Don Thomas d'Alburcy.

ANSELM: I know him indeed; and few men have known him better than I.

HARPAGON: What do I care about Don Thomas or Don Anyone! (*Seeing two candles burning,* HARPAGON *blows one out.*)

ANSELM: For Heaven's sake, let him speak. Let us see what he means.

VALÈRE: I mean that it is to him that I owe my birth.

ANSELM: Him?

VALÈRE: Yes.

ANSELM: Come, you are jesting. Get some other story which you can use better, and do not try to save yourself by such an imposture.

VALÈRE: Learn to speak more civilly. It is not an imposture, and I claim nothing which I cannot easily prove.

ANSELM: What? Do you dare to call yourself the son of Don Thomas d'Alburcy?

VALÈRE: Yes, I dare, and I am ready to maintain this truth against anyone.

ANSELM: His audacity is fantastic. Learn, to your confusion, that at least sixteen years ago the man of whom you speak perished at sea with his children and his wife while trying to save their lives from the cruel persecutions which accompanied the uprising in Naples, persecutions which caused the exile of several noble families.

VALÈRE: Yes, but learn to *your* confusion, that his son, seven years old, together with a servant, was saved from the shipwreck by a Spanish vessel, and it is this rescued son who speaks to you now. Learn, too, that the captain of the vessel, touched by my misfortune, took pity on me and brought me up as his own son; and that soldiering has been my profession ever since I could bear arms; and that I have recently learned that my father is not dead, as I had always believed; that, as I was passing through this city to find him, a heaven-sent accident allowed me to see the charming Elise; that this sight made me a slave of her beauty, and that the power of my love and the severity of her father made me decide to introduce myself into his house, and to send someone else in search of my parents.

ANSELM: What proofs—beyond your words—have you to assure us that this is not a fable constructed on a truth?

VALÈRE: The Spanish captain; a ruby seal which was my father's; an agate bracelet which my mother had put on my arm; old Pedro, the servant who was saved with me in the wreck.

MARIANE: Alas! I can vouch for your words; this is no imposture. All that you say proves clearly to me that you are my brother.

VALÈRE: You, my sister?

MARIANE: Yes, my heart was stirred the moment you began to speak. Our mother, who will be overjoyed to see you, has told me a thousand times of our family's misfortunes. Heaven did not let us perish either in that sad shipwreck, but it saved our lives only at the cost of our liberty, for pirates picked up my mother and me from the wreckage of our vessel. After ten years of slavery a happy accident gave us our freedom, and we returned to Naples, where we found all our property sold and no news about my father. We went on to Genoa, where my mother recovered some little scraps of a dissipated family inheritance. And from there, fleeing the barbarous injustice of her relatives, we came here, where she is now scarcely able to go on living.

ANSELM: Oh, Heaven, how great is the evidence of your power! And how plainly you show that you alone perform miracles. Embrace me, my children, and unite your joys with those of your father.

VALÈRE: You are our father?

MARIANE: It is you for whom my mother has wept so many years?

ANSELM: Yes, my daughter, yes, my son, I am Don Thomas d'Alburcy, whom Heaven rescued from the sea with all the money I had with me, and who, believing you all dead for over sixteen years, after a long journey prepared to seek the consolation of a new family with a gentle and prudent girl. The insecurities which I experienced in Naples made me renounce it for ever, and, having found means to sell all that I owned there, I settled here under the name of Anselm, endeavoring to forget the sorrows of this other name which caused me so much grief.

HARPAGON: Is this your son?

ANSELM: Yes.

HARPAGON: Then I hold you responsible for payment of the ten thousand écus he has stolen.

ANSELM: He? Robbed you?

HARPAGON: Yes, indeed.

VALÈRE: Who told you so?

HARPAGON: Jacques.

VALÈRE (*to* JACQUES): It's you who says so?

JACQUES: You can see that I say nothing.

HARPAGON: Yes. Here is the officer who took down the deposition.

VALÉRE: Can you believe me capable of so base an action?

HARPAGON: Capable or not capable, I want my money back.

(*Enter* CLÉANTE.)

CLÉANTE: Don't be troubled, father, and don't accuse any-one. I have learned something about your money, and I have come to tell you that if you let me wed Mariane, your money will be returned.

HARPAGON: Where is it?

CLÉANTE: Don't worry about it. It is in a place I can vouch for. Everything depends on me. It is for you to tell me what you decide; and you can choose either to give me Mariane or to lose your money box.

HARPAGON: Nothing has been taken out of it?

CLÉANTE: Not a thing. Make up your mind whether to accept this marriage and join your consent with that of her mother, who allows her to choose between the two of us.

MARIANE: But you do not know that this consent is not enough, and that Heaven has restored to me my brother (*pointing to* VALÈRE) and also (*pointing to* ANSELM) my father from whom you must get consent.

ANSELM: My children, Heaven did not restore me to you that I should thwart your desires. Monsieur Harpagon, you surely realize that a young girl's choice will fall on the son rather than on the father. Come, do not make people say what need not be heard; consent, as I do, to this double marriage.

HARPAGON: I must see my money box before I can decide.

CLÈANTE: You will see it safe and sound.

HARPAGON: I have no money to give my children for their marriage.

ANSELM: Well, I have enough for all. Don't worry about that.

HARPAGON: Will you pledge to pay the expenses for the marriages of these two?

ANSELM: Yes, I pledge it. Are you satisfied?

HARPAGON: Yes, provided that you give me a new suit of clothes for the wedding.

ANSELM: Agreed! Come, let us rejoice in the happiness this day has brought us.

OFFICER: One moment, gentlemen, one moment. Easy, if you please. Who is going to pay me for these depositions?

HARPAGON: We have nothing to do with your depositions.

OFFICER: Oh, but I don't intend to have drawn them up for nothing.

HARPAGON (*pointing to* JACQUES): For your payment, here is a man whom I give you to hang.

JACQUES: Ah, what can one do? They beat me for telling the truth, and they want to hang me for telling a lie.

ANSELM: Monsieur Harpagon, you must forgive him his hoax.

HARPAGON: Then will you pay the officer?

ANSELM: So be it. Come, let us go quickly to share our joy with your mother.

HARPAGON: And I, to see my darling money box.

John Gay:

THE BEGGAR'S OPERA

When the Puritans in the middle of the seventeenth century abolished the English monarchy and replaced it with the Commonwealth, they banned the staging of plays, announcing that "all stage-players are hereby declared to be, and are, and shall be taken to be, rogues." But in 1656 William D'Avenant circumvented the injunction against the theater by calling his *Siege of Rhodes* an opera, "a story sung in recitative music." When the monarchy was restored in 1660, the drama again began to flourish, but the operatic tradition remained, and in the early eighteenth century Italian opera gained popularity in England. The foreign form, however, met opposition from English literati, and John Gay's *Beggar's Opera* (1728) is partly a burlesque of the new importation. Setting the words of his songs to popular English, Irish, and Scottish tunes, Gay (1685-1732) wrote a musical play which offered a comic contrast to the high-flown Italian fare.

When we witness a comedy, Charles Lamb wrote, "the whole is a passing pageant, where we should sit as unconcerned at the issues, for life or death, as at a battle of the frogs and mice." Where in tragedy, he explains, the actor must convince us of the truth of the role, in comedy we ought to be fully conscious that villainy is merely *acted* villainy. Because fear is incompatible with amused laughter (we might note here that nervous and hysterical laughter have nothing to do with the laughter of comedy), a stage villain cannot be both terrifying and funny; his threats are grotesque rather than dire. Similarly, because pity interferes with amusement, a stage beggar cannot be too realistic; we must not feel, for example, that he is actually famished or shivering in his rags. The comic actor often has a mannered style which continually prevents us from taking his role too seriously. One has only to think of Harpo Marx or Charlie Chaplin to realize that the comic presentation of poverty is very different from poverty itself.

229

John Gay's *Beggar's Opera* has often been praised for its
vivid picture of London life in the early eighteenth century,
but the piece is primarily a comedy and not a sociological
document. For one thing, the characters not only speak more
cleverly than actual people of that or any other period, but
they frequently burst into song in a most unrealistic manner.
Although the bulk of operatic literature is tragic, opera is,
parodoxically, especially suited to comedy because it is so unrealistic—so *obviously* stylized—an art. Qualities which sometimes bother an inexperienced spectator at serious opera—the
elephantine heroine, for example, whose beauty and grace is
the subject of the dying hero's lengthy aria—can add to the
fun of comic opera. The world created by comedy must be
real enough to have some meaning for us, yet it must be
unreal enough for us to laugh at it rather than be oppressed
by it. In *The Beggar's Opera* we find a sufficiently plausible
London inhabited by persons who bear a relation to our
neighbors (the first audiences recognized in Peachum, the
gang's organizer, Robert Walpole, the prime minister), yet
we surely do not feel that we are looking at an exact dupli-
cate of life as it is or ever was. The citizens of Gay's world
not only sing and speak well, but they have standards which
strike us as obviously absurd. In Gay's comic world Mrs.
Peachum is pleased that her young servant, Filch, is getting a
good education as a thief; her husband, Peachum (informer),
is righteously indignant with lawyers because "they don't care
that anybody should get a clandestine livelihood but themselves." And young Polly Peachum has offended her parents
by marrying—and, to make matters worse, marrying not for
honor or money but for love. "Love him!" shouts her outraged mother, "worse and worse! I thought the girl had been
better bred."

Yet the world of *The Beggar's Opera* is not merely a fanciful realm with no relation to our own. It has its own strict
code of manners, and this code bears a curious similarity to
our rules of behavior—yet with a difference. Peachum, like
any businessman, is pleased that Black Moll "is very active
and industrious," and he is indignant that Tom Gagg is "a
lazy dog." But the comedy of the situation is that Moll is a
thieving prostitute, and Tom a crook. The characters in Gay's
world commend industry and activity, as we usually do, but
their industry and activity are applied to practices which we
consider immoral, thus suggesting that thieves and business-
men are one. Early in the nineteenth century William Hazlitt
considered the play a profoundly moral piece, and was willing
to "hazard a conjecture that the acting of the Beggar's Opera
a certain number of nights every year since it was first brought

out, has done more towards putting down the practice of highway robbery, than all the gibbets that ever were erected." His contemporary, Samuel Taylor Coleridge, however, was filled with "horror and disgust" when he saw the play. Hazlitt overstressed the moral effect, Coleridge seems to have overstressed the immorality; as the stage history of the play suggests, Peachum's world has entertained rather than frightened or disturbed or demoralized generations of theatergoers. The play is full of talk about hangings, yet the talk amuses us as talk about a real hanging would not. If it is the job of the comic artist to picture our follies, it is also his job to picture them in such a way that they entertain us. *The Beggar's Opera* had dozens of imitations (including *Polly*, by Gay himself), but none succeeded so well in depicting a world which is at once recognizable and yet "over the hills and far away."

The Beggar's Opera

PEACHUM
LOCKIT
MACHEATH
FILCH
JEMMY TWITCHER
CROOK-FINGER'D JACK
WAT DREARY
ROBIN OF BAGSHOT   } *Macheath's Gang*
NIMMING NED
HARRY PADINGTON
MATT OF THE MINT
BEN BUDGE
BEGGAR
PLAYER
MRS. PEACHUM
POLLY PEACHUM
LUCY LOCKIT
DIANA TRAPES
MRS. COAXER
DOLLY TRULL
MRS. VIXEN
BETTY DOXY
JENNY DIVER   } *Women of the Town*
MRS. SLAMMEKIN
SUKY TAWDRY
MOLLY BRAZEN
CONSTABLES, DRAWER, TURNKEY, &c.

INTRODUCTION

(BEGGAR, PLAYER)

BEGGAR: If Poverty be a Title to Poetry, I am sure No-body can dispute mine. I own myself of the Company of Beggars; and I make one at their Weekly Festivals at St. Giles. I have a small Yearly Salary for my Catches, and am welcome to a Dinner there whenever I please, which is more than most Poets can say.

PLAYER: As we live by the Muses, 'tis but Gratitude in us to encourage Poetical Merit where-ever we find it. The Muses, contrary to all other Ladies, pay no Distinction to Dress, and never partially mistake the Pertness of Embroidery for Wit, nor the Modesty of Want for Dulness. Be the Author who he will, we push his Play as far as it will go. So (though you are in Want) I wish you Success heartily.

BEGGAR: This Piece I own was originally writ for the celebrating the Marriage of James Chanter and Moll Lay, two most excellent Ballad-Singers. I have introduc'd the Similes that are in all your celebrated Operas: The Swallow, the Moth, the Bee, the Ship, the Flower, &c. Besides, I have a Prison Scene which the Ladies always reckon charmingly pathetick. As to the Parts, I have observ'd such a nice Impartiality to our two Ladies, that it is impossible for either of them to take Offence. I hope I may be forgiven, that I have not made my Opera throughout unnatural, like those in vogue; for I have no Recitative: Excepting this, as I have consented to have neither Prologue nor Epilogue, it must be allow'd an Opera in all its forms. The Piece indeed hath been heretofore frequently represented by our selves in our great Room at St. Giles's, so that I cannot too often acknowledge your Charity in bringing it now on the Stage.

PLAYER: But I see 'tis time for us to withdraw; the Actors are preparing to begin. Play away the Overture. (*Exeunt.*)

233

ACT I

SCENE I

(PEACHUM'S *House.*)

PEACHUM *sitting at a table with a large book of accounts before him*

AIR

Through all the Employments of Life
Each Neighbour abuses his Brother;
Whore and Rogue they call Husband and Wife:
All Professions be-rogue one another.
The Priest calls the Lawyer a Cheat,
The Lawyer be-knaves the Divine;
And the Statesman, because he's so great,
Thinks his Trade as honest as mine.

A Lawyer is an honest Employment, so is mine. Like me too he acts in a double Capacity, both against Rogues and for 'em; for 'tis but fitting that we should protect and encourage Cheats, since we live by them.

SCENE II

PEACHUM, FILCH

FILCH: Sir, Black Moll hath sent word her Tryal comes on in the Afternoon, and she hopes you will order Matters so as to bring her off.

PEACHUM: Why, she may plead her Belly[1] at worst; to my Knowledge she hath taken care of that Security. But as the Wench is very active and industrious, you may satisfy her that I'll soften the Evidence.

FILCH: Tom Gagg, Sir, is found guilty.

PEACHUM: A lazy Dog! When I took him the time before, I told him what he would come to if he did not mend his Hand. This is Death without Reprieve. I may venture to Book him. (*Writes.*) For Tom Gagg, forty Pounds. Let Betty Sly know that I'll save her from Transportation, for I can get more by her staying in England.

FILCH: Betty hath brought more Goods into our Lock[2] to-

[1] Pregnant women were not executed.
[2] A cant word for a warehouse where stolen goods are kept.

234

year than any five of the Gang; and in truth, 'tis a pity to lose so good a Customer.

PEACHUM: If none of the Gang take her off, she may, in the common course of Business, live a Twelve-month longer. I love to let Women scape. A good Sportsman always lets the Hen Partridges fly, because the breed of the Game depends upon them. Besides, here the Law allows us no Reward; there is nothing to be got by the Death of Women—except our Wives.

FILCH: Without dispute, she is a fine Woman! 'Twas to her I was oblig'd for my Education, and (to say a bold Word) she hath train'd up more young Fellows to the Business than the Gaming-table.

PEACHUM: Truly, Filch, thy Observation is right. We and the Surgeons are more beholden to Women than all the Professions besides.

AIR

FILCH: *'Tis Woman that seduces all Mankind,*
By her we first were taught the wheedling Arts:
Her very Eyes can cheat; when most she's kind,
She tricks us of our Money with our Hearts.
For her, like Wolves by night we roam for Prey,
And practise ev'ry Fraud to bribe her Charms;
For Suits of Love, like Law, are won by Pay,
And Beauty must be fee'd into our Arms.

PEACHUM: But make haste to Newgate, Boy, and let my Friends know what I intend; for I love to make them easy one way or other.

FILCH: When a Gentleman is long kept in suspence, Penitence may break his Spirit ever after. Besides, Certainty gives a Man a good Air upon his Tryal, and makes him risque another without Fear or Scruple. But I'll away, for 'tis a Pleasure to be the Messenger of Comfort to Friends in Affliction.

SCENE III

PEACHUM

But 'tis now high time to look about me for a decent Execution against next Sessions. I hate a lazy Rogue, by whom one can get nothing 'til he is hang'd. A Register of the Gang, (*Reading.*) "Crook-finger'd Jack." A Year and a half in the Service; Let me see how much the Stock owes to his Industry; one, two, three, four, five Gold Watches, and

seven Silver ones. A mighty clean-handed Fellow! Sixteen
Snuff-boxes, five of them of true Gold. Six dozen of Handkerchiefs, four silver-hilted Swords, half a dozen of Shirts, three
Tye-Perriwigs, and a Piece of Broad Cloth. Considering these
are only the Fruits of his leisure Hours, I don't know a pret-
tier Fellow, for no Man alive hath a more engaging Presence
of Mind upon the Road. "Wat Dreary, alias Brown Will," an
irregular Dog, who hath an underhand way of disposing of
his Goods. I'll try him only for a Sessions or two longer upon
his good Behaviour. "Harry Padington," a poor petty-larceny
Rascal, without the least Genius; that Fellow, though he were
to live these six Months, will never come to the Gallows with
any Credit. "Slippery Sam;" he goes off the next Sessions, for
the Villain hath the Impudence to have views of following
his Trade as a Taylor, which he calls an honest Employment.
"Mat of the Mint;" listed not above a Month ago, a promising
sturdy Fellow, and diligent in his way; somewhat too bold
and hasty, and may raise good Contributions on the Publick,
if he does not cut himself short by Murder. "Tom Tipple" a
guzzling soaking Sot, who is always too drunk to stand himself, or to make others stand. A Cart is absolutely necessary
for him. "Robin of Bagshot, alias Gorgon, alias Bluff Bob,
alias Carbuncle, alias Bob Booty."

SCENE IV

PEACHUM, MRS. PEACHUM

MRS. PEACHUM: What of Bob Booty, Husband? I hope
nothing bad hath betided him. You know, my Dear, he's a
favourite Customer of mine. 'Twas he made me a Present of
this Ring.

PEACHUM: I have set his Name down in the Black-List,
that's all, my Dear; he spends his Life among Women, and
as soon as his Money is gone, one or other of the Ladies will
hang him for the Reward, and there's forty Pound lost to us
for-ever.

MRS. PEACHUM: You know, my Dear, I never meddle in
matters of Death; I always leave those Affairs to you. Women
indeed are bitter bad Judges in these cases, for they are so
partial to the Brave that they think every Man handsome who
is going to the Camp or the Gallows.

AIR

If any Wench Venus's Girdle wear,
  Though she be never so ugly;
Lillys and Roses will quickly appear,

And her Face look wond'rous smuggly.
Beneath the left Ear so fit but a Cord,
(A Rope so charming a Zone is!)
The Youth in his Cart hath the Air of a Lord,
And we cry, There dies an Adonis!

But really, Husband, you should not be too hard-hearted, for you never had a finer, braver set of Men than at present. We have not had a Murder among them all, these seven Months. And truly, my Dear, that is a great Blessing.

PEACHUM: What a dickens is the Woman always a whimpring about Murder for? No Gentleman is ever look'd upon the worse for killing a Man in his own Defence; and if Business cannot be carried on without it, what would you have a Gentleman do?

MRS. PEACHUM: If I am in the wrong, my Dear, you must excuse me, for No-body can help the Frailty of an over-scrupulous Conscience.

PEACHUM: Murder is as fashionable a Crime as a Man can be guilty of. How many fine Gentlemen have we in Newgate every Year, purely upon that Article! If they have wherewithal to persuade the Jury to bring it in Manslaughter, what are they the worse for it? So, my Dear, have done upon this Subject. Was Captain Macheath here this Morning, for the Bank-notes he left with you last Week?

MRS. PEACHUM: Yes, my Dear; and though the Bank hath stopt Payment, he was so cheerful and so agreeable! Sure there is not a finer Gentleman upon the Road than the Captain! If he comes from Bagshot at any reasonable Hour he hath promis'd to make one this Evening with Polly and me, and Bob Booty, at a Party of Quadrille. Pray, my Dear, is the Captain rich?

PEACHUM: The Captain keeps too good Company ever to grow rich. Marybone[1] and the Chocolate-houses are his undoing. The Man that proposes to get Money by Play should have the Education of a fine Gentleman, and be train'd up to it from his Youth.

MRS. PEACHUM: Really, I am sorry upon Polly's Account the Captain hath not more Discretion. What business hath he to keep Company with Lords and Gentlemen? he should leave them to prey upon one another.

PEACHUM: Upon Polly's Account! What, a Plague, does the Woman mean?—Upon Polly's Account!

MRS. PEACHUM: Captain Macheath is very fond of the Girl.

PEACHUM: And what then?

[1] A gambling resort.

MRS. PEACHUM: If I have any Skill in the Ways of Women, I am sure Polly thinks him a very pretty Man.

PEACHUM: And what then? You would not be so mad to have the Wench marry him! Gamesters and Highwaymen are generally very good to their Whores, but they are very Devils to their Wives.

MRS. PEACHUM: But if Polly should be in love, how should we help her, or how can she help herself? Poor Girl, I am in the utmost Concern about her.

AIR

If Love the Virgin's Heart invade,
How, like a Moth, the simple Maid
Still plays about the Flame!
If soon she be not made a Wife,
Her Honour's sing'd, and then for Life,
She's—what I dare not name.

PEACHUM: Look ye, Wife. A handsome Wench in our way of Business is as profitable as at the Bar of a Temple Coffee-House, who looks upon it as her livelihood to grant every Liberty but one. You see I would indulge the Girl as far as prudently we can. In any thing, but Marriage! After that, my Dear, how shall we be safe? Are we not then in her Husband's Power? For a Husband hath the absolute Power over all a Wife's Secrets but her own. If the Girl had the Discretion of a Court Lady, who can have a dozen young Fellows at her Ear without complying with one, I should not matter it; but Polly is Tinder, and a Spark will at once set her on a Flame. Married! If the Wench does not know her own Profit, sure she knows her own Pleasure better than to make herself a Property! My Daughter to me should be, like a Court Lady to a Minister of State, a Key to the whole Gang. Married! If the Affair is not already done, I'll terrify her from it, by the Example of our Neighbours.

MRS. PEACHUM: May-hap, my Dear, you may injure the Girl. She loves to imitate the fine Ladies, and she may only allow the Captain Liberties in the View of Interest.

PEACHUM: But 'tis your Duty, my Dear, to warn the Girl against her Ruin, and to instruct her how to make the most of her Beauty. I'll go to her this moment, and sift her. In the mean time, Wife, rip out the Coronets and Marks of these dozen of Cambric Handkerchiefs, for I can dispose of them this Afternoon to a Chap in the City.

SCENE V

MRS. PEACHUM

Never was a Man more out of the way in an Argument than my Husband! Why must our Polly, forsooth, differ from her Sex, and love only her Husband? And why must Polly's Marriage, contrary to all Observation, make her the less followed by other Men? All Men are Thieves in Love, and like a Woman the better for being another's Property.

AIR

A Maid is like the golden Oar,
Which hath Guineas intrinsical in't,
Whose Worth is never known, before
It is try'd and imprest in the Mint.

A Wife's like a Guinea in Gold,
Stampt with the Name of her Spouse;
Now here, now there; is bought, or is sold;
And is current in every House.

SCENE VI

MRS. PEACHUM, FILCH

MRS. PEACHUM: Come hither, Filch. I am as fond of this Child, as though my Mind misgave me he were my own. He hath as fine a Hand at picking a Pocket as a Woman, and is as nimble-finger'd as a Juggler. If an unlucky Session does not cut the Rope of thy Life, I pronounce, Boy, thou wilt be a great Man in History. Where was your Post last Night, my Boy?

FILCH: I ply'd at the Opera, Madam; and considering 'twas neither dark nor rainy, so that there was no great Hurry in getting Chairs and Coaches, made a tolerable hand on't. These seven Handkerchiefs, Madam.

MRS. PEACHUM: Colour'd ones, I see. They are of sure Sale from our Warehouse at Redress among the Seamen.

FILCH: And this Snuff-box.

MRS. PEACHUM: Set in Gold! A pretty Encouragement this to a young Beginner.

FILCH: I had a fair tug at a charming Gold Watch. Pox take the Taylors for making the Fobs so deep and narrow! It stuck by the way, and I was forc'd to make my Escape under a Coach. Really, Madam, I fear I shall be cut off in the Flower of my Youth, so that every now and then (since I was pumpt) I have thoughts of taking up and going to Sea.

MRS. PEACHUM: You should go to Hockley in the Hole, and to Marybone, Child, to learn Valour. These are the Schools that have bred so many brave Men. I thought, Boy, by this time, thou hadst lost Fear as well as Shame. Poor Lad! how little does he know as yet of the Old-Bailey! For the first Fact I'll insure thee from being hang'd; and going to Sea, Filch, will come time enough upon a Sentence of Transportation. But now, since you have nothing better to do, ev'n go to your Book, and learn your Catechism; for really a Man makes but an ill Figure in the Ordinary's[1] Paper, who cannot give a satisfactory Answer to his Questions. But, hark you, my Lad. Don't tell me a Lye; for you know I hate a Lyar. Do you know of any thing that hath past between Captain Macheath and our Polly?

FILCH: I beg you, Madam, don't ask me; for I must either tell a Lye to you or to Miss Polly; for I promis'd her I would not tell.

MRS. PEACHUM: But when the Honour of our Family is concern'd—

FILCH: I shall lead a sad Life with Miss Polly, if ever she come to know that I told you. Besides, I would not willingly forfeit my own Honour by betraying any body.

MRS. PEACHUM: Yonder comes my Husband and Polly. Come, Filch, you shall go with me into my own Room, and tell me the whole Story. I'll give thee a glass of a most delicious Cordial that I keep for my own drinking.

SCENE VII

PEACHUM, POLLY

POLLY: I know as well as any of the fine Ladies how to make the most of my self and of my Man too. A Woman knows how to be mercenary, though she hath never been in a Court or at an Assembly. We have it in our Natures, Papa. If I allow Captain Macheath some trifling Liberties, I have this Watch and other visible Marks of his Favour to show for it. A Girl who cannot grant some Things, and refuse what is most material, will make but a poor hand of her Beauty, and soon be thrown upon the Common.

AIR

Virgins are like the fair Flower in its Lustre,
Which in the Garden enamels the Ground;
Near it the Bees in Play flutter and cluster,
And gaudy Butterflies frolick around.

[1] Chaplain's.

But, when once pluck'd, 'tis no longer alluring,
To Covent-Garden 'tis sent, (as yet sweet,)
There fades, and shrinks, and grows past all enduring,
Rots, stinks, and dies, and is trod under feet.

PEACHUM: You know, Polly, I am not against your toying and trifling with a Customer in the way of Business, or to get out a Secret, or so. But if I find out that you have play'd the fool and are married, you Jade you, I'll cut your Throat, Hussy. Now you know my Mind.

SCENE VIII

PEACHUM, POLLY, MRS. PEACHUM

AIR

MRS. PEACHUM, *in a very great Passion*

Our Polly is a sad Slut! nor heeds what we taught her.
I wonder any Man alive will ever rear a Daughter!
For she must have both Hoods and Gowns, and Hoops to
*   swell her Pride.*
With Scarfs and Stays, and Gloves and Lace; and she will
*   have Men beside;*
And when she's drest with Care and Cost, all-tempting, fine
*   and gay,*
As Men should serve a Cowcumber, she flings herself away.
*   Our Polly is a sad Slut, &c.*

You Baggage! you Hussy! you inconsiderate Jade! had you been hang'd, it would not have vex'd me, for that might have been your Misfortune; but to do such a mad thing by Choice! The Wench is married, Husband.

PEACHUM: Married! The Captain is a bold man, and will risque any thing for Money; to be sure he believes her a Fortune. Do you think your Mother and I should have liv'd comfortably so long together, if ever we had been married? Baggage!

MRS. PEACHUM: I knew she was always a proud Slut; and now the Wench hath play'd the Fool and married, because forsooth she would do like the Gentry. Can you support the expence of a Husband, Hussy, in gaming, drinking and whoring? have you Money enough to carry on the daily Quarrels of Man and Wife about who shall squander most? There are not many Husbands and Wifes, who can bear the Charges of plaguing one another in a handsome way. If you must be married, could you introduce no-body into our Family but a Highwayman? Why, thou foolish Jade, thou wilt be as ill-us'd, and as much neglected, as if thou hadst married a Lord!

PEACHUM: Let not your Anger, my Dear, break through the Rules of Decency, for the Captain looks upon himself in the Military Capacity, as a Gentleman by his Profession. Besides what he hath already, I know he is in a fair way of getting, or of dying; and both these ways, let me tell you, are most excellent Chances for a Wife. Tell me, Hussy, are you ruin'd or no?

MRS. PEACHUM: With Polly's Fortune, she might very well have gone off to a Person of Distinction. Yes, that you might, you pouting Slut!

PEACHUM: What, is the Wench dumb? Speak, or I'll make you plead by squeezing out an Answer from you. Are you really bound Wife to him, or are you only upon liking? (*Pinches her.*)

POLLY: Oh! (*Screaming.*)

MRS. PEACHUM: How the Mother is to be pitied who hath handsome Daughters! Locks, Bolts, Bars, and Lectures of Morality are nothing to them: They break through them all. They have as much Pleasure in cheating a Father and Mother, as in cheating at Cards.

PEACHUM: Why, Polly, I shall soon know if you are married, by Macheath's keeping from our House.

AIR

POLLY: *Can Love be controul'd by Advice?*
Will Cupid our Mothers obey?
Though my Heart were as frozen as Ice,
  At his Flame 'twould have melted away.

When he kist me so closely he prest,
  'Twas so sweet that I must have comply'd:
So I thought it both safest and best
  To marry, for fear you should chide.

MRS. PEACHUM: Then all the Hopes of our Family are gone for ever and ever!

PEACHUM: And Macheath may hang his Father and Mother-in-Law, in hope to get into their Daughter's Fortune.

POLLY: I did not marry him (as 'tis the Fashion) cooly and deliberately for Honour or Money. But, I love him.

MRS. PEACHUM: Love him! worse and worse! I thought the Girl had been better bred. Oh Husband, Husband! her Folly makes me mad! my Head swims! I'm distracted! I can't support myself—Oh! (*Faints.*)

PEACHUM: See, Wench, to what a Condition you have reduc'd your poor Mother! a Glass of Cordial, this instant.

How the poor Woman takes it to Heart!

(POLLY *goes out, and returns with it.*)

Ah, Hussy, now this is the only Comfort your Mother has left!

POLLY: Give her another Glass, Sir; my Mama drinks double the Quantity whenever she is out of Order. This, you see, fetches her.

MRS. PEACHUM: The Girl shows such a Readiness, and so much Concern, that I could almost find in my Heart to forgive her.

AIR

O Polly, you might have toy'd and kist.
By keeping Men off, you keep them on.
  POLLY: *But he so teaz'd me,*
      And he so pleas'd me,
What I did, you must have done.

MRS. PEACHUM: Not with a Highwayman.—You sorry Slut!

PEACHUM: A Word with you, Wife. 'Tis no new thing for a Wench to take a Man without consent of Parents. You know 'tis the Frailty of Woman, my Dear.

MRS. PEACHUM: Yes, indeed, the Sex is frail. But the first time a Woman is frail, she should be somewhat nice methinks, for then or never is the time to make her Fortune. After that, she hath nothing to do but to guard herself from being found out, and she may do what she pleases.

PEACHUM: Make your self a little easy; I have a Thought shall soon set all Matters again to rights. Why so melancholy, Polly? since what is done cannot be undone, we must all endeavour to make the best of it.

MRS. PEACHUM: Well, Polly; as far as one Woman can forgive another, I forgive thee.—Your Father is too fond of you, Hussy.

POLLY: Then all my Sorrows are at an end.

MRS. PEACHUM: A mighty likely Speech in troth, for a Wench who is just married!

AIR

  POLLY: *I, like a Ship in Storms, was tost;*
Yet afraid to put in to Land;
For seiz'd in the Port the Vessel's lost,
Whose Treasure is contreband.
    The Waves are laid,
    My Duty's paid.

O Joy beyond Expression!
Thus, safe a-shore,
I ask no more,
My All is in my Possession.

PEACHUM: I hear Customers in t'other Room; Go, talk
with 'em, Polly; but come to us again, as soon as they are
gone.—But, heark ye, Child, if 'tis the Gentleman who was
here Yesterday about the Repeating-Watch; say, you believe
we can't get Intelligence of it, till to-morrow. For I lent it to
Suky Straddle, to make a Figure with it to-night at a Tavern
in Drury-Lane. If t'other Gentleman calls for the Silver-
hilted Sword; you know Beetle-brow'd Jemmy hath it on, and
he doth not come from Tunbridge till Tuesday Night; so that
it cannot be had till then.

SCENE IX

PEACHUM, MRS. PEACHUM

PEACHUM: Dear Wife, be a little pacified. Don't let your
Passion run away with your Senses. Polly, I grant you, hath
done a rash thing.

MRS. PEACHUM: If she had had only an Intrigue with the
Fellow, why the very best Families have excus'd and huddled
up a Frailty of that sort. 'Tis Marriage, Husband, that makes
it a blemish.

PEACHUM: But Money, Wife, is the true Fuller's Earth
for Reputations, there is not a Spot or a Stain but what it
can take out. A rich Rogue now-a-days is fit Company for
any Gentleman; and the World, my Dear, hath not such a
Contempt for Roguery as you imagine. I tell you, Wife, I
can make this Match turn to our Advantage.

MRS. PEACHUM: I am very sensible, Husband, that Captain Macheath is worth Money, but I am in doubt whether
he hath not two or three Wives already, and then if he should
dye in a Session or two, Polly's Dower would come into
Dispute.

PEACHUM: That, indeed, is a Point which ought to be
consider'd.

AIR

A Fox may steal your Hens, Sir,
A Whore your Health and Pence, Sir,
Your Daughter rob your Chest, Sir,
Your Wife may steal your Rest, Sir,
*   A Thief your Goods and Plate.*
But this is all but picking;

With Rest, Pence, Chest and Chicken,
It ever was decreed, Sir,
If Lawyer's Hand is fee'd, Sir,
    He steals your whole Estate.

The Lawyers are bitter Enemies to those in our Way. They don't care that any Body should get a Clandestine Livelihood but themselves.

SCENE X

MRS. PEACHUM, PEACHUM, POLLY

POLLY: 'Twas only Nimming Ned. He brought in a Damask Window-Curtain, a Hoop-Petticoat, a Pair of Silver Candlesticks, a Perriwig, and one Silk Stocking, from the Fire that happen'd last Night.

PEACHUM: There is not a Fellow that is cleverer in his way, and saves more Goods out of the Fire than Ned. But now, Polly, to your Affair; for Matters must not be left as they are. You are married then, it seems?

POLLY: Yes, Sir.

PEACHUM: And how do you propose to live, Child?

POLLY: Like other Women, Sir, upon the Industry of my Husband.

MRS. PEACHUM: What, is the Wench turn'd Fool? A Highwayman's Wife, like a Soldier's, hath as little of his Pay, as of his Company.

PEACHUM: And had not you the common Views of a Gentlewoman in your Marriage, Polly?

POLLY: I don't know what you mean, Sir.

PEACHUM: Of a Jointure, and of being a Widow.

POLLY: But I love him, Sir: how then could I have Thoughts of parting with him?

PEACHUM: Parting with him! Why, that is the whole Scheme and Intention of all Marriage Articles. The comfortable Estate of Widow-hood, is the only hope that keeps up a Wife's Spirits. Where is the Woman who would scruple to be a Wife, if she had it in her Power to be a widow whenever she pleas'd? If you have any Views of this sort, Polly, I shall think the Match not so very unreasonable.

POLLY: How I dread to hear your Advice! Yet I must beg you to explain yourself.

PEACHUM: Secure what he hath got, have him peach'd the next Sessions, and then at once you are made a rich Widow.

POLLY: What, murder the Man I love! The Blood runs cold at my Heart with the very Thought of it.

PEACHUM: Fye, Polly! What hath Murder to do in the

Affair? Since the thing sooner or later must happen, I dare
say, the Captain himself would like that we should get the
Reward for his Death sooner than a Stranger. Why, Polly, the
Captain knows, that as 'tis his Employment to rob, so 'tis ours
to take Robbers; every Man in his Business. So that there is
no Malice in the Case.

MRS. PEACHUM: Ay, Husband, now you have nick'd the
Matter. To have him peach'd is the only thing could ever
make me forgive her.

AIR

> POLLY: *Oh, ponder well! be not severe;*
> *So save a wretched Wife!*
> *For on the Rope that hangs my Dear*
> *Depends poor Polly's Life.*

MRS. PEACHUM: But your Duty to your Parents, Hussy,
obliges you to hang him. What would many a Wife give for
such an Opportunity!

POLLY: What is a Jointure, what is Widow-hood to me? I
know my Heart. I cannot survive him.

AIR

> *The Turtle thus with plaintive crying,*
> *Her Lover dying,*
> *The Turtle thus with plaintive crying,*
> *Laments her Dove.*
> *Down she drops quite spent with sighing,*
> *Pair'd in Death, as pair'd in Love.*

Thus, Sir, it will happen to your poor Polly.

MRS. PEACHUM: What, is the Fool in love in earnest then? I
hate thee for being particular: Why, Wench, thou art a Shame
to thy very Sex.

POLLY: But hear me, Mother.—If you ever lov'd——

MRS. PEACHUM: Those cursed Playbooks she reads have
been her Ruin. One Word more, Hussy, and I shall knock
your Brains out, if you have any.

PEACHUM: Keep out of the way, Polly, for fear of Mischief,
and consider of what is propos'd to you.

MRS. PEACHUM: Away, Hussy. Hang your Husband, and be
dutiful.

SCENE XI

MRS. PEACHUM, PEACHUM, POLLY *listning*

MRS. PEACHUM: The Thing, Husband, must and shall be

done. For the sake of Intelligence we must take other Measures, and have him peach'd the next Session without her Consent. If she will not know her Duty, we know ours.

PEACHUM: But really, my Dear, it grieves one's Heart to take off a great Man. When I consider his Personal Bravery, his fine Stratagem, how much we have already got by him, and how much more we may get, methinks I can't find in my Heart to have a Hand in his Death. I wish you could have made Polly undertake it.

MRS. PEACHUM: But in a Case of Necessity—our own Lives are in danger.

PEACHUM: Then, indeed, we must comply with the Customs of the World, and make Gratitude give way to Interest.—He shall be taken off.

MRS. PEACHUM: I'll undertake to manage Polly.

PEACHUM: And I'll prepare Matters for the Old-Baily.

SCENE XII

POLLY: Now I'm a Wretch, indeed.—Methinks I see him already in the Cart, sweeter and more lovely than the Nosegay in his Hand!—I hear the Crowd extolling his Resolution and Intrepidity!—What Vollies of Sighs are sent from the Windows of Holborn, that so comely a Youth should be brought to disgrace!—I see him at the Tree! The whole Circle are in Tears!—even Butchers weep!—Jack Ketch himself hesitates to perform his Duty, and would be glad to lose his Fee, by a Reprieve. What then will become of Polly!—As yet I may inform him of their Design, and aid him in his Escape.—It shall be so.—But then he flies, absents himself, and I bar my self from his dear, dear Conversation! That too will distract me.—If he keep out of the way, my Papa and Mama may in time relent, and we may be happy.—If he stays, he is hang'd, and then he is lost for ever!—He intended to lye conceal'd in my Room, 'till the Dusk of the Evening: If they are abroad, I'll this Instant let him out, lest some Accident should prevent him. (*Exit, and returns.*)

SCENE XIII

POLLY, MACHEATH

AIR

MACHEATH: *Pretty Polly, say,*
When I was away,
Did your Fancy never stray
To some newer Lover?

POLLY: *Without Disguise,*
Heaving Sighs,
Doating Eyes,
My constant Heart discover.
Fondly let me loll!
MACHEATH: *O pretty, pretty Poll.*

POLLY: And are *you* as fond as ever, my Dear?

MACHEATH: Suspect my Honour, my Courage, suspect any thing but my Love.—May my Pistols miss Fire, and my Mare slip her Shoulder while I am pursu'd, if I ever forsake thee!

POLLY: Nay, my Dear, I have no Reason to doubt you, for I find in the Romance you lent me, none of the great Heroes were ever false in Love.

AIR

MACHEATH: *My Heart was so free,*
It rov'd like the Bee,
'Till Polly my Passion requited;
I sipt each Flower,
I chang'd ev'ry Hour,
But here ev'ry Flower is United.

POLLY: Were you sentenc'd to Transportation, sure, my Dear, you could not leave me behind you—could you?

MACHEATH: Is there any Power, any Force that could tear me from thee? You might sooner tear a Pension out of the Hands of a Courtier, a Fee from a Lawyer, a pretty Woman from a Looking-glass, or any Woman from Quadrille.—But to tear me from thee is impossible!

AIR

Were I laid on Greenland's Coast
And in my Arms embrac'd my Lass;
Warm amidst eternal Frost,
Too soon the Half Year's Night would pass.
POLLY: *Were I sold on Indian Soil,*
Soon as the burning Day was clos'd,
I could mock the sultry Toil,
When on my Charmer's Breast repos'd.
MACHEATH: *And I would love you all the Day,*
POLLY: *Every Night would kiss and play,*
MACHEATH: *If with me you'd fondly stray*
POLLY: *Over the Hills and far away.*

POLLY: Yes, I would go with thee. But oh!—how shall I speak it? I must be torn from thee. We must part.

MACHEATH: How! Part!

POLLY: We must, we must.—My Papa and Mama are set against thy Life. They now, even now are in Search after thee. They are preparing Evidence against thee. Thy Life depends upon a Moment.

AIR

> *O what Pain it is to part!*
> *Can I leave thee, can I leave thee?*
> *O what Pain it is to part!*
> *Can thy Polly ever leave thee?*
> *But lest Death my Love should thwart,*
> *And bring thee to the fatal Cart,*
> *Thus I tear thee from my bleeding Heart!*
> *Fly hence, and let me leave thee.*

One Kiss and then—one Kiss—begone—farewell.

MACHEATH: My Hand, my Heart, my Dear, is so rivited to thine, that I cannot unloose my Hold.

POLLY: But my Papa may intercept thee, and then I should lose the very glimmering of Hope. A few Weeks, perhaps, may reconcile us all. Shall thy Polly hear from thee?

MACHEATH: Must I then go?

POLLY: And will not Absence change your Love?

MACHEATH: If you doubt it, let me stay—and be hang'd.

POLLY: O how I fear! how I tremble!—Go—but when Safety will give you leave, you will be sure to see me again; for 'till then Polly is wretched.

AIR

(*Parting, and looking back at each other with fondness; he at one Door, she at the other.*)

> MACHEATH: *The Miser thus a Shilling sees,*
> *Which he's oblig'd to pay,*
> *With Sighs resigns it by degrees,*
> *And fears 'tis gone for aye.*
>
> POLLY: *The Boy, thus, when his Sparrow's flown,*
> *The Bird in Silence eyes;*
> *But soon as out of Sight 'tis gone,*
> *Whines, whimpers, sobs and cries.*

ACT II

SCENE I.—*A Tavern near Newgate*

JEMMY TWITCHER, CROOK-FINGER'D JACK, WAT DREARY, ROBIN OF BAGSHOT, NIMMING NED, HENRY PADINGTON, MATT OF THE MINT, BEN BUDGE, *and the rest of the* GANG, *at the Table, with Wine, Brandy and Tobacco.*

BEN: But pr'ythee, Matt, what is become of thy Brother Tom? I have not seen him since my Return from Transportation.

MATT: Poor Brother Tom had an Accident this time Twelvemonth, and so clever a made Fellow he was, that I could not save him from those fleaing Rascals the Surgeons; and now, poor Man, he is among the Otamys[1] at Surgeon's Hall.

BEN: So it seems, his Time was come.

JEMMY: But the present Time is ours, and no Body alive hath more. Why are the Laws levell'd at us? are we more dishonest than the rest of Mankind? What we win, Gentlemen, is our own by the Law of Arms, and the Right of Conquest.

JACK: Where shall we find such another Set of practical Philosophers, who to a Man are above the Fear of Death?

WAT: Sound Men, and true!

ROBIN: Of try'd Courage, and indefatigable Industry!

NED: Who is there here that would not dye for his Friend?

HARRY: Who is there here that would betray him for his Interest?

MATT: Show me a Gang of Courtiers that can say as much.

BEN: We are for a just Partition of the World, for every Man hath a Right to enjoy Life.

MATT: We retrench the Superfluities of Mankind. The World is avaritious, and I hate Avarice. A covetous fellow, like a Jackdaw, steals what he was never made to enjoy, for the sake of hiding it. These are the Robbers of Mankind, for Money was made for the Free-hearted and Generous, and where is the injury of taking from another, what he hath not the Heart to make use of?

JEMMY: Our several Stations for the Day are fixt. Good luck attend us all. Fill the Glasses.

AIR

MATT: *Fill ev'ry Glass, for Wine inspires us,*
And fires us
With Courage, Love and Joy.

[1] Anatomized bodies.

Women and Wine should Life employ.
Is there ought else on Earth desirous?
CHORUS: *Fill ev'ry Glass, &c.*

SCENE II

To them enter MACHEATH

MACHEATH: Gentlemen, well met. My Heart hath been with you this Hour; but an unexpected Affair hath detain'd me. No Ceremony, I beg you.

MATT: We were just breaking up to go upon Duty. Am I to have the Honour of taking the Air with you, Sir, this Evening upon the Heath? I drink a Dram now and then with the Stage-Coachmen in the way of Friendship and Intelligence; and I know that about this Time there will be Passengers upon the Western Road, who are worth speaking with.

MACHEATH: I was to have been of that Party—but—

MATT: But what, Sir?

MACHEATH: Is there any man who suspects my Courage?

MATT: We have all been witnesses of it.

MACHEATH: My Honour and Truth to the Gang?

MATT: I'll be answerable for it.

MACHEATH: In the Division of our Booty, have I ever shown the least Marks of Avarice or Injustice?

MATT: By these Questions something seems to have ruffled you. Are any of us suspected?

MACHEATH: I have a fixt Confidence, Gentlemen, in you all, as Men of Honour, and as such I value and respect you. Peachum is a Man that is useful to us.

MATT: Is he about to play us any foul Play? I'll shoot him through the Head.

MACHEATH: I beg you, Gentlemen, act with Conduct and Discretion. A Pistol is your last resort.

MATT: He knows nothing of this Meeting.

MACHEATH: Business cannot go on without him. He is a Man who knows the World, and is a necessary Agent to us. We have had a slight Difference, and till it is accommodated I shall be oblig'd to keep out of his way. Any private Dispute of mine shall be of no ill consequence to my Friends. You must continue to act under his Direction, for the moment we break loose from him, our Gang is ruin'd.

MATT: As a Bawd to a Whore, I grant you, he is to us of great Convenience.

MACHEATH: Make him believe I have quitted the Gang, which I can never do but with Life. At our private Quarters I will continue to meet you. A Week or so will probably reconcile us.

MATT: Your Instructions shall be observ'd. 'Tis now high time for us to repair to our several Duties; so till the Evening at our Quarters in Moor-fields we bid you farewell.

MACHEATH: I shall wish my self with you. Success attend you.

(*Sits down melancholy at the Table.*)

AIR

MATT: *Let us take the Road.*
Hark! I hear the sound of Coaches!
The hour of Attack approaches,
    To your Arms, brave Boys, and load.
    See the Ball I hold!
Let the Chymists toil like Asses,
Our fire their fire surpasses,
    And turns all our Lead to Gold.

(*The* GANG, *rang'd in the Front of the Stage, load their Pistols, and stick them under their Girdles; then go off singing the first Part in Chorus.*)

SCENE III

MACHEATH, DRAWER

MACHEATH: What a Fool is a fond Wench! Polly is most confoundedly bit.—I love the Sex. And a Man who loves Money, might as well be contented with one Guinea, as I with one Woman. The Town perhaps hath been as much oblig'd to me, for recruiting it with free-hearted Ladies, as to any Recruiting Officer in the Army. If it were not for us and the other Gentlemen of the Sword, Drury-Lane would be uninhabited.

AIR

If the Heart of a Man is deprest with Cares,
The Mist is dispell'd when a Woman appears;
Like the Notes of a Fiddle, she sweetly, sweetly
Raises the Spirits, and charms our Ears.
    Roses and Lillies her Cheeks disclose,
    But her ripe Lips are more sweet than those.
        Press her,
        Caress her
        With Blisses,
        Her Kisses
Dissolve us in Pleasure, and soft Repose.

I must have Women. There is nothing unbends the Mind like them. Money is not so strong a Cordial for the Time. Drawer.

(*Enter* DRAWER.)

Is the Porter gone for all the Ladies, according to my directions?

DRAWER: I expect him back every Minute. But you know, Sir, you sent him as far as Hockley in the Hole, for three of the Ladies, for one in Vinegar Yard, and for the rest of them somewhere about Lewkner's Lane. Sure some of them are below, for I hear the Barr Bell. As they come I will show them up. Coming, coming.

SCENE IV

MACHEATH, MRS. COAXER, DOLLY TRULL, MRS. VIXEN, BETTY DOXY, JENNY DIVER, MRS. SLAMMEKIN, SUKY TAWDRY, *and* MOLLY BRAZEN.

MACHEATH: Dear Mrs. Coaxer, you are welcome. You look charmingly to-day. I hope you don't want the Repairs of Quality, and lay on Paint.—Dolly Trull! kiss me, you Slut; are you as amorous as ever, Hussy? You are always so taken up with stealing Hearts, that you don't allow your self Time to steal any thing else.—Ah Dolly, thou wilt ever be a Coquette! —Mrs. Vixen, I'm yours, I always lov'd a Woman of Wit and Spirit; they make charming Mistresses, but plaguy Wives.— Betty Doxy! Come hither, Hussy. Do you drink as hard as ever? You had better stick to good Wholesome Beer; for in troth, Betty, Strong-Waters will in time ruin your Constitution. You should leave those to your Betters.—What! and my pretty Jenny Diver too! As prim and demure as ever! There is not any Prude, though ever so high bred, hath a more sanctify'd Look, with a more mischievous Heart. Ah! thou art a dear artful Hypocrite.—Mrs. Slammekin! as careless and genteel as ever! all you fine Ladies, who know your own Beauty, affect an Undress.—But see, here's Suky Tawdry come to contradict what I was saying. Every thing she gets one way she lays out upon her Back. Why Suky, you must keep at least a dozen Tallymen. Molly Brazen! (*She kisses him.*) That's well done. I love a free-hearted Wench. Thou hast a most agreeable Assurance, Girl, and art as willing as a Turtle. —But hark! I hear musick. The Harper is at the Door. If Musick be the Food of Love, play on. E'er you seat your selves, Ladies, what think you of a Dance? Come in.

(*Enter* HARPER.)

Play the French Tune, that Mrs. Slammekin was so fond of.
(*A Dance à la ronde in the French Manner; near the End of it this Song and Chorus.*)

AIR

Youth's the Season made for Joys,
Love is then our Duty,
She alone who that employs,
Well deserves her Beauty.
Let's be gay,
While we may,
Beauty's a Flower, despis'd in decay.
Youth's the Season, &c.

Let us drink and sport to-day,
Ours is not to-morrow.
Love with Youth flies swift away,
Age is nought but Sorrow.
Dance and sing,
Time's on the Wing,
Life never knows the return of Spring.
CHORUS: *Let us drink, &c.*

MACHEATH: Now, pray Ladies, take your Places. Here Fellow (*Pays the* HARPER.), Bid the Drawer bring us more Wine. (*Exit* HARPER.) If any of the Ladies chuse Ginn, I hope they will be so free to call for it.

JENNY: You look as if you meant me. Wine is strong enough for me. Indeed, Sir, I never drink Strong-Waters, but when I have the Cholic.

MACHEATH: Just the Excuse of the fine Ladies! Why, a Lady of Quality is never without the Cholic. I hope, Mrs. Coaxer, you have had good Success of late in your Visits among the Mercers.

MRS. COAXER: We have so many Interlopers—Yet with Industry, one may still have a little Picking. I carried a silver flower'd Lute-string, and a Piece of black Padesoy to Mr. Peachum's Lock but last Week.

MRS. VIXEN: There's Molly Brazen hath the Ogle of a Rattle-Snake. She rivetted a Linnen-draper's Eye so fast upon her, that he was nick'd of three Pieces of Cambric before he could look off.

BRAZEN: Oh dear Madam!—But sure nothing can come up to your handling of Laces! And then you have such a sweet deluding Tongue! To cheat a Man is nothing; but the Woman must have fine Parts indeed who cheats a Woman!

MRS. VIXEN: Lace, Madam, lyes in a small Compass, and is

of easy Conveyance. But you are apt, Madam, to think too well of your Friends.

MRS. COAXER: If any Woman hath more Art than another, to be sure, 'tis Jenny Diver. Though her Fellow be never so agreeable, she can pick his Pocket as cooly, as if Money were her only Pleasure. Now that is a Command of the Passions uncommon in a Woman!

JENNY: I never go to the Tavern with a Man, but in the View of Business. I have other Hours, and other sort of Men for my Pleasure. But had I your Address, Madam—

MACHEATH: Have done with your Compliments, Ladies; and drink about: You are not so fond of me, Jenny, as you use to be.

JENNY: 'Tis not convenient, Sir, to show my Fondness among so many Rivals. 'Tis your own Choice, and not the warmth of my Inclination that will determine you.

AIR

Before the Barn-door crowing,
  The Cock by Hens attended,
His Eyes around him throwing,
  Stands for a while suspended.
Then One he singles from the Crew,
  And cheers the happy Hen;
With how do you do, and how do you do,
  And how do you do again.

MACHEATH: Ah Jenny! thou art a dear Slut.

TRULL: Pray, Madam, were you ever in keeping?

TAWDRY: I hope, Madam, I ha'n been so long upon the Town, but I have met with some good Fortune as well as my Neighbours.

TRULL: Pardon me, Madam, I meant no harm by the Question; 'twas only in the way of Conversation.

TAWDRY: Indeed, Madam, if I had not been a Fool, I might have liv'd very handsomely with my last Friend. But upon his missing five Guineas, he turn'd me off. Now I never suspected he had counted them.

MRS. SLAMMEKIN: Who do you look upon, Madam, as your best sort of Keepers?

TRULL: That, Madam, is thereafter as they be.

MRS. SLAMMEKIN: I, Madam, was once kept by a Jew; and bating their Religion, to Women they are a good sort of People.

TAWDRY: Now for my part, I own I like an old Fellow: for we always make them pay for what they can't do.

MRS. VIXEN: A spruce Prentice, let me tell you, Ladies, is

no ill thing, they bleed freely. I have sent at least two or three dozen of them in my time to the Plantations.

JENNY: But to be sure, Sir, with so much good Fortune as you have had upon the Road, you must be grown immensely rich.

MACHEATH: The Road, indeed, hath done me justice, but the Gaming-Table hath been my ruin.

AIR

JENNY: *The Gamesters and Lawyers are Jugglers alike,*
If they meddle your All is in danger.
Like Gypsies, if once they can finger a Souse,
Your Pockets they pick, and they pilfer your House,
And give your Estate to a Stranger.

These are the Tools of a Man of Honour.
Cards and Dice are only fit for cowardly
Cheats, who prey upon their Friends.
(*She takes up his Pistol.* TAWDRY *takes up the other.*)

TAWDRY: This, Sir, is fitter for your Hand. Besides your Loss of Money, 'tis a Loss to the Ladies. Gaming takes you off from Women. How fond could I be of you! but before Company, 'tis ill bred.

MACHEATH: Wanton Hussies!

JENNY: I must and will have a Kiss to give my Wine a zest.
(*They take him about the Neck, and make Signs to* PEACHUM *and* CONSTABLES, *who rush in upon him.*)

SCENE V

To them, PEACHUM *and* CONSTABLES

PEACHUM: I seize you, Sir, as my Prisoner.

MACHEATH: Was this well done, Jenny?—Women are Decoy Ducks; who can trust them! Beasts, Jades, Jilts, Harpies, Furies, Whores!

PEACHUM: Your Case, Mr. Macheath, is not particular. The greatest Heroes have been ruin'd by Women. But, to do them justice, I must own they are a pretty sort of Creatures, if we could trust them. You must now, Sir, take your leave of the Ladies, and if they have a Mind to make you a Visit, they will be sure to find you at home. The Gentleman, Ladies, lodges in Newgate. Constables, wait upon the Captain to his Lodgings.

AIR

MACHEATH: *At the Tree I shall suffer with pleasure,*
At the Tree I shall suffer with pleasure,
     Let me go where I will,
     In all kinds of Ill,
PEACHUM: Ladies, I'll take care the Reckoning shall be
discharg'd.

I shall find no such Furies as these are.
(*Exit* MACHEATH, *guarded with* PEACHUM *and* CONSTABLES.)

SCENE VI

The WOMEN *remain*

MRS. VIXEN: Look ye, Mrs. Jenny, though Mr. Peachum
may have made a private Bargain with you and Suky Tawdry
for betraying the Captain, as we were all assisting, we ought
all to share alike.

MRS. COAXER: I think Mr. Peachum, after so long an acquaintance, might have trusted me as well as Jenny Diver.

MRS. SLAMMEKIN: I am sure at least three Men of his
hanging, and in a Year's time too (if he did me justice)
should be set down to my account.

TRULL: Mrs. Slammekin, that is not fair. For you know one
of them was taken in Bed with me.

JENNY: As far as a Bowl of Punch or a Treat, I believe Mrs.
Suky will join with me.—As for any thing else, Ladies, you
cannot in conscience expect it.

MRS. SLAMMEKIN: Dear Madam—
TRULL: I would not for the World—
MRS. SLAMMEKIN: 'Tis impossible for me—
TRULL: As I hope to be sav'd, Madam—
MRS. SLAMMEKIN: Nay, then I must stay here all Night—
TRULL: Since you command me.

(*Exeunt with great Ceremony.*)

SCENE VII.—*Newgate*

LOCKIT, TURNKEYS, MACHEATH, CONSTABLES

LOCKIT: Noble Captain, you are welcome. You have not
been a Lodger of mine this Year and half. You know the
custom, Sir. Garnish,[1] Captain, Garnish. Hand me down those
Fetters there.

MACHEATH: Those, Mr. Lockit, seem to be the heaviest of

[1] A bribe.

the whole sett. With your leave, I should like the further pair better.

LOCKIT: Look ye, Captain, we know what is fittest for our Prisoners. When a Gentleman uses me with Civility, I always do the best I can to please him.—Hand them down I say.—We have them of all Prices, from one Guinea to ten, and 'tis fitting every Gentleman should please himself.

MACHEATH: I understand you, Sir. (*Gives Money.*) The Fees here are so many, and so exorbitant, that few Fortunes can bear the Expense of getting off handsomly, or of dying like a Gentleman.

LOCKIT: Those, I see, will fit the Captain better.—Take down the further Pair. Do but examine them, Sir.—Never was better work.—How genteely they are made!—They will fit as easy as a Glove, and the nicest Man in England might not be asham'd to wear them. (*He puts on the Chains.*) If I had the best Gentleman in the Land in my Custody I could not equip him more handsomly. And so, Sir—I now leave you to your private Meditations.

SCENE VIII

MACHEATH

AIR

Man may escape from Rope and Gun
Nay, some have out-liv'd the Doctor's Pill;
Who takes a Woman must be undone,
    That Basilisk is sure to kill.
The Fly that sips Treacle is lost in the Sweets,
So he that tastes Woman, Woman, Woman,
    He that tastes Woman, Ruin meets.

To what a woful plight have I brought my self! Here must I (all day long, 'till I am hang'd) be confin'd to hear the Reproaches of a Wench who lays her Ruin at my Door.—I am in the Custody of her Father, and to be sure if he knows of the matter, I shall have a fine time on't betwixt this and my Execution.—But I promis'd the Wench Marriage.—What signifies a Promise to a Woman? Does not Man in Marriage itself promise a hundred things that he never means to perform? Do all we can, Women will believe us; for they look upon a Promise as an Excuse for following their own Inclinations.—But here comes Lucy, and I cannot get from her.—Wou'd I were deaf!

SCENE IX

LUCY: You base Man you,—how can you look me in the Face after what hath past between us?—See here, perfidious Wretch, how I am forc'd to bear about the load of Infamy you have laid upon me.—O Macheath! thou hast robb'd me of my Quiet—to see thee tortur'd would give me pleasure.

AIR

Thus when a good Huswife sees a Rat
In her Trap in the Morning taken,
With pleasure her Heart goes pit a pat,
In Revenge for her loss of Bacon.
Then she throws him
To the Dog or Cat,
To be worried, crush'd and shaken.

MACHEATH: Have you no Bowels, no Tenderness, my dear Lucy, to see a Husband in these Circumstances?

LUCY: A Husband!

MACHEATH: In ev'ry respect but the Form, and that, my Dear, may be said over us at any time.—Friends should not insist upon Ceremonies. From a Man of honour, his Word is as good as his Bond.

LUCY: 'Tis the pleasure of all you fine Men to insult the Women you have ruin'd.

AIR

How cruel are the Traytors,
Who lye and swear in jest,
To cheat unguarded Creatures
Of Virtue, Fame, and Rest!
Whoever steals a Shilling,
Through shame the Guilt conceals:
In Love the perjur'd Villain
With Boasts the Theft reveals.

MACHEATH: The very first opportunity, my Dear, (have but patience) you shall be my Wife in whatever manner you please.

LUCY: Insinuating Monster! And so you think I know nothing of the Affair of Miss Polly Peachum.—I could tear thy Eyes out!

MACHEATH: Sure Lucy, you can't be such a Fool as to be jealous of Polly!

LUCY: Are you not married to her, you Brute, you?

MACHEATH: Married! Very good. The Wench gives it out only to vex thee, and to ruin me in thy good Opinion. 'Tis true, I go to the House; I chat with the Girl, I kiss her, I say a thousand things to her (as all Gentlemen do) that mean nothing, to divert my self; and now the silly Jade hath set it about that I am married to her, to let me know what she would be at. Indeed, my dear Lucy, these violent Passions may be of ill consequence to a Woman in your condition.

LUCY: Come, come, Captain, for all your Assurance, you know that Miss Polly hath put it out of your power to do me the Justice you promis'd me.

MACHEATH: A jealous Woman believes ev'ry thing her Passion suggests. To convince you of my Sincerity, if we can find the Ordinary, I shall have no scruples of making you my Wife; and I know the consequence of having two at a time.

LUCY: That you are only to be hang'd, and so get rid of them both.

MACHEATH: I am ready, my dear Lucy, to give you satisfaction—if you think there is any in Marriage.—What can a Man of Honour say more?

LUCY: So then it seems, you are not married to Miss Polly.

MACHEATH: You know, Lucy, the Girl is prodigiously conceited. No Man can say a civil thing to her, but (like other fine Ladies) her Vanity makes her think he's her own for ever and ever.

AIR

The first time at the Looking-glass
The Mother sets her Daughter,
The Image strikes the smiling Lass
With Self-love ever after.
Each time she looks, she, fonder grown,
Thinks ev'ry Charm grows stronger.
But alas, vain Maid, all Eyes but your own
Can see you are not younger.

When Women consider their own Beauties, they are all alike unreasonable in their demands; for they expect their Lovers should like them as long as they like themselves.

LUCY: Yonder is my Father—perhaps this way we may light upon the Ordinary, who shall try if you will be as good as your Word.—For I long to be made an honest Woman.

SCENE X

PEACHUM, LOCKIT *with an Account-Book*

LOCKIT: In this last Affair, Brother Peachum, we are agreed. You have consented to go halves in Macheath.

PEACHUM: We shall never fall out about an Execution.—
But as to that Article, pray how stands our last Year's
account?

LOCKIT: If you will run your Eye over it, you'll find 'tis
fair and clearly stated.

PEACHUM: This long Arrear of the Government is very hard
upon us! Can it be expected that we should hang our
Acquaintance for nothing, when our Betters will hardly save
theirs without being paid for it? Unless the People in employment pay better, I promise them for the future, I shall let
other Rogues live besides their own.

LOCKIT: Perhaps, Brother, they are afraid these matters
may be carried too far. We are treated too by them with Contempt, as if our Profession were not reputable.

PEACHUM: In one respect indeed, our Employment may be
reckon'd dishonest, because, like Great Statesmen, we encourage those who betray their Friends.

LOCKIT: Such Language, Brother, any where else, might
turn to your prejudice. Learn to be more guarded, I beg you.

AIR

When you censure the Age,
Be cautious and sage,
Lest the Courtiers offended should be:
If you mention Vice or Bribe,
'Tis so pat to all the Tribe;
Each crys—That was levell'd at me.

PEACHUM: Here's poor Ned Clincher's Name, I see. Sure,
Brother Lockit, there was a little unfair proceeding in Ned's
case: for he told me in the Condemn'd Hold, that for Value
receiv'd you had promis'd him a Session or two longer without Molestation.

LOCKIT: Mr. Peachum—This is the first time my Honour
was ever call'd in Question.

PEACHUM: Business is at an end—if once we act dishonour-
ably.

LOCKIT: Who accuses me?

PEACHUM: You are warm, Brother.

LOCKIT: He that attacks my Honour, attacks my Livelyhood.—And this Usage—Sir—is not to be born.

PEACHUM: Since you provoke me to speak—I must tell you
too, that Mrs. Coaxer charges you with defrauding her of her
Information-Money, for the apprehending of curl-pated Hugh.
Indeed, indeed, Brother, we must punctually pay our Spies,
or we shall have no Information.

LOCKIT: Is this Language to me, Sirrah—who have sav'd you from the Gallows, Sirrah! (*Collaring each other.*)

PEACHUM: If I am hang'd, it shall be for ridding the World of an arrant Rascal.

LOCKIT: This Hand shall do the office of the Halter you deserve, and throttle you—you Dog!—

PEACHUM: Brother, Brother—We are both in the Wrong— We shall be both Losers in the Dispute—for you know we have it in our Power to hang each other. You should not be so passionate.

LOCKIT: Nor you so provoking.

PEACHUM: 'Tis our mutual Interest; 'tis for the Interest of the World we should agree. If I said any thing, Brother, to the Prejudice of your Character, I ask pardon.

LOCKIT: Brother Peachum—I can forgive as well as resent. —Give me your Hand. Suspicion does not become a Friend.

PEACHUM: I only meant to give you occasion to justifie yourself: But I must now step home, for I expect the Gentleman about this Snuff-box, that Filch nimm'd two Nights ago in the Park. I appointed him at this hour.

SCENE XI

LOCKIT, LUCY

LOCKIT: Whence come you, Hussy?

LUCY: My Tears might answer that Question.

LOCKIT: You have then been whimpering and fondling, like a Spaniel, over the Fellow that hath abus'd you.

LUCY: One can't help Love; one can't cure it. 'Tis not in my Power to obey you, and hate him.

LOCKIT: Learn to bear your Husband's Death like a reasonable Woman. 'Tis not the fashion, now-a-days, so much as to affect Sorrow upon these Occasions. No Woman would ever marry, if she had not the Chance of Mortality for a Release. Act like a Woman of Spirit, Hussy, and thank your Father for what he is doing.

AIR

LUCY: *Is then his Fate decreed, Sir?*
Such a Man can I think of quitting?
When first we met, so moves me yet,
O see how my Heart is splitting!

LOCKIT: Look ye, Lucy—There is no saving him.—So, I think you must ev'n do like other Widows—Buy your self Weeds, and be cheerful.

AIR

You'll think e'er many Days ensue
This Sentence not severe;
I hang your Husband, Child, 'tis true,
But with him hang your Care.
Twang dang dillo dee.

Like a good Wife, go moan over your dying Husband. That, Child, is your Duty—Consider, Girl, you can't have the Man and the Money too—so make yourself as easy as you can, by getting all you can from him.

SCENE XII

LUCY, MACHEATH

LUCY: Though the Ordinary was out of the way to-day I hope, my Dear, you will, upon the first opportunity, quiet my Scruples—Oh Sir!—my Father's hard Heart is not to be soften'd, and I am in the utmost Despair.

MACHEATH: But if I could raise a small Sum—Would not twenty Guineas, think you, move him?—Of all the Arguments in the way of Business, the Perquisite is the most prevailing.—Your Father's Perquisites for the Escape of Prisoners must amount to a considerable Sum in the Year. Money well tim'd, and properly apply'd, will do any thing.

AIR

If you at an Office solicit your Due,
And would not have Matters neglected;
You must quicken the Clerk with the perquisite too,
To do what his Duty directed.
Or would you the Frowns of a Lady prevent,
She too has this palpable Failing
The Perquisite softens her into Consent;
That Reason with all is prevailing.

LUCY: What Love or Money can do shall be done: for all my Comfort depends upon your Safety.

SCENE XIII

LUCY, MACHEATH, POLLY

POLLY: Where is my dear Husband?—Was a Rope ever intended for this Neck!—O let me throw my Arms about it, and throttle thee with Love!—Why dost thou turn away from me?—'Tis thy Polly—'Tis thy Wife.

MACHEATH: Was ever such an unfortunate Rascal as I am!

LUCY: Was there ever such another Villain!

POLLY: O Macheath! was it for this we parted? Taken! Imprison'd! Try'd! Hang'd!—cruel Reflection! I'll stay with thee 'till Death—no Force shall tear thy dear Wife from thee now. —What means my Love?—Not one kind Word! not one kind Look! think what thy Polly suffers to see thee in this Condition.

AIR

> *Thus when the Swallow, seeking Prey,*
> *Within the Sash is closely pent,*
> *His Consort, with bemoaning Lay,*
> *Without sits pining for th' Event.*
> *Her chatt'ring Lovers all around her skim;*
> *She heeds them not (poor Bird!), her Soul's with him.*

MACHEATH: I must disown her. (*Aside.*) The Wench is distracted.

LUCY: Am I then bilk'd of my Virtue? Can I have no Reparation? Sure Men were born to lye, and Women to believe them! O Villain! Villain!

POLLY: Am I not thy Wife—Thy Neglect of me, thy Aversion to me too severely proves it.—Look on me.—Tell me, am I not thy Wife?

LUCY: Perfidious Wretch!

POLLY: Barbarous Husband!

LUCY: Hadst thou been hang'd five Months ago, I had been happy.

POLLY: And I too—If you had been kind to me 'till Death, it would not have vex'd me. And that's no very unreasonable Request, (though from a Wife) to a Man who hath not above seven or eight Days to live.

LUCY: Art thou then married to another? Hast thou two Wives, Monster?

MACHEATH: If Women's Tongues can cease for an Answer —hear me.

LUCY: I won't.—Flesh and Blood can't bear my Usage.

POLLY: Shall I not claim my own? Justice bids me speak.

AIR

> MACHEATH: *How happy could I be with either,*
> *Were t'other dear Charmer away!*
> *But while you thus teaze me together,*
> *To neither a Word will I say;*
> *But tol de rol, &c.*

POLLY: Sure, my Dear, there ought to be some Preference shown to a Wife! At least she may claim the Appearance of it. He must be distracted with his Misfortunes, or he could not use me thus!

LUCY: O Villain, Villain! thou hast deceiv'd me—I could even inform against thee with Pleasure. Not a Prude wishes more heartily to have Facts against her intimate Acquaintance, than I now wish to have Facts against thee. I would have her Satisfaction, and they should all out.

AIR

POLLY: *I'm bubbled.*[1]
LUCY: *. . . I'm bubbled.*
POLLY: *Oh how I am troubled!*
LUCY: *Bambouzled, and bit!*
POLLY: *. . . My Distresses are doubled.*
LUCY: *When you come to the Tree, should the Hangman refuse,*
These Fingers, with Pleasure, could fasten the Noose.
POLLY: *I'm bubbled, &c.*

MACHEATH: Be pacified, my dear Lucy—This is all a Fetch of Polly's, to make me desperate with you in case I get off. If I am hang'd, she would fain have the Credit of being thought my Widow—Really, Polly, this is no time for a Dispute of this sort; for whenever you are talking of Marriage, I am thinking of Hanging.

POLLY: And hast thou the Heart to persist in disowning me?

MACHEATH: And hast thou the Heart to persist in persuading me that I am married? Why Polly, dost thou seek to aggravate my Misfortunes?

LUCY: Really, Miss Peachum, you but expose yourself. Besides, 'tis barbarous in you to worry a Gentleman in his Circumstances.

AIR

POLLY: *Cease your Funning;*
Force or Cunning
Never shall my Heart trapan.[2]
All these Sallies
Are but Malice
To seduce my constant Man.
'Tis most certain,
By their flirting

[1] Cheated.   [2] Beguile.

> *Women oft' have Envy shown;*
> *Pleas'd, to ruin*
> *Others wooing;*
> *Never happy in their own!*

POLLY: Decency, Madam, methinks might teach you to behave yourself with some Reserve with the Husband, while his Wife is present.

MACHEATH: But seriously, Polly, this is carrying the Joke a little too far.

LUCY: If you are determin'd, Madam, to raise a Disturbance in the Prison, I shall be oblig'd to send for the Turnkey to show you the Door. I am sorry, Madam, you force me to be so ill-bred.

POLLY: Give me leave to tell you, Madam: These forward Airs don't become you in the least, Madam. And my Duty, Madam, obliges me to stay with my Husband, Madam.

AIR

> LUCY: *Why how now, Madam Flirt?*
> *If you thus must chatter;*
> *And are for flinging Dirt,*
> *Let's try for best can spatter;*
> *Madam Flirt!*
> POLLY: *Why how now, saucy Jade;*
> *Sure the Wench is Tipsy!*
> *How can you see me made* (*to him*)
> *The Scoff of such a Gipsy?*
> *Saucy Jade!* (*to her.*)

SCENE XIV

LUCY, MACHEATH, POLLY, PEACHUM

PEACHUM: Where's my Wench? Ah Hussy! Hussy!—Come you home, you Slut; and when your Fellow is hang'd, hang yourself, to make your Family some amends.

POLLY: Dear, dear Father, do not tear me from him— I must speak; I have more to say to him—Oh! twist thy Fetters about me, that he may not haul me from thee!

PEACHUM: Sure all Women are alike! If ever they commit the Folly, they are sure to commit another by exposing themselves—Away—Not a Word more—You are my Prisoner now, Hussy.

AIR

> POLLY: *No Power on Earth can e'er divide,*
> *The Knot that Sacred Love hath ty'd.*

When Parents draw against our Mind,
The True-love's Knot they faster bind.
Oh, oh ray, oh Amborah—oh, oh, &c.
          (*Holding* MACHEATH, PEACHUM *pulling her.*)

SCENE XV

LUCY, MACHEATH

MACHEATH: I am naturally compassionate, Wife; so that I could not use the Wench as she deserv'd; which made you at first suspect there was something in what she said.

LUCY: Indeed, my Dear, I was strangely puzzled.

MACHEATH: If that had been the Case, her Father would never have brought me into this Circumstance—No, Lucy,—I had rather dye than be false to thee.

LUCY: How happy am I, if you say this from your Heart! For I love thee so, that I could sooner bear to see thee hang'd than in the Arms of another.

MACHEATH: But couldst thou bear to see me hang'd?

LUCY: O Macheath, I can never live to see that Day.

MACHEATH: You see, Lucy, in the Account of Love you are in my debt, and you must now be convinc'd that I rather chuse to die than be another's.—Make me, if possible, love thee more, and let me owe my Life to thee—If you refuse to assist me, Peachum and your Father will immediately put me beyond all means of Escape.

LUCY: My Father, I know, hath been drinking hard with the Prisoners: and I fancy he is now taking his Nap in his own Room—if I can procure the Keys, shall I go off with thee, my Dear?

MACHEATH: If we are together, 'twill be impossible to lye conceal'd. As soon as the Search begins to be a little cool, I will send to thee—'Till then my Heart is thy Prisoner.

LUCY: Come then, my dear Husband—owe thy Life to me—and though you love me not—be grateful—But that Polly runs in my Head strangely.

MACHEATH: A Moment of time may make us unhappy for-ever.

AIR

LUCY: *I like the Fox shall grieve,*
    Whose Mate hath left her side,
Whom Hounds, from Morn to Eve,
    Chase o'er the Country wide.

Where can my Lover hide?
    Where cheat the weary Pack?
If Love be not his Guide,
    He never will come back!

ACT III

SCENE I.—*Newgate*

LOCKIT, LUCY

LOCKIT: To be sure, Wench, you must have been aiding and abetting to help him to this Escape.

LUCY: Sir, here hath been Peachum and his Daughter Polly, and to be sure they know the Ways of Newgate as well as if they had been born and bred in the Place all their Lives. Why must all your Suspicion light upon me?

LOCKIT: Lucy, Lucy, I will have none of these shuffling Answers.

LUCY: Well then—If I know any Thing of him I wish I may be burnt!

LOCKIT: Keep your Temper, Lucy, or I shall pronounce you guilty.

LUCY: Keep yours, Sir,—I do wish I may be burnt. I do—And what can I say more to convince you?

LOCKIT: Did he tip handsomely?—How much did he come down with? Come Hussy, don't cheat your Father; and I shall not be angry with you—Perhaps, you have made a better Bargain with him than I could have done—How much, my good Girl?

LUCY: You know, Sir, I am fond of him, and would have given Money to have kept him with me.

LOCKIT: Ah Lucy! thy Education might have put thee more upon thy Guard; for a Girl in the Bar of an Alehouse is always besieg'd.

LUCY: Dear Sir, mention not my Education—for 'twas to that I owe my Ruin.

AIR

When young at the Bar you first taught me to score,
And bid me be free of my Lips, and no more;
I was kiss'd by the Parson, the Squire, and the Sot.
When the Guest was departed, the Kiss was forgot.
But his Kiss was so sweet, and so closely he prest,
That I languish'd and pin'd till I granted the rest.

If you can forgive me, Sir, I will make a fair Confession, for to be sure he hath been a most barbarous Villain to me.

LOCKIT: And so you have let him escape, Hussy—Have you?

LUCY: When a Woman loves, a kind Look, a tender Word can persuade her to any thing—And I could ask no other Bribe.

LOCKIT: Thou wilt always be a vulgar Slut, Lucy.—If you would not be look'd upon as a Fool, you should never do any thing but upon the Foot of Interest. Those that act otherwise are their own Bubbles.

LUCY: But Love, Sir, is a Misfortune that may happen to the most discreet Woman, and in Love we are all Fools alike.—Notwithstanding all he swore, I am now fully convinc'd that Polly Peachum is actually his Wife.—Did I let him escape, (Fool that I was!) to go to her?—Polly will wheedle herself into his Money, and then Peachum will hang him, and cheat us both.

LOCKIT: So I am to be ruin'd, because forsooth, you must be in Love!—a very pretty Excuse!

LUCY: I could murder that impudent happy Strumpet:—I gave him his Life, and that Creature enjoys the Sweets of it.—Ungrateful Macheath!

AIR

My Love is all Madness and Folly,
 Alone I lye,
 Toss, tumble, and cry,
What a happy Creature is Polly!
Was e'er such a Wretch as I!
With Rage I redden like Scarlet,
That my dear inconstant Varlet,
 Stark blind to my Charms,
 Is lost in the Arms
Of that Jilt, that inveigling Harlot!
 Stark blind to my Charms,
 Is lost in the Arms
Of that Jilt, that inveigling Harlot!
This, this my Resentment alarms.

LOCKIT: And so, after all this Mischief, I must stay here to be entertain'd with your catterwauling, Mistress Puss!—Out of my sight, wanton Strumpet! you shall fast and mortify yourself into Reason, with now and then a little handsome Discipline to bring you to your Senses.—Go.

SCENE II

LOCKIT

Peachum then intends to outwit me in this Affair; but I'll be even with him—The Dog is leaky in his Liquor, so I'll ply him that way, get the Secret from him, and turn this Affair to my own Advantage.—Lions, Wolves, and Vulturs don't live together in Herds, Droves or Flocks.—Of all Animals of Prey, Man is the only sociable one. Every one of us preys upon his Neighbour, and yet we herd together.—Peachum is my Companion, my Friend—According to the Custom of the World, indeed, he may quote thousands of Precedents for cheating me—And shall not I make use of the Privilege of Friendship to make him a Return?

AIR

Thus Gamesters united in Friendship are found,
Though they know that their Industry all is a Cheat;
They flock to their Prey at the Dice-Box's Sound,
And join to promote one another's Deceit.
 But if by mishap
 They fail of a Chap,
To keep in their Hands, they each other entrap.
Like Pikes, lank with Hunger, who miss of their Ends,
They bite their Companions, and prey on their Friends.

Now, Peachum, you and I, like honest Tradesmen, are to have a fair Tryal which of us two can over-reach the other.—Lucy.

(*Enter* LUCY.)

Are there any of Peachum's People now in the House?
LUCY: Filch, Sir, is drinking a Quartern of Strong-Waters in the next Room with Black Moll.
LOCKIT: Bid him come to me.

SCENE III

LOCKIT, FILCH

LOCKIT: Why, Boy, thou lookest as if thou wert half starv'd; like a shotten Herring.[1]
FILCH: One had need have the Constitution of a Horse to go through the Business.—Since the favourite Child-getter was disabled by a Mis-hap, I have pick'd up a little Money by helping the Ladies to a Pregnancy against their being call'd down to Sentence.—But if a Man cannot get an honest Livelyhood any easier way, I am sure, 'tis what I can't undertake for another Session.
LOCKIT: Truly, if that great Man should tip off, 'twould be an irreparable Loss. The Vigour and Prowess of a Knight Errant never sav'd half the Ladies in Distress that he hath

---

[1] Herring that has spawned.

done.—But, Boy, can'st thou tell me where thy Master is to be found?

FILCH: At his Lock,[1] Sir, at the Crooked Billet.

LOCKIT: Very well.—I have nothing more with you. (*Exit* FILCH.) I'll go to him there, for I have many important Affairs to settle with him; and in the way of those Transactions, I'll artfully get into his Secret.—So that Macheath shall not remain a Day longer out of my Clutches.

SCENE IV

MACHEATH *in a fine tarnish'd Coat,* BEN BUDGE, MATT OF THE MINT

MACHEATH: I am sorry, Gentlemen, the Road was so barren of Money. When my Friends are in Difficulties, I am always glad that my Fortune can be serviceable to them. (*Gives them Money.*) You see, Gentlemen, I am not a meer Court Friend, who professes every thing and will do nothing.

AIR

The Modes of the Court so common are grown,
   That a true Friend can hardly be met;
Friendship for Interest is but a Loan,
   Which they let out for what they can get.
      'Tis true, you find
      Some Friends so kind,
Who will give you good Counsel themselves to defend.
      In sorrowful Ditty,
      They promise, they pity,
But shift you for Money, from Friend to Friend.

But we, Gentlemen, have still Honour enough to break through the Corruptions of the World.—And while I can serve you, you may command me.

BEN: It grieves my Heart that so generous a Man should be involv'd in such Difficulties, as oblige him to live with such ill Company, and herd with Gamesters.

MATT: See the Partiality of Mankind!—One Man may steal a Horse, better than another look over a Hedge—Of all Mechanics, of all servile Handy-crafts-men, a Gamester is the vilest. But yet, as many of the Quality are of the Profession, he is admitted amongst the politest Company. I wonder we are not more respected.

[1] A Cant Word, signifying a Warehouse where stolen Goods are deposited.

MACHEATH: There will be deep Play to-night at Marybone, and consequently Money may be pick'd up upon the Road. Meet me there, and I'll give you the Hint who is worth Setting.

MATT: The Fellow with a brown Coat with a narrow Gold Binding, I am told, is never with·ut Money.

MACHEATH: What do you mean, Matt?—Sure you will not think of meddling with him!—He's a good honest kind of a Fellow, and one of us.

BEN: To be sure, Sir, we will put our selves under your Direction.

MACHEATH: Have an Eye upon the Money-Lenders.— A Rouleau,[1] or two, would prove a pretty sort of an Expedition. I hate Extortion.

MATT: Those Rouleaus are very pretty Things.—I hate your Bank Bills.—There is such a Hazard in putting them off.

MACHEATH: There is a certain Man of Distinction, who in his Time hath nick'd me out of a great deal of the Ready. He is in my Cash, Ben;—I'll point him out to you this Evening, and you shall draw upon him for the Debt.—The Company are met; I hear the Dice-box in the other Room. So, Gentlemen, your Servant. You'll meet me at Marybone.

Scene V

(PEACHUM'S *Lock: A Table with Wine, Brandy, Pipes and Tobacco*)

PEACHUM, LOCKIT

LOCKIT: The Coronation Account,[2] Brother Peachum, is of so intricate a Nature, that I believe it will never be settled.

PEACHUM: It consists indeed of a great Variety of Articles. —It was worth to our People, in Fees of different Kinds, above ten Instalments.[3]—This is part of the Account, Brother, that lies open before us.

LOCKIT: A Lady's Tail of rich Brocade—that, I see, is dispos'd of.

PEACHUM: To Mrs. Diana Trapes, the Tally-woman, and she will make a good Hand on't in Shoes and Slippers, to trick out young Ladies, upon their going into Keeping.—

LOCKIT: But I don't see any Article of the Jewels.

PEACHUM: Those are so well known, that they must be sent abroad—You'll find them enter'd under the Article of

---

[1] A roll of gold coins.
[2] The thefts from the crowd assembled at the recent coronation of George II.
[3] Public installations of the Lord Mayor.

Exportation.—As for the Snuff-Boxes, Watches, Swords, &c.
—I thought it best to enter them under their several Heads.

LOCKIT: Seven and twenty Women's Pockets compleat;
with the several things therein contain'd; all Seal'd, Number'd, and enter'd.

PEACHUM: But, Brother, it is impossible for us now to
enter upon this Affair.—We should have the whole Day
before us.—Besides, the Account of the last Half Year's
Plate is in a Book by it self, which lies at the other Office.

LOCKIT: Bring us then more Liquor.—To-day shall be
for Pleasure—To-morrow for Business.—Ah Brother, those
Daughters of ours are two slippery Hussies—Keep a watchful Eye upon Polly, and Macheath in a Day or two shall be
our own again.

AIR

> LOCKIT: *What Gudgeons are we Men!*
> *Ev'ry Woman's easy Prey.*
> *Though we have felt the Hook, agen*
> *We bite and they betray.*
> *The Bird that hath been trapt,*
> *When he hears his calling Mate,*
> *To her he flies, again he's clapt*
> *Within the wiry Grate.*

PEACHUM: But what signifies catching the Bird, if your
Daughter Lucy will set open the Door of the Cage?

LOCKIT: If Men were answerable for the Follies and
Frailties of their Wives and Daughters, no Friends could
keep a good Correspondence together for two Days.—This is
unkind of you, Brother; for among good Friends, what they
say or do goes for nothing.

(*Enter a* SERVANT.)

SERVANT: Sir, here's Mrs. Diana Trapes wants to speak
with you.

PEACHUM: Shall we admit her, Brother Lockit?

LOCKIT: By all means—She's a good Customer, and a
fine-spoken Woman—And a Woman who drinks and talks
so freely, will enliven the Conversation.

PEACHUM: Desire her to walk in. (*Exit* SERVANT.)

SCENE VI

PEACHUM, LOCKIT, MRS. TRAPES

PEACHUM: Dear Mrs. Dye, your Servant—One may know
by your Kiss, that your Ginn is excellent.

MRS. TRAPES: I was always very curious[1] in my Liquors.

LOCKIT: There is no perfum'd Breath like it—I have been long acquainted with the Flavour of those Lips—Han't I, Mrs. Dye?

MRS. TRAPES: Fill it up.—I take as large Draughts of Liquor, as I did of Love.—I hate a Flincher in either.

AIR

In the Days of my Youth I could bill like a Dove, fa, la,
*   la, &c.*
Like a Sparrow at all times was ready for Love, fa, la, la, &c.
The Life of all Mortals in Kissing should pass,
Lip to Lip while we're young—then the Lip to the Glass,
*   fa, &c.*

But now, Mr. Peachum, to our Business.—If you have Blacks of any kind, brought in of late, Mantoes—Velvet Scarfs—Petticoats—Let it be what it will—I am your Chap —for all my Ladies are very fond of Mourning.

PEACHUM: Why, look ye, Mrs. Dye—you deal so hard with us, that we can afford to give the Gentlemen, who venture their Lives for the Goods, little or nothing.

MRS. TRAPES: The hard Times oblige me to go very near in my Dealing.—To be sure, of late Years I have been a great Sufferer by the Parliament.—Three thousand Pounds would hardly make me amends.—The Act for destroying the Mint,[2] was a severe Cut upon our Business—'Till then, if a Customer stept out of the way—we knew where to have her—No doubt you know Mrs. Coaxer—there's a Wench now ('till to-day) with a good Suit of Cloaths of mine upon her Back, and I could never set Eyes upon her for three Months together.—Since the Act too against Imprisonment for small Sums, my Loss there too hath been very considerable, and it must be so, when a Lady can borrow a handsome Petticoat, or a clean Gown, and I not have the least Hank[8] upon her! And, o' my conscience, now-a-days most Ladies take a Delight in cheating, when they can do it with Safety.

PEACHUM: Madam, you had a handsome Gold Watch of us t'other Day for seven Guineas.—Considering we must have our Profit—To a Gentleman upon the Road, a Gold Watch will be scarce worth the taking.

MRS. TRAPES: Consider, Mr. Peachum, that Watch was remarkable, and not of very safe Sale.—If you have any

---

[1] Fastidious.

[2] A sanctuary formerly frequented by debtors; abolished by Parliament in 1723.

[8] Hold.

black Velvet Scarfs—they are a handsome Winter-wear; and take with most Gentlemen who deal with my Customers.— 'Tis I that put the Ladies upon a good Foot. 'Tis not Youth or Beauty that fixes their Price. The Gentlemen always pay according to their Dress, from half a Crown to two Guineas; and yet those Hussies make nothing of bilking of me.—Then, too, allowing for Accidents.—I have eleven fine Customers now down under the Surgeon's Hands,—what with Fees and other Expences, there are great Goings-out, and no Comings-in, and not a Farthing to pay for at least a Month's cloath-ing.—We run great Risques—great Risques indeed.

PEACHUM: As I remember, you said something just now of Mrs. Coaxer.

MRS. TRAPES: Yes, Sir.—To be sure I stript her of a Suit of my own Cloaths about two hours ago; and have left her as she should be, in her Shift, with a Lover of hers at my House. She call'd him up Stairs, as he was going to Mary-bone in a Hackney Coach.—And I hope, for her own sake and mine, she will perswade the Captain to redeem her, for the Captain is very generous to the Ladies.

LOCKIT: What Captain?

MRS. TRAPES: He thought I did not know him—An inti-mate Acquaintance of yours, Mr. Peachum—Only Captain Macheath—as fine as a Lord.

PEACHUM: To-morrow, dear Mrs. Dye, you shall set your own Price upon any of the Goods you like—We have at least half a dozen Velvet Scarfs, and all at your service. Will you give me leave to make you a Present of this Suit of Night-cloaths for your own wearing?—But are you sure it is Captain Macheath?

MRS. TRAPES: Though he thinks I have forgot him, no Body knows him better. I have taken a great deal of the Captain's Money in my Time at second-hand, for he always lov'd to have his Ladies well drest.

PEACHUM: Mr. Lockit and I have a little business with the Captain;—You understand me—and we will satisfye you for Mrs. Coaxer's Debt.

LOCKIT: Depend upon it—we will deal like Men of Honour.

MRS. TRAPES: I don't enquire after your Affairs—so what-ever happens, I wash my Hands on't.—It hath always been my Maxim, that one Friend should assist another—But if you please—I'll take one of the Scarfs home with me. 'Tis always good to have something in Hand.

LUCY

Jealousy, Rage, Love and Fear are at once tearing me to pieces. How I am weather-beaten and shatter'd with distresses!

AIR

I'm like a Skiff on the Ocean tost,
 Now high, now low, with each Billow born,
With her Rudder broke, and her Anchor lost,
 Deserted and all forlorn.
While thus I lye rolling and tossing all Night,
That Polly lyes sporting on Seas of Delight!
 Revenge, Revenge, Revenge,
Shall appease my restless Sprite.

I have the Rats-bane ready.—I run no Risque; for I can lay her Death upon the Ginn, and so many dye of that naturally that I shall never be call'd in Question.—But say, I were to be hang'd—I never could be hang'd for any thing that would give me greater Comfort, than the poysoning that Slut.

(*Enter* FILCH.)

FILCH: Madam, here's our Miss Polly come to wait upon you.
LUCY: Show her in.

SCENE VIII

LUCY, POLLY

LUCY: Dear Madam, your Servant.—I hope you will pardon my Passion, when I was so happy to see you last.—I was so overrun with the Spleen, that I was perfectly out of my self. And really when one hath the Spleen, every thing is to be excus'd by a Friend.

AIR

When a Wife's in her Pout
(As she's sometimes, no doubt;)
 The good Husband as meek as a Lamb,
 Her Vapours to still,
 First grants her her Will,
 And the quieting Draught is a Dram.
Poor Man! And the quieting Draught is a Dram.

—I wish all our Quarrels might have so comfortable a Reconciliation.

POLLY: I have no Excuse for my own Behaviour, Madam, but my Misfortunes.—And really, Madam, I suffer too upon your Account.

LUCY: But, Miss Polly—in the way of Friendship, will you give me leave to propose a Glass of Cordial to you?

POLLY: Strong-Waters are apt to give me the Head-ache— I hope, Madam, you will excuse me.

LUCY: Not the greatest Lady in the Land could have better in her Closet, for her own private drinking.—You seem mighty low in Spirits, my Dear.

POLLY: I am sorry, Madam, my Health will not allow me to accept of your Offer.—I should not have left you in the rude Manner I did when we met last, Madam, had not my Papa haul'd me away so unexpectedly—I was indeed somewhat provok'd, and perhaps might use some Expressions that were disrespectful.—But really, Madam, the Captain treated me with so much Contempt and Cruelty, that I deserv'd your Pity, rather than your Resentment.

LUCY: But since his Escape, no doubt all Matters are made up again.—Ah Polly! Polly! 'tis I am the unhappy Wife; and he loves you as if you were only his Mistress.

POLLY: Sure, Madam, you cannot think me so happy as to be the Object of your Jealousy.—A Man is always afraid of a Woman who loves him too well—so that I must expect to be neglected and avoided.

LUCY: Then our Cases, my dear Polly, are exactly alike. Both of us indeed have been too fond.

AIR

POLLY: *A Curse attends that Woman's Love,*
Who always would be pleasing.
LUCY: *The Pertness of the billing Dove,*
Like tickling, is but teazing.
POLLY: *What then in Love can Woman do?*
LUCY: *If we grow fond, they shun us.*
POLLY: *And when we fly them, they pursue.*
LUCY: *But leave us when they've won us.*

LUCY: Love is so very whimsical in both Sexes, that it is impossible to be lasting.—But my Heart is particular, and contradicts my own Observation.

POLLY: But really, Mistress Lucy, by his last Behaviour, I think I ought to envy you.—When I was forc'd from him, he did not shew the least Tenderness.—But perhaps, he hath a Heart not capable of it.

AIR

Among the Men, Coquets we find,
Who Court by turns all Woman-kind;
And we grant all their Hearts desir'd,
When they are flatter'd, and admir'd.

The Coquets of both Sexes are Self-lovers, and that is a
Love no other whatever can dispossess. I fear, my dear Lucy,
our Husband is one of those.

LUCY: Away with these melancholy Reflections,—indeed,
my dear Polly, we are both of us a Cup too low.—Let me
prevail upon you, to accept of my Offer.

AIR

Come, sweet Lass,
Let's banish Sorrow
'Till To-morrow;
Come, sweet Lass,
Let's take a chirping Glass.
Wine can clear
The Vapours of Despair;
And make us light as Air;
Then drink, and banish Care.

I can't bear, Child, to see you in such low Spirits.—And I
must persuade you to what I know will do you good.—
I shall now soon be even with the hypocritical Strumpet.
(*Aside.*)

SCENE IX

POLLY

POLLY: All this wheedling of Lucy cannot be for nothing.
—At this time too! when I know she hates me!—The Dis-
sembling of a Woman is always the Fore-runner of Mischief.
—By pouring Strong-Waters down my Throat, she thinks to
pump some Secrets out of me—I'll be upon my Guard, and
won't taste a Drop of her Liquor, I'm resolv'd.

SCENE X

LUCY, *with Strong-Waters;* POLLY

LUCY: Come, Miss Polly.

POLLY: Indeed, Child, you have given yourself trouble to
no purpose.—You must, my Dear, excuse me.

LUCY: Really, Miss Polly, you are so squeamishly affected about taking a Cup of Strong-Waters as a Lady before Company. I vow, Polly, I shall take it monstrously ill if you refuse me.—Brandy and Men (though Women love them never so well) are always taken by us with some Reluctance —unless 'tis in private.

POLLY: I protest, Madam, it goes against me.—What do I see! Macheath again in Custody!—Now every glimm'ring of Happiness is lost. (*Drops the Glass of Liquor on the Ground.*)

LUCY: Since things are thus, I'm glad the Wench hath escap'd: for by this Event, 'tis plain, she was not happy enough to deserve to be poison'd. (*Aside.*)

SCENE XI

LOCKIT, MACHEATH, PEACHUM, LUCY, POLLY

LOCKIT: Set your Heart to rest, Captain.—You have neither the Chance of Love or Money for another Escape,— for you are order'd to be call'd down upon your Tryal immediately.

PEACHUM: Away, Hussies!—This is not a time for a Man to be hamper'd with his Wives.—You see, the Gentleman is in Chains already.

LUCY: O Husband, Husband, my heart long'd to see thee; but to see thee thus distracts me!

POLLY: Will not my dear Husband look upon his Polly? Why hadst thou not flown to me for Protection? with me thou hadst been safe.

AIR

POLLY: *Hither, dear Husband, turn your Eyes.*
LUCY: *Bestow one Glance to cheer me.*
POLLY: *Think with that Look, thy Polly dyes.*
LUCY: *O shun me not—but hear me.*
POLLY: *'Tis Polly sues.*
LUCY: *. . . 'Tis Lucy speaks.*
POLLY: *Is thus true Love requited?*
LUCY: *My Heart is bursting.*
POLLY: *. . . Mine too breaks.*
LUCY: *Must I*
POLLY: *. . . Must I be slighted?*

MACHEATH: What would you have me say, Ladies?—You see, this Affair will soon be at an end, without my disobliging either of you.

PEACHUM: But the settling this Point, Captain, might prevent a Law-suit between your two Widows.

AIR

MACHEATH: *Which way shall I turn me?—How can I decide?*
Wives, the Day of our Death, are as fond as a Bride.
One Wife is too much for most Husbands to hear,
But two at a time there's no Mortal can bear.
This way, and that way, and which way I will,
What would comfort the one, t'other Wife would take ill.

POLLY: But if his own Misfortunes have made him insensible to mine—A Father sure will be more compassionate.—Dear, dear Sir, sink the material Evidence, and bring him off at his Tryal—Polly upon her Knees begs it of you.

AIR

When my Hero in Court appears,
And stands arraign'd for his Life;
Then think of poor Polly's Tears;
For Ah! Poor Polly's his Wife.
Like the Sailor he holds up his Hand,
Distrest on the dashing Wave.
To die a dry Death at Land,
Is as bad as a watry Grave.
And alas, poor Polly!
Alack, and well-a-day!
Before I was in Love,
Oh! every Month was May.

LUCY: If Peachum's Heart is harden'd, sure you, Sir, will have more Compassion on a Daughter.—I know the Evidence is in your Power.—How then can you be a Tyrant to me?

(*Kneeling.*)

AIR

When he holds up his Hand arraign'd for his Life,
O think of your Daughter, and think I'm his Wife!
What are Cannons, or Bombs, or clashing of Swords?
For Death is more certain by Witnesses Words.
Then nail up their Lips; that dread Thunder allay;
And each Month of my Life will hereafter be May.

LOCKIT: Macheath's time is come, Lucy.—We know our own Affairs, therefore let us have no more Whimpering or Whining.

PEACHUM: Set your Heart at rest, Polly.—Your Husband is to dye to-day.—Therefore, if you are not already provided, 'tis high time to look about for another. There's Comfort for you, you Slut.

LOCKIT: We are ready, Sir, to conduct you to the Old-Baily.

AIR

MACHEATH: *The Charge is prepar'd; The Lawyers are met,*
    The Judges all rang'd (a terrible Show!)
    I go, undismay'd.—For Death is a Debt,
    A Debt on demand.—So, take what I owe.
        Then farewell, my Love—Dear Charmers,
            adieu.
    Contented I die—'Tis the better for you.
    Here ends all Dispute the rest of our Lives.
    For this way at once I please all my Wives.

Now, Gentlemen, I am ready to attend you.

SCENE XII

LUCY, POLLY, FILCH

POLLY: Follow them, Filch, to the Court. And when the Tryal is over, bring me a particular Account of his Behaviour, and of every thing that happen'd.—You'll find me here with Miss Lucy. (*Exit* FILCH.) But why is all this Musick?

LUCY: The Prisoners, whose Tryals are put off till next Session, are diverting themselves.

POLLY: Sure there is nothing so charming as Musick! I'm fond of it to distraction!—But alas!—now, all Mirth seems an Insult upon my Affliction.—Let us retire, my dear Lucy, and indulge our Sorrows.—The noisy Crew, you see, are coming upon us. (*Exeunt.*)

(*A Dance of Prisoners in Chains, &c.*)

SCENE XIII

(*The Condemn'd Hold*)

MACHEATH, *in a melancholy Posture*

AIR

O cruel, cruel, cruel Case!
Must I suffer this Disgrace?

AIR

Of all the Friends in time of Grief,
When threatning Death looks grimmer,
Not one so sure can bring Relief,
As this best Friend, a Brimmer. (Drinks.)

AIR

Since I must swing,—I scorn, I scorn to wince or whine.
(Rises.)
AIR

But now again my Spirits sink;
I'll raise them high with Wine. (Drinks a Glass of Wine.)

AIR

But Valour the stronger grows,
The stronger Liquor we're drinking.
And how can we feel our Woes,
When we've lost the Trouble of Thinking? (Drinks.)

AIR

If thus—A Man can die
Much bolder with Brandy. (Pours out a Bumper of Brandy.)

AIR

So I drink off this Bumper.—And now I can stand the Test.
And my Comrades shall see, that I die as brave as the Best.
(Drinks.)
AIR

But can I leave my pretty Hussies,
Without one Tear, or tender Sigh?

AIR

Their Eyes, their Lips, their Busses
Recall my Love.—Ah, must I die?

282

Since Laws were made for ev'ry Degree,
To curb Vice in others, as well as me,
I wonder we han't better Company,
Upon Tyburn Tree!
But Gold from Law can take out the Sting;
And if rich Men like us were to swing,
'Twould thin the Land, such Numbers to string
Upon Tyburn Tree!

JAILOR: Some Friends of yours, Captain, desire to be admitted.—I leave you together.

Scene XIV

MACHEATH, BEN BUDGE, MATT OF THE MINT

MACHEATH: For my having broke Prison, you see, Gentlemen, I am order'd immediate Execution.—The Sheriffs Officers, I believe, are now at the Door.—That Jemmy Twitcher should peach me, I own surpriz'd me!—'Tis a plain Proof that the World is all alike, and that even our Gang can no more trust one another than other People. Therefore, I beg you, Gentlemen, look well to yourselves, for in all probability you may live some Months longer.

MATT: We are heartily sorry, Captain, for your Misfortune.—But 'tis what we must all come to.

MACHEATH: Peachum and Lockit, you know, are infamous Scoundrels. Their Lives are as much in your Power, as yours are in theirs.—Remember your dying Friend!—'Tis my last Request.—Bring those Villains to the Gallows before you, and I am satisfied.

MATT: We'll do't.

JAILOR: Miss Polly and Miss Lucy intreat a Word with you.

MACHEATH: Gentlemen, Adieu.

Scene XV

LUCY, MACHEATH, POLLY

MACHEATH: My dear Lucy—My dear Polly—Whatsoever hath past between us is now at an end.—If you are fond of marrying again, the best Advice I can give you, is to Ship yourselves off for the West-Indies, where you'll have a fair chance of getting a Husband a-piece; or by good Luck, two or three, as you like best.

POLLY: How can I support this Sight!

LUCY: There is nothing moves one so much as a great Man in Distress.

LUCY: *Would I might be hang'd!*

POLLY: *. . . And I would so too!*

LUCY: *To be hang'd with you.*

POLLY: *. . . My Dear, with you.*

MACHEATH: *O Leave me to Thought! I fear! I doubt!*
I tremble! I droop!—See, my Courage is out. (*Turns up the empty Bottle.*)

POLLY: *No token of Love?*

MACHEATH: *. . . See, my Courage is out.* (*Turns up the empty Pot.*)

LUCY: *No token of Love?*

POLLY: *. . . Adieu.*

LUCY: *. . . Farewell.*

MACHEATH: *But hark! I hear the Toll of the Bell.*

CHORUS: *Tol de rol lol, &c.*

JAILOR: Four Women more, Captain, with a Child a-piece!
See, here they come.

(*Enter* WOMEN *and* CHILDREN.)

MACHEATH: What—four Wives more!—This is too much.—
Here—tell the Sheriffs Officers I am ready. (*Exit* MACHEATH
guarded.)

SCENE XVI

To them, Enter PLAYER *and* BEGGAR

PLAYER: But, honest Friend, I hope you don't intend that
Macheath shall be really executed.

BEGGAR: Most certainly, Sir.—To make the Piece perfect,
I was for doing strict poetical Justice.—Macheath is to be
hang'd; and for the other Personages of the Drama, the
Audience must have suppos'd they were all either hang'd
or transported.

PLAYER: Why then, Friend, this is a down-right deep
Tragedy. The Catastrophe is manifestly wrong, for an Opera
must end happily.

BEGGAR: Your Objection, Sir, is very just; and is easily
remov'd. For you must allow, that in this kind of Drama, 'tis
no matter how absurdly things are brought about.—So—
you Rabble there—run and cry a Reprieve—let the Prisoner be brought back to his Wives in Triumph.

PLAYER: All this we must do, to comply with the Taste
of the Town.

BEGGAR: Through the whole Piece you may observe such a similitude of Manners in high and low Life, that it is difficult to determine whether (in the fashionable Vices) the fine Gentlemen imitate the Gentlemen of the Road, or the Gentlemen of the Road the fine Gentlemen.—Had the Play remain'd as I at first intended, it would have carried a most excellent Moral. 'Twould have shown that the lower Sort of People have their Vices in a degree as well as the Rich: And that they are punish'd for them.

SCENE XVII

To them, MACHEATH *with* RABBLE, *&c.*

MACHEATH: So, it seems, I am not left to my Choice, but must have a Wife at last.—Look ye, my Dears, we will have no Controversie now. Let us give this Day to Mirth, and I am sure she who thinks herself my Wife will testifie her Joy by a Dance.

ALL: Come, a Dance—a Dance.

MACHEATH: Ladies, I hope you will give me leave to present a Partner to each of you. And (if I may without Offence) for this time, I take Polly for mine.—And for Life, you Slut,—for we were really marry'd.—As for the rest—But at present keep your own Secret. (*To* POLLY.)

A DANCE

AIR

Thus I stand like the Turk, *with his Doxies around;*
From all Sides their Glances his Passion confound;
For black, brown, and fair, his Inconstancy burns,
And the different Beauties subdue him by turns:
Each calls forth her Charms, to provoke his Desires:
Though willing to all, with but one he retires.
But think of this Maxim, and put off your Sorrow,
The Wretch of To-day, may be happy To-morrow.
CHORUS: *But think of this Maxim, &c.*

Oscar Wilde:

THE IMPORTANCE OF BEING EARNEST

At a dinner where some guests were discussing the stock problem of whether Hamlet's madness is genuine or feigned, Oscar Wilde (1856-1900) laughed off the whole argument by announcing his intention of writing a treatise, "Are Hamlet's Commentators Really Mad or only Pretending to Be?" To attempt to analyze so light a comedy as Wilde's *The Importance of Being Earnest* (1895) is to run the risk of appearing mad, or at least very foolish, and therefore it may be best to skirt around the play and finally approach it through Wilde's own comments.

Wilde was the self-appointed high priest of England's Aesthetic Movement, an artistic movement which saw art as an end in itself and as independent of all morality. Asked whether a book could be immoral, Wilde countered that it could be far worse—it could be badly written. But Wilde's quarrel with moralizing art was partly aimed at freeing the artist not from ethics but from a particular system of aesthetics. He insisted that the poet's imagination be unfettered by the real world about him, and he claimed that the poet transcends everyday existence. While it is true that Wilde sometimes proceeded to write pieces which either have no relation to morality or which seem approvingly to describe ideas and situations uncongenial to most of society, his basic view that art is superior to life can be related to some eminently acceptable theories of art. In the Renaissance, for example, Sir Philip Sidney insisted that the poets depict a golden world whereas we fallen mortals live only in a brazen one. The world of the poet, Sidney says, is not a mere copy of what we see about us (why copy what is clear to every eye?) but is a superior view, an imaginative view of life as it *should* be rather than life as it is. Sidney's concept is highly moral, but we should note that in essence it defends the poet from the hack job of depicting the world about him and places high value on the poet's imagination.

The poet, Sidney insists, in forsaking our world, is showing us the nobler world of his visions.

The artist's nobler world is the subject of Wilde's clever —perhaps too clever, for the over-all point is easily lost under a heap of glittering wit—essay, *The Decay of Lying*. Wilde attacks realism—the production in art of life as it is to the naked eye—and insists that the artist has a higher function than to mirror nature. Life, Wilde claims, is merely the raw material of art. "The moment Art surrenders its imaginative medium it surrenders everything. As a method Realism is a complete failure." Wilde is especially close to Sidney when he insists that art ought not to copy nature, but rather that nature ought to copy art. Such a statement is shocking (Wilde, who had a good deal of the child in him, would have been disappointed if we were not shocked), but upon reflection we realize that nature (including, of course, mankind) does indeed imitate art, though unfortunately the art is usually bad. To take a crude example, we might note that Hollywood movies do not copy our homes and attitudes, but that, on the contrary, we sometimes strive to copy the movies. Small boys emulate Hopalong Cassidy, housewives strive for Audrey Hepburn's disarming ingenuousness, and men go undershirtless when Clark Gable does. This is only to say that while movies and TV do not exactly mirror our lives, we often strive to live up to the idealized world which these media reveal to us. If we may now use Wilde's word and say that the movies lie, we can perhaps say with him that "Lying, the telling of beautiful untrue things, is the proper aim of art." This view is narrow, but we might grant that such lying is the aim of some art.

Wilde's lying, thus vaguely defined, can be brought near to Sidney's golden world, but we must admit that the kinds of things that Wilde lied about are not the kinds of things that Sidney would aim for. Take the talk in *The Importance of Being Earnest*. None of us is as witty as Algernon or Jack, though we should all like to be. Yet the talk is inconsequential, and, however impressive from a writer's point of view, if we all strove to imitate it the world would probably not be a better place. The epigrams which crackle throughout the play rely chiefly on inverting clichés, and are closer to nonsense than to profound criticisms of our society. "Since her poor husband's death, I never saw a woman so altered," Lady Bracknell says of Lady Harbury; "she looks quite twenty years younger." Nonsense of this sort, of course, often amuses, perhaps because, as Schopenhauer says, "it is diverting to see Reason, that strict, untiring, troublesome governess, for once convicted of inadequacy."

Wilde's quips on marriage, idleness, and so forth may
occasionally criticize Victorian society and imply that a
better world is possible, but in general they are the pointless jests (rather like Groucho Marx's "I'd horsewhip you
if I had a horse") of a world which is delightful—so long
as it is kept at a distance on the stage.

The Importance of Being Earnest is often called a farce,
and the pigeonhole is at least as suited to it as is any other
compartment. A farce (from the Latin verb meaning "to
stuff" because "farces" were at first jokes or skits shoved
into a play) relies for its humor chiefly on situation rather
than on character. Plays dealing with mistaken identity,
where the humor consists mostly in enjoying, say, the spectacle of a tramp erroneously and deferentially treated as a
millionaire, are likely to be farcical. But if we think of
farce as necessarily crude, we must get another word or
(and this is the preferable alternative) alter our concept,
for, as Sir Max Beerbohm says in a review of *The Importance*, this play is different from all other farces, and
funnier, because of "the humorous contrast between its style
and matter." Its basic situations are the material of farce,
but no other farce has such polish.

The play has a philosophy, too, Wilde solemnly told a
reporter.

"Do you think the critics will understand your new play?"
"I hope not."

"What sort of play are we to expect?"

"It is exquisitely trivial, a delicate bubble of fancy, and
it has its philosophy."

"Its philosophy?"

"That we should treat all the trivial things of life seriously, and all the serious things of life with sincere and
studied triviality." How seriously or trivially we are to take
this pronouncement—and the play—will be left to the reader.
Incidentally, Wilde pretended, at least, to take his plays
trivially. "Most of them," he said, "are the results of bets."

The Importance of Being Earnest

A Trivial Comedy for Serious People

Characters

JOHN WORTHING, J.P.
ALGERNON MONCRIEFF
REV. CANON CHASUBLE, D.D.
MERRIMAN, *butler*
LANE, *manservant*
LADY BRACKNELL
HON. GWENDOLEN FAIRFAX
CECILY CARDEW
MISS PRISM, *governess*

ACT I

(*Morning-room in Algernon's flat in Half-Moon Street. The room is luxuriously and artistically furnished. The sound of a piano is heard in the adjoining room.*

LANE *is arranging afternoon tea on the table, and after the music has ceased,* ALGERNON *enters.*)

ALGERNON: Did you hear what I was playing, Lane?

LANE: I didn't think it polite to listen, sir.

ALGERNON: I'm sorry for that, for your sake. I don't play accurately—any one can play accurately—but I play with wonderful expression. As far as the piano is concerned, sentiment is my forte. I keep science for Life.

LANE: Yes, sir.

ALGERNON: And, speaking of the science of Life, have you got the cucumber sandwiches cut for Lady Bracknell?

LANE: Yes, sir. (*Hands them on a salver.*)

ALGERNON: (*Inspects them, takes two, and sits down on the sofa.*) Oh! . . . by the way, Lane, I see from your book that on Thursday night, when Lord Shoreman and Mr. Worthing were dining with me, eight bottles of champagne are entered as having been consumed.

LANE: Yes, sir; eight bottles and a pint.

ALGERNON: Why is it that at a bachelor's establishment the servants invariably drink the champagne? I ask merely for information.

LANE: I attribute it to the superior quality of the wine, sir. I have often observed that in married households the champagne is rarely of a first-rate brand.

ALGERNON: Good heavens! Is marriage so demoralizing as that?

LANE: I believe it *is* a very pleasant state, sir. I have had very little experience of it myself up to the present. I have only been married once. That was in consequence of a misunderstanding between myself and a young person.

ALGERNON (*languidly*): I don't know that I am much interested in your family life, Lane.

LANE: No, sir; it is not a very interesting subject. I never think of it myself.

ALGERNON: Very natural, I am sure. That will do, Lane, thank you.

LANE: Thank you, sir.

(LANE *goes out.*)

ALGERNON: Lane's views on marriage seem somewhat lax. Really, if the lower orders don't set us a good example, what on earth is the use of them? They seem, as a class, to have absolutely no sense of moral responsibility.

(*Enter* LANE.)

LANE: Mr. Ernest Worthing.

(*Enter* JACK. LANE *goes out.*)

ALGERNON: How are you, my dear Ernest? What brings you up to town?

JACK: Oh, pleasure, pleasure! What else should bring one anywhere? Eating as usual, I see, Algy!

ALGERNON (*stiffly*): I believe it is customary in good society to take some slight refreshment at five o'clock. Where have you been since last Thursday?

JACK (*sitting down on the sofa*): In the country.

ALGERNON: What on earth do you do there?

JACK (*pulling off his gloves*): When one is in town one amuses oneself. When one is in the country one amuses other people. It is excessively boring.

ALGERNON: And who are the people you amuse?

JACK (*airily*): Oh, neighbours, neighbours.

ALGERNON: Got nice neighbours in your part of Shropshire?

JACK: Perfectly horrid! Never speak to one of them.

ALGERNON: How immensely you must amuse them! (*Goes over and takes sandwich.*) By the way, Shropshire is your county, is it not?

JACK: Eh? Shropshire? Yes, of course. Hallo! Why all these cups? Why cucumber sandwiches? Why such reckless extravagance in one so young? Who is coming to tea?

ALGERNON: Oh! merely Aunt Augusta and Gwendolen.

JACK: How perfectly delightful!

ALGERNON: Yes, that is all very well; but I am afraid Aunt Augusta won't quite approve of your being here.

JACK: May I ask why?

ALGERNON: My dear fellow, the way you flirt with Gwendolen is perfectly disgraceful. It is almost as bad as the way Gwendolen flirts with you.

JACK: I am in love with Gwendolen. I have come up to town expressly to propose to her.

ALGERNON: I thought you had come up for pleasure? . . . I call that business.

JACK: How utterly unromantic you are!

ALGERNON: I really don't see anything romantic in proposing. It is very romantic to be in love. But there is nothing romantic about a definite proposal. Why, one may be accepted. One usually is, I believe. Then the excitement is all over. The very essence of romance is uncertainty. If ever I get married, I'll certainly try to forget the fact.

JACK: I have no doubt about that, dear Algy. The Divorce Court was specially invented for people whose memories are so curiously constituted.

ALGERNON: Oh! there is no use speculating on that subject. Divorces are made in Heaven—(JACK *puts out his hand to take a sandwich.* ALGERNON *at once interferes.*) Please don't touch the cucumber sandwiches. They are ordered specially for Aunt Augusta. (*Takes one and eats it.*)

JACK: Well, you have been eating them all the time.

ALGERNON: That is quite a different matter. She is my aunt. (*Takes plate from below.*) Have some bread and butter. The bread and butter is for Gwendolen. Gwendolen is devoted to bread and butter.

JACK (*advancing to table and helping himself*): And very good bread and butter it is too.

ALGERNON: Well, my dear fellow, you need not eat as if you were going to eat it all. You behave as if you were married to her already. You are not married to her already, and I don't think you ever will be.

JACK: Why on earth do you say that?

ALGERNON: Well, in the first place, girls never marry the men they flirt with. Girls don't think it right.

JACK: Oh, that is nonsense!

ALGERNON: It isn't. It is a great truth. It accounts for the extraordinary number of bachelors that one sees all over the place. In the second place, I don't give my consent.

JACK: Your consent!

ALGERNON: My dear fellow, Gwendolen is my first cousin. And before I allow you to marry her, you will have to clear up the whole question of Cecily. (*Rings bell.*)

JACK: Cecily! What on earth do you mean? What do you mean, Algy, by Cecily! I don't know any one of the name of Cecily.

(*Enter* LANE.)

ALGERNON: Bring me that cigarette case Mr. Worthing left in the smoking-room the last time he dined here.

LANE: Yes, sir.

(LANE *goes out.*)

JACK: Do you mean to say you have had my cigarette case all this time? I wish to goodness you had let me know. I have been writing frantic letters to Scotland Yard about it. I was very nearly offering a large reward.

ALGERNON: Well, I wish you would offer one. I happen to be more than usually hard up.

JACK: There is no good offering a large reward now that the thing is found.

(*Enter* LANE *with the cigarette case on a salver.* ALGERNON *takes it at once.* LANE *goes out.*)

ALGERNON: I think that is rather mean of you, Ernest, I must say. (*Opens case and examines it.*) However, it makes no matter, for, now that I look at the inscription inside, I find that the thing isn't yours after all.

JACK: Of course it's mine. (*Moving to him.*) You have seen me with it a hundred times, and you have no right whatsoever to read what is written inside. It is a very ungentlemanly thing to read a private cigarette case.

ALGERNON: Oh! it is absurd to have a hard and fast rule about what one should read and what one shouldn't. More than half of modern culture depends on what one shouldn't read.

JACK: I am quite aware of the fact, and I don't propose to discuss modern culture. It isn't the sort of thing one should talk of in private. I simply want my cigarette case back.

ALGERNON: Yes; but this isn't your cigarette case. This cigarette case is a present from someone of the name of Cecily, and you said you didn't know anyone of that name.

JACK: Well, if you want to know, Cecily happens to be my aunt.

ALGERNON: Your aunt!

JACK: Yes. Charming old lady she is, too. Lives at Tunbridge Wells. Just give it back to me, Algy.

ALGERNON (*retreating to back of sofa*): But why does she call herself little Cecily if she is your aunt and lives at Tunbridge Wells. (*Reading.*) "From little Cecily with her fondest love."

JACK (*moving to sofa and kneeling upon it*): My dear fellow, what on earth is there in that? Some aunts are tall, some aunts are not tall. That is a matter that surely an aunt may be allowed to decide for herself. You seem to think that every aunt should be exactly like your aunt! That is absurd. For Heaven's sake give me back my cigarette case. (*Follows* ALGERNON *round the room.*)

ALGERNON: Yes. But why does your aunt call you her uncle? "From little Cecily, with her fondest love to her dear Uncle Jack." There is no objection, I admit, to an aunt being a small aunt, but why an aunt, no matter what her size may be, should call her own nephew her uncle, I can't quite make out. Besides, your name isn't Jack at all; it is Ernest.

JACK: It isn't Ernest; it's Jack.

ALGERNON: You have always told me it was Ernest. I have introduced you to every one as Ernest. You answer to the name of Ernest. You look as if your name was Ernest. You are the most earnest-looking person I ever saw in my life. It is perfectly absurd your saying that your name isn't Ernest. It's on your cards. Here is one of them (*taking it from case*). "Mr. Ernest Worthing, B.4, The Albany." I'll keep this as a proof that your name is Ernest if ever you attempt to deny it to me, or to Gwendolen, or to any one else. (*Puts the card in his pocket.*)

JACK: Well, my name is Ernest in town and Jack in the country, and the cigarette case was given to me in the country.

ALGERNON: Yes, but that does not account for the fact that your small Aunt Cecily, who lives at Tunbridge Wells, calls you her dear uncle. Come, old boy, you had much better have the thing out at once.

JACK: My dear Algy, you talk exactly as if you were a dentist. It is very vulgar to talk like a dentist when one isn't a dentist. It produces a false impression.

ALGERNON: Well, that is exactly what dentists always do. Now, go on! Tell me the whole thing. I may mention that I have always suspected you of being a confirmed and secret Bunburyist; and I am quite sure of it now.

JACK: Bunburyist? What on earth do you mean by a Bunburyist?

ALGERNON: I'll reveal to you the meaning of that incomparable expression as soon as you are kind enough to inform me why you are Ernest in town and Jack in the country.

JACK: Well, produce my cigarette case first.

ALGERNON: Here it is. (*Hands cigarette case.*) Now produce your explanation, and pray make it improbable. (*Sits on sofa.*)

JACK: My dear fellow, there is nothing improbable about my explanation at all. In fact it's perfectly ordinary. Old Mr. Thomas Cardew, who adopted me when I was a little boy, made me in his will guardian to his granddaughter, Miss Cecily Cardew. Cecily, who addresses me as her uncle from motives of respect that you could not possibly appreciate, lives at my place in the country under the charge of her admirable governess, Miss Prism.

ALGERNON: Where is that place in the country, by the way?

JACK: That is nothing to you, dear boy. You are not going to be invited. . . . I may tell you candidly that the place is not in Shropshire.

ALGERNON: I suspected that, my dear fellow! I have Bunburyed all over Shropshire on two separate occasions. Now, go on. Why are you Ernest in town and Jack in the country?

JACK: My dear Algy, I don't know whether you will be able to understand my real motives. You are hardly serious enough. When one is placed in the position of guardian, one has to adopt a very high moral tone on all subjects. It's one's duty to do so. And as a high moral tone can hardly be said to conduce very much to either one's health or one's happiness, in order to get up to town I have always pretended to have a younger brother of the name of Ernest, who lives in the Albany, and gets into the most dreadful scrapes. That, my dear Algy, is the whole truth pure and simple.

ALGERNON: The truth is rarely pure and never simple. Modern life would be very tedious if it were either, and modern literature a complete impossibility!

JACK: That wouldn't be at all a bad thing.

ALGERNON: Literary criticism is not your forte, my dear fellow. Don't try it. You should leave that to people who haven't been at a University. They do it so well in the daily papers. What you really are is a Bunburyist. I was quite right in saying you were a Bunburyist. You are one of the most advanced Bunburyists I know.

JACK: What on earth do you mean?

ALGERNON: You have invented a very useful younger brother called Ernest, in order that you may be able to come up to town as often as you like. I have invented an invaluable permanent invalid called Bunbury, in order that I may be able to go down into the country whenever I choose. Bunbury is perfectly invaluable. If it wasn't for Bunbury's extraordinary bad health, for instance, I wouldn't be able to dine with you at Willis's to-night, for I have been really engaged to Aunt Augusta for more than a week.

JACK: I haven't asked you to dine with me anywhere to-night.

ALGERNON: I know. You are absurdly careless about sending out invitations. It is very foolish of you. Nothing annoys people so much as not receiving invitations.

JACK: You had much better dine with your Aunt Augusta.

ALGERNON: I haven't the smallest intention of doing anything of the kind. To begin with, I dined there on Monday, and once a week is quite enough to dine with one's own relations. In the second place, whenever I do dine there I am always treated as a member of the family, and sent down with either no woman at all, or two. In the third place, I know perfectly well whom she will place me next to, to-night. She will place me next Mary Farquhar, who always flirts with her own husband across the dinner-table. That is not very pleasant. Indeed, it is not even decent . . . and that sort of thing is enormously on the increase. The amount of women in London who flirt with their own husbands is perfectly scandalous. It looks so bad. It is simply washing one's clean linen in public. Besides, now that I know you to be a confirmed Bunburyist I naturally want to talk to you about Bunburying. I want to tell you the rules.

JACK: I'm not a Bunburyist at all. If Gwendolen accepts me, I am going to kill my brother, indeed I think I'll kill him in any case. Cecily is a little too much interested in him. It is rather a bore. So I am going to get rid of Ernest. And I strongly advise you to do the same with Mr. . . . with your invalid friend who has the absurd name.

ALGERNON: Nothing will induce me to part with Bunbury, and if you ever get married, which seems to me extremely problematic, you will be very glad to know Bunbury. A man who marries without knowing Bunbury has a very tedious time of it.

JACK: That is nonsense. If I marry a charming girl like Gwendolen, and she is the only girl I ever saw in my life that I would marry, I certainly won't want to know Bunbury.

ALGERNON: Then your wife will. You don't seem to realize, that in married life three is company and two is none.

JACK (*sententiously*): That, my dear young friend, is the theory that the corrupt French Drama has been propounding for the last fifty years.

ALGERNON: Yes; and that the happy English home has proved in half the time.

JACK: For heaven's sake, don't try to be cynical. It's perfectly easy to be cynical.

ALGERNON: My dear fellow, it isn't easy to be anything nowadays. There's such a lot of beastly competition about. (*The sound of an electric bell is heard.*) Ah! that must be Aunt Augusta. Only relatives, or creditors, ever ring in that Wagnerian manner. Now, if I get her out of the way for ten minutes, so that you can have an opportunity for proposing to Gwendolen, may I dine with you to-night at Willis's?

JACK: I suppose so, if you want to.

ALGERNON: Yes, but you must be serious about it. I hate

people who are not serious about meals. It is so shallow of them.

(*Enter* LANE.)

LANE: Lady Bracknell and Miss Fairfax.

(ALGERNON *goes forward to meet them. Enter* LADY BRACK-NELL *and* GWENDOLEN.)

LADY BRACKNELL: Good afternoon, dear Algernon, I hope you are behaving very well.

ALGERNON: I'm feeling very well, Aunt Augusta.

LADY BRACKNELL: That's not quite the same thing. In fact the two things rarely go together. (*Sees* JACK *and bows to him with icy coldness.*) ·

ALGERNON (*to* GWENDOLEN): Dear me, you are smart!

GWENDOLEN: I am always smart! Am I not, Mr. Worthing?

JACK: You're quite perfect, Miss Fairfax.

GWENDOLEN: Oh! I hope I am not that. It would leave no room for developments, and I intend to develop in many directions. (GWENDOLEN *and* JACK *sit down together in the corner.*)

LADY BRACKNELL: I'm sorry if we are a little late, Algernon, but I was obliged to call on dear Lady Harbury. I hadn't been there since her poor husband's death. I never saw a woman so altered; she looks quite twenty years younger. And now I'll have a cup of tea and one of those nice cucumber sandwiches you promised me.

ALGERNON: Certainly, Aunt Augusta. (*Goes over to tea-table.*)

LADY BRACKNELL: Won't you come and sit here, Gwendolen?

GWENDOLEN: Thanks, mamma, I'm quite comfortable where I am.

ALGERNON (*picking up empty plate in horror*): Good heavens! Lane! Why are there no cucumber sandwiches? I ordered them specially.

LANE (*gravely*): There were no cucumbers in the market this morning, sir. I went down twice.

ALGERNON: No cucumbers!

LANE: No, sir. Not even for ready money.

ALGERNON: That will do, Lane, thank you.

LANE: Thank you, sir. (*Goes out.*)

ALGERNON: I am greatly distressed, Aunt Augusta, about there being no cucumbers, not even for ready money.

LADY BRACKNELL: It really makes no matter, Algernon.

I had some crumpets with Lady Harbury, who seems to me to be living entirely for pleasure now.

ALGERNON: I hear her hair has turned quite gold from grief.

LADY BRACKNELL: It certainly has changed its colour. From what cause I, of course, cannot say. (ALGERNON *crosses and hands tea*.) Thank you. I've quite a treat for you to-night, Algernon. I am going to send you down with Mary Farquhar. She is such a nice woman, and so attentive to her husband. It's delightful to watch them.

ALGERNON: I am afraid, Aunt Augusta, I shall have to give up the pleasure of dining with you to-night after all.

LADY BRACKNELL (*frowning*): I hope not, Algernon. It would put my table completely out. Your uncle would have to dine upstairs. Fortunately he is accustomed to that.

ALGERNON: It is a great bore, and, I need hardly say, a terrible disappointment to me, but the fact is I have just had a telegram to say that my poor friend Bunbury is very ill again. (*Exchanges glances with* JACK.) They seem to think I should be with him.

LADY BRACKNELL: It is very strange. This Mr. Bunbury seems to suffer from curiously bad health.

ALGERNON: Yes; poor Bunbury is a dreadful invalid.

LADY BRACKNELL: Well, I must say, Algernon, that I think it is high time that Mr. Bunbury made up his mind whether he was going to live or to die. This shilly-shallying with the question is absurd. Nor do I in any way approve of the modern sympathy with invalids. I consider it morbid. Illness of any kind is hardly a thing to be encouraged in others. Health is the primary duty of life. I am always telling that to your poor uncle, but he never seems to take much notice . . . as far as any improvement in his ailments goes. I should be much obliged if you would ask Mr. Bunbury, from me, to be kind enough not to have a relapse on Saturday, for I rely on you to arrange my music for me. It is my last reception, and one wants something that will encourage conversation, particularly at the end of the season when every one has practically said whatever they had to say, which, in most cases, was probably not much.

ALGERNON: I'll speak to Bunbury, Aunt Augusta, if he is still conscious, and I think I can promise you he'll be all right by Saturday. Of course the music is a great difficulty. You see, if one plays good music, people don't listen, and if one plays bad music, people don't talk. But I'll run over the programme I've drawn out, if you will kindly come into the next room for a moment.

LADY BRACKNELL: Thank you, Algernon. It is very thoughtful of you. (*Rising, and following* ALGERNON.) I'm sure the programme will be delightful, after a few expurgations. French songs I cannot possibly allow. People always seem to think that they are improper, and either look shocked, which is vulgar, or laugh, which is worse. But German sounds a thoroughly respectable language, and, indeed I believe is so. Gwendolen, you will accompany me.

GWENDOLEN: Certainly, mamma.

(LADY BRACKNELL *and* ALGERNON *go into the music-room;* GWENDOLEN *remains behind.*)

JACK: Charming day it has been, Miss Fairfax.

GWENDOLEN: Pray don't talk to me about the weather, Mr. Worthing. Whenever people talk to me about the weather, I always feel quite certain that they mean something else. And that makes me so nervous.

JACK: I do mean something else.

GWENDOLEN: I thought so. In fact, I am never wrong.

JACK: And I would like to be allowed to take advantage of Lady Bracknell's temporary absence. . . .

GWENDOLEN: I would certainly advise you to do so. Mamma has a way of coming back suddenly into a room that I have often had to speak to her about.

JACK (*nervously*): Miss Fairfax, ever since I met you I have admired you more than any girl . . . I have ever met since . . . I met you.

GWENDOLEN: Yes, I am quite aware of the fact. And I often wish that in public, at any rate, you had been more demonstrative. For me you have always had an irresistible fascination. Even before I met you I was far from indifferent to you. (JACK *looks at her in amazement.*) We live, as I hope you know, Mr. Worthing, in an age of ideals. The fact is constantly mentioned in the more expensive monthly magazines, and has reached the provincial pulpits, I am told; and my ideal has always been to love some one of the name of Ernest. There is something in that name that inspires absolute confidence. The moment Algernon first mentioned to me that he had a friend called Ernest, I knew I was destined to love you.

JACK: You really love me, Gwendolen?

GWENDOLEN: Passionately!

JACK: Darling! You don't know how happy you've made me.

GWENDOLEN: My own Ernest!

JACK: But you don't really mean to say that you couldn't love me if my name wasn't Ernest?

GWENDOLEN: But your name is Ernest.

JACK: Yes, I know it is. But supposing it was something else? Do you mean to say you couldn't love me then?

GWENDOLEN (*glibly*): Ah! that is clearly a metaphysical speculation, and like most metaphysical speculations has very little reference at all to the actual facts of real life, as we know them.

JACK: Personally, darling, to speak quite candidly, I don't much care about the name of Ernest. . . . I don't think the name suits me at all.

GWENDOLEN: It suits you perfectly. It is a divine name. It has a music of its own. It produces vibrations.

JACK: Well, really, Gwendolen, I must say that I think there are lots of other much nicer names. I think Jack, for instance, a charming name.

GWENDOLEN: Jack? . . . No, there is very little music in the name Jack, if any at all, indeed. It does not thrill. It produces absolutely no vibrations. . . . I have known several Jacks, and they all, without exception, were more than usually plain. Besides, Jack is a notorious domesticity for John! And I pity any woman who is married to a man called John. She would probably never be allowed to know the entrancing pleasure of a single moment's solitude. The only really safe name is Ernest.

JACK: Gwendolen, I must get christened at once—I mean we must get married at once. There is no time to be lost.

GWENDOLEN: Married, Mr. Worthing?

JACK (*astounded*): Well . . . surely. You know that I love you, and you led me to believe, Miss Fairfax, that you were not absolutely indifferent to me.

GWENDOLEN: I adore you. But you haven't proposed to me yet. Nothing has been said at all about marriage. The subject has not even been touched on.

JACK: Well . . . may I propose to you now?

GWENDOLEN: I think it would be an admirable opportunity. And to spare you any possible disappointment, Mr. Worthing, I think it only fair to tell you quite frankly beforehand that I am fully determined to accept you.

JACK: Gwendolen!

GWENDOLEN: Yes, Mr. Worthing, what have you got to say to me?

JACK: You know what I have got to say to you.

GWENDOLEN: Yes, but you don't say it.

JACK: Gwendolen, will you marry me? (*Goes on his knees.*)

GWENDOLEN: Of course I will, darling. How long you have

been about it! I am afraid you have had very little experience in how to propose.

JACK: My own one, I have never loved any one in the world but you.

GWENDOLEN: Yes, but men often propose for practice. I know my brother Gerald does. All my girl-friends tell me so. What wonderfully blue eyes you have, Ernest! They are quite, quite blue. I hope you will always look at me just like that, especially when there are other people present.

(*Enter* LADY BRACKNELL.)

LADY BRACKNELL: Mr. Worthing! Rise sir, from this semi-recumbent posture. It is most indecorous.

GWENDOLEN: Mamma! (*He tries to rise; she restrains him.*) I must beg you to retire. This is no place for you. Besides, Mr. Worthing has not quite finished yet.

LADY BRACKELL: Finished what, may I ask?

GWENDOLEN: I am engaged to Mr. Worthing, mamma. (*They rise together.*)

LADY BRACKNELL: Pardon me, you are not engaged to any one. When you do become engaged to some one, I, or your father, should his health permit him, will inform you of the fact. An engagement should come on a young girl as a surprise, pleasant or unpleasant, as the case may be. It is hardly a matter that she could be allowed to arrange for herself. . . . And now I have a few questions to put to you, Mr. Worthing. While I am making these inquiries, you, Gwendolen, will wait for me below in the carriage.

GWENDOLEN (*reproachfully*): Mamma!

LADY BRACKNELL: In the carriage, Gwendolen! (GWENDOLEN *goes to the door. She and* JACK *blow kisses to each other behind* LADY BRACKNELL'S *back.* LADY BRACKNELL *looks vaguely about as if she could not understand what the noise was. Finally turns round.*) Gwendolen, the carriage!

GWENDOLEN: Yes, mamma. (*Goes out, looking back at* JACK.)

LADY BRACKNELL (*sitting down*): You can take a seat, Mr. Worthing.

(*Looks in her pocket for note-book and pencil.*)

JACK: Thank you, Lady Bracknell, I prefer standing.

LADY BRACKNELL (*pencil and note-book in hand*): I feel bound to tell you that you are not down on my list of eligible young men, although I have the same list as the dear Duchess of Bolton has. We work together, in fact. However, I am quite ready to enter your name, should your answers be what a really affectionate mother requires. Do you smoke?

JACK: Well, yes, I must admit I smoke.

LADY BRACKNELL: I am glad to hear it. A man should always have an occupation of some kind. There are far too many idle men in London as it is. How old are you?

JACK: Twenty-nine.

LADY BRACKNELL: A very good age to be married at. I have always been of opinion that a man who desires to get married should know either everything or nothing. Which do you know?

JACK (*after some hesitation*): I know nothing, Lady Bracknell.

LADY BRACKNELL: I am pleased to hear it. I do not approve of anything that tampers with natural ignorance. Ignorance is like a delicate exotic fruit; touch it and the bloom is gone. The whole theory of modern education is radically unsound. Fortunately in England, at any rate, education produces no effect whatsoever. If it did, it would prove a serious danger to the upper classes, and probably lead to acts of violence in Grosvenor Square. What is your income?

JACK: Between seven and eight thousand a year.

LADY BRACKNELL (*makes a note in her book*): In land, or in investments?

JACK: In investments, chiefly.

LADY BRACKNELL: That is satisfactory. What between the duties expected of one during one's lifetime, and the duties exacted from one after one's death, land has ceased to be either a profit or a pleasure. It gives one position, and prevents one from keeping it up. That's all that can be said about land.

JACK: I have a country house with some land, of course, attached to it, about fifteen hundred acres, I believe; but I don't depend on that for my real income. In fact, as far as I can make out, the poachers are the only people who make anything out of it.

LADY BRACKNELL: A country house! How many bedrooms? Well, that point can be cleared up afterwards. You have a town house, I hope? A girl with a simple, unspoiled nature, like Gwendolen, could hardly be expected to reside in the country.

JACK: Well, I own a house in Belgrave Square, but it is let by the year to Lady Bloxham. Of course, I can get it back whenever I like, at six months' notice.

LADY BRACKNELL: Lady Bloxham? I don't know her.

JACK: Oh, she goes about very little. She is a lady considerably advanced in years.

LADY BRACKNELL: Ah, nowadays that is no guarantee of respectability of character. What number in Belgrave Square?

JACK: 149.

LADY BRACKNELL (*shaking her head*): The unfashionable side. I thought there was something. However, that could easily be altered.

JACK: Do you mean the fashion, or the side?

LADY BRACKNELL (*sternly*): Both, if necessary, I presume. What are your politics?

JACK: Well, I am afraid I really have none. I am a Liberal Unionist.

LADY BRACKNELL: Oh, they count as Tories. They dine with us. Or come in the evening, at any rate. Now to minor matters. Are your parents living?

JACK: I have lost both my parents.

LADY BRACKNELL: To lose one parent, Mr. Worthing, may be regarded as a misfortune; to lose both looks like carelessness. Who was your father? He was evidently a man of some wealth. Was he born in what the Radical papers call the purple of commerce, or did he rise from the ranks of the aristocracy?

JACK: I am afraid I really don't know. The fact is, Lady Bracknell, I said I had lost my parents. It would be nearer the truth to say that my parents seem to have lost me. . . . I don't actually know who I am by birth. I was . . . well, I was found.

LADY BRACKNELL: Found!

JACK: The late Mr. Thomas Cardew, an old gentleman of a very charitable and kindly disposition, found me, and gave me the name of Worthing, because he happened to have a first-class ticket for Worthing in his pocket at the time. Worthing is a place in Sussex. It is a seaside resort.

LADY BRACKNELL: Where did the charitable gentleman who had a first-class ticket for this seaside resort find you?

JACK (*gravely*): In a hand-bag.

LADY BRACKNELL: A hand-bag?

JACK (*very seriously*): Yes, Lady Bracknell. I was in a hand-bag—a somewhat large, black leather hand-bag, with handles to it—an ordinary hand-bag in fact.

LADY BRACKNELL: In what locality did this Mr. James, or Thomas, Cardew come across this ordinary hand-bag?

JACK: In the cloak-room at Victoria Station. It was given to him in mistake for his own.

LADY BRACKNELL: The cloak-room at Victoria Station?

JACK: Yes. The Brighton line.

LADY BRACKNELL: The line is immaterial. Mr. Worthing, I confess I feel somewhat bewildered by what you have just told me. To be born, or at any rate bred, in a hand-bag, whether it had handles or not, seems to me to display a contempt for the ordinary decencies of family life that reminds one of the worst excesses of the French Revolution. And I presume you know what that unfortunate movement led to? As for the particular locality in which the hand-bag was found, a cloak-room at a railway station might serve to conceal a social indiscretion—has probably, indeed, been used for that purpose before now—but it could hardly be regarded as an assured basis for a recognized position in good society.

JACK: May I ask you then what you would advise me to do? I need hardly say I would do anything in the world to ensure Gwendolen's happiness.

LADY BRACKNELL: I would strongly advise you, Mr. Worthing, to try and acquire some relations as soon as possible, and to make a definite effort to produce at any rate one parent, of either sex, before the season is quite over.

JACK: Well, I don't see how I could possibly manage to do that. I can produce the hand-bag at any moment. It is in my dressing-room at home. I really think that should satisfy you, Lady Bracknell.

LADY BRACKNELL: Me, sir! What has it to do with me? You can hardly imagine that I and Lord Bracknell would dream of allowing our only daughter—a girl brought up with the utmost care—to marry into a cloak-room, and form an alliance with a parcel. Good morning, Mr. Worthing!

(LADY BRACKNELL *sweeps out in majestic indignation.*)

JACK: Good morning! (ALGERNON, *from the other room, strikes up the Wedding March.* JACK *looks perfectly furious, and goes to the door.*) For goodness' sake don't play that ghastly tune, Algy! How idiotic you are!

(*The music stops and* ALGERNON *enters cheerily.*)

ALGERNON: Didn't it go off all right, old boy? You don't mean to say Gwendolen refused you? I know it is a way she has. She is always refusing people. I think it is most ill-natured of her.

JACK: Oh, Gwendolen is as right as a trivet. As far as she is concerned, we are engaged. Her mother is perfectly unbearable. Never met such a Gorgon. . . . I don't really know what a Gorgon is like, but I am quite sure that Lady Bracknell is one. In any case, she is a monster, without being a myth, which is rather unfair. . . . I beg your pardon, Algy, I suppose I shouldn't talk about your own aunt in that way before you.

ALGERNON: My dear boy, I love hearing my relations abused. It is the only thing that makes me put up with them at all. Relations are simply a tedious pack of people, who haven't got the remotest knowledge of how to live, nor the smallest instinct about when to die.

JACK: Oh, that is nonsense!

ALGERNON: It isn't!

JACK: Well, I won't argue about the matter. You always want to argue about things.

ALGERNON: That is exactly what things were originally made for.

JACK: Upon my word, if I thought that, I'd shoot myself. . . . (*A pause.*) You don't think there is any chance of Gwendolen becoming like her mother in about a hundred and fifty years, do you, Algy?

ALGERNON: All women become like their mothers. That is their tragedy. No man does. That's his.

JACK: Is that clever?

ALGERNON: It is perfectly phrased! and quite as true as any observation in civilized life should be.

JACK: I am sick to death of cleverness. Everybody is clever nowadays. You can't go anywhere without meeting clever people. The thing has become an absolute public nuisance. I wish to goodness we had a few fools left.

ALGERNON: We have.

JACK: I should extremely like to meet them. What do they talk about?

ALGERNON: The fools? Oh! about the clever people, of course.

JACK: What fools.

ALGERNON: By the way, did you tell Gwendolen the truth about your being Ernest in town, and Jack in the country?

JACK (*in a very patronizing manner*): My dear fellow, the truth isn't quite the sort of thing one tells to a nice, sweet, refined girl. What extraordinary ideas you have about the way to behave to a woman!

ALGERNON: The only way to behave to a woman is to make love to her, if she is pretty, and to someone else, if she is plain.

JACK: Oh, that is nonsense.

ALGERNON: What about your brother? What about the profligate Ernest?

JACK: Oh, before the end of the week I shall have got rid of him. I'll say he died in Paris of apoplexy. Lots of people die of apoplexy, quite suddenly, don't they?

ALGERNON: Yes, but it's hereditary, my dear fellow. It's

a sort of thing that runs in families. You had much better say a severe chill.

JACK: You are sure a severe chill isn't hereditary, or anything of that kind?

ALGERNON: Of course it isn't!

JACK: Very well, then. My poor brother Ernest is carried off suddenly, in Paris, by a severe chill. That gets rid of him.

ALGERNON: But I thought you said that . . . Miss Cardew was a little too much interested in your poor brother Ernest? Won't she feel his loss a good deal?

JACK: Oh, that is all right. Cecily is not a silly romantic girl, I am glad to say. She has got a capital appetite, goes long walks, and pays no attention at all to her lessons.

ALGERNON: I would rather like to see Cecily.

JACK: I will take very good care you never do. She is excessively pretty, and she is only just eighteen.

ALGERNON: Have you told Gwendolen yet that you have an excessively pretty ward who is only just eighteen?

JACK: Oh! one doesn't blurt these things out to people. Cecily and Gwendolen are perfectly certain to be extremely great friends. I'll bet you anything you like that half an hour after they have met, they will be calling each other sister.

ALGERNON: Women only do that when they have called each other a lot of other things first. Now, my dear boy, if we want to get a good table at Willis's, we really must go and dress. Do you know it is nearly seven?

JACK (*irritably*): Oh! it always is nearly seven.

ALGERNON: Well, I'm hungry.

JACK: I never knew you when you weren't. . . .

ALGERNON: What shall we do after dinner? Go to a theatre?

JACK: Oh no! I loathe listening.

ALGERNON: Well, let us go to the Club?

JACK: Oh, no! I hate talking.

ALGERNON: Well, we might trot round to the Empire at ten?

JACK: Oh, no! I can't bear looking at things. It is so silly.

ALGERNON: Well, what shall we do?

JACK: Nothing!

ALGERNON: It is awfully hard work doing nothing. However, I don't mind hard work where there is no definite object of any kind.

(*Enter* LANE.)

LANE: Miss Fairfax.

(*Enter* GWENDOLEN. LANE *goes out*.)

ALGERNON: Gwendolen, upon my word!

GWENDOLEN: Algy, kindly turn your back. I have something very particular to say to Mr. Worthing.

ALGERNON: Really, Gwendolen, I don't think I can allow this at all.

GWENDOLEN: Algy, you always adopt a strictly immoral attitude towards life. You are not quite old enough to do that. (ALGERNON *retires to the fire-place.*)

JACK: My own darling!

GWENDOLEN: Ernest, we may never be married. From the expression on mamma's face I fear we never shall. Few parents nowadays pay any regard to what their children say to them. The old-fashioned respect for the young is fast dying out. Whatever influence I ever had over mamma, I lost at the age of three. But although she may prevent us from becoming man and wife, and I may marry someone else, and marry often, nothing that she can possibly do can alter my eternal devotion to you.

JACK: Dear Gwendolen!

GWENDOLEN: The story of your romantic origin, as related to me by mamma, with unpleasing comments, has naturally stirred the deeper fibres of my nature. Your Christian name has an irresistible fascination. The simplicity of your character makes you exquisitely incomprehensible to me. Your town address at the Albany I have. What is your address in the country?

JACK: The Manor House, Woolton, Hertfordshire.

(ALGERNON, *who has been carefully listening, smiles to himself, and writes the address on his shirt-cuff. Then picks up the Railway Guide.*)

GWENDOLEN: There is a good postal service, I suppose? It may be necessary to do something desperate. That of course will require serious consideration. I will communicate with you daily.

JACK: My own one!

GWENDOLEN: How long do you remain in town?

JACK: Till Monday.

GWENDOLEN: Good! Algy, you may turn round now.

ALGERNON: Thanks, I've turned round already.

GWENDOLEN: You may also ring the bell.

JACK: You will let me see you to your carriage, my own darling?

GWENDOLEN: Certainly.

JACK (*to* LANE, *who now enters*): I will see Miss Fairfax out.

LANE: Yes, sir. (JACK *and* GWENDOLEN *go off.*)

(LANE *presents several letters on a salver to* ALGERNON. *It is to be surmised that they are bills, as* ALGERNON, *after looking at the envelopes, tears them up.*)

ALGERNON: A glass of sherry, Lane.
LANE: Yes, sir.
ALGERNON: To-morrow, Lane, I'm going Bunburying.
LANE: Yes, sir.
ALGERNON: I shall probably not be back till Monday. You can put up my dress clothes, my smoking jacket, and all the Bunbury suits . . .
LANE: Yes, sir. (*Handing sherry.*)
ALGERNON: I hope to-morrow will be a fine day, Lane.
LANE: It never is, sir.
ALGERNON: Lane, you're a perfect pessimist.
LANE: I do my best to give satisfaction, sir.

(*Enter* JACK. LANE *goes off.*)

JACK: There's a sensible, intellectual girl! the only girl I ever cared for in my life. (ALGERNON *is laughing immoderately.*) What on earth are you so amused at?
ALGERNON: Oh, I'm a little anxious about poor Bunbury, that is all.
JACK: If you don't take care, your friend Bunbury will get you into a serious scrape some day.
ALGERNON: I love scrapes. They are the only things that are never serious.
JACK: Oh, that's nonsense, Algy. You never talk anything but nonsense.
ALGERNON: Nobody ever does.

(JACK *looks indignantly at him, and leaves the room.* ALGERNON *lights a cigarette, reads his shirt-cuff, and smiles.*)

ACT II

(*Garden at the Manor House. A flight of grey stone steps leads up to the house. The garden, an old-fashioned one, full of roses. Time of year, July. Basket chairs, and a table covered with books, are set under a large yew-tree.*)

(MISS PRISM *discovered seated at the table.* CECILY *is at the back, watering flowers.*)

MISS PRISM (*calling*): Cecily, Cecily! Surely such a utilitarian occupation as the watering of flowers is rather Moulton's duty than yours? Especially at a moment when intellectual pleasures await you. Your German grammar is on the table. Pray open it at page fifteen. We will repeat yesterday's lesson.

CECILY (*coming over very slowly*): But I don't like German. It isn't at all a becoming language. I know perfectly well that I look quite plain after my German lesson.

MISS PRISM: Child, you know how anxious your guardian is that you should improve yourself in every way. He laid particular stress on your German, as he was leaving for town yesterday. Indeed, he always lays stress on your German when he is leaving for town.

CECILY: Dear Uncle Jack is so very serious! Sometimes he is so serious that I think he cannot be quite well.

MISS PRISM (*drawing herself up*): Your guardian enjoys the best of health, and his gravity of demeanour is especially to be commended in one so comparatively young as he is. I know no one who has a higher sense of duty and responsibility.

CECILY: I suppose that is why he often looks a little bored when we three are together.

MISS PRISM: Cecily! I am surprised at you. Mr. Worthing has many troubles in his life. Idle merriment and triviality would be out of place in his conversation. You must remember his constant anxiety about that unfortunate young man his brother.

CECILY: I wish Uncle Jack would allow that unfortunate young man, his brother, to come down here sometimes. We might have a good influence over him, Miss Prism. I am sure you certainly would. You know German, and geology, and things of that kind influence a man very much. (CECILY *begins to write in her diary.*)

MISS PRISM (*shaking her head*): I do not think that even I could produce any effect on a character that according to his own brother's admission is irretrievably weak and vacillating. Indeed I am not sure that I would desire to reclaim him. I am not in favour of this modern mania for turning bad people into good people at a moment's notice. As a man sows so let him reap. You must put away your diary, Cecily. I really don't see why you should keep a diary at all.

CECILY: I keep a diary in order to enter the wonderful secrets of my life. If I didn't write them down, I should probably forget all about them.

MISS PRISM: Memory, my dear Cecily, is the diary that we all carry about with us.

CECILY: Yes, but it usually chronicles the things that have never happened, and couldn't possibly have happened. I believe that Memory is responsible for nearly all the three-volume novels that Mudie sends us.

MISS PRISM: Do not speak slightingly of the three-volume novel, Cecily. I wrote one myself in earlier days.

CECILY: Did you really, Miss Prism? How wonderfully clever you are! I hope it did not end happily? I don't like novels that end happily. They depress me so much.

MISS PRISM: The good ended happily, and the bad unhappily. That is what Fiction means.

CECILY: I suppose so. But it seems very unfair. And was your novel ever published?

MISS PRISM: Alas! no. The manuscript unfortunately was abandoned. (CECILY *starts*.) I used the word in the sense of lost or mislaid. To your work, child, these speculations are profitless.

CECILY (*smiling*): But I see dear Dr. Chasuble coming up through the garden.

MISS PRISM (*rising and advancing*): Dr. Chasuble! This is indeed a pleasure.

(*Enter* CANON CHASUBLE.)

CHASUBLE: And how are we this morning? Miss Prism, you are, I trust, well?

CECILY: Miss Prism has just been complaining of a slight headache. I think it would do her so much good to have a short stroll with you in the Park, Dr. Chasuble.

MISS PRISM: Cecily, I have not mentioned anything about a headache.

CECILY: No, dear Miss Prism, I know that, but I felt instinctively that you had a headache. Indeed I was thinking about that, and not about my German lesson, when the Rector came in.

CHASUBLE: I hope, Cecily, you are not inattentive.

CECILY: Oh, I am afraid I am.

CHASUBLE: That is strange. Were I fortunate enough to be Miss Prism's pupil, I would hang upon her lips. (MISS PRISM *glares*.) I spoke metaphorically.—My metaphor was drawn from bees. Ahem! Mr. Worthing, I suppose, has not returned from town yet?

MISS PRISM: We do not expect him till Monday afternoon.

CHASUBLE: Ah yes, he usually likes to spend his Sunday in London. He is not one of those whose sole aim is enjoyment, as, by all accounts, that unfortunate young man his brother seems to be. But I must not disturb Egeria and her pupil any longer.

MISS PRISM: Egeria? My name is Laetitia, Doctor.

CHASUBLE (*bowing*): A classical allusion merely, drawn from the Pagan authors. I shall see you both no doubt at Evensong?

MISS PRISM: I think, dear Doctor, I will have a stroll with you. I find I have a headache after all, and a walk might do it good.

CHASUBLE: With pleasure, Miss Prism, with pleasure. We might go as far as the schools and back.

MISS PRISM: That would be delightful. Cecily, you will read your Political Economy in my absence. The chapter on the Fall of the Rupee you may omit. It is somewhat too sensational. Even these metallic problems have their melodramatic side.

(*Goes down the garden with* DR. CHASUBLE.)

CECILY (*picks up books and throws them back on table*): Horrid Political Economy! Horrid Geography! Horrid, horrid German!

(*Enter* MERRIMAN *with a card on a salver.*)

MERRIMAN: Mr. Ernest Worthing has just driven over from the station. He has brought his luggage with him.

CECILY (*takes the card and reads it*): "Mr. Ernest Worthing, B.4, The Albany, W." Uncle Jack's brother! Did you tell him Mr. Worthing was in town?

MERRIMAN: Yes, Miss. He seemed very much disappointed. I mentioned that you and Miss Prism were in the garden. He said he was anxious to speak to you privately for a moment.

CECILY: Ask Mr. Ernest Worthing to come here. I suppose you had better talk to the housekeeper about a room for him.

MERRIMAN: Yes, Miss. (MERRIMAN *goes off.*)

CECILY: I have never met any really wicked person before. I feel rather frightened. I am so afraid he will look just like every one else.

(*Enter* ALGERNON, *very gay and debonnair.*)

He does!

ALGERNON (*raising his hat*): You are my little cousin Cecily, I'm sure.

CECILY: You are under some strange mistake. I am not little. In fact, I believe I am more than usually tall for my age. (ALGERNON *is rather taken aback.*) But I am your cousin Cecily. You, I see from your card, are Uncle Jack's brother, my cousin Ernest, my wicked cousin Ernest.

ALGERNON: Oh! I am not really wicked at all, Cousin Cecily. You mustn't think that I am wicked.

CECILY: If you are not, then you have certainly been deceiving us all in a very inexcusable manner. I hope you have not been leading a double life, pretending to be wicked and being really good all the time. That would be hypocrisy.

ALGERNON (*looks at her in amazement*): Oh! Of course I have been rather reckless.

CECILY: I am glad to hear it.

ALGERNON: In fact, now you mention the subject, I have been very bad in my own small way.

CECILY: I don't think you should be so proud of that, though I am sure it must have been very pleasant.

ALGERNON: It is much pleasanter being here with you.

CECILY: I can't understand how you are here at all. Uncle Jack won't be back till Monday afternoon.

ALGERNON: That is a great disappointment. I am obliged to go up by the first train on Monday morning. I have a business appointment that I am anxious . . . to miss!

CECILY: Couldn't you miss it anywhere but in London?

ALGERNON: No: the appointment is in London.

CECILY: Well, I know, of course, how important it is not to keep a business engagement, if one wants to retain any sense of the beauty of life, but still I think you had better wait till Uncle Jack arrives. I know he wants to speak to you about your emigrating.

ALGERNON: About my what?

CECILY: Your emigrating. He has gone up to buy your outfit.

ALGERNON: I certainly wouldn't let Jack buy my outfit. He has no taste in neckties at all.

CECILY: I don't think you will require neckties. Uncle Jack is sending you to Australia.

ALGERNON: Australia! I'd sooner die.

CECILY: Well, he said at dinner on Wednesday night, that you would have to choose between this world, the next world, and Australia.

ALGERNON: Oh, well! The accounts I have received of Australia and the next world are not particularly encouraging. This world is good enough for me, Cousin Cecily.

CECILY: Yes, but are you good enough for it?

ALGERNON: I'm afraid I'm not that. That is why I want you to reform me. You might make that your mission, if you don't mind, cousin Cecily.

CECILY: I'm afraid I've no time, this afternoon.

ALGERNON: Well, would you mind my reforming myself this afternoon?

CECILY: It is rather Quixotic of you. But I think you should try.

ALGERNON: I will. I feel better already.

CECILY: You are looking a little worse.

ALGERNON: That is because I am hungry.

CECILY: How thoughtless of me. I should have remembered that when one is going to lead an entirely new life, one requires regular and wholesome meals. Won't you come in?

ALGERNON: Thank you. Might I have a buttonhole first? I never have any appetite unless I have a buttonhole first.

CECILY: A Maréchal Niel? (*Picks up scissors.*)

ALGERNON: No, I'd sooner have a pink rose.

CECILY: Why? (*Cuts a flower.*)

ALGERNON: Because you are like a pink rose, Cousin Cecily.

CECILY: I don't think it can be right for you to talk to me like that. Miss Prism never says such things to me.

ALGERNON: Then Miss Prism is a short-sighted old lady. (CECILY *puts the rose in his buttonhole.*) You are the prettiest girl I ever saw.

CECILY: Miss Prism says that all good looks are a snare.

ALGERNON: They are a snare that every sensible man would like to be caught in.

CECILY: Oh, I don't think I would care to catch a sensible man. I shouldn't know what to talk to him about.

(*They pass into the house.* MISS PRISM *and* DR. CHASUBLE *return.*)

MISS PRISM: You are too much alone, dear Dr. Chasuble. You should get married. A misanthrope I can understand— a womanthrope, never!

CHASUBLE (*with a scholar's shudder*): Believe me, I do not deserve so neologistic a phrase. The precept as well as the practice of the Primitive Church was distinctly against matrimony.

MISS PRISM (*sententiously*): That is obviously the reason why the Primitive Church has not lasted up to the present day. And you do not seem to realize, dear Doctor, that by persistently remaining single, a man converts himself into a permanent public temptation. Men should be more careful; this very celibacy leads weaker vessels astray.

CHASUBLE: But is a man not equally attractive when married?

MISS PRISM: No married man is ever attractive except to his wife.

CHASUBLE: And often, I've been told, not even to her.

MISS PRISM: That depends on the intellectual sympathies of the woman. Maturity can always be depended on. Ripeness can be trusted. Young women are green. (DR. CHASUBLE *starts.*) I spoke horticulturally. My metaphor was drawn from fruits. But where is Cecily?

CHASUBLE: Perhaps she followed us to the schools.

(*Enter* JACK *slowly from the back of the garden. He is dressed in the deepest mourning, with crepe hatband and black gloves.*)

MISS PRISM: Mr. Worthing!

CHASUBLE: Mr. Worthing?

MISS PRISM: This is indeed a surprise. We did not look for you till Monday afternoon.

JACK (*shakes* MISS PRISM'S *hand in a tragic manner*): I have returned sooner than I expected. Dr. Chasuble, I hope you are well?

CHASUBLE: Dear Mr. Worthing, I trust this garb of woe does not betoken some terrible calamity?

JACK: My brother.

MISS PRISM: More shameful debts and extravagance?

CHASUBLE: Still leading his life of pleasure?

JACK (*shaking his head*): Dead!

CHASUBLE: Your brother Ernest dead?

JACK: Quite dead.

MISS PRISM: What a lesson for him! I trust he will profit by it.

CHASUBLE: Mr. Worthing, I offer you my sincere condolence. You have at least the consolation of knowing that you were always the most generous and forgiving of brothers.

JACK: Poor Ernest! He had many faults, but it is a sad, sad blow.

CHASUBLE: Very sad indeed. Were you with him at the end?

JACK: No. He died abroad; in Paris, in fact. I had a telegram last night from the manager of the Grand Hotel.

CHASUBLE: Was the cause of death mentioned?

JACK: A severe chill, it seems.

MISS PRISM: As a man sows, so shall he reap.

CHASUBLE (*raising his hand*): Charity, dear Miss Prism, charity! None of us are perfect. I myself am peculiarly susceptible to draughts. Will the interment take place here?

JACK: No. He seems to have expressed a desire to be buried in Paris.

CHASUBLE: In Paris! (*Shakes his head.*) I fear that hardly points to any very serious state of mind at the last. You would no doubt wish me to make some slight allusion to this tragic domestic affliction next Sunday. (JACK *presses his hand convulsively.*) My sermon on the meaning of the manna in the wilderness can be adapted to almost any occasion, joyful, or, as in the present case, distressing. (*All sigh.*) I have preached it at harvest celebrations, christenings, confirmations, on days of humiliation and festal days. The last time I delivered it was in the Cathedral, as a charity sermon on behalf of the Society for the Prevention of Discontent among the Upper Orders. The Bishop, who was present, was much struck by some of the analogies I drew.

JACK: Ah! that reminds me, you mentioned christenings I think, Dr. Chasuble? I suppose you know how to christen all right? (DR. CHASUBLE *looks astounded.*) I mean, of course, you are continually christening, aren't you?

MISS PRISM: It is, I regret to say, one of the Rector's most constant duties in this parish. I have often spoken to the poorer classes on the subject. But they don't seem to know what thrift is.

CHASUBLE: But is there any particular infant in whom you are interested, Mr. Worthing? Your brother was, I believe, unmarried, was he not?

JACK: Oh yes.

MISS PRISM (*bitterly*): People who live entirely for pleasure usually are.

JACK: But it is not for any child, dear Doctor. I am very fond of children. No! the fact is, I would like to be christened myself, this afternoon, if you have nothing better to do.

CHASUBLE: But surely, Mr. Worthing, you have been christened already?

JACK: I don't remember anything about it.

CHASUBLE: But have you any grave doubts on the subject?

JACK: I certainly intend to have. Of course I don't know if the thing would bother you in any way, or if you think I am a little too old now.

CHASUBLE: Not at all. The sprinkling, and, indeed, the immersion of adults is a perfectly canonical practice.

JACK: Immersion!

CHASUBLE: You need have no apprehensions. Sprinkling is all that is necessary, or indeed I think advisable. Our weather is so changeable. At what hour would you wish the ceremony performed?

JACK: Oh, I might trot round about five if that would suit you.

CHASUBLE: Perfectly, perfectly! In fact I have two similar ceremonies to perform at that time. A case of twins that occurred recently in one of the outlying cottages on your own estate. Poor Jenkins the carter, a most hard-working man.

JACK: Oh! I don't see much fun in being christened along with other babies. It would be childish. Would half-past five do?

CHASUBLE: Admirably! Admirably! (*Takes out watch.*) And now, dear Mr. Worthing, I will not intrude any longer into a house of sorrow. I would merely beg you not to be too much bowed down by grief. What seem to us bitter trials are often blessings in disguise.

MISS PRISM: This seems to me a blessing of an extremely obvious kind.

(*Enter* CECILY *from the house.*)

CECILY: Uncle Jack! Oh, I am pleased to see you back. But what horrid clothes you have got on. Do go and change them.

MISS PRISM: Cecily!

CHASUBLE: My child! My child! (CECILY *goes towards* JACK; *he kisses her brow in a melancholy manner.*)

CECILY: What is the matter, Uncle Jack? Do look happy! You look as if you had toothache, and I have got such a surprise for you. Who do you think is in the dining-room? Your brother!

JACK: Who?

CECILY: Your brother Ernest. He arrived about half an hour ago.

JACK: What nonsense! I haven't got a brother.

CECILY: Oh, don't say that. However badly he may have behaved to you in the past he is still your brother. You couldn't be so heartless as to disown him. I'll tell him to come out. And you will shake hands with him, won't you, Uncle Jack? (*Runs back into the house.*)

CHASUBLE: These are very joyful tidings.

MISS PRISM: After we had all been resigned to his loss, his sudden return seems to me peculiarly distressing.

JACK: My brother is in the dining-room? I don't know what it all means. I think it is perfectly absurd.

(*Enter* ALGERNON *and* CECILY *hand in hand. They come slowly up to* JACK.)

JACK: Good heavens! (*Motions* ALGERNON *away.*)

ALGERNON: Brother John, I have come down from town to tell you that I am very sorry for all the trouble I have given you, and that I intend to lead a better life in the future. (JACK *glares at him and does not take his hand.*)

CECILY: Uncle Jack, you are not going to refuse your own brother's hand?

JACK: Nothing will induce me to take his hand. I think his coming down here disgraceful. He knows perfectly well why.

CECILY: Uncle Jack, do be nice. There is some good in everyone. Ernest has just been telling me about his poor invalid friend Mr. Bunbury whom he goes to visit so often. And surely there must be much good in one who is kind to an invalid, and leaves the pleasures of London to sit by a bed of pain.

JACK: Oh! he has been talking about Bunbury, has he?

CECILY: Yes, he has told me all about poor Mr. Bunbury, and his terrible state of health.

JACK: Bunbury! Well, I won't have him talk to you about Bunbury or about anything else. It is enough to drive one perfectly frantic.

ALGERNON: Of course I admit that the faults were all on my side. But I must say that I think that Brother John's coldness to me is peculiarly painful. I expected a more enthusiastic welcome, especially considering it is the first time I have come here.

CECILY: Uncle Jack, if you don't shake hands with Ernest I will never forgive you.

JACK: Never forgive me?

CECILY: Never, never, never!

JACK: Well, this is the last time I shall ever do it. (*Shakes hands with* ALGERNON *and glares.*)

CHASUBLE: It's pleasant, is it not, to see so perfect a reconciliation? I think we might leave the two brothers together.

MISS PRISM: Cecily, you will come with us.

CECILY: Certainly, Miss Prism. My little task of reconciliation is over.

CHASUBLE: You have done a beautiful action to-day, dear child.

MISS PRISM: We must not be premature in our judgements.

CECILY: I feel very happy. (*They all go off except* JACK *and* ALGERNON.)

JACK: You young scoundrel, Algy, you must get out of this place as soon as possible. I don't allow any Bunburying here.

(*Enter* MERRIMAN.)

MERRIMAN: I have put Mr. Ernest's things in the room next to yours, sir. I suppose that is all right?

JACK: What?

MERRIMAN: Mr. Ernest's luggage, sir. I have unpacked it and put it in the room next to your own.

JACK: His luggage?

MERRIMAN: Yes, sir. Three portmanteaus, a dressing-case, two hat-boxes, and a large luncheon-basket.

ALGERNON: I am afraid I can't stay more than a week this time.

JACK: Merriman, order the dog-cart at once. Mr. Ernest has been suddenly called back to town.

MERRIMAN: Yes, sir. (*Goes back into the house.*)

ALGERNON: What a fearful liar you are, Jack. I have not been called back to town at all.

JACK: Yes, you have.

ALGERNON: I haven't heard any one call me.

JACK: Your duty as a gentleman calls you back.

ALGERNON: My duty as a gentleman has never interfered with my pleasures in the smallest degree.

JACK: I can quite understand that.

ALGERNON: Well, Cecily is a darling.

JACK: You are not to talk of Miss Cardew like that. I don't like it.

ALGERNON: Well, I don't like your clothes. You look perfectly ridiculous in them. Why on earth don't you go up and change? It is perfectly childish to be in deep mourning for a man who is actually staying for a whole week with you in your house as a guest. I call it grotesque.

JACK: You are certainly not staying with me for a whole week as a guest or anything else. You have got to leave . . . by the four-five train.

ALGERNON: I certainly won't leave you so long as you are in mourning. It would be most unfriendly. If I were in mourning you would stay with me, I suppose. I should think it very unkind if you didn't.

JACK: Well, will you go if I change my clothes?

ALGERNON: Yes, if you are not too long. I never saw anybody take so long to dress, and with such little result.

JACK: Well, at any rate, that is better than being always over-dressed as you are.

ALGERNON: If I am occasionally a little over-dressed, I make up for it by being always immensely over-educated.

JACK: Your vanity is ridiculous, your conduct an outrage, and your presence in my garden utterly absurd. However, you have got to catch the four-five, and I hope you will have a pleasant journey back to town. This Bunburying, as you call it, has not been a great success for you.

(*Goes into the house.*)

ALGERNON: I think it has been a great success. I'm in love with Cecily, and that is everything.

(*Enter* CECILY *at the back of the garden. She picks up the can and begins to water the flowers.*)

But I must see her before I go, and make arrangements for another Bunbury. Ah, there she is.

CECILY: Oh, I merely came back to water the roses. I thought you were with Uncle Jack.

ALGERNON: He's gone to order the dog-cart for me.

CECILY: Oh, is he going to take you for a nice drive?

ALGERNON: He's going to send me away.

CECILY: Then have we got to part?

ALGERNON: I am afraid so. It's a very painful parting.

CECILY: It is always painful to part from people whom one has known for a very brief space of time. The absence of old friends one can endure with equanimity. But even a momentary separation from any one to whom one has just been introduced is almost unbearable.

ALGERNON: Thank you.

(*Enter* MERRIMAN.)

MERRIMAN: The dog-cart is at the door, sir.

(ALGERNON *looks appealingly at* CECILY.)

CECILY: It can wait, Merriman . . . for . . . five minutes.

MERRIMAN: Yes, miss.

(*Exit* MERRIMAN.)

ALGERNON: I hope, Cecily, I shall not offend you if I state quite frankly and openly that you seem to me to be in every way the visible personification of absolute perfection.

CECILY: I think your frankness does you great credit, Ernest. If you will allow me, I will copy your remarks into my diary. (*Goes over to table and begins writing in diary.*)

ALGERNON: Do you really keep a diary? I'd give anything to look at it. May I?

CECILY: Oh no. (*Puts her hand over it.*) You see, it is simply a very young girl's record of her own thoughts and impressions, and consequently meant for publication. When it appears in volume form I hope you will order a copy. But pray, Ernest, don't stop. I delight in taking down from dictation. I have reached "absolute perfection." You can go on. I am quite ready for more.

ALGERNON (*somewhat taken aback*): Ahem! Ahem!

CECILY: Oh, don't cough, Ernest. When one is dictating one should speak fluently and not cough. Besides, I don't know how to spell a cough. (*Writes as* ALGERNON *speaks.*)

ALGERNON (*speaking very rapidly*): Cecily, ever since I first looked upon your wonderful and incomparable beauty, I have dared to love you wildly, passionately, devotedly, hopelessly.

CECILY: I don't think that you should tell me that you love me wildly, passionately, devotedly, hopelessly. Hopelessly doesn't seem to make much sense, does it?

ALGERNON: Cecily.

(*Enter* MERRIMAN.)

MERRIMAN: The dog-cart is waiting, sir.

ALGERNON: Tell it to come round next week, at the same hour.

MERRIMAN (*looks at* CECILY, *who makes no sign*): Yes, sir.

(MERRIMAN *retires*.)

CECILY: Uncle Jack would be very much annoyed if he knew you were staying on till next week, at the same hour.

ALGERNON: Oh, I don't care about Jack. I don't care for anybody in the whole world but you. I love you, Cecily. You will marry me, won't you?

CECILY: You silly boy! Of course. Why, we have been engaged for the last three months.

ALGERNON: For the last three months?

CECILY: Yes, it will be exactly three months on Thursday.

ALGERNON: But how did we become engaged?

CECILY: Well, ever since dear Uncle Jack first confessed to us that he had a younger brother who was very wicked and bad, you of course have formed the chief topic of conversation between myself and Miss Prism. And of course a man who is much talked about is always very attractive. One feels there must be something in him, after all. I daresay it was foolish of me, but I fell in love with you, Ernest.

ALGERNON: Darling. And when was the engagement actually settled?

CECILY: On the 14th of February last. Worn out by your entire ignorance of my existence, I determined to end the matter one way or the other, and after a long struggle with myself I accepted you under this dear old tree here. The next day I bought this little ring in your name, and this is the little bangle with the true lovers' knot I promised you always to wear.

ALGERNON: Did I give you this? It's very pretty, isn't it?

CECILY: Yes, you've wonderfully good taste, Ernest. It's the excuse I've always given for your leading such a bad life.

And this is the box in which I keep all your dear letters. (*Kneels at table, opens box, and produces letters tied up with blue ribbon.*)

ALGERNON: My letters! But, my own sweet Cecily, I have never written you any letters.

CECILY: You need hardly remind me of that, Ernest. I remember only too well that I was forced to write your letters for you. I wrote always three times a week, and sometimes oftener.

ALGERNON: Oh, do let me read them, Cecily?

CECILY: Oh, I couldn't possibly. They would make you far too conceited. (*Replaces box.*) The three you wrote me after I had broken off the engagement are so beautiful, and so badly spelled, that even now I can hardly read them without crying a little.

ALGERNON: But was our engagement ever broken off?

CECILY: Of course it was. On the 22nd of last March. You can see the entry if you like. (*Shows diary.*) "To-day I broke off my engagement with Ernest. I feel it is better to do so. The weather still continues charming."

ALGERNON: But why on earth did you break it off? What had I done? I had done nothing at all. Cecily, I am very much hurt indeed to hear you broke it off. Particularly when the weather was so charming.

CECILY: It would hardly have been a really serious engagement if it hadn't been broken off at least once. But I forgave you before the week was out.

ALGERNON (*crossing to her, and kneeling*): What a perfect angel you are, Cecily.

CECILY: You dear romantic boy. (*He kisses her, she puts her fingers through his hair*). I hope your hair curls naturally, does it?

ALGERNON: Yes, darling, with a little help from others.

CECILY: I am so glad.

ALGERNON: You'll never break off our engagement again, Cecily?

CECILY: I don't think I could break it off now that I have actually met you. Besides, of course, there is the question of your name.

ALGERNON: Yes, of course. (*Nervously.*)

CECILY: You must not laugh at me, darling, but it had always been a girlish dream of mine to love some one whose name was Ernest. (ALGERNON *rises*, CECILY *also.*) There is something in that name that seems to inspire absolute confidence. I pity any poor married woman whose husband is not called Ernest.

ALGERNON: But, my dear child, do you mean to say you could not love me if I had some other name?

CECILY: But what name?

ALGERNON: Oh, any name you like—Algernon—for instance . . .

CECILY: But I don't like the name of Algernon.

ALGERNON: Well, my own dear, sweet, loving little darling, I really can't see why you should object to the name of Algernon. It is not at all a bad name. In fact, it is rather an aristocratic name. Half of the chaps who get into the Bankruptcy Court are called Algernon. But seriously, Cecily . . . (*moving to her*) if my name was Algy, couldn't you love me?

CECILY (*rising*): I might respect you, Ernest, I might admire your character, but I fear that I should not be able to give you my undivided attention.

ALGERNON: Ahem! Cecily! (*Picking up hat.*) Your Rector here is, I suppose, thoroughly experienced in the practice of all the rites and ceremonials of the Church?

CECILY: Oh, yes. Dr. Chasuble is a most learned man. He has never written a single book, so you can imagine how much he knows.

ALGERNON: I must see him at once on a most important christening—I mean on most important business.

CECILY: Oh!

ALGERNON: I shan't be away more than half an hour.

CECILY: Considering that we have been engaged since February the 14th, and that I only met you to-day for the first time, I think it is rather hard that you should leave me for so long a period as half an hour. Couldn't you make it twenty minutes?

ALGERNON: I'll be back in no time. (*Kisses her and rushes down the garden.*)

CECILY: What an impetuous boy he is! I like his hair so much. I must enter his proposal in my diary.

(*Enter* MERRIMAN.)

MERRIMAN: A Miss Fairfax just called to see Mr. Worthing. On very important business, Miss Fairfax states.

CECILY: Isn't Mr. Worthing in his library?

MERRIMAN: Mr. Worthing went over in the direction of the Rectory some time ago.

CECILY: Pray ask the lady to come out here; Mr. Worthing is sure to be back soon. And you can bring tea.

MERRIMAN: Yes, Miss.

(*Goes out.*)

CECILY: Miss Fairfax! I suppose one of the many good elderly women who are associated with Uncle Jack in some of his philanthropic work in London. I don't quite like women who are interested in philanthropic work. I think it is so forward of them.

(*Enter* MERRIMAN.)

MERRIMAN: Miss Fairfax.

(*Enter* GWENDOLEN. *Exit* MERRIMAN.)

CECILY (*advancing to meet her*): Pray let me introduce myself to you. My name is Cecily Cardew.

GWENDOLEN: Cecily Cardew? (*Moving to her and shaking hands.*) What a very sweet name! Something tells me that we are going to be great friends. I like you already more than I can say. My first impressions of people are never wrong.

CECILY: How nice of you to like me so much after we have known each other such a comparatively short time. Pray sit down.

GWENDOLEN (*still standing up*): I may call you Cecily, may I not?

CECILY: With pleasure!

GWENDOLEN: And you will always call me Gwendolen, won't you?

CECILY: If you wish.

GWENDOLEN: Then that is all quite settled, is it not?

CECILY: I hope so. (*A pause. They both sit down together.*)

GWENDOLEN: Perhaps this might be a favourable opportunity for my mentioning who I am. My father is Lord Bracknell. You have never heard of papa, I suppose?

CECILY: I don't think so.

GWENDOLEN: Outside the family circle, papa, I am glad to say, is entirely unknown. I think that is quite as it should be. The home seems to me to be the proper sphere for the man. And certainly once a man begins to neglect his domestic duties he becomes painfully effeminate, does he not? And I don't like that. It makes men so very attractive. Cecily, mamma, whose views on education are remarkably strict, has brought me up to be extremely shortsighted; it is part of her system; so do you mind my looking at you through my glasses?

CECILY: Oh! not at all, Gwendolen. I am very fond of being looked at.

GWENDOLEN (*after examining* CECILY *carefully through a lorgnette*): You are here on a short visit, I suppose.

CECILY: Oh no! I live here.

GWENDOLEN (*severely*): Really? Your mother, no doubt, or some female relative of advanced years, resides here also?

CECILY: Oh no! I have no mother, nor, in fact, any relations.

GWENDOLEN: Indeed?

CECILY: My dear guardian, with the assistance of Miss Prism, has the arduous task of looking after me.

GWENDOLEN: Your guardian?

CECILY: Yes, I am Mr. Worthing's ward.

GWENDOLEN: Oh! It is strange he never mentioned to me that he had a ward. How secretive of him! He grows more interesting hourly. I am not sure, however, that the news inspires me with feelings of unmixed delight. (*Rising and going to her.*) I am very fond of you, Cecily; I have liked you ever since I met you! But I am bound to state that now that I know that you are Mr. Worthing's ward, I cannot help expressing a wish you were—well, just a little older than you seem to be—and not quite so very alluring in appearance. In fact, if I may speak candidly—

CECILY: Pray do! I think that whenever one has anything unpleasant to say, one should always be quite candid.

GWENDOLEN: Well, to speak with perfect candour, Cecily, I wish that you were fully forty-two, and more than usually plain for your age. Ernest has a strong upright nature. He is the very soul of truth and honour. Disloyalty would be as impossible to him as deception. But even men of the noblest possible moral character are extremely susceptible to the influence of the physical charms of others. Modern, no less than Ancient History, supplies us with many most painful examples of what I refer to. If it were not so, indeed, History would be quite unreadable.

CECILY: I beg your pardon, Gwendolen, did you say Ernest?

GWENDOLEN: Yes.

CECILY: Oh, but it is not Mr. Ernest Worthing who is my guardian. It is his brother—his elder brother.

GWENDOLEN (*sitting down again*): Ernest never mentioned to me that he had a brother.

CECILY: I am sorry to say they have not been on good terms for a long time.

GWENDOLEN: Ah! that accounts for it. And now that I think of it I have never heard any man mention his brother. The subject seems distasteful to most men. Cecily, you have lifted a load from my mind. I was growing almost anxious. It would have been terrible if any cloud had come across a friendship like ours, would it not? Of course you are quite, quite sure that it is not Mr. Ernest Worthing who is your guardian?

CECILY: Quite sure. (*A pause.*) In fact, I am going to be his.

GWENDOLEN (*inquiringly*): I beg your pardon?

CECILY (*rather shy and confidingly*): Dearest Gwendolen, there is no reason why I should make a secret of it to you. Our little country newspaper is sure to chronicle the fact next week. Mr. Ernest Worthing and I are engaged to be married.

GWENDOLEN (*quite politely, rising*): My darling Cecily, I think there must be some slight error. Mr. Ernest Worthing is engaged to me. The announcement will appear in the *Morning Post* on Saturday at the latest.

CECILY (*very politely, rising*): I am afraid you must be under some misconception. Ernest proposed to me exactly ten minutes ago. (*Shows diary.*)

GWENDOLEN (*examines diary through her lorgnette carefully*): It is very curious, for he asked me to be his wife yesterday afternoon at 5:30. If you would care to verify the incident, pray do so. (*Produces diary of her own.*) I never travel without my diary. One should always have something sensational to read in the train. I am so sorry, dear Cecily, if it is any disappointment to you, but I am afraid I have the prior claim.

CECILY: It would distress me more than I can tell you, dear Gwendolen, if it caused you any mental or physical anguish, but I feel bound to point out that since Ernest proposed to you he clearly has changed his mind.

GWENDOLEN (*meditatively*): If the poor fellow has been entrapped into any foolish promise I shall consider it my duty to rescue him at once, and with a firm hand.

CECILY (*thoughtfully and sadly*): Whatever unfortunate entanglement my dear boy may have got into, I will never reproach him with it after we are married.

GWENDOLEN: Do you allude to me, Miss Cardew, as an entanglement? You are presumptuous. On an occasion of this kind it becomes more than a moral duty to speak one's mind. It becomes a pleasure.

CECILY: Do you suggest, Miss Fairfax, that I entrapped Ernest into an engagement? How dare you? This is no time for wearing the shallow mask of manners. When I see a spade I call it a spade.

GWENDOLEN (*satirically*): I am glad to say that I have never seen a spade. It is obvious that our social spheres have been widely different.

(*Enter* MERRIMAN, *followed by the footman. He carries a*

salver, table cloth, and plate stand. CECILY *is about to retort. The presence of the servants exercises a restraining influence, under which both girls chafe.*)

MERRIMAN: Shall I lay tea here as usual, Miss?

CECILY (*sternly, in a calm voice*): Yes, as usual. (MERRIMAN *begins to clear table and lay cloth. A long pause.* CECILY *and* GWENDOLEN *glare at each other.*)

GWENDOLEN: Are there many interesting walks in the vicinity, Miss Cardew?

CECILY: Oh! yes! a great many. From the top of one of the hills quite close one can see five counties.

GWENDOLEN: Five counties! I don't think I should like that; I hate crowds.

CECILY (*sweetly*): I suppose that is why you live in town? (GWENDOLEN *bites her lip, and beats her foot nervously with her parasol.*)

GWENDOLEN (*looking round*): Quite a well-kept garden this is, Miss Cardew.

CECILY: So glad you like it, Miss Fairfax.

GWENDOLEN: I had no idea there were any flowers in the country.

CECILY: Oh, flowers are as common here, Miss Fairfax, as people are in London.

GWENDOLEN: Personally I cannot understand how anybody manages to exist in the country, if anybody who is anybody does. The country always bores me to death.

CECILY: Ah! This is what the newspapers call agricultural depression, is it not? I believe the aristocracy are suffering very much from it just at present. It is almost an epidemic amongst them, I have been told. May I offer you some tea, Miss Fairfax?

GWENDOLEN (*with elaborate politeness*): Thank you. (*Aside.*) Detestable girl! But I require tea!

CECILY (*sweetly*): Sugar?

GWENDOLEN (*superciliously*): No, thank you. Sugar is not fashionable any more. (CECILY *looks angrily at her, takes up the tongs and puts four lumps of sugar into the cup.*)

CECILY (*severely*): Cake or bread and butter?

GWENDOLEN (*in a bored manner*): Bread and butter, please. Cake is rarely seen at the best houses nowadays.

CECILY (*cuts a very large slice of cake and puts it on the tray*): Hand that to Miss Fairfax.

(MERRIMAN *does so, and goes out with footman.* GWENDOLEN *drinks the tea and makes a grimace. Puts down cup at once, reaches out her hand to the bread and butter, looks at it, and finds it is cake. Rises in indignation.*)

GWENDOLEN: You have filled my tea with lumps of sugar, and though I asked most distinctly for bread and butter, you have given me cake. I am known for the gentleness of my disposition, and the extraordinary sweetness of my nature, but I warn you, Miss Cardew, you may go too far.

CECILY (*rising*): To save my poor, innocent, trusting boy from the machinations of any other girl there are no lengths to which I would not go.

GWENDOLEN: From the moment I saw you I distrusted you. I felt that you were false and deceitful. I am never deceived in such matters. My first impressions of people are invariably right.

CECILY: It seems to me, Miss Fairfax, that I am trespassing on your valuable time. No doubt you have many other calls of a similar character to make in the neighbourhood.

(*Enter* JACK.)

GWENDOLEN (*catching sight of him*): Ernest! My own Ernest!

JACK: Gwendolen! Darling! (*Offers to kiss her.*)

GWENDOLEN (*drawing back*): A moment! May I ask if you are engaged to be married to this young lady? (*Points to* CECILY.)

JACK (*laughing*): To dear little Cecily! Of course not! What could have put such an idea into your pretty little head?

GWENDOLEN: Thank you. You may! (*Offers her cheek.*)

CECILY (*very sweetly*): I knew there must be some misunderstanding, Miss Fairfax. The gentleman whose arm is at present round your waist is my dear guardian, Mr. John Worthing.

GWENDOLEN: I beg your pardon?

CECILY: This is Uncle Jack.

GWENDOLEN (*receding*): Jack! Oh!

(*Enter* ALGERNON.)

CECILY: Here is Ernest.

ALGERNON (*goes straight over to* CECILY *without noticing anyone else*): My own love! (*Offers to kiss her.*)

CECILY (*drawing back*): A moment, Ernest! May I ask you —are you engaged to be married to this young lady?

ALGERNON (*looking round*): To what young lady? Good heavens! Gwendolen!

CECILY: Yes: to good heavens, Gwendolen, I mean to Gwendolen.

ALGERNON (*laughing*): Of course not! What could have put such an idea into your pretty little head?

CECILY: Thank you. (*Presenting her cheek to be kissed.*) You may. (ALGERNON *kisses her.*)

GWENDOLEN: I felt there was some slight error, Miss Cardew. The gentleman who is now embracing you is my cousin, Mr. Algernon Moncrieff.

CECILY (*breaking away from Algernon*): Algernon Moncrieff! Oh! (*The two girls move towards each other and put their arms round each other's waists as if for protection.*)

CECILY: Are you called Algernon?

ALGERNON: I cannot deny it.

CECILY: Oh!

GWENDOLEN: Is your name really John?

JACK (*standing rather proudly*): I could deny it if I liked. I could deny anything if I liked. But my name certainly is John. It has been John for years.

CECILY (*to* GWENDOLEN): A gross deception has been practised on both of us.

GWENDOLEN: My poor wounded Cecily!

CECILY: My sweet wronged Gwendolen!

GWENDOLEN (*slowly and seriously*): You will call me sister, will you not? (*They embrace.* JACK *and* ALGERNON *groan and walk up and down.*)

CECILY (*rather brightly*): There is just one question I would like to be allowed to ask my guardian.

GWENDOLEN: An admirable idea! Mr. Worthing, there is just one question I would like to be permitted to put to you. Where is your brother Ernest? We are both engaged to be married to your brother Ernest, so it is a matter of some importance to us to know where your brother Ernest is at present.

JACK (*slowly and hesitatingly*): Gwendolen—Cecily—it is very painful for me to be forced to speak the truth. It is the first time in my life that I have ever been reduced to such a painful position, and I am really quite inexperienced in doing anything of the kind. However, I will tell you quite frankly that I have no brother Ernest. I have no brother at all. I never had a brother in my life, and I certainly have not the smallest intention of ever having one in the future.

CECILY (*surprised*): No brother at all?

JACK (*cheerily*): None!

GWENDOLEN (*severely*): Had you never a brother of any kind?

JACK (*pleasantly*): Never. Not even of any kind.

GWENDOLEN: I am afraid it is quite clear, Cecily, that neither of us is engaged to be married to anyone.

CECILY: It is not a very pleasant position for a young girl suddenly to find herself in. Is it?

GWENDOLEN: Let us go into the house. They will hardly venture to come after us there.

CECILY: No, men are so cowardly, aren't they?

(*They retire into the house with scornful looks.*)

JACK: This ghastly state of things is what you call Bunbury-ing, I suppose?

ALGERNON: Yes, and a perfectly wonderful Bunbury it is. The most wonderful Bunbury I have ever had in my life.

JACK: Well, you've no right whatsoever to Bunbury here.

ALGERNON: That is absurd. One has a right to Bunbury any-where one chooses. Every serious Bunburyist knows that.

JACK: Serious Bunburyist? Good heavens!

ALGERNON: Well, one must be serious about something, if one wants to have any amusement in life. I happen to be serious about Bunburying. What on earth you are serious about I haven't got the remotest idea. About everything, I should fancy. You have such an absolutely trivial nature.

JACK: Well, the only small satisfaction I have in the whole of this wretched business is that your friend Bunbury is quite exploded. You won't be able to run down to the country quite so often as you used to do, dear Algy. And a very good thing too.

ALGERNON: Your brother is a little off colour, isn't he, dear Jack? You won't be able to disappear to London quite so frequently as your wicked custom was. And not a bad thing either.

JACK: As for your conduct towards Miss Cardew, I must say that your taking in a sweet, simple, innocent girl like that is quite inexcusable. To say nothing of the fact that she is my ward.

ALGERNON: I can see no possible defence at all for your deceiving a brilliant, clever, thoroughly experienced young lady like Miss Fairfax. To say nothing of the fact that she is my cousin.

JACK: I wanted to be engaged to Gwendolen, that is all. I love her.

ALGERNON: Well, I simply wanted to be engaged to Cecily. I adore her.

JACK: There is certainly no chance of your marrying Miss Cardew.

ALGERNON: I don't think there is much likelihood, Jack, of you and Miss Fairfax being united.

JACK: Well, that is no business of yours.

ALGERNON: If it was my business, I wouldn't talk about it. (*Begins to eat muffins.*) It is very vulgar to talk about one's business. Only people like stockbrokers do that, and then merely at dinner parties.

JACK: How you can sit there, calmly eating muffins when we are in this horrible trouble, I can't make out. You seem to me to be perfectly heartless.

ALGERNON: Well, I can't eat muffins in an agitated manner. The butter would probably get on my cuffs. One should always eat muffins quite calmly. It is the only way to eat them.

JACK: I say it's perfectly heartless your eating muffins at all, under the circumstances.

ALGERNON: When I am in trouble, eating is the only thing that consoles me. Indeed, when I am in really great trouble, as any one who knows me intimately will tell you, I refuse everything except food and drink. At the present moment I am eating muffins because I am unhappy. Besides, I am particularly fond of muffins. (*Rising.*)

JACK (*rising*): Well, there is no reason why you should eat them all in that greedy way. (*Takes muffins from Algernon.*)

ALGERNON (*offering tea-cake*): I wish you would have tea-cake instead. I don't like tea-cake.

JACK: Good heavens! I suppose a man may eat his own muffins in his own garden.

ALGERNON: But you have just said it was perfectly heartless to eat muffins.

JACK: I said it was perfectly heartless of you, under the circumstances. That is a very different thing.

ALGERNON: That may be. But the muffins are the same. (*He seizes the muffin-dish from* JACK.)

JACK: Algy, I wish to goodness you would go.

ALGERNON: You can't possibly ask me to go without having some dinner. It's absurd. I never go without my dinner. No one ever does, except vegetarians and people like that. Besides I have just made arrangements with Dr. Chasuble to be christened at a quarter to six under the name of Ernest.

JACK: My dear fellow, the sooner you give up that nonsense the better. I made arrangements this morning with Dr. Chasuble to be christened myself at 5:30, and I naturally will take the name of Ernest. Gwendolen would wish it. We can't both be christened Ernest. It's absurd. Besides, I have a perfect right to be christened if I like. There is no evidence at all that I have ever been christened by anybody. I should think it extremely probable I never was, and so does Dr. Chasuble. It is entirely different in your case. You have been christened already.

ALGERNON: Yes, but I have not been christened for years.

JACK: Yes, but you have been christened. That is the important thing.

ALGERNON: Quite so. So I know my constitution can stand it. If you are not quite sure about your ever having been christened, I must say I think it rather dangerous your venturing on it now. It might make you very unwell. You can hardly have forgotten that someone very closely connected with you was very nearly carried off this week in Paris by a severe chill.

JACK: Yes, but you said yourself that a severe chill was not hereditary.

ALGERNON: It usen't to be, I know—but I daresay it is now. Science is always making wonderful improvements in things.

JACK (*picking up the muffin-dish*): Oh, that is nonsense; you are always talking nonsense.

ALGERNON: Jack, you are at the muffins again! I wish you wouldn't. There are only two left. (*Takes them.*) I told you I was particularly fond of muffins.

JACK: But I hate tea-cake.

ALGERNON: Why on earth then do you allow tea-cake to be served up for your guests? What ideas you have of hospitality!

JACK: Algernon! I have already told you to go. I don't want you here. Why don't you go!

ALGERNON: I haven't quite finished my tea yet! and there is still one muffin left. (JACK *groans, and sinks into a chair.* ALGERNON *still continues eating.*)

ACT III

(*Morning-room at the Manor House.* GWENDOLEN *and* CECILY *are at the window, looking out into the garden.*)

GWENDOLEN: The fact that they did not follow us at once into the house, as any one else would have done, seems to me to show that they have some sense of shame left.

CECILY: They have been eating muffins. That looks like repentance.

GWENDOLEN (*after a pause*): They don't seem to notice us at all. Couldn't you cough?

CECILY: But I haven't got a cough.

GWENDOLEN: They're looking at us. What effrontery!

CECILY: They're approaching. That's very forward of them.

GWENDOLEN: Let us preserve a dignified silence.

CECILY: Certainly. It's the only thing to do now.

(*Enter* JACK *followed by* ALGERNON. *They whistle some dreadful popular air from a British Opera.*)

GWENDOLEN: This dignified silence seems to produce an unpleasant effect.

CECILY: A most distasteful one.

GWENDOLEN: But we will not be the first to speak.

CECILY: Certainly not.

GWENDOLEN: Mr. Worthing, I have something very particular to ask you. Much depends on your reply.

CECILY: Gwendolen, your common sense is invaluable. Mr. Moncrieff, kindly answer me the following question. Why did you pretend to be my guardian's brother?

ALGERNON: In order that I might have an opportunity of meeting you.

CECILY (to GWENDOLEN): That certainly seems a satisfactory explanation, does it not?

GWENDOLEN: Yes, dear, if you can believe him.

CECILY: I don't. But that does not affect the wonderful beauty of his answer.

GWENDOLEN: True. In matters of grave importance, style, not sincerity, is the vital thing. Mr. Worthing, what explanation can you offer to me for pretending to have a brother? Was it in order that you might have an opportunity of coming up to town to see me as often as possible?

JACK: Can you doubt it, Miss Fairfax?

GWENDOLEN: I have the gravest doubts upon the subject. But I intend to crush them. This is not the moment for German scepticism. (Moving to CECILY.) Their explanations appear to be quite satisfactory, especially Mr. Worthing's. That seems to me to have the stamp of truth upon it.

CECILY: I am more than content with what Mr. Moncrieff said. His voice alone inspires one with absolute credulity.

GWENDOLEN: Then you think we should forgive them?

CECILY: Yes. I mean no.

GWENDOLEN: True! I had forgotten. There are principles at stake that one cannot surrender. Which of us should tell them? The task is not a pleasant one.

CECILY: Could we not both speak at the same time?

GWENDOLEN: An excellent idea! I nearly always speak at the same time as other people. Will you take the time from me?

CECILY: Certainly. (GWENDOLEN beats time with uplifted finger.)

GWENDOLEN and CECILY (speaking together): Your Christian names are still an insuperable barrier. That is all!

JACK and ALGERNON (speaking together): Our Christian names! Is that all? But we are going to be christened this afternoon.

GWENDOLEN (*to* JACK): For my sake you are prepared to do this terrible thing?

JACK: I am.

CECILY (*to* ALGERNON): To please me you are ready to face this fearful ordeal?

ALGERNON: I am!

GWENDOLEN: How absurd to talk of the equality of the sexes! Where questions of self-sacrifice are concerned, men are infinitely beyond us.

JACK: We are. (*Clasps hands with* ALGERNON.)

CECILY: They have moments of physical courage of which we women know absolutely nothing.

GWENDOLEN (*to* JACK): Darling!

ALGERNON (*to* CECILY): Darling! (*They fall into each other's arms.*)

(*Enter* MERRIMAN. *When he enters he coughs loudly, seeing the situation.*)

MERRIMAN: Ahem! Ahem! Lady Bracknell.

JACK: Good heavens!

(*Enter* LADY BRACKNELL. *The couples separate in alarm. Exit* MERRIMAN.)

LADY BRACKNELL: Gwendolen! What does this mean?

GWENDOLEN: Merely that I am engaged to be married to Mr. Worthing, mamma.

LADY BRACKNELL: Come here. Sit down. Sit down immediately. Hesitation of any kind is a sign of mental decay in the young, of physical weakness in the old. (*Turns to* JACK.) Apprised, sir, of my daughter's sudden flight by her trusty maid, whose confidence I purchased by means of a small coin, I followed her at once by a luggage train. Her unhappy father is, I am glad to say, under the impression that she is attending a more than usually lengthy lecture by the University Extension Scheme on the Influence of a permanent income on Thought. I do not propose to undeceive him. Indeed I have never undeceived him on any question. I would consider it wrong. But of course, you will clearly understand that all communication between yourself and my daughter must cease immediately from this moment. On this point, as indeed on all points, I am firm.

JACK: I am engaged to be married to Gwendolen, Lady Bracknell!

LADY BRACKNELL: You are nothing of the kind, sir. And now as regards Algernon! . . . Algernon!

ALGERNON: Yes, Aunt Augusta.

LADY BRACKNELL: May I ask if it is in this house that your invalid friend Mr. Bunbury resides?

ALGERNON (*stammering*): Oh! No! Bunbury doesn't live here. Bunbury is somewhere else at present. In fact, Bunbury is dead.

LADY BRACKNELL: Dead! When did Mr. Bunbury die? His death must have been extremely sudden.

ALGERNON (*airily*): Oh! I killed Bunbury this afternoon. I mean poor Bunbury died this afternoon.

LADY BRACKNELL: What did he die of?

ALGERNON: Bunbury? Oh, he was quite exploded.

LADY BRACKNELL: Exploded! Was he the victim of a revolutionary outrage? I was not aware that Mr. Bunbury was interested in social legislation. If so, he is well punished for his morbidity.

ALGERNON: My dear Aunt Augusta, I mean he was found out! The doctors found out that Bunbury could not live, that is what I mean—so Bunbury died.

LADY BRACKNELL: He seems to have had great confidence in the opinion of his physicians. I am glad, however, that he made up his mind at the last to some definite course of action, and acted under proper medical advice. And now that we have finally got rid of this Mr. Bunbury, may I ask, Mr. Worthing, who is that young person whose hand my nephew Algernon is now holding in what seems to me a peculiarly unnecessary manner?

JACK: That lady is Miss Cecily Cardew, my ward. (LADY BRACKNELL *bows coldly to* CECILY.)

ALGERNON: I am engaged to be married to Cecily, Aunt Augusta.

LADY BRACKNELL: I beg your pardon?

CECILY: Mr. Moncrieff and I are engaged to be married, Lady Bracknell.

LADY BRACKNELL (*with a shiver, crossing to the sofa and sitting down*): I do not know whether there is anything peculiarly exciting in the air of this particular part of Hertfordshire, but the number of engagements that go on seems to me considerably above the proper average that statistics have laid down for our guidance. I think some preliminary inquiry on my part would not be out of place. Mr. Worthing, is Miss Cardew at all connected with any of the larger railway stations in London? I merely desire information. Until yesterday I had no idea that there were any families or persons whose origin was a Terminus. (JACK *looks perfectly furious, but restrains himself.*)

JACK (*in a cold, clear voice*): Miss Cardew is the granddaughter of the late Mr. Thomas Cardew of 149 Belgrave Square, S.W.; Gervase Park, Dorking, Surrey; and the Sporran, Fifeshire, N.B.

LADY BRACKNELL: That sounds not unsatisfactory. Three addresses always inspire confidence, even in tradesmen. But what proof have I of their authenticity?

JACK: I have carefully preserved the Court Guides of the period. They are open to your inspection, Lady Bracknell.

LADY BRACKNELL (*grimly*): I have known strange errors in that publication.

JACK: Miss Cardew's family solicitors are Messrs. Markby, Markby, and Markby.

LADY BRACKNELL: Markby, Markby, and Markby? A firm of the very highest position in their profession. Indeed I am told that one of the Mr. Markbys is occasionally to be seen at dinner parties. So far I am satisfied.

JACK (*very irritably*): How extremely kind of you, Lady Bracknell! I have also in my possession, you will be pleased to hear, certificates of Miss Cardew's birth, baptism, whooping cough, registration, vaccination, confirmation, and the measles; both the German and the English variety.

LADY BRACKNELL: Ah! A life crowded with incident, I see; though perhaps somewhat too exciting for a young girl. I am not myself in favour of premature experiences. (*Rises, looks at her watch.*) Gwendolen! the time approaches for our departure. We have not a moment to lose. As a matter of form, Mr. Worthing, I had better ask you if Miss Cardew has any little fortune?

JACK: Oh! about a hundred and thirty thousand pounds in the Funds. That is all. Good-bye, Lady Bracknell. So pleased to have seen you.

LADY BRACKNELL (*sitting down again*): A moment, Mr. Worthing. A hundred and thirty thousand pounds! And in the Funds! Miss Cardew seems to me a most attractive young lady, now that I look at her. Few girls of the present day have any really solid qualities, any of the qualities that last, and improve with time. We live, I regret to say, in an age of surfaces. (*To* CECILY.) Come over here, dear. (CECILY *goes across.*) Pretty child! your dress is sadly simple, and your hair seems almost as Nature might have left it. But we can soon alter all that. A thoroughly experienced French maid produces a really marvellous result in a very brief space of time. I remember recommending one to young Lady Lancing, and after three months her own husband did not know her.

JACK: And after six months nobody knew her.

LADY BRACKNELL (*glares at Jack for a few moments. Then bends, with a practised smile, to* CECILY): Kindly turn round, sweet child. (CECILY *turns completely round.*) No, the side view is what I want. (CECILY *presents her profile.*) Yes, quite as I expected. There are distinct social possibilities in your profile. The two weak points in our age are its want of principle and its want of profile. The chin a little higher, dear. Style largely depends on the way the chin is worn. They are worn very high, just at present. Algernon!

ALGERNON: Yes, Aunt Augusta!

LADY BRACKNELL: There are distinct social possibilities in Miss Cardew's profile.

ALGERNON: Cecily is the sweetest, dearest, prettiest girl in the whole world. And I don't care twopence about social possibilities.

LADY BRACKNELL: Never speak disrespectfully of Society, Algernon. Only people who can't get into it do that. (*To* CECILY.) Dear child, of course you know that Algernon has nothing but his debts to depend upon. But I do not approve of mercenary marriages. When I married Lord Bracknell I had no fortune of any kind. But I never dreamed for a moment of allowing that to stand in my way. Well, I suppose I must give my consent.

ALGERNON: Thank you, Aunt Augusta.

LADY BRACKNELL: Cecily, you may kiss me!

CECILY (*kisses her*): Thank you, Lady Bracknell.

LADY BRACKNELL: You may also address me as Aunt Augusta for the future.

CECILY: Thank you, Aunt Augusta.

LADY BRACKNELL: The marriage, I think, had better take place quite soon.

ALGERNON: Thank you, Aunt Augusta.

CECILY: Thank you, Aunt Augusta.

LADY BRACKNELL: To speak frankly, I am not in favour of long engagements. They give people the opportunity of finding out each other's character before marriage, which I think is never advisable.

JACK: I beg your pardon for interrupting you, Lady Bracknell, but this engagement is quite out of the question. I am Miss Cardew's guardian, and she cannot marry without my consent until she comes of age. That consent I absolutely decline to give.

LADY BRACKNELL: Upon what grounds, may I ask? Algernon is an extremely, I may almost say an ostentatiously, eligible young man. He has nothing, but he looks everything. What more can one desire?

JACK: It pains me very much to have to speak frankly to you, Lady Bracknell, about your nephew, but the fact is that I do not approve at all of his moral character. I suspect him of being untruthful. (ALGERNON *and* CECILY *look at him in indignant amazement*.)

LADY BRACKNELL: Untruthful! My nephew Algernon? Impossible! He is an Oxonian.

JACK: I fear there can be no possible doubt about the matter. This afternoon during my temporary absence in London on an important question of romance, he obtained admission to my house by means of the false pretence of being my brother. Under an assumed name he drank, I've just been informed by my butler, an entire pint bottle of my Perrier-Jouet, Brut, '89; wine I was specially reserving for myself. Continuing his disgraceful deception, he succeeded in the course of the afternoon in alienating the affections of my only ward. He subsequently stayed to tea, and devoured every single muffin. And what makes his conduct all the more heartless is, that he was perfectly well aware from the first that I have no brother, that I never had a brother, and that I don't intend to have a brother, not even of any kind. I distinctly told him so myself yesterday afternoon.

LADY BRACKNELL: Ahem! Mr. Worthing, after careful consideration I have decided entirely to overlook my nephew's conduct to you.

JACK: That is very generous of you, Lady Bracknell. My own decision, however, is unalterable. I decline to give my consent.

LADY BRACKNELL (*to* CECILY): Come here, sweet child. (CECILY *goes over.*) How old are you, dear?

CECILY: Well, I am really only eighteen, but I always admit to twenty when I go to evening parties.

LADY BRACKNELL: You are perfectly right in making some slight alteration. Indeed, no woman should ever be quite accurate about her age. It looks so calculating. . . . (*In a meditative manner.*) Eighteen, but admitting to twenty at evening parties. Well, it will not be very long before you are of age and free from the restraints of tutelage. So I don't think your guardian's consent is, after all, a matter of any importance.

JACK: Pray excuse me, Lady Bracknell, for interrupting you again, but it is only fair to tell you that according to the terms of her grandfather's will Miss Cardew does not come legally of age till she is thirty-five.

LADY BRACKNELL: That does not seem to me to be a grave objection. Thirty-five is a very attractive age. London society is full of women of the very highest birth who have, of their own free choice, remained thirty-five for years. Lady Dumbleton is an instance in point. To my own knowledge she has been thirty-five ever since she arrived at the age of forty, which was many years ago now. I see no reason why our dear Cecily should not be even still more attractive at the age you mention than she is at present. There will be a large accumulation of property.

CECILY: Algy, could you wait for me till I was thirty-five?

ALGERNON: Of course I could, Cecily. You know I could.

CECILY: Yes, I felt it instinctively, but I couldn't wait all that time. I hate waiting even five minutes for anybody. It always makes me rather cross. I am not punctual myself, I know, but I do like punctuality in others, and waiting, even to be married, is quite out of the question.

ALGERNON: Then what is to be done, Cecily?

CECILY: I don't know, Mr. Moncrieff.

LADY BRACKNELL: My dear Mr. Worthing, as Miss Cardew states positively that she cannot wait till she is thirty-five—a remark which I am bound to say seems to me to show a somewhat impatient nature—I would beg of you to reconsider your decision.

JACK: But my dear Lady Bracknell, the matter is entirely in your own hands. The moment you consent to my marriage with Gwendolen, I will most gladly allow your nephew to form an alliance with my ward.

LADY BRACKNELL (*rising and drawing herself up*): You must be quite aware that what you propose is out of the question.

JACK: Then a passionate celibacy is all that any of us can look forward to.

LADY BRACKNELL: That is not the destiny I propose for Gwendolen. Algernon, of course, can choose for himself. (*Pulls out her watch.*) Come, dear (GWENDOLEN *rises*), we have already missed five, if not six, trains. To miss any more might expose us to comment on the platform.

(*Enter* DR. CHASUBLE.)

CHASUBLE: Everything is quite ready for the christenings.

LADY BRACKNELL: The christenings, sir! Is not that somewhat premature?

CHASUBLE (*looking rather puzzled, and pointing to* JACK *and* ALGERNON): Both these gentlemen have expressed a desire for immediate baptism.

LADY BRACKNELL: At their age? The idea is grotesque and irreligious! Algernon, I forbid you to be baptized. I will not hear of such excesses. Lord Bracknell would be highly displeased if he learned that that was the way in which you wasted your time and money.

CHASUBLE: Am I to understand then that there are to be no christenings at all this afternoon?

JACK: I don't think that, as things are now, it would be of much practical value to either of us, Dr. Chasuble.

CHASUBLE: I am grieved to hear such sentiments from you, Mr. Worthing. They savour of the heretical views of the Anabaptists, views that I have completely refuted in four of my unpublished sermons. However, as your present mood seems to be one peculiarly secular, I will return to the church at once. Indeed, I have just been informed by the pew-opener that for the last hour and a half Miss Prism has been waiting for me in the vestry.

LADY BRACKNELL (*starting*): Miss Prism! Did I hear you mention a Miss Prism?

CHASUBLE: Yes, Lady Bracknell. I am on my way to join her.

LADY BRACKNELL: Pray allow me to detain you for a moment. This matter may prove to be one of vital importance to Lord Bracknell and myself. Is this Miss Prism a female of repellent aspect, remotely connected with education?

CHASUBLE (*somewhat indignantly*): She is the most cultivated of ladies, and the very picture of respectability.

LADY BRACKNELL: It is obviously the same person. May I ask what position she holds in your household?

CHASUBLE (*severely*): I am a celibate, madam.

JACK (*interposing*): Miss Prism, Lady Bracknell, has been for the last three years Miss Cardew's esteemed governess and valued companion.

LADY BRACKNELL: In spite of what I hear of her, I must see her at once. Let her be sent for.

CHASUBLE (*looking off*): She approaches; she is nigh.

(*Enter* MISS PRISM *hurriedly.*)

MISS PRISM: I was told you expected me in the vestry, dear Canon. I have been waiting for you there for an hour and three-quarters. (*Catches sight of* LADY BRACKNELL, *who has fixed her with a stony glare.* MISS PRISM *grows pale and quails. She looks anxiously round as if desirous to escape.*)

LADY BRACKNELL (*in a severe, judicial voice*): Prism! (MISS PRISM *bows her head in shame.*) Come here, Prism! (MISS PRISM *approaches in a humble manner.*) Prism! Where is that baby? (*General consternation. The Canon starts back in horror.* ALGERNON *and* JACK *pretend to be anxious to shield* CECILY *and* GWENDOLEN *from hearing the details of a terrible public scandal.*) Twenty-eight years ago, Prism, you left Lord Bracknell's house, Number 104, Upper Grosvenor Square, in charge of a perambulator that contained a baby of the male sex. You never returned. A few weeks later, through the elaborate investigations of the Metropolitan police, the perambulator was discovered at midnight standing by itself in a remote corner of Bayswater. It contained the manuscript of a three-volume novel of more than usually revolting sentimentality. (MISS PRISM *starts in involuntary indignation.*) But the baby was not there. (*Every one looks at* MISS PRISM.) Prism! Where is that baby? (*A pause.*)

MISS PRISM: Lady Bracknell, I admit with shame that I do not know. I only wish I did. The plain facts of the case are these. On the morning of the day you mention, a day that is for ever branded on my memory, I prepared as usual to take the baby out in its perambulator. I had also with me a somewhat old, but capacious hand-bag in which I had intended to place the manuscript of a work of fiction that I had written during my few unoccupied hours. In a moment of mental abstraction, for which I can never forgive myself, I deposited the manuscript in the bassinette and placed the baby in the hand-bag.

JACK (*who has been listening attentively*): But where did you deposit the hand-bag?

MISS PRISM: Do not ask me, Mr. Worthing.

JACK: Miss Prism, this is a matter of no small importance to me. I insist on knowing where you deposited the hand-bag that contained that infant.

MISS PRISM: I left it in the cloak-room of one of the larger railway stations in London.

JACK: What railway station?

MISS PRISM (*quite crushed*): Victoria. The Brighton line. (*Sinks into a chair.*)

JACK: I must retire to my room for a moment. Gwendolen, wait here for me.

GWENDOLEN: If you are not too long, I will wait here for you all my life. (*Exit* JACK *in great excitement.*)

CHASUBLE: What do you think this means, Lady Bracknell?

LADY BRACKNELL: I dare not even suspect, Dr. Chasuble. I need hardly tell you that in families of high position strange coincidences are not supposed to occur. They are hardly considered the thing.

(*Noises heard overhead as if some one was throwing trunks about. Every one looks up.*)

CECILY: Uncle Jack seems strangely agitated.

CHASUBLE: Your guardian has a very emotional nature.

LADY BRACKNELL: This noise is extremely unpleasant. It sounds as if he was having an argument. I dislike arguments of any kind. They are always vulgar, and often convincing.

CHASUBLE (*looking up*): It has stopped now. (*The noise is redoubled.*)

LADY BRACKNELL: I wish he would arrive at some conclusion.

GWENDOLEN: This suspense is terrible. I hope it will last.

(*Enter* JACK *with a hand-bag of black leather in his hand.*)

JACK (*rushing over to* MISS PRISM): Is this the hand-bag, Miss Prism? Examine it carefully before you speak. The happiness of more than one life depends on your answer.

MISS PRISM (*calmly*): It seems to be mine. Yes, here is the injury it received through the upsetting of a Gower Street omnibus in younger and happier days. Here is the stain on the lining caused by the explosion of a temperance beverage, an incident that occurred at Leamington. And here, on the lock, are my initials. I had forgotten that in an extravagant mood I had had them placed there. The bag is undoubtedly mine. I am delighted to have it so unexpectedly restored to me. It has been a great inconvenience being without it all these years.

JACK (*in a pathetic voice*): Miss Prism, more is restored to you than this hand-bag. I was the baby you placed in it.

MISS PRISM (*amazed*): You?

JACK (*embracing her*): Yes . . . mother!

MISS PRISM (*recoiling in indignant astonishment*): Mr. Worthing. I am unmarried!

JACK: Unmarried! I do not deny that is a serious blow. But after all, who has the right to cast a stone against one who has suffered? Cannot repentance wipe out an act of folly? Why should there be one law for men, and another for women? Mother, I forgive you. (*Tries to embrace her again.*)

MISS PRISM (*still more indignant*): Mr. Worthing, there is some error. (*Pointing to* LADY BRACKNELL.) There is the lady who can tell you who you really are.

JACK (*after a pause*): Lady Bracknell, I hate to seem inquisitive, but would you kindly inform me who I am?

LADY BRACKNELL: I am afraid that the news I have to give you will not altogether please you. You are the son of my poor sister, Mrs. Moncrieff, and consequently Algernon's elder brother.

JACK: Algy's elder brother! Then I have a brother after all. I knew I had a brother! I always said I had a brother! Cecily—how could you have ever doubted that I had a brother? (*Seizes hold of* ALGERNON.) Dr. Chasuble, my unfortunate brother. Miss Prism, my unfortunate brother. Gwendolen, my unfortunate brother. Algy, you young scoundrel, you will have to treat me with more respect in the future. You have never behaved to me like a brother in all your life.

ALGERNON: Well, not till to-day, old boy, I admit. I did my best, however, though I was out of practice.

(*Shakes hands.*)

GWENDOLEN (*to* JACK): My own! But what own are you? What is your Christian name, now that you have become some one else?

JACK: Good heavens! . . . I had quite forgotten that point. Your decision on the subject of my name is irrevocable, I suppose?

GWENDOLEN: I never change, except in my affections.

CECILY: What a noble nature you have, Gwendolen!

JACK: Then the question had better be cleared up at once. Aunt Augusta, a moment. At the time when Miss Prism left me in the hand-bag, had I been christened already?

LADY BRACKNELL: Every luxury that money could buy, including christening, had been lavished on you by your fond and doting parents.

JACK: Then I was christened! That is settled. Now, what name was I given? Let me know the worst.

LADY BRACKNELL: Being the eldest son you were naturally christened after your father.

JACK (*irritably*): Yes, but what was my father's Christian name?

LADY BRACKNELL (*meditatively*): I cannot at the present moment recall what the General's Christian name was. But I have no doubt he had one. He was eccentric, I admit. But only in later years. And that was the result of the Indian climate, and marriage, and indigestion, and other things of that kind.

JACK: Algy! Can't you recollect what our father's Christian name was?

ALGERNON: My dear boy, we were never even on speaking terms. He died before I was a year old.

JACK: His name would appear in the Army Lists of the period, I suppose, Aunt Augusta?

LADY BRACKNELL: The General was essentially a man of peace, except in his domestic life. But I have no doubt his name would appear in any military directory.

JACK: The Army Lists of the last forty years are here. These delightful records should have been my constant study. (*Rushes to bookcase and tears the books out.*) M. Generals . . . Mallam, Maxbohm, Magley—what ghastly names they have—Markby, Migsby, Mobbs, Moncrieff! Lieutenant 1840,

Captain, Lieutenant-Colonel, Colonel, General 1869, Christian names, Ernest John. (*Puts book very quietly down and speaks quite calmly.*) I always told you, Gwendolen, my name was Ernest, didn't I? Well, it is Ernest after all. I mean it naturally is Ernest.

LADY BRACKNELL: Yes, I remember now that the General was called Ernest. I knew I had some particular reason for disliking the name.

GWENDOLEN: Ernest! My own Ernest! I felt from the first that you could have no other name!

JACK: Gwendolen, it is a terrible thing for a man to find out suddenly that all his life he has been speaking nothing but the truth. Can you forgive me?

GWENDOLEN: I can. For I feel that you are sure to change.

JACK: My own one!

CHASUBLE (*to* MISS PRISM): Laetitia! (*Embraces her.*)

MISS PRISM (*enthusiastically*): Frederick! At last!

ALGERNON: Cecily! (*Embraces her.*) At last!

JACK: Gwendolen! (*Embraces her.*) At last!

LADY BRACKNELL: My nephew, you seem to be displaying signs of triviality.

JACK: On the contrary, Aunt Augusta, I've now realized for the first time in my life the vital Importance of Being Earnest.

TABLEAU

Anton Chekhov:

UNCLE VANYA

It is embarrassing to talk about Chekhov's art because he himself so clearly saw the futility of much critical writing: "For twenty-five years," he told his fellow-dramatist Gorky, "I have read criticisms of my work, and don't remember a single remark of value, or one word of valuable advice." The basic criticism which Chekhov (1860-1904) encountered, and which dominated most of the comments on his work until recent years—indeed, it is occasionally uttered even today—is that nothing ever happens in any of his plays. If we think that drama must depict intrigue and counter-intrigue, to say nothing of secret passageways and long-lost relatives, we will surely find Chekhov's plays deficient in plot. At first glance they seem merely to record scraps of frustrated conversation, and if we believe that a hodgepodge of aimless talk is typically Russian, we should bear in mind that Chekhov's plays were not immediately popular with his own countrymen. To take a specific instance, Leo Tolstoi found Chekhov pointless. "You are good, Anton Pavlovitch," he told Chekhov after seeing a performance of *Uncle Vanya,* "but your plays are bad all the same. . . . I cannot bear Shakespeare, you know, but your plays are even worse. Shakespeare, for all that, takes the reader by the neck and leads him to a certain goal, and does not let him turn aside. And where is one to go with your heroes? From the sofa where they are lying to the closet and back again." Tolstoi's dislike of Shakespeare (based in part on his odd assumption that the best art is the most popular, and that therefore peasant tunes are superior to Shakespeare's plays) perhaps allows us to discount much of his dramatic criticism, but his description of Chekhov is still considered valid by many.

Chekhov would be the first to admit that he does not seize his audience by the neck and lead it to a goal. He sought to imitate life, and life, he said, does not consist of people who shoot themselves but rather of people who eat, drink, talk

344

foolishly, and do *not* shoot themselves. The curse of drama, he came to believe, was that dramatists were more concerned with art than with life, and that they worried more about artistic movements than about the human nature which they ought to depict. In the first act of *The Sea Gull* (1896) a foolish young playwright insists that we need "new forms of expression"; in the final act, however, he has learned that "it is not a question of forms new or old, but of ideas that must pour freely from the author's heart, without his bothering his head about any forms whatsoever." Chekhov's distrust of "staginess" does not, however, result in a mere transcription of life as any of us sees it. Why, after all, should an artist bother simply to depict life realistically? An audience will hardly pay to see in the theater exactly what it daily sees outside. If art simply holds the mirror up to nature, why not look at nature rather than at its reflection in the mirror? Chekhov does more than merely transcribe the images we see and the sounds we hear. For one thing, when he begins and ends the play where he does—when he decides to imitate *this* rather than *that* slice of life—he is making an artistic choice. And by juxtaposing particular characters at particular moments, he achieves a picture more vivid than that which real life affords. Chekhov's "realism" is not mere photographic reporting, but is rather like the "realism" of Melanesian primitive artists who make "X-ray drawings." These drawings of animals show not only the outer contours but also the bones and inner organs, for the artists believe that their job is to portray the animal as it really is, not merely as it appears to the eye. Chekhov does not tell us a great deal about characters' external appearance, but through carefully chosen dialogue and situations he reveals their inner life.

If one is looking for a heavily plotted and obviously organized play, with action neatly balanced, one can turn to Chekhov's *The Wood Demon* (1889), the play which he later rewrote and turned into *Uncle Vanya* (1899). In *The Wood Demon* a man commits suicide, a married woman leaves her husband and then returns to him, and two young couples are finally united to make the play fit the conventional formula summarized by Lord Byron:

> All tragedies are finish'd by a death,
> All comedies are ended by a marriage.

But in *Uncle Vanya* all of these actions are eliminated. Life, however, has been added. In place of unbelievable characters who act only in accordance with the demands of an improbable plot, we have characters who resemble people about us, so astutely drawn that they make us see more clearly our neighbors and ourselves. These new characters are not heroes, not villains, but persons in whom virtues and vices are mingled. The characters in Chekhov's mature works are often idiosyncratic, but, as Dr. Astroff tells Uncle Vanya, "I used to think that every fool was out of his senses, but now I see that lack of sense is a man's normal state." Chekhov depicts ordinary men who are serious and egotistical—and therefore laughable. As a realist he does not isolate and heighten one aspect of life in order to make his work purely comic or tragic; he subtitles his play "Scenes from Country Life." In Plato's *Symposium* we read that Socrates compelled two Greek playwrights to admit that he who has skill as a tragic dramatist must also have skill as a comic dramatist. Shakespeare alone has left great works of both kinds which can substantiate that claim. But Chekhov shows a genius for both genres within single works. He captures both the comic and the tragic views of life; Vanya is not a tragic figure, nor a fool, but a mixture, sad and a little foolish, too. There is, for example, something pathetically comic when, having realized that he has drudged his life away in haggling over the price of cheese and peas so that a pompous brother-in-law could write worthless pamphlets, Uncle Vanya shouts: "If I had lived a normal life I might have become another Schopenhauer or Dostoieffski." Here, Uncle Johnny (Vanya is a diminutive of Ivan or John, and the name itself suggests childishness) could hardly be more pathetic—or funnier.

Despite the common criticism that nothing "happens" in Chekhov's plays, a great deal happens in *Uncle Vanya*. Near the end of the play, Vanya says to his brother-in-law, Professor Serebrakoff, "Everything will be as before." But between the raising of the curtain and this statement we see and hear such things as make us realize that nothing can be as before. The fretful people manufactured by Chekhov give us an insight into the pathetic comicality of man's illusions. At the end, Chekhov's comedy has afforded us a more accurate view of life. "Art," as Picasso somewhere says, "is a lie that makes us realize the truth."

Uncle Vanya

Scenes from Country Life

TRANSLATED BY MARIAN FELL

Characters

ALEXANDER SEREBRAKOFF, *a retired professor.*
HELENA, *his wife, twenty-seven years old.*
SONIA, *his daughter by a former marriage.*
MME. VOITSKAYA, *widow of a privy councilor, and mother of*
      Serebrakoff's first wife.
IVAN (VANYA) VOITSKI, *her son.*
MICHAEL ASTROFF, *a doctor.*
ILIA (WAFFLES) TELEGIN, *an impoverished landowner.*
MARINA, *an old nurse.*
A WORKMAN.

The scene is laid on SEREBRAKOFF'S *country place.*

ACT I

(*A country house on a terrace. In front of it a garden. In an avenue of trees, under an old poplar, stands a table set for tea, with a samovar, etc. Some benches and chairs stand near the table. On one of them is lying a guitar. A hammock is swung near the table. It is three o'clock in the afternoon of a cloudy day.*)

(MARINA, *a quiet, gray-haired, little old woman, is sitting at the table knitting a stocking.* ASTROFF *is walking up and down near her.*)

MARINA (*pouring some tea into a glass*): Take a little tea, my son.

ASTROFF (*Takes the glass from her unwillingly.*): Somehow, I don't seem to want any.

MARINA: Then will you have a little vodka instead?

ASTROFF: No, I don't drink vodka every day, and besides, it is too hot now. (*A pause.*) Tell me, nurse, how long have we known each other?

MARINA (*thoughtfully*): Let me see, how long is it? Lord—help me to remember. You first came here, into our parts—let me think—when was it? Sonia's mother was still alive—it was two winters before she died; that was eleven years ago—(*thoughtfully*) perhaps more.

ASTROFF: Have I changed much since then?

MARINA: Oh, yes. You were handsome and young then, and now you are an old man and not handsome any more. You drink, too.

ASTROFF: Yes, ten years have made me another man. And why? Because I am overworked. Nurse, I am on my feet from dawn till dusk. I know no rest; at night I tremble under my blankets for fear of being dragged out to visit some one who is sick; I have toiled without repose or a day's freedom since I have known you; could I help growing old? And then, existence is tedious, anyway; it is a senseless, dirty business, this life, and goes heavily. Every one about here is silly, and after living with them for two or three years one grows silly oneself. It is inevitable. (*Twisting his mustache*) See what a long mustache I have grown. A foolish, long mustache. Yes, I am as silly as the rest, nurse, but not as stupid; no, I have not grown stupid. Thank God, my brain is not addled yet, though my feelings have grown numb. I ask nothing, I need nothing, I love no one, unless it is yourself alone. (*He kisses her head.*) I had a nurse just like you when I was a child.

MARINA: Don't you want a bite of something to eat?

ASTROFF: No. During the third week of Lent I went to the epidemic at Malitskoi. It was eruptive typhoid. The peasants were all lying side by side in their huts, and the calves and pigs were running about the floor among the sick. Such dirt there was, and smoke! Unspeakable! I slaved among those people all day, not a crumb passed my lips, but when I got home there was still no rest for me; a switchman was carried in from the railroad; I laid him on the operating table and he went and died in my arms under chloroform, and then my feelings that should have been deadened awoke again, my conscience tortured me as if I had killed the man. I sat down and closed my eyes—like this—and thought: will our descendants two hundred years from now, for whom we are breaking the road, remember to give us a kind word? No, nurse, they will forget.

MARINA: Man is forgetful, but God remembers.

ASTROFF: Thank you for that. You have spoken the truth.

(*Enter* VOITSKI *from the house. He has been asleep after dinner and looks rather disheveled. He sits down on the bench and straightens his collar.*)

VOITSKI: H'm. Yes. (*A pause.*) Yes.

ASTROFF: Have you been asleep?

VOITSKI: Yes, very much so. (*He yawns.*) Ever since the professor and his wife have come, our daily life seems to have jumped the track. I sleep at the wrong time, drink wine, and eat all sorts of messes for luncheon and dinner. It isn't wholesome. Sonia and I used to work together and never had an idle moment, but now Sonia works alone and I only eat and drink and sleep. Something is wrong.

MARINA (*Shakes her head.*): Such a confusion in the house! The professor gets up at twelve, the samovar is kept boiling all the morning, and everything has to wait for him. Before they came we used to have dinner at one o'clock, like everybody else, but now we have it at seven. The professor sits up all night writing and reading, and suddenly, at two o'clock, there goes the bell! Heavens, what is that? The professor wants some tea! Wake the servants, light the samovar! Lord, what disorder!

ASTROFF: Will they be here long?

VOITSKI: A hundred years! The professor has decided to make his home here.

MARINA: Look at this now! The samovar has been on the table for two hours, and they are all out walking!

VOITSKI: All right, don't get excited; here they come.

(*Voices are heard approaching.* SEREBRAKOFF, HELENA, SONIA, *and* TELEGIN *come in from the depths of the garden, returning from their walk.*)

SEREBRAKOFF: Superb! Superb! What beautiful views!
TELEGIN: They are wonderful, your Excellency.
SONIA: Tomorrow we shall go into the woods, shall we, papa?
VOITSKI: Ladies and gentlemen, tea is ready.
SEREBRAKOFF: Won't you please be good enough to send my tea into the library? I still have some work to finish.
SONIA: I am sure you will love the woods.

(HELENA, SEREBRAKOFF, *and* SONIA *go into the house.* TELEGIN *sits down at the table beside* MARINA.)

VOITSKI: There goes our learned scholar on a hot, sultry day like this, in his overcoat and goloshes and carrying an umbrella!
ASTROFF: He is trying to take good care of his health.
VOITSKI: How lovely she is! How lovely! I have never in my life seen a more beautiful woman.
TELEGIN: Do you know, Marina, that as I walk in the fields or in the shady garden, as I look at this table here, my heart swells with unbounded happiness. The weather is enchanting, the birds are singing, we are all living in peace and content-ment—what more could the soul desire? (*Takes a glass of tea.*)
VOITSKI (*dreaming*): Such eyes—a glorious woman!
ASTROFF: Come, Ivan, tell us something.
VOITSKI (*indolently*): What shall I tell you?
ASTROFF: Haven't you any news for us?
VOITSKI: No, it is all stale. I am just the same as usual, or perhaps worse, because I have become lazy. I don't do any-thing now but croak like an old raven. My mother, the old magpie, is still chattering about the emancipation of woman, with one eye on her grave and the other on her learned books, in which she is always looking for the dawn of a new life.
ASTROFF: And the professor?
VOITSKI: The professor sits in his library from morning till night, as usual—
> "Straining the mind, wrinkling the brow,
> We write, write, write,
> Without respite
> Or hope of praise in the future or now."

Poor paper! He ought to write his autobiography; he would make a really splendid subject for a book! Imagine it, the life of a retired professor, as stale as a piece of hardtack, tortured by gout, headaches, and rheumatism, his liver bursting with jealousy and envy, living on the estate of his first wife, although he hates it, because he can't afford to live in town. He is everlastingly whining about his hard lot, though, as a matter of fact, he is extraordinarily lucky. He is the son of a common deacon and has attained the professor's chair, become the son-in-law of a senator, is called "your Excellency," and so on. But I'll tell you something; the man has been writing on art for twenty-five years, and he doesn't know the very first thing about it. For twenty-five years he has been chewing on other men's thoughts about realism, naturalism, and all such foolishness; for twenty-five years he has been reading and writing things that clever men have long known and stupid ones are not interested in; for twenty-five years he has been making his imaginary mountains out of mole-hills. And just think of the man's self-conceit and presumption all this time! For twenty-five years he has been masquerading in false clothes and has now retired, absolutely unknown to any living soul; and yet see him! stalking across the earth like a demi-god!

ASTROFF: I believe you envy him.

VOITSKI: Yes, I do. Look at the success he has had with women! Don Juan himself was not more favored. His first wife, who was my sister, was a beautiful, gentle being, as pure as the blue heaven there above us, noble, great-hearted, with more admirers than he has pupils, and she loved him as only beings of angelic purity can love those who are as pure and beautiful as themselves. His mother-in-law, my mother, adores him to this day, and he still inspires a sort of worshipful awe in her. His second wife is, as you see, a brilliant beauty; she married him in his old age and has surrendered all the glory of her beauty and freedom to him. Why? What for?

ASTROFF: Is she faithful to him?

VOITSKI: Yes, unfortunately she is.

ASTROFF: Why "unfortunately"?

VOITSKI: Because such fidelity is false and unnatural, root and branch. It sounds well, but there is no logic in it. It is thought immoral for a woman to deceive an old husband whom she hates, but quite moral for her to strangle her poor youth in her breast and banish every vital desire from her heart.

TELEGIN (*in a tearful voice*): Vanya, I don't like to hear you talk so. Listen, Vanya; every one who betrays husband or wife is faithless, and could also betray his country.

VOITSKI (*crossly*): Turn off the tap, Waffles.

TELEGIN: No, allow me, Vanya. My wife ran away with a lover on the day after our wedding, because my exterior was unprepossessing. I have never failed in my duty since then. I love her and am true to her to this day. I help her all I can and have given my fortune to educate the daughter of herself and her lover. I have forfeited my happiness, but I have kept my pride. And she? Her youth has fled, her beauty has faded according to the laws of nature, and her lover is dead. What has she kept?

(HELENA *and* SONIA *come in; after them comes* MME. VOITSKAYA *carrying a book. She sits down and begins to read. Some one hands her a glass of tea which she drinks without looking up.*)

SONIA (*hurriedly, to the* NURSE): There are some peasants waiting out there. Go and see what they want. I shall pour the tea. (*Pours out some glasses of tea.*)

(MARINA *goes out.* HELENA *takes a glass and sits drinking in the hammock.*)

ASTROFF: I have come to see your husband. You wrote me that he had rheumatism and I know not what else, and that he was very ill, but he appears to be as lively as a cricket.

HELENA: He had a fit of the blues yesterday evening and complained of pains in his legs, but he seems all right again today.

ASTROFF: And I galloped over here twenty miles at breakneck speed! No matter, though, it is not the first time. Once here, however, I am going to stay until tomorrow, and at any rate sleep *quantum satis.*

SONIA: Oh, splendid! You so seldom spend the night with us. Have you had dinner yet?

ASTROFF: No.

SONIA: Good. So you will have it with us. We dine at seven now. (*Drinks her tea.*) This tea is cold!

TELEGIN: Yes, the samovar has grown cold.

HELENA: Don't mind, Monsieur Ivan, we will drink cold tea, then.

TELEGIN: I beg your pardon, my name is not Ivan, but Ilia, ma'am——Ilia Telegin, or Waffles, as I am sometimes called on account of my pock-marked face. I am Sonia's godfather, and his Excellency, your husband, knows me very well. I now live with you, ma'am, on this estate, and perhaps you will be so good as to notice that I dine with you every day.

SONIA: He is our great help, our right-hand man. (*tenderly*) Dear godfather, let me pour you some tea.

MME. VOITSKAYA: Oh! Oh!

SONIA: What is it, grandmother?

MME. VOITSKAYA: I forgot to tell Alexander—I have lost my memory—I received a letter today from Paul Alexevitch in Kharkoff. He has sent me a new pamphlet.

ASTROFF: Is it interesting?

MME. VOITSKAYA: Yes, but strange. He refutes the very theories which he defended seven years ago. It is appalling!

VOITSKI: There is nothing appalling about it. Drink your tea, mamma.

MME. VOITSKAYA: It seems you never want to listen to what I have to say. Pardon me, Jean, but you have changed so in the last year that I hardly know you. You used to be a man of settled convictions and had an illuminating personality——

VOITSKI: Oh, yes. I had an illuminating personality, which illuminated no one. (*A pause.*) I had an illuminating personality! You couldn't say anything more biting. I am forty-seven years old. Until last year I endeavored, as you do now, to blind my eyes by your pedantry to the truths of life. But now— Oh, if you only knew! If you knew how I lie awake at night, heartsick and angry, to think how stupidly I have wasted my time when I might have been winning from life everything which my old age now forbids.

SONIA: Uncle Vanya, how dreary!

MME. VOITSKAYA (*to her son*): You speak as if your former convictions were somehow to blame, but you yourself, not they, were at fault. You have forgotten that a conviction, in itself, is nothing but a dead letter. You should have done something.

VOITSKI: Done something! Not every man is capable of being a writer *perpetuum mobile* like your Herr Professor.

MME. VOITSKAYA: What do you mean by that?

SONIA (*imploringly*): Mother! Uncle Vanya! I entreat you!

VOITSKI: I am silent. I apologize and am silent. (*A pause.*)

HELENA: What a fine day! Not too hot. (*A pause.*)

VOITSKI: A fine day to hang oneself.

(TELEGIN *tunes the guitar.* MARINA *appears near the house, calling the chickens.*)

MARINA: Chick, chick, chick!

SONIA: What did the peasants want, nurse?

MARINA: The same old thing, the same old nonsense. Chick, chick, chick!

SONIA: Why are you calling the chickens?

MARINA: The speckled hen has disappeared with her chicks. I am afraid the crows have got her.

(TELEGIN *plays a polka. All listen in silence. Enter* WORK-MAN.)

WORKMAN: Is the doctor here? (*To* ASTROFF) Excuse me, sir, but I have been sent to fetch you.

ASTROFF: Where are you from?

WORKMAN: The factory.

ASTROFF (*annoyed*): Thank you. There is nothing for it, then, but to go. (*Looking around him for his cap*) Damn it, this is annoying!

SONIA: Yes, it is too bad, really. You must come back to dinner from the factory.

ASTROFF: No, I won't be able to do that. It will be too late. Now where, where— (*To the* WORKMAN) Look here, my man, get me a glass of vodka, will you? (*The* WORKMAN *goes out.*) Where—where— (*Finds his cap.*) One of the characters in Ostroff's plays is a man with a long mustache and short wits, like me. However, let me bid you good-bye, ladies and gentlemen. (*To* HELENA.) I should be really delighted if you would come to see me some day with Miss Sonia. My estate is small, but if you are interested in such things I should like to show you a nursery and seed-bed whose like you will not find within a thousand miles of here. My place is surrounded by government forests. The forester is old and always ailing, so I superintend almost all the work myself.

HELENA: I have always heard that you were very fond of the woods. Of course one can do a great deal of good by helping to preserve them, but does not that work interfere with your real calling?

ASTROFF: God alone knows what a man's real calling is.

HELENA: And do you find it interesting?

ASTROFF: Yes, very.

VOITSKI (*sarcastically*): Oh, extremely!

HELENA: You are still young, not over thirty-six or seven, I should say, and I suspect that the woods do not interest you as much as you say they do. I should think you would find them monotonous.

SONIA: No, the work is thrilling. Dr. Astroff watches over the old woods and sets out new plantations every year, and he has already received a diploma and a bronze medal. If you will listen to what he can tell you, you will agree with him entirely. He says that forests are the ornaments of the earth, that they teach mankind to understand beauty and attune his mind to lofty sentiments. Forests temper a stern climate, and in countries where the climate is milder, less strength is wasted in the battle with nature, and the people are kind and gentle. The inhabitants of such countries are handsome, tractable, sensitive, graceful in speech and gesture.

Their philosophy is joyous, art and science blossom among them, their treatment of women is full of exquisite nobility——

VOITSKI (*laughing*): Bravo! Bravo! All that is very pretty, but it is also unconvincing. So my friend (*to* ASTROFF), you must let me go on burning firewood in my stoves and building my sheds of planks.

ASTROFF: You can burn peat in your stoves and build your sheds of stone. Oh, I don't object, of course, to cutting wood from necessity, but why destroy the forests? The woods of Russia are trembling under the blows of the axe. Millions of trees have perished. The homes of the wild animals and birds have been desolated; the rivers are shrinking, and many beautiful landscapes are gone forever. And why? Because men are too lazy and stupid to stoop down and pick up their fuel from the ground. (*To* HELENA) Am I not right, Madame? Who but a stupid barbarian could burn so much beauty in his stove and destroy that which he cannot make? Man is endowed with reason and the power to create, so that he may increase that which has been given him, but until now he has not created, but demolished. The forests are disappearing, the rivers are running dry, the game is exterminated, the climate is spoiled, and the earth becomes poorer and uglier every day. (*To* VOITSKI) I read irony in your eye; you do not take what I am saying seriously, and—and—after all, it may very well be nonsense. But when I pass peasant-forests that I have preserved from the axe, or hear the rustling of the young plantations set out with my own hands, I feel as if I had had some small share in improving the climate, and that if mankind is happy a thousand years from now I will have been a little bit responsible for their happiness. When I plant a little birch tree and then see it budding into young green and swaying in the wind, my heart swells with pride and I—(*Sees the* WORKMAN, *who is bringing him a glass of vodka on a tray.*) However—(*he drinks*) I must be off. Probably it is all nonsense, anyway. Good-bye.

(*He goes toward the house.* SONIA *takes his arm and goes with him.*)

SONIA: When are you coming to see us again?

ASTROFF: I can't say.

SONIA: In a month?

(ASTROFF *and* SONIA *go into the house.* HELENA *and* VOITSKI *walk over to the terrace.*)

HELENA: You have behaved shockingly again. Ivan, what sense was there in teasing your mother and talking about *perpetuum mobile*? And at breakfast you quarreled with Alexander again. Really, your behavior is too petty.

VOITSKI: But if I hate him?

HELENA: You hate Alexander without reason; he is like every one else, and no worse than you are.

VOITSKI: If you could only see your face, your gestures! Oh, how tedious your life must be.

HELENA: It is tedious, yes, and dreary! You all abuse my husband and look on me with compassion; you think, "Poor woman, she is married to an old man." How well I understand your compassion! As Astroff said just now, see how you thoughtlessly destroy the forests, so that there will soon be none left. So you also destroy mankind, and soon fidelity and purity and self-sacrifice will have vanished with the woods. Why cannot you look calmly at a woman unless she is yours? Because, the doctor was right, you are all possessed by a devil of destruction; you have no mercy on the woods or the birds or on women or on one another.

VOITSKI: I don't like your philosophy.

HELENA: That doctor has a sensitive, weary face—an interesting face. Sonia evidently likes him, and she is in love with him, and I can understand it. This is the third time he has been here since I have come, and I have not had a real talk with him yet or made much of him. He thinks I am disagreeable. Do you know, Ivan, the reason you and I are such friends? I think it is because we are both lonely and unfortunate. Yes, unfortunate. Don't look at me in that way, I don't like it.

VOITSKI: How can I look at you otherwise when I love you? You are my joy, my life, and my youth. I know that my chances of being loved in return are infinitely small, do not exist, but I ask nothing of you. Only let me look at you, listen to your voice——

HELENA: Hush, some one will overhear you. (*They go toward the house.*)

VOITSKI (*following her*): Let me speak to you of my love, do not drive me away, and this alone will be my greatest happiness!

HELENA: Ah! This is agony!

(TELEGIN *strikes the strings of his guitar and plays a polka.* MME. VOITSKAYA *writes something on the leaves of her pamphlet.*)

ACT II

(*The dining-room of* SEREBRAKOFF's *house. It is night. The tapping of the* WATCHMAN's *rattle is heard in the garden.* SEREBRAKOFF *is dozing in an armchair by an open window and* HELENA *is sitting beside him, also half asleep.*)

SEREBRAKOFF (*rousing himself*): Who is here? Is it you, Sonia?

HELENA: It is I.

SEREBRAKOFF: Oh, it is you, Helene. This pain is intolerable.

HELENA: Your shawl has slipped down. (*She wraps up his legs in the shawl.*) Let me shut the window.

SEREBRAKOFF: No, leave it open; I am suffocating. I dreamt just now that my left leg belonged to some one else, and it hurt so that I woke. I don't believe this is gout, it is more like rheumatism. What time is it?

HELENA: Half-past twelve. (*A pause.*)

SEREBRAKOFF: I want you to look for Batushka's works in the library tomorrow. I think we have him.

HELENA: What is that?

SEREBRAKOFF: Look for Batushka tomorrow morning; we used to have him, I remember. Why do I find it so hard to breathe?

HELENA: You are tired; this is the second night you have had no sleep.

SEREBRAKOFF: They say that Turgenieff got angina of the heart from gout. I am afraid I am getting angina too. Oh, damn this horrible, accursed old age! Ever since I have been old I have been hateful to myself, and I am sure, hateful to you all as well.

HELENA: You speak as if we were to blame for your being old.

SEREBRAKOFF: I am more hateful to you than to any one.

(HELENA *gets up and walks away from him, sitting down at a distance.*)

SEREBRAKOFF: You are quite right, of course. I am not an idiot; I can understand you. You are young and healthy and beautiful, and longing for life, and I am an old dotard, almost a dead man already. Don't I know it? Of course I see that it is foolish for me to live so long, but wait! I shall soon set you all free. My life cannot drag on much longer.

HELENA: You are overtaxing my powers of endurance. Be quiet, for God's sake!

SEREBRAKOFF: It appears that, thanks to me, everybody's power of endurance is being overtaxed; everybody is miserable, only I am blissfully triumphant. Oh, yes, of course!

HELENA: Be quiet! You are torturing me.

SEREBRAKOFF: I torture everybody. Of course.

HELENA (*weeping*): This is unbearable! Tell me, what is it you want me to do?

SEREBRAKOFF: Nothing.

HELENA: Then be quiet, please.

SEREBRAKOFF: It is funny that everybody listens to Ivan

and his old idiot of a mother, but the moment I open my lips you all begin to feel ill-treated. You can't even stand the sound of my voice. Even if I am hateful, even if I am a selfish tyrant, haven't I the right to be one at my age? Haven't I deserved it? Haven't I, I ask you, the right to be respected, now that I am old?

HELENA: No one is disputing your rights. (*The window slams in the wind.*) The wind is rising, I must shut the window. (*She shuts it.*) We shall have rain in a moment. Your rights have never been questioned by anybody.

(*The* WATCHMAN *in the garden sounds his rattle.*)

SEREBRAKOFF: I have spent my life working in the interests of learning. I am used to my library and the lecture hall and to the esteem and admiration of my colleagues. Now I suddenly find myself plunged in this wilderness, condemned to see the same stupid people from morning till night and listen to their futile conversation. I want to live; I long for success and fame and the stir of the world, and here I am an exile! Oh, it is dreadful to spend every moment grieving for the lost past, to see the success of others and sit here with nothing to do but to fear death. I cannot stand it! It is more than I can bear. And you will not even forgive me for being old!

HELENA: Wait, have patience; I shall be old myself in four or five years.

(SONIA *comes in.*)

SONIA: Father, you sent for Dr. Astroff, and now when he comes you refuse to see him. It is not nice to give a man so much trouble for nothing.

SEREBRAKOFF: What do I care about your Astroff? He understands medicine about as well as I understand astronomy.

SONIA: We can't send for the whole medical faculty, can we, to treat your gout?

SEREBRAKOFF: I won't talk to that madman!

SONIA: Do as you please. It's all the same to me. (*She sits down.*)

SEREBRAKOFF: What time is it?

HELENA: One o'clock.

SEREBRAKOFF: It is stifling in here. Sonia, hand me that bottle on the table.

SONIA: Here it is.

(*She hands him a bottle of medicine.*)

SEREBRAKOFF (*crossly*): No, not that one! Can't you understand me? Can't I ask you to do a thing?

SONIA: Please don't be captious with me. Some people may

like it, but you must spare me, if you please, because I don't.
Besides, I haven't the time; we are cutting the hay tomorrow
and I must get up early.

(VOITSKI *comes in dressed in a long gown and carrying
a candle.*)

VOITSKI: A thunderstorm is coming up. (*The lightning
flashes.*) There it is! Go to bed, Helena and Sonia. I have
come to take your place.

SEREBRAKOFF (*frightened*): No, no, no! Don't leave me
alone with him! Oh, don't. He will begin to lecture me.

VOITSKI: But you must give them a little rest. They have
not slept for two nights.

SEREBRAKOFF: Then let them go to bed, but you go away
too! Thank you. I implore you to go. For the sake of our
former friendship do not protest against going. We will talk
some other time——

VOITSKI: Our former friendship! Our former——

SONIA: Hush, Uncle Vanya!

SEREBRAKOFF (*to his wife*): My darling, don't leave me
alone with him. He will begin to lecture me.

VOITSKI: This is ridiculous.

(MARINA *comes in carrying a candle.*)

SONIA: You must go to bed, nurse, it is late.

MARINA: I haven't cleared away the tea things. Can't go
to bed yet.

SEREBRAKOFF: No one can go to bed. They are all worn
out, only I enjoy perfect happiness.

MARINA: (*goes up to* SEREBRAKOFF *and speaks tenderly.*)
What's the matter, master? Does it hurt? My own legs are
aching too, oh, so badly. (*Arranges his shawl about his legs.*)
You have had this illness such a long time. Sonia's dead
mother used to stay awake with you too, and wear herself
out for you. She loved you dearly. (*A pause.*) Old people
want to be pitied as much as young ones, but nobody cares
about them somehow. (*She kisses* SEREBRAKOFF'S *shoulder.*)
Come, master, let me give you some linden-tea and warm
your poor feet for you. I shall pray to God for you.

SEREBRAKOFF (*touched*): Let us go, Marina.

MARINA: My own feet are aching so badly, oh, so badly!
(*She and* SONIA *begin to lead* SEREBRAKOFF *out.*) Sonia's
mother used to wear herself out with sorrow and weeping.
You were still little and foolish then, Sonia. Come, come,
master.

(SEREBRAKOFF, SONIA, *and* MARINA *go out.*)

HELENA: I am absolutely exhausted by him, and can hardly
stand.

VOITSKI: You are exhausted by him, and I am exhausted by my own self. I have not slept for three nights.

HELENA: Something is wrong in this house. Your mother hates everything but her pamphlets and the professor; the professor is vexed, he won't trust me, and fears you; Sonia is angry with her father, and with me, and hasn't spoken to me for two weeks! I am at the end of my strength, and have come near bursting into tears at least twenty times today. Something is wrong in this house.

VOITSKI: Leave speculating alone.

HELENA: You are cultured and intelligent, Ivan, and you surely understand that the world is not destroyed by villains and conflagrations, but by hate and malice and all this spiteful tattling. It is your duty to make peace, and not to growl at everything.

VOITSKI: Help me first to make peace with myself. My darling! (*Seizes her hand.*)

HELENA: Let go! (*She drags her hand away.*) Go away!

VOITSKI: Soon the rain will be over, and all nature will sigh and awake refreshed. Only I am not refreshed by the storm. Day and night the thought haunts me like a fiend, that my life is lost forever. My past does not count, because I frittered it away on trifles, and the present has so terribly miscarried! What shall I do with my life and my love? What is to become of them? This wonderful feeling of mine will be wasted and lost as a ray of sunlight is lost that falls into a dark chasm, and my life will go with it.

HELENA: I am as it were benumbed when you speak to me of your love, and I don't know how to answer you. Forgive me, I have nothing to say to you. (*She tries to go out.*) Good night!

VOITSKI (*Barring the way.*): If you only knew how I am tortured by the thought that beside me in this house is another life that is being lost forever—it is yours! What are you waiting for? What accursed philosophy stands in your way? Oh, understand, understand——

HELENA (*looking at him intently*): Ivan, you are drunk!

VOITSKI: Perhaps. Perhaps.

HELENA: Where is the doctor?

VOITSKI: In there, spending the night with me. Perhaps I am drunk, perhaps I am; nothing is impossible.

HELENA: Have you just been drinking together? Why do you do that?

VOITSKI: Because in that way I get a taste of life. Let me do it, Helena!

HELENA: You never used to drink, and you never used to talk so much. Go to bed, I am tired of you.

VOITSKI (*falling on his knees before her*): My sweetheart, my beautiful one——

HELENA (*angrily*): Leave me alone! Really, this has become too disagreeable.

(HELENA *goes out. A pause.*)

VOITSKI (*alone*): She is gone! I met her first ten years ago, at her sister's house, when she was seventeen and I was thirty-seven. Why did I not fall in love with her then and propose to her? It would have been so easy! And now she would have been my wife. Yes, we would both have been waked tonight by the thunderstorm, and she would have been frightened, but I would have held her in my arms and whispered: "Don't be afraid! I am here." Oh, enchanting dream, so sweet that I laugh to think of it. (*He laughs.*) But my God! My head reels! Why am I so old? Why won't she understand me? I hate all that rhetoric of hers, that morality of indolence, that absurd talk about the destruction of the world— (*A pause.*) Oh, how I have been deceived! For years I have worshiped that miserable gout-ridden professor. Sonia and I have squeezed this estate dry for his sake. We have bartered our butter and curds and peas like misers, and have never kept a morsel for ourselves, so that we could scrape enough pennies together to send to him. I was proud of him and of his learning; I received all his words and writings as inspired, and now? Now he has retired, and what is the total of his life? A blank! He is absolutely unknown, and his fame has burst like a soap-bubble. I have been deceived; I see that now, basely deceived.

(ASTROFF *comes in. He has his coat on, but is without his waistcoat or collar, and is slightly drunk.* TELEGIN *follows him, carrying a guitar.*)

ASTROFF: Play!

TELEGIN: But every one is asleep.

ASTROFF: Play!

(TELEGIN *begins to play softly.*)

ASTROFF: Are you alone here? No women about?

(*Sings with his arms akimbo.*)

"The hut is cold, the fire is dead;
Where shall the master lay his head?"

The thunderstorm woke me. It was a heavy shower. What time is it?

VOITSKI: The devil only knows.

ASTROFF: I thought I heard Helena's voice.

VOITSKI: She was here a moment ago.

ASTROFF: What a beautiful woman! (*Looking at the medicine bottles on the table*) Medicine, is it? What a variety we have; prescriptions from Moscow, from Kharkoff, from Tula!

Why, he has been pestering all the towns of Russia with his gout! Is he ill, or simply shamming?

VOITSKI: He is really ill.

ASTROFF: What is the matter with you tonight? You seem sad. Is it because you are sorry for the professor?

VOITSKI: Leave me alone.

ASTROFF: Or in love with the professor's wife?

VOITSKI: She is my friend.

ASTROFF: Already?

VOITSKI: What do you mean by "already"?

ASTROFF: A woman can only become a man's friend after having first been his acquaintance and then his beloved— then she becomes his friend.

VOITSKI: What vulgar philosophy!

ASTROFF: What do you mean? Yes, I must confess I am getting vulgar, but then, you see, I am drunk. I usually only drink like this once a month. At such times my audacity and temerity know no bounds. I feel capable of anything. I attempt the most difficult operations and do them magnificently. The most brilliant plans for the future take shape in my head. I am no longer a poor fool of a doctor, but mankind's greatest benefactor. I evolve my own system of philosophy and all of you seem to crawl at my feet like so many insects or microbes. (*To* TELEGIN) Play, Waffles!

TELEGIN: My dear boy, I would with all my heart, but do listen to reason; everybody in the house is asleep.

ASTROFF: Play!

(TELEGIN *plays softly.*)

ASTROFF: I want a drink. Come, we still have some brandy left. And then, as soon as it is day, you will come home with me.

(*He sees* SONIA, *who comes in at that moment.*)

ASTROFF: I beg your pardon, I have no collar on.

(*He goes out quickly, followed by* TELEGIN.)

SONIA: Uncle Vanya, you and the doctor have been drinking! The good fellows have been getting together! It is all very well for him, he has always done it, but why do you follow his example? It looks dreadful at your age.

VOITSKI: Age has nothing to do with it. When real life is wanting one must create an illusion. It is better than nothing.

SONIA: Our hay is all cut and rotting in these daily rains, and here you are busy creating illusions! You have given up the farm altogether. I have done all the work alone until I am at the end of my strength— (*Frightened*) Uncle! Your eyes are full of tears!

VOITSKI: Tears? Nonsense, there are no tears in my eyes. You looked at me then just as your dead mother used to,

my darling—— (*He eagerly kisses her face and hands.*)
My sister, my dearest sister, where are you now? Ah, if you
only knew, if you only knew!

SONIA: If she only knew what, Uncle?

VOITSKI: My heart is bursting. It is awful. No matter,
though. I must go. (*He goes out.*)

SONIA: (*Knocks at the door.*) Dr. Astroff! Are you awake?
Please come here for a minute.

ASTROFF (*Behind the door*): In a moment.

(*He appears in a few seconds. He has put on his collar
and waistcoat.*)

ASTROFF: What do you want?

SONIA: Drink as much as you please yourself, if you don't
find it revolting, but I implore you not to let my uncle do
it. It is bad for him.

ASTROFF: Very well; we won't drink any more. I am going
home at once. That is settled. It will be dawn by the time
the horses are harnessed.

SONIA: It is still raining; wait till morning.

ASTROFF: The storm is blowing over. This is only the edge
of it. I must go. And please don't ask me to come and see
your father any more. I tell him he has gout, and he says
it is rheumatism. I tell him to lie down, and he sits up. Today
he refused to see me at all.

SONIA: He has been spoilt. (*She looks in the sideboard.*)
Won't you have a bite to eat?

ASTROFF: Yes, please. I believe I will.

SONIA: I love to eat at night. I am sure we shall find
something here. They say that he has made a great many
conquests in his life, and that the women have spoiled him.
Here is some cheese for you.

(*They stand eating by the sideboard.*)

ASTROFF: I haven't eaten anything today. Your father
has a very difficult nature. (*He takes a bottle out of the
sideboard.*) May I? (*He pours himself a glass of vodka.*)
We are alone here, and I can speak frankly. Do you know,
I could not stand living in this house for even a month? This
atmosphere would stifle me. There is your father, entirely
absorbed in his books, and his gout; there is your Uncle
Vanya with his hypochondria, your grandmother, and finally,
your stepmother——

SONIA: What about her?

ASTROFF: A human being should be entirely beautiful: the

face, the clothes, the mind, the thoughts. Your stepmother is, of course, beautiful to look at, but don't you see? She does nothing but sleep and eat and walk and bewitch us, and that is all. She has no responsibilities, everything is done for her—am I not right? And an idle life can never be a pure one. (*A pause.*) However, I may be judging her too severely. Like your Uncle Vanya, I am discontented, and so we are both grumblers.

SONIA: Aren't you satisfied with life?

ASTROFF: I like life as life, but I hate and despise it in a little Russian country village, and as far as my own personal life goes, by heaven! there is absolutely no redeeming feature about it. Haven't you noticed if you are riding through a dark wood at night and see a little light shining ahead, how you forget your fatigue and the darkness and the sharp twigs that whip your face? I work, that you know—as no one else in the country works. Fate beats me on without rest; at times I suffer unendurably and I see no light ahead. I have no hope; I do not like people. It is long since I have loved any one.

SONIA: You love no one?

ASTROFF: Not a soul. I only feel a sort of tenderness for your old nurse for old-times' sake. The peasants are all alike; they are stupid and live in dirt, and the educated people are hard to get along with. One gets tired of them. All our good friends are petty and shallow and see no farther than their own noses; in one word, they are dull. Those that have brains are hysterical, devoured with a mania for self-analysis. They whine, they hate, they pick faults everywhere with unhealthy sharpness. They sneak up to me sideways, look at me out of a corner of the eye, and say: "That man is a lunatic," "That man is a wind-bag." Or, if they don't know what else to label me with, they say I am strange. I like the woods; that is strange. I don't eat meat; that is strange, too. Simple, natural relations between man and man or man and nature do not exist.

(*He tries to go out;* SONIA *prevents him.*)

SONIA: I beg you, I implore you, not to drink any more!

ASTROFF: Why not?

SONIA: It is so unworthy of you. You are well-bred, your voice is sweet, you are even—more than any one I know—handsome. Why do you want to resemble the common people that drink and play cards? Oh, don't, I beg you! You always say that people do not create anything, but only destroy what heaven has given them. Why, oh, why, do

you destroy yourself? Oh, don't, I implore you not to! I
entreat you!

ASTROFF: (*Gives her his hand.*) I won't drink any more.

SONIA: Promise me.

ASTROFF: I give you my word of honor.

SONIA: (*Squeezing his hand.*) Thank you.

ASTROFF: I have done with it. You see, I am perfectly
sober again, and so I shall stay till the end of my life. (*He
looks at his watch.*) But, as I was saying, life holds nothing
for me; my race is run. I am old, I am tired, I am trivial;
my sensibilities are dead. I could never attach myself to
any one again. I love no one, and—never shall! Beauty alone
has the power to touch me still. I am deeply moved by it.
Helena could turn my head in a day if she wanted to, but
that is not love, that is not affection——

(*He shudders and covers his face with his hands.*)

SONIA: What is it?

ASTROFF: Nothing. During Lent one of my patients died
under chloroform.

SONIA: It is time to forget that. (*A pause.*) Tell me,
doctor, if I had a friend or a younger sister, and if you knew
that she, well—loved you, what would you do?

ASTROFF (*shrugging his shoulders*): I don't know. I don't
think I should do anything. I should make her understand
that I could not return her love—however, my mind is not
bothered about those things now. I must start at once if I
am ever to get off. Good-bye, my dear girl. At this rate
we shall stand here talking till morning. (*He shakes hands
with her.*) I shall go out through the sitting-room, because
I am afraid your uncle might detain me. (*He goes out.*)

SONIA (*alone*): Not a word! His heart and soul are still
locked from me, and yet for some reason I am strangely
happy. I wonder why? (*She laughs with pleasure.*) I told
him that he was well-bred and handsome and that his voice
was sweet. Was that a mistake? I can still feel his voice
vibrating in the air; it caresses me. (*Wringing her hands.*)
Oh! how terrible it is to be plain! I am plain, I know it.
As I came out of church last Sunday I overheard a woman
say, "She is a dear, noble girl, but what a pity she is so
ugly!" So ugly!

(*Helena comes in and throws open the window.*)

HELENA: The storm is over. What delicious air! (*A pause.*)
Where is the doctor?

SONIA: He has gone. (*A pause.*)

HELENA: Sonia!

SONIA: Yes?

HELENA: How much longer are you going to sulk at me? We have not hurt each other. Why not be friends? We have had enough of this.

SONIA: I myself—(*She embraces* HELENA.) Let us make peace.

HELENA: With all my heart. (*They are both moved.*)

SONIA: Has papa gone to bed?

HELENA: No, he is sitting up in the drawing-room. Heaven knows what reason you and I had for not speaking to each other for weeks. (*Sees the open sideboard.*) Who left the sideboard open?

SONIA: Dr. Astroff has just had supper.

HELENA: There is some wine. Let us seal our friendship.

SONIA: Yes, let us.

HELENA: Out of one glass. (*She fills a wine-glass.*) So we are friends, are we?

SONIA: Yes. (*They drink and kiss each other.*) I have long wanted to make friends, but somehow, I was ashamed to. (*She weeps.*)

HELENA: Why are you crying?

SONIA: I don't know. It is nothing.

HELENA: There, there, don't cry. (*She weeps.*) Silly! Now I am crying too. (*A pause.*) You are angry with me because I seem to have married your father for his money, but don't believe the gossip you hear. I swear to you I married him for love. I was fascinated by his fame and learning. I know now that it was not real love, but it seemed real at the time. I am innocent, and yet your clever, suspicious eyes have been punishing me for an imaginary crime ever since my marriage.

SONIA: Peace, peace! Let us forget the past.

HELENA: You must not look so at people. It is not becoming to you. You must trust people, or life becomes impossible.

SONIA: Tell me truly, as a friend, are you happy?

HELENA: Truly, no.

SONIA: I knew it. One more question: do you wish your husband were young?

HELENA: What a child you are! Of course I do. Go on, ask something else.

SONIA: Do you like the doctor?

HELENA: Yes, very much indeed.

SONIA (*laughing*): I have a stupid face, haven't I? He has

just gone out, and his voice is still in my ears; I hear his step; I see his face in the dark window. Let me say all I have in my heart! But no, I cannot speak of it so loudly. I am ashamed. Come to my room and let me tell you there. I seem foolish to you, don't I? Talk to me of him.

HELENA: What can I say?

SONIA: He is clever. He can do everything. He can cure the sick, and plant woods.

HELENA: It is not a question of medicine and woods, my dear, he is a man of genius. Do you know what that means? It means he is brave, profound, and of clear insight. He plants a tree and his mind travels a thousand years into the future, and he sees visions of the happiness of the human race. People like him are rare and should be loved. What if he does drink and act roughly at times? A man of genius cannot be a saint in Russia. There he lives, cut off from the world by cold and storm and endless roads of bottomless mud, surrounded by a rough people who are crushed by poverty and disease, his life one continuous struggle, with never a day's respite; how can a man live like that for forty years and keep himself sober and unspotted? (*Kissing* SONIA.) I wish you happiness with all my heart; you deserve it. (*She gets up.*) As for me, I am a worthless, futile woman. I have always been futile; in music, in love, in my husband's house—in a word, in everything. When you come to think of it, Sonia, I am really very, very unhappy. (*Walks excitedly up and down.*) Happiness can never exist for me in this world. Never. Why do you laugh?

SONIA: (*Laughing and covering her face with her hands.*) I am so happy, so happy!

HELENA: I want to hear music. I might play a little.

SONIA: Oh, do, do! (*She embraces her.*) I could not possibly go to sleep now. Do play!

HELENA: Yes, I will. Your father is still awake. Music irritates him when he is ill, but if he says I may, then I shall play a little. Go, Sonia, and ask him.

SONIA: Very well.

(*She goes out. The* WATCHMAN'S *rattle is heard in the garden.*)

HELENA: It is long since I have heard music. And now, I shall sit and play, and weep like a fool. (*Speaking out of the window.*) Is that you rattling out there, Ephim?

VOICE OF THE WATCHMAN: It is I.

HELENA: Don't make such a noise. Your master is ill.

VOICE OF THE WATCHMAN: I am going away this minute. (*Whistles a tune.*)
SONIA: (*Comes back.*) He says, no.

ACT III

(*The drawing-room of* SEREBRAKOFF'S *house. There are three doors: one to the right, one to the left, and one in the center of the room.* VOITSKI *and* SONIA *are sitting down.* HELENA *is walking up and down, absorbed in thought.*)

VOITSKI: We were asked by the professor to be here at one o'clock. (*Looks at his watch.*) It is now a quarter to one. It seems he has some communication to make to the world.
HELENA: Probably a matter of business.
VOITSKI: He never had any business. He writes twaddle, grumbles, and eats his heart out with jealousy; that's all he does.
SONIA (*reproachfully*): Uncle!
VOITSKI: All right. I beg your pardon. (*He points to* HELENA.) Look at her. Wandering up and down from sheer idleness. A sweet picture, really.
HELENA: I wonder you are not bored, droning on in the same key from morning till night. (*Despairingly*) I am dying of this tedium. What shall I do?
SONIA (*shrugging her shoulders*): There is plenty to do if you would.
HELENA: For instance?
SONIA: You could help run this place, teach the children, care for the sick—isn't that enough? Before you and papa came, Uncle Vanya and I used to go to market ourselves to deal in flour.
HELENA: I don't know anything about such things, and besides, they don't interest me. It is only in novels that women go out and teach and heal the peasants; how can I suddenly begin to do it?
SONIA: How can you live here and not do it? Wait awhile, you will get used to it all. (*Embraces her.*) Don't be sad, dearest. (*Laughing.*) You feel miserable and restless, and can't seem to fit into this life, and your restlessness is catching. Look at Uncle Vanya, he does nothing now but haunt you like a shadow, and I have left my work today to come here and talk with you. I am getting lazy, and don't want to go on with it. Dr. Astroff hardly ever used to come here; it was all we could do to persuade him to visit us once a month, and now he has abandoned his forestry and his practice, and comes every day. You must be a witch.

VOITSKI: Why should you languish here? Come, my dearest, my beauty, be sensible! The blood of a nixie runs in your veins. Oh, won't you let yourself be one? Give your nature the reins for once in your life; fall head over ears in love with some other water sprite and plunge down head first into a deep pool, so that the Herr Professor and all of us may have our hands free again.

HELENA (*angrily*): Leave me alone! How cruel you are! (*She tries to go out.*)

VOITSKI (*preventing her*): There, there, my beauty, I apologize. (*He kisses her hand.*) Forgive me.

HELENA: Confess that you would try the patience of an angel.

VOITSKI: As a peace offering I am going to fetch some flowers which I picked for you this morning: some autumn roses, beautiful, sorrowful roses. (*He goes out.*)

SONIA: Autumn roses, beautiful, sorrowful roses!

(*She and* HELENA *stand looking out of the window.*)

HELENA: September already! How shall we live through the long winter here? (*A pause.*) Where is the doctor?

SONIA: He is writing in Uncle Vanya's room. I am glad Uncle Vanya has gone out, I want to talk to you about something.

HELENA: About what?

SONIA: About what?

(*She lays her head on* HELENA'S *breast.*)

HELENA (*stroking her hair*): There, there, that will do. Don't, Sonia.

SONIA: I am ugly!

HELENA: You have lovely hair.

SONIA: Don't say that! (*She turns to look at herself in the glass.*) No, when a woman is ugly they always say she has beautiful hair or eyes. I have loved him now for six years; I have loved him more than one loves one's mother. I seem to hear him beside me every moment of the day. I feel the pressure of his hand on mine. If I look up, I seem to see him coming, and as you see, I run to you to talk of him. He is here every day now, but he never looks at me, he does not notice my presence. It is agony. I have absolutely no hope, no, no hope. Oh, my God! Give me strength to endure. I prayed all last night. I often go up to him and speak to him and look into his eyes. My pride is

gone. I am not mistress of myself. Yesterday I told Uncle
Vanya. I couldn't control myself, and all the servants know
it. Every one knows that I love him.

HELENA: Does he?

SONIA: No, he never notices me.

HELENA (*thoughtfully*): He is a strange man. Listen, Sonia,
will you allow me to speak to him? I shall be careful, only
hint. (*A pause.*) Really, to be in uncertainty all these years!
Let me do it! (SONIA *nods an affirmative.*) Splendid! It will
be easy to find out whether he loves you or not. Don't be
ashamed, sweetheart, don't worry. I shall be careful; he will
not notice a thing. We only want to find out whether it is
yes or no, don't we? (*A pause.*) And if it is no, then he
must keep away from here, is that so? (SONIA *nods.*) It will
be easier not to see him any more. We won't put off the
examination an instant. He said he had a sketch to show
me. Go and tell him at once that I want to see him.

SONIA (*in great excitement*): Will you tell me the whole
truth?

HELENA: Of course I will. I am sure that no matter what
it is, it will be easier for you to bear than this uncertainty.
Trust to me, dearest.

SONIA: Yes, yes. I shall say that you want to see his
sketch. (*She starts out, but stops near the door and looks
back.*) No, it is better not to know—and yet—there may
be hope.

HELENA: What do you say?

SONIA: Nothing. (*She goes out.*)

HELENA (*alone*): There is no greater sorrow than to know
another's secret when you cannot help them. (*In deep
thought.*) He is obviously not in love with her, but why
shouldn't he marry her? She is not pretty, but she is so
clever and pure and good, she would make a splendid wife
for a country doctor of his years. (*A pause.*) I can
understand how the poor child feels. She lives here in this
desperate loneliness with no one around her except these
colorless shadows that go mooning about talking nonsense and
knowing nothing except that they eat, drink, and sleep.
Among them appears from time to time this Dr. Astroff, so
different, so handsome, so interesting, so charming. It is
like seeing the moon rise on a dark night. Oh, to surrender
oneself to his embrace! To lose oneself in his arms! I am
a little in love with him myself! Yes, I am lonely without
him, and when I think of him I smile. That Uncle Vanya
says I have the blood of a nixie in my veins: "Give rein to
your nature for once in your life!" Perhaps it is right that
I should. Oh, to be free as a bird, to fly away from all your

sleepy faces and your talk and forget that you have existed
at all! But I am a coward, I am afraid; my conscience torments me. He comes here every day now. I can guess why,
and feel guilty already; I should like to fall on my knees
at Sonia's feet and beg her forgiveness, and weep.

(*Astroff comes in carrying a portfolio.*)

ASTROFF: How do you do? (*Shakes hands with her.*) Do
you want to see my sketch?

HELENA: Yes, you promised to show me what you had
been doing. Have you time now?

ASTROFF: Of course I have!

(*He lays the portfolio on the table, takes out the sketch
and fastens it to the table with thumbtacks.*)

ASTROFF: Where were you born?

HELENA (*helping him*): In St. Petersburg.

ASTROFF: And educated?

HELENA: At the Conservatory there.

ASTROFF: You don't find this life very interesting, I dare
say?

HELENA: Oh, why not? It is true I don't know the country
very well, but I have read a great deal about it.

ASTROFF: I have my own desk there in Ivan's room. When
I am absolutely too exhausted to go on I drop everything
and rush over here to forget myself in this work for an
hour or two. Ivan and Miss Sonia sit rattling at their count-
ing-boards, the cricket chirps, and I sit beside them and
paint, feeling warm and peaceful. But I don't permit myself
this luxury very often, only once a month. (*Pointing to the
picture.*) Look there! That is a map of our country as it was
fifty years ago. The green tints, both dark and light, represent forests. Half the map, as you see, is covered with it.
Where the green is striped with red the forests were inhabited
by elk and wild goats. Here on this lake lived great flocks
of swans and geese and ducks; as the old men say, there
was a power of birds of every kind. Now they have vanished like a cloud. Beside the hamlets and villages, you
see, I have dotted down here and there the various settle-
ments, farms, hermit's caves, and water-mills. This country carried a great many cattle and horses, as you can
see by the quantity of blue paint. For instance, see how
thickly it lies in this part; there were great herds of them
here, an average of three horses to every house. (*A pause.*)
Now, look lower down. This is the country as it was twenty-
five years ago. Only a third of the map is green now with
forests. There are no goats left and no elk. The blue paint is

lighter, and so on, and so on. Now we come to the third part; our country as it appears today. We still see spots of green, but not much. The elk, the swans, the black-cock have disappeared. It is, on the whole, the picture of a regular and slow decline which it will evidently only take about ten or fifteen more years to complete. You may perhaps object that it is the march of progress, that the old order must give place to the new, and you might be right if roads had been run through these ruined woods, or if factories and schools had taken their place. The people then would have become better educated and healthier and richer, but as it is, we have nothing of the sort. We have the same swamps and mosquitoes; the same disease and want; the typhoid, the diphtheria, the burning villages. We are confronted by the degradation of our country, brought on by the fierce struggle for existence of the human race. It is the consequence of the ignorance and unconsciousness of starving, shivering, sick humanity that, to save its children, instinctively snatches at everything that can warm it and still its hunger. So it destroys everything it can lay its hands on, without a thought for the morrow. And almost everything has gone, and nothing has been created to take its place. (*Coldly.*) But I see by your face that I am not interesting you.

HELENA: I know so little about such things!

ASTROFF: There is nothing to know. It simply isn't interesting, that's all.

HELENA: Frankly, my thoughts were elsewhere. Forgive me! I want to submit you to a little examination, but I am embarrassed and don't know how to begin.

ASTROFF: An examination?

HELENA: Yes, but quite an innocent one. Sit down. (*They sit down.*) It is about a certain young girl I know. Let us discuss it like honest people, like friends, and then forget what has passed between us, shall we?

ASTROFF: Very well.

HELENA: It is about my step-daughter, Sonia. Do you like her?

ASTROFF: Yes, I respect her.

HELENA: Do you like her—as a woman?

ASTROFF (*slowly*): No.

HELENA: One more word, and that will be the last. You have not noticed anything?

ASTROFF: No, nothing.

HELENA (*taking his hand*): You do not love her. I see that in your eyes. She is suffering. You must realize that, and not come here any more.

ASTROFF: My sun has set, yes, and then I haven't the time.

(*Shrugging his shoulders*) Where shall I find time for such things? (*He is embarrassed.*)

HELENA: Bah! What an unpleasant conversation! I am as out of breath as if I had been running three miles uphill. Thank heaven, that is over! Now let us forget everything as if nothing had been said. You are sensible. You understand. (*A pause.*) I am actually blushing.

ASTROFF: If you had spoken a month ago I might perhaps have considered it, but now—(*He shrugs his shoulders.*) Of course, if she is suffering—but I cannot understand why you had to put me through this examination. (*He searches her face with his eyes, and shakes his finger at her.*) Oho, you are wily!

HELENA: What does this mean?

ASTROFF (*laughing*): You are a wily one! I admit that Sonia is suffering, but what does this examination of yours mean? (*He prevents her from retorting, and goes on quickly.*) Please don't put on such a look of surprise; you know perfectly well why I come here every day. Yes, you know perfectly why and for whose sake I come! Oh, my sweet tigress! don't look at me in that way; I am an old bird!

HELENA (*perplexed*): A tigress? I don't understand you.

ASTROFF: Beautiful, sleek tigress, you must have your victims! For a whole month I have done nothing but seek you eagerly. I have thrown over everything for you, and you love to see it. Now then, I am sure you knew all this without putting me through your examination. (*Crossing his arms and bowing his head.*) I surrender. Here you have me—now, eat me.

HELENA: You have gone mad!

ASTROFF: You are afraid!

HELENA: I am a better and stronger woman than you think me. Good-bye. (*She tries to leave the room.*)

ASTROFF: Why good-bye? Don't say good-bye, don't waste words. Oh, how lovely you are—what hands! (*He kisses her hands.*)

HELENA: Enough of this! (*She frees her hands.*) Leave the room! You have forgotten yourself.

ASTROFF: Tell me, tell me, where can we meet tomorrow? (*He puts his arm around her.*) Don't you see that we must meet, that it is inevitable?

(*He kisses her.* VOITSKI *comes in carrying a bunch of roses; and stops in the doorway.*)

HELENA (*without seeing* VOITSKI): Have pity! Leave me. (*Lays her head on* ASTROFF'S *shoulder.*) Don't! (*She tries to break away from him.*)

ASTROFF (*holding her by the waist*): Be in the forest tomorrow at two o'clock. Will you? Will you?

HELENA (*sees* VOITSKI): Let me go! (*Goes to the window deeply embarrassed.*) This is appalling!

VOITSKI (*Throws the flowers on a chair, and speaks in great excitement, wiping his face with his handkerchief.*) Nothing—yes, yes, nothing.

ASTROFF: The weather is fine today, my dear Ivan; the morning was overcast and looked like rain, but now the sun is shining again. Honestly, we have had a very fine autumn, and the wheat is looking fairly well. (*Puts his map back into the portfolio.*) But the days are growing short. (*Exit.*)

HELENA (*Goes quickly up to* VOITSKI.): You must do your best; you must use all your power to get my husband and myself away from here today! Do you hear? I say, this very day!

VOITSKI (*wiping his face*): Oh! Ah! Oh! All right! I—Helena, I saw everything!

HELENA (*in great agitation*): Do you hear me? I must leave here this very day.

(SEREBRAKOFF, SONIA, MARINA, *and* TELEGIN *come in.*)

TELEGIN: I am not very well myself, your Excellency. I have been limping for two days, and my head——

SEREBRAKOFF: Where are the others? I hate this house. It is a regular labyrinth. Every one is always scattered through the twenty-six enormous rooms; one never can find a soul. (*Rings.*) Ask my wife and Madame Voitskaya to come here!

HELENA: I am here already.

SEREBRAKOFF: Please, all of you, sit down.

SONIA (*goes up to* HELENA *and asks anxiously*): What did he say?

HELENA: I'll tell you later.

SONIA: You are moved. (*Looking quickly and inquiringly into her face*) I understand; he said he would not come here any more. (*A pause.*) Tell me, did he? (HELENA *nods.*)

SEREBRAKOFF (*to* TELEGIN): One can, after all, become reconciled to being an invalid, but not to this country life. The ways of it stick in my throat and I feel exactly as if I had been whirled off the earth and landed on a strange planet. Please be seated, ladies and gentlemen. Sonia! (SONIA *does not hear. She is standing with her head bowed sadly forward on her breast.*) Sonia! (*A pause.*) She does not hear me. (*To* MARINA) Sit down too, nurse. (MARINA *sits down and begins to knit her stocking.*) I crave your indulgence, ladies and gentlemen; hang your ears, if I may say so, on the peg of attention. (*He laughs.*)

VOITSKI (*agitated*): Perhaps you do not need me—may I be excused?

SEREBRAKOFF: No, you are needed now more than any one.

VOITSKI: What is it you want of me?

SEREBRAKOFF: You—but what are you angry about? If it is anything I have done, I ask you to forgive me.

VOITSKI: Oh, drop that and come to business; what do you want? (MME. VOITSKAYA *comes in.*)

SEREBRAKOFF: Here is mother. Ladies and gentlemen, I shall begin. I have asked you to assemble here, my friends, in order to discuss a very important matter. I want to ask you for your assistance and advice, and knowing your unfailing amiability I think I can count on both. I am a bookworm and a scholar, and am unfamiliar with practical affairs. I cannot, I find, dispense with the help of well-informed people such as you, Ivan, and you, Telegin, and you, mother. The truth is, *manet omnes una nox*, that is to say, our lives are in the hands of God, and as I am old and ill, I realize that the time has come for me to dispose of my property in regard to the interests of my family. My life is nearly over, and I am not thinking of myself, but I have a young wife and daughter. (*A pause.*) I cannot continue to live in the country; we were not made for country life, and yet we cannot afford to live in town on the income derived from this estate. We might sell the woods, but that would be an expedient we could not resort to every year. We must find some means of guaranteeing to ourselves a certain more or less fixed yearly income. With this object in view, a plan has occurred to me which I now have the honor of presenting to you for your consideration. I shall only give you a rough outline, avoiding all details. Our estate does not pay on an average more than two per cent on the money invested in it. I propose to sell it. If we then invest our capital in bonds, it will earn us four to five per cent, and we should probably have a surplus over of several thousand roubles, with which we could buy a summer cottage in Finland——

VOITSKI: Hold on! Repeat what you just said; I don't think I heard you quite right.

SEREBRAKOFF: I said we would invest the money in bonds and buy a cottage in Finland with the surplus.

VOITSKI: No, not Finland—you said something else.

SEREBRAKOFF: I propose to sell this place.

VOITSKI: Aha! That was it! So you are going to sell the place? Splendid. The idea is a rich one. And what do you propose to do with my old mother and me and with Sonia here?

SEREBRAKOFF: That will be decided in due time. We can't
do everything at once.

VOITSKI: Wait! It is clear that until this moment I have
never had a grain of sense in my head. I have always been
stupid enough to think that the estate belonged to Sonia.
My father bought it as a wedding present for my sister, and
I foolishly imagined that as our laws were made for Russians and not Turks, my sister's estate would come down
to her child.

SEREBRAKOFF: Of course it is Sonia's. Has any one denied
it? I don't want to sell it without Sonia's consent; on the
contrary, what I am doing is for Sonia's good.

VOITSKI: This is absolutely incomprehensible. Either I have
gone mad or—or——

MME. VOITSKAYA: Jean, don't contradict Alexander. Trust
to him; he knows better than we do what is right and what
is wrong.

VOITSKI: I shan't. Give me some water. (*He drinks.*) Go
ahead! Say anything you please—anything!

SEREBRAKOFF: I can't imagine why you are so upset.
I don't pretend that my scheme is an ideal one, and if you
all object to it I shall not insist. (*A pause.*)

TELEGIN (*with embarrassment*): I not only nourish feelings of respect toward learning, your Excellency, but I am
also drawn to it by family ties. My brother Gregory's wife's
brother, whom you may know; his name is Constantine Lake-
demonoff, and he used to be a magistrate——

VOITSKI: Stop, Waffles. This is business; wait a bit, we
will talk of that later. (*To* SEREBRAKOFF) There now, ask
him what he thinks; this estate was bought from his uncle.

SEREBRAKOFF: Ah! Why should I ask questions? What
good would it do?

VOITSKI: The price was ninety-five thousand roubles. My
father paid seventy and left a debt of twenty-five. Now listen!
This place could never have been bought had I not re-
nounced my inheritance in favor of my sister, whom I
deeply loved—and what is more, I worked for ten years
like an ox, and paid off the debt.

SEREBRAKOFF: I regret ever having started this conversation.

VOITSKI: Thanks entirely to my own personal efforts, the
place is entirely clear of debts, and now, when I have grown
old, you want to throw me out, neck and crop!

SEREBRAKOFF: I can't imagine what you are driving at.

VOITSKI: For twenty-five years I have managed this place,
and have sent you the returns from it like the most honest
of servants, and you have never given me one single word

of thanks for my work, not one—neither in my youth nor now. You allowed me a meager salary of five hundred roubles a year, a beggar's pittance, and have never even thought of adding a rouble to it.

SEREBRAKOFF: What did I know about such things, Ivan? I am not a practical man and don't understand them. You might have helped yourself to all you wanted.

VOITSKI: Yes, why did I not steal? Don't you all despise me for not stealing, when it would have been only justice? And I should not now have been a beggar!

MME. VOITSKAYA (*sternly*): Jean!

TELEGIN (*agitated*): Vanya, old man, don't talk in that way. Why spoil such pleasant relations? (*He embraces him.*) Do stop!

VOITSKI: For twenty-five years I have been sitting here with my mother like a mole in a burrow. Our every thought and hope was yours and yours only. By day we talked with pride of you and your work, and spoke your name with veneration; our nights we wasted reading the books and papers which my soul now loathes.

TELEGIN: Don't, Vanya, don't. I can't stand it.

SEREBRAKOFF (*wrathfully*): What under heaven do you want, anyway?

VOITSKI: We used to think of you as almost superhuman, but now the scales have fallen from my eyes and I see you as you are! You write on art without knowing anything about it. Those books of yours which I used to admire are not worth one copper kopeck. You are a hoax!

SEREBRAKOFF: Can't any one make him stop? I am going!

HELENA: Ivan, I command you to stop this instant! Do you hear me?

VOITSKI: I refuse! (SEREBRAKOFF *tries to get out of the room, but* VOITSKI *bars the way.*) Wait! I have not done yet! You have wrecked my life. I have never lived. My best years have gone for nothing, have been ruined, thanks to you. You are my most bitter enemy!

TELEGIN: I can't stand it; I can't stand it. I am going. (*He goes out in great excitement.*)

SEREBRAKOFF: But what do you want! What earthly right have you to use such language to me? Ruination! If this estate is yours, then take it, and let me be ruined!

HELENA: I am going away out of this hell this minute. (*Shrieks.*) This is too much!

VOITSKI: My life has been a failure. I am clever and brave and strong. If I had lived a normal life I might have become another Schopenhauer or Dostoieffski. I am losing my head! I am going crazy! Mother, I am in despair! Oh, mother!

MME. VOITSKAYA (*sternly*): Listen, Alexander!

(SONIA *falls on her knees beside the* NURSE *and nestles against her.*)

SONIA: Oh, nurse, nurse!

VOITSKI: Mother! What shall I do? But no, don't speak! I know what to do. (*To* SEREBRAKOFF) And you will understand me!

(*He goes out through the door in the center of the room and* MME. VOITSKAYA *follows him.*)

SEREBRAKOFF: Tell me, what on earth is the matter? Take this lunatic out of my sight! I cannot possibly live under the same roof with him. His room (*he points to the center door*) is almost next door to mine. Let him take himself off into the village or into the wing of the house, or I shall leave here at once. I cannot stay in the same house with him.

HELENA (*to her husband*): We are leaving today; we must get ready at once for our departure.

SEREBRAKOFF: What a perfectly dreadful man!

SONIA (*On her knees beside the* NURSE *and turning to her father. She speaks with emotion.*): You must be kind to us, papa. Uncle Vanya and I are so unhappy! (*Controlling her despair*) Have pity on us. Remember how Uncle Vanya and Granny used to copy and translate your books for you every night—every, every night. Uncle Vanya has toiled without rest; he would never spend a penny on us, we sent it all to you. We have not eaten the bread of idleness. I am not saying this as I should like to, but you must understand us, papa, you must be merciful to us.

HELENA (*very excited, to her husband*): For heaven's sake, Alexander, go and have a talk with him—explain!

SEREBRAKOFF: Very well, I shall have a talk with him, but I won't apologize for a thing. I am not angry with him, but you must confess that his behavior has been strange, to say the least. Excuse me, I shall go to him.

(*He goes out through the center door.*)

HELENA: Be gentle with him; try to quiet him. (*She follows him out.*)

SONIA (*nestling nearer to* MARINA): Nurse, oh, nurse!

MARINA: It's all right, my baby. When the geese have cackled they will be still again. First they cackle and then they stop.

SONIA: Nurse!

MARINA: You are trembling all over, as if you were freezing. There, there, little orphan baby, God is merciful. A little linden-tea, and it will all pass away. Don't cry, my sweetest.

(*Looking angrily at the door in the center of the room*) See, the geese have all gone now. The devil take them!

(*A shot is heard,* HELENA *screams behind the scenes.* SONIA *shudders.*)

MARINA: Bang! What's that?

SEREBRAKOFF (*Comes in reeling with terror.*): Hold him! hold him! He has gone mad!

(HELENA *and* VOITSKI *are seen struggling in the doorway.*)

HELENA (*trying to wrest the revolver from him*): Give it to me; give it to me, I tell you!

VOITSKI: Let me go, Helena, let me go! (*He frees himself and rushes in, looking everywhere for* SEREBRAKOFF.) Where is he? Ah, there he is! (*He shoots at him. A pause.*) I didn't get him? I missed again? (*Furiously*) Damnation! Damnation! To hell with him!

(*He flings the revolver on the floor, and drops helpless into a chair.* SEREBRAKOFF *stands as if stupefied.* HELENA *leans against the wall, almost fainting.*)

HELENA: Take me away! Take me away! I can't stay here— I can't!

VOITSKI (*in despair*): Oh, what shall I do? What shall I do?

SONIA (*softly*): Oh, nurse, nurse!

ACT IV

(VOITSKI'S *bedroom, which is also his office. A table stands near the window; on it are ledgers, letter scales, and papers of every description. Near by stands a smaller table belonging to* ASTROFF, *with his paints and drawing materials. On the wall hangs a cage containing a starling. There is also a map of Africa on the wall, obviously of no use to anybody. There is a large sofa covered with buckram. A door to the left leads into an inner room; one to the right leads into the front hall, and before this door lies a mat for the peasants with their muddy boots to stand on. It is an autumn evening. The silence is profound.* TELEGIN *and* MARINA *are sitting facing one another, winding wool.*)

TELEGIN: Be quick, Marina, or we shall be called away to say good-bye before you have finished. The carriage has already been ordered.

MARINA (*trying to wind more quickly*): I am a little tired.

TELEGIN: They are going to Kharkoff to live.

MARINA: They do well to go.

TELEGIN: They have been frightened. The professor's wife won't stay here an hour longer. "If we are going at all, let's be off," says she, "we shall go to Kharkoff and look about us, and then we can send for our things." They are traveling light. It seems, Marina, that fate has decreed for them not to live here.

MARINA: And quite rightly. What a storm they have just raised! It was shameful!

TELEGIN: It was indeed. The scene was worthy of the brush of Aibazofski.

MARINA: I wish I'd never laid eyes on them. (*A pause.*) Now we shall have things as they were again: tea at eight, dinner at one, and supper in the evening; everything in order as decent folks, as Christians like to have it. (*Sighs.*) It is a long time since I have eaten noodles.

TELEGIN: Yes, we haven't had noodles for ages. (*A pause.*) Not for ages. As I was going through the village this morning, Marina, one of the shop-keepers called after me, "Hi! you hanger-on!" I felt it bitterly.

MARINA: Don't pay the least attention to them, master; we are all dependents on God. You and Sonia and all of us. Every one must work, no one can sit idle. Where is Sonia?

TELEGIN: In the garden with the doctor, looking for Ivan. They fear he may lay violent hands on himself.

MARINA: Where is his pistol?

TELEGIN (*whispers*): I hid it in the cellar.

(VOITSKI *and* ASTROFF *come in.*)

VOITSKI: Leave me alone! (*To* MARINA *and* TELEGIN) Go away! Go away and leave me to myself, if but for an hour. I won't have you watching me like this!

TELEGIN: Yes, yes, Vanya. (*He goes out on tiptoe.*)

MARINA: The gander cackles; ho! ho! ho! (*She gathers up her wool and goes out.*)

VOITSKI: Leave me by myself!

ASTROFF: I would, with the greatest pleasure. I ought to have gone long ago, but I shan't leave you until you have returned what you took from me.

VOITSKI: I took nothing from you.

ASTROFF: I am not jesting, don't detain me, I really must go.

VOITSKI: I took nothing of yours.

ASTROFF: You didn't? Very well, I shall have to wait a little longer, and then you will have to forgive me if I resort to force. We shall have to bind you and search you. I mean what I say.

VOITSKI: Do as you please. (*A pause.*) Oh, to make such

a fool of myself! To shoot twice and miss him both times!
I shall never forgive myself.

ASTROFF: When the impulse came to shoot, it would have
been as well had you put a bullet through your own head.

VOITSKI (*shrugging his shoulders*): Strange! I attempted
murder, and am not going to be arrested or brought to trial.
That means they think me mad. (*With a bitter laugh.*) Me!
I am mad, and those who hide their worthlessness, their dull-
ness, their crying heartlessness behind a professor's mask,
are sane! Those who marry old men and then deceive them
under the noses of all, are sane! I saw you kiss her; I saw
you in each other's arms!

ASTROFF: Yes, sir, I did kiss her; so there. (*He puts his
thumb to his nose.*)

VOITSKI (*his eyes on the door*): No, it is the earth that is
mad, because she still bears us on her breast.

ASTROFF: That is nonsense.

VOITSKI: Well? Am I not a madman, and therefore irre-
sponsible? Haven't I the right to talk nonsense?

ASTROFF: This is a farce! You are not mad; you are simply
a ridiculous fool. I used to think every fool was out of his
senses, but now I see that lack of sense is a man's normal
state, and you are perfectly normal.

VOITSKI (*Covers his face with his hands.*): Oh! if you knew
how ashamed I am! These piercing pangs of shame are like
nothing on earth. (*In an agonized voice.*) I can't endure
them! (*He leans against the table.*) What can I do? What
can I do?

ASTROFF: Nothing.

VOITSKI: You must tell me something! Oh, my God! I am
forty-seven years old. I may live to sixty; I still have thirteen years before me; an eternity! How shall I be able to
endure life for thirteen years? What shall I do? How can
I fill them? Oh, don't you see? (*He presses* ASTROFF'S *hand
convulsively.*) Don't you see, if only I could live the rest of
my life in some new way! If I could only wake some still,
bright morning and feel that life had begun again; that the
past was forgotten and had vanished like smoke. (*He weeps.*)
Oh, to begin life anew! Tell me, tell me how to begin.

ASTROFF (*crossly*): What nonsense! What sort of a new
life can you and I look forward to? We can have no hope.

VOITSKI: None?

ASTROFF: None. Of that I am convinced.

VOITSKI: Tell me what to do. (*He puts his hand to his
heart.*) I feel such a burning pain here.

ASTROFF (*shouts angrily*): Stop! (*Then, more gently*)
It may be that posterity, which will despise us for our blind

and stupid lives, will find some road to happiness; but we—
you and I—have but one hope, the hope that we may be
visited by visions, perhaps by pleasant ones, as we lie resting
in our graves. (*Sighing*) Yes, brother, there were only two
respectable, intelligent men in this county, you and I. Ten
years or so of this life of ours, this miserable life, have
sucked us under, and we have become as contemptible and
petty as the rest. But don't try to talk me out of my purpose!
Give me what you took from me, will you?

VOITSKI: I took nothing from you.

ASTROFF: You took a little bottle of morphine out of my
medicine-case. (*A pause.*) Listen! If you are positively determined to make an end to yourself, go into the woods and
shoot yourself there. Give up the morphine, or there will be
a lot of talk and guesswork; people will think I gave it
to you. I don't fancy having to perform a post-mortem on
you. Do you think I should find it interesting?

(SONIA *comes in.*)

VOITSKI: Leave me alone.

ASTROFF (*to* SONIA): Sonia, your uncle has stolen a bottle
of morphine out of my medicine-case and won't give it up.
Tell him that his behavior is—well, unwise. I haven't time,
I must be going.

SONIA: Uncle Vanya, did you take the morphine?

ASTROFF: Yes, he took it. (*A pause.*) I am absolutely sure.

SONIA: Give it up! Why do you want to frighten us?
(*Tenderly*) Give it up, Uncle Vanya! My misfortune is
perhaps even greater than yours, but I am not plunged in
despair. I endure my sorrow, and shall endure it until my
life comes to a natural end. You must endure yours, too.
(*A pause.*) Give it up! Dear, darling Uncle Vanya. Give
it up! (*She weeps.*) You are so good, I am sure you will
have pity on us and give it up. You must endure your sorrow, Uncle Vanya; you must endure it.

(VOITSKI *takes a bottle from the drawer of the table and
hands it to* ASTROFF.)

VOITSKI: There it is! (*to* SONIA) And now, we must get
to work at once; we must do something, or else I shall not
be able to endure it.

SONIA: Yes, yes, to work! As soon as we have seen them
off we shall go to work. (*She nervously straightens out the
papers on the table.*) Everything is in a muddle!

ASTROFF (*putting the bottle in his case, which he straps
together*): Now I can be off.

(HELENA *comes in.*)

HELENA: Are you here, Ivan? We are starting in a moment. Go to Alexander, he wants to speak to you.

SONIA: Go, Uncle Vanya. (*She takes* VOITSKI'S *arm.*) Come, you and papa must make peace; that is absolutely necessary.

(SONIA *and* VOITSKI *go out.*)

HELENA: I am going away. (*She gives* ASTROFF *her hand.*) Good-bye.

ASTROFF: So soon?

HELENA: The carriage is waiting.

ASTROFF: Good-bye.

HELENA: You promised me you would go away yourself today.

ASTROFF: I have not forgotten. I am going at once. (*A pause.*) Were you frightened? Was it so terrible?

HELENA: Yes.

ASTROFF: Couldn't you stay? Couldn't you? Tomorrow—in the forest——

HELENA: No. It is all settled, and that is why I can look you so bravely in the face. Our departure is fixed. One thing I must ask of you: don't think too badly of me; I should like you to respect me.

ASTROFF: Ah! (*With an impatient gesture*) Stay, I implore you! Confess that there is nothing for you to do in this world. You have no object in life; there is nothing to occupy your attention, and sooner or later your feelings must master you. It is inevitable. It would be better if it happened not in Kharkoff or in Kursk, but here, in nature's lap. It would then at least be poetical, even beautiful. Here you have the forest, the houses half in ruins that Turgenieff writes of.

HELENA: How comical you are! I am angry with you and yet I shall always remember you with pleasure. You are interesting and original. You and I will never meet again, and so I shall tell you—why should I conceal it?—that I am just a little in love with you. Come, one more last pressure of our hands, and then let us part good friends. Let us not bear each other any ill will.

ASTROFF (*pressing her hand*): Yes, go. (*Thoughtfully*) You seem to be sincere and good, and yet there is something strangely disquieting about all your personality. No sooner did you arrive here with your husband than every one whom you found busy and actively creating something was forced to drop his work and give himself up for the whole summer to your husband's gout and yourself. You and he have infected us with your idleness. I have been swept off my feet; I have not put my hand to a thing for weeks, during which sickness has been running its course unchecked among the people, and the peasants have been pasturing their cattle in my woods and young plantations. Go where you will, you and your husband will always carry destruction in your train. I am joking of course, and yet I am strangely sure that had you stayed here we should have been overtaken by the most immense desolation. I would have gone to my ruin, and you—you would not have prospered. So go! È finita la commedia!

HELENA (*snatching a pencil off* ASTROFF'S *table, and hiding it with a quick movement.*) I shall take this pencil for memory!

ASTROFF: How strange it is. We meet, and then suddenly it seems that we must part forever. That is the way in this world. As long as we are alone, before Uncle Vanya comes in with a bouquet—allow me—to kiss you good-bye—may I? (*He kisses her on the cheek.*) So! Splendid!

HELENA: I wish you every happiness. (*She glances about her.*) For once in my life, I shall! and scorn the consequences! (*She kisses him impetuously, and they quickly part.*) I must go.

ASTROFF: Yes, go. If the carriage is there, then start at once. (*They stand listening.*)

ASTROFF: È finita!

(VOITSKI, SEREBRAKOFF, MME. VOITSKAYA *with her book,* TELEGIN, *and* SONIA *come in.*)

SEREBRAKOFF (*to* VOITSKI): Shame on him who bears malice for the past. I have gone through so much in the last few hours that I feel capable of writing a whole treatise on the conduct of life for the instruction of posterity. I gladly accept your apology, and myself ask your forgiveness.

(*He kisses* VOITSKI *three times.* HELENA *embraces* SONIA.)

VOITSKI: You will regularly receive the same amount as before. Everything will be as before.

SEREBRAKOFF (*kissing* MME. VOITSKAYA'S *hand*): Mother!

MME. VOITSKAYA (*kissing him*): Have your picture taken, Alexander, and send me one. You know how dear you are to me.

TELEGIN: Good-bye, your Excellency. Don't forget us.

SEREBRAKOFF (*kissing his daughter*): Good-bye, good-bye all. (*Shaking hands with* ASTROFF) Many thanks for your pleasant company. I have a deep regard for your opinions and your enthusiasm, but let me, as an old man, give one word of advice at parting: do something, my friend! Work! Do something! (*They all bow.*) Good luck to you all.

(*He goes out followed by* MME. VOITSKAYA *and* SONIA.)

VOITSKI (*kissing* HELENA'S *hand fervently*): Good-bye—forgive me. I shall never see you again!

HELENA (*touched*): Good-bye, dear boy.

(*She lightly kisses his head as he bends over her hand, and goes out.*)

ASTROFF: Tell them to bring my carriage around too, Waffles.

TELEGIN: All right, old man.

(ASTROFF *and* VOITSKI *are left behind alone.* ASTROFF *collects his paints and drawing materials on the table and packs them away in a box.*)

ASTROFF: Why don't you go to see them off?

VOITSKI: Let them go! I—I can't go out there. I feel too sad. I must go to work on something at once. To work! To work!

(*He rummages through his papers on the table. A pause. The tinkling of bells is heard as the horses trot away.*)

ASTROFF: They have gone! The professor, I suppose, is glad to go. He couldn't be tempted back now by a fortune.

(MARINA *comes in.*)

MARINA: They have gone. (*She sits down in an armchair and knits her stocking.*)

(SONIA *comes in wiping her eyes.*)

SONIA: They have gone. God be with them. (*To her uncle.*) And now, Uncle Vanya, let us do something!

VOITSKI: To work! To work!

SONIA: It is long, long, since you and I have sat together at this table. (*She lights a lamp on the table.*) No ink! (*She takes the inkstand to the cupboard and fills it from an ink-bottle.*) How sad it is to see them go!

(MME. VOITSKAYA *comes slowly in.*)

MME. VOITSKAYA: They have gone.

(*She sits down and at once becomes absorbed in her book.*)

(SONIA *sits down at the table and looks through an account book.*)

SONIA: First, Uncle Vanya, let us write up the accounts.

They are in a dreadful state. Come, begin. You take one and I will take the other.

VOITSKI: In account with—— (*They sit silently writing.*)

MARINA (*yawning*): The sand-man has come.

ASTROFF: How still it is. Their pens scratch, the cricket sings; it is so warm and comfortable. I hate to go.

(*The tinkling of bells is heard.*)

ASTROFF: My carriage has come. There now remains but to say good-bye to you, my friends, and to my table here, and then—away! (*He puts the map into the portfolio.*)

MARINA: Don't hurry away; sit a little longer with us.

ASTROFF: Impossible.

VOITSKI (*writing*): And carry forward from the old debt two seventy-five——

(WORKMAN *comes in.*)

WORKMAN: Your carriage is waiting, sir.

ASTROFF: All right. (*He hands the* WORKMAN *his medicine-case, portfolio, and box.*) Look out, don't crush the portfolio!

WORKMAN: Very well, sir. (*Exit.*)

SONIA: When shall we see you again?

ASTROFF: Hardly before next summer. Probably not this winter, though, of course, if anything should happen you will let me know. (*He shakes hands with them.*) Thank you for your kindness, for your hospitality, for everything! (*He goes up to* MARINA *and kisses her head.*) Good-bye, old nurse!

MARINA: Are you going without your tea?

ASTROFF: I don't want any, nurse.

MARINA: Won't you have a drop of vodka?

ASTROFF (*hesitatingly*): Yes, I might.

(MARINA *goes out.*)

ASTROFF (*after a pause*): My off-wheeler has gone lame for some reason. I noticed it yesterday when Peter was taking him to water.

VOITSKI: You should have him re-shod.

ASTROFF: I shall have to go around by the blacksmith's on my way home. It can't be avoided. (*He stands looking up at the map of Africa hanging on the wall.*) I suppose it is roasting hot in Africa now.

VOITSKI: Yes, I suppose it is.

(MARINA *comes back carrying a tray on which are a glass of vodka and a piece of bread.*)

MARINA: Help yourself. (ASTROFF *drinks.*) To your good health! (*She bows deeply.*) Eat your bread with it.

ASTROFF: No, I like it so. And now, good-bye. (*To* MA-
RINA.) You needn't come out to see me off, nurse.

(*He goes out.* SONIA *follows him with a candle to light him
to the carriage.* MARINA *sits down in her armchair.*)

VOITSKI (*writing*): On the 2d of February, twenty pounds
of butter; on the 16th, twenty pounds of butter again. Buck-
wheat flour——— (*A pause. Bells are heard tinkling.*)

MARINA: He has gone. (*A pause.*)

(SONIA *comes in and sets the candlestick on the table.*)

SONIA: He has gone.

VOITSKI (*adding and writing*): Total, fifteen—twenty-
five—

(SONIA *sits down and begins to write.*)

MARINA (*yawning*): Oh, ho! The Lord have mercy.

(TELEGIN *comes in on tiptoe, sits down near the door, and
begins to tune his guitar.*)

VOITSKI (*to* SONIA, *stroking her hair*): Oh, my child, I am
so miserable; if you only knew how miserable I am!

SONIA: What can we do? We must live our lives. (*A
pause.*) Yes, we shall live, Uncle Vanya. We shall live
through the long procession of days before us, and through
the long evenings; we shall patiently bear the trials that
fate imposes on us; we shall work for others without rest,
both now and when we are old; and when our last hour
comes we shall meet it humbly, and there, beyond the grave,
we shall say that we have suffered and wept, that our life
was bitter, and God will have pity on us. Ah, then, dear, dear
Uncle, we shall see that bright and beautiful life; we shall
rejoice and look back upon our sorrow here; a tender smile—
and—we shall rest. I have faith, Uncle, fervent, passionate
faith. (SONIA *kneels down before her uncle and lays her head
on his hands. She speaks in a weary voice.*) We shall rest.
(TELEGIN *plays softly on the guitar.*) We shall rest. We shall
hear the angels. We shall see heaven shining like a jewel. We
shall see all evil and all our pain sink away in the great compassion that shall enfold the world. Our life will be as peaceful and tender and sweet as a caress. I have faith; I have
faith. (*She wipes away her tears.*) My poor, poor Uncle
Vanya, you are crying! (*Weeping.*) You have never known
what happiness was, but wait, Uncle Vanya, wait! We shall
rest. (*She embraces him.*) We shall rest. (*The* WATCHMAN'S
rattle is heard in the garden; TELEGIN *plays softly;* MME.
VOITSKAYA *writes something on the margin of her pamphlet;*
MARINA *knits her stocking.*) We shall rest.

George Bernard Shaw:

ARMS AND THE MAN

Though *Arms and the Man* (1894), Shaw's fourth attempt at playwriting, was at first a financial failure, it is unquestionably a theatrical success. It was a great hit on the first night, but the actors, encouraged by the laughter, later played broadly for laughs and thus succeeded in killing much of the humor. The first night, however, was marked not only by a restrained (and therefore successful) performance, but by a more personal triumph of Shaw's. At the end of the play he appeared onstage in response to the applause; as the cheers died down a solitary "boo" came from the gallery. "My dear fellow," Shaw (1856-1950) replied pleasantly, "I quite agree with you; but what are we two against so many?" The night was Shaw's, and the line was so successful that seventeen years later when someone booed at another of his plays, GBS is reported to have used it again with equal success.

The play's subsequent failure, however, was probably due not merely to the actors but to the audience. The British public had not yet learned to laugh at military heroics, and its ears still rang with Tennyson's glorification of the Light Brigade which bravely did its duty and annihilated itself. Gilbert and Sullivan had, in *The Pirates of Penzance,* however, begun to chip away the gilt which covers the unpleasant idea of dying in battle:

> Go, ye heroes, go to glory.
> Though you die in combat gory
> Ye shall live in song and story.
> Go to immortality.
> Go to death, and go to slaughter;
> Die, and every Cornish daughter
> With her tears your grave shall water.
> Go, ye heroes, go and die!

But Gilbert and Sullivan were considered jesters, not social critics. Nine weeks after the opening of *Arms and the Man*, Shaw himself pointed out in an essay in *The New Review* that no one confused H.M.S. *Pinafore* with a real ship, but he insisted that *Arms and the Man* realistically portrays a real war. How unreceptive the public was to a play which pooh-poohed heroics and showed a soldier who preferred chocolates to cartridges can be seen in the comment by the Prince of Wales (later Edward VII) that the author was mad, and a statement was circulated that "His Royal Highness regretted that the play should have shown so disrespectful an attitude as was betrayed by the character of the chocolate-cream soldier."

Many in the first audiences which saw *Arms and the Man* concluded that the play was a libel on heroism; Captain Bluntschli's insistence that it is a soldier's duty "to live as long as we can, and kill as many of the enemy as we can," was regarded as the central point of the drama. Bluntschli's line was shocking, for in imperial England one did not proclaim, in effect, that a soldier's duty is not to die for his country but to make the enemy soldier die for his. But the play is less about war than about the pseudo-romance of war, and perhaps we can generalize and say it is an attack not on war but on dangerous (and silly) romantic ideas. Battles are not usually won by patriotic brainless heroes; they are won by clever men. Similarly, successful marriages cannot be based on a woman's infatuation with a clean uniform and a handsome profile. The romance of war is one of Shaw's targets; the romance of romance is another.

Like most comedy, *Arms and the Man* criticizes foibles, and, like most comic authors, Shaw assumes that man's behavior ought to be rational. But we should here note an important way in which Shavian comedy differs from most other comedy. Most comic dramatists poke fun at the individual who deviates from society's norm. The assumption is, this is to say, that society is rational and that the occasional deviant (the miser, the jealous husband, the braggart) is irrational and ought to behave like the majority. Shaw's plays, however, generally make fun of society as a whole and insist that only the deviant is rational. In *Arms and the Man*, for instance, Captain Bluntschli is at odds with the conventional view, but Shaw goes on to demonstrate that Bluntschli is sensible and that the conventional view is foolish. Although Shaw's plays thus differ from most comedies, they are nevertheless allied to traditional comedy in their insistence that deviations from reason are absurd.

Society's irrationality is caricatured in the aristocrats who in the beginning are opposed to Bluntschli. Raina and Sergius hold the conventional romantic view of war, and Bluntschli

at first appears absurd. But as the play progresses we see that
Bluntschli's view is sound and that the heroic view of war is,
though prevalent, unsound. Shaw is thus not merely standing
ideas on their head for the sake of a momentary laugh, as,
say, Wilde does when he solemnly proclaims that divorces are
made in heaven. Rather, Shaw dramatizes the absurdity of
some commonly accepted concepts and seriously suggests
that a whole army except for one man *can* be out of step.
Beneath the tomfoolery, Shaw is often in earnest; he wants
us to see life as it really is and not as our preconceptions tell
us it should or must be. An oculist once told him, Shaw
wrote, that he had normal vision, but when he assumed his
sight was like most people's, the oculist explained that Shaw
was highly fortunate because only a small minority has
normal vision. His mind, Shaw went on to say, was in this
sense normal: though untypical, it was undamaged and saw
clearly the fuzzy minds of his contemporaries.

But life as Shaw says it is may not be life as it really is;
Shaw's view may be as one-sided as that of the romanticists
he depicts. His countryman, William Butler Yeats (who could
not quite be called Shaw's friend, for he quoted approvingly
Wilde's observation that "Mr. Bernard Shaw has no enemies
but is intensely disliked by all his friends") found Shaw's
realistic view not only offensive but unlifelike: "I listened to
Arms and the Man with admiration and hatred. It seemed
to me inorganic, logical straightness and not the crooked road
of life, yet I stood aghast before its energy." Perhaps Shaw's
rational view, then, is as false and one-sided as the one-
sided view of a comic figure. His anti-romantic vision, his
"logical straightness," is, one might say with Yeats, cold,
mechanistic, unlifelike—and amusing. "I had a nightmare,"
Yeats wrote, after seeing Shaw's *Arms and the Man*, "that I
was haunted by a sewing-machine, that clicked and shone,
but the incredible thing was that the machine smiled, smiled
perpetually."

Arms and the Man

A PLEASANT PLAY

Characters

RAINA PETKOFF, *a young Bulgarian lady.*
CATHERINE PETKOFF, *her mother.*
LOUKA, *the Petkoffs' maid.*
CAPTAIN BLUNTSCHLI, *a Swiss officer in the Serbian army.*
A RUSSIAN OFFICER *in the Bulgarian army.*
NICOLA, *the Petkoffs' butler.*
PETKOFF, *Raina's father, a major in the Bulgarian army.*
SERGIUS SARANOFF, *Raina's fiancé, a major in the Bulgarian
army.*

ACT I

(*Night: A lady's bedchamber in Bulgaria, in a small town near the Dragoman Pass, late in November in the year 1885. Through an open window with a little balcony a peak of the Balkans, wonderfully white and beautiful in the starlit snow, seems quite close at hand, though it is really miles away. The interior of the room is not like anything to be seen in the west of Europe. It is half rich Bulgarian, half cheap Viennese. Above the head of the bed, which stands against a little wall cutting off the left hand corner of the room, is a painted wooden shrine, blue and gold, with an ivory image of Christ, and a light hanging before it in a pierced metal ball suspended by three chains. The principal seat, placed towards the other side of the room and opposite the window, is a Turkish otto-man. The counterpane and hangings of the bed, the window curtains, the little carpet, and all the ornamental textile fabrics in the room are oriental and gorgeous; the paper on the walls is occidental and paltry. The washstand, against the wall on the side nearest the ottoman and window, consists of an en-amelled iron basin with a pail beneath it in a painted metal frame, and a single towel on the rail at the side. The dressing table, between the bed and the window, is a common pine table, covered with a cloth of many colours, with an expensive toilet mirror on it. The door is on the side nearest the bed; and there is a chest of drawers between. This chest of drawers is also covered by a variegated native cloth; and on it there is a pile of paper backed novels, a box of chocolate creams, and a miniature easel with a large photograph of an extremely handsome officer, whose lofty bearing and magnetic glance can be felt even from the portrait. The room is lighted by a candle on the chest of drawers, and another on the dressing table with a box of matches beside it.*

The window is hinged doorwise and stands wide open. Out-side, a pair of wooden shutters, opening outwards, also stand open. On the balcony a young lady, intensely conscious of the romantic beauty of the night, and of the fact that her own youth and beauty are part of it, is gazing at the snowy Bal-kans. She is in her nightgown, well covered by a long mantle of furs, worth, on a moderate estimate, about three times the furniture of the room.

Her reverie is interrupted by her mother, CATHERINE PET-KOFF, *a woman over forty, imperiously energetic, with mag-nificent black hair and eyes, who might be a very splendid specimen of the wife of a mountain farmer, but is determined*

*to be a Viennese lady, and to that end wears a fashionable
tea gown on all occasions.*)

CATHERINE (*entering hastily, full of good news*): Raina!
(*She pronounces it Rah-eena, with the stress on the ee.*)
Raina! (*She goes to the bed, expecting to find* RAINA *there.*)
Why, where——? (RAINA *looks into the room.*) Heavens, child!
are you out in the night air instead of in your bed? Youll
catch your death. Louka told me you were asleep.

RAINA (*dreamily*): I sent her away. I wanted to be alone.
The stars are so beautiful! What is the matter?

CATHERINE: Such news! There has been a battle.

RAINA (*her eyes dilating*): Ah! (*She comes eagerly to*
CATHERINE.)

CATHERINE: A great battle at Slivnitza! A victory! And it
was won by Sergius.

RAINA (*with a cry of delight*): Ah! (*They embrace raptur-
ously.*) Oh, mother! (*Then, with sudden anxiety*) is father
safe?

CATHERINE: Of course! he sends me the news. Sergius is
the hero of the hour, the idol of the regiment.

RAINA: Tell me, tell me. How was it? (*Ecstatically*) Oh,
mother! mother! mother! (*She pulls her mother down on the
ottoman; and they kiss one another frantically.*)

CATHERINE (*with surging enthusiasm*): You cant guess
how splendid it is. A cavalry charge! think of that! He defied
our Russian commanders—acted without orders—led a
charge on his own responsibility—headed it himself—was the
first man to sweep through their guns. Cant you see it, Raina:
our gallant splendid Bulgarians with their swords and eyes
flashing, thundering down like an avalanche and scattering
the wretched Serbs and their dandified Austrian officers like
chaff. And you! you kept Sergius waiting a year before you
would be betrothed to him. Oh, if you have a drop of Bulgarian blood in your veins, you will worship him when he
comes back.

RAINA: What will he care for my poor little worship after
the acclamations of a whole army of heroes? But no matter:
I am so happy! so proud! (*She rises and walks about excitedly.*) It proves that all our ideas were real after all.

CATHERINE (*indignantly*): Our ideas real! What do you
mean?

RAINA: Our ideas of what Sergius would do. Our patriotism.
Our heroic ideals. I sometimes used to doubt whether they
were anything but dreams. Oh, what faithless little creatures
girls are! When I buckled on Sergius's sword he looked so
noble: it was treason to think of disillusion or humiliation or

failure. And yet—and yet—(*She sits down again suddenly.*) Promise me youll never tell him.

CATHERINE: Dont ask me for promises until I know what I'm promising.

RAINA: Well, it came into my head just as he was holding me in his arms and looking into my eyes, that perhaps we only had our heroic ideas because we are so fond of reading Byron and Pushkin, and because we were so delighted with the opera that season at Bucharest. Real life is so seldom like that! indeed never, as far as I knew it then. (*Remorsefully*) Only think, mother: I doubted him: I wondered whether all his heroic qualities and his soldiership might not prove mere imagination when he went into a real battle. I had an uneasy fear that he might cut a poor figure there beside all those clever officers from the Tsar's court.

CATHERINE: A poor figure! Shame on you! The Serbs have Austrian officers who are just as clever as the Russians; but we have beaten them in every battle for all that.

RAINA (*laughing and snuggling against her mother*): Yes: I was only a prosaic little coward. Oh, to think that it was all true! that Sergius is just as splendid and noble as he looks! that the world is really a glorious world for women who can see its glory and men who can act its romance! What happiness! what unspeakable fulfillment!

(*They are interrupted by the entry of* LOUKA, *a handsome proud girl in a pretty Bulgarian peasant's dress with double apron, so defiant that her servility to* RAINA *is almost insolent. She is afraid of* CATHERINE, *but even with her goes as far as she dares.*)

LOUKA: If you please, madam, all the windows are to be closed and the shutters made fast. They say there may be shooting in the streets. (RAINA *and* CATHERINE *rise together, alarmed.*) The Serbs are being chased right back through the pass; and they say they may run into the town. Our cavalry will be after them; and our people will be ready for them, you may be sure, now theyre running away. (*She goes out on the balcony, and pulls the outside shutters to; then steps back into the room.*)

CATHERINE (*businesslike, housekeeping instincts aroused*): I must see that everything is made safe downstairs.

RAINA: I wish our people were not so cruel. What glory is there in killing wretched fugitives?

CATHERINE: Cruel! Do you suppose they would hesitate to kill you—or worse?

RAINA (*to* LOUKA): Leave the shutters so that I can just close them if I hear any noise.

CATHERINE (*authoritatively, turning on her way to the door*): Oh no, dear: you must keep them fastened. You would be sure to drop off to sleep and leave them open. Make them fast, Louka.

LOUKA: Yes, madam. (*She fastens them.*)

RAINA: Dont be anxious about me. The moment I hear a shot, I shall blow out the candles and roll myself up in bed with my ears well covered.

CATHERINE: Quite the wisest thing you can do, my love. Goodnight.

RAINA: Goodnight. (*Her emotion comes back for a moment.*) Wish me joy. (*They kiss.*) This is the happiest night of my life—if only there are no fugitives.

CATHERINE: Go to bed, dear; and dont think of them. (*She goes out.*)

LOUKA (*secretly to* RAINA): If you would like the shutters open, just give them a push like this (*she pushes them: they open: she pulls them to again.*) One of them ought to be bolted at the bottom; but the bolt's gone.

RAINA (*with dignity, reproving her*): Thanks, Louka; but we must do what we are told. (LOUKA *makes a grimace.*) Goodnight.

LOUKA (*carelessly*): Goodnight. (*She goes out, swaggering.*)

(RAINA, *left alone, takes off her fur cloak and throws it on the ottoman. Then she goes to the chest of drawers, and adores the portrait there with feelings that are beyond all expression. She does not kiss it or press it to her breast, or shew it any mark of bodily affection; but she takes it in her hands and elevates it, like a priestess.*)

RAINA (*looking up at the picture*): Oh, I shall never be unworthy of you any more, my soul's hero: never, never, never. (*She replaces it reverently. Then she selects a novel from the little pile of books. She turns over the leaves dreamily; finds her page; turns the book inside out at it; and, with a happy sigh, gets into bed and prepares to read herself to sleep. But before abandoning herself to fiction, she raises her eyes once more, thinking of the blessed reality, and murmurs.*) My hero! my hero!

(*A distant shot breaks the quiet of the night. She starts, listening; and two more shots, much nearer, follow, startling her so that she scrambles out of bed, and hastily blows out the candle on the chest of drawers. Then, putting her fingers in her ears, she runs to the dressing table, blows out the light there, and hurries back to bed in the dark, nothing being visible but the glimmer of the light in the pierced ball before the image, and the starlight seen through the slits at the top of the shutters. The firing breaks out again: there is a startling fusillade quite close at hand. Whilst it is still echoing, the shutters disappear, pulled open from without; and for an instant the rectangle of snowy starlight flashes out with the figure of a man silhouetted in black upon it. The shutters close immediately; and the room is dark again. But the silence is now broken by the sound of panting. Then there is a scratch; and the flame of a match is seen in the middle of the room.)*

RAINA (*crouching on the bed*): Who's there? (*The match is out instantly.*) Who's there? Who is that?

A MAN'S VOICE (*in the darkness, subduedly, but threateningly*): Sh—sh! Dont call out; or youll be shot. Be good; and no harm will happen to you. (*She is heard leaving her bed, and making for the door.*) Take care: it's no use trying to run away.

RAINA: But who—

THE VOICE (*warning*): Remember: if you raise your voice my revolver will go off. (*Commandingly*) Strike a light and let me see you. Do you hear. (*Another moment of silence and darkness as she retreats to the chest of drawers. Then she lights a candle; and the mystery is at an end. He is a man of about 35, in a deplorable plight, bespattered with mud and blood and snow, his belt and the strap of his revolver case keeping together the torn ruins of the blue tunic of a Serbian artillery officer. All that the candlelight and his unwashed unkempt condition make it possible to discern is that he is of middling stature and undistinguished appearance, with strong neck and shoulders, roundish obstinate looking head covered with short crisp bronze curls, clear quick eyes and good brows and mouth, hopelessly prosaic nose like that of a strong minded baby, trim soldierlike carriage and energetic manner, and with all his wits about him in spite of his desperate predicament: even with a sense of the humor of it, without, however, the least intention of trifling with it or throwing away a chance. Reckoning up what he can guess about* RAINA: *her age, her social position, her character, and the extent to which she is frightened, he continues, more politely but still most determinedly*) Excuse my disturbing you; but you recognize my uniform? Serb! If I'm caught I shall be killed. (*Menacingly*) Do you understand that?

RAINA: Yes.

THE MAN: Well, I dont intend to get killed if I can help it. (*Still more formidably*) Do you understand that? (*He locks the door quickly but quietly.*)

RAINA (*disdainfully*): I suppose not. (*She draws herself up superbly, and looks him straight in the face, adding, with cutting emphasis*) Some soldiers, I know, are afraid to die.

THE MAN (*with grim goodhumor*): All of them, dear lady, all of them, believe me. It is our duty to live as long as we can. Now, if you raise an alarm—

RAINA (*cutting him short*): You will shoot me. How do you know that *I* am afraid to die?

THE MAN (*cunningly*): Ah; but suppose I dont shoot you, what will happen then? A lot of your cavalry will burst into this pretty room of yours and slaughter me here like a pig; for I'll fight like a demon: they shant get me into the street to amuse themselves with: I know what they are. Are you prepared to receive that sort of company in your present undress? (RAINA, *suddenly conscious of her nightgown, instinctively shrinks and gathers it more closely about her neck. He watches her and adds pitilessly*) Hardly presentable, eh? (*She turns to the ottoman. He raises his pistol instantly, and cries*) Stop! (*She stops.*) Where are you going?

RAINA (*with dignified patience*): Only to get my cloak.

THE MAN (*passing swiftly to the ottoman and snatching the cloak*): A good idea! I'll keep the cloak; and you'll take care that nobody comes in and sees you without it. This is a better weapon than the revolver: eh? (*He throws the pistol down on the ottoman.*)

RAINA (*revolted*): It is not the weapon of a gentleman!

THE MAN: It's good enough for a man with only you to stand between him and death. (*As they look at one another for a moment,* RAINA *hardly able to believe that even a Serbian officer can be so cynically and selfishly unchivalrous, they are startled by a sharp fusillade in the street. The chill of imminent death hushes the man's voice as he adds*) Do you hear? If you are going to bring those blackguards in on me you shall receive them as you are.

(*Clamor and disturbance. The pursuers in the street batter at the house door, shouting,* Open the door! Open the door! Wake up, will you! *A man servant's voice calls to them angrily from within,* This is Major Petkoff's house: you cant come in here; *but a renewal of the clamor, and a torrent of blows on the door, end with his letting a chain down with a clank, followed by a rush of heavy footsteps and a din of triumphant yells, dominated at last by the voice of* CATHERINE, *indignantly addressing an officer with* What does this mean, sir? Do you know where you are? *The noise subsides suddenly.*)

LOUKA (*outside, knocking at the bedroom door*): My lady! my lady! get up quick and open the door. If you dont they will break it down.

(*The fugitive throws up his head with the gesture of a man who sees that it is all over with him, and drops the manner he has been assuming to intimidate* RAINA.)

THE MAN (*sincerely and kindly*): No use, dear: I'm done for. (*Flinging the cloak to her*) Quick! wrap yourself up: they're coming.

RAINA: Oh, thank you. (*She wraps herself up with intense relief.*)

THE MAN (*between his teeth*): Don't mention it.

RAINA (*anxiously*): What will you do?

THE MAN (*grimly*): The first man in will find out. Keep out of the way; and don't look. It wont last long; but it will not be nice. (*He draws his sabre and faces the door, waiting.*)

RAINA (*impulsively*): I'll help you. I'll save you.

THE MAN: You cant.

RAINA: I can. I'll hide you. (*She drags him towards the window.*) Here! behind the curtains.

THE MAN (*yielding to her*): There's just half a chance, if you keep your head.

RAINA (*drawing the curtain before him*): S-sh! (*She makes for the ottoman.*)

THE MAN (*putting out his head*): Remember——

RAINA (*running back to him*): Yes?

THE MAN:——nine soldiers out of ten are born fools.

RAINA: Oh! (*She draws the curtain angrily before him.*)

THE MAN (*looking out at the other side*): If they find me, I promise you a fight: a devil of a fight.

(*She stamps at him. He disappears hastily. She takes off her cloak, and throws it across the foot of the bed. Then, with a sleepy, disturbed air, she opens the door.* LOUKA *enters excitedly.*)

LOUKA: One of those beasts of Serbs has been seen climbing up the waterpipe to your balcony. Our men want to search for him; and they are so wild and drunk and furious. (*She makes for the other side of the room to get as far from the door as possible.*) My lady says you are to dress at once and to—(*She sees the revolver lying on the ottoman, and stops, petrified.*)

RAINA (*as if annoyed at being disturbed*): They shall not search here. Why have they been let in?

CATHERINE (*coming in hastily*): Raina, darling, are you safe? Have you seen anyone or heard anything?

RAINA: I heard the shooting. Surely the soldiers will not dare come in here?

CATHERINE: I have found a Russian officer, thank Heaven: he knows Sergius. (*Speaking through the door to someone outside*) Sir: will you come in now. My daughter will receive you.

(*A young Russian officer, in Bulgarian uniform, enters, sword in hand.*)

OFFICER (*with soft feline politeness and stiff military carriage*): Good evening, gracious lady. I am sorry to intrude; but there is a Serb hiding on the balcony. Will you and the gracious lady your mother please to withdraw whilst we search?

RAINA (*petulantly*): Nonsense, sir: you can see that there is no one on the balcony. (*She throws the shutters wide open and stands with her back to the curtain where the man is hidden, pointing to the moonlit balcony. A couple of shots are fired right under the window; and a bullet shatters the glass opposite* RAINA, *who winks and gasps, but stands her ground; whilst* CATHERINE *screams, and* THE OFFICER, *with a cry of* Take care! *rushes to the balcony.*)

THE OFFICER (*on the balcony, shouting savagely down to the street*): Cease firing there, you fools: do you hear? Cease firing, damn you! (*He glares down for a moment; then turns to* RAINA, *trying to resume his polite manner.*) Could anyone have got in without your knowledge? Were you asleep?

RAINA: No: I have not been to bed

THE OFFICER (*impatiently, coming back into the room*): Your neighbors have their heads so full of runaway Serbs that they see them everywhere. (*Politely*) Gracious lady: a thousand pardons. Goodnight. (*Military bow, which* RAINA *returns coldly. Another to* CATHERINE, *who follows him out.*)

(RAINA *closes the shutters. She turns and sees* LOUKA, *who has been watching the scene curiously.*)

RAINA: Don't leave my mother, Louka, until the soldiers go away.

(LOUKA *glances at* RAINA, *at the ottoman, at the curtain; then purses her lips secretively, laughs insolently, and goes out.* RAINA, *highly offended by this demonstration, follows her to the door, and shuts it behind her with a slam, locking it violently. The man immediately steps out from behind the curtain, sheathing his sabre. Then, dismissing the danger from his mind in a businesslike way, he comes affably to* RAINA.)

THE MAN: A narrow shave; but a miss is as good as a mile. Dear young lady: your servant to the death. I wish for your sake I had joined the Bulgarian army instead of the other one. I am not a native Serb.

RAINA (*haughtily*): No: you are one of the Austrians who set the Serbs on to rob us of our national liberty, and who officer their army for them. We hate them!

THE MAN: Austrian! not I. Dont hate me, dear young lady. I am a Swiss, fighting merely as a professional soldier. I joined the Serbs because they came first on the road from Switzerland. Be generous: youve beaten us hollow.

RAINA: Have I not been generous?

THE MAN: Noble! Heroic! But I'm not saved yet. This particular rush will soon pass through; but the pursuit will go on all night by fits and starts. I must take my chance to get off in a quiet interval. (*Pleasantly*) You dont mind my waiting just a minute or two, do you?

RAINA (*putting on her most genteel society manner*): Oh, not at all. Wont you sit down?

THE MAN: Thanks. (*He sits on the foot of the bed.*)

(RAINA *walks with studied elegance to the ottoman and sits down. Unfortunately she sits on the pistol, and jumps up with a shriek. The man, all nerves, shies like a frightened horse to the other side of the room.*)

THE MAN (*irritably*): Dont frighten me like that. What is it?

RAINA: Your revolver! It was staring that officer in the face all the time. What an escape!

THE MAN (*vexed at being unnecessarily terrified*): Oh, is that all?

RAINA (*staring at him rather superciliously as she conceives a poorer and poorer opinion of him, and feels proportionately more and more at her ease*): I am sorry I frightened you. (*She takes up the pistol and hands it to him.*) Pray take it to protect yourself against me.

THE MAN (*grinning wearily at the sarcasm as he takes the pistol*): No use, dear young lady; there's nothing in it. It's not loaded. (*He makes a grimace at it, and drops it despairingly into his revolver case.*)

RAINA: Load it by all means.

THE MAN: Ive no ammunition. What use are cartridges in battle? I always carry chocolate instead; and I finished the last cake of that hours ago.

RAINA (*outraged in her most cherished ideals of manhood*): Chocolate! Do you stuff your pockets with sweets—like a schoolboy—even in the field?

THE MAN (*grinning*): Yes: isnt it contemptible? (*Hungrily*) I wish I had some now.

RAINA: Allow me. (*She sails away scornfully to the chest of drawers, and returns with the box of confectionery in her hand.*) I am sorry I have eaten them all except these. (*She offers him the box.*)

THE MAN (*ravenously*): Youre an angel! (*He gobbles the contents.*) Creams! Delicious! (*He looks anxiously to see whether there are any more. There are none: he can only scrape the box with his fingers and suck them. When that nourishment is exhausted he accepts the inevitable with pathetic goodhumor, and says, with grateful emotion*) Bless you, dear lady! You can always tell an old soldier by the inside of his holsters and cartridge boxes. The young ones carry pistols and cartridges: the old ones, grub. Thank you. (*He hands back the box. She snatches it contemptuously from him and throws it away. He shies again, as if she had meant to strike him.*) Ugh! Dont do things so suddenly, gracious lady. It's mean to revenge yourself because I frightened you just now.

RAINA (*loftily*): Frighten me! Do you know, sir, that though I am only a woman, I think I am at heart as brave as you.

THE MAN: I should think so. You havnt been under fire for three days as I have. I can stand two days without shewing it much; but no man can stand three days: I'm as nervous as a mouse. (*He sits down on the ottoman, and takes his head in his hands.*) Would you like to see me cry?

RAINA (*alarmed*): No.

THE MAN: If you would, all you have to do is to scold me just as if I were a little boy and you my nurse. If I were in camp now, theyd play all sorts of tricks on me.

RAINA (*a little moved*): I'm sorry. I wont scold you. (*Touched by the sympathy in her tone, he raises his head and looks gratefully at her: she immediately draws back and says stiffly*): You must excuse me: our soldiers are not like that. (*She moves away from the ottoman.*)

THE MAN: Oh yes they are. There are only two sorts of soldiers: old ones and young ones. I've served fourteen years: half of your fellows never smelt powder before. Why, how is it that youve just beaten us? Sheer ignorance of the art of war, nothing else. (*Indignantly*) I never saw anything so unprofessional.

RAINA (*ironically*): Oh! was it unprofessional to beat you?

THE MAN: Well, come! is it professional to throw a regiment of cavalry on a battery of machine guns, with the dead certainty that if the guns go off not a horse or man will

ever get within fifty yards of the fire? I couldn't believe my
eyes when I saw it.

RAINA (*eagerly turning to him, as all her enthusiasm and
her dreams of glory rush back on her*): Did you see the
great cavalry charge? Oh, tell me about it. Describe it to me.

THE MAN: You never saw a cavalry charge, did you?

RAINA: How could I?

THE MAN: Ah, perhaps not. No: of course not! Well, it's
a funny sight. It's like slinging a handful of peas against a
window pane: first one comes; then two or three close behind him; and then all the rest in a lump.

RAINA (*her eyes dilating as she raises her clasped hands
ecstatically*): Yes, first One! the bravest of the brave!

THE MAN (*prosaically*): Hm! you should see the poor
devil pulling at his horse.

RAINA: Why should he pull at his horse?

THE MAN (*impatient of so stupid a question*): It's running
away with him, of course: do you suppose the fellow wants
to get there before the others and be killed? Then they all
come. You can tell the young ones by their wildness and
their slashing. The old ones come bunched up under the
number one guard: they know that theyre mere projectiles,
and that it's no use trying to fight. The wounds are mostly
broken knees, from the horses cannoning together.

RAINA: Ugh! But I dont believe the first man is a coward.
I know he is a hero!

THE MAN (*goodhumoredly*): Thats what youd have said if
youd seen the first man in the charge today.

RAINA (*breathless, forgiving him everything*): Ah, I knew
it! Tell me. Tell me about him.

THE MAN: He did it like an operatic tenor. A regular
handsome fellow, with flashing eyes and lovely moustache,
shouting his war-cry and charging like Don Quixote at the
windmills. We did laugh.

RAINA: You dared to laugh!

THE MAN: Yes; but when the sergeant ran up as white as
a sheet, and told us theyd sent us the wrong ammunition,
and that we couldnt fire a round for the next ten minutes,
we laughed at the other side of our mouths. I never felt so
sick in my life; though Ive been in one or two very tight
places. And I hadnt even a revolver cartridge: only chocolate. We'd no bayonets: nothing. Of course, they just cut us
to bits. And there was Don Quixote flourishing like a drum
major, thinking he'd done the cleverest thing ever known,
whereas he ought to be courtmartialled for it. Of all the
fools ever let loose on a field of battle, that man must be

the very maddest. He and his regiment simply committed suicide; only the pistol missed fire: thats all.

RAINA (*deeply wounded, but steadfastly loyal to her ideals*): Indeed! Would you know him again if you saw him?

THE MAN: Shall I ever forget him!

(*She again goes to the chest of drawers. He watches her with a vague hope that she may have something more for him to eat. She takes the portrait from its stand and brings it to him.*)

RAINA: That is a photograph of the gentleman—the patriot and hero—to whom I am betrothed.

THE MAN (*recognizing it with a shock*): I'm really very sorry. (*Looking at her*) Was it fair to lead me on? (*He looks at the portrait again.*) Yes: thats Don Quixote: not a doubt of it. (*He stifles a laugh.*)

RAINA (*quickly*): Why do you laugh?

THE MAN (*apologetic, but still greatly tickled*): I didnt laugh, I assure you. At least I didnt mean to. But when I think of him charging the windmills and imagining he was doing the finest thing—(*He chokes with suppressed laughter.*)

RAINA (*sternly*): Give me back the portrait, sir.

THE MAN (*with sincere remorse*): Of course. Certainly. I'm really very sorry. (*He hands her the picture. She deliberately kisses it and looks him straight in the face before returning to the chest of drawers to replace it. He follows her, apologizing.*) Perhaps I'm quite wrong, you know: no doubt I am. Most likely he had got wind of the cartridge business somehow, and knew it was a safe job.

RAINA: That is to say, he was a pretender and a coward! You did not dare say that before.

THE MAN (*with a comic gesture of despair*): It's no use, dear lady: I cant make you see it from the professional point of view. (*As he turns away to get back to the ottoman, a couple of distant shots threaten renewed trouble.*)

RAINA (*sternly, as she sees him listening to the shots*): So much the better for you!

THE MAN (*turning*): How?

RAINA: You are my enemy; and you are at my mercy. What would I do if I were a professional soldier?

THE MAN: Ah, true, dear young lady: youre always right. I know how good youve been to me: to my last hour I shall remember those three chocolate creams. It was unsoldierly; but it was angelic.

RAINA (*coldly*): Thank you. And now I will do a soldierly thing. You cannot stay here after what you have just said about my future husband; but I will go out on the balcony and see whether it is safe for you to climb down into the street. (*She turns to the window.*)

THE MAN (*changing countenance*): Down that waterpipe! Stop! Wait! I cant! I darent! The very thought of it makes me giddy. I came up it fast enough with death behind me. But to face it now in cold blood—! (*He sinks on the ottoman.*) It's no use: I give up: I'm beaten. Give the alarm. (*He drops his head on his hands in the deepest dejection.*)

RAINA (*disarmed by pity*): Come: dont be disheartened. (*She stoops over him almost maternally: he shakes his head.*) Oh, you are a very poor soldier: a chocolate cream soldier! Come, cheer up! it takes less courage to climb down than to face capture: remember that.

THE MAN (*dreamily, lulled by her voice*): No: capture only means death; and death is sleep: oh, sleep, sleep, sleep, undisturbed sleep! Climbing down the pipe means doing something—exerting myself—thinking! Death ten times over first.

RAINA (*softly and wonderingly, catching the rhythm of his weariness*): Are you as sleepy as that?

THE MAN: Ive not had two hours undisturbed sleep since I joined. I havnt closed my eyes for forty-eight hours.

RAINA (*at her wit's end*): But what am I to do with you?

THE MAN (*staggering up, roused by her desperation*): Of course. I must do something. (*He shakes himself; pulls himself together; and speaks with rallied vigor and courage.*) You see, sleep or no sleep, hunger or no hunger, tired or not tired, you can always do a thing when you know it must be done. Well, that pipe must be got down: (*he hits himself on the chest*) do you hear that, you chocolate cream soldier? (*He turns to the window.*)

RAINA (*anxiously*): But if you fall?

THE MAN: I shall sleep as if the stones were a feather bed. Goodbye. (*He makes boldly for the window; and his hand is on the shutter when there is a terrible burst of firing in the street beneath.*)

RAINA (*rushing to him*): Stop! (*She seizes him recklessly, and pulls him quite round.*) Theyll kill you.

THE MAN (*coolly, but attentively*): Never mind: this sort of thing is all in my day's work. I'm bound to take my chance. (*Decisively*) Now do what I tell you. Put out the candle; so that they shant see the light when I open the shutters. And keep away from the window, whatever you do. If they see me theyre sure to have a shot at me.

RAINA (*clinging to him*): Theyre sure to see you: it's bright moonlight. I'll save you. Oh, how can you be so indifferent! You want me to save you, dont you?

THE MAN: I really dont want to be troublesome. (*She shakes him in her impatience.*) I am not indifferent, dear young lady, I assure you. But how is it to be done?

RAINA: Come away from the window. (*She takes him firmly back to the middle of the room. The moment she releases him he turns mechanically towards the window again. She seizes him and turns him back, exclaiming*) Please! (*He becomes motionless, like a hypnotized rabbit, his fatigue gaining fast on him. She releases him, and addresses him patronizingly.*) Now listen. You must trust to our hospitality. You do not yet know in whose house you are. I am a Petkoff.

THE MAN: A pet what?

RAINA (*rather indignantly*): I mean that I belong to the family of the Petkoffs, the richest and best known in our country.

THE MAN: Oh, yes, of course. I beg your pardon. The Petkoffs, to be sure. How stupid of me!

RAINA: You know you never heard of them until this moment. How can you stoop to pretend!

THE MAN: Forgive me: I'm too tired to think; and the change of subject was too much for me. Dont scold me.

RAINA: I forgot. It might make you cry. (*He nods, quite seriously. She pouts and then resumes her patronizing tone.*) I must tell you that my father holds the highest command of any Bulgarian in our army. He is (*proudly*) a Major.

THE MAN (*pretending to be deeply impressed*): A Major! Bless me! Think of that!

RAINA: You shewed great ignorance in thinking that it was necessary to climb up to the balcony because ours is the only private house that has two rows of windows. There is a flight of stairs inside to get up and down by.

THE MAN: Stairs! How grand! You live in great luxury indeed, dear young lady.

RAINA: Do you know what a library is?

THE MAN: A library? A roomful of books?

RAINA: Yes. We have one, the only one in Bulgaria.

THE MAN: Actually a real library! I should like to see that.

RAINA (*affectedly*): I tell you these things to shew you that you are not in the house of ignorant country folk who would kill you the moment they saw your Serbian uniform, but among civilized people. We go to Bucharest every year for the opera season; and I have spent a whole month in Vienna.

THE MAN: I saw that, dear young lady. I saw at once that you knew the world.

RAINA: Have you ever seen the opera of Ernani?

THE MAN: Is that the one with the devil in it in red velvet, and a soldiers' chorus?

RAINA (*contemptuously*): No!

THE MAN (*stifling a heavy sigh of weariness*): Then I dont know it.

RAINA: I thought you might have remembered the great scene where Ernani, flying from his foes just as you are to-night, takes refuge in the castle of his bitterest enemy, an old Castilian noble. The noble refuses to give him up. His guest is sacred to him.

THE MAN (*quickly, waking up a little*): Have your people got that notion?

RAINA (*with dignity*): My mother and I can understand that notion, as you call it. And if instead of threatening me with your pistol as you did you had simply thrown yourself as a fugitive on our hospitality, you would have been as safe as in your father's house.

THE MAN: Quite sure?

RAINA (*turning her back on him in disgust*): Oh, it is useless to try to make you understand.

THE MAN: Dont be angry: you see how awkward it would be for me if there was any mistake. My father is a very hospitable man: he keeps six hotels; but I couldnt trust him as far as that. What about your father?

RAINA: He is away at Slivnitza fighting for his country. I answer for your safety. There is my hand in pledge of it. Will that reassure you? (*She offers him her hand.*)

THE MAN (*looking dubiously at his own hand*): Better not touch my hand, dear young lady. I must have a wash first.

RAINA (*touched*): That is very nice of you. I see that you are a gentleman.

THE MAN (*puzzled*): Eh?

RAINA: You must not think I am surprised. Bulgarians of really good standing—people in our position—wash their hands nearly every day. So you see I can appreciate your delicacy. You may take my hand. (*She offers it again.*)

THE MAN (*kissing it with his hands behind his back*): Thanks, gracious young lady: I feel safe at last. And now would you mind breaking the news to your mother? I had better not stay here secretly longer than is necessary.

RAINA: If you will be so good as to keep perfectly still whilst I am away.

THE MAN: Certainly. (*He sits down on the ottoman.*)

(RAINA *goes to the bed and wraps herself in the fur cloak. His eyes close. She goes to the door. Turning for a last look at him, she sees that he is dropping off to sleep.*)

RAINA (*at the door*): You are not going asleep, are you?

(*He murmurs inarticulately: she runs to him and shakes him.*) Do you hear? Wake up: you are falling asleep.

THE MAN: Eh? Falling aslee—? Oh no: not the least in the world: I was only thinking. It's all right: I'm wide awake.

RAINA (*severely*): Will you please stand up while I am away. (*He rises reluctantly.*) All the time, mind.

THE MAN (*standing unsteadily*): Certainly. Certainly: you may depend on me.

(RAINA *looks doubtfully at him. He smiles weakly. She goes reluctantly, turning again at the door, and almost catching him in the act of yawning. She goes out.*)

THE MAN (*drowsily*): Sleep, sleep, sleep, sleep, slee—(*The words trail off into a murmur. He wakes again with a shock on the point of falling.*) Where am I? Thats what I want to know: where am I? Must keep awake. Nothing keeps me awake except danger: remember that: (*intently*) danger, danger, danger, dan—(*trailing off again: another shock*) Wheres danger? Mus' find it. (*He starts off vaguely round the room in search of it.*) What am I looking for? Sleep—danger—dont know. (*He stumbles against the bed.*) Ah yes: now I know. All right now. I'm to go to bed, but not to sleep. Be sure not to sleep, because of danger. Not to lie down either, only sit down. (*He sits on the bed. A blissful expression comes into his face.*) Ah! (*With a happy sigh he sinks back at full length; lifts his boots into the bed with a final effort; and falls fast asleep instantly.*)

(CATHERINE *comes in, followed by* RAINA.)

RAINA (*looking at the ottoman*): He's gone! I left him here.

CATHERINE: Here! Then he must have climbed down from the—

RAINA (*seeing him*): Oh! (*She points.*)

CATHERINE (*scandalized*): Well! (*She strides to the bed,* RAINA *following until she is opposite her on the other side.*) He's fast asleep. The brute!

RAINA (*anxiously*): Sh!

CATHERINE (*shaking him*): Sir! (*Shaking him again, harder*) Sir!! (*Vehemently, shaking very hard*) Sir!!!

RAINA (*catching her arm*): Dont, mamma; the poor darling is worn out. Let him sleep.

CATHERINE (*letting him go, and turning amazed to* RAINA): The poor darling! Raina!!! (*She looks sternly at her daughter.*)

(*The man sleeps profoundly.*)

ACT II

(*The sixth of March, 1886. In the garden of* MAJOR PET-
KOFF'S *house. It is a fine spring morning: the garden looks
fresh and pretty. Beyond the paling the tops of a couple of
minarets can be seen, shewing that there is a valley there,
with the little town in it. A few miles further the Balkan
mountains rise and shut in the landscape. Looking towards
them from within the garden, the side of the house is seen
on the left, with a garden door reached by a little flight of
steps. On the right the stable yard, with its gateway, en-
croaches on the garden. There are fruit bushes along the
paling and house, covered with washing spread out to dry.
A path runs by the house, and rises by two steps at the
corner, where it turns out of sight. In the middle, a small
table, with two bent wood chairs at it, is laid for breakfast
with Turkish coffee pot, cups, rolls, etc.; but the cups have
been used and the bread broken. There is a wooden garden
seat against the wall on the right.*

LOUKA, *smoking a cigaret, is standing between the table
and the house, turning her back with angry disdain on a man
servant who is lecturing her. He is a middle-aged man of
cool temperament and low but clear and keen intelligence,
with the complacency of the servant who values himself on
his rank in servitude, and the imperturbability of the accurate calculator who has no illusions. He wears a white
Bulgarian costume: jacket with embroidered border, sash,
wide knickerbockers, and decorated gaiters. His head is
shaved up to the crown, giving him a high Japanese forehead. His name is* NICOLA.)

NICOLA: Be warned in time, Louka: mend your manners.
I know the mistress. She is so grand that she never dreams
that any servant could dare be disrespectful to her; but if
she once suspects that you are defying her, out you go.

LOUKA: I do defy her. I will defy her. What do I care
for her?

NICOLA: If you quarrel with the family, I never can marry
you. It's the same as if you quarrelled with me!

LOUKA: You take her part against me, do you?

NICOLA (*sedately*): I shall always be dependent on the
good will of the family. When I leave their service and
start a shop in Sofia, their custom will be half my capital:
their bad word would ruin me.

LOUKA: You have no spirit. I should like to catch them
saying a word against me!

NICOLA (*pityingly*): I should have expected more sense from you, Louka. But youre young: youre young!

LOUKA: Yes; and you like me the better for it, dont you? But I know some family secrets they wouldnt care to have told, young as I am. Let them quarrel with me if they dare!

NICOLA (*with compassionate superiority*): Do you know what they would do if they heard you talk like that?

LOUKA: What could they do?

NICOLA: Discharge you for untruthfulness. Who would believe any stories you told after that? Who would give you another situation? Who in this house would dare be seen speaking to you ever again? How long would your father be left on his little farm? (*She impatiently throws away the end of her cigaret, and stamps on it.*) Child: you dont know the power such high people have over the like of you and me when we try to rise out of our poverty against them. (*He goes close to her and lowers his voice.*) Look at me, ten years in their service. Do you think I know no secrets? I know things about the mistress that she wouldnt have the master know for a thousand levas. I know things about him that she wouldnt let him hear the last of for six months if I blabbed them to her. I know things about Raina that would break off her match with Sergius if—

LOUKA (*turning on him quickly*): How do you know? I never told you!

NICOLA (*opening his eyes cunningly*): So thats your little secret, is it? I thought it might be something like that. Well, you take my advice and be respectful; and make the mistress feel that no matter what you know or dont know, she can depend on you to hold your tongue and serve the family faithfully. Thats what they like; and thats how youll make most out of them.

LOUKA (*with searching scorn*): You have the soul of a servant, Nicola.

NICOLA (*complacently*): Yes: thats the secret of success in service.

(*A loud knocking with a whip handle on a wooden door is heard from the stable yard.*)

MALE VOICE OUTSIDE: Hollo! Hollo there! Nicola!

LOUKA: Master! back from the war!

NICOLA (*quickly*): My word for it, Louka, the war's over. Off with you and get some fresh coffee. (*He runs out into the stable yard.*)

LOUKA (*as she collects the coffee pot and cups on the tray, and carries it into the house*): Youll never put the soul of a servant into me.

(MAJOR PETKOFF *comes from the stable yard, followed by* NICOLA. *He is a cheerful, excitable, insignificant, unpolished man of about fifty, naturally unambitious except as to his income and his importance in local society, but just now greatly pleased with the military rank which the war has thrust on him as a man of consequence in his town. The fever of plucky patriotism which the Serbian attack roused in all the Bulgarians has pulled him through the war; but he is obviously glad to be home again.*)

PETKOFF (*pointing to the table with his whip*): Breakfast out here, eh?

NICOLA: Yes, sir. The mistress and Miss Raina have just gone in.

PETKOFF (*sitting down and taking a roll*): Go in and say Ive come; and get me some fresh coffee.

NICOLA: It's coming, sir. (*He goes to the house door.* LOUKA, *with fresh coffee, a clean cup, and a brandy bottle on her tray, meets him.*) Have you told the mistress?

LOUKA: Yes: she's coming.

(NICOLA *goes into the house.* LOUKA *brings the coffee to the table.*)

PETKOFF: Well: the Serbs havnt run away with you, have they?

LOUKA: No, sir.

PETKOFF: Thats right. Have you brought me some cognac?

LOUKA (*putting the bottle on the table*): Here, sir.

PETKOFF: Thats right. (*He pours some into his coffee.*)

(CATHERINE, *who, having at this early hour made only a very perfunctory toilet, wears a Bulgarian apron over a once brilliant but now half worn-out dressing gown, and a colored handkerchief tied over her thick black hair, comes from the house with Turkish slippers on her bare feet, looking astonishingly handsome and stately under all the circumstances.* LOUKA *goes into the house.*)

CATHERINE: My dear Paul: what a surprise for us! (*She stoops over the back of his chair to kiss him.*) Have they brought you fresh coffee?

PETKOFF: Yes: Louka's been looking after me. The war's over. The treaty was signed three days ago at Bucharest; and the decree for our army to demobilize was issued yesterday.

CATHERINE (*springing erect, with flashing eyes*): Paul: have you let the Austrians force you to make peace?

PETKOFF (*submissively*): My dear: they didnt consult me. What could *I* do? (*She sits down and turns away from him.*) But of course we saw to it that the treaty was an honorable one. It declares peace—

CATHERINE (*outraged*): Peace!

PETKOFF (*appeasing her*):—but not friendly relations: remember that. They wanted to put that in; but I insisted on its being struck out. What more could I do?

CATHERINE: You could have annexed Serbia and made Prince Alexander Emperor of the Balkans. Thats what I would have done.

PETKOFF: I dont doubt it in the least, my dear. But I should have had to subdue the whole Austrian Empire first; and that would have kept me too long away from you. I missed you greatly.

CATHERINE (*relenting*): Ah! (*She stretches her hand affectionately across the table to squeeze his.*)

PETKOFF: And how have you been, my dear?

CATHERINE: Oh, my usual sore throats: thats all.

PETKOFF (*with conviction*): That comes from washing your neck every day. Ive often told you so.

CATHERINE: Nonsense, Paul!

PETKOFF (*over his coffee and cigaret*): I dont believe in going too far with these modern customs. All this washing cant be good for the health; it's not natural. There was an Englishman at Philippopolis who used to wet himself all over with cold water every morning when he got up. Disgusting! It all comes from the English: their climate makes them so dirty that they have to be perpetually washing themselves. Look at my father! he never had a bath in his life; and he lived to be ninety-eight, the healthiest man in Bulgaria. I dont mind a good wash once a week to keep up my position; but once a day is carrying the thing to a ridiculous extreme.

CATHERINE: You are a barbarian at heart still, Paul. I hope you behaved yourself before all those Russian officers.

PETKOFF: I did my best. I took care to let them know that we have a library.

CATHERINE: Ah; but you didnt tell them that we have an electric bell in it? I have had one put up.

PETKOFF: Whats an electric bell?

CATHERINE: You touch a button; something tinkles in the kitchen; and then Nicola comes up.

PETKOFF: Why not shout for him?

CATHERINE: Civilized people never shout for their servants. Ive learnt that while you were away.

PETKOFF: Well, I'll tell you something Ive learnt too. Civilized people dont hang out their washing to dry where visitors can see it: so youd better have all that (*indicating the clothes on the bushes*) put somewhere else.

CATHERINE: Oh, thats absurd, Paul: I don't believe really refined people notice such things.

SERGIUS (*knocking at the stable gates*): Gate, Nicola!

PETKOFF: Theres Sergius. (*Shouting*) Hollo, Nicola!

CATHERINE: Oh, dont shout, Paul: it really isnt nice.

PETKOFF: Bosh! (*He shouts louder than before*): Nicola!

NICOLA (*appearing at the house door*): Yes, sir.

PETKOFF: Are you deaf? Dont you hear Major Saranoff knocking? Bring him round this way. (*He pronounces the name with the stress on the second syllable: Sarahnoff.*)

NICOLA: Yes, Major. (*He goes into the stable yard.*)

PETKOFF: You must talk to him, my dear, until Raina takes him off our hands. He bores my life out about our not promoting him. Over my head, if you please.

CATHERINE: He certainly ought to be promoted when he marries Raina. Besides, the country should insist on having at least one native general.

PETKOFF: Yes; so that he could throw away whole brigades instead of regiments. It's no use, my dear: he hasnt the slightest chance of promotion until we're quite sure that the peace will be a lasting one.

NICOLA (*at the gate, announcing*): Major Sergius Saranoff! (*He goes into the house and returns presently with a third chair, which he places at the table. He then withdraws.*)

MAJOR SERGIUS SARANOFF, *the original of the portrait in* RAINA'S *room, is a tall romantically handsome man, with the physical hardihood, the high spirit, and the susceptible imagination of an untamed mountaineer chieftain. But his remarkable personal distinction is of a characteristically civilized type. The ridges of his eyebrows, curving with an interrogative twist round the projections at the outer corners; his jealously observant eye; his nose, thin, keen, and apprehensive in spite of the pugnacious high bridge and large nostril; his assertive chin would not be out of place in a Parisian salon, shewing that the clever imaginative barbarian has an acute critical faculty which has been thrown into intense activity by the arrival of western civilization in the Balkans. The result is precisely what the advent of nineteenth century thought first produced in England: to wit, Byronism. By his brooding on the perpetual failure, not only of others, but of himself, to live up to his ideals; by his consequent cynical scorn for humanity; by his jejune credulity as to the absolute validity of his concepts and the unworthiness of the world in disregarding them; by his wincings and mockeries under the sting of the petty disillusions which every hour spent among men brings to his sensitive observation, he has acquired the half tragic, half ironic air, the mysterious moodiness, the suggestion of a strange and terrible history that has left nothing but undying remorse, by which Childe Harold fascinated the grandmothers of his English contemporaries. It is clear that here or nowhere is* RAINA's *ideal hero.* CATHERINE *is hardly less enthusiastic about him than her daughter, and much less reserved in shewing her enthusiasm. As he enters from the stable gate, she rises effusively to greet him.* PETKOFF *is distinctly less disposed to make a fuss about him.*)

PETKOFF: Here already, Sergius! Glad to see you.

CATHERINE: My dear Sergius! (*She holds out both her hands.*)

SERGIUS (*kissing them with scrupulous gallantry*): My dear mother, if I may call you so.

PETKOFF (*drily*): Mother-in-law, Sergius: mother-in-law! Sit down; and have some coffee.

SERGIUS: Thank you: none for me. (*He gets away from the table with a certain distaste for* PETKOFF'S *enjoyment of it, and posts himself with conscious dignity against the rail of the steps leading to the house.*)

CATHERINE: You look superb. The campaign has improved you, Sergius. Everybody here is mad about you. We were all wild with enthusiasm about that magnificent cavalry charge.

SERGIUS (*with grave irony*): Madam: it was the cradle and the grave of my military reputation.

CATHERINE: How so?

SERGIUS: I won the battle the wrong way when our worthy Russian generals were losing it the right way. In short, I upset their plans, and wounded their self-esteem. Two Cossack colonels had their regiments routed on the most correct principles of scientific warfare. Two major-generals got killed strictly according to military etiquette. The two colonels are now major-generals; and I am still a simple major.

CATHERINE: You shall not remain so, Sergius. The women are on your side; and they will see that justice is done you.

SERGIUS: It is too late. I have only waited for the peace to send in my resignation.

PETKOFF (*dropping his cup in his amazement*): Your resignation!

CATHERINE: Oh, you must withdraw it!

SERGIUS (*with resolute measured emphasis, folding his arms*): I never withdraw.

PETKOFF (*vexed*): Now who could have supposed you were going to do such a thing?

SERGIUS (*with fire*): Everyone that knew me. But enough of myself and my affairs. How is Raina; and where is Raina?

RAINA (*suddenly coming round the corner of the house and standing at the top of the steps in the path*): Raina is here.

(*She makes a charming picture as they turn to look at her. She wears an underdress of pale green silk, draped with an overdress of thin ecru canvas embroidered with gold. She is crowned with a dainty eastern cap of gold tinsel. Sergius goes impulsively to meet her. Posing regally, she presents her hand: he drops chivalrously on one knee and kisses it.*)

PETKOFF (*aside to* CATHERINE, *beaming with parental pride*): Pretty, isnt it? She always appears at the right moment.

CATHERINE (*impatiently*): Yes; she listens for it. It is an abominable habit.

(SERGIUS *leads* RAINA *forward with splendid gallantry. When they arrive at the table, she turns to him with a bend of the head: he bows; and thus they separate, he coming to his place and she going behind her father's chair.*)

RAINA (*stooping and kissing her father*): Dear father! Welcome home!

PETKOFF (*patting her cheek*): My little pet girl. (*He kisses her. She goes to the chair left by* NICOLA *for* SERGIUS, *and sits down.*)

CATHERINE: And so youre no longer a soldier, Sergius.

SERGIUS: I am no longer a soldier. Soldiering, my dear madam, is the coward's art of attacking mercilessly when you are strong, and keeping out of harm's way when you are weak. That is the whole secret of successful fighting. Get your enemy at a disadvantage; and never, on any account, fight him on equal terms.

PETKOFF: They wouldnt let us make a fair stand-up fight of it. However, I suppose soldiering has to be a trade like any other trade.

SERGIUS: Precisely. But I have no ambition to shine as a tradesman; so I have taken the advice of that bagman of a captain that settled the exchange of prisoners with us at Pirot, and given it up.

PETKOFF: What! that Swiss fellow? Sergius: I've often thought of that exchange since. He over-reached us about those horses.

SERGIUS: Of course he over-reached us. His father was a hotel and livery stable keeper; and he owed his first step to his knowledge of horse-dealing. (*With mock enthusiasm*) Ah, he was a soldier: every inch a soldier! If only I had bought the horses for my regiment instead of foolishly leading it into danger, I should have been a field-marshal now!

CATHERINE: A Swiss? What was he doing in the Serbian army?

PETKOFF: A volunteer, of course: keen on picking up his profession. (*Chuckling*) We shouldnt have been able to begin fighting if these foreigners hadnt shewn us how to do it: we knew nothing about it; and neither did the Serbs. Egad, there'd have been no war without them!

RAINA: Are there many Swiss officers in the Serbian Army?

PETKOFF: No. All Austrians, just as our officers were all Russians. This was the only Swiss I came across. I'll never trust a Swiss again. He humbugged us into giving him fifty ablebodied men for two hundred worn out chargers. They werent even eatable!

SERGIUS: We were two children in the hands of that consummate soldier, Major: simply two innocent little children.

RAINA: What was he like?

CATHERINE: Oh, Raina, what a silly question!

SERGIUS: He was like a commercial traveller in uniform. Bourgeois to his boots!

PETKOFF (*grinning*): Sergius: tell Catherine that queer story his friend told us about how he escaped after Slivnitza. You remember. About his being hid by two women.

SERGIUS (*with bitter irony*): Oh yes: quite a romance! He was serving in the very battery I so unprofessionally charged. Being a thorough soldier, he ran away like the rest of them, with our cavalry at his heels. To escape their sabres he climbed a waterpipe and made his way into the bedroom of a young Bulgarian lady. The young lady was enchanted by his persuasive commercial traveller's manners. She very modestly entertained him for an hour or so, and then called in her mother lest her conduct should appear unmaidenly. The old lady was equally fascinated; and the fugitive was sent on his way in the morning, disguised in an old coat belonging to the master of the house, who was away at the war.

RAINA (*rising with marked stateliness*): Your life in the camp has made you coarse, Sergius. I did not think you would have repeated such a story before me. (*She turns away coldly.*)

CATHERINE (*also rising*): She is right, Sergius. If such women exist, we should be spared the knowledge of them.

PETKOFF: Pooh! nonsense! what does it matter?

SERGIUS (*ashamed*): No, Petkoff: I was wrong. (*To* RAINA, *with earnest humility*): I beg your pardon. I have behaved

abominably. Forgive me, Raina. (*She bows reservedly.*) And
you too, madam. (CATHERINE *bows graciously and sits down.
He proceeds solemnly, again addressing* RAINA.) The glimpses I have had of the seamy side of life during the last few
months have made me cynical; but I should not have brought
my cynicism here: least of all into your presence, Raina.
I—(*Here, turning to the others, he is evidently going to
begin a long speech when the Major interrupts him.*)

PETKOFF: Stuff and nonsense, Sergius! Thats quite enough
fuss about nothing: a soldier's daughter should be able to
stand up without flinching to a little strong conversation.
(*He rises.*) Come: it's time for us to get to business. We have
to make up our minds how those three regiments are to get
back to Philippopolis: theres no forage for them on the Sofia
route. (*He goes towards the house.*) Come along. (SERGIUS *is
about to follow him when* CATHERINE *rises and intervenes.*)

CATHERINE: Oh, Paul, cant you spare Sergius for a few
moments? Raina has hardly seen him yet. Perhaps I can help
you to settle about the regiments.

SERGIUS (*protesting*): My dear madam, impossible: you—

CATHERINE (*stopping him playfully*): You stay here, my
dear Sergius: theres no hurry. I have a word or two to say
to Paul. (SERGIUS *instantly bows and steps back.*) Now, dear
(*taking* PETKOFF'S *arm*): come and see the electric bell.

PETKOFF: Oh, very well, very well.

(*They go into the house together affectionately.* SERGIUS,
left alone with RAINA, *looks anxiously at her, fearing that she
is still offended. She smiles, and stretches out her arms to
him.*)

SERGIUS (*hastening to her*): Am I forgiven?

RAINA (*placing her hands on his shoulders as she looks up
at him with admiration and worship*): My hero! My king!

SERGIUS: My queen! (*He kisses her on the forehead.*)

RAINA: How I have envied you, Sergius! You have been
out in the world, on the field of battle, able to prove yourself
there worthy of any woman in the world; whilst I have had
to sit at home inactive—dreaming—useless—doing nothing
that could give me the right to call myself worthy of
any man.

SERGIUS: Dearest: all my deeds have been yours. You
inspired me. I have gone through the war like a knight in
a tournament with his lady looking down at him!

RAINA: And you have never been absent from my
thoughts for a moment. (*Very solemnly*) Sergius: I think
we two have found the higher love. When I think of you,

I feel that I could never do a base deed, or think an ignoble thought.

SERGIUS: My lady and my saint! (*He clasps her reverently.*)

RAINA (*returning his embrace*): My lord and my—

SERGIUS: Sh—sh! Let me be the worshipper, dear. You little know how unworthy even the best man is of a girl's pure passion!

RAINA: I trust you. I love you. You will never disappoint me, Sergius. (LOUKA *is heard singing within the house. They quickly release each other.*) I cant pretend to talk indifferently before her: my heart is too full. (LOUKA *comes from the house with her tray. She goes to the table, and begins to clear it, with her back turned to them.*) I will get my hat; and then we can go out until lunch time. Wouldnt you like that?

SERGIUS: Be quick. If you are away five minutes, it will seem five hours. (RAINA *runs to the top of the steps, and turns there to exchange looks with him and wave him a kiss with both hands. He looks after her with emotion for a moment; then turns slowly away, his face radiant with the loftiest exaltation. The movement shifts his field of vision, into the corner of which there now comes the tail of* LOUKA'S *double apron. His attention is arrested at once. He takes a stealthy look at her, and begins to twirl his moustache mischievously, with his left hand akimbo on his hip. Finally, striking the ground with his heels in something of a cavalry swagger, he strolls over to the other side of the table, opposite her, and says*) Louka: do you know what the higher love is?

LOUKA (*astonished*): No, sir.

SERGIUS: Very fatiguing thing to keep up for any length of time, Louka. One feels the need of some relief after it.

LOUKA (*innocently*): Perhaps you would like some coffee, sir? (*She stretches her hand across the table for the coffee pot.*)

SERGIUS (*taking her hand*): Thank you, Louka.

LOUKA (*pretending to pull*): Oh, sir, you know I didnt mean that. I'm surprised at you!

SERGIUS (*coming clear of the table and drawing her with him*): I am surprised at myself, Louka. What would Sergius, the hero of Slivnitza, say if he saw me now? What would Sergius, the apostle of the higher love, say if he saw me now? What would the half dozen Sergiuses who keep popping in and out of this handsome figure of mine say if they caught us here? (*Letting go her hand and slipping his arm dexterously round her waist*) Do you consider my figure handsome, Louka?

LOUKA: Let me go, sir. I shall be disgraced. (*She struggles: he holds her inexorably.*) Oh, will you let go?

SERGIUS (*looking straight into her eyes*): No.

LOUKA: Then stand back where we cant be seen. Have you no common sense?

SERGIUS: Ah! thats reasonable. (*He takes her into the stable yard gateway, where they are hidden from the house.*)

LOUKA (*plaintively*): I may have been seen from the windows: Miss Raina is sure to be spying about after you.

SERGIUS (*stung: letting her go*): Take care, Louka. I may be worthless enough to betray the higher love; but do not you insult it.

LOUKA (*demurely*): Not for the world, sir, I'm sure. May I go on with my work, please, now?

SERGIUS (*again putting his arm round her*): You are a provoking little witch, Louka. If you were in love with me, would you spy out of windows on me?

LOUKA: Well, you see, sir, since you say you are half a dozen different gentlemen all at once, I should have a great deal to look after.

SERGIUS (*charmed*): Witty as well as pretty. (*He tries to kiss her.*)

LOUKA (*avoiding him*): No: I dont want your kisses. Gentlefolk are all alike: you making love to me behind Miss Raina's back; and she doing the same behind yours.

SERGIUS (*recoiling a step*): Louka!

LOUKA: It shews how little you really care.

SERGIUS (*dropping his familiarity, and speaking with freezing politeness*): If our conversation is to continue, Louka, you will please remember that a gentleman does not discuss the conduct of the lady he is engaged to with her maid.

LOUKA: It's so hard to know what a gentleman considers right. I thought from your trying to kiss me that you had given up being so particular.

SERGIUS (*turning from her and striking his forehead as he comes back into the garden from the gateway*): Devil! devil!

LOUKA: Ha! ha! I expect one of the six of you is very like me, sir; though I am only Miss Raina's maid. (*She goes back to her work at the table, taking no further notice of him.*)

SERGIUS (*speaking to himself*): Which of the six is the real man? thats the question that torments me. One of them is a hero, another a buffoon, another a humbug, another perhaps a bit of a blackguard. (*He pauses, and looks furtively at* LOUKA *as he adds, with deep bitterness*) And one, at least, is a coward: jealous, like all cowards. (*He goes to the table.*) Louka.

LOUKA: Yes?

SERGIUS: Who is my rival?

LOUKA: You shall never get that out of me, for love or money.

SERGIUS: Why?

LOUKA: Never mind why. Besides, you would tell that I told you; and I should lose my place.

SERGIUS (*holding out his right hand in affirmation*): No! on the honor of a—(*He checks himself; and his hand drops, nerveless, as he concludes sardonically*)—of a man capable of behaving as I have been behaving for the last five minutes. Who is he?

LOUKA: I dont know. I never saw him. I only heard his voice through the door of her room.

SERGIUS: Damnation! How dare you?

LOUKA (*retreating*): Oh, I mean no harm: youve no right to take up my words like that. The mistress knows all about it. And I tell you that if that gentleman ever comes here again, Miss Raina will marry him, whether he likes it or not. I know the difference between the sort of manner you and she put on before one another and the real manner.

(SERGIUS *shivers as if she had stabbed him. Then, setting his face like iron, he strides grimly to her, and grips her above the elbows with both hands.*)

SERGIUS: Now listen you to me.

LOUKA (*wincing*): Not so tight: youre hurting me.

SERGIUS: That doesnt matter. You have stained my honor by making me a party to your eavesdropping. And you have betrayed your mistress.

LOUKA (*writhing*): Please—

SERGIUS: That shews that you are an abominable little clod of common clay, with the soul of a servant. (*He lets her go as if she were an unclean thing, and turns away, dusting his hands of her, to the bench by the wall, where he sits down with averted head, meditating gloomily.*)

LOUKA (*whimpering angrily with her hands up her sleeves, feeling her bruised arms*): You know how to hurt with your tongue as well as with your hands. But I dont care, now Ive found out that whatever clay I'm made of, youre made of the same. As for her, she's a liar; and her fine airs are a cheat; and I'm worth six of her. (*She shakes the pain off hardily; tosses her head; and sets to work to put the things on the tray.*)

(*He looks doubtfully at her. She finishes packing the tray, and laps the cloth over the edges, so as to carry all out together. As she stoops to lift it, he rises.*)

SERGIUS: Louka! (*She stops and looks defiantly at him.*)

A gentleman has no right to hurt a woman under any circumstances. (*With profound humility, uncovering his head*) I beg your pardon.

LOUKA: That sort of apology may satisfy a lady. Of what use is it to a servant?

SERGIUS (*rudely crossed in his chivalry, throws it off with a bitter laugh, and says slightingly*): Oh! you wish to be paid for the hurt! (*He puts on his shako, and takes some money from his pocket.*)

LOUKA (*her eyes filling with tears in spite of herself*): No: I want my hurt made well.

SERGIUS (*sobered by her tone*): How?

(*She rolls up her left sleeve; clasps her arm with the thumb and fingers of her right hand; and looks down at the bruise. Then she raises her head and looks straight at him. Finally, with a superb gesture, she presents her arm to be kissed. Amazed, he looks at her; at the arm; at her again; hesitates; and then, with shuddering intensity, exclaims* Never! *and gets away as far as possible from her.*

Her arm drops. Without a word, and with unaffected dignity, she takes her tray, and is approaching the house when RAINA *returns, wearing a hat and jacket in the height of the Vienna fashion of the previous year, 1885.* LOUKA *makes way proudly for her, and then goes into the house.*)

RAINA: I'm ready. Whats the matter? (*Gaily*) Have you been flirting with Louka?

SERGIUS (*hastily*): No, no. How can you think such a thing?

RAINA (*ashamed of herself*): Forgive me, dear: it was only a jest. I am so happy today.

(*He goes quickly to her, and kisses her hand remorsefully.* CATHERINE *comes out and calls to them from the top of the steps.*)

CATHERINE (*coming down to them*): I am sorry to disturb you, children; but Paul is distracted over those three regiments. He doesnt know how to send them to Philippopolis; and he objects to every suggestion of mine. You must go and help him, Sergius. He is in the library.

RAINA (*disappointed*): But we are just going out for a walk.

SERGIUS: I shall not be long. Wait for me just five minutes. (*He runs up the steps to the door.*)

RAINA (*following him to the foot of the steps and looking up at him with timid coquetry*): I shall go round and wait in full view of the library windows. Be sure you draw father's

attention to me. If you are a moment longer than five minutes, I shall go in and fetch you, regiments or no regiments.

SERGIUS (*laughing*): Very well. (*He goes in.*)

(RAINA *watches him until he is out of her sight. Then,
with a perceptible relaxation of manner, she begins to pace
up and down the garden in a brown study.*)

CATHERINE: Imagine their meeting that Swiss and hearing
the whole story! The very first thing your father asked for
was the old coat we sent him off in. A nice mess you have
got us into!

RAINA (*gazing thoughtfully at the gravel as she walks*):
The little beast!

CATHERINE: Little beast! What little beast?

RAINA: To go and tell! Oh, if I had him here, I'd cram him
with chocolate creams til he couldnt ever speak again!

CATHERINE: Dont talk such stuff. Tell me the truth, Raina.
How long was he in your room before you came to me?

RAINA (*whisking round and recommencing her march in
the opposite direction*): Oh, I forget.

CATHERINE: You cannot forget! Did he really climb up
after the soldiers were gone: or was he there when that
officer searched the room?

RAINA: No. Yes: I think he must have been there then.

CATHERINE: You think! Oh, Raina! Raina! Will anything
ever make you straightforward? If Sergius finds out, it will
be all over between you.

RAINA (*with cool impertinence*): Oh, I know Sergius is
your pet. I sometimes wish you could marry him instead
of me. You would just suit him. You would pet him, and
spoil him, and mother him to perfection.

CATHERINE (*opening her eyes very widely indeed*): Well,
upon my word!

RAINA (*capriciously: half to herself*): I always feel a longing to do or say something dreadful to him—to shock his
propriety—to scandalize the five senses out of him. (*To
CATHERINE, perversely*) I dont care whether he finds out
about the chocolate cream soldier or not. I half hope he
may. (*She again turns and strolls flippantly away up the
path to the corner of the house.*)

CATHERINE: And what should I be able to say to your
father, pray?

RAINA (*over her shoulder, from the top of the two steps*):
Oh, poor father! As if he could help himself! (*She turns the
corner and passes out of sight.*)

CATHERINE (*looking after her, her fingers itching*): Oh, if
you were only ten years younger! (LOUKA *comes from the*

house with a salver, which she carries hanging down by her side.) Well?

LOUKA: Theres a gentleman just called, madam. A Serbian officer.

CATHERINE *(flaming)*: A Serb! And how dare he—*(checking herself bitterly)*: Oh, I forgot. We are at peace now. I suppose we shall have them calling every day to pay their compliments. Well: if he is an officer why dont you tell your master? He is in the library with Major Saranoff. Why do you come to me?

LOUKA: But he asks for you, madam. And I dont think he knows who you are: he said the lady of the house. He gave me this little ticket for you. *(She takes a card out of her bosom; puts it on the salver; and offers it to CATHERINE).*

CATHERINE *(reading)*: "Captain Bluntschli"? Thats a German name.

LOUKA: Swiss, madam, I think.

CATHERINE *(with a bound that makes LOUKA jump back)*: Swiss! What is he like?

LOUKA *(timidly)*: He has a big carpet bag, madam.

CATHERINE: Oh Heavens! he's come to return the coat. Send him away: say we're not at home: ask him to leave his address and I'll write to him. Oh stop: that will never do. Wait! *(She throws herself into a chair to think it out. LOUKA waits.)* The master and Major Saranoff are busy in the library, arnt they?

LOUKA: Yes, madam.

CATHERINE *(decisively)*: Bring the gentleman out here at once. *(Peremptorily)*: And be very polite to him. Dont delay. Here *(impatiently snatching the salver from her)*: leave that here; and go straight back to him.

LOUKA: Yes, madam *(going.)*

CATHERINE: Louka!

LOUKA *(stopping)*: Yes, madam.

CATHERINE: Is the library door shut?

LOUKA: I think so, madam.

CATHERINE: If not, shut it as you pass through.

LOUKA: Yes, madam *(going).*

CATHERINE: Stop *(LOUKA stops.)* He will have to go that way *(indicating the gate of the stable yard.)* Tell Nicola to bring his bag here after him. Dont forget.

LOUKA *(surprised)*: His bag?

CATHERINE: Yes: here: as soon as possible. *(Vehemently)* Be quick! *(LOUKA runs into the house. CATHERINE snatches her apron off and throws it behind a bush. She then takes up the salver and uses it as a mirror, with the result that the handkerchief tied round her head follows the apron. A touch to her hair and a shake to her dressing gown make her pre-*

sentable.) Oh, how? how? how can a man be such a fool! Such a moment to select! (LOUKA *appears at the door of the house, announcing* Captain Bluntschli. *She stands aside at the top of the steps to let him pass before she goes in again. He is the man of the midnight adventure in* RAINA'S *room, clean, well brushed, smartly uniformed, and out of trouble, but still unmistakably the same man. The moment* LOUKA'S *back is turned,* CATHERINE *swoops on him with impetuous, urgent, coaxing appeal.*) Captain Bluntschli: I am very glad to see you; but you must leave this house at once. (*He raises his eyebrows.*) My husband has just returned with my future son-in-law; and they know nothing. If they did, the consequences would be terrible. You are a foreigner: you do not feel our national animosities as we do. We still hate the Serbs: the effect of the peace on my husband has been to make him feel like a lion baulked of his prey. If he discovers our secret, he will never forgive me; and my daughter's life will hardly be safe. Will you, like the chivalrous gentleman and soldier you are, leave at once before he finds you here?

BLUNTSCHLI (*disappointed, but philosophical*): At once, gracious lady. I only came to thank you and return the coat you lent me. If you will allow me to take it out of my bag and leave it with your servant as I pass out, I need detain you no further. (*He turns to go into the house.*)

CATHERINE (*catching him by the sleeve*): Oh, you must not think of going back that way. (*Coaxing him across to the stable gates*) This is the shortest way out. Many thanks. So glad to have been of service to you. Goodbye.

BLUNTSCHLI: But my bag?

CATHERINE: It shall be sent on. You will leave me your address.

BLUNTSCHLI: True. Allow me. (*He takes out his cardcase, and stops to write his address, keeping* CATHERINE *in an agony of impatience. As he hands her the card,* PETKOFF, *hatless, rushes from the house in a fluster of hospitality, followed by* SERGIUS.)

PETKOFF (*as he hurries down the steps*): My dear Captain Bluntschli—

CATHERINE: Oh Heavens! (*She sinks on the seat against the wall.*)

PETKOFF (*too preoccupied to notice her as he shakes* BLUNTSCHLI'S *hand heartily*): Those stupid people of mine thought I was out here, instead of in the—haw!—library (*he cannot mention the library without betraying how proud he is of it*). I saw you through the window. I was wondering why you didnt come in. Saranoff is with me: you remember him, dont you?

SERGIUS (*saluting humorously, and then offering his hand*

with great charm of manner): Welcome, our friend the enemy!

PETKOFF: No longer the enemy, happily. (*Rather anxiously*) I hope youve called as a friend, and not about horses or prisoners.

CATHERINE: Oh, quite as a friend, Paul. I was just asking Captain Bluntschli to stay to lunch; but he declares he must go at once.

SERGIUS (*sardonically*): Impossible, Bluntschli. We want you here badly. We have to send on three cavalry regiments to Philippopolis; and we dont in the least know how to do it.

BLUNTSCHLI (*suddenly attentive and businesslike*): Philippopolis? The forage is the trouble, I suppose.

PETKOFF (*eagerly*): Yes: thats it. (*To* SERGIUS) He sees the whole thing at once.

BLUNTSCHLI: I think I can shew you how to manage that.

SERGIUS: Invaluable man! Come along! (*Towering over* BLUNTSCHLI, *he puts his hand on his shoulder and takes him to the steps,* PETKOFF *following.*)

(RAINA *comes from the house as* BLUNTSCHLI *puts his foot on the first step.*)

RAINA: Oh! The chocolate cream soldier!

(BLUNTSCHLI *stands rigid.* SERGIUS, *amazed, looks at* RAINA, *then at* PETKOFF, *who looks back at him and then at his wife.*)

CATHERINE (*with commanding presence of mind*): My dear Raina, dont you see that we have a guest here? Captain Bluntschli: one of our new Serbian friends.

(RAINA *bows:* BLUNTSCHLI *bows.*)

RAINA: How silly of me! (*She comes down into the centre of the group, between* BLUNTSCHLI *and* PETKOFF.) I made a beautiful ornament this morning for the ice pudding; and that stupid Nicola has just put down a pile of plates on it and spoilt it. (*To* BLUNTSCHLI, *winningly*) I hope you didnt think that you were the chocolate cream soldier, Captain Bluntschli.

BLUNTSCHLI (*laughing*): I assure you I did. (*Stealing a whimsical glance at her*) Your explanation was a relief.

PETKOFF (*suspiciously, to* RAINA): And since when, pray, have you taken to cooking?

CATHERINE: Oh, whilst you were away. It is her latest fancy.

PETKOFF (*testily*): And has Nicola taken to drinking? He used to be careful enough. First he shews Captain

Bluntschli out here when he knew quite well I was in the library; and then he goes downstairs and breaks Raina's chocolate soldier. He must—(NICOLA *appears at the top of the steps with the bag. He descends; places it respectfully before* BLUNTSCHLI; *and waits for further orders. General amazement.* NICOLA, *unconscious of the effect he is producing, looks perfectly satisfied with himself. When* PETKOFF *recovers his power of speech, he breaks out at him with*) Are you mad, Nicola?

NICOLA (*taken aback*): Sir?

PETKOFF: What have you brought that for?

NICOLA: My lady's orders, major. Louka told me that—

CATHERINE (*interrupting him*): My orders! Why should I order you to bring Captain Bluntschli's luggage out here? What are you thinking of, Nicola?

NICOLA (*after a moment's bewilderment, picking up the bag as he addresses* BLUNTSCHLI *with the very perfection of servile discretion*): I beg your pardon, captain, I am sure. (*To* CATHERINE): My fault, madame: I hope youll overlook it. (*He bows, and is going to the steps with the bag, when* PETKOFF *addresses him angrily.*)

PETKOFF: Youd better go and slam that bag, too, down on Miss Raina's ice pudding! (*This is too much for* NICOLA. *The bag drops from his hand almost on his master's toes, eliciting a roar of*) Begone, you butter-fingered donkey.

NICOLA (*snatching up the bag, and escaping into the house*): Yes, Major.

CATHERINE: Oh, never mind. Paul: dont be angry.

PETKOFF (*blustering*): Scoundrel! He's got out of hand while I was away. I'll teach him. Infernal blackguard! The sack next Saturday! I'll clear out the whole establishment— (*He is stifled by the caresses of his wife and daughter, who hang round his neck, petting him.*)

CATHERINE		Now, now, now, it
	(*together*):	
RAINA		Wow, wow, wow:

mustnt be angry. He meant
not on your first day at home.

no harm. Be good to please
I'll make another ice pudding.

me, dear. Sh-sh-sh-sh!
Tch-ch-ch!

PETKOFF (*yielding*): Oh well, never mind. Come, Bluntschli: lets have no more nonsense about going away. You know very well youre not going back to Switzerland yet. Until you do go back youll stay with us.

RAINA: Oh, do, Captain Bluntschli.

PETKOFF (*to* CATHERINE): Now, Catherine: it's of you he's afraid. Press him: and he'll stay.

CATHERINE: Of course I shall be only too delighted if (*appealingly*) Captain Bluntschli really wishes to stay. He knows my wishes.

BLUNTSCHLI (*in his driest military manner*): I am at madam's orders.

SERGIUS (*cordially*): That settles it!

PETKOFF (*heartily*): Of course!

RAINA: You see you must stay.

BLUNTSCHLI (*smiling*): Well, if I must, I must.

(*Gesture of despair from* CATHERINE.)

ACT III

(*In the library after lunch. It is not much of a library. Its literary equipment consists of a single fixed shelf stocked with old paper covered novels, broken backed, coffee stained, torn and thumbed; and a couple of little hanging shelves with a few gift books on them: the rest of the wall space being occupied by trophies of war and the chase. But it is a most comfortable sitting room. A row of three large windows shews a mountain panorama, just now seen in one of its friendliest aspects in the mellowing afternoon light. In the corner next the right hand window a square earthenware stove, a perfect tower of glistening pottery, rises nearly to the ceiling and guarantees plenty of warmth. The ottoman is like that in* RAINA'S *room, and similarly placed; and the window seats are luxurious with decorated cushions. There is one object, however, hopelessly out of keeping with its surroundings. This is a small kitchen table, much the worse for wear, fitted as a writing table with an old canister full of pens, an eggcup filled with ink, and a deplorable scrap of heavily used pink blotting paper.*

At the side of this table, which stands to the left of anyone facing the window, BLUNTSCHLI *is hard at work with a couple of maps before him, writing orders. At the head of it sits* SERGIUS, *who is supposed to be also at work, but is actually gnawing the feather of a pen, and contemplating* BLUNT-SCHLI'S *quick, sure, businesslike progress with a mixture of envious irritation at his own incapacity and awestruck wonder at an ability which seems to him almost miraculous, though its prosaic character forbids him to esteem it.* THE MAJOR *is comfortably established on the ottoman, with a newspaper in his hand and the tube of his hookah within easy reach.* CATHERINE *sits at the stove, with her back to them, em-*

broidering. RAINA, *reclining on the divan, is gazing in a daydream out at the Balkan landscape, with a neglected novel in her lap.*

The door is on the same side as the stove, farther from the window. The button of the electric bell is at the opposite side, behind BLUNTSCHLI.)

PETKOFF (*looking up from his paper to watch how they are getting on at the table*): Are you sure I cant help in any way, Bluntschli?

BLUNTSCHLI (*without interrupting his writing or looking up*): Quite sure, thank you. Saranoff and I will manage it.

SERGIUS (*grimly*): Yes: we'll manage it. He finds out what to do; draws up the orders; and I sign em. Division of labor! (BLUNTSCHLI *passes him a paper.*) Another one? Thank you. (*He plants the paper squarely before him; sets his chair carefully parallel to it; and signs with his cheek on his elbow and his protruded tongue following the movements of his pen.*) This hand is more accustomed to the sword than to the pen.

PETKOFF: It's very good of you, Bluntschli: it is indeed, to let yourself be put upon in this way. Now are you quite sure I can do nothing?

CATHERINE (*in a low warning tone*): You can stop interrupting, Paul.

PETKOFF (*starting and looking round at her*): Eh? Oh! Quite right, my love: Quite right. (*He takes his newspaper up again, but presently lets it drop.*) Ah, you havnt been campaigning, Catherine: you dont know how pleasant it is for us to sit here, after a good lunch, with nothing to do but enjoy ourselves. Theres only one thing I want to make me thoroughly comfortable.

CATHERINE: What is that?

PETKOFF: My old coat. I'm not at home in this one: I feel as if I were on parade.

CATHERINE: My dear Paul, how absurd you are about that old coat! It must be hanging in the blue closet where you left it.

PETKOFF: My dear Catherine, I tell you Ive looked there. Am I to believe my own eyes or not? (CATHERINE *rises and crosses the room to press the button of the electric bell.*) What are you shewing off that bell for? (*She looks at him majestically, and silently resumes her chair and her needlework.*) My dear: if you think the obstinacy of your sex can make a coat out of two old dressing gowns of Raina's, your waterproof, and my mackintosh, youre mistaken. Thats exactly what the blue closet contains at present.

(NICOLA *presents himself.*)

CATHERINE: Nicola: go to the blue closet and bring your master's old coat here: the braided one he wears in the house.

NICOLA: Yes, madame. (*He goes out.*)

PETKOFF: Catherine.

CATHERINE: Yes, Paul.

PETKOFF: I bet you any piece of jewellery you like to order from Sofia against a week's housekeeping money that the coat isnt there.

CATHERINE: Done, Paul!

PETKOFF (*excited by the prospect of a gamble*): Come: heres an opportunity for some sport. Wholl bet on it? Bluntschli: I'll give you six to one.

BLUNTSCHLI (*imperturbably*): It would be robbing you, Major. Madame is sure to be right. (*Without looking up, he passes another batch of papers to* SERGIUS.)

SERGIUS (*also excited*): Bravo, Switzerland! Major: I bet my best charger against an Arab mare for Raina that Nicola finds the coat in the blue closet.

PETKOFF (*eagerly*): Your best char—

CATHERINE (*hastily interrupting him*): Don't be foolish, Paul. An Arabian mare will cost you 50,000 levas.

RAINA (*suddenly coming out of her picturesque revery*): Really, mother, if you are going to take the jewellery, I don't see why you should grudge me my Arab.

(NICOLA *comes back with the coat, and brings it to* PET-KOFF, *who can hardly believe his eyes.*)

CATHERINE: Where was it, Nicola?

NICOLA: Hanging in the blue closet, madame.

PETKOFF: Well, I am d—

CATHERINE (*stopping him*): Paul!

PETKOFF: I could have sworn it wasnt there. Age is beginning to tell on me. I'm getting hallucinations. (*To* NICOLA) Here: help me to change. Excuse me, Bluntschli. (*He begins changing coats,* NICOLA *acting as valet.*) Remember: I didnt take that bet of yours, Sergius. Youd better give Raina that Arab steed yourself, since youve roused her expectations. Eh, Raina? (*He looks round at her; but she is again rapt in the landscape. With a little gush of parental affection and pride, he points her out to them, and says*) She's dreaming, as usual.

SERGIUS: Assuredly she shall not be the loser.

PETKOFF: So much the better for her. *I* shant come off so cheaply, I expect. (*The change is now complete.* NICOLA *goes out with the discarded coat.*) Ah, now I feel at home at last. (*He sits down and takes his newspaper with a grunt of relief.*)

BLUNTSCHLI (*to* SERGIUS, *handing a paper*): Thats the last order.

PETKOFF (*jumping up*): What! Finished?

BLUNTSCHLI: Finished.

PETKOFF (*with childlike envy*): Havnt you anything for me to sign?

BLUNTSCHLI: Not necessary. His signature will do.

PETKOFF (*inflating his chest and thumping it*): Ah well, I think weve done a thundering good day's work. Can I do anything more?

BLUNTSCHLI: You had better both see the fellows that are to take these. (SERGIUS *rises*.) Pack them off at once; and shew them that Ive marked on the orders the time they should hand them in by. Tell them that if they stop to drink or tell stories—if theyre five minutes late, theyll have the skin taken off their backs.

SERGIUS (*stiffening indignantly*): I'll say so. (*He strides to the door.*) And if one of them is man enough to spit in my face for insulting him, I'll buy his discharge and give him a pension. (*He goes out.*)

BLUNTSCHLI (*confidentially*): Just see that he talks to them properly, Major, will you?

PETKOFF (*officiously*): Quite right, Bluntschli, quite right. I'll see to it. (*He goes to the door importantly, but hesitates on the threshold.*) By the bye, Catherine, you may as well come too. Theyll be far more frightened of you than of me.

CATHERINE (*putting down her embroidery*): I daresay I had better. You would only splutter at them. (*She goes out,* PETKOFF *holding the door for her and following her.*)

BLUNTSCHLI: What an army! They make cannons out of cherry trees; and the officers send for their wives to keep discipline! (*He begins to fold and docket the papers.*)

(RAINA, *who has risen from the divan, marches slowly down the room with her hands clasped behind her, and looks mischievously at him.*)

RAINA: You look ever so much nicer than when we last met. (*He looks up, surprised.*) What have you done to yourself?

BLUNTSCHLI: Washed; brushed; good night's sleep and breakfast. Thats all.

RAINA: Did you get back safely that morning?

BLUNTSCHLI: Quite, thanks.

RAINA: Were they angry with you for running away from Sergius's charge?

BLUNTSCHLI (*grinning*): No: they were glad; because theyd all just run away themselves.

RAINA (*going to the table, and leaning over it towards him*): It must have made a lovely story for them: all that about me and my room.

BLUNTSCHLI: Capital story. But I only told it to one of them: a particular friend.

RAINA: On whose discretion you could absolutely rely?

BLUNTSCHLI: Absolutely.

RAINA: Hm! He told it all to my father and Sergius the day you exchanged the prisoners. (*She turns away and strolls carelessly across to the other side of the room.*)

BLUNTSCHLI (*deeply concerned, and half incredulous*): No! You dont mean that, do you?

RAINA (*turning, with sudden earnestness*): I do indeed. But they dont know that it was in this house you took refuge. If Sergius knew, he would challenge you and kill you in a duel.

BLUNTSCHLI: Bless me! then dont tell him.

RAINA: Please be serious, Captain Bluntschli. Can you not realize what it is to me to deceive him? I want to be quite perfect with Sergius: no meanness, no smallness, no deceit. My relation to him is the one really beautiful and noble part of my life. I hope you can understand that.

BLUNTSCHLI (*sceptically*): You mean that you wouldnt like him to find out that the story about the ice pudding was a—a—a—You know.

RAINA (*wincing*): Ah, dont talk of it in that flippant way. I lied: I know it. But I did it to save your life. He would have killed you. That was the second time I ever uttered a false-hood. (BLUNTSCHLI *rises quickly and looks doubtfully and somewhat severely at her.*) Do you remember the first time?

BLUNTSCHLI: I! No. Was I present?

RAINA: Yes; and I told the officer who was searching for you that you were not present.

BLUNTSCHLI: True. I should have remembered it.

RAINA (*greatly encouraged*): Ah, it is natural that you should forget it first. It cost you nothing: it cost me a lie! A lie!

(*She sits down on the ottoman, looking straight before her with her hands clasped round her knee.* BLUNTSCHLI, *quite touched, goes to the ottoman with a particularly reassuring and considerate air, and sits down beside her.*)

BLUNTSCHLI: My dear young lady, dont let this worry you. Remember: I'm a soldier. Now what are the two things that happen to a soldier so often that he comes to think nothing of them? One is hearing people tell lies (RAINA *recoils*): the other is getting his life saved in all sorts of ways by all sorts of people.

RAINA (*rising in indignant protest*): And so he becomes a creature incapable of faith and of gratitude.

BLUNTSCHLI (*making a wry face*): Do you like gratitude? I dont. If pity is akin to love, gratitude is akin to the other thing.

RAINA: Gratitude! (*Turning on him*) If you are incapable of gratitude you are incapable of any noble sentiment. Even animals are grateful. Oh, I see now exactly what you think of me! You were not surprised to hear me lie. To you it was something I probably did every day! every hour! That is how men think of women. (*She paces the room tragically.*)

BLUNTSCHLI (*dubiously*): Theres reason in everything. You said youd told only two lies in your whole life. Dear young lady: isnt that rather a short allowance? I'm quite a straightforward man myself; but it wouldn't last me a whole morning.

RAINA (*staring haughtily at him*): Do you know, sir, that you are insulting me?

BLUNTSCHLI: I cant help it. When you strike that noble attitude and speak in that thrilling voice, I admire you; but I find it impossible to believe a single word you say.

RAINA (*superbly*): Captain Bluntschli!

BLUNTSCHLI (*unmoved*): Yes?

RAINA (*standing over him, as if she could not believe her senses*): Do you mean what you said just now? Do you know what you said just now?

BLUNTSCHLI: I do.

RAINA (*gasping*): I! I!!!! (*She points to herself incredulously, meaning "I, Raina Petkoff tell lies!" He meets her gaze unflinchingly. She suddenly sits down beside him, and adds, with a complete change of manner from the heroic to a babyish familiarity*) How did you find me out?

BLUNTSCHLI (*promptly*): Instinct, dear young lady. Instinct, and experience of the world.

RAINA (*wonderingly*): Do you know, you are the first man I ever met who did not take me seriously?

BLUNTSCHLI: You mean, dont you, that I am the first man that has ever taken you quite seriously?

RAINA: Yes: I suppose I do mean that. (*Cosily, quite at her ease with him*) How strange it is to be talked to in such a way! You know, Ive always gone on like that.

BLUNTSCHLI: You mean the—?

RAINA: I mean the noble attitude and the thrilling voice. (*They laugh together.*) I did it when I was a tiny child to my nurse. She believed in it. I do it before my parents. They believe in it. I do it before Sergius. He believes in it.

BLUNTSCHLI: Yes: he's a little in that line himself, isnt he?

RAINA (*startled*): Oh! Do you think so?

BLUNTSCHLI: You know him better than I do.

RAINA: I wonder—I wonder is he? If I thought that—!
(*Discouraged*) Ah, well; what does it matter? I suppose, now
youve found me out, you despise me.

BLUNTSCHLI (*warmly, rising*): No, my dear young lady,
no, no, no a thousand times. It's part of your youth: part of
your charm. I'm like all the rest of them: the nurse, your
parents, Sergius: I'm your infatuated admirer.

RAINA (*pleased*): Really?

BLUNTSCHLI (*slapping his breast smartly with his hand,
German fashion*): Hand aufs Herz! Really and truly.

RAINA (*very happy*): But what did you think of me for
giving you my portrait?

BLUNTSCHLI (*astonished*): Your portrait! You never gave
me your portrait.

RAINA (*quickly*): Do you mean to say you never got it?

BLUNTSCHLI: No. (*He sits down beside her, with renewed
interest, and says, with some complacency*) When did you
send it to me?

RAINA (*indignantly*): I did not send it to you. (*She turns
her head away, and adds, reluctantly*) It was in the pocket of
that coat.

BLUNTSCHLI (*pursing his lips and rounding his eyes*):
Oh-o-oh! I never found it. It must be there still.

RAINA (*springing up*): There still! for my father to find the
first time he puts his hand in his pocket! Oh, how could you
be so stupid?

BLUNTSCHLI (*rising also*): It doesnt matter: I suppose it's
only a photograph: how can he tell who it was intended for?
Tell him he put it there himself.

RAINA (*bitterly*): Yes: that is so clever! isnt it? (*Distractedly*) Oh! what shall I do?

BLUNTSCHLI: Ah, I see. You wrote something on it. That
was rash.

RAINA (*vexed almost to tears*): Oh, to have done such a
thing for you, who care no more—except to laugh at me—
oh! Are you sure nobody has touched it?

BLUNTSCHLI: Well, I cant be quite sure. You see, I couldnt
carry it about with me all the time: one cant take much
luggage on active service.

RAINA: What did you do with it?

BLUNTSCHLI: When I got through to Pirot I had to put it
in safe keeping somehow. I thought of the railway cloak
room; but thats the surest place to get looted in modern
warfare. So I pawned it.

RAINA: Pawned it!!!

BLUNTSCHLI: I know it doesnt sound nice: but it was much
the safest plan. I redeemed it the day before yesterday.

Heaven only knows whether the pawnbroker cleared out the pockets or not.

RAINA (*furious: throwing the words right into his face*): You have a low shopkeeping mind. You think of things that would never come into a gentleman's head.

BLUNTSCHLI (*phlegmatically*): Thats the Swiss national character, dear lady. (*He returns to the table.*)

RAINA: Oh, I wish I had never met you. (*She flounces away, and sits at the window fuming.*)

(LOUKA *comes in with a heap of letters and telegrams on her salver, and crosses, with her bold free gait, to the table. Her left sleeve is looped up to the shoulder with a brooch, shewing her naked arm, with a broad gilt bracelet covering the bruise.*)

LOUKA (*to* BLUNTSCHLI): For you. (*She empties the salver with a fling on to the table.*) The messenger is waiting. (*She is determined not to be civil to an enemy, even if she must bring him his letters.*)

BLUNTSCHLI (*to* RAINA): Will you excuse me: the last postal delivery that reached me was three weeks ago. These are the subsequent accumulations. Four telegrams: a week old. (*He opens one.*) Oho! Bad news!

RAINA (*rising and advancing a little remorsefully*): Bad news?

BLUNTSCHLI: My father's dead. (*He looks at the telegram with his lips pursed, musing on the unexpected change in his arrangements.* LOUKA *crosses herself hastily.*)

RAINA: Oh, how very sad!

BLUNTSCHLI: Yes: I shall have to start for home in an hour. He has left a lot of big hotels behind him to be looked after. (*He takes up a fat letter in a long blue envelope.*) Here's a whacking letter from the family solicitor. (*He puts out the enclosures and glances over them.*) Great Heavens! Seventy! Two hundred! (*In a crescendo of dismay*) Four hundred! Four thousand!! Nine thousand six hundred!!! What on earth am I to do with them all?

RAINA (*timidly*): Nine thousand hotels?

BLUNTSCHLI: Hotels nonsense. If you only knew! Oh, it's too ridiculous! Excuse me: I must give my fellow orders about starting. (*He leaves the room hastily, with the documents in his hand.*)

LOUKA (*knowing instinctively that she can annoy* RAINA *by disparaging* BLUNTSCHLI): He has not much heart, that Swiss. He has not a word of grief for his poor father.

RAINA (*bitterly*): Grief! A man who has been doing nothing but killing people for years! What does he care? What does any soldier care? (*She goes to the door, restraining her tears with difficulty.*)

LOUKA: Major Saranoff has been fighting too; and he has plenty of heart left. (RAINA, *at the door, draws herself up haughtily and goes out.*) Aha! I thought you wouldnt get much feeling out of your soldier. (*She is following* RAINA *when* NICOLA *enters with an armful of logs for the stove.*)

NICOLA (*grinning amorously at her*): Ive been trying all the afternoon to get a minute alone with you, my girl. (*His countenance changes as he notices her arm.*) Why, what fashion is that of wearing your sleeve, child?

LOUKA (*proudly*): My own fashion.

NICOLA: Indeed! If the mistress catches you, she'll talk to you. (*He puts the logs down, and seats himself comfortably on the ottoman.*)

LOUKA: Is that any reason why you should take it on yourself to talk to me?

NICOLA: Come! dont be contrairy with me. Ive some good news for you. (*She sits down beside him. He takes out some paper money.* LOUKA, *with an eager gleam in her eyes, tries to snatch it; but he shifts it quickly to his left hand, out of her reach.*) See! a twenty leva bill! Sergius gave me that, out of pure swagger. A fool and his money are soon parted. Theres ten levas more. The Swiss gave me that for backing up the mistress' and Raina's lies about him. He's no fool, he isnt. You should have heard old Catherine downstairs as polite as you please to me, telling me not to mind the Major being a little impatient; for they knew what a good servant I was—after making a fool and a liar of me before them all! The twenty will go to our savings; and you shall have the ten to spend if youll only talk to me so as to remind me I'm a human being. I get tired of being a servant occasionally.

LOUKA: Yes: sell your manhood for 30 levas, and buy me for 10! (*Rising scornfully*) Keep your money. You were born to be a servant. I was not. When you set up your shop you will only be everybody's servant instead of somebody's servant. (*She goes moodily to the table and seats herself regally in* SERGIUS's *chair.*)

NICOLA (*picking up his logs, and going to the stove*): Ah, wait til you see. We shall have our evenings to ourselves; and I shall be master in my own house, I promise you. (*He throws the logs down and kneels at the stove.*)

LOUKA: You shall never be master in mine.

NICOLA (*turning, still on his knees, and squatting down rather forlornly on his calves, daunted by her implacable disdain*): You have a great ambition in you, Louka. Remember: if any luck comes to you, it was I that made a woman of you.

LOUKA: You!

NICOLA (*scrambling up and going to her*): Yes, me. Who was it made you give up wearing a couple of pounds of false black hair on your head and reddening your lips and cheeks like any other Bulgarian girl! I did. Who taught you to trim your nails, and keep your hands clean, and be dainty about yourself, like a fine Russian lady! Me: do you hear that? me! (*She tosses her head defiantly; and he turns away, adding more coolly*) Ive often thought that if Raina were out of the way, and you just a little less of a fool and Sergius just a little more of one, you might come to be one of my grandest customers, instead of only being my wife and costing me money.

LOUKA: I believe you would rather be my servant than my husband. You would make more out of me. Oh, I know that soul of yours.

NICOLA (*going closer to her for greater emphasis*): Never you mind my soul; but just listen to my advice. If you want to be a lady, your present behaviour to me wont do at all, unless when we're alone. It's too sharp and impudent; and impudence is a sort of familiarity: it shews affection for me. And dont you try being high and mighty with me, either. Youre like all country girls: you think it's genteel to treat a servant the way I treat a stableboy. Thats only your ignorance; and dont you forget it. And dont be so ready to defy everybody. Act as if you expected to have your own way, not as if you expected to be ordered about. The way to get on as a lady is the same as the way to get on as a servant: youve got to know your place: thats the secret of it. And you may depend on me to know my place if you get promoted. Think over it, my girl. I'll stand by you: one servant should always stand by another.

LOUKA (*rising impatiently*): Oh, I must behave in my own way. You take all the courage out of me with your cold-blooded wisdom. Go and put those logs in the fire: thats the sort of thing you understand.

(*Before* NICOLA *can retort,* SERGIUS *comes in. He checks himself a moment on seeing* LOUKA; *then goes to the stove.*)

SERGIUS (*to* NICOLA): I am not in the way of your work, I hope.

NICOLA (*in a smooth, elderly manner*): Oh no, sir: thank you kindly. I was only speaking to this foolish girl about her habit of running up here to the library whenever she gets a chance, to look at the books. Thats the worst of her education, sir: it gives her habits above her station. (*To* LOUKA)

Make that table tidy, Louka, for the Major. (*He goes out sedately.*)

(LOUKA, *without looking at* SERGIUS, *pretends to arrange the papers on the table. He crosses slowly to her, and studies the arrangement of her sleeve reflectively.*)

SERGIUS: Let me see: is there a mark there? (*He turns up the bracelet and sees the bruise made by his grasp. She stands motionless, not looking at him: fascinated, but on her guard*): Ffff! Does it hurt?

LOUKA: Yes.

SERGIUS: Shall I cure it?

LOUKA (*instantly withdrawing herself proudly, but still not looking at him*): No. You cannot cure it now.

SERGIUS (*masterfully*): Quite sure? (*He makes a movement as if to take her in his arms.*)

LOUKA: Dont trifle with me, please. An officer should not trifle with a servant.

SERGIUS (*indicating the bruise with a merciless stroke of his forefinger*): That was no trifle, Louka.

LOUKA (*flinching; then looking at him for the first time*): Are you sorry?

SERGIUS (*with measured emphasis, folding his arms*): I am never sorry.

LOUKA (*wistfully*): I wish I could believe a man could be as unlike a woman as that. I wonder are you really a brave man?

SERGIUS (*unaffectedly, relaxing his attitude*): Yes: I am a brave man. My heart jumped like a woman's at the first shot; but in the charge I found that I was brave. Yes: that at least is real about me.

LOUKA: Did you find in the charge that the men whose fathers are poor like mine were any less brave than the men who are rich like you?

SERGIUS (*with bitter levity*): Not a bit. They all slashed and cursed and yelled like heroes. Psha! the courage to rage and kill is cheap. I have an English bull terrier who has as much of that sort of courage as the whole Bulgarian nation, and the whole Russian nation at its back. But he lets my groom thrash him, all the same. Thats your soldier all over! No, Louka: your poor men can cut throats; but they are afraid of their officers; they put up with insults and blows; they stand by and see one another punished like children: aye, and help to do it when they are ordered. And the officers!!! Well (*with a short harsh laugh*) I am an officer. Oh, (*fervently*) give me the man who will defy to the death any power on earth or in heaven that sets itself up against his own will and conscience: he alone is the brave man.

LOUKA: How easy it is to talk! Men never seem to me to grow up: they all have schoolboy's ideas. You dont know what true courage is.

SERGIUS (*ironically*): Indeed! I am willing to be instructed. (*He sits on the ottoman, sprawling magnificently.*)

LOUKA: Look at me! How much am I allowed to have my own will? I have to get your room ready for you: to sweep and dust, to fetch and carry. How could that degrade me if it did not degrade you to have it done for you? But (*with subdued passion*) if I were Empress of Russia, above everyone in the world, then!! Ah then, though according to you I could shew no courage at all, you should see, you should see.

SERGIUS: What would you do, most noble Empress?

LOUKA: I would marry the man I loved, which no other queen in Europe has the courage to do. If I loved you, though you would be as far beneath me as I am beneath you, I would dare to be the equal of my inferior. Would you dare as much if you loved me? No: if you felt the beginnings of love for me you would not let it grow. You would not dare: you would marry a rich man's daughter because you would be afraid of what other people would say of you.

SERGIUS (*bounding up*): You lie: it is not so, by all the stars! If I loved you, and I were the Tsar himself, I would set you on the throne by my side. You know that I love another woman, a woman as high above you as heaven is above earth. And you are jealous of her.

LOUKA: I have no reason to be. She will never marry you now. The man I told you of has come back. She will marry the Swiss.

SERGIUS (*recoiling*): The Swiss!

LOUKA: A man worth ten of you. Then you can come to me; and I will refuse you. You are not good enough for me. (*She turns to the door.*)

SERGIUS (*springing after her and catching her fiercely in his arms*): I will kill the Swiss; and afterwards I will do as I please with you.

LOUKA (*in his arms, passive and steadfast*): The Swiss will kill you, perhaps. He has beaten you in love. He may beat you in war.

SERGIUS (*tormentedly*): Do you think I believe that she— she! whose worst thoughts are higher than your best ones, is capable of trifling with another man behind my back?

LOUKA: Do you think she would believe the Swiss if he told her now that I am in your arms?

SERGIUS (*releasing her in despair*): Damnation! Oh, damnation! Mockery! mockery everywhere! everything I think is mocked by everything I do! (*He strikes himself frantically on the breast.*) Coward! liar! fool! Shall I kill myself like a man, or live and pretend to laugh at myself? (*She again turns to go.*) Louka! (*She stops near the door.*) Remember: you belong to me.

LOUKA (*turning*): What does that mean? An insult?

SERGIUS (*commandingly*): It means that you love me, and that I have had you here in my arms, and will perhaps have you there again. Whether that is an insult I neither know nor care: take it as you please. But (*vehemently*) I will not be a coward and a trifler. If I choose to love you, I dare marry you, in spite of all Bulgaria. If these hands ever touch you again, they shall touch my affianced bride.

LOUKA: We shall see whether you dare keep your word. And take care. I will not wait long.

SERGIUS (*again folding his arms and standing motionless in the middle of the room*): Yes: we shall see. And you shall wait my pleasure.

(BLUNTSCHLI, *much preoccupied, with his papers still in his hand, enters, leaving the door open for* LOUKA *to go out. He goes across to the table, glancing at her as he passes.* SERGIUS, *without altering his resolute attitude, watches him steadily.* LOUKA *goes out, leaving the door open.*

BLUNTSCHLI (*absently, sitting at the table as before, and putting down his papers*): Thats a remarkable-looking young woman.

SERGIUS (*gravely, without moving*): Captain Bluntschli.

BLUNTSCHLI: Eh?

SERGIUS: You have deceived me. You are my rival. I brook no rivals. At six o'clock I shall be in the drilling-ground on the Klissoura road, alone, on horseback, with my sabre. Do you understand?

BLUNTSCHLI (*staring, but sitting quite at his ease*): Oh, thank you: thats a cavalry man's proposal. I'm in the artillery; and I have the choice of weapons. If I go, I shall take a machine gun. And there shall be no mistake about the cartridges this time.

SERGIUS (*flushing, but with deadly coldness*): Take care, sir. It is not our custom in Bulgaria to allow invitations of that kind to be trifled with.

BLUNTSCHLI (*warmly*): Pooh! dont talk to me about Bulgaria. You dont know what fighting is. But have it your own way. Bring your sabre along. I'll meet you.

SERGIUS (*fiercely delighted to find his opponent a man of spirit*): Well said, Switzer. Shall I lend you my best horse?

BLUNTSCHLI: No: damn your horse! thank you all the same, my dear fellow. (RAINA *comes in, and hears the next sentence.*) I shall fight you on foot. Horseback's too dangerous; I dont want to kill you if I can help it.

RAINA (*hurrying forward anxiously*): I have heard what Captain Bluntschli said, Sergius. You are going to fight. Why? (SERGIUS *turns away in silence, and goes to the stove, where he stands watching her as she continues, to* BLUNTSCHLI) What about?

BLUNTSCHLI: I don't know: he hasn't told me. Better not interfere, dear young lady. No harm will be done: Ive often acted as sword instructor. He wont be able to touch me; and I'll not hurt him. It will save explanations. In the morning I shall be off home; and youll never see me or hear of me again. You and he will then make it up and live happily ever after.

RAINA (*turning away deeply hurt, almost with a sob in her voice*): I never said I wanted to see you again.

SERGIUS (*striding forward*): Ha! That is a confession.

RAINA (*haughtily*): What do you mean?

SERGIUS: You love that man!

RAINA (*scandalized*): Sergius!

SERGIUS: You allow him to make love to you behind my back, just as you treat me as your affianced husband behind his. Bluntschli: you knew our relations; and you deceived me. It is for that that I call you to account, not for having received favors *I* never enjoyed.

BLUNTSCHLI (*jumping up indignantly*): Stuff! Rubbish! I have received no favors. Why, the young lady doesnt even know whether I'm married or not.

RAINA (*forgetting herself*): Oh! (*Collapsing on the ottoman*) Are you?

SERGIUS: You see the young lady's concern, Captain Bluntschli. Denial is useless. You have enjoyed the privilege of being received in her own room, late at night—

BLUNTSCHLI (*interrupting him pepperily*): Yes, you blockhead! she received me with a pistol at her head. Your cavalry were at my heels. I'd have blown out her brains if she'd uttered a cry.

SERGIUS (*taken aback*): Bluntschli! Raina: is this true?

RAINA (*rising in wrathful majesty*): Oh, how dare you, how dare you?

BLUNTSCHLI: Apologize, man: apologize. (*He resumes his seat at the table.*)

SERGIUS (*with the old measured emphasis, folding his arms*): I never apologize!

RAINA (*passionately*): This is the doing of that friend of yours, Captain Bluntschli. It is he who is spreading this horrible story about me. (*She walks about excitedly.*)

BLUNTSCHLI: No: he's dead. Burnt alive.

RAINA (*stopping, shocked*): Burnt alive!

BLUNTSCHLI: Shot in the hip in a woodyard. Couldnt drag himself out. Your fellows' shells set the timber on fire and burnt him, with a half a dozen other poor devils in the same predicament.

RAINA: How horrible!

SERGIUS: And how ridiculous! Oh, war! war! the dream of patriots and heroes! A fraud, Bluntschli. A hollow sham, like love.

RAINA (*outraged*): Like love! You say that before me!

BLUNTSCHLI: Come, Saranoff: that matter is explained.

SERGIUS: A hollow sham, I say. Would you have come back here if nothing had passed between you except at the muzzle of your pistol? Raina is mistaken about your friend who was burnt. He was not my informant.

RAINA: Who then? (*Suddenly guessing the truth*) Ah, Louka! my maid! my servant! You were with her this morning all that time after—after—Oh, what sort of god is this I have been worshipping! (*He meets her gaze with sardonic enjoyment of her disenchantment. Angered all the more, she goes closer to him, and says, in a lower, intenser tone*) Do you know that I looked out of the window as I went upstairs, to have another sight of my hero; and I saw something I did not understand then. I know now that you were making love to her.

SERGIUS (*with grim humor*): You saw that?

RAINA: Only too well. (*She turns away, and throws herself on the divan under the centre window, quite overcome.*)

SERGIUS (*cynically*): Raina: our romance is shattered. Life's a farce.

BLUNTSCHLI (*to* RAINA, *whimsically*): You see: he's found himself out now.

SERGIUS (*going to him*): Bluntschli: I have allowed you to call me a blockhead. You may now call me a coward as well. I refuse to fight you. Do you know why?

BLUNTSCHLI: No; but it doesnt matter. I didnt ask the reason when you cried on; and I dont ask the reason now that you cry off. I'm a professional soldier! I fight when I have to, and am very glad to get out of it when I havnt to. Youre only an amateur: you think fighting's an amusement.

SERGIUS (*sitting down at the table, nose to nose with him*):

You shall hear the reason all the same, my professional. The reason is that it takes two men—real men—men of heart, blood and honor—to make a genuine combat. I could no more fight with you than I could make love to an ugly woman. Youve no magnetism: youre not a man: youre a machine.

BLUNTSCHLI (*apologetically*): Quite true, quite true. I always was that sort of chap. I'm very sorry.

SERGIUS: Psha!

BLUNTSCHLI: But now that youve found that life isnt a farce, but something quite sensible and serious, what further obstacle is there to your happiness?

RAINA (*rising*): You are very solicitous about my happiness and his. Do you forget his new love—Louka? It is not you that he must fight now, but his rival, Nicola.

SERGIUS: Rival!! (*Bouncing half across the room.*)

RAINA: Dont you know that theyre engaged?

SERGIUS: Nicola! Are fresh abysses opening? Nicola!

RAINA (*sarcastically*): A shocking sacrifice, isnt it? Such beauty! such intellect! such modesty! wasted on a middle-aged servant man. Really, Sergius, you cannot stand by and allow such a thing. It would be unworthy of your chivalry.

SERGIUS (*losing all self-control*): Viper! Viper! (*He rushes to and fro, raging.*)

BLUNTSCHLI: Look here, Saranoff: youre getting the worst of this.

RAINA (*getting angrier*): Do you realize what he has done, Captain Bluntschli? He has set this girl as a spy on us; and her reward is that he makes love to her.

SERGIUS: False! Monstrous!

RAINA: Monstrous! (*Confronting him*) Do you deny that she told you about Captain Bluntschli being in my room?

SERGIUS: No; but—

RAINA (*interrupting*): Do you deny that you were making love to her when she told you?

SERGIUS: No; but I tell you—

RAINA (*cutting him short contemptuously*): It is unnecessary to tell us anything more. That is quite enough for us. (*She turns away from him and sweeps majestically back to the window.*)

BLUNTSCHLI (*quietly, as* SERGIUS, *in an agony of mortification, sinks on the ottoman, clutching his averted head between his fists*): I told you you were getting the worst of it, Saranoff.

SERGIUS: Tiger cat!

RAINA (*running excitedly to* BLUNTSCHLI): You hear this man calling me names, Captain Bluntschli?

BLUNTSCHLI: What else can he do, dear lady? He must defend himself somehow. Come (*very persuasively*): dont quarrel. What good does it do?

(RAINA, *with a gasp, sits down on the ottoman, and after a vain effort to look vexedly at* BLUNTSCHLI, *falls a victim to her sense of humor, and actually leans back babyishly against the writhing shoulder of* SERGIUS.)

SERGIUS: Engaged to Nicola! Ha! ha! Ah well, Bluntschli, you are right to take this huge imposture of a world coolly.

RAINA (*quaintly to* BLUNTSCHLI, *with an intuitive guess at his state of mind*): I daresay you think us a couple of grown-up babies, dont you?

SERGIUS (*grinning savagely*): He does: he does. Swiss civilization nursetending Bulgarian barbarism, eh?

BLUNTSCHLI (*blushing*): Not at all, I assure you. I'm only very glad to get you two quieted. There! there! let's be pleasant and talk it over in a friendly way. Where is this other young lady?

RAINA: Listening at the door, probably.

SERGIUS (*shivering as if a bullet had struck him, and speaking with quiet but deep indignation*): I will prove that that, at least, is a calumny. (*He goes with dignity to the door and opens it. A yell of fury bursts from him as he looks out. He darts into the passage, and returns dragging in* LOUKA, *whom he flings violently against the table, exclaiming*) Judge her, Bluntschli. You, the cool impartial one: judge the eavesdropper.

(LOUKA *stands her ground, proud and silent.*)

BLUNTSCHLI (*shaking his head*): I mustnt judge her. I once listened myself outside a tent when there was a mutiny brewing. It's all a question of the degree of provocation. My life was at stake.

LOUKA: My love was at stake. I am not ashamed.

RAINA (*contemptuously*): Your love! Your curiosity, you mean.

LOUKA (*facing her and returning her contempt with interest*): My love, stronger than anything you can feel, even for your chocolate cream soldier.

SERGIUS (*with quick suspicion, to* LOUKA): What does that mean?

LOUKA (*fiercely*): It means—

SERGIUS (*interrupting her slightingly*): Oh, I remember: the ice pudding. A paltry taunt, girl!

(MAJOR PETKOFF *enters, in his shirtsleeves.*)

PETKOFF: Excuse my shirtsleeves, gentlemen. Raina: somebody has been wearing that coat of mine: I'll swear it. Somebody with a differently shaped back. It's all burst open at the sleeve. Your mother is mending it. I wish she'd make haste: I shall catch cold. (*He looks more attentively at them.*) Is anything the matter?

RAINA: No. (*She sits down at the stove, with a tranquil air.*)

SERGIUS: Oh no. (*He sits down at the end of the table, as at first.*)

BLUNTSCHLI (*who is already seated*): Nothing. Nothing.

PETKOFF (*sitting down on the ottoman in his old place*): Thats all right. (*He notices* LOUKA.) Anything the matter, Louka?

LOUKA: No, sir.

PETKOFF (*genially*): Thats all right. (*He sneezes*): Go and ask your mistress for my coat, like a good girl, will you?

(NICOLA *enters with the coat.* LOUKA *makes a pretence of having business in the room by taking the little table with the hookah away to the wall near the windows.*)

RAINA (*rising quickly as she sees the coat on* NICOLA'S *arm*): Here it is papa. Give it to me Nicola; and do you put some more wood on the fire. (*She takes the coat, and brings it to* THE MAJOR, *who stands up to put it on.* NICOLA *attends to the fire.*)

PETKOFF (*to* RAINA, *teasing her affectionately*): Aha! Going to be very good to poor old papa just for one day after his return from the wars, eh?

RAINA (*with solemn reproach*): Ah, how can you say that to me, father?

PETKOFF: Well, well, only a joke, little one. Come: give me a kiss. (*She kisses him.*) Now give me the coat.

RAINA: No: I am going to put it on for you. Turn your back. (*He turns his back and feels behind him with his arms for the sleeves. She dexterously takes the photograph from the pocket and throws it on the table before* BLUNTSCHLI, *who covers it with a sheet of paper under the very nose of* SERGIUS, *who looks on amazed, with his suspicions roused in the highest degree. She then helps* PETKOFF *on with his coat.*) There, dear! Now are you comfortable?

PETKOFF: Quite, little love. Thanks. (*He sits down; and* RAINA *returns to her seat near the stove.*) Oh, by the bye, Ive found something funny. Whats the meaning of this? (*He puts his hand into the picked pocket.*) Eh? Hallo! (*He tries the other pocket.*) Well, I could have sworn—! (*Much puzzled, he tries the breast pocket.*) I wonder—(*trying the original pocket.*) Where can it—? (*He rises, exclaiming*) Your mother's taken it!

RAINA (*very red*): Taken what?

PETKOFF: Your photograph, with the inscription: "Raina, to her Chocolate Cream Soldier: a Souvenir." Now you know theres something more in this than meets the eye; and I'm going to find it out. (*Shouting*) Nicola!

NICOLA (*coming to him*): Sir!

PETKOFF: Did you spoil any pastry of Miss Raina's this morning?

NICOLA: You heard Miss Raina say that I did, sir.

PETKOFF: I know that, you idiot. Was it true?

NICOLA: I am sure Miss Raina is incapable of saying anything that is not true, sir.

PETKOFF: Are you? Then I'm not. (*Turning to the others*) Come: do you think I dont see it all? (*He goes to* SERGIUS, *and slaps him on the shoulder.*) Sergius: youre the chocolate cream soldier, arnt you?

SERGIUS (*starting up*): I! A chocolate cream soldier! Certainly not.

PETKOFF: Not! (*He looks at them. They are all very serious and very conscious.*) Do you mean to tell me that Raina sends things like that to other men?

SERGIUS (*enigmatically*): The world is not such an innocent place as we used to think, Petkoff.

BLUNTSCHLI (*rising*): It's all right, Major. I'm the chocolate cream soldier. (PETKOFF *and* SERGIUS *are equally astonished.*) The gracious young lady saved my life by giving me chocolate creams when I was starving: shall I ever forget their flavour! My late friend Stolz told you the story at Pirot. I was the fugitive.

PETKOFF: You! (*He gasps.*) Sergius: do you remember how those two women went on this morning when we mentioned it? (SERGIUS *smiles cynically.* PETKOFF *confronts* RAINA *severely.*) Youre a nice young woman, arnt you?

RAINA (*bitterly*): Major Saranoff has changed his mind. And when I wrote that on the photograph, I did not know that Captain Bluntschli was married.

BLUNTSCHLI (*startled into vehement protest*): I'm not married.

RAINA (*with deep reproach*): You said you were.

BLUNTSCHLI: I did not. I positively did not. I never was married in my life.

PETKOFF (*exasperated*): Raina: will you kindly inform me, if I am not asking too much, which of these gentlemen you are engaged to?

RAINA: To neither of them. This young lady (*introducing*

LOUKA, *who faces them all proudly*) is the object of Major Saranoff's affections at present.

PETKOFF: Louka! Are you mad, Sergius? Why, this girl's engaged to Nicola.

NICOLA: I beg your pardon, sir. There is a mistake. Louka is not engaged to me.

PETKOFF: Not engaged to you, you scoundrel! Why, you had twenty-five levas from me on the day of your betrothal; and she had that gilt bracelet from Miss Raina.

NICOLA (*with cool unction*): We gave it out so, sir. But it was only to give Louka protection. She had a soul above her station; and I have been no more than her confidential servant. I intend, as you know, sir, to set up a shop later on in Sofia; and I look forward to her custom and recommendation should she marry into the nobility. (*He goes out with impressive discretion, leaving them all staring after him.*)

PETKOFF (*breaking the silence*): Well, I am—hm!

SERGIUS: This is either the finest heroism or the most crawling baseness. Which is it, Bluntschli?

BLUNTSCHLI: Never mind whether it's heroism or baseness. Nicola's the ablest man Ive met in Bulgaria. I'll make him manager of a hotel if he can speak French and German.

LOUKA (*suddenly breaking out at* SERGIUS): I have been insulted by everyone here. You set them the example. You owe me an apology.

(SERGIUS, *like a repeating clock of which the spring has been touched, immediately begins to fold his arms.*)

BLUNTSCHLI (*before he can speak*): It's no use. He never apologizes.

LOUKA: Not to you, his equal and his enemy. To me, his poor servant, he will not refuse to apologize.

SERGIUS (*approvingly*): You are right. (*He bends his knee in his grandest manner.*) Forgive me.

LOUKA: I forgive you. (*She timidly gives him her hand, which he kisses.*) That touch makes me your affianced wife.

SERGIUS (*springing up*): Ah! I forgot that.

LOUKA (*coldly*): You can withdraw if you like.

SERGIUS: Withdraw! Never! You belong to me. (*He puts his arm about her.*)

(CATHERINE *comes in and finds* LOUKA *in* SERGIUS' *arms, with all the rest gazing at them in bewildered astonishment.*)

CATHERINE: What does this mean?

(SERGIUS *releases* LOUKA.)

PETKOFF: Well, my dear, it appears that Sergius is going

to marry Louka instead of Raina. (*She is about to break out indignantly at him: he stops her by exclaiming testily*): Dont blame me: Ive nothing to do with it. (*He retreats to the stove.*)

CATHERINE: Marry Louka! Sergius: you are bound by your word to us!

SERGIUS (*folding his arms*) Nothing binds me.

BLUNTSCHLI (*much pleased by this piece of common sense*): Saranoff: your hand. My congratulations. These heroics of yours have their practical side after all. (*To* LOUKA): Gracious young lady: the best wishes of a good Republican! (*He kisses her hand, to* RAINA'S *great disgust, and returns to his seat.*)

CATHERINE: Louka: you have been telling stories.

LOUKA: I have done Raina no harm.

CATHERINE (*haughtily*): Raina!

(RAINA, *equally indignant, almost snorts at the liberty.*)

LOUKA: I have a right to call her Raina: she calls me Louka. I told Major Saranoff she would never marry him if the Swiss gentleman came back.

BLUNTSCHLI (*rising, much surprised*): Hallo!

LOUKA (*turning to* RAINA): I thought you were fonder of him than of Sergius. You know best whether I was right.

BLUNTSCHLI: What nonsense! I assure you, my dear Major, my dear Madame, the gracious young lady simply saved my life, nothing else. She never cared two straws for me. Why, bless my heart and soul, look at the young lady and look at me. She, rich, young, beautiful, with her imagination full of fairy princes and noble natures and cavalry charges and goodness knows what! And I, a commonplace Swiss soldier who hardly knows what a decent life is after fifteen years of barracks and battles: a vagabond, a man who has spoiled all his chances in life through an incurably romantic disposition, a man—

SERGIUS (*starting as if a needle had pricked him and interrupting* BLUNTSCHLI *in incredulous amazement*): Excuse me, Bluntschli: what did you say had spoiled your chances in life?

BLUNTSCHLI (*promptly*): An incurably romantic disposition. I ran away from home twice when I was a boy. I went into the army instead of into my father's business. I climbed the balcony of this house when a man of sense would have dived into the nearest cellar. I came sneaking back here to have another look at the young lady when any other man of my age would have sent the coat back—

PETKOFF: My coat!

BLUNTSCHLI:—yes: thats the coat I mean—would have sent it back and gone quietly home. Do you suppose I am the sort of fellow a young girl falls in love with? Why, look at our ages! I'm thirty-four: I dont suppose the young lady is much over seventeen. (*This estimate produces a marked sensation, all the rest turning and staring at one another. He proceeds innocently*): All that adventure which was life or death to me, was only a schoolgirl's game to her—chocolate creams and hide and seek. Heres the proof! (*He takes the photograph from the table.*) Now, I ask you, would a woman who took the affair seriously have sent me this and written on it "Raina, to her Chocolate Cream Soldier: a Souvenir"? (*He exhibits the photograph triumphantly, as if it settled the matter beyond all possibility of refutation.*)

PETKOFF: Thats what I was looking for. How the deuce did it get there? (*He comes from the stove to look at it, and sits down on the ottoman.*)

BLUNTSCHLI (*to* RAINA, *complacently*): I have put everything right, I hope, gracious young lady.

RAINA (*going to the table to face him*): I quite agree with your account of yourself. You are a romantic idiot. (BLUNTSCHLI *is unspeakably taken back.*) Next time, I hope you will know the difference between a schoolgirl of seventeen and a woman of twenty-three.

BLUNTSCHLI (*stupefied*): Twenty-three!

RAINA *snaps the photograph contemptuously from his hand; tears it up; throws the pieces in his face; and sweeps back to her former place.*)

SERGIUS (*with grim enjoyment of his rival's discomfiture*): Bluntschli: my one last belief is gone. Your sagacity is a fraud, like everything else. You have less sense than even I!

BLUNTSCHLI (*overwhelmed*): Twenty-three! Twenty-three!! (*He considers.*) Hm! (*Swiftly making up his mind and coming to his host*) In that case, Major Petkoff, I beg to propose formally to become a suitor for your daughter's hand, in place of Major Saranoff retired.

RAINA: You dare!

BLUNTSCHLI: If you were twenty-three when you said those things to me this afternoon, I shall take them seriously.

CATHERINE (*loftily polite*): I doubt, sir, whether you quite realize either my daughter's position or that of Major Sergius Saranoff, whose place you propose to take. The Petkoffs and the Saranoffs are known as the richest and most important families in the country. Our position is almost historical: we can go back for twenty years.

PETKOFF: Oh, never mind that, Catherine. (*To* BLUNT-

SCHLI) We should be most happy, Bluntschli, if it were only a question of your position; but hang it, you know, Raina is accustomed to a very comfortable establishment. Sergius keeps twenty horses.

BLUNTSCHLI: But who wants twenty horses? We're not going to keep a circus.

CATHERINE (*severely*): My daughter, sir, is accustomed to a first-rate stable.

RAINA: Hush, mother: youre making me ridiculous.

BLUNTSCHLI: Oh well, if it comes to a question of an establishment, here goes! (*He darts impetuously to the table; seizes the papers in the blue envelope; and turns to* SERGIUS.) How many horses did you say?

SERGIUS: Twenty, noble Switzer.

BLUNTSCHLI: I have two hundred horses. (*They are amazed.*) How many carriages?

SERGIUS: Three.

BLUNTSCHLI: I have seventy. Twenty-four of them will hold twelve inside, besides two on the box, without counting the driver and conductor. How many tablecloths have you?

SERGIUS: How the deuce do I know?

BLUNTSCHLI: Have you four thousand?

SERGIUS: No.

BLUNTSCHLI: I have. I have nine thousand six hundred pairs of sheets and blankets, with two thousand four hundred eider-down quilts. I have ten thousand knives and forks, and the same quantity of dessert spoons. I have three hundred servants. I have six palatial establishments, besides two livery stables, a tea garden, and a private house. I have four medals for distinguished services; I have the rank of an officer and the standing of a gentleman; and I have three native languages. Shew me any man in Bulgaria that can offer as much!

PETKOFF (*with childish awe*): Are you Emperor of Switzerland?

BLUNTSCHLI: My rank is the highest known in Switzerland: I am a free citizen.

CATHERINE: Then, Captain Bluntschli, since you are my daughter's choice—

RAINA (*mutinously*): He's not.

CATHERINE (*ignoring her*):—I shall not stand in the way of her happiness. (PETKOFF *is about to speak.*) That is Major Petkoff's feeling also.

PETKOFF: Oh, I shall be only too glad. Two hundred horses! Whew!

SERGIUS: What says the lady?

RAINA (*pretending to sulk*): The lady says that he can keep his tablecloths and his omnibuses. I am not here to be sold to the highest bidder. (*She turns her back on him.*)

BLUNTSCHLI: I wont take that answer. I appealed to you as a fugitive, a beggar, and a starving man. You accepted me. You gave me your hand to kiss, your bed to sleep in, and your roof to shelter me.

RAINA: I did not give them to the Emperor of Switzerland.

BLUNTSCHLI: Thats just what I say. (*He catches her by the shoulders and turns her face-to-face with him.*) Now tell us whom you did give them to.

RAINA (*succumbing with a shy smile*): To my chocolate cream soldier.

BLUNTSCHLI (*with a boyish laugh of delight*): Thatll do. Thank you. (*He looks at his watch and suddenly becomes businesslike.*) Time's up, Major. Youve managed those regiments so well that youre sure to be asked to get rid of some of the infantry of the Timok division. Send them home by way of Lom Palanka. Saranoff: dont get married until I come back: I shall be here punctually at five in the evening on Tuesday fortnight. Gracious ladies (*his heels click*) good evening. (*He makes them a military bow, and goes.*)

SERGIUS: What a man! Is he a man!

PART TWO

THE ESSAYS

G. K. Chesterton:

ON THE COMIC SPIRIT

Not so long ago the author of what was counted the wittiest of recent comedies produced another comedy, which was received with booing; and even, among those who would hardly descend to booing, received with boredom. As I have never seen either the play called a success or the play called a failure, I am naturally not going to pronounce on the merits of the playwright. But the contrast suggests certain considerations about the position of modern comedy which may do something to solve the riddle. Everybody agrees that the comedies in question are what is called "modern"; which seems to mean that they are comedies about cocktails and artificial complexions and people who walk about in a languid manner, when they are supposed to be taking part in a wild dance of liberty and the joy of life. In the recent case some apparently felt that the appearance of a film hero in blue pyjamas was a little absurd. To some of us, I grieve to say, the appearance of a film hero is always absurd, even when the film has wholly discoloured his sleeping-suit. But even to these too sensitive souls the hero is only felt to be absurd because he is supposed to be heroic. And that involves a truth which may have something to do with the reaction against this comedy. It might be stated by saying that, where there is flippancy, there cannot be irony.

It is obvious on the surface that all fun depends on some sort of solemnity. The Bishop of Rumti-foo is a funny figure because the Bishop of Rome is a serious figure. A horrible thought crosses my mind, at this moment, that perhaps there are some in the new world who know nothing of the Bishop of Rumti-foo and his missionary efforts; who may even look him up in a clerical directory or consult the atlas for the discovery of his diocese. I do not know how many people now read the *Bab Ballads;* but those who do will find many inventions much more amusing than any of the cocktail comedies.

To those who have ever known the work, it may possibly recall the particular figure, if I say that the Bishop of Rumti-foo had another link of association with the Bishop of Rome. His name was Peter. He preached to the cannibals of Rumti-foo and persuaded them to wear clothes: generally to wear his own cast clothes; so that each of those wild barbarians presented the appearance of an imperfectly or hastily attired Anglican bishop. But his most famous exploit was learning to dance; not at all in a languid modern manner, but in a wild and fantastic manner, to amuse the islanders of Rumti-foo. And this alone will serve to illustrate the contrast needed for comedy. It seemed very funny in the *Bab Ballads* that a bishop should fling himself about into wild attitudes like an acrobat; or indeed that a bishop should dance at all. But I imagine that there were high priests of old hieratic cults who really did dance at high solemnities, as David danced before the Ark. Those people did not think there was anything funny about a high priest dancing; because a high priest was simply a man who danced. And just as there is no fun in it when everything is serious, so there is no fun in it when everything is funny. A man who thinks the high priests of Rome and Rumti-foo equally absurd and antiquated, will not see any difference between them and the wild priest of the primitive cult; or between the dancing dervish and the dancing David. Some regard ecclesiastical emblems, last lumber of an abandoned barbarism, as things to be dismissed as grotesque and meaningless. And they would see very little difference between the insignia of the Bishop of Rumti-foo and the fetishes or totems of the tribe of savages among whom that excellent missionary discharged his mission. Suppose that we have really agreed to class clericalism with cannibalism. It will then be no longer possible to make fun of a bishop by imagining him clad (or unclad) like a cannibal. It will be impossible to make any more comic contrast than we should feel between the ways of the Sandwich Islanders and those of the Solomon Islanders. There will be no more comedy in the confusion than there would be in the confusion between one set of savages who baked their missionaries and another set of savages who boiled them. Where both are equally grotesque objects, there is no effect of the grotesque. There must be something serious that is respected, even in order that it may be satirized. There may be something amusing in a bishop's gaiters; but only because they are a bishop's. Take somebody who has never heard of a bishop and show him over a huge emporium which sells nothing but gaiters, and it is doubtful whether even the ten-thousandth gaiter which he takes up to gaze at will of itself move him to peals of mirth. Modern

comedy seems to be collecting gaiters and to have somehow
mislaid the bishop and consequently missed the joke.

Now, when we talk of the artificial and superficial character
of the old comedies, we do not mean exactly the same thing.
The comedies of Congreve or Sheridan did not, for the
moment, take the world seriously. But they did not describe a
world in which nobody took anything seriously. The respectable things were there, if only to be treated with disrespect.
Moreover, the respectable things were respected things. There
were a hundred indications that the things being mocked were
things that were generally and normally revered. A dialogue
of Congreve may be flippant, in the sense that he keeps
entirely on the surface. But he does not imply that there is no
solid ground under the surface. The old comedy is like a
scene of people dancing a minuet on a very polished floor; but
it is a polished oak floor. The new comedy is like a scene of
people dancing the Charleston on a sheet of ice—of very thin
ice. Both floors are very smooth; both floors are very slippery;
on both floors undignified accidents occur from time to time.
But we know that the Congreve character will not sink
through the floor; that the earth will not open and swallow
him; that he will not fall with a crash into the wine-cellar and
destroy dozens of fine old port. In the other case we feel that
the whole thing may dissolve; and there is nothing under that
hard and glittering ice except water; sometimes, I fear, rather
dirty water. But, anyhow, the old scoffer was dancing on
something solid, even if he was dancing on his mother's grave.
And the quaint old custom of paying some respect to graves,
and even to mothers, was necessary to the grotesque effect
even of that dance of death. But the comedy of ice melts
very easily into mere colourless water; and the mockers of
everything are really mockers of nothing. Unstable as water,
they shall not excel.

For in a world where everything is ridiculous, nothing can
be ridiculed. You cannot unmask a mask; when it is ad-
mittedly as hollow as a mask. You cannot turn a thing upside
down, if there is no theory about when it is right way up. If
life is really so formless that you cannot make head or tail
of it, you cannot pull its tail; and you certainly cannot make
it stand on its head. Now there is a certain degree of frivolity
that becomes formlessness. If the comic writer has not, at the
back of his mind, either his own theory of life which he thinks
right, or somebody else's theory of life which he thinks wrong,
or at least some negative notion that somebody is wrong in
thinking it wrong, he has really nothing to write about. He
attempts to produce a sort of comedy in which everybody is
indifferent to everything and to everybody else; but you cannot

create excitement by the collision of several different boredoms. Boredom is dangerously infectious; and has a way of spreading across the footlights. The reason is that there is not in the frivolity any touch of the serious, and therefore none of the satiric. The satirist is no longer set down to make fun of a bishop; he is set down all alone in the cold world to make fun of a gaiter. The old aesthetes used to explain that Art is unmoral, rather than immoral. It would be rather truer to say that Art can be immoral, but cannot be unmoral. Unmoral comedy is rapidly ceasing to be comic.

Bonamy Dobrée:

COMEDY

It is not surprising that no theory of comedy yet developed, from Aristotle to Meredith or M. Bergson, seems to cover all the ground; and for the purposes of this book it will be useful to distinguish three kinds of comedy, or at least three elements in comedy. This is not to elaborate a theory, but to provide a standpoint from which we may obtain a clearer view of the works we are about to consider.

1. *Critical Comedy*. The vast bulk of comedy is of the "critical" variety. What, for instance, was Aristophanes doing but "to laugh back into their senses 'revolting' sons and wives, to defend the orthodox faith against philosophers and men of science"? Menander, to judge from Terence, was doing the same kind of thing, as was Terence himself. This is the classical comedy from which much modern comedy is derived. It sets out definitely to correct manners by laughter; it strives to "cure excess."

This comedy, then, tends to repress eccentricity, exaggeration, any deviation from the normal: it wields the Meredithian "sword of common sense." It expresses the general feeling of the community, for which another name is morality; it is, to quote Meredith again, the "guardian of our civil fort," and it is significant that when comedy has been attacked, it has always been defended not on aesthetic but on moral grounds. But the defence has never been very successful, for the morality preached by comedy is not that of fierce ardour, of the passionate search after the utmost good, that in itself is excess, and subject for comedy (e.g. *Le Misanthrope*); but, as we continually find from Terence to the present day, it supports the happy mean, the comfortable life, the ideal of the *honnête homme*. Its lesson is to be righteous, but not to be

righteous overmuch, which in the mouths of those who hold
the doctrine becomes

> J'aime mieux un vice commode
> Qu'une fatigante vertu.

Its object is to damp enthusiasm, to prick illusions. It is in a
sense prig-drama; it flatters the vanity of the spectator, for
whose amusement the weaknesses of his friends are held
up. . . .

The foregoing may throw a light upon why it is that
comedy appears when it does. Comedy of this type is not a
phosphorescent gleam upon the surface of a decaying society,
but a conservative reaction against change. It is, in short, a
social corrective.

2. *"Free" Comedy.* There are, however, some comedies
which seem to produce quite a different effect in us, comedies
in which we feel no superiority, and which inculcate no
moral, but in which we seem to gain a release, not only from
what Lamb called the burden of our perpetual moral ques-
tioning, but from all things that appear to limit our powers.
Of this kind of comedy, the plays of Etherege and Regnard
are perhaps the best examples, though much of the laughter
of Aristophanes is evoked in the same way. Here we feel that
no values count, that there are no rules of conduct, hardly
laws of nature. Certainly no appeal, however indirect, is made
to our critical or moral faculties. We can disport ourselves
freely in a realm where nothing is accountable; all we need
to exact is that the touch shall be light enough. We take the
same delight in the vagaries of Sir Fopling Flutter as we do
at the sight of an absurdly gambolling calf. Judgement, except
the aesthetic, is out of place here. We are permitted to play
with life, which becomes a charming harlequinade without
being farce. It is all spontaneous and free, rapid and exhilarat-
ing; the least emotion, an appeal to common sense, and the
joyous illusion is gone.

I have named this comedy "free" because it depends upon
there being no valuations whatever; it is possible only in a
world where nothing matters, either because one has everything, or because one has nothing. Since it can afford to be
careless, it can be completely unmoral. . . .

3. *Great Comedy.* There is, however, a third comedy,
perilously near tragedy, in which the balance is so fine that it
seems sometimes as though it would topple over into the other
form, as in *Volpone* or *Le Misanthrope.* And here to leave
the instances definitely recognized as comedy, are not *Troilus
and Cressida* (Shakespeare's), *Measure for Measure,* and

All's Well that Ends Well also of this kind? Is not Mr. Shaw right in regarding *Coriolanus* as the greatest of Shakespeare's comedies? Indeed the really great figures of comic literature can hardly be thought of apart from their tragedy: who can regard the melancholy knight of La Mancha without pity, or disentangle the elements of the tales that beguiled the road to Canterbury?

The greatest comedy seems inevitably to deal with the disillusion of mankind, the bitterness of a Troilus or an Alceste, the failure of men to realize their most passionate desires. And does not this enable us to come to some conclusion as to what comedy really is? Cannot we see from the very periods in which it arises in its greatest forms with what aspect of humanity it needs must deal? It comes when the positive attitude has failed, when doubt is creeping in to undermine values, and men are turning for comfort to the very ruggedness of life, and laughing in the face of it all. "Je suis le rire en personne," says Maurice Sand's Polichinelle, "le rire triomphant, le rire du mal." There he represents "great" comedy.

For comedy does not give us anything in exchange for our loss. Tragedy moves us in such a way that life becomes rich and glowing, in spite of pain and all imaginable horror, perhaps because of them. In tragedy we are left in admiration of the grandiose spectacle of humanity stronger than its chains, and we are reconciled when a Cleopatra, hugging the asp, whispers:

> Peace, peace!
> Dost thou not see my baby at my breast
> That sucks the nurse asleep?

In tragedy we are made free by being taken outside the life of the senses into that of imaginative reality.

Comedy makes daily life livable in spite of folly and disillusion, but its vision, though as universal, is not that of tragedy, for it laughs at the spirit as much as at the flesh, and will not take sides. Tragedy is all that is commonly said of it, in depth, revelation, and grandeur; but comedy is not its opposite. The latter is not necessarily more distant from life, nor is it life apprehended through the mind rather than through the emotions. Neither is it the triumph of the angel in man over our body of the beast, as one has said, nor, to quote another, the triumph of the beast in man over the divine. It is nothing so fleeting as a triumph. It is "a recordation in man's soul" of his dual nature.

Goethe sought in art courage to face the battle of life. But it is doubtful if life is a battle, or a game, or a chaos through which we walk with slippery feet. And comedy gives us courage to face life without any standpoint; we need not regard it as a magnificent struggle nor as a puppet play; we need not view it critically nor feel heroically. We need only to feel humanly, for comedy shows us life, not at such a distance that we cannot but regard it coldly, but only so far as we may bring to it a ready sympathy freed from terror or too overwhelming a measure of pity.

Susanne K. Langer:

THE COMIC RHYTHM

The pure sense of life is the underlying feeling of comedy, developed in countless different ways. To give a general phenomenon one name is not to make all its manifestations one thing, but only to bring them conceptually under one head. Art does not generalize and classify; art sets forth the individuality of forms which discourse, being essentially general, has to suppress. The sense of life is always new, infinitely complex, therefore infinitely variable in its possible expressions. This sense, or "enjoyment" as Alexander would call it,[1] is the realization in direct feeling of what sets organic nature apart from inorganic: self-preservation, self-restoration, functional tendency, purpose. Life is teleological, the rest of nature is, apparently, mechanical; to maintain the pattern of vitality in a non-living universe is the most elementary instinctual purpose. An organism tends to keep its equilibrium amid the bombardment of aimless forces that beset it, to regain equilibrium when it has been disturbed, and to pursue a sequence of actions dictated by the need of keeping all its interdependent parts constantly renewed, their structure intact. Only organisms have needs; lifeless objects whirl or slide or tumble about, are shattered and scattered, stuck together, piled up, without showing any impulse to return to some pre-eminent condition and function. But living things strive to persist in a particular chemical balance, to maintain a particular temperature, to repeat particular functions, and to develop along particular lines, achieving a growth that seems to be preformed in their earliest, rudimentary, protoplasmic structure.

That is the basic biological pattern which all living things share: the round of conditioned and conditioning organic processes that produces the life rhythm. When this rhythm is

[1] S. Alexander, *Space, Time and Deity*. See Vol. I, p. 12.

disturbed, all activities in the total complex are modified by the break; the organism as a whole is out of balance. But, within a wide range of conditions, it struggles to retrieve its original dynamic form by overcoming and removing the obstacle, or if this proves impossible, it develops a slight variation of its typical form and activity and carries on life with a new balance of functions—in other words, it adapts itself to the situation. A tree, for instance, that is bereft of the sunshine it needs by the encroachment of other trees, tends to grow tall and thin until it can spread its own branches in the light. A fish that has most of its tail bitten off partly overcomes the disturbance of its locomotion patterns by growing new tissue, replacing some of the tail, and partly adapts to its new condition by modifying the normal uses of its fins, swimming effectively without trying to correct the list of its whole body in the water, as it did at first.

But the impulse to survive is not spent only in defense and accommodation; it appears also in the varying power of organisms to seize on opportunities. Consider how chimney swifts, which used to nest in crevasses among rocks, have exploited the products of human architecture, and how unfailingly mice find the warmth and other delights of our kitchens. All creatures live by opportunities, in a world fraught with disasters. That is the biological pattern in most general terms. . . .

Mankind has its rhythm of animal existence, too—the strain of maintaining a vital balance amid the alien and impartial chances of the world, complicated and heightened by passional desires. The pure sense of life springs from that basic rhythm, and varies from the composed well-being of sleep to the intensity of spasm, rage, or ecstasy. But the process of living is incomparably more complex for human beings than for even the highest animals; man's world is, above all, intricate and puzzling. The powers of language and imagination have set it utterly apart from that of other creatures. In human society an individual is not, like a member of a herd or a hive, exposed only to others that visibly or tangibly surround him, but is consciously bound to people who are absent, perhaps far away, at the moment. Even the dead may still play into his life. His awareness of events is far greater than the scope of his physical perceptions. Symbolic construction has made this vastly involved and extended world: and mental adroitness is his chief asset for exploiting it. The pattern of his vital feeling, therefore, reflects his deep emotional relation to those symbolic structures that are his realities, and his instinctual life modified in almost every way by thought—a brainy opportunism in face of an essentially dreadful universe.

This human life-feeling is the essence of comedy. It is at once religious and ribald, knowing and defiant, social and freakishly individual. The illusion of life which the comic poet creates is the oncoming future fraught with dangers and opportunities, that is, with physical or social events occurring by chance and building up the coincidences with which individuals cope according to their lights. This ineluctable future —ineluctable because its countless factors are beyond human knowledge and control—is Fortune. Destiny in the guise of Fortune is the fabric of comedy; it is developed by comic action, which is the upset and recovery of the protagonist's equilibrium, his contest with the world and his triumph by wit, luck, personal power, or even humorous, or ironical, or philosophical acceptance of mischance. Whatever the theme —serious and lyrical as in *The Tempest,* coarse slapstick as in the *Schwänke* of Hans Sachs, or clever and polite social satire—the immediate sense of life is the underlying feeling of comedy, and dictates its rhythmically structured unity, that is to say its organic form.

Comedy is an art form that arises naturally wherever people are gathered to celebrate life, in spring festivals, triumphs, birthdays, weddings, or initiations. For it expresses the elementary strains and resolutions of animate nature, the animal drives that persist even in human nature, the delight man takes in his special mental gifts that make him the lord of creation; it is an image of human vitality holding its own in the world amid the surprises of unplanned coincidence. The most obvious occasions for the performance of comedies are thanks or challenges to fortune. What justifies the term "Comedy" is not that the ancient ritual procession, the Comus, honoring the god of that name, was the source of this great art form— for comedy has arisen in many parts of the world, where the Greek god with his particular worship was unknown—but that the Comus was a fertility rite, and the god it celebrated a fertility god, a symbol of perpetual rebirth, eternal life. . . .

Because comedy abstracts, and reincarnates for our perception, the motion and rhythm of living, it enhances our vital feeling, much as the presentation of space in painting enhances our awareness of visual space. The virtual life on the stage is not diffuse and only half felt, as actual life usually is: virtual life, always moving visibly into the future, is intensified, speeded up, exaggerated; the exhibition of vitality rises to a breaking point, to mirth and laughter. We laugh in the theater at small incidents and drolleries which would hardly rate a chuckle off-stage. It is not for such psychological reasons that we go there to be amused, nor are we bound by rules of politeness to hide our hilarity, but these trifles at which we laugh are really funnier *where they occur* than they would be elsewhere; they are employed in the play, not merely brought in casually. They occur where the tension of dialogue or other action reaches a high point. As thought breaks into speech—as the wave breaks into form—vitality breaks into humor.

Humor is the brilliance of drama, a sudden heightening of the vital rhythm. A good comedy, therefore, builds up to every laugh; a performance that has been filled up with jokes at the indiscretion of the comedian or of his writer may draw a long series of laughs, yet leave the spectator without any clear impression of a very funny play. The laughs, moreover, are likely to be of a peculiar sameness, almost perfunctory, the formal recognition of a timely "gag."

The amoral character of the comic protagonist goes through the whole range of what may be called the comedy of laughter. Even the most civilized products of this art—plays that George Meredith would honor with the name of "comedy," because they provoke "thoughtful laughter"—do not present moral distinctions and issues, but only the ways of wisdom and of folly. Aristophanes, Menander, Molière—practically the only authors this most exacting of critics admitted as truly comic poets—are not moralists, yet they do not flout or deprecate morality; they have, literally, "no use" for moral principles—that is, they do not use them. Meredith, like practically all his contemporaries, labored under the belief that poetry must teach society lessons, and that comedy was valuable for what it revealed concerning the social order.[1] He tried hard to hold its exposé of foibles and vindication of common sense to an ethical standard, yet in his very efforts to justify its amoral personages he only admitted their amoral nature, and their simple relish for life, as when he said: "The heroines of comedy are like women of the world, not necessarily heartless from being clear-sighted. . . . Comedy is an

---

[1] His well-known little work is called *An Essay on Comedy, and the Uses of the Comic Spirit*. These uses are entirely non-artistic. Praising the virtues of "good sense" (which is whatever has survival value in the eyes of society), he says: "The French have a school of stately comedy to which they can fly for renovation whenever they have fallen away from it; and their having such a school is the main reason why, as John Stuart Mill pointed out, they know men and women more accurately than we do." And a few pages later: "The *Femmes Savantes* is a capital instance of the uses of comedy in teaching the world to understand what ails it. The French had felt the burden of this new nonsense [the fad of academic learning, new after the fad of excessive nicety and precision in speech, that had marked the *Précieuses*]; but they had to see the comedy several times before they were consoled in their suffering by seeing the cause of it exposed."

exhibition of their battle with men, and that of men with them. . . ."

There it is, in a nutshell: the contest of men and women—the most universal contest, humanized, in fact civilized, yet still the primitive joyful challenge, the self-preservation and self-assertion whose progress is the comic rhythm. . . .

The same impulse that drove people, even in prehistoric times, to enact fertility rites and celebrate all phases of their biological existence, sustains their eternal interest in comedy. It is in the nature of comedy to be erotic, risqué, and sensuous if not sensual, impious, and even wicked. This assures it a spontaneous emotional interest, yet a dangerous one: for it is easy and tempting to command an audience by direct stimulation of feeling and fantasy, not by artistic power. But where the formulation of feeling is really achieved, it probably reflects the whole development of mankind and man's world, for feeling is the intaglio image of reality. The sense of precariousness that is the typical tension of light comedy was undoubtedly developed in the eternal struggle with chance that every farmer knows only too well —with weather, blights, beasts, birds and beetles. The embarrassments, perplexities and mounting panic which characterize that favorite genre, comedy of manners, may still reflect the toils of ritual and taboo that complicated the caveman's existence. Even the element of aggressiveness in comic action serves to develop a fundamental trait of the comic rhythm—the deep cruelty of it, as all life feeds on life. There is no biological truth that feeling does not reflect, and that good comedy, therefore, will not be prone to reveal.

But the fact that the rhythm of comedy is the basic rhythm of life does not mean that biological existence is the "deeper meaning" of all its themes, and that to understand the play is to interpret all the characters as symbols and the story as a parable, a disguised rite of spring or fertility magic, performed four hundred and fifty times on Broadway. The stock characters are probably symbolic both in origin and in appeal. There are such independently symbolic factors, or residues of them, in all the arts,[1] but their value for art lies in the degree to which their significance can be "swallowed" by the single symbol, the art work. Not the derivation of personages and situations, but of the rhythm of "felt life" that the poet puts upon them, seems to me to be of artistic importance: the essential comic feeling, which is the sentient aspect of organic unity, growth, and self-preservation.

[1] E.g., the symbolization of the zodiac in some sacred architecture, of our bodily orientation in the picture plane, or of walking measure, a primitive measure of actual time, in music. But a study of such non-artistic symbolic functions would require a monograph.

Northrop Frye:

THE STRUCTURE OF COMEDY

Dramatic comedy, from which fictional comedy is mainly descended, has been remarkably tenacious of its structural principles and character types. Bernard Shaw remarked that a comic dramatist could get a reputation for daring originality by stealing his method from Molière and his characters from Dickens: if we were to read Menander and Aristophanes for Molière and Dickens the statement would be hardly less true, at least as a general principle. The earliest extant European comedy, Aristophanes' *The Acharnians,* contains the *miles gloriosus* or military braggart who is still going strong in Chaplin's *Great Dictator;* the Joxer Daly of O'Casey's *Juno and the Paycock* has the same character and dramatic function as the parasites of twenty-five hundred years ago, and the audiences of vaudeville, comic strips, and television programs still laugh at the jokes that were declared to be outworn at the opening of *The Frogs.*

The plot structure of Greek New Comedy, as transmitted by Plautus and Terence, in itself less a form than a formula, has become the basis for most comedy, especially in its more highly conventionalized dramatic form, down to our own day. It will be most convenient to work out the theory of comic construction from drama, using illustrations from fiction only incidentally. What normally happens is that a young man wants a young woman, that his desire is resisted by some opposition, usually paternal, and that near the end of the play some twist in the plot enables the hero to have his will. In this simple pattern there are several complex elements. In the first place, the movement of comedy is usually a movement from one kind of society to another. At the beginning of the play the obstructing characters are in charge of the play's society, and the audience recognizes that they are usurpers. At the end of the play the device in the plot that brings hero and heroine together causes a new society to crystallize around the hero, and the moment when this crystallization occurs is the point of resolution in the action, the comic discovery, *anagnorisis* or *cognitio.*

The appearance of this new society is frequently signalized by some kind of party or festive ritual, which either appears at the end of the play or is assumed to take place immediately afterward. Weddings are most common, and sometimes so many of them occur, as in the quadruple wedding at the end

of *As You Like It*, that they suggest also the wholesale pair-
ing off that takes place in a dance, which is another common
conclusion, and the normal one for the masque. The banquet
at the end of *The Taming of the Shrew* has an ancestry that
goes back to Greek Middle Comedy; in Plautus the audience
is sometimes jocosely invited to an imaginary banquet afterwards; Old Comedy, like the modern Christmas pantomime,
was more generous, and occasionally threw bits of food to the
audience. As the final society reached by comedy is the one
that the audience has recognized all along to be the proper
and desirable state of affairs, an act of communion with the
audience is in order. Tragic actors expect to be applauded as
well as comic ones, but nevertheless the word "plaudite" at
the end of a Roman comedy, the invitation to the audience
to form part of the comic society, would seem rather out of
place at the end of a tragedy. The resolution of comedy
comes, so to speak, from the audience's side of the stage; in
a tragedy it comes from some mysterious world on the
opposite side. In the movie, where darkness permits a more
erotically oriented audience, the plot usually moves toward
an act which, like death in Greek tragedy, takes place off-
stage, and is symbolized by a closing embrace.

The obstacles to the hero's desire, then, form the action of
the comedy, and the overcoming of them the comic resolution. The obstacles are usually parental, hence comedy often
turns on a clash between a son's and a father's will. Thus the
comic dramatist as a rule writes for the younger men in his
audience, and the older members of almost any society are
apt to feel that comedy has something subversive about it.
This is certainly one element in the social persecution of
drama, which is not peculiar to Puritans or even Christians,
as Terence in pagan Rome met much the same kind of
social opposition that Ben Jonson did. There is one scene in
Plautus where a son and father are making love to the same
courtesan, and the son asks his father pointedly if he really
does love mother. One has to see this scene against the back-
ground of Roman family life to understand its importance as
psychological release. Even in Shakespeare there are startling
outbreaks of baiting older men, and in contemporary movies
the triumph of youth is so relentless that the moviemakers
find some difficulty in getting anyone over the age of seventeen into their audiences.

The opponent to the hero's wishes, when not the father, is
generally someone who partakes of the father's closer relation to established society: that is, a rival with less youth
and more money. In Plautus and Terence he is usually either
the pimp who owns the girl, or a wandering soldier with a

supply of ready cash. The fury with which these characters are baited and exploded from the stage shows that they are father-surrogates, and even if they were not, they would still be usurpers, and their claim to possess the girl must be shown up as somehow fraudulent. They are, in short, impostors, and the extent to which they have real power implies some criticism of the society that allows them their power. In Plautus and Terence this criticism seldom goes beyond the immorality of brothels and professional harlots, but in Renaissance dramatists, including Jonson, there is some sharp observation of the rising power of money and the sort of ruling class it is building up.

The tendency of comedy is to include as many people as possible in its final society: the blocking characters are more often reconciled or converted than simply repudiated. Comedy often includes a scapegoat ritual of expulsion which gets rid of some irreconcilable character, but exposure and disgrace make for pathos, or even tragedy. *The Merchant of Venice* seems almost an experiment in coming as close as possible to upsetting the comic balance. If the dramatic role of Shylock is ever so slightly exaggerated, as it generally is when the leading actor of the company takes the part, it is upset, and the play becomes the tragedy of the Jew of Venice with a comic epilogue. *Volpone* ends with a great bustle of sentences to penal servitude and the galleys, and one feels that the deliverance of society hardly needs so much hard labor; but then *Volpone* is exceptional in being a kind of comic imitation of a tragedy, with the point of Volpone's *hybris* carefully marked.

The principle of conversion becomes clearer with characters whose chief function is the amusing of the audience. The original *miles gloriosus* in Plautus is a son of Jove and Venus who has killed an elephant with his fist and seven thousand men in one day's fighting. In other words, he is trying to put on a good show: the exuberance of his boasting helps to put the play over. The convention says that the braggart must be exposed, ridiculed, swindled, and beaten. But why should a professional dramatist, of all people, want so to harry a character who is putting on a good show—*his* show at that? When we find Falstaff invited to the final feast in *The Merry Wives*, Caliban reprieved, attempts made to mollify Malvolio, and Angelo and Parolles allowed to live down their disgrace, we are seeing a fundamental principle of comedy at work. The tendency of the comic society to include rather than exclude is the reason for the traditional importance of the parasite, who has no business to be at the final festival but is nevertheless there. The word "grace," with all its Renaissance overtones from the graceful courtier of Castiglione to the gracious God of Christianity, is a most important thematic word in Shakespearean comedy.

The action of comedy in moving from one social center to another is not unlike the action of a lawsuit, in which plaintiff and defendant construct different versions of the same situation, one finally being judged as real and the other as illusory. This resemblance of the rhetoric of comedy to the rhetoric of jurisprudence has been recognized from earliest times. A little pamphlet called the *Tractatus Coislinianus*, closely related to Aristotle's *Poetics*, which sets down all the essential facts about comedy in about a page and a half, divides the *dianoia* [theme, meaning] of comedy into two parts, opinion (*pistis*) and proof (*gnosis*). These correspond roughly to the usurping and the desirable societies respectively. Proofs (i.e., the means of bringing about the happier society) are subdivided into oaths, compacts, witnesses, ordeals (or tortures), and laws—in other words the five forms of material proof in law cases listed in the *Rhetoric*. We notice how often the action of a Shakespearean comedy begins with some absurd, cruel, or irrational law: the law of killing Syracusans in the *Comedy of Errors*, the law of compulsory marriage in *A Midsummer Night's Dream*, the law that confirms Shylock's bond, the attempts of Angelo to legislate people into righteousness, and the like, which the action of the comedy then evades or breaks. Compacts are as a rule the conspiracies formed by the hero's society; witnesses, such as overhearers of conversations or people with special knowledge (like the hero's old nurse with her retentive memory for birthmarks), are the commonest devices for bringing about the comic discovery. Ordeals (*basanoi*) are usually tests or touchstones of the hero's character: the Greek word also means touchstones, and seems to be echoed in Shakespeare's Bassanio whose ordeal it is to make a judgment on the worth of metals.

There are two ways of developing the form of comedy: one is to throw the main emphasis on the blocking characters; the other is to throw it forward on the scenes of discovery and reconciliation. One is the general tendency of comic irony, satire, realism, and studies of manners; the other is the tendency of Shakespearean and other types of romantic comedy. In the comedy of manners the main ethical interest falls as a rule on the blocking characters. The technical hero and heroine are not often very interesting people: the *adulescentes* of Plautus and Terence are all alike, as hard to tell apart in the dark as Demetrius and Lysander, who may be parodies of them. Generally the hero's character has the neutrality that enables him to represent a wish-fulfilment. It is very different with the miserly or ferocious parent, the boastful or foppish rival, or the other characters who stand in the way of the action. In Molière we have a simple but fully tested formula in which the ethical interest is focussed on a single blocking character, a heavy father, a miser, a misanthrope, a hypocrite, or a hypochrondriac. These are the figures that we remember, and the plays are usually named after them, but we can seldom remember all the Valentins and Angeliques who wriggle out of their clutches. In *The Merry Wives* the technical hero, a man named Fenton, has only a bit part, and this play has picked up a hint or two from Plautus's *Casina*, where the hero and heroine are not even brought on the stage at all. Fictional comedy, especially Dickens, often follows the same practice of grouping its interesting characters around a somewhat dullish pair of technical leads. Even Tom Jones, though far more fully realized, is still deliberately associated, as his commonplace name indicates, with the conventional and typical.

Comedy usually moves toward a happy ending, and the normal response of the audience to a happy ending is "this should be," which sounds like a moral judgment. So it is, except that it is not moral in the restricted sense, but social. Its opposite is not the villainous but the absurd, and comedy finds the virtues of Malvolio as absurd as the vices of Angelo. Molière's misanthrope, being committed to sincerity, which is a virtue, is morally in a strong position, but the audience soon realizes that his friend Philinte, who is ready to lie quite cheerfully in order to enable other people to preserve their self-respect, is the more genuinely sincere of the two. It is of course quite possible to have a moral comedy, but the result is often the kind of melodrama that we have described as comedy without humor, and which achieves its happy ending with a self-righteous tone that most comedy avoids. It is hardly possible to imagine a drama without conflict, and it is hardly possible to imagine a conflict without some kind of enmity. But just as love, including sexual love, is a very different thing from lust, so enmity is a very different thing from hatred. In tragedy, of course, enmity almost always includes hatred; comedy is different, and one feels that the social judgment against the absurd is closer to the comic norm than the moral judgment against the wicked.

The question then arises of what makes the blocking character absurd. Ben Jonson explained this by his theory of the "humor," the character dominated by what Pope calls a ruling passion. The humor's dramatic function is to express a state of what might be called ritual bondage. He is obsessed by his humor, and his function in the play is primarily to repeat his obsession. A sick man is not a humor, but a hypochondriac is, because, *qua* hypochondriac, he can never admit to good health, and can never do anything inconsistent with the role that he has prescribed for himself. A miser can do and say nothing that is not connected with the hiding of gold or saving of money. In *The Silent Woman*, Jonson's nearest approach to Molière's type of construction, the whole action recedes from the humor of Morose, whose determination to eliminate noise from his life produces so loquacious a comic action.

The principle of the humor is the principle that unincremental repetition, the literary imitation of ritual bondage, is funny. In a tragedy—*Oedipus Tyrannus* is the stock example —repetition leads logically to catastrophe. Repetition overdone or not going anywhere belongs to comedy, for laughter is partly a reflex, and like other reflexes it can be conditioned by a simple repeated pattern. In Synge's *Riders to the Sea* a mother, after losing her husband and five sons at sea, finally loses her last son, and the result is a very beautiful and moving play. But if it had been a full-length tragedy plodding glumly through the seven drownings one after another, the audience would have been helpless with unsympathetic laughter long before it was over. The principle of repetition as the basis of humor both in Jonson's sense and in ours is well known to the creators of comic strips, in which a character is established as a parasite, a glutton (often confined to one dish), or a shrew, and who begins to be funny after the point has been made every day for several months. Continuous comic radio programs, too, are much more amusing to habitués than to neophytes. The girth of Falstaff and the hallucinations of Quixote are based on much the same comic laws. Mr. E. M. Forster speaks with disdain of Dickens's Mrs. Micawber, who never says anything except that she will never desert Mr. Micawber: a strong contrast is marked here between the refined writer too finicky for popular formulas, and the major one who exploits them ruthlessly.

The humor in comedy is usually someone with a good deal of social prestige and power, who is able to force much of the play's society into line with his obsession. Thus the humor is intimately connected with the theme of the absurd or irrational law that the action of comedy moves toward breaking. It is significant that the central character of our earliest humor comedy, *The Wasps*, is obsessed by law cases: Shylock, too, unites a craving for the law with the humor of revenge. Often the absurd law appears as a whim of a bemused tyrant whose will is law, like Leontes or the humorous Duke Frederick in Shakespeare, who makes some arbitrary decision or rash promise: here law is replaced by "oath," also mentioned in the *Tractatus*. Or it may take the form of a sham Utopia, a society of ritual bondage constructed by an act of humorous or pedantic will, like the academic retreat in *Love's Labor's Lost*. This theme is also as old as Aristophanes, whose parodies of Platonic social schemes in *The Birds* and *Ecclesiazusae* deal with it.

The society emerging at the conclusion of comedy represents, by contrast, a kind of moral norm, or pragmatically free society. Its ideals are seldom defined or formulated: definition and formulation belong to the humors, who want predictable activity. We are simply given to understand that the newly-married couple will live happily ever after, or that at any rate they will get along in a relatively unhumorous and clear-sighted manner. That is one reason why the character of the successful hero is so often left undeveloped: his real life begins at the end of the play, and we have to believe him to be potentially a more interesting character than he appears to be. In Terence's *Adelphoi*, Demea, a harsh father, is contrasted with his brother Micio, who is indulgent. Micio being more liberal, he leads the way to the comic resolution, and converts Demea, but then Demea points out the indolence inspiring a good deal of Micio's liberality, and releases him from a complementary humorous bondage.

Thus the movement from *pistis* to *gnosis*, from a society controlled by habit, ritual bondage, arbitrary law and the older characters to a society controlled by youth and pragmatic freedom is fundamentally, as the Greek words suggest, a movement from illusion to reality. Illusion is whatever is fixed or definable, and reality is best understood as its negation: whatever reality is, it's not *that*. Hence the importance of the theme of creating and dispelling illusion in comedy: the illusions caused by disguise, obsession, hypocrisy, or unknown parentage.

The comic ending is generally manipulated by a twist in the plot. In Roman comedy the heroine, who is usually a slave or courtesan, turns out to be the daughter of somebody respectable, so that the hero can marry her without loss of face. The *cognitio* in comedy, in which the characters find out who their relatives are, and who is left of the opposite sex not a relative, and hence available for marriage, is one of the features of comedy that have never changed much: *The Confidential Clerk* indicates that it still holds the attention of dramatists. There is a brilliant parody of a *cognitio* at the end of *Major Barbara* (the fact that the hero of this play is a professor of Greek perhaps indicates an unusual affinity to the conventions of Euripides and Menander), where Undershaft is enabled to break the rule that he cannot appoint his son-in-law as successor by the fact that the son-in-law's own father married his deceased wife's sister in Australia, so that the son-in-law is his own first cousin as well as himself. It sounds complicated, but the plots of comedy often are complicated because there is something inherently absurd about complications. As the main character interest in comedy is so often focussed on the defeated characters, comedy regularly illustrates a victory of arbitrary plot over consistency of character. Thus, in striking contrast to tragedy, there can hardly be such a thing as inevitable comedy, as far as the action of the individual play is concerned. That is, we may know that the convention of comedy will make some kind of happy ending inevitable, but still for each play the dramatist must produce a distinctive "gimmick" or "weenie," to use two disrespectful Hollywood synonyms for *anagnorisis*. Happy endings do not impress us as true, but as desirable, and they are brought about by manipulation. The watcher of death and tragedy has nothing to do but sit and wait for the inevitable end; but something gets born at the end of comedy, and the watcher of birth is a member of a busy society.

The manipulation of plot does not always involve metamorphosis of character, but there is no violation of comic decorum when it does. Unlikely conversions, miraculous transformations, and providential assistance are inseparable from comedy. Further, whatever emerges is supposed to be there for good: if the curmudgeon becomes lovable, we understand that he will not immediately relapse again into his ritual habit. Civilizations which stress the desirable rather than the real, and the religious as opposed to the scientific perspective, think of drama almost entirely in terms of comedy. In the classical drama of India, we are told, the tragic ending was regarded as bad taste, much as the manipulated endings of comedy are regarded as bad taste by novelists interested in ironic realism.

The total *mythos* [narrative] of comedy, only a small part of which is ordinarily presented, has regularly what in music is called a ternary form: the hero's society rebels against the society of the *senex* and triumphs, but the hero's society is a Saturnalia, a reversal of social standards which recalls a golden age in the past before the main action of the play begins. Thus we have a stable and harmonious order disrupted by folly, obsession, forgetfulness, "pride and prejudice," or events not understood by the characters themselves, and then restored. Often there is a benevolent grandfather, so to speak, who overrules the action set up by the blocking humor and so links the first and third parts. An example is Mr. Burchell, the disguised uncle of the wicked squire, in *The Vicar of Wakefield*. A very long play, such as the Indian *Sakuntala*, may present all three phases; a very intricate one, such as many of Menander's evidently were, may indicate their outlines. But of course very often the first phase is not given at all: the audience simply understands an ideal state of affairs which it knows to be better than what is revealed in the play, and which it recognizes as like that to which the action leads. This ternary action is, ritually, like a contest of summer and winter in which winter occupies the middle action; psychologically, it is like the removal of a neurosis or blocking point and the restoring of an unbroken current of energy and memory.

BIBLIOGRAPHY

The following books represent a highly readable fraction of the enormous literature on the subject.

GENERAL

Auden, W. H. "Notes on the Comic," *The Dyer's Hand* (1962), pp. 57–71
Banham, Martin. *The Cambridge Guide to Theatre* (1995)
Bennett, Susan. *Theatre Audiences: A Theory of Production and Reception* (1990)
Bergson, Henri. "Laughter," in *Comedy*, ed. by Wylie Sypher (1956)
Clark, Barrett H., ed. *European Theories of the Drama*, rev. ed. (1947)
Cook, Albert S. *The Dark Voyage and the Golden Mean* (1949)
Cooper, Lane, *An Aristotelian Theory of Comedy* (1922)
Dover, K. J. *Aristophanic Comedy* (1972)
Feibleman, James. *Aesthetics* (1949)
Freud, Sigmund. *Wit and Its Relation to the Unconscious*, trans. by A. A. Brill (1916); reprinted in *Basic Writings of Sigmund Freud* (1938)
Harriott, Rosemary. *Aristophanes, Poet and Dramatist* (1986)
Koestler, Arthur. *Insight and Outlook* (1949)
Meredith, George. "An Essay on Comedy," in *Comedy*, ed. by Wylie Sypher (1956)
Monro, D. H. *Argument of Laughter* (1951)
Potts, L. J. *Comedy* (1949)
Sypher, Wylie. "The Meaning of Comedy," in *Comedy*, ed. by Wylie Sypher (1956)
Thompson, Alan Reynolds. *Anatomy of Drama*, 2nd ed. (1948)
Wimsatt, W. K., Jr. *English Stage Comedy* (1955)
Wimsatt, W. K., Jr., and Cleanth Brooks. *Literary Criticism: A Short History* (1957)

ARISTOPHANES

Hamilton, Edith. *The Greek Way* (1948)
Jaeger, Werner. *Paideia: The Ideals of Greek Culture*, 2nd ed. trans. by Gilbert Highet. Vol. I (1945)
Lever, Katherine. *The Art of Greek Comedy* (1956)

MACHIAVELLI

Bentley, Eric. "From Leo X to Pius XII," in *The Dramatic Event* (1954)
Gauss, Christian. Introduction to Machiavelli's *The Prince* (1952)
Kennard, Joseph Spencer. *The Italian Theatre*, 2 vols. (1932)
Wilkins, Ernest Hatch. *A History of Italian Literature* (1954)

SHAKESPEARE

Berry, Ralph. *Changing Styles in Shakespeare* (1981)
Draper, John. *The Twelfth Night of Shakespeare's Audience* (1950)
Harbage, Alfred B. *As They Liked It* (1947)
Novy, Marianne. *Love's Argument: Gender Relations in Shakespeare* (1984)
Salinger, Leo. *Shakespeare and the Traditions of Comedy* (1974)
Summers, Joseph. "The Masks of Twelfth Night," *University of Kansas City Review*, 22 (Autumn 1955): 25-32. Reprinted in *Shakespeare: Modern Essays in Criticism*, ed. by Leonard Dean (1957)

MOLIÈRE

Bermel, Albert. *Molière's Theatrical Bounty* (1990)
Guicharnaud, Jacques, ed. *Molière: A Collection of Critical Essays* (1964)
Moore, W. G. *Molière: A New Criticism* (1949)
Schwartz, I. A. *Commedia dell'Arte and Its Influence on French Comedy in the Seventeenth Century* (1933)

BIBLIOGRAPHY

Stoll, E. E. "The Comic Method," in *Shakespeare Studies, Historical and Comparative in Method*, rev. ed. (1942)
Turnell, Martin. *The Classical Moment* (1947)
Thompson, Alan Reynolds. *The Dry Mock: A Study of Iron in Drama* (1948)

GAY

Armens, Sven M. *John Gay, Social Critic* (1954)
Bateson, F. W. *English Comic Drama, 1700–1750* (1929)
Gagey, Edmund. *Ballad Opera* (1937)
Roberts, Edgar V. *The Beggar's Opera* (1969)

WILDE

Beerbohm, Max. *Around Theatres* (1953)
Bentley, Eric. *The Playwright as Thinker* (1946)
Donohue, Joseph, with Ruth Bergrren. *Oscar Wilde's The Importance of Being Earnest* (1995)
Ellmann, Richard. *Oscar Wilde* (1988)
Woodcock, George R. *The Paradox of Oscar Wilde* (1949)

CHEKHOV

Bentley, Eric. *In Search of Theater* (1953)
Gilman, Richard. *Anton Chekhov* (1995)
Magarshack, David. *Chekhov the Dramatist* (1952)
Peace, Richard. *Chekhov: A Study of the Four Major Plays* (1983)
Popkin, Henry. "Chekov—the Ironic Spectator," *Theatre Arts* (March 1952), pp. 17, 80
Stanislavski, Constantin. *My Life in Art*, trans. by J. J. Robbins (1956)
Styan, J. L. *Chekhov in Performance* (1971)

SHAW

Bentley, Eric. *Bernard Shaw* (rev. ed. 1957)
Berst, Charles A. *Bernard Shaw and the Art of Drama* (1973)
Henderson, Archibald. *George Bernard Shaw: Man of the Century* (1956)
Meisel, Martin. *Shaw and the Nineteenth-Century Drama* (1963)
Shaw, George Bernard. *Advice to a Young Critic, and Other Letters*, ed. by F. J. West (1955)

SIGNET ⓜ **MENTOR** ℗ **PLUME** (0451)/(0452)

Outstanding Contemporary Plays

☐ **WHO'S AFRAID OF VIRGINIA WOOLF? by Edward Albee.** The stunning play that has become a classic in our time. "A brilliantly original work of art—an excoriating theatrical experience, surging with shocks of recognition and dramatic fire."—*Newsweek*   (158717—$4.99)

☐ **THE AMERICAN DREAM and THE ZOO STORY by Edward Albee.** Two more critically acclaimed plays by the major American playwright, author of *Who's Afraid of Virginia Woolf?*   (166434—$4.99)

☐ **PLAYS FROM THE CONTEMPORARY BRITISH THEATER edited and with an Introduction by Brooks McNamara.** Includes *What the Butler Saw*, by Joe Orton; *The Changing Room*, by David Storey; *Plenty*, by David Hare; *Betrayal*, by Harold Pinter; *Pack of Lies*, by Hugh Whitemore; and *The Life and Adventures of Nicholas Nickleby*, adapted by David Edgar. This anthology is a valuable resource for students, actors, and all who love the contemporary stage.   (628519—$6.99)

☐ **AWAKE AND SINGING Edited and with an Introduction by Ellen Schiff.** This groundbreaking collection is the first to focus on plays written by Jews about Jews in America. These seven classics, produced between 1920 and 1960, brought explicit Jewish drama to the American stage. Taken together, all seven plays tell the story of the Jew in America struggling to assimilate yet pondering what being Jewish means.   (628691—$6.99)

Prices slightly higher in Canada
